American Mosaic

American Mosaic

MULTICULTURAL READINGS IN CONTEXT

SECOND EDITION

Barbara Roche Rico
Loyola Marymount University

Sandra Mano
University of California, Los Angeles

HOUGHTON MIFFLIN COMPANY BOSTON TORONTO
Geneva, Illinois   Palo Alto   Princeton, New Jersey

Sponsoring Editor George Kane
Editorial Assistant Bruce Cantley
Associate Project Editor Elena DiCesare
Editorial Assistant Stefanie Jacobs
Production/Design Coordinator Carol Merrigan
Senior Manufacturing Coordinator Marie Barnes

Cover design by Linda Manly Wade
Cover image by Javier Arevalo (Mexican, b. 1937), "Los Encuentros," 1991.
Watercolor on paper, $43^1/4 \times 51^1/2$ inches. Private Collection, Los Angeles, CA.
Courtesy of Iturralde Gallery, Los Angeles, CA.

For Our Students

Printed in the U.S.A.

Library of Congress Catalog Card Number: 94–76543

ISBN: 0–395–69313–6

Examination Copy ISBN: 0–395–71899–6

789-B-01 00 99

CREDITS

(Credits are continued on pages 681–685 which constitute an extension of the copyright page.)

CONTENTS

5 JAPANESE AMERICANS
In Camp, In Community   *289*

6 AFRICAN AMERICANS
The Struggle for Civil Rights   *359*

7 CHICANOS
Negotiating Political and Cultural Boundaries   *443*

8 AMERICAN INDIANS
Reclaiming Cultural Heritage   *527*

9 THE NEW IMMIGRANTS

Reviving, Reinventing, and Challenging the American Dream   *611*

PREFACE

Using a chronological framework, the second edition of *American Mosaic: Multicultural Readings in Context* celebrates diversity by presenting the writings of many ethnic groups at a particularly generative period in their histories. We believe that all students will be enriched by hearing these voices and by understanding the period in which the authors were writing. Moreover, students will come to appreciate the contributions these writers have made to American culture.

Each chapter reflects what we consider to be an important period in the development of a particular ethnic group, by using readings that are representative of the attitudes and concerns of that time. Our intention is to let the authors speak for themselves about issues important to them. Our desire is not to provide a comprehensive coverage of American ethnic literature and history, but instead to suggest the richness of the American experience. *American Mosaic* is designed to allow students to develop historical awareness and critical thinking skills while they study the development of literary, political, and cultural voices within our country. The new edition reinforces the strengths of the first edition. We have included twenty-two new selections; many of which have a more strongly critical or analytical focus. The final chapter addresses some more recent immigrant groups and their role in the continual reshaping of American culture.

We have begun our historical examination during the late nineteenth century. Clearly American culture did not begin at that point. American Indian groups had developed many forms of expressive cultural production—what some critics call oral literature—long before the coming of the Europeans. One can also find earlier examples of immigrant writings and the writings of the "forced immigrants," Africans brought here as slaves. The late 1800s is an important period to examine, though, because it marked three important developments: the large influx of immigrants primarily from Europe and Asia who came for religious and economic reasons; the altering of the parameters of American society through nativist groups, exclusionary laws, and the establishment of reservations; and the change in the national character brought about by the growth of cities and the migrations north of African Americans. Throughout the text we have tried to reflect not only the changes experienced by the ethnic groups, but also the interaction of given ethnic groups with the majority culture. As importantly, the readings selected illustrate how each group participated in the development and transformation of American culture.

To help students perceive the mosaic, we have presented in each chapter a combination of literary and historical material. The excerpt from the legal document included in each section suggests ways in which the dominant culture responded to each ethnic group. (These documents are, however, only a sampling; we urge students to explore further the legal context that can only be outlined in the chapter.) The readings themselves illustrate the emergence of multicultural voices. In addition to essays, we have included first person narratives, journalistic pieces, oratory, fiction, and poetic works, because we believe that expository essays alone do not reflect the richness of the literature that was produced. By concluding each chapter with an essay by a scholar who has extensively studied the culture of the group, we hope to illustrate how issues of culture can be explored across the disciplines.

The text's apparatus is designed to inform students and to encourage them to respond to and challenge what they read. Every chapter includes an introductory essay intended to be a starting point for discussion. Headnotes to the selections provide further background information. Pre-reading and post-reading questions foster critical thinking and allow students to respond creatively to the texts, both in class discussion and in writing. In this edition, each set of responding questions begins with a journal or in-class writing assignment, followed by a question inviting students to work collaboratively in small groups. The next two questions present essay topics which involve close re-reading of the text and ask students to incorporate their personal experience and outside information into their responses. Connecting questions at the end of the chapter have been reorganized so that those questions relating selections within a chapter precede questions that make connections to other chapters. Finally, suggestions for library research as well as lists of supplemental materials give students an opportunity to explore issues further.

From these encounters, students will, we hope, strengthen their abilities to think critically and to respond to what they read. They will come to see American culture not as a single monologic entity, but as an ongoing conversation involving many ethnic groups. And we trust they will find in the interplay of historical, literary, and cultural concerns an opportunity to assert their own voices.

Acknowledgments

We would like to thank the Research Program in Ethnic Studies administered by UCLA's Institute for American Cultures, Norris Hundley, Chair, and the Chicano Studies Research Center Faculty Advisory Committee, David Hayes-

Bautista, Chair, for the two-year grant that enabled both of us to undertake our research. We would also like to acknowledge a grant from the Rains Foundation administered through Loyola Marymount University, which provided additional support for this project. In addition, we thank the Loyola Marymount University Department of English, Linda Bannister, Chair, and the College of Liberal Arts, Sr. Mary Milligan, R.S.H.M., Dean, for their continued encouragement.

In the preparation of this text, we have received the help and encouragement of many colleagues and friends. Mike Rose has acted from the outset as a mentor, commenting on and encouraging us in our work. We also appreciate the support of Anne Marie Albertazzi, Héctor Calderón, Lee Carroll, Sandra Cisneros, Maria Cuevas, Robert Cullen, Michael Fried, Lucy Garza, Russell Leong, Graciela Limón, Kenneth Lincoln, Bonnie Lisle, Sharon Locy, Cathy Machado, Regina Mandanici, Berenice Mirenda, Steven Osborn, Louise Phelps, Manuel Rezende, Henrietta Rico, Mona Rivera, Alice Roy, A. LaVonne Brown Ruoff, Santiago Sia, Ted Simpson, Robin Strayhorn, Betty Takahashi, Tracey Thompson, Lucy Wilson, W. Ross Winterowd, Gail Wronsky, Fatima Wu, and Kelly Younger.

In addition, we would like to thank our reviewers. For the first edition: Poonam Arora, University of Michigan, Dearborn; Betty Bamberg, University of Southern California; John Bodnar, Indiana University, Bloomington; Ron Estes, St. Louis Community College at Forest Park; Donald Fixico, Western Michigan University; Eugene Howard, Bucks County Community College, PA; Jacquelyn Jackson, Middle Tennessee State University; Yolette Jones, Volunteer State Community College, TN; Malcolm Kiniry, Rutgers University, Newark, NJ; Rhonda Levine, University of California, Santa Barbara; Shirley Lim, University of California, Santa Barbara; Lois Marchino, University of Texas, El Paso; Beverly Moss, Ohio State University; Dottie Perry, Norfolk State University, VA; Georgia Rhoades, University of Louisville; Vicki Ruiz, University of California, Davis; Melita Schaum, University of Michigan, Dearborn; Lacreta Scott, Cerritos College; Joseph Skerrett, University of Massachusetts, Amherst; Bruce Southerd, East Carolina University, Greenville; Antonio Stevens-Arroyo, Brooklyn College, City University of New York; Franklin O. Sutton, Community College of Allegheny County, PA; Michael Vivion, University of Missouri, Kansas City; Linda Woodson, University of Texas, San Antonio; and Maria Elena Yepes, East Los Angeles College. For the second edition: Jeanne Anderson, University of Louisville; SDiane Bogus, DeAnza College; Diane Cogan, San Diego Mesa College; Lenore Navarro Dowling, Rio Hondo Community College; Ulrike Z. Jaeckel, University of Illinois at Chicago; Beatrice Kingston-Cataldo, College of Saint Elizabeth; Geraldine R. Lash, SUNY Technical College at Alfred; Edward Marx, City College of New York; Jim Murphy, Boston College, John T. Reilly, Loyola Marymount University; Jerry Shaw, The Wichita State University; Katharine Reid Stone, Georgia State University; Daphne Swabey, University of Michigan, Ann Arbor; Linda Woodson, University of Texas, San Antonio; and Kerry Candaele, Columbia University.

We owe special thanks to Ellen Darion, our development editor, whose encouragement helped to make the second edition a better book. At Houghton Mifflin we would also like to thank George Kane, Kristin Watts Peri, Bruce Cantley, Elena DiCesare, and Tracy Shaw. For their work on the first edition we thank Carolyn Potts, Lynn Walterick and Danielle Carbonneau.

We would like to add a special note of appreciation to our husbands, Morris Mano and Richard Rico, and our families, who have contributed so much to this book.

We dedicate this book to our students and to the memory of those who have nurtured us and helped us to shape our ideas.

B.R.R.
S.M.

American Mosaic

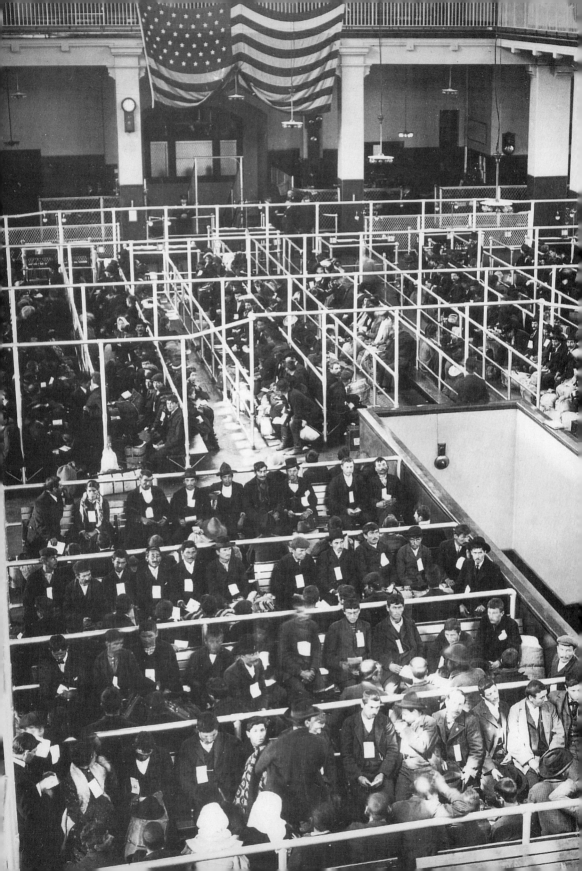

1

EARLY IMMIGRANTS

In Search of the Land of Milk and Honey

⌗

Above: Sweatshop in a Division Street tenement, New York City. Photographed by Jacob Riis. *(Jacob. A. Riis Collection/Museum of the City of New York)*

Opposite: Ellis Island, circa 1910. Newly arrived immigrants wait to be processed in the Great Hall, before being permitted entry into the U.S. *(William Williams Collection, United States History, Local History & Genealogy Division, The New York Public Library/Astor, Lenox and Tilden Foundations)*

SETTING THE HISTORICAL AND CULTURAL CONTEXT

In 1883, during the second great wave of immigration from Europe, Emma Lazarus wrote the now famous poem "The New Colossus"—a poem which gives voice to the promise of the Statue of Liberty:

"Keep, ancient lands, your storied pomp!" cries she
With silent lips. "Give me your tired, your poor,
Your huddled masses yearning to breathe free,
The wretched refuse of your teeming shore.
Send these, the homeless, tempest-tost to me,
I lift my lamp beside the golden door!"

The poem seemed so expressive of the American ideal that civic leaders had the words engraved at the foot of the Statue of Liberty to mark the dedication of that monument in 1883. In the rather florid language of the time, "The New Colossus" depicts the nation's role as a refuge for the poor and oppressed, a "golden door" open to all. Ironically, the publication of the poem and the national dedication of the monument coincided with the introduction of congressional legislation imposing greater restrictions on immigration. A look at the historical background of this period will trace the struggles of immigrants to achieve the opportunities promised them.

From its founding the United States has been a land of immigrants. With the exception of American Indians, all persons who consider themselves Americans have been immigrants or descendants of immigrants. From colonial times, the process of immigration and resettlement has been an ongoing one, but the nineteenth century witnessed two particular waves of immigration. From 1820 to 1860, social and economic conditions in Europe—urban overcrowding, economic depression, and a series of bad harvests—prompted thousands to emigrate. Most of these immigrants, Protestants and Catholics from northern and western Europe, settled in the urban areas of the northeast. A second wave of immigration occurred between 1880 and 1902, predominantly with Catholics from southern Europe and Jews from eastern Europe. In addition to economic and political factors, many of these immigrants were fleeing religious persecution. Many Jews, particularly those from Russia, needed to escape the violent anti-Semitic attacks known as *pogroms;* Armenians fled the oppressive regimes of the Turks.

Urged by advertisements and stories in European newspapers, as well as letters from friends and family members already settled in America, immigrants came to the United States expecting to find vast farmlands, theirs for the taking, and cities that would welcome even unskilled workers. The newcomers' expectations were often violated by the immigration process itself, the so-called Ellis Island experience, which has become a part of the nation's collective memory.

As soon as they arrived, immigrant families were detained at the immigration center for a series of debasing questions and medical examinations. They were asked their names and nationalities; if the names were long or too difficult for the immigration official to spell, they might be changed on the spot. Those who failed the mandatory medical examinations were subject to detention or immediate deportation; this often resulted in families being separated for long periods of time. Although more than three quarters of the people who attempted to immigrate were admitted to the country, the other 20 to 25 percent were sent back to their homelands.

New immigrants were vulnerable to exploitation, by both government officials and other immigrants themselves. An investigation of Ellis Island during Theodore Roosevelt's administration exposed the corrupt practices of some immigration officials and commercial enterprises that used unfair currency exchange rates to cheat immigrants. Unprincipled attorneys would claim to have the immigrants' best interests in mind, only to charge them exorbitant fees. As Constantine Panunzio reports, *padroni* or other middlemen would also take advantage of immigrants, promising them impressive employment opportunities that turned out to be "pick and shovel" work. But at other times earlier immigrants offered encouragement and support and worked to protect the newer immigrants' rights; Maxine Seller's essay recounts the efforts of three such immigrants to improve the quality of life for those who followed them.

After being admitted by immigration officials, most newcomers settled in the northeastern and midwestern states. Some took advantage of the Homestead Act of 1862, guaranteeing that those who lived on a parcel of land for five years could claim ownership of the land. Some worked in the mines. A larger percentage, however, settled in urban areas, where they established small shops or, more often, took jobs in factories. Many found work in the garment industry in New York City and the slaughterhouses and meatpacking firms in Chicago.

For most new immigrants, life in both urban and rural areas was more difficult than they had expected. In cities, they had to live in crowded apartments in tenement buildings, where sanitation, heat, and even light were at a premium. That poverty and deprivation is clearly visible in Anzia Yezierska's story "The Fat of the Land," where neighbors talk to each other across a narrow airshaft and children routinely fight over a potato. Typically, the landlords who profited from the renting space in tenements lived some distance from the structures and could thus remain comfortably oblivious to the conditions inside the tenements. It took the investigative work of photographers and writers such as Jacob Riis (1849–1914) in New York and John Spargo (1876–1966) in Chicago to make the public aware of these abuses. Those who settled in on the plains had it no easier, for they found themselves in a

continual battle with the elements, deprivation, and the despair of rural isolation, all depicted in the excerpt from Ole Edvart Rölvaag's *Giants in the
Earth*.

Working conditions were also substandard. Many urban immigrants
were forced to work in overcrowded sweatshops without adequate facilities.
Men often worked sixteen-hour shifts; everyone worked long hours for low
pay. By the mid-nineteenth century laws were passed to prohibit women
from working longer than ten hours at one time. But it was not until the
first decades of the twentieth century that child labor laws were passed to
protect the rights of children and to make the education of minors compulsory.

At first workers had little power to influence the conditions of their employment because they received little help from organized labor unions. The
unions, in turn, saw the immigrants as a threat because the immigrants were
sometimes brought in as contract laborers and had been used, often unwit-
tingly, to break up strikes. After a time, however, some of the unions began
to recognize the immigrant workers; the American Federation of Labor under the direction of the immigrant Samuel Gompers began to represent immigrant workers. In some urban areas there was competition between the unions that would admit immigrants and the unions that wanted to exclude
immigrants from the labor force. The Irish immigrant Elizabeth Gurley
Flynn, whose writing is included in this chapter, was a major force in the
American labor movement.

The struggle for acceptance by the unions, and thus for a more secure
place in the economy, mirrors the immigrants' struggle for a more secure
place in society. Many natives and other immigrants believed that newcomers
could best ensure their success in this country by becoming "Americanized,"
or incorporated into the mainstream American culture. This process, known
as "assimilation," usually involved gradually replacing the attitudes, mores,
and customs of one's own country of origin with the attitudes and customs
of one's new home. Writers, such as the philosopher John Dewey (1859–
1952) and the journalist Abraham Cahan (1860–1951), wrote essays and articles suggesting the importance of assimilating. The title of Israel Zangwill's
play, *The Melting Pot* (1908) provided a term for this process of assimilation,
which is still in use today. Other writings and cartoons of the period mocked
the "greenhorn," the person who, naively or not, clings to the trappings of
the Old Country. The educational system also contributed to the assimilation
process, not only by making the immigrants more familiar with English, but
also by indoctrinating in them the necessity of becoming Americanized.
David M. Fine's article in this chapter discusses the view of assimilation and
acculturation presented in many of the novels written by early immigrants.
The article also explains the way in which the expression "melting pot" has
often been misunderstood.

Assimilation was not accomplished, however, without loss and pain. In her story, "The Fat of the Land," Anzia Yezierska explores the cost of acculturation and economic success for an immigrant mother, her family, and friends. Acculturation often meant the loss of the comfort and sense of identity of the traditional way of life. In the story we see the main character's need for family rituals and old friends and we discover the alienation and self-doubt that assimilation can bring.

Even during this early period some social critics objected to the assimilationist view. Some who reviewed Zangwill's *The Melting Pot*, for example, objected to the intermarriage of a Jew and a Gentile that takes place at the play's end, for this would constitute a violation of Jewish law. And while some reformers such as Jacob Riis advocated assimilation, the Hull House founder Jane Addams (1860–1935) took a different view. Addams believed that for acculturation to be successful, a two-way exchange had to take place: not only would the immigrant learn the ways of the new country, but the new country would be enriched by cultural contributions made by the newcomer. Maxine S. Seller's essay illustrates how that ideal was fulfilled in the work of Josephine Zeman, an eastern European immigrant who was educated at Hull House and went on to become an important social worker, journalist, and advocate for the rights of other immigrants.

Although many writers and reformers celebrated the arrival of the newcomers, many other members of society did not. Indeed, during the 1880s, the period when the Statue of Liberty was becoming such an important symbol of invitation, much of the country's attention was given to exclusionist legislation and nativist doctrines, which promoted the rights and interests of inhabitants who considered themselves native to the United States over the rights and interests of immigrants. Ironically, these so-called native inhabitants were immigrants, too; they had simply arrived in this country earlier than those whom they were trying to keep out.

The rejection of immigrants took several forms. Some members of the labor force regarded immigrants as a source of competition for jobs. Others, even government officials, entertained stereotyped notions about immigrants, believing that some groups included dangerous radicals. Other nativists subscribed to a theory of eugenics, which asserted the innate superiority of some groups. Still others claimed that the national identity might be diluted if the country were allowed to become a melting pot. As a result of nativist pressure, Congress passed exclusionist legislation, establishing immigration quotas that favored Protestant immigrants from northern and western Europe over those with other religious beliefs and those from other areas. Congress also instituted a "head tax," a onetime charge for entering the country; each subsequent piece of exclusionist legislation was accompanied by an increase in the head tax.

Despite these obstacles, however, immigrants continued to come. They settled in urban areas, either working in factories or establishing small businesses. They formed civic organizations, built synagogues and churches, and dreamed of providing their children with better lives. As time passed, they began to exercise some political power, if not in Congress, at least at the municipal level. As important, by altering the economic structures of the country, they gave the social structures a new fluidity. They reduced the possibility that there would evolve in this country a rigid system of social class. In a very real way, the "huddled masses" of which Lazarus wrote made "the American dream" more than simply an expression.

BEGINNING: Pre-reading/Writing

Working in a group, use the knowledge you have gained from reading the introduction to this chapter or your own experience to list the possible reasons that immigrants flocked to America during the period between 1820 and 1920. Share your list with the class. How do you think these reasons compare with those motivating immigrants today?

The Bill of Rights comprises the first ten amendments to the Constitution of the United States. They resulted from an agreement between those who wanted a strong federal government and those who sought to restrict the power of that government. These amendments, added in 1791, were designed to prevent the federal government from making laws that violated such basic rights as freedom of speech, press, assembly, expression of religious faith, and trial by jury. The Supreme Court later extended the power of the Bill of Rights by applying the document to state governments as well.

The Bill of Rights clearly articulates the rights guaranteed to each individual. As such it has assumed a special importance for many immigrants who have fled repressive regimes or religious persecution in their homelands.

⚜

THE BILL OF RIGHTS

ARTICLES IN ADDITION TO, and Amendment of the Constitution of the United States of America, proposed by Congress, and ratified by the Legislatures of the several States, pursuant to the fifth Article of the original Constitution.

Art. I

Congress shall make no law respecting an establishment of religion, or prohibiting the free exercise thereof; or abridging the freedom of speech, or of the press; or the right of the people peaceably to assemble, and to petition the government for a redress of grievances.

Art. II

A well regulated Militia, being necessary to the security of a free State, the right of the people to keep and bear Arms, shall not be infringed.

Art. III

No Soldier shall, in time of peace be quartered in any house, without the consent of the Owner, nor in time of war, but in a manner to be prescribed by law.

Art. IV

The right of the people to be secure in their persons, houses, papers, and effects, against unreasonable searches and seizures, shall not be violated, and no Warrants shall issue, but upon probable cause, supported by Oath or affirmation, and particularly describing the place to be searched, and the persons or things to be seized.

Art. V

No person shall be held to answer for a capital, or otherwise infamous crime, unless on a presentment or indictment of a Grand Jury, except in cases arising in the land or naval forces, or in the Militia, when in actual service in time of War or public danger; nor shall any person be subject for the same offence to be twice put in jeopardy of life or limb; nor shall be compelled in any criminal case to be a witness against himself, nor be deprived of life, liberty, or property, without due process of law; nor shall private property be taken for public use, without just compensation.

Art. VI

In all criminal prosecutions, the accused shall enjoy the right to a speedy and public trial, by an impartial jury of the State and district wherein the crime shall have been committed, which district shall have been previously ascertained by law, and to be informed of the nature and cause of the accusation; to be confronted with the witnesses against him; to have compulsory process for obtaining witnesses in his favor, and to have the Assistance of Counsel for his defence.

Art. VII

In Suits at common law, where the value in controversy shall exceed twenty dollars, the right of trial by jury shall be preserved, and no fact tried by a jury, shall be otherwise re-examined in any Court of the United States, than according to the rules of the common law.

Art. VIII

Excessive bail shall not be required, nor excessive fines imposed, nor cruel and unusual punishments inflicted.

Art. IX

The enumeration in the Constitution, of certain rights, shall not be construed to deny or disparage others retained by the people.

Art. X

The powers not delegated to the United States by the Constitution, nor prohibited by it to the States, are reserved to the States respectively, or to the people. ✠

RESPONDING

1. Choose one of the provisions of the Bill of Rights that is particularly important to you. In a journal entry, explain in your own words what it promises or implies and why you chose it.

2. Working individually or in a group, rewrite all the provisions of the Bill of Rights in less technical language.

3. Choose one of the rights that you think would have been particularly important to early immigrants and write an essay explaining your choice. You may use information from the introduction to the chapter, other sources, and your own knowledge.

CONSTANTINE PANUNZIO

Constantine Panunzio, who was born in Bari, Italy, in 1884, arrived in the United States on July 3, 1902. After completing studies in theology at Wesleyan University, Boston University, and New York University, he earned a doctorate from the Brookings Institution in 1925. During the period between 1915 and 1920, Panunzio was active in the immigrant community, working at settlement houses and at the YMCA; in 1919 he became the superintendent of immigrant labor for the Interchurch World Movement. After 1920 he devoted most of his time to teaching, serving on the sociology faculty of several universities, including the State University of New York and the University of California, Los Angeles. Many of Panunzio's published works treated the issues of immigration and deportation. He died in 1964, at the age of seventy-nine.

Panunzio's book The Soul of an Immigrant *(1922) recounts the author's own experiences and celebrates his assimilation into his new culture. Despite the text's general optimism, the excerpt that follows tells of his struggles to find housing and work just after arriving in America.*

✠

IN THE AMERICAN STORM

Not that they starve, but starve so dreamlessly,
Not that they sow, but that they seldom reap,
Not that they serve, but have no gods to serve,
Not that they die, but that they die like sheep.
— VACHEL LINDSAY

1 THE *Francesco* put out to sea from Trapani, Sicily, on May 3, 1902, and a week or so later passed the Pillars of Hercules. Then she plunged into the wake of the trade winds and for about three weeks she sailed majestically before them like a gull, stirring not a sail all the while. Then followed a period of varying weather, which in turn was succeeded by a few days when the ocean was breathless and motionless. Frequently we could see whole schools of dolphins as they came to the surface, or monster whales spurting pillars of water into the air, a sight especially beautiful on calm moonlit nights.

2 The little brig had reached a distance of about three hundred miles from the coast of North America, when one day the very weight of heaven seemed to be pressing down upon her. The clouds were yellow, sullen and angry-looking; the air was breathless with pent-up power. As the day advanced the ba-

rometer went lower and lower, and with the approach of evening this invisible, uncontrollable power seemed to be seizing the little ship as if with mighty claws. The sea rumbled beneath her, the thick masses of clouds pressed closer upon her, the waters became deep-dyed black. At five-thirty we heard the call: "All hands on deck," and a few moments later: "All sails in but lower-topsail and jib." Climbing like monkeys after coconuts, we made short work of the task. We knew, however, that something more strenuous was coming. At six, just as the four bells were striking, the very bowels of sea and sky opened upon us with amazing suddenness and force. The seasoned Tuscan sailor, whose every word was wont to be an oath, struck with sudden fear, fell upon his knees by the bulwark and began to say his prayers. Some one kicked him as you would a dog. The moment the terrific gale struck the ship it tore the heavy lower-topsail and flapped it madly in the air as if it were a piece of tissue paper. The brave little ship beat pitifully beneath the gale; its mainroyalmast was broken like a reed; its cargo was shifted to one side like a handful of pebbles, and its hull sprung a leak. The blast was over in an hour or so, but all hands worked steadily for three days and nights to shift the cargo back in place, while four men were kept at the hand-pump night and day until we reached shore a week or more later.

Some years afterward an American friend, reflecting upon this incident as I had described it to him remarked, "That storm was indeed prophetic of your early experiences in America, was it not?" It may be that it was, and perhaps we shall soon discover the analogy as it appeared in my friend's mind.   3

On July 3rd, 1902, after a voyage of sixty-one days, the *Francesco* anchored in Boston Harbor. As the next day was the "Fourth," the city was already decked in festal array. The captain hastened to register his arrival. A boat was lowered, and I was ordered to take him ashore; thus it was my good fortune to be the first to touch land. "America!" I whispered to myself as I did so.   4

In a day or two the ship was towed to a pier in Charlestown, where it lay until its cargo of salt was unloaded and a cargo of lumber consigned to Montevideo was put on board of her.   5

In the meantime a desire had arisen within me to return home. There were several reasons for this. In the first place, it was becoming increasingly unpleasant for me to remain in the midst of that crew. It chanced that I was the only person on board hailing from southern Italy; the rest of the men were mostly Genoese, with one or two Tuscans. Now, the feeling of sectional provincialism between north and south Italy is still so strong, and the North always assumes such airs of superiority, that I had become the butt of every joke and the scapegoat of every occasion. This was becoming more and more unbearable, and as time went on I decided that my self-respect could not and would not stand it. To this was added the fact that the captain was one of those creatures who seem to be more brute than man, especially in dealing with youth. During that voyage he had more than once beaten me in a way that would have made the hardest punishments of my father blush. He was so cruel and unreasonable that before he left Boston several of the crew, including the first mate, left him.   6

7   In the face of these circumstances I began to think that if the captain would only let me go, I would return home. Accordingly, one day I went to him and very respectfully told him of my intention to return to Italy immediately if he would permit me, and would pay me the money which was due me. The stern, sea-hardened sailor brushed me aside without even an answer. A day or so later I again went to him; this time he drove me from his presence with a sharp kick. Whatever manhood there ever was in my being rose up and stood erect within me; with a determination as quick and as sharp as his kick had been, I decided I would now go at any cost.

8   I began to look about for ways and means to carry out my determination. On the pier was an elderly watchman, an Italian by birth, who had been in America for several years. To him I confided my difficulties. He was a sane and conservative man, cautious in giving advice. My desire was to find a ship which was returning to some European port. He did not know of any, but one evening he suggested that if worse came to worst, I could do some kind of work for a few days and thereby earn enough money to buy a third-class passage back to Naples, which at that time cost only fifty or sixty dollars. This gave me a new idea. I decided to take my destiny in my own hands and in some way find my way back to Italy. Two months had already passed since our arrival in Boston, and almost any day now the vessel would take to sea. If I were to act it must be now or never. I had been ashore twice and had become acquainted with a barber near the pier. To him I also confided my troubles, and he offered to keep my few belongings for me, should I finally decide to leave the ship.

9   Late in the evening of September 8, 1902, when the turmoil of the street traffic was subsiding, and the silence of the night was slowly creeping over the city, I took my sea chest, my sailor bag and all I had and set foot on American soil. I was in America. Of immigration laws I had not even a knowledge of their existence; of the English language I knew not a word; of friends I had none in Boston or elsewhere in America to whom I might turn for counsel or help. I had exactly fifty cents remaining out of a dollar which the captain had finally seen fit to give me. But as I was soon to earn money and return to Molfetta, I felt no concern.

10   My Charlestown barber friend took me in that first night with the distinct understanding that I could stay only one night. So the next morning bright and early, leaving all my belongings with the barber, I started out in search of a job. I roamed about the streets, not knowing where or to whom to turn. That day and the next four days I had one loaf of bread each day for food and at night, not having money with which to purchase shelter, I stayed on the recreation pier on Commercial Street. One night, very weary and lonely, I lay upon a bench and soon dozed off into a light sleep. The next thing I knew I cried out in bitter pain and fright. A policeman had stolen up to me very quietly and with his club had dealt me a heavy blow upon the soles of my feet. He drove me away, and I think I cried; I cried my first American cry. What became of me that night I cannot say. And the next day and the next. . . . I just roamed

aimlessly about the streets, between the Public Garden with its flowers and the water-side, where I watched the children at play, even as I had played at the water's brink in old Molfetta.

Those first five days in America have left an impression upon my mind which can never be erased with the years, and which gives me a most profound sense of sympathy for immigrants as they arrive. On the fifth day, by mere chance, I ran across a French sailor on the recreation pier. We immediately became friends. His name was Louis. Just to look at Louis would make you laugh. He was over six feet tall, lank, queer-shaped, freckle-faced, with small eyes and a crooked nose. I have sometimes thought that perhaps he was the "missing link" for which the scientist has been looking. Louis could not speak Italian; he had a smattering of what he called "italien," but I could not see it his way. On the other hand, I kept imposing upon his good nature by giving a nasal twang to Italian words and insisting on calling it "francese." We had much merriment. Two facts, however, made possible a mutual understanding. Both had been sailors and had traveled over very much of the same world; this made a bond between us. Then too, we had an instinctive knowledge of "esperanto," a strange capacity for gesticulation and facial contortion, which was always our last "hope" in making each other understand.

Not far from the recreation pier on which we met is located the Italian colony of "North End," Boston. To this Louis and I made our way, and to an Italian boarding house. How we happened to find it and to get in I do not now recall. It was a "three-room apartment" and the landlady informed us that she was already "full," but since we had no place to go, she would take us in. Added to the host that was already gathered there, our coming made fourteen people. At night the floor of the kitchen and the dining table were turned into beds. Louis and I were put to sleep in one of the beds with two other men, two facing north and two south. As I had slept all my life in a bed or bunk by myself this quadrupling did not appeal to me especially. But we could not complain. We had been taken in on trust, and the filth, the smells and the crowding together were a part of the trust.

We began to make inquiries about jobs and were promptly informed that there was plenty of work at "pick and shovel." We were also given to understand by our fellow-boarders that "pick and shovel" was practically the only work available to Italians. Now these were the first two English words I had heard and they possessed great charm. Moreover, if I were to earn money to return home and this was the only work available for Italians, they were very weighty words for me, and I must master them as soon and as well as possible and then set out to find their hidden meaning. I practised for a day or two until I could say "peek" and "shuvle" to perfection. Then I asked a fellow-boarder to take me to see what the work was like. He did. He led me to Washington Street, not far from the colony, where some excavation work was going on, and there I did see, with my own eyes, what the "peek" and "shuvle" were about. My heart sank within me, for I had thought it some form of office work; but I was game and since this was the only work available for Italians, and since I must have money to return home, I would take it up. After all, it was only a means to an end, and would last but a few days.

14 It may be in place here to say a word relative to the reason why this idea was prevalent among Italians at the time, and why so many Italians on coming to America find their way to what I had called "peek and shuvle." It is a matter of common knowledge, at least among students of immigration, that a very large percentage of Italian immigrants were "contadini" or farm laborers in Italy. American people often ask the question, "Why do they not go to the farms in this country?" This query is based upon the idea that the "contadini" were farmers in the sense in which we apply that word to the American farmer. The facts in the case are that the "contadini" were not farmers in that sense at all, but simply farm-laborers, more nearly serfs, working on landed estates and seldom owning their own land. Moreover, they are not in any way acquainted with the implements of modern American farming. Their farming tools consisted generally of a "zappa," a sort of wide mattock; an ax and the wooden plow of biblical times. When they come to America, the work which comes nearest to that which they did in Italy is not farming, or even farm labor, but excavation work. This fact, together with the isolation which inevitably would be theirs on an American farm, explains, in a large measure, why so few Italians go to the farm and why so many go into excavation work. There is another factor to be considered, and that is that the "padrone" perhaps makes a greater per capita percentage in connection with securing and managing workers for construction purposes than in any other line, and therefore he becomes a walking delegate about the streets of Italian colonies spreading the word that only "peek and shuvle" is available.

15 Now, though Louis and I had never done such work, because we were Italians we must needs adapt ourselves to it and go to work with "peek and shuvle." (I should have stated that Louis, desiring to be like the Romans while living with them, for the time being passed for an Italian.)

16 So we went out to hunt our first job in America. For several mornings Louis and I went to North Square, where there were generally a large number of men loitering in groups discussing all kinds of subjects, particularly the labor market. One morning we were standing in front of one of those infernal institutions which in America are permitted to bear the name of "immigrant banks," when we saw a fat man coming toward us. "Buon giorno, padrone," said one of the men. "Padrone?" said I to myself. Now the word "padrone" in Italy is applied to a proprietor, generally a respectable man, at least one whose dress and appearance distinguish him as a man of means. This man not only showed no signs of good breeding in his face, but he was unshaven and dirty and his clothes were shabby. I could not quite understand how he could be called "padrone." However, I said nothing, first because I wanted to get back home, and second because I wanted to be polite when I was in *American* society!

17 The "padrone" came up to our group and began to wax eloquent and to

gesticulate (both in Sicilian dialect) about the advantages of a certain job. I remember very clearly the points which he emphasized: "It is not very far, only twelve miles from Boston. For a few cents you can come back any time you wish, to see 'i parenti e gli amici,' your relatives and friends. The company has a 'shantee' in which you can sleep, and a 'storo' where you can buy your 'grosserie' all very cheap. 'Buona paga,'" he continued, "(Good pay), $1.25 per day, and you only have to pay me fifty cents a week for having gotten you this 'gooda jobba.' I only do it to help you and because you are my countrymen. If you come back here at six o'clock to-night with your bundles, I myself will take you out."

The magnanimity of this man impressed Louis and me very profoundly; we looked at each other and said, "Wonderful!" We decided we would go; so at the appointed hour we returned to the very spot. About twenty men finally gathered there and we were led to North Station. There we took a train to some suburban place, the name of which I have never been able to learn. On reaching our destination we were taken to the "shantee" where we were introduced to long open bunks filled with straw. These were to be our beds. The "storo" of which we had been told was at one end of the shanty. The next morning we were taken out to work. It was a sultry autumn day. The "peek" seemed to grow heavier at every stroke and the "shuvle" wider and larger in its capacity to hold the gravel. The second day was no better than the first, and the third was worse than the second. The work was heavy and monotonous to Louis and myself especially, who had never been "contadini" like the rest. The "padrone" whose magnanimity had so stirred us was little better than a brute. We began to do some simple figuring and discovered that when we had paid for our groceries at the "storo," for the privilege of sleeping in the shanty, and the fifty cents to the "padrone" for having been so condescending as to employ us, we would have nothing left but sore arms and backs. So on the afternoon of the third day Louis and I held a solemn conclave and decided to part company with "peek and shuvle,"—for ever. We left, without receiving a cent of pay, of course.

Going across country on foot we came to a small manufacturing village. We decided to try our luck at the factory, which proved to be a woolen mill, and found employment. Our work was sorting old rags and carrying them in wheelbarrows into a hot oven, in which the air was almost suffocating. Every time a person went in it he was obliged to run out as quickly as possible, for the heat was unbearable. Unfortunately for us, the crew was composed almost entirely of Russians, who hated us from the first day, and called us "dagoes." I had never heard the word before; I asked Louis if he knew its meaning, but he did not. In going in and out of the oven the Russians would crowd against us and make it hard for us to pass. One morning as I was coming out, four of the men hedged me in. I thought I would suffocate. I finally succeeded in pushing out, my hand having been cut in the rush of the wheelbarrows.

The superintendent of the factory had observed the whole incident. He was a very kindly man. From his light complexion I think he was a Swede. He came to my rescue, reprimanded the Russians, and led me to his office, where he bandaged my hand. Then he called Louis and explained the situation to us. The Russians looked upon us as intruders and were determined not to work side by side with "the foreigners," but to drive them out of the factory. Therefore, much as he regretted it, the superintendent was obliged to ask us to leave, since there were only two of us, as against the large number of Russians who made up his unskilled crew.

21   So we left. My bandaged hand hurt me, but my heart hurt more. This kind of work was hard and humiliating enough, but what went deeper than all else was the first realization that because of race I was being put on the road. And often since that day I have felt the cutting thrusts of race prejudice. They have been dealt by older immigrants, who are known as "Americans," as well as by more recent comers. All have been equally heart-rending and head-bending. I hold no grudge against any one; I realize that it is one of the attendant circumstances of our present nationalistic attitude the world over, and yet it is none the less saddening to the human heart. I have seen prejudice, like an evil shadow, everywhere. It lurks at every corner, on every street and in every mart. I have seen it in the tram and on the train; I have felt its dreaded power in school and college, in clubs and churches. It is an ever-present evil spirit, felt though unseen, wounding hearts, cutting souls. It passes on its poison like a serpent from generation to generation, and he who would see the fusion of the various elements into a truly American type must ever take into cognizance its presence in the hearts of some human beings. ✠

RESPONDING

1. In a journal entry, compare Panunzio's experiences in a new situation and country to the experience of your family when they first came to the United States or moved to another part of the country or to your own experience in any new environment.

2. Working individually or in a group, use examples from Panunzio's autobiography to illustrate how the storm he encountered on his journey to America was "indeed prophetic of [his] early experiences in America" (paragraph 3). Which of those conditions would you have found most intolerable?

3. Write an essay discussing Panunzio's attitude toward prejudice. Do you agree that prejudice "passes on its poison like a serpent from generation to generation" (paragraph 21)? And what do you think of Panunzio's statement "I hold no grudge against any one" (paragraph 21)? Is this an effective

response to prejudice or are there other strategies that might work better? Consider your own experience as well as the selection and any other relevant reading.

4. In an essay, compare Panunzio's experiences working in Boston in 1902 with the experiences of new immigrants today. Base your response on your own knowledge, observations, and reading as well as any news coverage, documentaries, or films you may have seen on this subject. How have employment opportunities and working conditions for new immigrants changed? Have they improved?

OLE EDVART RÖLVAAG

Ole Edvart Rölvaag was born in Norway in 1876. After immigrating in 1896, he spent his early years in this country working on his uncle's farm in South Dakota. He later earned undergraduate and advanced degrees from Augustana College (in South Dakota), St. Olaf College (in Minnesota), and the University of Oslo. From 1906 to 1931 Rölvaag served as professor of Norwegian letters and literature at St. Olaf College. His publications include Giants in the Earth: A Saga of the Prairie *(1924–1925, Norwegian; 1927, English);* Peder Victorious *(1929),* Their Father's God *(1931), and* Boat of Longings *(1933), published after his death in 1931.*

Giants in the Earth has been praised for its psychological realism and for the intensity with which it depicts a pioneer family's struggles with the isolation of their environment. The excerpt that follows explores the tensions experienced by the woman of the family, who is in many ways a reluctant pioneer.

✠

FACING THE GREAT DESOLATION

VI

1   THE DAYS WERE LONG for the boys during their father's absence. Ole soon tired of standing at the chopping block without the company of his brother; he idled aimlessly about, and made frequent errands into the house to see whether he couldn't hatch up something to break the monotony. Store-Hans wasn't much better off; the secret which his father had entrusted to him was certainly interesting; but it wasn't quite fascinating enough to hold its own with the vision of the ducks out there in the swamps. The father would surely bring something home from town to solve this problem; he and his brother ought to be over west reconnoitering every spare minute of the time. And now the Irish had all gone away, too; their sod huts were standing empty; there would be many curious things to look at and pry into! . . . Besides, their mother said so little these days; it was no fun to be with her any longer. Often when he spoke to her she was not there; she neither saw nor heard him, said only yes and no, which seemed to come from far away. . . . Probably she was brooding over the strange thing about to happen, Store-Hans told himself; he often looked wonderingly at her, thinking many thoughts beyond his years. . . . He remembered his father's words, and never left her for long, although it was very lonesome for him in the house.

A couple of days after the men's departure, she sent the boy over to Kjersti
to borrow a darning needle; she had hidden her own away so carefully that she
could not find it. Such things occurred commonly now; she would put something away, she could not remember where, and would potter around looking
for it without really searching; at last, she would forget altogether what she was
about, and would sit down with a peculiarly vacant look on her face; at such
times she seemed like a stranger. . . . Ole was sitting in the house that morning,
finishing a sling-shot which he had just made.

Suddenly Store-Hans came darting back with the needle; he had run until
he was all out of breath. He burst out with the strangest news, of Tönseten's
having killed a big animal; it was awfully big—almost like a bear! . . . Tönseten
said it *was* a bear, so it must be true! Tönseten and Kjersti were skinning him
right now; Kjersti had told him that if he would bring a pail, they could have
fresh meat for supper. Both boys immediately began pleading for permission to
go and see the animal; their mother scarcely answered; she gave them a pail and
asked them not to stay long.

The boys came running down the hill just as Kjersti was cutting up the
carcass; Tönseten was struggling with the hide, trying to stretch it on the barn
door; his mouth bristled with nails, his hands were bloody—he was a frightful
spectacle!

"What's that you've got?" asked Ole.

"Bear, my boy—bear!" . . . Tönseten wagged his head, took the nails out
of his mouth, and spat a gob of tobacco juice.

"Bear!" snorted Ole, scornfully.

"That's no bear!" put in Store-Hans, though less doubtingly.

"By George! boys, to-day he had to bite the dust!" . . .

"But there aren't any bears out here, I tell you!" Ole protested.

"Is that so—huh? . . . There isn't an animal living that you can't find out
here!" Tönseten spoke with such certainty that it was difficult for the boys to
gainsay him.

"Where did you get him?" Store-Hans asked.

"Out west of the Irish a little way. . . . There were two of 'em; they had
gone into the ground for the winter; this is the young one, you see—the old
mammy got away from me!"

"But you didn't have any gun!" was Ole's next objection.

"Better than that, my boy! . . . I went for him with the crowbar!" Tönseten
spat fiercely and looked at the boys. . . . "I smashed in his skull! . . . With that
old bar I'd tackle either a tiger or a rhinoceros!"

"What became of the old she-bear?" Ole asked, falling under the spell of
Tönseten's enthusiasm.

"She went north across the prairie, lickety-split! . . . Come here, now—take
some of these chunks of meat home with you. . . . This will make delicious stew,
let me tell you!"

18   "Is it fit to eat?" asked Store-Hans, still doubting.

19   "Fit to eat? No finer meat to be found than bear meat—don't you know that?"

20   The boys followed him over to where Kjersti was still cutting up the animal; it must have been a large carcass, for the cut meat made a sizable heap.

21   "Is it . . . is it really bear?" asked Ole, in a more humble tone.

22   "He's meaty enough for it! . . . Here, give me the pail; Beret needs some good, strengthening food. . . . Maybe you'll take a little to Sörrina, too; you can stop in with it on the way. . . . Careful—don't spill it, now!"

23   The boys loitered along on the way home; from time to time they had to put down the pail, in order to discuss this extraordinary event. . . . So there actually were bears slinking about this country! . . . If bears, there must be lions and tigers and other such wild beasts; this was worth while! . . . Suppose they were to go home and get Old Maria, hunt up the she-bear herself, and put a big bullet through her head? They thrilled with excitement. . . . "Do you dare to shoot her off?" Store-Hans demanded of his brother; Ole scowled ominously and clenched his fists. . . . "*I!* . . . I'd aim straight for her temple, and she'd drop deader than a herring!" . . . "Yes, aim at her *temple!*" Store-Hans advised soberly. "And if it's close range, you must draw the bead very fine!" . . . "Fine as a hair!" said Ole, excitedly.

24   They picked up the pail at last, and finally succeeded in reaching Sörine's, where there was another long delay; a detailed account had to be given of the marvellous feat which Tönseten had performed.

25   When they were about to leave Sofie came out and wanted to know if they weren't frightened; maybe the old mother bear was slinking about the prairie right now looking for her cub! The boys lingered to talk with her; they drew a glowing picture for the girl of how they were going home this minute to get Old Maria, and then go hunting for the she-bear herself . . . just watch them bring home a real roast pretty soon! . . . But weren't they scared? she asked. . . . "Scared?" exclaimed Store-Hans. . . . "Oh, fiddle-sticks!" cried Ole. "Only girls and old women get scared!"

26   Sofie only laughed; at which they affected a swaggering gruffness and tried to spit like Tönseten—but theirs wouldn't come brown. . . .

27   They were gone such a long time that their mother grew anxious; when they came over from Sörine's at last she stood outside the door watching for them. She had dressed And-Ongen, and was almost on the point of starting out to search; the boys were too preoccupied to notice this; Store-Hans spoke first:

28   "Just think, there's a big she-bear over there to the westward!" . . .

29   "We're going to take the gun and shoot her!" exclaimed Ole, gleefully.

30   "We'll aim straight for her temple!" Store-Hans assured his mother.

31   "Now we'll have plenty of bear meat!" continued Ole in the next breath, with absolute confidence.

32   The boys were all raging excitement; their mood frightened Beret still more; she grasped them frantically, one hand on the shoulder of each, and gave them

a hard shake. . . . They were to go inside this very minute, and take their books! They weren't going out of this house to-day! . . . "Go in, don't you hear me! . . . Go in!" . . .

. . . But this wasn't fair! Ole began reasoning with his mother; he used strong words, his eyes flaming. . . . Didn't she realize that there was a real bear over to the westward—a real full-grown *grizzly* bear! . . . Mother . . . please . . . *please!* . . . Dad wasn't home, but the gun was all loaded and ready; they could easily manage the rest of it! In an hour's time they would have that bear's hide! Store-Hans even thought that he could go straight to the lair. . . . *Right through the temple* they would put the bullet! . . . The boys carried on like a raging hurricane.

The mother had to use force to get them indoors. . . . "Go in, I say, and take your books! Can't you hear what I'm saying?" . . .

This was hard on them; they burst into the house like two mad bull calves; she had to repeat the order several times more before they finally submitted and began to hunt for their books. At last Ole snatched up the "Epitome," his brother the "Bible History." They sat down to read by the table in front of the window, in a state of mutinous rebellion.

Trouble soon arose. Each wanted the seat immediately in front of the window, where the most light fell; and neither would give up the position. A terrible battle broke out; Ole was the stronger, but his brother the quicker. On account of his age and size Ole considered himself the legitimate master of the house in the absence of his father, and therefore had the right to do anything; he now burst out with words which he had heard in the mouths of the men when something went wrong with their work. As soon as Store-Hans heard this he too began to use vile language; if Ole dared, he certainly did; he knew those words, and plenty more! . . . The boys kept up the scrimmage until they almost upset the table; their books suffered bad treatment and lay scattered about on the floor. And-Ongen watched them open-mouthed until she suddenly grew frightened and set up a howl.

Over by the stove the mother was washing the meat, putting it into a kettle which she had placed on the fire. . . . Although she heard every word, she kept on working in silence; but her face turned ashen grey.

When she had finished the task she went out hurriedly; in a moment she came back with a willow switch in her hand. Going straight over to the table, she began to lay about her with the switch; she seemed beside herself, struck out blindly, hit whatever she happened to aim at, and kept it up without saying a word. The switch whizzed and struck; shrieks of pain arose. The boys at once stopped fighting and gazed horror-stricken at their mother; they could not remember that she had ever laid a hand on them before. . . . And now there was such a strange, unnatural look in her eyes! . . .

They flew out on the floor to gather up their books, while the blows continued to rain down upon them; And-Ongen stood in the middle of the floor, screaming with terror. . . .

40   Not until the mother struck amiss, breaking the switch against the edge of the table, did she stop. . . . Suddenly she seemed to come to her senses; she left the child screaming in the middle of the floor, went out of the house, and was gone a long time. When she came back, she carried an armful of wood; she went over to the stove and fed the fire; then she picked up And-Ongen, and lay down on the bed with her. . . . The boys sat quietly at the table reading; neither of them had the courage to look up. . . .

41   The house seemed strangely still after the passage of the storm. Ole put his fingers into his ears to shut out the terrible silence; his brother began to read aloud. It was bad enough for Ole, but worse for Store-Hans; he now recalled clearly what his father had confided in him; he thought of his own solemn promise; here he had been away from the house nearly the whole day! He felt burning hot all over his body. . . . He had opened the book where it told about the choosing of the twelve disciples, and now he tried to read; but *that* wasn't the stuff for him just now! . . . He turned the pages forward to the story of Samson, and read it diligently; then to David and Goliath; then to the story about Joseph and his brethren. The last eased his heart somewhat. . . . Joseph was just the sort of boy that he longed to be!

42   Ole had felt ashamed at the sight of his mother bringing in the wood, though that was not his task; his brother was to be the hired girl! . . . Suddenly anger seized him; this time it certainly was the fault of Store-Hans—he should have given him the place! . . . He dragged himself through the *Third Article*, which he knew perfectly well already; when the tumult within him had somewhat subsided he sat there thinking of how shamefully Tönseten must have deceived them. . . . *He* kill a bear! It was nothing but a measly old badger! And now this nasty stuff was cooking on the stove—they were going to have it for supper! And mother was so angry that one would never dare to explain it to her! . . . There sat his younger brother, snuffling and reading his brains out; plain to be seen that he would never amount to anything! . . . Ole closed his book with a bang, got up, and went outdoors to chop more wood; but he did not dare to look at the bed as he passed. . . .

43   Store-Hans sat over his book until it grew so dark that he could no longer distinguish the letters. . . . From time to time he looked up; his mother lay on the bed perfectly still; he could not see her face; And-Ongen was fast asleep with her head high on the pillow. The boy rose quietly, looked around—then took an empty pail and went out for water. He left the pailful of water outside the door; then he brought Rosie and Injun and the two oxen into the stable, and tied them up for the night. He spoke loudly and gruffly to the animals; mother should hear that he was tending to business! . . . When he finally brought in the water his mother was up again; he could see nothing unusual about her.

44   . . . No, she hadn't been crying this time! The thought made Store-Hans so happy that he went straight to his brother, who was toiling over the chopping block as if possessed, and made friends with him again. The boys stayed outside

until it was pitch dark; they talked fast and nervously, about a multitude of things; but that which weighed most heavily on their hearts—the way their mother's face had looked when she whipped them—they could not mention.

Inside the house the lamp had been lit. And-Ongen toddled about the floor, busy over her own little affairs; the boys came in quietly and sat down to their books again; but very little reading was done now. . . . At last the kettle of meat that had been boiling on the stove was ready; the mother put the food on the table; the boys drew up, Ole somewhat reluctantly. . . . "You get that troll stuff down!" he whispered to his brother, making a wry face. To this command Store-Hans made no answer; he had stuck his spoon into a crack between the boards of the table; they were large, those cracks—he could see a broad section of floor when he laid his eye down close. The earthen floor had such a rich brown colour in the dim sheen of the lamp; the cracks in the table made stripes across the shadow down there; it looked pretty, too—and just then it had occurred to Store-Hans how nice it would be if they could only have the floor looking like that by daylight.

The mother filled the big bowl from the kettle and put it on the table; she had made a thick stew, with potatoes, carrots, and pieces of the meat; it looked appetizing enough but somehow the boys felt in no hurry to start. The mother came and sat down, bringing And-Ongen with her; the child was so delighted over the holiday fare they had to-night that she hurried to say grace.

She and the mother immediately began to eat; the boys no longer had an excuse to sit watching. Store-Hans dipped up a spoonful of stew, blew on it, closed his eyes, and gulped it down. Ole did the same, but coughed as if he had swallowed the wrong way; then he leaned under the table and spat it out. . . .

The mother asked quietly how they liked the supper. . . . At that, Ole could no longer restrain himself; he looked at his mother imploringly, and said in a tear-choked voice as he laid his spoon aside:

"It tastes like dog to me!"

To Store-Hans it seemed a shameful thing for Ole to speak that way of food which their mother had prepared for them; he swallowed spoonful after spoonful, while sweat poured from him.

"I have heard it said many times," the mother went on, quietly, "that bear meat is all right. . . . The stew has a tangy taste, I notice, but not so bad that it can't be eaten. . . . You'd better leave the meat if you don't like it."

"It isn't bear at all!" Ole blurted out.

"What?" cried the mother in alarm, lowering her spoon.

"It's only a lousy old badger! . . . I've heard dad say often that they aren't fit to eat!" . . .

"It's true, every word of it!" cried Store-Hans, suddenly feeling frightened and jamming his spoon farther down into the crack. . . . "I could tell it by his tail—Syvert had forgotten to cut it off! . . . Oh, I'm going to be sick—I can feel it coming!"

Beret got up, trembling in every limb; she took the bowl and carried it out

into the darkness; a long way from the house she emptied it on the ground;
And-Ongen cried and toddled after her. . . . The boys sat on the table glaring
reproachfully at each other; in the eyes of both blazed the same accusation:

57   "A nice mess you've made of things! Why didn't you keep your mouth
shut?"

58   The mother came in again; she set the empty kettle on the stove and scoured
it out carefully. . . .Then she cooked porridge for them, but when it was ready
she could eat nothing herself. . . .

59   . . . That night she hung still more clothes over the window than she had
the evening before. She sat up very late; it seemed as if she was unable to go to
bed.

VII

60   She had been lying awake a long time; sleep would not come. Her thoughts
drifted. . . .

61   . . . So it had come to this; they were no longer ashamed to eat troll food;
they even sent it from house to house, as lordly fare!

62   All night long as she tossed in bed, bitter revolt raged within her. *They
should not stay here through the winter!* . . . As soon as Per Hansa came home they
must start on the journey back east; he, too, ought to be able to see by this time
that they would all become wild beasts if they remained here much longer.
Everything human in them would gradually be blotted out. . . . They saw
nothing, learned nothing. . . . It would be even worse for their children—and
what of their children's children? . . . Couldn't he understand that if the Lord
God had intended these infinities to be peopled, He would not have left them
desolate down through all the ages . . . until now, when the end was near-
ing? . . .

63   After a while the bitterness of her revolt began to subside; her thoughts
became clear and shrewd, she tried to reason out the best way of getting back
to civilization. That night she did not sleep at all.

64   The next morning she got up earlier than usual, kindled the fire, got the
breakfast and waked the children. The food was soon prepared; first she poured
some water into the pot, put in a spoonful or two of molasses, and added a few
pieces of cinnamon; then she cut into bits the cold porridge from last night,
and put them into the big bowl; when the sweetened water was hot she poured
it over the porridge. . . . This was all they had—and no one asked for more.

65   While she ate she looked repeatedly at the big chest, trying to recall how
everything had been packed when they came out last summer. Where did she
keep all the things now? She had better get the packing done at once—then
that job would be out of the way when he came home. . . .

66   The greatest difficulty would be to obtain wagons. . . . Alas! those old
wagons! The smaller one he had taken apart and used in making the very table
around which they were now seated; as for the larger wagon, she knew only too

well that it would never hang together through the long journey back; only the other day she had heard Per Hansa mention that he intended to break it up, and see if he couldn't make something or other out of it. . . . Well—how to get the wagons would be his business! They certainly couldn't perish out here for want of a wagon or two! Was there not One who once upon a time had had mercy on a great city full of wicked people, only because one just human being interceded?

. . . One just human being. . . . Alas! . . . Beret sighed heavily and put her   67
hand up under her breast.

When there was no more porridge left in the bowl she rose, washed the   68
dish, and put it away on the shelf. Ole had nothing to do in the house that morning; he walked toward the door, motioning to his brother to follow; but Store-Hans shook his head. Then Ole went out; the other boy sat there looking at his mother, not knowing what to do, unhappy and heavy-hearted; he felt a sudden impulse to throw himself down on the floor and weep aloud.

The mother was pottering about at some trifles, her thoughts constantly   69
occupied with the idea of returning to civilization. Into her serious, grey-pale face, still soft and beautiful, had crept an expression of firmness and defiance; soon this aspect grew so marked that her face appeared to simulate anger, like that of one playing at being ferocious with a child.

As soon as she had finished her housework she went over to the big chest,   70
opened the lid, sank down on her knees beside it, and began to rearrange the contents. The task was quickly done; then she took the clothes from the last washing, folded them up, and laid them carefully in the chest; there weren't many clothes left now! He ought to realize that they would soon be naked if they stayed here much longer! And where were they to get money for everything they needed out here? . . . Beret stood up and looked around the room, trying to decide what to pack first. On the shelf above the window lay an old Bible, a gift to her from her grandfather; it was so old that it was hard to read now, because of the many changes the language had undergone since then; but it was the only one they had. This book had been in her family many generations; her great-grandfather had owned it before her grandfather; from her it should pass on to Store-Hans; thus she had always determined when she thought of the matter. On top of the Bible lay the hymn book, in which she had read a little every Sunday since their arrival here. . . .

She put both books in the chest.   71

Again Beret rose and glanced around the room. Perhaps she had better take   72
the school books, too; the boys were none too eager to use them; they might as well be excused for the rest of the day; either that day or the next the father would surely come. . . . She asked Store-Hans to bring the books to her so that she could pack them.

Not until then did the boy fully take in what his mother was doing; it   73
startled him so that for a moment he could not get up.

"Mother, what are you doing?" . . .   74

75   "We must begin to get ready!" . . . She sighed, and pressed her hands tightly under her burden; it was painful to her, stooping over so long at a time.

76   "Get ready? Are . . . are we going *away*?" . . . Store-Hans's throat contracted; his eyes stared big and terror-stricken at his mother.

77   "Why, yes, Hansy-boy—we had better be going back where people live before the winter is upon us," she told him, sadly.

78   The boy had risen, and now stood at the end of the table; he wanted to go to his mother but fear chained him to the spot; he stared at her with his mouth wide open. At last he got out:

79   "What will dad say?" . . . The words came accusingly but there were tears in them.

80   She looked at him like one in a dream; again she looked, but could not utter a word. . . . The sheer impossibility of what she was about to do was written as if in fire on the face and whole body of the boy—as if in rays that struck her, lighted everything up with an awful radiance, and revealed the utter futility of it all. . . . She turned slowly toward the chest, let down the lid, and sank on it in untold weariness. . . . Again the child stirred within her, kicking and twisting, so that she had to press her hand hard against it.

81   . . . O God! . . . now *he* was protesting, too! Was it only by ruthless sacrifice of life that this endless desolation could ever be peopled?

82   . . . "Thou canst not be so cruel!" she moaned. . . . "Demand not this awful sacrifice of a frail human being!" . . .

83   She rose slowly from the chest; as she walked across the floor and opened the door she felt as if she were dragging leaden weights. . . . Her gaze flitted fearfully toward the sky line—reached it, but dared not travel upward. . . .

84   Store-Hans remained at the end of the table, staring after her; he wanted to scream, but could not utter a sound. Then he ran to her, put his arms around her, and whispered hoarsely between sobs:

85   "Mother, are you . . . are you . . . getting sick now?"

86   Beret stroked the head that was pressed so hard against her side; it had such a vigorous, healthy warmth, the hair was soft and pleasant to the touch; she had to run her fingers through it repeatedly. . . . Then she stooped over and put her arm around the boy; his response to her embrace was so violent that it almost choked her. . . . O God! how sorely she needed some one to be kind to her now! . . . She was weeping; Store-Hans, too, was struggling with wild, tearing sobs. Little And-Ongen, who could not imagine what the two were doing over there by the door, came toddling to them and gazed up into their faces; then she opened her mouth wide, brought her hand up to it, and shrieked aloud. . . . At that moment Ole came running down the hill, his feet flying against the sky, and shouted out to them:

87   "They are coming! . . . Get the coffee on!"

88   . . .Gone was the boy like a gust of wind; he threw himself on the pony and galloped away to meet the returning caravan.

89   Beret and Store-Hans had both sprung to their feet and stood looking across

the prairie. . . . Yes, there they were, away off to the southeast! . . . And now Store-Hans, also, forgot himself; he glanced imploringly into his mother's face, his eyes eagerly questioning:

"Would it be safe to leave you while I run to meet dad?" 90

She smiled down into the eager face—a benign, spreading smile. 91

"Don't worry about me. . . . Just run along." . . . 92

VIII

The father sat at the table eating, with And-Ongen on his knee, the boys stood 93 opposite him, listening enthusiastically to the story of his adventures along the way; the mother went to and fro between the stove and the table. There was an enchanting joyousness about Per Hansa to-day which coloured all he said; no matter how much he told, it always sounded as if he were keeping back the best till later on. This had a positively intoxicating effect on the boys; it made them impatient and eager for more, and caused a steady flood of fresh questions.

Even Beret was smiling, though her hand trembled. 94

At last the boys had to give an account of how they had managed affairs at 95 home. When, after much teasing and banter, Per Hansa had finally heard the whole absurd story—it came little by little, in disjointed outbursts—of Tönseten and the bear, and their ill-starred badger stew of the night before, he laughed until the tears came and he had to stop eating. His mirth was so free and hearty that the boys, too, began to see the real fun of the incident, and joined in boisterously. Beret stood over by the stove, listening to it all; their infectious merriment carried her away, but at the same time she had to wipe her eyes. . . . She was glad that she had remembered to take out of the chest the things that she had begun to pack awhile before!

"Come here, Store-Hans," said the father, still laughing. "What's that across 96 the back of your neck?"

The question caught the boy unawares; he ran over and stood beside his 97 father.

"Why, it's a big red welt! . . . Have you been trying to hang yourself, boy?" 98

Store-Hans turned crimson; he suddenly remembered the fearful blows of 99 last night.

Ole glanced quickly at his mother. . . . "Oh, pshaw!" he said with a manly 100 air. . . . "That was only Hans and me fighting!"

"Ah-ha!" exclaimed the father, with another laugh. "So that's the way you 101 two have been acting while I was away? Mother couldn't manage you, eh? . . . Well, now you'll soon be dancing to a different tune; we've got so much work on our hands that there won't be any peace here day or night. . . . Thanks for good food, Beret-girl!"

He got up, took the boys with him, and began to carry things in from the 102 wagon. Most of the load they stored away in the house; some extra things, however, had to find a temporary place in the stable.

103   At length Per Hansa brought in a small armful of bottles and set them on the table.

104   "Come here, Beret-girl of mine! You have earned a good drink, and a good drink you shall have!" . . . . He went over to the water pail with the coffee cup from which he had just been drinking, rinsed it out with a little water, and emptied it on the floor; then he poured out a good half cupful of whisky and offered it to her. She put out her hand as if to push him away. . . . . Yes, indeed, she would have to take it, he told her, putting his arm around her waist and lifting the cup to her lips. She took the cup and emptied it in one draught. . . . . "There, that's a good little wife! . . . . You're going to have just another little drop!" He went to the table again and poured out a second drink, but not so much this time. "Two legs, and one for each! Just drink it down! . . . And now you take care of the bottles!"

105   That was a busy day in the humble dwelling of Per Hansa. First of all, he had promised a load of potatoes to the Hallings, who waited back east somewhere under a bleak sky, without even a potato peeling to put in their pot; he must carry food to them. When Beret heard how poorly things were in that hut—about the woman with the drawn cheeks and the starved look in her eyes—she straightway began to hurry him up; he must go while he had the horses and wagon here. Couldn't he get started to-day?

106   "Not so hasty there, my girl, not so hasty!" laughed Per Hansa, his face beaming. . . . . "I'm not going to sleep with any *Halling woman* to-night—that I can tell you!"

107   Now he was his old irresistible self again. How strong, how precious to her, he seemed! . . . She felt a loving impulse to grasp his hair and shake him. . . .

108   Ole was immediately put to work knitting the net. The father had already knitted four fathoms of it, by the light of the camp fire the night before; he had sat up working over the net long after the others had turned in. . . . The boys grew wild with enthusiasm at the sight of the net; were they going fishing in the Sioux River? Both of them immediately began begging to be taken along. . . . "Just keep your fingers moving, Olamand—hurry them up, I tell you!" . . . The father made a great mystery of it, and refused to give any further explanation.

109   As for himself and Store-Hans, they busied themselves over the lime; it was all carried inside and placed in a corner where no moisture could reach it. The preparations for the mixing required a good deal of work; the first thing was to make a wooden box sufficiently tight to hold water. Well, there was plenty of lumber now, at any rate! Per Hansa built the box and carried it down to the creek; there he placed it under water, hoping that it would swell enough to be tight by the time he needed it.

110   Evening fell all too soon on a wonderfully busy and joyful day. The boys were at last in bed, fast asleep.

But Per Hansa had no time for rest; to-night that net simply had to be 111 finished. He finally made Beret go to bed, but she wasn't a bit sleepy; she lay there talking to him and filling the shuttles whenever they were empty. He explained fully to her how he intended to use the net; first he would set it in the Sioux River as he passed by there to-morrow; he knew of just the place; he would leave it there until he came back from the Hallings'. Unless the cards were stacked against him he would bring back a nice mess of fish. . . . That, however, wasn't his great plan with the net, he told her; but she mustn't say a word about this to the boys. It was to be a big surprise for them; they were such brave fellows! The fact of the matter was, he planned to catch *ducks* with that net; that had been the real reason for his buying the twine; there would be other fare than badger stew in this hut, he would just let her know, if the weather only held a few days more!

All at once it occurred to Beret that she had forgotten to cover up the 112 windows to-night; she smiled to herself at the discovery. . . . What was the need of it, anyway? Cover the windows . . . what nonsense! . . . She smiled again, feeling a languorous drowsiness creep over her.

Per Hansa knit away on the net, chatting happily with her as he worked; a 113 confident ring of joy sounded in all he said. He had fastened the net to the bedpost, just as her father always had done. She listened peacefully to his warm, cheerful voice, which after a while began to sound more distant, like the indolent swish and gurgle of lapping ocean waves on a fair summer's night. Gradually she was borne away on this sound, and slept the whole night through without stirring.

When she awoke next morning Per Hansa, still fully dressed, lay beside 114 her, over against the wall; he evidently had thrown himself down to rest only a little while before. Light was creeping into the room; directly in front of the bed lay a big white heap of something. . . . Those careless boys—had they thrown their clothes on the floor again? . . . She stooped over to pick the clothes up and put them on the bench; she grasped hold of the heap—and it was a new net, sheeted and fully rigged, as a new net ought to be!

. . . Poor man!—he must have sat up all night! . . . She spread the quilt 115 carefully over him.

That morning Beret took some of the precious white flour and made a batch 116 of pancakes. He deserved to have one good meal before he went away again!

He left right after breakfast. Beret worked industriously throughout the day, 117 while many thoughts came and went. . . . It must be her destiny, this! There was One who governed all things. . . . He knew what was best, and against His will it was useless to struggle! . . .

. . . Often that day she went to the window to look eastward. Every time 118 she looked, it seemed to be growing darker over there. . . .

. . . That evening she again covered the window. . . . ✠ 119

RESPONDING

1. Analyze Beret's response to the boys' fight. What pressures produced her reaction? What was she thinking and feeling when she "left the child screaming in the middle of the floor, went out of the house, and was gone a long time" (paragraph 40)? Imagine that your journal is Beret's diary and write an entry about the event.

2. Working in two groups, discuss the behaviors and duties Ole and Store-Hans expect from women and men. One group should list these behaviors for women; the other should do the same for men. Put the lists on the board. Discuss the gender roles the children have internalized. Are they the same for men and women?

3. Write an essay comparing Beret's and Per Hansa's attitudes to life in the wilderness. How do you explain the differences? Some factors to consider are personal temperament, gender, upbringing, activities, responsibilities, ambitions, and expectations for the future.

4. Beret has great difficulty with life on the prairie. Using your own knowledge, describe the pioneer heroine so often portrayed in stories and film. In an essay, compare her character and behavior with Beret's. What might account for the differences between Beret and the pioneer heroine?

ANZIA YEZIERSKA

Anzia Yezierska was born in Poland in 1885, the daughter of a Talmudic scholar. Her family immigrated to the United States during the 1890s. After attending night school, she graduated from the Teachers College of Columbia University in 1904. Her publications include The Free Vacation House *(1915),* "The Fat of the Land" *(1919),* Salome of the Tenements *(1922),* Children of Loneliness *(1923),* The Bread Givers *(1925),* The Arrogant Beggar *(1927),* All I Could Never Be *(1932), and* The Red Ribbon on a White Horse *(1950).* "The Fat of the Land" *was awarded the O. Henry Prize for the best story of 1919; Yezierska's other literary prizes included the 1929–1930 Zora Gale Fellowship at the University of Wisconsin and two awards from the National Institute of Arts and Letters (1962 and 1965).*

In the early part of Yezierska's career, her work enjoyed great popularity. She was friendly with many of the leading intellectuals of the day, including the philosopher John Dewey. In 1918 she was invited to Hollywood by film producer Sam Goldwyn to adapt one of her stories for the screen. Later in her life Yezierska had more difficulty getting her work published. She died in 1970.

Many of Yezierska's works explore elements of the immigrant experience. The selection that follows depicts the life of an immigrant from two perspectives—during the period just after she settles in this country and twenty-five years later—and invites us to compare the quality of her life and her assessment of her place in the world from those perspectives. The story also raises interesting questions about the expectations placed on immigrant parents by their children.

⁜

THE FAT OF THE LAND

IN AN AIR-SHAFT so narrow that you could touch the next wall with your bare hands, Hanneh Breineh leaned out and knocked on her neighbor's window.   1

"Can you loan me your wash-boiler for the clothes?" she called.   2

Mrs. Pelz threw up the sash.   3

"The boiler? What's the matter with yours again? Didn't you tell me you had it fixed already last week?"   4

"A black year on him, the robber, the way he fixed it! If you have no luck in this world, then it's better not to live. There I spent out fifteen cents to stop up one hole, and it runs out another. How I ate out my gall bargaining with   5 him he should let it down to fifteen cents! He wanted yet a quarter, the swindler. Gottuniu! My bitter heart on him for every penny he took from me for nothing!"

6   "You got to watch all those swindlers, or they'll steal the whites out of your eyes," admonished Mrs. Pelz. "You should have tried out your boiler before you paid him. Wait a minute till I empty out my dirty clothes in a pillow-case; then I'll hand it to you."

7   Mrs. Pelz returned with the boiler and tried to hand it across to Hanneh Breineh, but the soap-box refrigerator on the window-sill was in the way.

8   "You got to come in for the boiler yourself," said Mrs. Pelz.

9   "Wait only till I tie my Sammy on to the high-chair he shouldn't fall on me again. He's so wild that ropes won't hold him."

10 Hanneh Breineh tied the child in the chair, stuck a pacifier in his mouth, and went in to her neighbor. As she took the boiler Mrs. Pelz said:

11 "Do you know Mrs. Melker ordered fifty pounds of chicken for her daughter's wedding? And such grand chickens! Shining like gold! My heart melted in me just looking at the flowing fatness of those chickens."

12 Hanneh Breineh smacked her thin, dry lips, a hungry gleam in her sunken eyes.

13 "Fifty pounds!" she gasped. "It ain't possible. How do you know?"

14 "I heard her with my own ears. I saw them with my own eyes. And she said she will chop up the chicken livers with onions and eggs for an appetizer, and then she will buy twenty-five pounds of fish, and cook it sweet and sour with raisins, and she said she will bake all her shtrudels on pure chicken fat."

15 "Some people work themselves up in the world," sighed Hanneh Breineh. "For them is America flowing with milk and honey. In Savel Mrs. Melker used to get shriveled up from hunger. She and her children used to live on potato-peelings and crusts of dry bread picked out from the barrels; and in America she lives to eat chicken, and apple shtrudels soaking in fat."

16 "The world is a wheel always turning," philosophized Mrs. Pelz. "Those who were high go down low, and those who've been low go up higher. Who will believe me here in America that in Poland I was a cook in a banker's house? I handled ducks and geese every day. I used to bake coffee-cake with cream so thick you could cut it with a knife."

17 "And do you think I was a nobody in Poland?" broke in Hanneh Breineh, tears welling in her eyes as the memories of her past rushed over her. "But what's the use of talking? In America money is everything. Who cares who my father or grandfather was in Poland? Without money I'm a living dead one. My head dries out worrying how to get for the children the eating a penny cheaper."

18 Mrs. Pelz wagged her head, a gnawing envy contracting her features.

19 "Mrs. Melker had it good from the day she came," she said, begrudgingly. "Right away she sent all her children to the factory, and she began to cook meat

for dinner every day. She and her children have eggs and buttered rolls for breakfast each morning like millionaires."

A sudden fall and a baby's scream, and the boiler dropped from Hanneh   20
Breineh's hands as she rushed into her kitchen, Mrs. Pelz after her. They found the high-chair turned on top of the baby.

"Gewalt! Save me! Run for a doctor!" cried Hanneh Breineh, as she dragged   21
the child from under the high-chair. "He's killed! He's killed! My only child! My precious lamb!" she shrieked as she ran back and forth with the screaming infant.

Mrs. Pelz snatched little Sammy from the mother's hands.   22

"Meshugneh! What are you running around like a crazy, frightening the   23
child? Let me see. Let me tend to him. He ain't killed yet." She hastened to the sink to wash the child's face, and discovered a swelling lump on his forehead. "Have you a quarter in your house?" she asked.

"Yes, I got one," replied Hanneh Breineh, climbing on a chair. "I got to   24
keep it on a high shelf where the children can't get it."

Mrs. Pelz seized the quarter Hanneh Breineh handed down to her.   25

"Now pull your left eyelid three times while I'm pressing the quarter, and   26
you'll see the swelling go down."

Hanneh Breineh took the child again in her arms, shaking and cooing over   27
it and caressing it.

"Ah-ah-ah, Sammy! Ah-ah-ah-ah, little lamb! Ah-ah-ah, little bird! Ah-ah-   28
ah-ah, precious heart! Oh, you saved my life; I thought he was killed," gasped Hanneh Breineh, turning to Mrs. Pelz. "Oi-i!" she sighed, "a mother's heart! Always in fear over her children. The minute anything happens to them all life goes out of me. I lose my head and I don't know where I am any more."

"No wonder the child fell," admonished Mrs. Pelz. "You should have a red   29
ribbon or red beads on his neck to keep away the evil eye. Wait. I got something in my machine-drawer."

Mrs. Pelz returned, bringing the boiler and a red string, which she tied   30
about the child's neck while the mother proceeded to fill the boiler.

A little later Hanneh Breineh again came into Mrs. Pelz's kitchen, holding   31
Sammy in one arm and in the other an apronful of potatoes. Putting the child down on the floor, she seated herself on the unmade kitchen-bed and began to peel the potatoes in her apron.

"Woe to me!" sobbed Hanneh Breineh. "To my bitter luck there ain't no   32
end. With all my other troubles, the stove got broke. I lighted the fire to boil the clothes, and it's to get choked with smoke. I paid rent only a week ago, and the agent don't want to fix it. A thunder should strike him! He only comes for the rent, and if anything has to be fixed, then he don't want to hear nothing."

"Why comes it to me so hard?" went on Hanneh Breineh, the tears   33
streaming down her cheeks. "I can't stand it no more. I came into you for a minute to run away from my troubles. It's only when I sit myself down to peel

potatoes or nurse the baby that I take time to draw a breath, and beg only for death."

34 Mrs. Pelz, accustomed to Hanneh Breineh's bitter outbursts, continued her scrubbing.

35 "Ut!" exclaimed Hanneh Breineh, irritated at her neighbor's silence, "what are you tearing up the world with your cleaning? What's the use to clean up when everything only gets dirty again?"

36 "I got to shine up my house for the holidays."

37 "You've got it so good nothing lays on your mind but to clean your house. Look on this little blood-sucker," said Hanneh Breineh, pointing to the wizened child, made prematurely solemn from starvation and neglect. "Could anybody keep that brat clean? I wash him one minute, and he is dirty the minute after." Little Sammy grew frightened and began to cry. "Shut up!" ordered the mother, picking up the child to nurse it again. "Can't you see me take a rest for a minute?"

38 The hungry child began to cry at the top of its weakened lungs.

39 "Na, na, you glutton." Hanneh Breineh took out a dirty pacifier from her pocket and stuffed it into the baby's mouth. The grave, pasty-faced infant shrank into a panic of fear, and chewed the nipple nervously, clinging to it with both his thin little hands.

40 "For what did I need yet the sixth one?" groaned Hanneh Breineh, turning to Mrs. Pelz. "Wasn't it enough five mouths to feed? If I didn't have this child on my neck, I could turn myself around and earn a few cents." She wrung her hands in a passion of despair. "Gottuniu! The earth should only take it before it grows up!"

41 "Shah! Shah!" reproved Mrs. Pelz. "Pity yourself on the child. Let it grow up already so long as it is here. See how frightened it looks on you." Mrs. Pelz took the child in her arms and petted it. "The poor little lamb! What did it done you should hate it so?"

42 Hanneh Breineh pushed Mrs. Pelz away from her.

43 "To whom can I open the wounds of my heart?" she moaned. "Nobody has pity on me. You don't believe me, nobody believes me until I'll fall down like a horse in the middle of the street. Oi weh! Mine life is so black for my eyes! Some mothers got luck. A child gets run over by a car, some fall from a window, some burn themselves up with a match, some get choked with diphtheria; but no death takes mine away."

44 "God from the world, stop cursing!" admonished Mrs. Pelz. "What do you want from the poor children? Is it their fault that their father makes small wages? Why do you let it all out on them?" Mrs. Pelz sat down beside Hanneh Breineh. "Wait only till your children get old enough to go to the shop and earn money," she consoled. "Push only through those few years while they are yet small; your sun will begin to shine; you will live on the fat of the land, when they begin to bring you in the wages each week."

45 Hanneh Breineh refused to be comforted.

"Till they are old enough to go to the shop and earn money they'll eat the 46
head off my bones," she wailed. "If you only knew the fights I got by each meal.
Maybe I gave Abe a bigger piece of bread than Fanny. Maybe Fanny got a little
more soup in her plate than Jake. Eating is dearer than diamonds. Potatoes went
up a cent on a pound, and milk is only for millionaires. And once a week, when
I buy a little meat for the Sabbath, the butcher weighs it for me like gold, with
all the bones in it. When I come to lay the meat out on a plate and divide it
up, there ain't nothing to it but bones. Before, he used to throw me in a piece
of fat extra or a piece of lung, but now you got to pay for everything, even for
a bone to the soup."

"Never mind; you'll yet come out from all your troubles. Just as soon as 47
your children get old enough to get their working papers the more children
you got, the more money you'll have."

"Why should I fool myself with the false shine of hope? Don't I know it's 48
already my black luck not to have it good in this world? Do you think American
children will right away give everything they earn to their mother?"

"I know what is with you the matter," said Mrs. Pelz. "You didn't eat yet 49
to-day. When it is empty in the stomach, the whole world looks black. Come,
only let me give you something good to taste in the mouth; that will freshen
you up." Mrs. Pelz went to the cupboard and brought out the saucepan of gefülte
fish that she had cooked for dinner and placed it on the table in front of Hanneh
Breineh. "Give a taste my fish," she said, taking one slice on a spoon, and
handing it to Hanneh Breineh with a piece of bread. "I wouldn't give it to you
on a plate because I just cleaned up my house, and I don't want to dirty up
more dishes."

"What, am I stranger you should have to serve me on a plate yet!" cried 50
Hanneh Breineh, snatching the fish in her trembling fingers.

"Oi weh! How it melts through all the bones!" she exclaimed, brightening 51
as she ate. "May it be for good luck to us all!" she exulted, waving aloft the last
precious bite.

Mrs. Pelz was so flattered that she even ladled up a spoonful of gravy. 52

"There is a bit of onion and carrot in it," she said, as she handed it to her 53
neighbor.

Hanneh Breineh sipped the gravy drop by drop, like a connoisseur sipping 54
wine.

"Ah-h-h! A taste of that gravy lifts me up to heaven!" As she disposed 55
leisurely of the slice of onion and carrot she relaxed and expanded and even
grew jovial. "Let us wish all our troubles on the Russian Czar! Let him burst
with our worries for rent! Let him get shriveled with our hunger for bread! Let
his eyes dry out of his head looking for work!"

"Shah! I'm forgetting from everything," she exclaimed, jumping up. "It 56
must be eleven or soon twelve, and my children will be right away out of school
and fall on me like a pack of wild wolves. I better quick run to the market and
see what cheaper I can get for a quarter."

57   Because of the lateness of her coming, the stale bread at the nearest bakeshop was sold out, and Hanneh Breineh had to trudge from shop to shop in search of the usual bargain, and spent nearly an hour to save two cents.

58   In the meantime the children returned from school, and, finding the door locked, climbed through the fire-escape, and entered the house through the window. Seeing nothing on the table, they rushed to the stove. Abe pulled a steaming potato out of the boiling pot, and so scalded his fingers that the potato fell to the floor; whereupon the three others pounced on it.

59   "It was my potato," cried Abe, blowing his burned fingers, while with the other hand and his foot he cuffed and kicked the three who were struggling on the floor. A wild fight ensued, and the potato was smashed under Abe's foot amid shouts and screams. Hanneh Breineh, on the stairs, heard the noise of her famished brood, and topped their cries with curses and invectives.

60   "They are here already, the savages! They are here already to shorten my life! They heard you all over the hall, in all the houses around!"

61   The children, disregarding her words, pounced on her market-basket, shouting ravenously: "Mamma, I'm hungry! What more do you got to eat?"

62   They tore the bread and herring out of Hanneh Breineh's basket and devoured it in starved savagery, clamoring for more.

63   "Murderers!" screamed Hanneh Breineh, goaded beyond endurance. "What are you tearing from me my flesh? From where should I steal to give you more? Here I had already a pot of potatoes and a whole loaf of bread and two herrings, and you swallowed it down in the wink of an eye. I have to have Rockefeller's millions to fill your stomachs."

64   All at once Hanneh Breineh became aware that Benny was missing. "Oi weh!" she burst out, wringing her hands in a new wave of woe, "where is Benny? Didn't he come home yet from school?"

65   She ran out into the hall, opened the grime-coated window, and looked up and down the street; but Benny was nowhere in sight.

66   "Abe, Jake, Fanny, quick, find Benny!" entreated Hanneh Breineh, as she rushed back into the kitchen. But the children, anxious to snatch a few minutes' play before the school-call, dodged past her and hurried out.

67   With the baby on her arm, Hanneh Breineh hastened to the kindergarten.

68   "Why are you keeping Benny here so long?" she shouted at the teacher as she flung open the door. "If you had my bitter heart, you would send him home long ago and not wait until I got to come for him."

69   The teacher turned calmly and consulted her record-cards.

70   "Benny Safron? He wasn't present this morning."

71   "Not here?" shrieked Hanneh Breineh. "I pushed him out myself he should go. The children didn't want to take him, and I had no time. Woe is me! Where is my child?" She began pulling her hair and beating her breast as she ran into the street.

72   Mrs. Pelz was busy at a pushcart, picking over some spotted apples, when

she heard the clamor of an approaching crowd. A block off she recognized Hanneh Breineh, her hair disheveled, her clothes awry, running toward her with her yelling baby in her arms, the crowd following.

"Friend mine," cried Hanneh Breineh, falling on Mrs. Pelz's neck, "I lost   73
my Benny, the best child of all my children." Tears streamed down her red, swollen eyes as she sobbed. "Benny! mine heart, mine life! Oi-i-i!"

Mrs. Pelz took the frightened baby out of the mother's arms.   74

"Still yourself a little! See how you're frightening your child."   75

"Woe to me! Where is my Benny? Maybe he's killed already by a car. Maybe   76
he fainted away from hunger. He didn't eat nothing all day long. Gottuniu! Pity yourself on me!"

She lifted her hands full of tragic entreaty.   77

"People, my child! Get me my child! I'll go crazy out of my head! Get me   78
my child, or I'll take poison before your eyes!"

"Still yourself a little!" pleaded Mrs. Pelz.   79

"Talk not to me!" cried Hanneh Breineh, wringing her hands. "You're   80
having all your children. I lost mine. Every good luck comes to other people. But I didn't live yet to see a good day in my life. Mine only joy, mine Benny, is lost away from me."

The crowd followed Hanneh Breineh as she wailed through the streets,   81
leaning on Mrs. Pelz. By the time she returned to her house the children were back from school; but seeing that Benny was not there, she chased them out in the street, crying:

"Out of here, you robbers, gluttons! Go find Benny!" Hanneh Breineh   82
crumpled into a chair in utter prostration. "Oi weh! he's lost! Mine life; my little bird; mine only joy! How many nights I spent nursing him when he had the measles! And all that I suffered for weeks and months when he had the whooping-cough! How the eyes went out of my head till I learned him how to walk, till I learned him how to talk! And such a smart child! If I lost all the others, it wouldn't tear me so by the heart."

She worked herself up into such a hysteria, crying, and tearing her hair,   83
and hitting her head with her knuckles, that at last she fell into a faint. It took some time before Mrs. Pelz, with the aid of neighbors, revived her.

"Benny, mine angel!" she moaned as she opened her eyes.   84

Just then a policeman came in with the lost Benny.   85

"Na, na, here you got him already!" said Mrs. Pelz. "Why did you carry   86
on so for nothing? Why did you tear up the world like a crazy?"

The child's face was streaked with tears as he cowered, frightened and   87
forlorn. Hanneh Breineh sprang toward him, slapping his cheeks, boxing his ears, before the neighbors could rescue him from her.

"Woe on your head!" cried the mother. "Where did you lost yourself? Ain't   88
I got enough worries on my head than to go around looking for you? I didn't have yet a minute's peace from that child since he was born!"

89   "See a crazy mother!" remonstrated Mrs. Pelz, rescuing Benny from another beating. "Such a mouth! With one breath she blesses him when he is lost, and with the other breath she curses him when he is found."

90   Hanneh Breineh took from the window-sill a piece of herring covered with swarming flies, and putting it on a slice of dry bread, she filled a cup of tea that had been stewing all day, and dragged Benny over to the table to eat.

91   But the child, choking with tears, was unable to touch the food.

92   "Go eat!" commanded Hanneh Breineh. "Eat and choke yourself eating!"

93   "Maybe she won't remember me no more. Maybe the servant won't let me in," thought Mrs. Pelz, as she walked by the brownstone house on Eighty-Fourth Street where she had been told Hanneh Breineh now lived. At last she summoned up enough courage to climb the steps. She was all out of breath as she rang the bell with trembling fingers. "Oi weh! even the outside smells riches and plenty! Such curtains! And shades on all windows like by millionaires! Twenty years ago she used to eat from the pot to the hand, and now she lives in such a palace."

94   A whiff of steam-heated warmth swept over Mrs. Pelz as the door opened, and she saw her old friend of the tenements dressed in silk and diamonds like a being from another world.

95   "Mrs. Pelz, is it you!" cried Hanneh Breineh, overjoyed at the sight of her former neighbor. "Come right in. Since when are you back in New York?"

96   "We came last week," mumbled Mrs. Pelz, as she was led into a richly carpeted reception-room.

97   "Make yourself comfortable. Take off your shawl," urged Hanneh Breineh.

98   But Mrs. Pelz only drew her shawl more tightly around her, a keen sense of her poverty gripping her as she gazed, abashed by the luxurious wealth that shone from every corner.

99   "This shawl covers up my rags," she said, trying to hide her shabby sweater.

100   "I'll tell you what; come right into the kitchen," suggested Hanneh Breineh. "The servant is away for this afternoon, and we can feel more comfortable there. I can breathe like a free person in my kitchen when the girl has her day out."

101   Mrs. Pelz glanced about her in an excited daze. Never in her life had she seen anything so wonderful as a white-tiled kitchen, with its glistening porcelain sink and the aluminum pots and pans that shone like silver.

102   "Where are you staying now?" asked Hanneh Breineh, as she pinned an apron over her silk dress.

103   "I moved back to Delancey Street, where we used to live," replied Mrs. Pelz, as she seated herself cautiously in a white enameled chair.

104   "Oi weh! What grand times we had in that old house when we were neighbors!" sighed Hanneh Breineh, looking at her old friend with misty eyes.

105   "You still think on Delancey Street? Haven't you more high-class neighbors uptown here?"

106   "A good neighbor is not to be found every day," deplored Hanneh Breineh.

"Uptown here, where each lives in his own house, nobody cares if the person next door is dying or going crazy from loneliness. It ain't anything like we used to have it in Delancey Street, when we could walk into one another's rooms without knocking, and borrow a pinch of salt or a pot to cook in."

Hanneh Breineh went over to the pantry-shelf. 107

"We are going to have a bite right here on the kitchen-table like on 108
Delancey Street. So long there's no servant to watch us we can eat what we please."

"Oi! How it waters my mouth with appetite, the smell of the herring and 109
onion!" chuckled Mrs. Pelz, sniffing the welcome odors with greedy pleasure.

Hanneh Breineh pulled a dish-towel from the rack and threw one end of 110
it to Mrs. Pelz.

"So long as there's no servant around, we can use it together for a napkin. 111
It's dirty, anyhow. How it freshens up my heart to see you!" she rejoiced as she poured out her tea into a saucer. "If you would only know how I used to beg my daughter to write for me a letter to you; but these American children, what is to them a mother's feelings?"

"What are you talking!" cried Mrs. Pelz. "The whole world rings with you 112
and your children. Everybody is envying you. Tell me how began your luck?"

"You heard how my husband died with consumption," replied Hanneh 113
Breineh. "The five hundred dollars lodge money gave me the first lift in life, and I opened a little grocery store. Then my son Abe married himself to a girl with a thousand dollars. That started him in business, and now he has the biggest shirt-waist factory on West Twenty-Ninth Street."

"Yes, I heard your son had a factory." Mrs. Pelz hesitated and stammered; 114
"I'll tell you the truth. What I came to ask you—I thought maybe you would beg your son Abe if he would give my husband a job."

"Why not?" said Hanneh Breineh. "He keeps more than five hundred 115
hands. I'll ask him if he should take in Mr. Pelz."

"Long years on you, Hanneh Breineh! You'll save my life if you could only 116
help my husband get work."

"Of course my son will help him. All my children like to do good. My 117
daughter Fanny is a milliner on Fifth Avenue, and she takes in the poorest girls in her shop and even pays them sometimes while they learn the trade." Hanneh Breineh's face lit up, and her chest filled with pride as she enumerated the successes of her children. "And my son Benny he wrote a play on Broadway and he gave away more than a hundred free tickets for the first night."

"Benny! The one who used to get lost from home all the time? You always 118
did love that child more than all the rest. And what is Sammy your baby doing?"

"He ain't a baby no longer. He goes to college and quarterbacks the football 119
team. They can't get along without him.

"And my son Jake, I nearly forgot him. He began collecting rent in 120
Delancey Street, and now he is boss of renting the swellest apartment-houses on Riverside Drive."

121   "What did I tell you? In America children are like money in the bank," purred Mrs. Pelz, as she pinched and patted Hanneh Breineh's silk sleeve. "Oi weh! How it shines from you! You ought to kiss the air and dance for joy and happiness. It is such a bitter frost outside; a pail of coal is so dear, and you got it so warm with steam heat. I had to pawn my feather bed to have enough for the rent, and you are rolling in money."

122   "Yes, I got it good in some ways, but money ain't everything," sighed Hanneh Breineh.

123   "You ain't yet satisfied?"

124   "But here I got no friends," complained Hanneh Breineh.

125   "Friends?" queried Mrs. Pelz. "What greater friend is there on earth than the dollar?"

126   "Oi! Mrs. Pelz; if you could only look into my heart! I'm so choked up! You know they say a cow has a long tongue, but can't talk." Hanneh Breineh shook her head wistfully, and her eyes filmed with inward brooding. "My children give me everything from the best. When I was sick, they got me a nurse by day and one by night. They bought me the best wine. If I asked for dove's milk, they would buy it for me; but—but—I can't talk myself out in their language. They want to make me over for an American lady, and I'm different." Tears cut their way under her eyelids with a pricking pain as she went on: "When I was poor, I was free, and could holler and do what I like in my own house. Here I got to lie still like a mouse under a broom. Between living up to my Fifth-Avenue daughter and keeping up with the servants, I am like a sinner in the next world that is thrown from one hell to another." The doorbell rang, and Hanneh Breineh jumped up with a start.

127   "Oi weh! It must be the servant back already!" she exclaimed, as she tore off her apron. "Oi weh! Let's quickly put the dishes together in a dish-pan. If she sees I eat on the kitchen table, she will look on me like the dirt under her feet."

128   Mrs. Pelz seized her shawl in haste.

129   "I better run home quick in my rags before your servant sees me."

130   "I'll speak to Abe about the job," said Hanneh Breineh, as she pushed a bill into the hand of Mrs. Pelz, who edged out as the servant entered.

131   "I'm having fried potato lotkes special for you, Benny," said Hanneh Breineh, as the children gathered about the table for the family dinner given in honor of Benny's success with his new play. "Do you remember how you used to lick the fingers from them?"

132   "Oh, mother!" reproved Fanny. "Anyone hearing you would think we were still in the pushcart district."

133   "Stop your nagging, sis, and let ma alone," commanded Benny, patting his mother's arm affectionately. "I'm home only once a month. Let her feed me what she pleases. My stomach is bomb-proof."

"Do I hear that the President is coming to your play?" said Abe, as he 134
stuffed a napkin over his diamond-studded shirt-front.

"Why shouldn't he come?" returned Benny. "The critics say it's the greatest 135
antidote for the race hatred created by the war. If you want to know, he is
coming to-night; and what's more, our box is next to the President's."

"Nu, mammeh," sallied Jake, "did you ever dream in Delancey Street that 136
we should rub sleeves with the President?"

"I always said that Benny had more head than the rest of you," replied the 137
mother.

As the laughter died away, Jake went on: 138

"Honor you are getting plenty; but how much mezummen does this play 139
bring you? Can I invest any of it in real estate for you?"

"I'm getting ten per cent royalties of the gross receipts," replied the youthful 140
playwright.

"How much is that?" queried Hanneh Breineh. 141

"Enough to buy up all your fish-markets in Delancey Street," laughed Abe 142
in good-natured raillery at his mother.

Her son's jest cut like a knife-thrust in her heart. She felt her heart ache 143
with the pain that she was shut out from their successes. Each added triumph
only widened the gulf. And when she tried to bridge this gulf by asking
questions, they only thrust her back upon herself.

"Your fame has even helped me get my hat trade solid with the Four 144
Hundred," put in Fanny. "You bet I let Mrs. Van Suyden know that our box is
next to the President's. She said she would drop in to meet you. Of course she
let on to me that she hadn't seen the play yet, though my designer said she saw
her there on the opening night."

"Oh, Gosh, the toadies!" sneered Benny. "Nothing so sickens you with 145
success as the way people who once shoved you off the sidewalk come crawling
to you on their stomachs begging you to dine with them."

"Say, that leading man of yours he's some class!" cried Fanny. "That's the 146
man I'm looking for. Will you invite him to supper after the theater?"

The playwright turned to his mother. 147

"Say, ma," he said, laughingly, "how would you like a real actor for a 148
son-in-law?"

"She should worry," mocked Sam. "She'll be discussing with him the future 149
of the Greek drama. Too bad it doesn't happen to be Warfield, or mother could
give him tips on the 'Auctioneer.'"

Jake turned to his mother with a covert grin. 150

"I guess you'd have no objection if Fanny got next to Benny's leading man. 151
He makes at least fifteen hundred a week. That wouldn't be such a bad addition
to the family, would it?"

Again the bantering tone stabbed Hanneh Breineh. Everything in her began 152
to tremble and break loose.

153   "Why do you ask me?" she cried, throwing her napkin into her plate. "Do I count for a person in this house? If I'll say something, will you even listen to me? What is to me the grandest man that my daughter could pick out? Another enemy in my house! Another person to shame himself from me!" She swept in her children in one glance of despairing anguish as she rose from the table. "What worth is an old mother to American children? The President is coming to-night to the theater, and none of you asked me to go." Unable to check the rising tears, she fled toward the kitchen and banged the door.

154   They all looked at one another guiltily.

155   "Say, sis," Benny called out sharply, "what sort of frame-up is this? Haven't you told mother that she was to go with us to-night?"

156   "Yes—I—" Fanny bit her lips as she fumbled evasively for words. "I asked her if she wouldn't mind my taking her some other time."

157   "Now you have made a mess of it!" fumed Benny. "Mother'll be too hurt to go now."

158   "Well, I don't care," snapped Fanny. "I can't appear with mother in a box at the theater. Can I introduce her to Mrs. Van Suyden? And suppose your leading man should ask to meet me?"

159   "Take your time, sis. He hasn't asked yet," scoffed Benny.

160   "The more reason I shouldn't spoil my chances. You know mother. She'll spill the beans that we come from Delancey Street the minute we introduce her anywhere. Must I always have the black shadow of my past trailing after me?"

161   "But have you no feelings for mother?" admonished Abe.

162   "I've tried harder than all of you to do my duty. I've *lived* with her." She turned angrily upon them. "I've borne the shame of mother while you bought her off with a present and a treat here and there. God knows how hard I tried to civilize her so as not to have to blush with shame when I take her anywhere. I dressed her in the most stylish Paris models, but Delancey Street sticks out from every inch of her. Whenever she opens her mouth, I'm done for. You fellows had your chance to rise in the world because a man is free to go up as high as he can reach up to; but I, with all my style and pep, can't get a man my equal because a girl is always judged by her mother."

163   They were silenced by her vehemence, and unconsciously turned to Benny.

164   "I guess we all tried to do our best for mother," said Benny, thoughtfully. "But wherever there is growth, there is pain and heartbreak. The trouble with us is that the ghetto of the Middle Ages and the children of the twentieth century have to live under one roof, and—"

165   A sound of crashing dishes came from the kitchen, and the voice of Hanneh Breineh resounded through the dining-room as she wreaked her pent-up fury on the helpless servant.

166   "Oh, my nerves! I can't stand it any more! There will be no girl again for another week!" cried Fanny.

167   "Oh, let up on the old lady," protested Abe. "Since she can't take it out on us any more, what harm is it if she cusses the servants?"

"If you fellows had to chase around employment agencies, you wouldn't see 168
anything funny about it. Why can't we move into a hotel that will do away with
the need of servants altogether?"

"I got it better," said Jake, consulting a notebook from his pocket. "I have 169
on my list an apartment on Riverside Drive where there's only a small kitchenette; but we can do away with the cooking, for there is a dining service in
the building."

The new Riverside apartment to which Hanneh Breineh was removed by her 170
socially ambitious children was for the habitually active mother an empty desert
of enforced idleness. Deprived of her kitchen, Hanneh Breineh felt robbed of
the last reason for her existence. Cooking and marketing and puttering busily
with pots and pans gave her an excuse for living and struggling and bearing up
with her children. The lonely idleness of Riverside Drive stunned all her senses
and arrested all her thoughts. It gave her that choked sense of being cut off
from air, from life, from everything warm and human. The cold indifference,
the each-for-himself look in the eyes of the people about her were like stinging
slaps in the face. Even the children had nothing real or human in them. They
were starched and stiff miniatures of their elders.

But the most unendurable part of the stifling life on Riverside Drive was 171
being forced to eat in the public dining-room. No matter how hard she tried
to learn polite table manners, she always found people staring at her, and her
daughter rebuking her for eating with the wrong fork or guzzling the soup or
staining the cloth.

In a fit of rebellion Hanneh Breineh resolved never to go down to the public 172
dining-room again, but to make use of the gas-stove in the kitchenette to cook
her own meals. That very day she rode down to Delancey Street and purchased a new market-basket. For some time she walked among the haggling
pushcart venders, relaxing and swimming in the warm waves of her old familiar
past.

A fish-peddler held up a large carp in his black, hairy hand and waved it 173
dramatically:

"Women! Women! Fourteen cents a pound!" 174

He ceased his raucous shouting as he saw Hanneh Breineh in her rich attire 175
approach his cart.

"How much?" she asked, pointing to the fattest carp. 176

"Fifteen cents, lady," said the peddler, smirking as he raised his price. 177

"Swindler! Didn't I hear you call fourteen cents?" shrieked Hanneh 178
Breineh, exultingly, the spirit of the penny chase surging in her blood. Diplomatically, Hanneh Breineh turned as if to go, and the fisherman seized her
basket in frantic fear.

"I should live; I'm losing money on the fish, lady," whined the peddler. "I'll 179
let it down to thirteen cents for you only."

"Two pounds for a quarter, and not a penny more," said Hanneh Breineh, 180 thrilling again with the rare sport of bargaining, which had been her chief joy in the good old days of poverty.

181   "Nu, I want to make the first sale for good luck." The peddler threw the fish on the scale.

182   As he wrapped up the fish, Hanneh Breineh saw the driven look of worry in his haggard eyes, and when he counted out the change from her dollar, she waved it aside. "Keep it for your luck," she said, and hurried off to strike a new bargain at a pushcart of onions.

183   Hanneh Breineh returned triumphantly with her purchases. The basket under her arm gave forth the old, homelike odors of herring and garlic, while the scaly tail of a four-pound carp protruded from its newspaper wrapping. A gilded placard on the door of the apartment-house proclaimed that all merchandise must be delivered through the trade entrance in the rear; but Hanneh Breineh with her basket strode proudly through the marble-paneled hall and rang nonchalantly for the elevator.

184   The uniformed hall-man, erect, expressionless, frigid with dignity, stepped forward:

185   "Just a minute, madam. I'll call a boy to take up your basket for you."

186   Hanneh Breineh, glaring at him, jerked the basket savagely from his hands. "Mind your own business!" she retorted. "I'll take it up myself. Do you think you're a Russian policeman to boss me in my own house?"

187   Angry lines appeared on the countenance of the representative of social decorum.

188   "It is against the rules, madam," he said, stiffly.

189   "You should sink into the earth with all your rules and brass buttons. Ain't this America? Ain't this a free country? Can't I take up in my own house what I buy with my own money?" cried Hanneh Breineh, reveling in the opportunity to shower forth the volley of invectives that had been suppressed in her for the weeks of deadly dignity of Riverside Drive.

190   In the midst of this uproar Fanny came in with Mrs. Van Suyden. Hanneh Breineh rushed over to her, crying:

191   "This bossy policeman won't let me take up my basket in the elevator."

192   The daughter, unnerved with shame and confusion, took the basket in her white-gloved hand and ordered the hall-boy to take it around to the regular delivery entrance.

193   Hanneh Breineh was so hurt by her daughter's apparent defense of the hall-man's rules that she utterly ignored Mrs. Van Suyden's greeting and walked up the seven flights of stairs out of sheer spite.

194   "You see the tragedy of my life?" broke out Fanny, turning to Mrs. Van Suyden.

195   "You poor child! You go right up to your dear, old lady mother, and I'll come some other time."

196   Instantly Fanny regretted her words. Mrs. Van Suyden's pity only roused her wrath the more against her mother.

197   Breathless from climbing the stairs, Hanneh Breineh entered the apartment

just as Fanny tore the faultless millinery creation from her head and threw it on the floor in a rage.

"Mother, you are the ruination of my life! You have driven away Mrs. Van Suyden, as you have driven away all my best friends. What do you think we got this apartment for but to get rid of your fish smells and your brawls with the servants? And here you come with a basket on your arm as if you had just landed from steerage! And this afternoon, of all times, when Benny is bringing his leading man to tea. When will you ever stop disgracing us?" 198

"When I'm dead," said Hanneh Breineh, grimly. "When the earth will cover me up, then you'll be free to go your American way. I'm not going to make myself over for a lady on Riverside Drive. I hate you and all your swell friends. I'll not let myself be choked up here by you or by that hall-boss policeman that is higher in your eyes than your own mother." 199

"So that's your thanks for all we've done for you?" cried the daughter. 200

"All you've done for me!" shouted Hanneh Breineh. "What have you done for me? You hold me like a dog on a chain! It stands in the Talmud; some children give their mothers dry bread and water and go to heaven for it, and some give their mother roast duck and go to Gehenna because it's not given with love." 201

"You want me to love you yet?" raged the daughter. "You knocked every bit of love out of me when I was yet a kid. All the memories of childhood I have is your everlasting cursing and yelling that we were gluttons." 202

The bell rang sharply, and Hanneh Breineh flung open the door. 203

"Your groceries, ma'am," said the boy. 204

Hanneh Breineh seized the basket from him, and with a vicious fling sent it rolling across the room, strewing its contents over the Persian rugs and inlaid floor. Then seizing her hat and coat, she stormed out of the apartment and down the stairs. 205

Mr. and Mrs. Pelz sat crouched and shivering over their meager supper when the door opened, and Hanneh Breineh in fur coat and plumed hat charged into the room. 206

"I come to cry out to you my bitter heart," she sobbed. "Woe is me! It is so black for my eyes!" 207

"What is the matter with you, Hanneh Breineh?" cried Mrs. Pelz in bewildered alarm. 208

"I am turned out of my own house by the brass-buttoned policeman that bosses the elevator. Oi-i-i-i! Weh-h-h-h! What have I from my life? The whole world rings with my son's play. Even the President came to see it, and I, his mother, have not seen it yet. My heart is dying in me like in a prison," she went on wailing. "I am starved out for a piece of real eating. In that swell restaurant is nothing but napkins and forks and lettuce-leaves. There are a dozen plates to every bite of food. And it looks so fancy on the plate, but it's nothing but straw in the mouth. I'm starving, but I can't swallow down their American eating." 209

"Hanneh Breineh," said Mrs. Pelz, "you are sinning before God. Look on 210 your fur coat; it alone would feed a whole family for a year. I never had yet a piece of fur trimming on a coat, and you are in fur from the neck to the feet. I never had yet a piece of feather on a hat, and your hat is all feathers."

211 "What are you envying me?" protested Hanneh Breineh. "What have I from all my fine furs and feathers when my children are strangers to me? All the fur coats in the world can't warm up the loneliness inside my heart. All the grandest feathers can't hide the bitter shame in my face that my children shame themselves from me."

212 Hanneh Breineh suddenly loomed over them like some ancient, heroic figure of the Bible condemning unrighteousness.

213 "Why should my children shame themselves from me? From where did they get the stuff to work themselves up in the world? Did they get it from the air? How did they get all their smartness to rise over the people around them? Why don't the children of born American mothers write my Benny's plays? It is I, who never had a chance to be a person, who gave him the fire in his head. If I would have had a chance to go to school and learn the language, what couldn't I have been? It is I and my mother and my mother's mother and my father and father's father who had such a black life in Poland; it is our choked thoughts and feelings that are flaming up in my children and making them great in America. And yet they shame themselves from me!"

214 For a moment Mr. and Mrs. Pelz were hypnotized by the sweep of her words. Then Hanneh Breineh sank into a chair in utter exhaustion. She began to weep bitterly, her body shaking with sobs.

215 "Woe is me! For what did I suffer and hope on my children? A bitter old age—my end. I'm so lonely!"

216 All the dramatic fire seemed to have left her. The spell was broken. They saw the Hanneh Breineh of old, ever discontented, ever complaining even in the midst of riches and plenty.

217 "Hanneh Breineh," said Mrs. Pelz, "the only trouble with you is that you got it too good. People will tear the eyes out of your head because you're complaining yet. If I only had your fur coat! If I only had your diamonds! I have nothing. You have everything. You are living on the fat of the land. You go right back home and thank God that you don't have any bitter lot."

218 "You got to let me stay here with you," insisted Hanneh Breineh. "I'll not go back to my children except when they bury me. When they will see my dead face, they will understand how they killed me."

219 Mrs. Pelz glanced nervously at her husband. They barely had enough covering for their one bed; how could they possibly lodge a visitor?

220 "I don't want to take up your bed," said Hanneh Breineh. "I don't care if I have to sleep on the floor or on the chairs, but I'll stay here for the night."

221 Seeing that she was bent on staying, Mr. Pelz prepared to sleep by putting a few chairs next to the trunk, and Hanneh Breineh was invited to share the rickety bed with Mrs. Pelz.

222 The mattress was full of lumps and hollows. Hanneh Breineh lay cramped

and miserable, unable to stretch out her limbs. For years she had been accustomed to hair mattresses and ample woolen blankets, so that though she covered herself with her fur coat, she was too cold to sleep. But worse than the cold were the creeping things on the wall. And as the lights were turned low, the mice came through the broken plaster and raced across the floor. The foul odors of the kitchen-sink added to the night of horrors.

"Are you going back home?" asked Mrs. Pelz, as Hanneh Breineh put on her hat and coat the next morning. *223*

"I don't know where I'm going," she replied, as she put a bill into Mrs. Pelz's hand. *224*

For hours Hanneh Breineh walked through the crowded ghetto streets. She realized that she no longer could endure the sordid ugliness of her past, and yet she could not go home to her children. She only felt that she must go on and on. *225*

In the afternoon a cold, drizzling rain set in. She was worn out from the sleepless night and hours of tramping. With a piercing pain in her heart she at last turned back and boarded the subway for Riverside Drive. She had fled from the marble sepulcher of the Riverside apartment to her old home in the ghetto; but now she knew that she could not live there again. She had outgrown her past by the habits of years of physical comforts, and these material comforts that she could no longer do without choked and crushed the life within her. *226*

A cold shudder went through Hanneh Breineh as she approached the apartment-house. Peering through the plate glass of the door she saw the face of the uniformed hall-man. For a hesitating moment she remained standing in the drizzling rain, unable to enter, and yet knowing full well that she would have to enter. *227*

Then suddenly Hanneh Breineh began to laugh. She realized that it was the first time she had laughed since her children had become rich. But it was the hard laugh of bitter sorrow. Tears streamed down her furrowed cheeks as she walked slowly up the granite steps. *228*

"The fat of the land!" muttered Hanneh Breineh, with a choking sob as the hall-man with immobile face deferentially swung open the door—"the fat of the land!" ✤ *229*

RESPONDING

1. We see Hanneh Brieneh from the author's point of view, but the other characters in the story see her differently. Imagine that you are one of her children and write a letter to a friend explaining your mother's behavior. Or write a journal entry about a time when you were torn between loyalty to a parent, sibling, or friend and embarrassment about his or her behavior in front of someone you wanted to impress.

2. Working individually or in a group, write a moral to this story. Share the morals in class. Consider whether the main character learns something. If the answer is yes, what does she learn?

3. Write an essay comparing Hanneh Breineh's life before and after her husband's death. Consider both her physical and emotional circumstances.

4. Hanneh Breineh's friend and old neighbor Mrs. Pelz says that in America money is everything and "What greater friend is there on earth than the dollar" (paragraph 125). She believes that the only trouble with Hanneh Breineh is that she "got it too good" (paragraph 217). Do you agree or disagree? Support your argument with evidence from the story as well as from your own experience.

Elizabeth Gurley Flynn

*The author and labor organizer Elizabeth Gurley Flynn (1890–1964) was
the child of Irish political and economic refugees. From her teenage years,
Flynn showed much of the same activism, devoting most of her life to calling
attention to poverty and deprivation and what she perceived as the other
injustices of capitalism. In 1906 she helped organize the Industrial Workers
of the World; she later became a prominent figure in the Workers Defense
Union and helped found the American Civil Liberties Union in 1920. She
continued to be involved in controversial political activities even into her old
age. In 1961 she became the first woman to chair the American Communist
Party. Her publications include* Women in the War *(1942),* Women Have
a Date with Destiny *(1944),* The Plot to Gag America *(1950),* Communists and the People *(1953), and* I Speak My Own Piece: Autobiography of "The Rebel Girl" *(1955).*

The excerpt that follows, taken from I Speak My Own Piece, *addresses
both the political and economic factors that caused her family to leave Ireland
and the poverty that turn-of-the-century immigrants often found in American
cities.*

⌗

From I SPEAK MY OWN PIECE

By birth I am a New Englander, though not of Mayflower stock. My ancestors
were "immigrants and revolutionists"—from the Emerald Isle. I was born in
1890, at the end of a most tragic century for "that most distressful country,"
which had suffered under British rule for over 700 years. There was an uprising
in each generation in Ireland, and forefathers of mine were in every one of
them. The awareness of being Irish came to us as small children, through
plaintive song and heroic story. The Irish people fought to wrest their native
soil from foreign landlords, to speak their native Gaelic tongue, to worship in
the church of their choice, to have their own schools, to be independent and
self-governing. As children, we drew in a burning hatred of British rule with
our mother's milk. Until my father died, at over eighty, he never said *England*
without adding, "God damn her!" Before I was ten I knew of the great heroes—
Robert Emmet, Wolfe Tone, Michael Davitt, Parnell, and O'Donovan Rossa,
who was chained hand and foot, like a dog, and had to eat from a tin plate on
the floor of a British prison.

When the French army landed at Killalla Bay in 1798, on an expedition
planned by Wolfe Tone, to help free Ireland, all four of my great grandfathers— 2

Gurley, Flynn, Ryan and Conneran—joined them. They were members of the Society of United Irishmen, dedicated to set up an Irish Republic. Fired with enthusiasm over the French revolution and the success of the American colonies, they were determined to follow their examples. Young Irishmen for miles around dropped their potato digging when they heard "the French are in the Bay." The French armed the Irish, who had only pikes for weapons, and together they defeated the British garrison at Castlebar. The story is that Paddy Flynn of Mayo County, known far and wide as "Paddy the Rebel," led the French eighteen miles around through the mountains, to attack the British from the rear. The Irish revolution was finally crushed in a sea of blood by General Cornwallis, who had surrendered to George Washington at Yorktown.

3   A reign of horrible terror and reprisal against the Irish followed—floggings, executions, massacres, exile. Paddy Flynn lay in a ditch near his home all night till he heard that a baby was born. Then he was "On the run!" again with a price on his head, fed and protected by the peasants, like hundreds of his countrymen. Others fled to France, some came to the Americas, others were shipped to Australian penal colonies. Irish songs reflect this period—"Who dares to speak of '98?" and "Here's a memory to the friends that are gone, boys—gone!" Paddy slipped around the hills he knew so well. Once he lay in the center of a ripe wheatfield, while the peasants, knowing he was there, slowly cut and reaped all around him, and the British soldiers rode past, looking for rebels. Finally he reached the home of his foster brother, who was a landlord, but one who had a loyalty to the son of his peasant wet-nurse, and with whom he grew up as a lad. So he hid him away safely in the barn.

4   But my bold adventurous great-grandfather-to-be had a gun, a blunderbuss it was called, that "shot a hatful of bullets." He couldn't resist taking aim at the wild geese as they flew over. A "loyal" (pro-British) weaver heard the shot and came after him with a shuttle board, demanding his surrender. "A fine challenge!" cried Paddy, and shot the king's spokesman. A neighbor digging peat nearby threw down his spade and rushed to town spreading the news: "Paddy Flynn is in the bog shooting yeomen!" All his friends rushed to his aid while the British sent out a searching party. But he was over the hills and far away again. After several years, pardons (amnesty) were granted, and he came home to live to a ripe old age. He had two wives and eighteen children, who later scattered as immigrants to all continents. When he was dying, his last words were—"I want to see the French land on this coast once more!"

5   My grandfather, Tom Flynn, was one of the many sons of Paddy the Rebel. He was arrested in Ireland as a boy of sixteen, when caught fishing for salmon on a Sunday morning, at an hour when everybody was expected to be in church. The river was considered the private property of the landlord. Enraged because hungry people could not have the fish for food in a famine year, Tom Flynn threw lime in the water so the fish floated bellies up, dead, to greet the gentry. Then he ran away to America. His widowed mother, with her other children, followed during the '40's. The widow Conneran, with her large family had come

earlier in the '30's. They travelled on small sailing vessels that took three months, carrying their own pots and pans and doing their cooking on board. The ships were crowded and unsanitary. Cholera would break out and some were to be held in quarantine in St. John's, New Brunswick. Tom, who was there to meet his family, hired a row boat and rescued a brother and sister and as many others as he could load in the boat. He laid them in the bottom, covered them over and started away. A guard shouted, "What have ye there?" Tom boldly replied, "Fish, do you want some?" The guard replied, "No, just keep away from here!" which Tom gladly did, with a hearty "Go to Hell!" which was ever on his lips for a British uniform.

Life was hard and primitive for these early Irish immigrants in isolated settlements in the state of Maine. Grandfather Tom Flynn worked in lumber camps, on building railroads, as an expert river man driving logs, and in granite quarries of Maine and New Hampshire. The climate was more rigorous than their own mild country. The work was harder than agriculture in Ireland. So many died from tuberculosis that it was called "the Irish disease." 6

Undoubtedly "stonecutter's consumption" was what we know today as silicosis. Grandfather Flynn had an obsession against living in another man's house. He built a new cabin wherever he moved by setting up a keg of whiskey and inviting all hands to help him. He became an American citizen in 1856. He voted for Abraham Lincoln in 1860. He married my grandmother at Machias, Maine, where my father was born in 1859. She was little and pretty and had a violent temper. (That's where we get it, Sister Kathie says.) 7

Grandfather died of consumption in 1877 at Pennacook, New Hampshire, then Fisherville, where he is buried. He was only forty-nine years old. He was ever a fighter for freedom, in the spirit of his father. Dissatisfied with the bad living and working conditions, the lack of education for his children, and the prejudice and discrimination against the Irish, he at one time joined with others in an expedition to overthrow the Canadian government and set up a republic there. They captured an armory from the surprised Canadian militia and then got drunk to celebrate. But when they had to return across the border for lack of supplies, their leaders were arrested by the American authorities. Again in 1870 and '71 my father remembered that similar attempted raids were made on Canada. Gay, fighting old Paddy the Rebel has lived on, even unto the third generation. . . . 8

The Irish who came to this country around the middle of the last century were far from happy. They sought but had not found freedom from religious and political persecution, nor a chance to earn a decent livelihood for their families. My father was very bitter about the hard conditions which prevailed here in his youth among the Irish. They were principally employed at manual labor—building railroads, canals, roads, and in mines and quarries. They lived in shanty towns, even in New York City. One such—consisting of 20,000 inhabitants—was located in what is now Central Park. They were excluded from the better residential areas. In my father's youth there were many signs on empty 9 houses and factories seeking help: "No Irish Need Apply." They were ridiculed by the Protestant Yankees for their "Papist" religion, for their large families, their fighting and drinking—called dirty, ignorant, superstitious, lazy, and what not, as each immigrant group in turn has been similarly maligned. Nor were the Irish united. Bloody battles occurred in my father's youth between Catholic Irish and Orangemen, who were Protestant Irish. A narrow canal was pointed out to me in Lowell, Massachusetts, by an old man who said: "That stream was once red with blood after a battle between Orangemen and Catholics."

10   However, the Irish had one advantage which other immigrants did not share—they did not have to learn to speak English. They more easily became citizens. My father commented bitterly: "They soon become foremen, straw bosses, policemen and politicians, and forget the Irish traditions of struggle for freedom!" While this was true of many, it was an exaggeration. The majority of the Irish Americans remained workers—on the waterfront, in mining, transport, maritime, in the building trades, and in other basic industries. They played a heroic part in early American labor history—in the Knights of Labor, the Western Federation of Miners, and the American Federation of Labor. William Sylvis, Peter Maguire, Terence V. Powderly, Kate Mullaney, Leonora O'Reilly, T. B. Barry, John Collins, Martin A. Foran, J. P. McDonald, John Sincey—are a few of the Irish names appearing in early labor history. In fact, in the beginnings of organizing labor they defied their church to be union members. Finally, yielding to the inevitable, the Catholic Church gave its blessing to trade unionism in 1891. Terence V. Powderly in his autobiography, *The Path I Trod*, has an interesting chapter, "Ecclesiastic Opposition," in which he tells of his struggles to defend the Knights of Labor, of which he was the head, against the attacks of priests, bishops and archbishops. Cardinal Gibbons, in his recommendations to the Pope not to condemn the Knights of Labor, saw the danger to the church in the growing cleavage between it and the mass of Catholic workers, who were joining unions.

11   My father, who was then a laborer in the quarries, met my mother in the mid '80's. There were tight social lines drawn between the "lace curtain" Irish of my mother's family and the "shanty Irish" of my father's family. The difficulties he had in courting my mother are indicated by the fact that neither Gurleys nor Flynns came to their wedding. My father was determined to leave the quarry. All but one of his male relatives had died as a result of working there. My father carried the mark of the quarry to his grave. When he was a young boy, working in a quarry in Maine, carrying tools, the sight of one eye was destroyed by a flying chip of granite. He lived to be over eighty, "thanks to Mama," we always said, who encouraged him in his ambition. He had a keen mathematical mind and through self-study and tutoring, he passed the entry examinations at Dartmouth College in Hanover, New Hampshire. He attended the Thayer School of Engineering and made excellent progress. One of his classmates, later a professor at Ann Arbor, Michigan, told me of how he remembered Tom Flynn poring over his book in the failing light of evening, finally taking it to the window to catch the last rays of the sun.

He was suspended from college for a short interval, because he refused to   12
give information as to who attended a secret meeting of Catholic students, who
were organizing to protest the denial of the right of Catholic students to attend
Catholic services. The New York *World* of that day had an article commending
his stand, the student body supported him, and he was reinstated. I thought
proudly of this family precedent in December, 1952, over sixty-five years later,
when I entered the Women's House of Detention in New York City, to serve
a thirty days' sentence for contempt of court, for refusal to "name names." His
brother Pat died of consumption shortly before my father was to graduate. Pat
was the breadwinner for his mother and three sisters, who demanded that Tom
now go to work. His money gave out, trying to divide with them, and he was
compelled to leave college. He was sufficiently grounded, however, so that he
worked from then on as a civil engineer.

When he married, his family was highly indignant, but Mama remained at   13
work, partially solving the economic problem for a few years. My father got
work in 1896 in Manchester, New Hampshire, as a civil engineer for the
Manchester Street Railroad Company, which was laying a track for a new mode
of transportation, since torn up to make way for buses. "Frogs" and switches
were his specialty then. This was eighteen miles south of Concord, and we
moved there. Here he took his first flyer into politics. He ran independently
for City Engineer. He had joined the "Ancient Order of Hibernians" (A.O.H.)
and marched in the St. Patrick's Day parade. He sported white gloves and a
green sash over his shoulder, with golden harps and green shamrocks on it. We
children were terribly impressed. We organized parades and pranced around in
that sash till we wore it out. Undoubtedly he got the Irish vote but it was not
enough to elect him. He was convinced that he lost because he was Irish and
looked around for a job outside of New England. He took a poorly paid
map-making job in Cleveland, Ohio. It was an uncertain, seasonal type of work.
Collecting his pay in full depended upon how many orders the canvassers
received for the finished atlases. Sometimes the operating companies failed or
were fly-by-night concerns and in the end nothing was forthcoming. Somebody
was always "owing Papa money."

Yet he worked hard, was out tramping around in all kinds of weather, with   14
his small hand-drafting board, plotting in with red and blue pencils the streets,
houses, etc. He worked at this for years, making maps of Cleveland, Boston,
Baltimore, Newark, Trenton, Kentucky, Nova Scotia and many other places. At
first we moved around as his jobs changed, from Concord to Manchester, to
Cleveland, to Adams, Massachusetts, and finally to New York City. Our greatest
fear was "Papa losing his job!" We enjoyed our peaceful life with Mama when
she gave us all her attention. We knew that there would be no money when he
was at home all day, and that he would become increasingly irritable and
explosive. We were selfishly happy when Papa got a new job and went off to
another town. . . .

We finally arrived in New York City at the turn of the century—in 1900.   15
My mother was tired of moving around and decided here we would stay. Our

school terms had been interrupted and what little furniture we possessed was being smashed up in moving around. We came to Aunt Mary, a widow and a tailoress, who lived with her five children in the South Bronx. Soon they found a flat for us nearby. It was on the inside facing an airshaft, gas-lit, with cold water. The only heat was the kitchen stove. We three older children cried, we refused to unpack our toys, and were as heart-sick for the green hills of New England as any lonely immigrants for their pleasant native lands. We missed the fields, the flowers, the cows, and beautiful Greylock Mountain we had seen from our window. We hated the big crowded dirty city, where now our playgrounds were empty lots with neither grass nor trees. The flats where we lived, at 833 East 133rd St., are still in use, for "welfare families," I understand, although for a while they were condemned and boarded up.

16   We were horrified, too, at the conditions we had never met in our travels elsewhere—the prevalence of pests in the old slum houses—mice, rats, cockroaches and bedbugs. My poor mother carried on a desperate struggle to rid us of these parasites. And then something horrible happened to us in school— pediculosis is the scientific term—"lousy" the children called it. One child can infect a whole classroom, as every teacher knows. Yet often you will hear a smug prosperous person say: "Well, at least the poor can keep clean." I remember my friend, Rose Pastor Stokes, answering a woman who said this: "Did your mother ever look at a nickel in her hand and decide between a loaf of bread and a cake of soap? Well, mine did!" To be clean requires soap, hot water, changes of underwear, stockings and handkerchiefs, enough sheets and pillow cases and heat in the bathroom. We had none of these in periods of stark poverty. Mama washed our underwear clothes at night to be ready for the next morning.

17   On cold winter days we'd huddle in the kitchen and shut off the rest of the house. We would do our lessons by a kerosene lamp, when the gas was shut off for non-payment. We'd undress in the kitchen, scurry to the cold bedrooms, all the children sleeping in one bed, where we put our coats over us to keep us warm. We might as well have lived on an isolated farm in the Dakotas for all the good the benefits of the great city did us then. Bill collectors harassed my gentle mother—the landlord, the gas man, the milk man, the grocer. Once she bought us an encyclopedia, on the installment plan. But she couldn't keep up the payments and our hearts were broken when we lost the beautiful books we treasured so highly.

18   Our front windows of this long tunnel-like apartment faced the smoky roundhouse of the New York, New Haven and Hartford Railroad. The great engines would chug in day and night and blow off steam there. Many railroad workers lived in the area. In particularly bad times they would throw off chunks of coal and then look the other way when local children came to pick up coal around the roundhouse. There were many accidents to railroad workers. Widows lived around us who had lost their husbands on that dangerous road, and their children starved while the road fought sometimes for years against paying damages.

There were many small factories, veritable sweatshops in the neighborhood, 19
where children went to work as early as the law allowed and even younger. They
made paper boxes, pencils, shirts, handkerchiefs (at three dollars a week and
bring your own thread). There were larger factories employing adult labor—
piano and refrigerator factories, a drug plant, and others. Mothers worked too
and many children were left alone. Sometimes babies fell out of windows; one
boy was killed when a huge sewer pipe rolled over him; a widow's only son fell
from a swaying pole in a backyard, where he was putting up a clothes line and
was killed. Children lost legs on the railroad and under trucks on the streets.
The wife of the corner saloon-keeper made huge kettles of soup for free lunch
and sent bowls of it around to the poorest families. People helped each other
as best they could. Truly, as some philosopher said, "Poverty is like a strange
and terrible country. Only those who have been there can really speak of it with
knowledge."

An unforgettable tragedy of our childhood was the burning of the excursion 20
boat, the "General Slocum," in 1904. It had left the Lower East Side loaded
with women and children on a Sunday school picnic of the Lutheran Church.
When it reached Hellgate, a pot of fat upset and the kitchen took fire. The
captain tried to reach a dock at 138th Street. By then the boat was an inferno.
A thousand people died as a result of burns or drowning. The local undertakers'
establishments were full of bodies. The Alexander Avenue Police Station was a
temporary morgue, where grief-stricken fathers and husbands rushed up from
the East Side to claim their dead. It was heartrending to all of us in the
neighborhood, like a disaster in a mining town. Investigation showed that the
boat was an old firetrap, with inadequate fire-fighting equipment and life-pre-
servers. The Captain, who did his best, was sent to prison, which cleared the
company of responsibility for negligence. It was considered one of the worst
marine disasters up to that time. The lives of working-class mothers and
children were sacrificed to greed and corruption. ✠

RESPONDING

1. In a journal entry, discuss the phrase "No Irish Need Apply." Why do you
   think people used this phrase? What does it suggest about conditions in
   America during the mid-1850s? Are you aware of similar phrases and
   situations that exist today for some groups?

2. Working individually or in a group, construct a time line depicting important events in the author's family history in Ireland and America. If you are
   able, add events in your own family history to the time line. Compare your
   family's situation to that of the Flynns.

3. Write an essay describing the character of Tom Flynn. Pay particular attention to the adjectives you use to describe him. Support your description with evidence from the reading.

4. Flynn reports that conditions in the New York slums were horrendous; she refutes the attitude often expressed by prosperous people that the poor should at least be able to keep clean. Journalist Jacob Riis, however, quotes a report on slum conditions at the time that says, "The proprietors frequently urged the filthy habits of the tenants as an excuse for the condition of their property, utterly losing sight of the fact that it was the tolerance of those habits which was the real evil, and that for this they themselves were alone responsible." In an essay that expresses your opinion, supported by evidence from the reading, discuss who is responsible for slum conditions: landlords, tenants, society in general.

DAVID M. FINE

David M. Fine is a professor of history at California State University at Long Beach. He has studied the history and literature of American immigrant groups for many years. His publications include The City, the Immigrant, and American Fiction, 1820–1920 *(1977) and* Los Angeles in Fiction *(1984), which he edited.*

    The essay that follows explores the way in which early immigrant writers viewed assimilation. It discusses the controversies, both within and outside the immigrant community, about the interpretation of the term "melting pot" and the degree to which newcomers should be expected to assimilate.

✜

ATTITUDES TOWARD ACCULTURATION IN THE ENGLISH FICTION OF THE JEWISH IMMIGRANT, 1900–1917

WHEN THE JEWISH IMMIGRANT began to write novels in the language of his adopted land, it was both natural and inevitable that his subject should have been his own adjustment to America. Having the leisure to write fiction meant having achieved some measure of success in America, and, as might be expected, the process the immigrant novelists characteristically described was one of assimilation and accommodation with the dominant culture. We are given most often an account of his own interpretation of "Americanization," a concept which could mean either the shedding of Old World customs and the absorption of native habits or the broader melting pot fusion of Old and New World culture. Rarely did cultural pluralism, or "cosmopolitanism"—the idea advanced by Horace Kallen[1] that America existed as a confederation of culturally-distinct national and ethnic groups—play a part in the fiction written by the first generation immigrant, except as an idea to be rejected: the writer's own experience had moved in an opposite direction.

    Like so many of the immigrant autobiographies which appeared during the period, the novels written by immigrant Jews had a hopeful message to preach. In a period characterized by the mounting distrust of foreigners and the suspicion that the newer arrivals from eastern Europe were unassimilable, these novels were optimistic affirmations of immigrant assimilability. There were exceptions, of course—among them Abraham Cahan's *The Rise of David Levinsky*

1

2

---

1. Horace Kallen (1882–1974), German-born American teacher, editor, translator.

and Sidney Nyburg's *The Chosen People*. We would like to contrast these two novels with others written by Jewish writers, particularly Elias Tobenkin, Ezra Brudno, and Edward Steiner, at the same time placing the immigrant novel within the larger cultural context of assimilation attitudes which prevailed in these years.

3   Although they were not the largest of the "new immigrant" groups, the Jews produced most of the period's immigrant fiction.[2] Like other large groups from southern and eastern Europe the Jews were motivated to emigrate for a variety of reasons, but to a greater extent than with the other groups, repression provided the spur. As a result, they brought a sizeable number of educated men with them and thus were able to achieve culturally in the first generation what other groups had to wait until the second and third generations to achieve. Moreover, since many were fleeing Czarist oppression, there were relatively few "birds of passage." In far greater proportion than other immigrants they planned to remain in America, so that the whole question of acculturation was a crucial one.

4   To some Jews acculturation meant sloughing off of Old World habits and embracing Christian American values. No better testament to this assimilation ideal exists than the autobiography of Mary Antin, *The Promised Land*, which created something of a literary sensation when it appeared in 1912. Her story tells of the girl who emigrated in 1894 at the age of thirteen from Polotsk, Russia, to Boston. In Russia she had been a stranger in her own land, a victim of Christian maliciousness and persecution. In America she is made to feel at home, and, encouraged to adopt the ways of her new land, she is reborn as an entirely new person: "I was born, I have lived, and I have been made over. . . . I am absolutely other than the person whose story I have to tell. . . . My life I still have to live; her life ended when mine began.[3]

5   To Danish-born journalist Jacob Riis, whose autobiography, *The Making of an American*, was written in much the same spirit as Miss Antin's, the clannishness of the recent immigrants stood as one of the chief stumbling blocks to acculturation. While he recognized that the tenement building and the sweat shop system were major factors which fostered the immigrant's cultural isolation, he pointed out to readers of *How the Other Half Lives* (1890) that some immigrant groups had risen from the ghettos rapidly, while others had stubbornly resisted Americanization. As the immigrant who made it in America, he had little patience with foreigners who were slow to adopt native ways. His sympathies diminished in proportion to the immigrants' obstinacy in clinging to Old World manners and traditions. The Russian Jews were to him among

---

2. Between 1881 and 1917 some four million Italians came to America as compared to two million East European Jews. Moses Rischin, *The Promised City: New York's Jews, 1900–1911* (Cambridge, Massachusetts: 1962), p. 20; Harvey Wish, *Society and Thought in Modern America: A Social and Intellectual History of the American People from 1865* (New York: 1962), pp. 242, 248. [Author's note]
3. Mary Antin, *The Promised Land* (Boston: 1912), p. xi. [Author's note]

the most recalcitrant of the new immigrants, standing "where the new day that dawned on Calvary left them, stubbornly refusing to see the light."[4]

The immigrant novelist whose works came closest to advocating the kind of assimilation Mary Antin and Jacob Riis were recommending was Russian-born Elias Tobenkin. In *Witte Arrives* (1916), he describes the Americanization of Emile Witte (born Wittowski), who emigrates as a youth from Russia and after attending a Western university becomes a commercial and artistic success as a journalist, while his father remains a peddler in America, too rooted in Old World habits to become Americanized. So thoroughly has Witte been made over that his articles on domestic issues, we are told, have an "Emersonian flavor" and that most readers "would have placed the writer of such articles as none other than a scion of one of the oldest American families."[5]

Witte seals his "arrival" at the end of the novel by marrying a Gentile girl of wealthy, old New England stock, after his Jewish wife dies. His transformation from bewildered alien to successful citizen seems much too facile but for the fact that, like Tobenkin, Witte arrived in America as a young boy and grew up in the rural West and not in the urban ghetto. He became Americanized not as Mary Antin had, by erasing the stigmata of the past but as Jacob Riis had, by channeling his talents into the mainstream of the middle-class American reform movement, by putting his journalistic skills to the service of broad, native, democratic ideals.

The reviewers praised *Witte Arrives*, some likening it to *The Promised Land*, others reading it—or misreading it—as an affirmation of the melting pot, ignoring the implications of fusing contained in the metaphor. Typical of the latter view was the comment of H. W. Boynton, who wrote in *Bookman* that "the main picture of the ardent young alien becoming in a brief score of years a loyal thoroughgoing American is of a sort to stiffen our faith in the melting pot." A reviewer for *Nation*, commenting a year and a half later on Tobenkin's next novel, *The House of Conrad*, reminded readers of *Witte Arrives:* "It was the story of the melting pot, of a young Russian who came to this country in boyhood and made himself at least as American as the Americans."[6]

Such remarks illustrate the looseness with which the term "melting pot" was used during the period. As Philip Gleason has indicated in his essay on the melting pot in the *American Quarterly*, the term was employed in these years to denote almost any view toward assimilation favored by those using it.[7] During the war years, with the fear of divided loyalties and the suspicion of all but "100

4. Jacob Riis, *How the Other Half Lives: Studies Among the Tenements of New York* (New York: 1892), p. 112. [Author's note]

5. Elias Tobenkin, *Witte Arrives* (New York: 1916), p. 293. [Author's note]

6. H. W. Boynton, "Witte Arrives," *Bookman*, XLIV (October, 1916), 183; "Dreams and the Main Chance," *Nation*, CVI (March 14, 1918), 295–296. For other reviews of *Witte Arrives* see *New York Times Book Review*, August 1916, 334; Edward Hale, "Recent Fiction," *Dial*, LXI (September 21, 1916), 194; and "Witte Arrives," *Nation*, CIII (September 28, 1916), 304–305. [Author's note]

7. Philip Gleason, "The Melting Pot: Symbol of Fusion or Confusion?" *American Quarterly*, XVI (Spring, 1964), 20–46. [Author's note]

percent Americans," the traditional optimistic view that the melting pot was working to produce a stronger America by blending the best elements of Old and New World cultures lost ground to the view that the function of the pot was to purge the "foreign dross" and "impurities" from the immigrant. In the popular mind the melting pot was identified more and more closely with indoctrination. As a result of this shift in the meaning of the term, those liberal critics who rejected narrow Americanization as a cultural ideal tended also to reject the melting pot, with its connotations of conformity and standardization. One of these critics was Randolph Bourne. Following the lead of Horace Kallen, Bourne rejected fusion altogether as either a realistic possibility or a desirable goal and called for an ethnically diverse, "Trans-National" America.[8] Writing in the *Dial* in 1918, Bourne sarcastically denounced what he called the "insistant smugness" of Tobenkin's *The House of Conrad*, which again emphasized the theme of assimilation and identified success with the absorption of native ideals.[9]

10   Acculturation in the novels of Elias Tobenkin and in the immigrant auto-biography of Mary Antin presumes movement in one direction only: the immigrant sheds his past and adjusts to his adopted land. Missing from such statements is the traditional attitude that cultural blending is a two-way process, that Old World culture is needed to enrich the nation. This attitude found expression at the turn of the century in the settlement ideals of Jane Addams and in the journalistic sketches of Hutchins Hapgood. In her work at Chicago's Hull House and in her writing, Miss Addams, daughter of a prominent Midwestern family, concentrated on what the native American can gain from the "gifts" of the newcomers, and instead of premising her urban reform program on the rapid Americanization of the immigrants, as Riis was doing, she urged them to retain the rich folk traditions of their former lives and share them with Americans.[10] Hapgood, product of one of America's oldest families (his ancestors arrived at Massachusetts Bay in the 1640's), looked to the new immigrants to supply cultural and spiritual values to a nation caught up in getting and spending. Like his brother Norman, who became an authority on New York's Yiddish theater before taking over the editorship of *Collier's Weekly*, "Hutch" was infatuated with the Lower East Side ghetto which he came to know as a New York reporter, working alongside Abraham Cahan on Lincoln Steffens' *Commercial Advertiser*. *The Spirit of the Ghetto* (1902), a collection of Hapgood's journalistic pieces, remains a moving if sentimental tribute to the cultural richness of New York's Lower East Side. In contrast to Jacob Riis, whose

8. Randolph Bourne, "Trans-National America," *Atlantic Monthly*, CXVIII (July 1916), 86–97. For Horace Kallen's position, see "Democracy Versus the Melting Pot," *Nation*, C (1915), 217–220. A more recent statement by Kallen is contained in *Culture Pluralism and the American Idea: An Essay in Social Philosophy* (Philadelphia: 1956). [Author's note]
9. Randolph Bourne, "Clipped Wings," *Dial*, LXIV (April 11, 1918), 358–359. [Author's note]
10. See, for instance, her address, "The Objective Value of a Social Settlement," in *Philanthropy and Social Progress: Seven Essays* (New York: 1893), pp. 27–40, and her *Twenty Years at Hull House* (New York: 1910), especially p. 246. [Author's note]

concern for slum reform and Americanization led him to sketch the ghetto's derelicts, paupers, and street arabs, Hapgood sketched its artists, poets, and scholars. Riis examined its crowded tenements, saloons, and stale beer dives; Hapgood its theaters, schools, and coffee houses.

By addressing themselves not merely to what the immigrants could gain by becoming Americans but to what America could gain by keeping its immigrant ports open, Jane Addams and Hutchins Hapgood brought forward into the urban-industrial age the traditional belief that the New World is a place of new men, and that the national character would continue to be modified by those who chose to come here.

The term "melting pot," used to describe the fusing of Old and New World cultures on American soil, was given currency by the English novelist-playwright Israel Zangwill, who used it as the title of his successful 1908 play about immigrant life in New York. The play concerns a young musician who has fled from Kishinev to his uncle's flat in New York following the pogrom in which his parents had been massacred before his eyes. Dedicated to the ideal of the melting pot, he composes an "American Symphony" which will passionately proclaim his faith in his new life. He is never allowed to forget the past, however; he carries as a reminder a Russian bullet in his shoulder and is given to hysterical paranoiac outbursts. The play's conflict arises when, incredulously, he learns that his fiancée, a non-Jewish Russian immigrant, is the daughter of the Czarist officer who led the Kishinev massacre. By the end of the play, though, his love for Vera and his ecstatic vision of America as a land where ancient hatreds can be put aside, prove stronger than the anguish of the past. At the opposite extreme from David's almost neurotic obsession with the melting pot is the cultural pluralism of the boy's uncle, Mendel Quixano, who rigorously opposes his nephew's marriage to a Christian girl even before he learns of Vera's past. The Jews, he argues, have survived in captivity and in the Diaspora only because they have sustained a separate identity and have refused to merge with the dominant culture. Assimilation would spell the death of the Jewish people.

Mendel's position had considerable support among America's immigrant Jews. Those who had fled the pogroms of Russia came to America not to be fused into a different culture but in order to be free to retain old beliefs, customs, and cultural identity. Opposition to melting pot blending came not only from Orthodox Jews and Zionists, but from many of those immigrants who had reached maturity in eastern Europe during the eighties and who retained the vivid memory of Czarist persecution. Such elders of the immigrant community were unwilling to give up their loyalty to Old World traditions which satisfied social and emotional as well as religious needs.[11] *The American Hebrew*, an important organ of the older, more assimilated German Jews, voiced the feelings of at least part of the ghetto when it said of Zangwill:

11. Solomon Liptzin, *Generation of Decision* (New York: 1958), pp. 175–176. [Author's note]

Certain it is that no man who has felt so distinctly the heart-beats of the great Jewish masses can be expected to be taken seriously if he proposes Assimilation as the solution of the Jewish problem. Not for this did prophets sing and martyrs die.[12]

14 Opinion among "arrived" Jews was divided. Louis Marshall, president of the American Jewish Committee and one of the most influential Jews in American life, wrote that "the melting pot, as advanced by Zangwill, produces mongrelization . . . our struggles should be not to create a hybrid civilization, but preserve the best elements that constitute the civilization we are still seeking, the civilization of universal brotherhood."[13] On the other hand, President Roosevelt's Secretary of Labor and Commerce, Oscar Straus, the highest ranking Jew in government, reportedly shared with the President an enthusiasm for the play's optimistic message of fusion.[14]

15 In the years just prior to the premiere of Zangwill's play two novels written by immigrants, Ezra Brudno's *The Fugitive* (1904) and Edward Steiner's *The Mediator* (1907), affirmed the melting pot credo in a manner quite similar to Zangwill's. The novels are remarkably alike and can conveniently be described together. Both tell of Russian-Jewish youths, victims of Old World persecution who come to America with apocalyptic visions of the reunification of Jew and Christian. The faith in the healing power of the New World both authors wrote into their novels had its roots in their own successful public careers in America. Brudno, born in Lithuania in 1879, attended Yale University and went on to a prominent legal career. Steiner, a convert to Christianity, was born in Vienna in 1866, taught theology and sociology at Grinnell College in Iowa, and authored several books on immigration.

16 The early chapters of both novels are devoted to the Old World childhood of the protagonists. Both young men are raised in Christian environments. Brudno's hero, Israel Rusakoff, the son of an Orthodox Jew falsely convicted of the ritual slaughter of a Christian girl, is adopted by a Russian landowner who it later turns out—in one of the ironic coincidences which plague this fiction—is the repentant betrayer of the boy's father. Steiner's hero, Samuel Cohen, has been raised by a Catholic nurse following the death of his mother. So awed is he by the beauty and pomp of Catholicism he enters a monastery to study for the priesthood, only to abandon his vocation when he witnesses a brutal pogrom perpetrated in the name of Christianity. Both youths conclude that Christianity is a false sanctuary, that they cannot escape their pasts, that their destinies have been shaped by their heritage. Yet to return to the Orthodoxy of their fathers

12. Quoted in "Mr. Zangwill's New Dramatic Gospel," *Current Literature*, XLV (December, 1908), 672. [Author's note]
13. Charles Reznikoff, ed., *Louis Marshall: Champion of Liberty* (New York: 1957) p. 809. [Author's note]
14. *Current Literature, loc. cit.*, p. 671. [Author's note]

is as impossible as to reject their birthright completely. Old World Judaism—particularly in Brudno's novel—is rendered in its most medieval, oriental, and reactionary aspects.

In both works the flight to America is a flight from forms of oppression 17 imposed by both Jew and Christian, but in the ghetto of New York's Lower East Side, they find further oppression. To indicate the debasement of the European Jew in the New World ghetto, both Brudno and Steiner employ the device, so common to the immigrant novel, of allowing figures from the protagonists' Old World past to reappear: prominent Russian Jews, forced to flee following the 1881 assassination of the Czar, turn up as sweatshop workers; former Talmudic scholars become Yankee "dandies" or "allrightniks." The usual metamorphosis places the Jew behind a sewing machine, tyrannized by the German-Jewish "sweater." Conventionally, the Americanized "uptown" German Jew is the villain in the fiction of the ghetto, both in these novels produced by immigrants and in the popular native-drawn sketches of immigrant life which were then appearing in the magazines. Between the poles of rigid Old World piety and traditionalism and New World secularism and materialism, the heroes of Brudno and Steiner seek to define their American and Jewish identities. To reconcile Old World and New, Russian and German, Jew and Gentile, becomes their mission.

Steiner's "mediator" assumes a more active role in bringing about the 18 rapprochement of the two worlds. Having been raised in a monastery and having fled with the traumatic recognition of the gulf between Christian teaching and Christian practice, he became an evangelist on the East Side, proclaiming the true spirit of Christ to Jew and Gentile. He is aided by the patrician philanthropist Mr. Bruce, but the mission he sets for himself is a broader one than the simple conversion advocated by Bruce. The conflict between the two men, which dominates the later chapters of the novel, centers on the distinction between the rival interpretations of Americanization, that is, one-sided assimilation with the dominant population group as against the more liberal melting pot ideal. Bruce seeks to Americanize the Jewish immigrant by converting him to Christianity; Samuel Cohen seeks to fuse the two faiths, preserving the highest ideals of both.

The protagonists in both novels confirm their roles as cultural mediators 19 by marrying Gentile women. Brudno's hero, like Zangwill's, marries the daughter of his Old World enemy. Thus the marriage which has been forbidden in the Old World is sanctioned in the New. Steiner's hero weds the daughter of the missionary with whom he has joined forces. As in *Witte Arrives*, *The Melting Pot*, and *The Fugitive*, the union of the Jewish male with the Gentile woman—either a native-born aristocrat or the daughter of the Jew's Old World betrayer—provides the symbolism for the reconciliation of Old and New World. Marriage to a Christian American is both the badge signifying the immigrant's successful "arrival" and the broader symbol of the possibilities for cultural fusion in America.

20   The most interesting comment on the solution Steiner's mediator presents comes from another novel about a self-styled mediator written ten years later. In *The Chosen People* (1917) Sydney Nyburg, a Baltimore lawyer and grandson of a Dutch Jewish immigrant, tells the story of Philip Graetz, rabbi of an affluent urban synagogue who conceives his divinely-appointed mission to be the mediator between the Americanized, "uptown" German Jews of his own congregation and the recently-arrived "downtown" Russian Jews of the city's ghetto. Steiner's mediator sought to bring together Jew and Gentile; Nyburg's wants to join the two worlds of Jews in America. In both novels the clash is between the values of the Old World and those of the New; in both the protagonist is a self-appointed "prophet of peace," who, upheld by a visionary melting pot credo, directs his rhetoric to the fusion of two diverse worlds. The difference is that not only is Graetz singularly unfit for his chosen task, but the task itself is shown to be beyond the possibility of attainment by any single man. What the world needs, Graetz learns, is not the prophet with his abstract plea for justice, but the pragmatic bargainer—the tough-minded realist, who, if he cannot make the uptown Jew love his downtown brothers, can, at least, keep him from exploiting their labor.

21   Graetz's teacher and foil in the novel is a cynical, Russian-born labor attorney, David Gordon. In the strike which serves in the novel as a focus for the struggle between uptown and downtown, the workers of the ghetto are able to achieve better working conditions not because Graetz has convinced the industrialists of his congregation of their selfishness, but because Gordon has marshalled an army of workers willing to challenge the Jewish plutocracy. To Gordon, the two worlds of Jews cannot be kept from fighting as long as they occupy opposite poles in a capitalistic, individualistic society. His own solution is Zionism, which he feels will bind all Jews together in the building of their own society. Like the cultural pluralists, he believes that the Jews can stay alive only by defining their identity outside the value system of America. At the other extreme are the German Jews of Graetz's congregation, who embrace their Americanization ardently and are embarrassed by the persistence of Old World habits in the Russian Jews. They live in fear that the vast presence of the newcomers will undermine their own hard-won position in Christian America, and yet because they rely on the cheap labor force supplied by the recent immigrant, they have a vested interest in perpetuating his ignorance.

22   *The Chosen People* was a needed antidote to the facile affirmation of assimilation and the melting pot offered by such immigrant writers as Tobenkin, Brudno, and Steiner. Labor warfare between uptown German and downtown Russian Jews in Baltimore served Nyburg well as a vehicle for examining the broader question of the cultural gulf between older and newer Americans in the early years of the twentieth century. Abraham Cahan's major novel, *The Rise of David Levinsky*, appeared within a few months of *The Chosen People* and a few reviewers, pairing the two in their columns, noted the thematic parallels.

23   Levinsky's "rise" in America is an ironic one, for it is achieved at the expense

of what is deepest and truest in him. He has realized the American dream of material success, but the victory is hollow. His life has been a dismal failure, he recognizes from his millionaire's perspective, because his outer achievements fail to satisfy his inner hunger.

The Rise of David Levinsky restates the theme which occupied Cahan in his earlier, shorter fiction. Throughout his tales of Jewish immigrant life in New York City, the Diaspora, a central and definitive historical fact in the Jewish experience, dominates the consciousness of the immigrant protagonists. His heroes are painfully aware of their exile, and whatever outer success they achieve in America, they are never permitted to forget what they have lost. This is Cahan's reply to the novels of acculturation with their glib, optimistic generalizations about cultural reconciliation and fusion. Under the pressure of New World experience, Old World values totter but never collapse entirely, for his protagonists are both unable and unwilling to extricate themselves from the grip of the past. Yearning for the past becomes one of the inescapable conditions—and, indeed, positive forces—in their lives. "The gloomiest past is dearer than the brightest present," Levinsky confesses.[15] And even Jake Podkovnik, Cahan's "Yekl," the flashy "allrightnik" and the most vulgar of his Americanizers, sees his Old World past as "a charming tale, which he was neither willing to banish from his memory nor reconcile with the actualities of his American present."[16] As Cahan's heroes outwardly assimilate into American life, they become increasingly alienated from themselves. The outer self comes into conflict with the inner self, which cannot and will not be stilled.

The result is loneliness, ennui, and guilt. In the no-man's land in which Cahan's heroes reside, there are no enduring loves or happy marriages. There are no unions with native-born aristocratic Gentile women to symbolize the melting pot blending of Old and New World. Nor are marriages or friendships from the Old World permitted to continue in the New. Yekl divorces his Russian wife for the perfumed, gaudy Mamie Fein. Levinsky, despite his great wealth, is rejected by three women. The widowed Asriel Stroom in "The Imported Bridegroom" (1898) is denied the old-age dream of seeing his Americanized daughter married to a pious Talmudic scholar. In Cahan's many other stories which deal with love and marriage in the ghetto, only one, "A Ghetto Wedding," seems to offer the prospect of a permanent, fulfilling liaison. Contacts with the past are always unnerving. Yekl sends to Russia for his family but is embarrassed by his wife's appearance at Ellis Island and forces her to remove the traditional wig which identifies her as a "greenhorn." Levinsky is always uncomfortable in the presence of Old World figures. In one scene he is unable—or unwilling—to leave a street car to offer aid to a destitute man he sees and recognizes as a fellow student from his boyhood in Russia. In a mood of nostalgia near the end of the novel he arranges a reunion with a "ship brother" twenty-five years after

15. Abraham Cahan, *The Rise of David Levinsky* (New York: 1917), p. 526. [Author's note]
16. Abraham Cahan, *Yekl, A Tale of the New York Ghetto* (New York: 1896), p. 54. [Author's note]

he and the other man, a tailor, arrived from Europe, but the affair is spoiled by mutual distrust and embarrassment, and Levinsky is made to feel guilty for his success. Throughout the book when faces from the past reappear, he is unable to contend with his mixed feelings of hostility and compassion. The faces remind him of all that he has striven to eliminate from his mind—his near starvation, the brutal death of his mother, the bitter Czarist oppression—and yet he cannot help identifying with these people, and he yearns for their company.

26   The conditions of Levinsky's present life have made it impossible for him to bridge the gulf to the past he yearns for, yet, paradoxically, he is never far removed from the past. Loneliness, hunger, and alienation have been so firmly stamped on his character since his boyhood, they seem the most authentic parts of him. And while he cries on the one hand for an end to his sorrows, the sorrows seem to have their own kind of value. Through his meteoric rise his inner identity has remained essentially unchanged. Neither the thorough Americanization prescribed by Mary Antin, Jacob Riis, and Elias Tobenkin, nor the cultural fusion urged by Jane Addams, Ezra Brudno, and Edward Steiner are, in the end, realizable states in Cahan's fictional world. With *The Rise of David Levinsky* the novel of immigrant acculturation is no longer the story of easy faith. David Levinsky, immigrant and entrepreneur, finds emptiness at the end of the American dream.[17]

27   It seems appropriately ironic that 1917, the year America entered the war and passed its first major immigration restriction law, should mark the publication of the two most probing novels of immigration acculturation. At the height of the xenophobia engendered by the foreign crisis, Sidney Nyburg and Abraham Cahan, the one a third-generation and the other a first-generation American, wrote the period's most compelling fictional accounts of the Jewish immigrant in urban America. *The Chosen People* and *The Rise of David Levinsky* stand apart from and above the other novels of immigrant acculturation in having resisted ideological formulas and doctrinaire solutions and in having succeeded in portraying realistically the ironies, complexities, and dilemmas of cultural assimilation. The setting for the conflict between Old and New World in both works is the urban industrial arena because it was here that older and newer Americans so often clashed. The industrial conflict served as a metaphor for the broader, more fundamental cultural conflict. Rabbi Philip Graetz, ideologically

17. Our discussion of *The Rise of David Levinsky* follows the general lines of Isaac Rosenfeld's essay, "America, the Land of the Sad Millionaire," *Commentary*, XIV (August, 1952), 131–135. For a different approach see David Singer, "David Levinsky's Fall: A Note on the Liebman Thesis," *American Quarterly*, XIX (Winter, 1967), 696–697. Beginning with the thesis of Professor Charles Liebman that East European Jewish immigrants to America were not, in the main, Orthodox Jews as is commonly assumed, Singer attempts to demonstrate that Levinsky had rejected his Old World piety long before emigrating and that such gestures as cutting his earlocks in America are not to be interpreted as signs of his loss of faith but of his desire for cultural assimilation and social acceptance. For a recent account of Cahan's career and a discussion of his fiction, including the earlier magazine version of Levinsky, see Ronald Sanders, *The Downtown Jews: Portraits of an Immigrant Generation* (New York: 1969). [Author's note]

linked with the affluent industrialists of his congregation, discovered a deeper identity with the exploited proletariat of the ghetto. David Levinsky, whose outer identity shifted with his changing fortunes, discovered that his inner identity was inescapable.

One of the conclusions to be drawn from a study of the immigrant novel is that it is dangerous to assume that the foreign-born writer, because he lived through the process of adjustment, would necessarily produce the most trenchant accounts of the process. Some immigrant writers seemed more to reflect what they had read than what they had experienced. Conventions which they absorbed from the popular ghetto melodramas appearing in the journals—stock figures like the malevolent German Jewish sweater and the fiery young ghetto idealist, for instance—and the ideological doctrines of the reformers and the social theorists proved irresistible. In the novels of Elias Tobenkin, Ezra Brudno, and Edward Steiner, the psychological complexities of acculturation are evaded in favor of overly-enthusiastic affirmations of Americanization. As immigrants who succeeded in America, they used the novel, as Mary Antin used autobiography, to chant the praises of their adopted land. While all the immigrant novelists of the period described the disparity between the expectations and the actualities of America, between the "imagined" and the "real" America, only Cahan among them pursued the psychological implications of that disparity, its permanent cost to the psyche. Only Cahan, among the pre–World War I, first-generation Jewish American novelists, refused to turn his immigrant heroes into propagandists or preachers, refused to blink his eyes as he faced the chasm which lay between Old World values and New World experience. ✤

28

RESPONDING

1. Fine introduces Nyburg's *The Chosen People* as a "vehicle for examining the broader question of the cultural gulf between older and newer Americans in the early years of the twentieth century" (paragraph 22). Describe the gulf that existed then. Do you believe such a gulf exists today? Write a journal entry explaining your point of view and supporting it with evidence from your reading and your own experience.

2. An important issue, still the subject of controversy, is whether new immigrants should strive for assimilation or strive to maintain cultural pluralism. Working individually or in a group, define the concepts of assimilation and cultural pluralism. Write an essay discussing the implications of each for the individual immigrant. You may support your points with examples from the readings or from personal knowledge and experience.

3. Using information from Fine's article, write an essay defining and tracing the history of the term "melting pot." Why might critics object to the image of America as a melting pot? What other image might replace it?

4. How does the melting-pot image that many Americans have advocated for so many years fit into a society that wants to encourage cultural diversity? Write an essay arguing that America should or should not try to be a melting pot.

MAXINE S. SELLER

Maxine S. Seller, an expert in immigration history and ethnic life, was born in 1935 in Wilmington, North Carolina. She received her B.A. from Bryn Mawr College in 1956 and her doctorate from the University of Pennsylvania in 1965. Seller has taught history and education at various institutions, including Temple University, Bucks County Community College, and the State University of New York at Buffalo. She has written To Seek America: A History of Ethnic Life in the United States *(1977) and edited two essay collections,* Immigrant Women *(1981) and* Ethnic Theater in the United States *(1982).*

Seller's essay "Beyond the Stereotype" not only details the contribution of three generally unnoticed immigrant activists, it also suggests ways in which historians need to challenge the stereotyped, and often inaccurate, ways in which the role of immigrant women is too often portrayed.

⁜

BEYOND THE STEREOTYPE:

A NEW LOOK AT THE IMMIGRANT WOMAN, 1880–1924

MUCH HAS BEEN WRITTEN about the achievements and experiences of the men who came to the United States from Southern and Eastern Europe between 1880 and 1924. Much less has been written, however, about the achievements and experiences of the immigrant women of this period. It is my opinion that the relative lack of material about immigrant women is not the result of a lack of activity on the part of these women. Rather, it is the result of the persistence of old, negative stereotypes, stereotypes making it appear that women did little worth writing about.

According to her native born contemporaries, the immigrant woman from Southern or Eastern Europe spent her life "confined within the four walls of her home and chained to her household routine."[1] According to a librarian, "(Immigrant) women are left behind in intelligence by the father and children. They do not learn English; they do not keep up with other members of the family."[2] The political influence of the foreign born woman was supposedly nil,

---

1. John Palmer Gavit, *Americans By Choice*, Harper and Row 1922. Reprinted in *Americanization Studies: The Acculturation of Immigrant Groups into American Society.* Patterson Smith, Montclair, New Jersey, 1971, p. 318.
2. Gavit, p. 319.

both before and after the passage of the Women's Suffrage Amendment. As one observer put it, "The foreign born woman plays directly in American politics a part somewhat, but not much, more important than that played by snakes in the zoology of Ireland."[3] In summary, the native born who saw all immigrants as a threat to the American way of life, saw the immigrant woman in particular as backward, ignorant, and degraded. She was considered excellent raw material for the "uplift" programs of social workers and home missionary societies, but good for little else. To fervent advocates of Americanization of the immigrant mother was a "natural obstructionist" whose eventual death would enable the family to "move on much more victoriously to Americanization."[4]

3   These negative stereotypes from the early twentieth century have continued to influence our view of the immigrant woman. The second or third generation ethnic comedian romanticizes her as Super-Mom, a domestic wonder woman who solved the problems of the world with steaming bowls of chicken soup, spaghetti, or other appropriate ethnic food. Those less steeped in nostalgia are likely to think of her, if at all, as a shadowy, kerchiefed figure absorbed in the not very efficient care of a cluttered tenement apartment and an unending stream of offspring. If she had ambition, it was for her children, never for herself. Her own horizons were limited to the corner grocery and the parish church.

4   Historians, like others, have been influenced by these stereotypes. They have also been influenced by the knowledge that Southern and Eastern European immigrant groups usually had, and still have, a patriarchal family structure. Many share the general bias of our society that the activities of women are less important than those of men. Even in recent works on ethnic history far fewer women than men are mentioned by name, and women's organizations and activities are rarely treated as fully as the corresponding organizations and activities of men.

5   Is the stereotyped picture of the immigrant woman an accurate reflection of reality? There were women who did conform to the stereotype, but significant numbers did not. Women of energy and ability stepped outside the traditionally feminine spheres of home and child care to make a variety of contributions to their ethnic communities and to American life in general. Immigrant women built social, charitable, and educational institutions that spanned the neighborhood and the nation. They established day care centers, restaurants, hotels, employment agencies, and legal aid bureaus. They wrote novels, plays, and poetry. They campaigned for a variety of causes, from factory legislation to birth control, from cleaner streets to cleaner government.[5]

3. Gavit, p. 318.

4. The Second Annual Report of the Commission of Immigration and Housing of California, California State Printing Office, San Francisco, 1916, pp. 151–2. See also Albert Kennedy and Robert Woods, *Handbook of Settlements*, Russell Sage Foundation, New York, 1911, pp. 16, 37, 191, 211, 245.

5. Information about immigrant women's organizations can be found in Sophonisba Breckenridge, *New Homes for Old* and John Daniels, *America Via the Neighborhood*, both reprinted in *Americanization Studies: The Acculturation of Immigrant Groups into American Society*, Patterson Smith, Montclair, New

To illustrate the range of these activities, I will begin this paper with case studies of three non-traditional women, each from a different ethnic background, each making her contribution in a different area: Antonietta Pisanelli Alessandro, a founder of professional Italian theater in the United States; Josephine Humpel Zeman, Bohemian journalist, lecturer, and feminist; and Rose Pesotta, Russian Jewish labor organizer. After sketching the career of each of these undeservedly obscure women, I will explore how, coming from patriarchal ethnic cultures, they were able to achieve what they did. Then, by discussing briefly the activities of other immigrant women, I will show that these three were not unique. So many women's lives, traditional as well as nontraditional, departed from the stereotype in so many ways that much more research in this area is needed. As ethnic historian Rudolph Vecoli recently observed, the history of the immigrant woman remains to be written.[6]

Antonietta Pisanelli Alessandro came from Naples to New York as a child.[7] As a young woman, she made her living singing, dancing, and acting in the major eastern cities. She made her New York debut at an Italian benefit in Giambelli Hall. Then, as there were no professional Italian theaters in New York, she and some colleagues organized several. Personal tragedy marred her career, however; first her mother died, then her husband, then one of her two children.

With her remaining young son and few other resources but her ingenuity, she arrived in San Francisco in 1904. She assembled a group of amateur performers, rented a ramshackled hall, and opened an Italian theater. According to an early patron, the settings were so crude they were liable to fall apart at any moment—as were the actors. But the performance earned $150. By the time the fire department closed the building, Pisanelli was able to open the more substantial Cafe Pisanelli Family Circle, a combination theater, club, opera house, and cafe. Featuring the finest actors and singers imported from Italy, the Circle was soon known as the liveliest theater in San Francisco. Through road tours as well as home performances, Antonietta Pisanelli Alessandro and her company brought Italian drama and Italian music, from folk songs to opera, to Italian Americans and others throughout the country.

Josephine Humpel Zeman was born in Bohemia (Czechoslavakia) in 1870

Jersey, 1971. Examples of individual women active in public life are Teofila Samolinska, Polish poet, dramatist, and community organizer; Anzia Yezierska, Jewish author of short stories and novels; and Mrs. Mantura Frangierea, Lebanese businesswoman and advocate for the early Arabic community of Boston. Perhaps the best known national figure was Emma Goldman, spokeswoman for unpopular causes such as anarchism, labor reform, birth control, and the complete equality of women. Of course there were many more.

6. Rudolph J. Vecoli, "European Americans: From Immigrants to Ethics," *The Reinterpretation of American History and Culture*, edited by William H. Cartwright and Richard L. Watson, Jr., National Council for the Social Studies, Washington, D.C., 1973, p. 104.

7. For a full account of Antonietta Pisanelli Alessandro's career, see Lawrence Estavan, *The Italian Theater in San Francisco*, United States Works Progress Administration, North California District, San Francisco, 1939. Typescript copy is available at the Lincoln Center Theater Library in New York City.

and immigrated to Chicago as a young girl.[8] There she met Mary Ingersoll, a social worker at Hull House who became, in Humpel's words, "my second mother." Recognizing the young girl's ability, Mary Ingersoll helped her learn English and get an education. In 1895 Josephine Humpel Zeman was a member of the staff of Hull House, devoting her time to the study of the Bohemian community of Chicago. She was especially sensitive to the problems of women. In a published Hull House paper she complained that "nothing whatsoever has been done for the Bohemian working woman. No one has deemed her worthy of any effort. This is an interesting fact; for as long as these hundreds of thousands of girls shall be unorganized and uninformed, they will always be a great stumbling block in the path of the working women of Chicago."[9]

10   As social worker, author, journalist, and lecturer (both in her native language and in English) Josephine Zeman showed her concern for the welfare of immigrants, of women, and of all who were at the bottom of the nation's socio-economic pyramid. She wrote articles for the ethnic press, for American magazines such as *Commons*, and for the United States Industrial Commission on Immigration and Education. According to the Library of Congress catalog, a Josephine Zeman, presumably Josephine Humpel Zeman, wrote two novels, *The Victim Triumphs: A Panorama of Modern Society* published by Dillingham in 1903, and *My Crime*, published by Ogelvie in 1907. Thomas Capek, who described Zeman's career in his *History of the Czechs in the United States*, did not mention these novels, however, raising the question of whether she did in fact write them. He does mention her social critique of the United States, *America in Its True Light*, published in Prague in 1903. The book contained lectures she delivered on a tour to some thirty towns in Bohemia, and Silesia. Zeman's most important work was the founding of the Chicago-based Bohemian feminist journal *Zemske Listy, The Woman's Gazette*, in 1894. Written, edited, and even printed by an exclusively female staff, the paper circulated throughout the United States. Avoiding the household hints and beauty advice common to most women's publications, the paper stressed the need to improve the lot of the working woman and campaigned for the adoption of the Women's Suffrage Amendment.[10]

11   Rose Pesotta was born in 1896 in the Ukraine, in the pale of settlement where Russian Jews were forced by law to live.[11] At the age of seventeen she came to New York City, where her older sister, who had emigrated earlier, got her a job in a garment factory. Familiar with the ideas of various peasant and

---

8. Information on Josephine Humpel Zeman can be found in Thomas Capek, *The Czechs in America*, Houghton Mifflin Company, New York, 1920. I received additional information from the Balch Institute in Philadelphia, for which I am grateful to the Institute's bibliographer, Glen Skillen.

9. Josephine Humpel Zeman, "The Bohemian People in Chicago," *Hull House Maps and Papers*, Boston, 1895. Reprinted by Arno Press, New York, 1970, p. 120.

10. Emily Balch, *Our Slavic Fellow Citizens*, Charities Publications Committee, New York, 1910, p. 384.

11. For an account of Pesotta's career, see her autobiography, Rose Pesotta, *Bread Upon the Waters*, Dodd, Mead & Company, New York, 1945.

worker revolutionary groups in Russia, Pesotta joined Waistmakers Local 25 of the International Ladies Garment Workers Union almost immediately. On May Day, 1914 she marched with her co-workers in a mass parade past the scene of the Triangle Waist Factory fire—an industrial disaster in which 126 garment workers, mostly immigrant girls like herself, burned to death.

Inspired by stories of the great labor battles of the recent past and by the distress of working people she saw all around her, Pesotta became actively involved in the organizational work of her union. She learned English at night school and continued her education, under the auspices of the Union, at Brookwood Labor College and at the Bryn Mawr Summer School for Working Girls. According to Pesotta, the aim of the latter institution was "to stimulate an active and continuous interest in the problems of our economic life which vitally concern industrial women as wage earners."[12]

The Bryn Mawr Summer School realized its aim: Pesotta began by working to organize her fellow workers in New York, many of whom, like herself, were Jewish immigrants. Soon she was also organizing Italians and other workers of a wide variety of ethnic backgrounds. She traveled from coast to coast, unionizing garment workers in Los Angeles, San Francisco, Montreal, San Juan, and wherever else her services were needed. During the Great Depression of the 1930s she helped organize automobile and rubber workers also. She traveled in Europe and, upon her return, rallied aid for the cause of the Spanish Loyalists. In recognition of her valuable services, she was elected a vice president of the International Ladies Garment Workers Union for three consecutive terms. Rejecting the suggestion of a fourth term in 1944, she pointed out that a union with 300,000 members, 85% of whom were women, should have more than one token woman, herself, on its executive committee.[13]

The lives of Antonietta Pisanelli Alessandro, Josephine Humpel Zeman, and Rose Pesotta were not confined within the limits of customary women's activities. Why did these three women break with tradition? In the first place, like millions of other working women, immigrant and native born, they could not afford the luxury of full-time domesticity. Alessandro was a widow with a child to support when she opened her first theater in San Francisco. An "unfortunate" marriage made it necessary for Zeman to support herself. Pesotta, too, worked throughout her life to earn her own living.

For all three of these women, however, economic necessity was a less important motivating force than their inner drives to do meaningful and challenging work in the larger world. Antoinetta Alessandro began organizing theaters in New York while her first husband was still alive and continued to run her theater in San Francisco after a second marriage relieved her of the necessity to earn her living. Even before she left Russia, Rose Pesotta had decided that the traditional woman's life would not meet her needs. In her own

12. Pesotta, p. 15.
13. Pesotta, p. 395.

words, "I can see no future for myself except to marry some young man returned from his four years of military service and be a housewife. That is not enough. . . . In America things are different. A decent middle class girl can work without disgrace."[14]

16 In each of these women motivation was matched by energy and ability. Alessandro impressed all who met her with her business acumen and resourcefulness, as well as with her unfailing charm. A fellow journalist dubbed Zeman "Mrs. General," a derisive acknowledgement of her forceful manner.[15] A colleague and former teacher described Pesotta as "possessing built-in energy . . . talk with her a few minutes as casually as you may and strength is poured into you, as when a depleted battery is connected to a generator."[16]

17 All three of these women came from ethnic backgrounds in which men were the dominant sex and women were relegated to domestic duties. Why, then, despite their obvious abilities, did they aspire to non-traditional careers in the first place? The journey to America opened new possibilities to these women, as it did to all immigrants. Still, early twentieth century America was scarcely more liberal than Europe in the roles it assigned to women. Also, by the time these three women arrived in the United States, their personalities and aspirations had already been shaped by old world environments. Undoubtedly there must be intensive investigation on the status of women in the mother countries if the immigrant woman is to be fully understood. Even a cursory investigation reveals, however, that there were cross currents in European ethnic cultures that supported the achievements of women like Alessandro, Zeman, and Pesotta.

18 Alessandro grew up in Southern Italy, where women were taught to be subservient to their fathers, husbands, uncles, brothers, even their male cousins. Still, Southern Italian women were respected, even revered, in their roles as mothers—perhaps because of the religious veneration of Mary as the mother of Jesus, or perhaps because of the critical economic importance of their work in a society where livelihood was marginal. Whatever the reasons, an Italian family could survive the death of the father, but not that of the mother.[17]

19 Alessandro was not above utilizing the respect due her as an Italian mother when it was to her advantage to do so. On one occasion, a road tour audience in St. Louis threatened to riot in the theater because of a misunderstanding about the program. (They had expected the opera *Carmen* instead of the folk song with a similar name that was actually presented.) Alesandro restored peace and probably saved the building from being torn apart by putting her young son on stage to sing "Wait Til the Sun Shines, Nellie"—while her husband

---

14. Pesotta, p. 9.
15. Capek, p. 275.
16. Pesotta, p. vii.
17. Leonard Covello, *The Social Background of the Italian-American School Child*, Ph.D. Thesis, New York University, 1944. E. J. Brill, Leiden, 1967, p. 210.

slipped out of the back door to safety carrying with him the evening's cash receipts.

According to an old Slavic proverb, "the man who does not beat his wife   20
is not a man." According to another, "one man is worth more than ten women." Women in the more remote areas of the Balkans were used, along with the animals, to carry the heavy burdens.[18] The Slavic societies of Eastern Europe were far from monolithic, however, in their views on religion, sex, or anything else. Josephine Humpel Zeman was from Bohemia, an area with a long tradition of opposition to established religious and political institutions.[19] The rationalism of Bohemian "free thinkers" was notorious both in the United States and in Europe, and provided a hospitable atmosphere for the radical social ideas and non-traditional behavior of someone like Josephine Zeman. Indeed, her lectures on feminism and social reform may have seemed less shocking in Bohemia than in Chicago.

Rose Pesotta, too, could find support for her chosen life work from within   21
her own ethnic tradition. Sex roles were sharply defined in East European Jewish society, but not in precisely the same way as in Anglo Saxon society. In theory at least, the Jewish man was most admired for his religious scholarship rather than for his physical prowess or his economic achievement. It was not uncommon for a pious Jewish man to spend all his time in religious study, while his wife assumed full responsibility for earning the family livelihood. Thus, many East European Jewish women from religious backgrounds were at home in the world of the marketplace.[20]

In addition, by the turn of the century some young women had come under   22
the influence of two new secular philosophies, socialism and zionism, both of which emphasized the equality of the sexes and offered a new range of roles for women. In 1880 Russia opened its universities to women. Although the government allowed few Jewish women to take advantage of this opportunity, increasing numbers found their way to some secular education. The "new" Jewish woman, intellectual, aggressive, and self-sufficient, brought her new lifestyle with her to the United States. According to journalist Hutchins Hapgood, who described the Jewish quarter of New York City in 1902,

> there are successful female dentists, physicians, writers, and even lawyers by the score in East Broadway who have attained financial independence through their industry and intelligence. They are ambitious to a degree and often direct the careers of their husbands. . . . There is more than one case on record where a

18. Gerald Gilbert Govorchin, *Americans from Yugoslavia*, University of Florida Press, Gainesville, 1961, pp. 188–189.
19. Kenneth Miller, *The Czech-Slovaks in America*, George H. Doran Company, New York, 1922, pp. 128–130.
20. Mark Zborowski and Elizabeth Herzog, *Life Is with People: The Culture of the Shtetl*, New York, Schocken, 1962, p. 131.

girl has compelled her recalcitrant lover to learn law, medicine, or dentistry, or submit to being jilted by her. . . . The description of this type of woman seems rather cold and forbidding in the telling, but such an impression is misleading. . . . The women . . . are strikingly interesting because of their warm temperaments. . . .[21]

23   Certainly the old, limiting stereotypes of immigrant women do not apply to Alesandro, Zeman, and Pesotta. These three women were unusually able, but, as already suggested, they were not unique. The same combination of talents, motivations, necessities, and opportunities that turned these three to activities outside the traditional woman's sphere acted upon other immigrant women as well.

24   As many historians have noted, more men than women immigrated to the United States between 1880 and 1924, husbands often coming first and then sending for their wives and children. Still, surprisingly large numbers of single women did immigrate independently. Between 1912 and 1917, half a million single women under the age of thirty entered the United States. Many, like Rose Pesotta, were in their teens. Of 120,000 Polish women who came during this period, 84,000 were under the age of twenty-one.[22] Undoubtedly some came to join fiancés, but others came entirely on their own. For them, the act of immigration itself was a breach of the stereotype.

25   In a family unit or on their own, immigrant women frequently became part of the labor force. In 1910 about a million and a quarter foreign born women were gainfully employed. Thus, contrary to the stereotype of the homebound immigrant woman, large numbers spent the greater part of their time somewhere other than in their own homes. Nor was this necessarily a new experience. The economic pressures that stimulated immigration had already forced tens of thousands of East European women into day labor fields or in the homes of the large landowners. Thus, even before immigration, many women were working outside the traditional family unit, beyond the immediate supervision of father or husband.

26   The women of Southern Italy were kept closer to home than their Slavic counterparts, but here too, economic pressures were causing breaks in the traditional patterns even before immigration. In the United States most Italian families preferred to have their women work at home, but the need to earn more money drove increasing numbers into the garment factories. So many entered the clothing industry that the Women's Trade Union League of New

21. Hutchins Hapgood, *The Spirit of the Ghetto: Studies of the Jewish Quarter of New York*, 1902. Schocken paperback edition, New York, 1965.
22. Grace Abbott, *The Immigrant and the Community*, The Century Company, New York, 1921, pp. 55.

York found it worthwhile to establish a special Italian committee to organize Italian working women.[23]

Working outside the home did not always—or even often—lead to a new lifestyle. But the ability to earn money could be a first step toward change. New economic power among women caused an enormous change in the lifestyle of at least one immigrant group—those from the Middle East. Arabic immigrant men, who often earned their living peddling lace, underwear, and notions from door to door, discovered that their wives had easier access to American homes than they did. Arabic wives learned English quickly by peddling with or for their husbands. As the family fortunes advanced, some became active partners in large commercial enterprises. Such women moved in one generation from a subordinate, almost cloistered life in the old country to economic and social equality with their husbands in the United States and positions of importance in their communities.[24]

Whether an immigrant woman worked outside of her home or not, other aspects of life in the United States tended to break up traditional patterns. American courts could be appealed to prevent some of the abuses, such as repeated wife beating, against which there was no legal redress in many old world cultures. According to male Ukrainian immigrants, "the laws here are made for women."[25] In Middle Eastern societies the education and even the social life of the children had been controlled by their father. In the United States teachers, doctors, and social workers supported the mother in assuming control of these areas.[26]

Neighborhood problems pulled immigrant women into activities not traditionally associated with their homemaking and childbearing roles—politics, for example. An Italian woman, newly arrived in a Chicago neighborhood, was appalled at the presence of open ditches, a hazard to her young children. At the suggestion of a settlement worker, she canvassed the neighborhood to see how many other children were similarly endangered. Her survey led to a formal complaint to city hall, and the offending ditches were covered.[27]

Nor was this an isolated case. In Chicago Bohemian women organized to protest the use of open garbage wagons in their neighborhood. After the passing of the Nineteenth Amendment, Poles, Bohemians, and other immigrant women in Chicago helped organize a women's civic league, which registered five thousand women voters and campaigned against corrupt city administration.

23. Rudolph Glanz, *Jew and Italian, Historic Group Relations and the New Immigration 1881–1924,* New York, 1971, p. 47.
24. Sabia F. Haddad, "The Woman's Role in Socialization of Syrian-Americans in Chicago," *The Arab-American: Studies in Assimilation,* edited by Elaine Hogopian and Ann Paden. Medina University Press International, Wilmett, 1969, pp. 89–97.
25. Breckenridge, p. 215.
26. Haddad, pp. 97–100.
27. Daniels, p. 213.

J. Joseph Huthmacher suggests that the success of Progressive Era reforms in urban states like Massachusetts and New York was at least partly the result of immigrant political pressure.[28] More investigation is needed on the role of immigrant women in these reforms.

31   In a study of today's working-class women, Nancy Seifer suggests that "When a wife comes home after testifying at a City Council hearing, from a meeting of the local school or hospital board, or from helping to out-maneuver a local politician or win a vote for day care in her union, she is changing the balance of power in her marriage in the most fundamental way, often without realizing it."[29] Did the pioneering ventures of immigrant women into the public life of their day have a similar effect on their marriages?

32   Immigrant women created a great variety of local organizations, sometimes with the aid of second generation women of their own ethnic group or sympathetic social workers from nearby settlements and sometimes entirely on their own. Singing societies and other cultural associations were common, but there were many others. In New York City a group of Finnish domestic servants pooled their money to rent a small apartment for use on their days off. Within a few years the Finnish Women's Cooperative Home, as it was called, grew into a four story building with sleeping accommodations for forty, lounges, clubrooms, a library, a restaurant, and an employment bureau—still owned and operated by the women themselves.[30] In Buffalo an immigrant Jewish women's club based on a settlement house bought and remodeled an old home where they established a day care center for their own children and the children of others.[31]

33   Slovenes, Lithuanians, Poles, Ukrainians, Lebanese, Syrians, Jews, and other immigrant women formed organizations that often expanded to include regions, or even the entire nation, to pursue charitable and educational work among the women of their own communities. Some of these groups functioned as auxiliaries to men's organizations. Others were independent. The Polish National Alliance, for example, was organized as one unit in which men and women were to be equal members. In practice, however, the Polish women discovered themselves an ineffective minority in a male dominated organization. A group of women decided, therefore, to establish a completely independent organization, The Polish Women's Alliance, so that Polish women could develop their own self-confidence and leadership ability.[32]

34   The varied and wide ranging activities of ethnic women's organizations are an appropriate subject for more intensive investigation. The Polish Women's

28. J. Joseph Huthmacher, "Urban Liberalism and the Age of Reform," *Mississippi Valley Historical Review XLIX* (September 1962), pp. 231–241.
29. Nancy Seifer, *Absent From the Majority*, National Project on Ethnic America, American Jewish Committee, 1973, p. 45.
30. Daniels, pp. 78–81.
31. Daniels, pp. 185–186.
32. Breckenridge, pp. 205–209.

Protective League gave free legal advice and other aid to Polish working women.[33] The Ukrainian Women's Alliance published a magazine offering its members information on homemaking, childcare, and women's suffrage.[34] The Lithuanian Women's Alliance provided insurance policies as well as social and educational programs.[35] Syrian, Lebanese, and Armenian women's groups had a virtual monopoly of social and charitable services within their communities. Another group of immigrant women whose contributions were great, and often overlooked, are the members of religious orders. Among these women were capable organizers and administrators of badly needed schools, hospitals, orphanages, and other social service institutions.

Contrary to the view expressed in the old stereotypes, then, many immigrant women had interests and commitments that extended beyond the care of their own homes and families. But what of those who did not? What of the very traditional wife and mother who had neither the time, the energy, the self-assurance, nor perhaps even the desire to participate in public life. The negative stereotypes are unfair to her too. They are unfair because they confuse illiteracy with ignorance and poverty with personal degradation. The woman who fed and clothed a large family on five dollars a week—to the astonishment of the social worker trained in home economics—may have been illiterate, but she was certainly not ignorant. The woman who worked a twelve hour night shift in a foundry and cared for her family and several boarders during the day had no time for the so-called "finer" things in life, but she was not therefore a degraded human being. To survive at all she must have possessed enormous inner resources.

Nor was the uneducated, homebound immigrant woman necessarily politically naive. While many women, like many men, sold their votes or did not vote at all, others were remarkably conscientious and astute. According to Jane Addams, Italian women who came in to vote knew more about the city's problems than their husbands, who were often away on construction or railroad jobs six months of the year. Addams writes of an illiterate Irish woman whom she was allowed to help at the voting booth in a Chicago municipal election. "The first proposition was about bonds for a new hospital. The Irish woman said, 'Is the same bunch to spend the money that run the hospital we have now? Then I am against it'. . . . There were ten propositions to be acted upon. I was scrupulous not to influence her: Yet on nine of them she voted from her own common sense just as the Municipal League and the City Club had recommended as the result of painstaking research."[36]

Undoubtedly life was too much for some immigrant women. Broken homes, physical and mental illness, despair, even suicide were all too often present in

---

33. Breckenridge, p. 294.
34. Breckenridge, p. 215.
35. Breckenridge, p. 214.
36. Gavit, p. 324.

the ethnic ghetto. The amazing thing is that, given the cultural shock of immigration and the problems of poverty, and discrimination, and survival in urban slums, so many women were able to keep themselves and their families from being defeated. An early social worker, Katherine Anthony, described one such woman, a Hungarian immigrant, Mrs. Mary Grubinsky. Mr. Grubinsky worked in a furniture factory. The couple had seven children. Mrs. Grubinsky worked "a day here, half a day there" returning to her jobs within a month after the birth of each of her children.

> In addition she helps her husband with chair caning, makes the children's clothes, mends for her own family and also for hire, cooks, washes, irons, scrubs, tends her window boxes, minds the children of a neighbor who is doing a day's work, fetches ice from the brewery where it is thrown away, forages for kindling around warehouses, runs to the school when the teacher summons her—but a list of all that Mrs. Grubinsky does in the course of a week would be quite impossible. In her home nothing is lost. Even the feathers from a Thanksgiving turkey were made into cushions and dust brushes.[37]

38 It would be understandable if such a busy woman would lag behind the rest of her family in learning English and adjusting to the United States. But according to Katherine Anthony, this was not the case with Mary Grubinsky.

> She takes the lead in Americanizing her husband and family. She insisted they move from a two to a three room apartment to have a sitting room. . . . Sees to it the girls have proper clothes, white shoes for confirmation. In these matters Mrs. Grubinsky feels that she must decide and that Martin must accommodate himself.

39 Like Alesandro, Humpel, and Pesotta, Mary Grubinsky was unusually capable. But also like them, she was not unique.

40 In conclusion, the current interest in ethnicity occurring simultaneously with the new interest in the history of women makes this an opportune time for scholars to take a new look at the immigrant woman. "Forgotten" women, who like Alessandro, Humpel, and Pesotta, played an important role in the public life of their communities can be rediscovered by a careful study of the ethnic press and the papers of ethnic institutions (especially women's groups), labor unions, settlement houses, and political parties. The experiences of these women should become an integral part of our understanding of immigration history.

41 So, too, should the experiences of the more traditional women whose lives,

37. Katherine Anthony, *Mothers Who Must Earn*, New York, 1914, pp. 186–190.

like that of Mary Grubinsky, were centered around care of the home and the family. These women constituted too varied and complex a group to be ignored or dismissed with an inherited negative stereotype. More can be learned about them from their letters and diaries (where these exist), from the records of charities, hospitals, courts and other institutions, and from demographic sources such as census tracts and school surveys. Letters-to-the-editor columns in the ethnic press can be useful, as can the short stories, novels, and poetry of perspective immigrant writers.[38] Research is needed on the impact of immigration and acculturation on the lives of all immigrant women, on the institution of marriage, and on child-rearing practices.

In conclusion, sources are available for the study of the Southern and Eastern European immigrant woman. With the use of some ingenuity on the part of historians, many more can probably be uncovered. It is time to begin writing the story of the immigrant woman—beyond the stereotype. ✥

42

RESPONDING

1. Write a journal entry describing an immigrant woman. You might talk about a family member, someone else you know, or someone you have read about. Does this woman fit the stereotype Seller describes?

2. Working individually or in a group, examine the current expectations for women in your culture or another culture with which you are familiar. Compare these with the expectations for women in one of the cultures Seller discusses.

3. List the relevant factors that influenced the lives of Antonietta Pisanelli Alesandro, Josephine Humpel Zeman, and Rose Pesotta. Write an essay comparing their experiences. Consider whether all three are the products of similar backgrounds. What factors or events facilitated their choices? Was each a product of a unique culture?

4. Seller's position is that the negative stereotype of immigrant women is incorrect. How do you think this stereotype came about? What might its function have been? Support your argument with evidence from the reading, outside information, and your own experience. Refer to your journal entry to get started.

---

38. See, for example, the works of Anzia Yezierska, *Hungry Hearts, The Bread Winners, Salome of the Tenements,* and *All I Could Never Be.*

⊞

CONNECTING

Critical Thinking and Writing

1. Write an essay that explores the difficulties of adjusting to life in a new country. You can use examples from the readings as well as personal experience.

2. Compare characters from two stories in this section to show the variety of ways early immigrants reacted to the challenges of living in a new country. Analyze the circumstances and the personal qualities of the characters to explain their methods of coping.

3. An American clergyman, Canon Barnett, stated that "the things which make men alike are finer and better than the things that keep them apart, and that these basic likenesses, if they are properly accentuated, easily transcend the less essential differences of race, language, creed and tradition." Agree or disagree with this statement using evidence from the readings in this section as well as your own experience.

4. Research your own family history and write the story of your family's journey to the United States and their experiences when they arrived in this country. If you are interested in writing a family history but are an American Indian or are unable to find out anything about your family's initial immigration, record the circumstances in which your family moved to the place where they currently live.

5. First- and second-generation Americans often criticize new immigrants for failing to learn English and failing to adopt their way of doing things. They often cite their own parents or grandparents as examples of immigrants who easily assimilated. Write an essay supporting or refuting the idea that early immigrant groups were more easily absorbed into the country than recent ones. Use examples from your own knowledge and experience as well as evidence from the readings in this chapter.

6. Seller describes a prevalent negative stereotype of immigrant women. Argue that the women portrayed in the other readings in this section are or are not modeled on the stereotype.

7. Design your own essay topic that analyzes or compares some aspect that relates two or more of the readings in this chapter.

8. For some immigrants, Ellis Island was an "Island of Tears," for others "The House of Freedom." Explain the significance of the two names and discuss the selection process that took place at Ellis Island. Was the American government too harsh in its treatment of arriving immigrants? What rationale might there have been for the selection process?

9. Write an essay discussing the difficulties and misunderstandings that can occur between foreign-born parents and children raised in America. Support your points with examples from at least two readings in the text as well as from your own knowledge and experience. Some readings that particularly focus on this theme are "The Fat of the Land" and "Facing the Great Desolation" from Chapter 1, and *No-no Boy* from Chapter 5.

10. Discuss the problems European immigrants faced at the turn of the century such as poor working and living conditions, difficulty learning the language, lack of government support, and prejudice against new immigrants. Compare their hardships with those of other immigrant groups such as the Japanese, Chinese, Puerto Ricans, or Chicanos.

11. Evidence of folk beliefs and practices occurs in some of the readings when the characters prepare love potions, wear charms to ward off evil, or behave in certain ways to avoid bad luck. Compare folk beliefs that appear in stories such as "The Fat of the Land" (in Chapter 1) and "Love Medicine" (in Chapter 7) with those in your own culture. Argue that such beliefs and practices are or are not an important part of all or most cultures.

For Further Research

1. Review current immigration laws and compare them to laws at the turn of the century. Some issues to consider are the ways in which attitudes have changed as the country has become more populated, who currently makes up the largest group of immigrants, whether certain groups are more welcome than others, and what policies we should have in the future.

2. Research social legislation to protect children and adults in the United States at the turn of the century. Some questions to consider include (a) What were the child labor laws? (b) Was there compulsory education? (c) Were unemployment benefits available? (d) Were working conditions regulated? (e) Was there a minimum wage? Expand this topic by comparing the working person's rights at the turn of the century with those rights today. What laws have been enacted to guarantee those rights?

REFERENCES AND ADDITIONAL SOURCES

Addams, Jane. *Twenty Years at Hull House: with Autobiographical Notes.* New York: Macmillan, 1910, 1967.

——. *Forty Years at Hull House.* New York: Macmillan, 1935.

Barolini, Helen. *The Dream Book: An Anthology of Writings by Italian American Women.* New York: Schocken, 1985.

Cahan, Abraham. *The Education of Abraham Cahan.* Trans. Leo Stein et al. Philadelphia: Jewish Publication Society of America, 1969.

Dunne, Finley Peter. *Observations by Mr. Dooley.* New York: R. H. Russell, 1902; Harper, 1906.

Ferraro, Thomas. *Ethnic Passages: Literary Immigrants in Twentieth-Century America.* Chicago: University of Chicago Press, 1993.

Fine, David M. *The City, the Immigrant and American Fiction, 1880–1920.* Metuchen, N.J.: Scarecrow, 1977.

Glenn, Susan Anita. *Daughters of the Shtetl: Life and Labor in the Immigrant Generation.* Ithaca: Cornell University Press, 1990.

Handlin, Oscar. *Race and Nationality in American Life.* Garden City, N.Y.: Doubleday, 1957.

——. *Uprooted: The Epic Story of the Great Migrations that Made the American People.* Boston: Little, Brown, 1951. New York: Grosset & Dunlap, 1957.

Heinze, Andrew R. *Adapting to Abundance: Jewish Immigrants, Mass Consumption, and the Search for American Identity.* New York: Columbia University Press, 1990.

Hoerder, Dirk, ed. *American Labor and Immigration History, 1877–1920s: Recent European Research.* Urbana: University of Illinois Press, 1983.

Jones, Maldwyn Allen. *American Immigration.* Chicago: University of Chicago Press, 1960. 2nd ed. 1992.

Kraut, Alan M. *The Huddled Masses: The Immigrant in American Society, 1880–1921.* Arlington Heights, Ill.: Harlan Davidson, 1982.

Luebke, Frederick C. *Germans in the New World: Essays in the History of Immigration.* Urbana: University of Illinois Press, 1990.

Marcuson, Lewis R. *The Stage Immigrant: The Irish, Italians, and Jews in American Drama, 1920–1960.* New York: Garland, 1990.

Miller, Kerby A. *Emigrants and Exiles: Ireland and the Irish Exodus to North America.* New York: Oxford University Press, 1985.

Miller, Wayne Charles. *A Gathering of Ghetto Writers: Irish, Italian, Jewish, Black, and Puerto Rican.* New York: NYU Press, 1972.

2

CHINESE IMMIGRANTS

The Lure of the Gold Mountain

Above: Chinese immigrants building the transcontinental railroad, circa 1866. *(Asian American Studies Library, University of California at Berkeley)*
Opposite: Chinese immigrants detained at the Angel Island Immigrants Station. *(California Historical Society, San Francisco. FN-18240)*

SETTING THE HISTORICAL AND CULTURAL CONTEXT

IN A POEM WRITTEN BY a Chinese immigrant, we hear a warning to others who might want to follow: "Return to the old country quickly/to avoid going astray." This poem and much of the other writing of the period of early Chinese immigration establishes a clear contrast between the promise of the Gold Mountain—the term applied by the Chinese to California or, more generally, to America itself—and its actual cost in human terms. Although "Gold Mountain" was generally interpreted as a land of opportunity offering an escape from the poverty of China, the term could also suggest more than financial success. Many immigrants planned to return to China after spending some time in the United States; the journey to the Gold Mountain provided each sojourner with an opportunity to improve his social position at home. But too often, the promise was illusory. As the Gold Mountain poems reprinted in this chapter suggest, immigrants, rather than finding riches, found themselves victims of prejudice who were often treated like criminals. Despite these pressures, however, immigrants did more than endure: they helped to enrich the cultural development of the United States. In order to understand these pressures and the Chinese immigrant community's response to them, we need to examine briefly the circumstances of the immigrants' arrival in America.

Although there were a few earlier Chinese immigrants, the Chinese first arrived in the United States in great numbers between 1849 and 1870. Most came from the area of Kwangtung, a province on China's south coast, noted as a commercial rather than agricultural region. Because it was a port city, its residents were kept informed about distant events through contacts from around the world. After hearing about the Gold Rush in California, many citizens decided to leave Kwangtung to seek new opportunities for success in America. A large percentage of those who emigrated were the young males who had left their families behind, hoping to return within a few years with their newly acquired prosperity.

Emigration often involved a good deal of hardship. Until 1860 the act of emigration itself violated both Chinese custom and the emperor's laws; those apprehended were subject to capital punishment. Moreover, life aboard ship was often a test of one's endurance—quarters were cramped, and food supplies were often inadequate. For many immigrants the struggle was not over once they had arrived in California; like the newcomers discussed in chapter one, the Chinese immigrants usually had to undergo a series of medical tests and interrogation sessions at immigration headquarters. As Sui Sin Far's story "In the Land of the Free" and Connie Young Yu's essay about her grandmother make clear, the process itself, with its apparently arbitrary laws, made immigrants vulnerable to lengthy periods of separation from their children and other forms of exploitation.

During the first twenty years of Chinese immigration, many new arrivals moved quickly from the coast to jobs inland. Generally, they served first as contract workers, working to repay managers for the costs of their passage. Although a small number of Chinese workers found employment in New England or in the South, most remained in the West, journeying inland to the gold mines of the Sierra Nevada mountains. Many worked in the mines; others provided laundry and cooking services in the mining camps.

Although there were profits to be made, the Chinese in the mining camps also experienced many problems. Maxine Hong Kingston's narrative reveals the dehumanizing nature of the work required of the sojourners, who were sent down the mountains in baskets to plant explosives and later sent into the mines, "biting like rats into the earth." Furthermore, the tensions between immigrants and whites at the worksite sometimes became violent.

In the larger society, Chinese immigrant workers were subjected to unfair legislation. Discriminatory taxes, later ruled unconstitutional by the Supreme Court, were levied by the State of California upon the income of the Chinese workers. Despite these obstacles, many Chinese contributed significantly to the labor force. They earned the praise of business and governmental leaders alike for their ability to perform difficult and dangerous labor. In 1871, for example, a United States commission designated to report on the mining industry praised the efficiency and courage of Chinese immigrant workers.

After the Gold Rush had ended, some immigrants found work in other kinds of mines, but a much larger number were employed in building the transcontinental railroad. Railroad executives were so impressed by the efficiency of the Chinese workers and the quality of their work that they sent emissaries to Kwangtung province to recruit additional workers. During the last years of the construction (1865–1869), the great majority of railroad construction workers were Chinese immigrants. When the final piece of track connecting the eastern with the western railroads had been put into place, the Chinese workers were acknowledged to have made an important contribution to the growth of the nation. Yet this recognition was not without a certain irony, which Hong Kingston makes clear as she explores conflicts between agency and ownership, self-sacrifice and reward. Moreover, as the selection from Pardee Lowe's "Father and Glorious Descendants" suggests, an individual's success is often determined less by his or her own ambition than by the judgments and prejudices of others.

When the railroad construction project was over, Chinese immigrants turned to other enterprises. Some moved to the San Joaquin Valley, where they applied their skills to a large land reclamation project. Others working in agriculture helped to cultivate California's citrus crops and to develop new strains of fruit. Other immigrants settled on the coast, where they worked to establish fisheries. By the 1870s, however, the large majority of Chinese immigrants had settled in urban areas.

The most important of these urban areas during the nineteenth century was San Francisco's Chinatown. This section underwent dramatic growth during the period following the completion of the Union Pacific Railway. Chinatown offered a place to live during times when immigrants were able to find work in the larger society. It also offered a place of refuge during times of persecution. When immigrants were forced out of other areas of employment, Chinatown provided them with a place where they could establish their own small businesses and enterprises.

But Chinatown was more than a refuge. It was a social, political, and cultural center. By the mid-1850s it had its own theater. By the 1890s Chinatown had, in addition to its many bookstores and locally published periodicals, the first bilingual daily newspaper in the nation. Chinatown also had its own literary societies and political, fraternal, and social organizations. Other Chinatowns developed in other urban centers as settlers moved down the California coast and took the railroad east to New York and Boston.

Like many other communities settled right after the Gold Rush, Chinatown also had its share of the social problems of the time, specifically prostitution, gambling, and the opium trade. The circumstances of the immigrants' lives sometimes exacerbated common problems. The immigrants' resort to prostitutes can be partially attributed to state and federal laws barring men from having their wives join them or from marrying non-Asians.

Although Chinatown provided immigrants with a community based on shared language and tradition, Chinatown could offer little protection from the virulent anti-Chinese sentiment that became more pronounced at the end of the nineteenth century. This backlash was in part the result of an economic depression. With the mines exhausted and railroad construction completed, there was less work for the pool of available laborers. The railroad the Chinese immigrants had helped to construct added to their problems by bringing to the West Coast many workers who were not able to find work in the east. As in other periods, those who were unemployed sometimes blamed their situation not on the economics of the day but on the immigrants, who sometimes would work for a cheaper wage. As a result of the widely held prejudices of the time, Chinese immigrants continued to be scapegoated for economic problems that were out of their control.

The prevalent atmosphere allowed nativist and protectionist organizations to be formed throughout the west. These groups exerted pressure on government officials at all levels to exclude the Chinese immigrants who were already settled from employment and to bar new immigrants from entering the country. Ironically, this call for sanctions was sometimes led by persons who had themselves immigrated to this country, the most notable example being Denis Kearney, an Irish immigrant who founded the Workingmen's Party. This San Francisco–based organization had as its goal the exclusion of Asian workers from American commerce.

The media intensified the exclusionary sentiments. Historians have been able to trace antiimmigrant news stories as early as Civil War times—the *New York Times*, for example, ran a series of purported news stories in the

1860s warning about the influx of immigrants. By the 1890s, western papers such as the *San Francisco Chronicle* began to sensationalize the issue further by advertising and covering in depth the rallies and other media events organized by nativist and protectionist factions such as the Workingmen's Party.

The pressure exerted by media and special-interest groups was felt by many politicians of the period. Some ran on nativist or exclusionary platforms; others became more exclusionary with time. Leland Stanford, who as the head of the Central Pacific Railroad had praised Chinese workers, became more exclusionary when he served as California governor and United States senator.

Exclusionary legislation was passed on the local, state, and federal levels. In San Francisco, for example, schools were ordered to be racially segregated. In addition to making the Chinese subject to discriminatory taxes, the State of California passed laws prohibiting Asians from obtaining business licenses or owning real estate. On the federal level, the Scott Act prohibited Chinese laborers from entering the country and prevented those immigrants who had returned to China from being readmitted to the United States.

The most serious piece of discriminatory legislation passed during this period, however, was the federal Chinese Exclusion Act of 1882. This prohibited most Chinese nationals from entering the United States. President Taft vetoed the act, but it passed over his veto. After the passage of this act, some immigrants were able to enter the country from Mexico or Canada; a small number of others claimed to be from those categories of immigrants exempted by the Chinese Exclusion Act. Generally, however, the Chinese Exclusion Act virtually halted immigration to the United States from China until 1943.

The passage of the Chinese Exclusion Act was particularly deplorable, given the way in which the Chinese government had welcomed American nationals as early as the 1840s. Indeed, in 1841 the Chinese had granted rather extensive rights to American citizens coming to China. These rights were granted unilaterally: the Americans were not required to reciprocate. By the time the first treaty was to expire, though, the negotiators representing the Chinese government insisted that their subjects be guaranteed certain basic rights. The Burlingame Treaty, negotiated in 1868, provided Chinese nationals with the immigration and employment rights accorded to persons from "a most favored nation." The Chinese Exclusion Act was thus a clear violation of the Burlingame Treaty.

After the passage of the Chinese Exclusion Act, those Chinese nationals who attempted to enter the United States legally were routinely detained for questioning; after 1910 they were held at Angel Island in San Francisco Bay. During their detention at Angel Island, they were examined and questioned about their status. Those who were able to convince the examiners of their right to be in the country were admitted; those who were not were deported. The process of examining immigrants often took months. Whatever the duration, detainees had to live in squalid quarters and eat substandard food.

Family members were separated by gender for the duration of the stay, and detainees were allowed no visitors. Even though the facility was declared "uninhabitable" as early as 1920, it remained in operation until the 1940s. Inmates protested these living conditions in poems written on the barrack walls. These works, first transcribed in 1910, provide a record of the suffering endured by many Chinese nationals. Often in these poems the promise of America is contrasted with the intolerant atmosphere that immigrants were forced to confront.

The Chinese Exclusion Act was renewed in 1890 and remained in effect until 1943. It was not until that late date that the American government's treatment of immigrants from China began to change; even then, this change was due less to a change of heart than a change in strategic priorities. As the United States's entry into World War II became more probable, American military strategists sought to strengthen the nation's alliances in Asia. Improvement of relations with China thus became extremely important. The repeal of the Chinese Exclusion Act in 1943 was thus a part of the nation's attempt to improve its international strategic position.

During the first years after the repeal, though, only a token number of Chinese—approximately one hundred—were allowed to immigrate each year. In 1945 immigration laws were relaxed somewhat to allow the foreign spouses of American soldiers to immigrate. Another law, passed in 1947, allowed approximately one thousand Chinese nationals entry into the country. During the next forty years these numbers increased with the easing of American immigration restrictions and the change of government in China. Some Chinese fled the country after the Communists' victory in 1949; others left during the Cultural Revolution of the 1960s and 1970s. More recently, Chinese young people who came to the United States to study sought and were granted political asylum after the massacre at Tiananmen Square in 1989. Like the immigrants who proceeded them, the Chinese immigrants of the last forty years have not only revitalized Chinatowns across the nation, but they have strengthened the quality of American life.

BEGINNING: Pre-reading/Writing

Working in a group, use your knowledge of early Chinese immigrants gained from the introduction to this chapter, other books or media, and personal experience to try to construct profiles of some of the first Chinese immigrants to California. Consider sex, age, marital status, economic status, skills or profession, and reasons for immigrating. Share your profiles with the class. What type of person do you think would have made the journey from China to a foreign land in the mid-1800s?

The Chinese Exclusion Act barred Chinese nationals, with very few exceptions, from entering the United States. For the first time in American history, immigrants were excluded because of their country of origin. Congress passed the Act after much lobbying by nativist and protectionist groups such as Denis Kearney's Workingmen's Party. The Chinese Exclusion Act was later renewed and remained in effect until 1943.

⁜

From THE CHINESE EXCLUSION ACT

May 6, 1882. CHAP. 126.—An act to execute certain treaty stipulations relating to Chinese.

WHEREAS, IN THE OPINION OF THE Government of the United States the coming   1
of Chinese laborers to this country endangers the good order of certain localities within the territory thereof: Therefore,

Be it enacted by the Senate and House of Representatives of the United States of   2
America in Congress assembled, That from and after the expiration of ninety days next after the passage of this act, and until the expiration of ten years next after the passage of this act, the coming of Chinese laborers to the United States be, and the same is hereby, suspended; and during such suspension it shall not be lawful for any Chinese laborer to come, or, having so come after the expiration of said ninety days, to remain within the United States.

SEC. 2. That the master of any vessel who shall knowingly bring within the   3
United States on such vessel, and land or permit to be landed, any Chinese laborer, from any foreign port or place, shall be deemed guilty of a misdemeanor, and on conviction thereof shall be punished by a fine of not more than five hundred dollars for each and every such Chinese laborer so brought, and may also be imprisoned for a term not exceeding one year.

SEC. 3. That the two foregoing sections shall not apply to Chinese laborers   4
who were in the United States on the seventeenth day of November, eighteen hundred and eighty, or who shall have come into the same before the expiration of ninety days next after the passage of this act, and who shall produce to such master before going on board such vessel, and shall produce to the collector of the port in the United States at which such vessel shall arrive, the evidence hereinafter in this act required of his being one of the laborers in this section mentioned; nor shall the two foregoing sections apply to the case of any master whose vessel, being bound to a port not within the United States, shall come within the jurisdiction of the United States by reason of being in distress or in stress of weather, or touching at any port of the United States on its voyage to

any foreign port or place: *Provided,* That all Chinese laborers brought on such vessel shall depart with the vessel on leaving port.

April 29, 1902. CHAP. 641.—An act to prohibit the coming into and to regulate the residence within the United States, its Territories, and all territory under its jurisdiction, and the District of Columbia, of Chinese and persons of Chinese descent.

5 *Be it enacted by the Senate and House of Representatives of the United States of America in Congress assembled,* That all laws now in force prohibiting and regulating the coming of Chinese persons, and persons of Chinese descent, into the United States, and the residence of such persons therein, including sections five, six, seven, eight, nine, ten, eleven, thirteen, and fourteen of the Act entitled "An Act to prohibit the coming of Chinese laborers into the United States" approved September thirteenth, eighteen hundred and eighty-eight, be, and the same are hereby, re-enacted, extended, and continued so far as the same are not inconsistent with treaty obligations, until otherwise provided by law, and said laws shall also apply to the island territory under the jurisdiction of the United States, and prohibit the immigration of Chinese laborers, not citizens of the United States, from such island territory to the mainland territory of the United States, whether in such island territory at the time of cession or not, and from one portion of the island territory of the United States to another portion of said island territory: *Provided, however,* That said laws shall not apply to the transit of Chinese laborers from one island to another island of the same group; and any islands within the jurisdiction of any State or the District of Alaska shall be considered a part of the mainland under this section.

6 Sᴇᴄ. 2. That the Secretary of the Treasury is hereby authorized and empowered to make and prescribe, and from time to time to change, such rules and regulations not inconsistent with the laws of the land as he may deem necessary and proper to execute the provisions of this Act and of the Acts hereby extended and continued and of the treaty of December eighth, eighteen hundred and ninety-four, between the United States and China, and with the approval of the President to appoint such agents as he may deem necessary for the efficient execution of said treaty and said Acts.

7 Sᴇᴄ. 3. That nothing in the provisions of this Act or any other Act shall be construed to prevent, hinder, or restrict any foreign exhibitor, representative, or citizen of any foreign nation, or the holder, who is a citizen of any foreign nation, of any concession or privilege from any fair or exposition authorized by Act of Congress from bringing into the United States, under contract, such mechanics, artisans, agents, or other employees, natives of their respective foreign countries, as they or any of them may deem necessary for the purpose of making preparation for installing or conducting their exhibits or of preparing for installing or conducting any business authorized or permitted under or by virtue of or pertaining to any concession or privilege which may have been or

may be granted by any said fair or exposition in connection with such exposition, under such rules and regulations as the Secretary of the Treasury may prescribe, both as to the admission and return of such person or persons.

SEC. 4. That it shall be the duty of every Chinese laborer, other than a citizen, rightfully in, and entitled to remain in any of the insular territory of the United States (Hawaii excepted) at the time of the passage of this Act, to obtain within one year thereafter a certificate of residence in the insular territory wherein he resides, which certificate shall entitle him to residence therein, and upon failure to obtain such certificate as herein provided he shall be deported from such insular territory; and the Philippine Commission is authorized and required to make all regulations and provisions necessary for the enforcement of this section in the Philippine Islands, including the form and substance of the certificate of residence so that the same shall clearly and sufficiently identify the holder thereof and enable officials to prevent fraud in the transfer of the same: *Provided, however*, That if said Philippine Commission shall find that it is impossible to complete the registration herein provided for within one year from the passage of this Act, said Commission is hereby authorized and empowered to extend the time for such registration for a further period not exceeding one year.

Approved, April 29, 1902. ✤

RESPONDING

1. Imagine that you are a Chinese immigrant in San Francisco in the late 1800s with a wife in China. Write a letter to your wife explaining the impact of the Chinese Exclusion Act on your life.

2. Using material from the introduction to this chapter, your own knowledge, or sources in your school library, gather information to answer the following questions:
   a. Why were the Chinese invited to the United States in the 1800s?
   b. How many laborers were imported from China?
   c. On what projects did they primarily work?
   Working individually or in a group, use the information gained from the research into the importation of laborers to speculate about the reactions of other groups already in the West.

3. Write an essay discussing the ways in which the Exclusion Act of 1882 tried to curtain Chinese immigration. Discuss the effect the passage of this act might have had on the Chinese view of America as a land of opportunity.

From **THE GOLD MOUNTAIN POEMS**

The Gold Mountain poems are anonymous works written by some of the earliest Chinese immigrants to the United States. It was not until several generations later that the poems were edited by Marlon K. Hom and published by the University of California Press.

These three poems express the hardship and discrimination the immigrants faced when arriving in America.

✛

欲覓蠅頭利。窮鄉沒作置。(一)
乘危履險走花旗(一)。遇着稅員盤詰汝(二)
稍忘記。撥(三)禁荒島裡。
好漢真無用武地。不能一步越雷池。

(一) 花旗：美國
(二) 稅員：參看歌#1
(三) 撥：驅逐

JSGJ I.5a

In search of a pin-head gain,
I was idle in an impoverished village.
I've risked a perilous journey to come to the Flowery
　Flag Nation.
Immigration officers interrogated me:
And, just for a slight lapse of memory,
I am deported, and imprisoned in this barren
　mountain.
A brave man cannot use his might here,
And he can't take one step beyond the confines.

家貧柴米恵。貸本來金山(一)。
關員審問脱身難。撥往埃崙(三)。
到此間。闇室長嗟嘆。
國弱被人多辱慢。儼然畜類任摧殘。

（一）金山：美國
（二）撥：參看歌#3
（三）埃崙：音譯「島」；
指天使島

JSGJ I.14a

At home I was in poverty,
　constantly worried about firewood and rice.
I borrowed money
　to come to Gold Mountain.
Immigration officers cross-examined me;
　no way could I get through.
Deported to this island,
　like a convicted criminal.
Here—
Mournful sighs fill the gloomy room.
A nation weak; her people often humiliated
Like animals, tortured and destroyed at others'
　whim.

自由爲國例。何事學專制。
不持公理美人兮。困我監牢嚴密睇(一)
狼虎差。橫行更欲噬。
罪及無辜真惡抵(二)。幾時出獄開心懷。

（二）（一）
睇：：參看歌 #10
惡抵：：難以抵受；參看歌 #10

JSGJ I.13b

So, liberty is your national principle;
Why do you practice autocracy?
You don't uphold justice, you Americans,
You detain me in prison, guard me closely.
Your officials are wolves and tigers,
All ruthless, all wanting to bite me.
An innocent man implicated, such an injustice!
When can I get out of this prison and free
    my mind? ✣

RESPONDING

1. Unlike most of the poetry in this book, these poems were not written by professional poets who wanted to publish their work but by immigrants who used poetry as a way of understanding their own experiences and expressing their feelings about them. Write a poem about some experience that affected you strongly, or write a journal entry discussing the benefits of writing as an emotional outlet.

2. Working in groups, discuss the attitude of the speakers in each of these poems. How does each feel about the United States government? Report your findings to the class.

3. We don't know exactly why the speaker in the second poem is imprisoned. Using material from the chapter introduction and your own knowledge,

write your own story about the circumstances that might have caused him to be "deported to this island, like a convicted criminal."

4. Drawing on your knowledge, the chapter introduction, or sources in the library, write a letter from a government official to a San Francisco newspaper justifying the speaker's imprisonment. Or write an editorial for a San Francisco newspaper condemning the treatment of prisoners held on Angel Island.

SUI SIN FAR

Sui Sin Far is a pseudonym assumed by the writer Edith Maude Eaton. Born in 1867, Edith Eaton was the eldest of fourteen children of a Chinese mother and an English father. Her earliest jobs included work in stenography and in the advertising department of a railroad company. Most of her stories were published in such magazines as The Overland Monthly, Century, *and* Good Housekeeping. *She died in 1909.*

The stories of Sui Sin Far are among the first works published by an Asian-American author. "In the Land of the Free," which explores the consequences of the immigration process for one family, also depicts the family's vulnerability to exploitation by unscrupulous people.

IN THE LAND OF THE FREE

I

1   "SEE, LITTLE ONE—the hills in the morning sun. There is thy home for years to come. It is very beautiful and thou wilt be very happy there."

2   The Little One looked up into his mother's face in perfect faith. He was engaged in the pleasant occupation of sucking a sweetmeat; but that did not prevent him from gurgling responsively.

3   "Yes, my olive bud; there is where thy father is making a fortune for thee. Thy father! Oh, wilt thou not be glad to behold his dear face. 'Twas for thee I left him."

4   The Little One ducked his chin sympathetically against his mother's knee. She lifted him on to her lap. He was two years old, a round, dimple-cheeked boy with bright brown eyes and a sturdy little frame.

5   "Ah! Ah! Ah! Ooh! Ooh! Ooh!" puffed he, mocking a tugboat steaming by.

6   San Francisco's waterfront was lined with ships and steamers, while other craft, large and small, including a couple of white transports from the Philippines, lay at anchor here and there off shore. It was some time before the *Eastern Queen* could get docked, and even after that was accomplished, a lone Chinaman who had been waiting on the wharf for an hour was detained that much longer by men with the initials U.S.C. on their caps, before he could board the steamer and welcome his wife and child.

7   "This is thy son," announced the happy Lae Choo.

8   Hom Hing lifted the child, felt of his little body and limbs, gazed into his

face with proud and joyous eyes; then turned inquiringly to a customs officer at his elbow.

"That's a fine boy you have there," said the man. "Where was he born?" 9

"In China," answered Hom Hing, swinging the Little One on his right 10 shoulder, preparatory to leading his wife off the steamer.

"Ever been to America before?" 11

"No, not he," answered the father with a happy laugh. 12

The customs officer beckoned to another. 13

"This little fellow," said he, "is visiting America for the first time." 14

The other customs officer stroked his chin reflectively. 15

"Good day," said Hom Hing. 16

"Wait!" commanded one of the officers. "You cannot go just yet." 17

"What more now?" asked Hom Hing. 18

"I'm afraid," said the customs officer, "that we cannot allow the boy to go 19 ashore. There is nothing in the papers that you have shown us—your wife's papers and your own—having any bearing upon the child."

"There was no child when the papers were made out," returned Hom Hing. 20 He spoke calmly; but there was apprehension in his eyes and in his tightening grip on his son.

"What is it? What is it?" quavered Lae Choo, who understood a little 21 English.

The second customs officer regarded her pityingly. 22

"I don't like this part of the business," he muttered. 23

The first officer turned to Hom Hing and in an official tone of voice, said: 24

"Seeing that the boy has no certificate entitling him to admission to this 25 country you will have to leave him with us."

"Leave my boy!" exclaimed Hom Hing. 26

"Yes; he will be well taken care of, and just as soon as we can hear from 27 Washington, he will be handed over to you."

"But," protested Hom Hing, "he is my son." 28

"We have no proof," answered the man with a shrug of his shoulders; "and 29 even if so we cannot let him pass without orders from the Government."

"He is my son," reiterated Hom Hing, slowly and solemnly. "I am a Chinese 30 merchant and have been in business in San Francisco for many years. When my wife told to me one morning that she dreamed of a green tree with spreading branches and one beautiful red flower growing thereon, I answered her that I wished my son to be born in our country, and for her to prepare to go to China. My wife complied with my wish. After my son was born my mother fell sick and my wife nursed and cared for her; then my father, too, fell sick, and my wife also nursed and cared for him. For twenty moons my wife care for and nurse the old people, and when they did they bless her and my son, and I send for her to return to me. I had no fear of trouble. I was a Chinese merchant and my son was my son."

31   "Very good, Hom Hing," replied the first officer. "Nevertheless, we take your son."

32   "No, you not take him; he my son too."

33   It was Lae Choo. Snatching the child from his father's arms she held and covered him with her own.

34   The officers conferred together for a few moments; then one drew Hom Hing aside and spoke in his ear.

35   Resignedly Hom Hing bowed his head, then approached his wife. "'Tis the law," said he, speaking in Chinese, "and 'twill be but for a little while—until tomorrow's sun arises."

36   "You, too," reproached Lae Choo in a voice eloquent with pain. But accustomed to obedience she yielded the boy to her husband, who in turn delivered him to the first officer. The Little One protested lustily against the transfer; but his mother covered her face with her sleeve and his father silently led her away. Thus was the law of the land complied with.

II

37   Day was breaking. Lae Choo, who had been awake all night, dressed herself, then awoke her husband.

38   "'Tis the morn," she cried. "Go, bring our son."

39   The man rubbed his eyes and arose upon his elbow so that he could see out of the window. A pale star was visible in the sky. The petals of a lily in a bowl on the windowsill were unfurled.

40   "'Tis not yet time," said he, laying his head down again.

41   "Not yet time. Ah, all the time that I lived before yesterday is no so much as the time that has been since my Little One was taken from me."

42   The mother threw herself down beside the bed and covered her face.

43   Hom Hing turned on the light, and touching his wife's bowed head with a sympathetic hand inquired if she had slept.

44   "Slept!" she echoed, weepingly. "Ah, how could I close my eyes with my arms empty of the little body that has filled them every night for more than twenty moons! You do not know—man—what it is to miss the feel of the little fingers and the little toes and the soft round limbs of your little one. Even in the darkness his darling eyes used to shine up to mine, and often have I fallen into slumber with his pretty babble at my ear. And now, I see him not; I touch him not; I hear him not. My baby, my little fat one!"

45   "Now! Now! Now!" consoled Hom Hing, patting his wife's shoulder reassuringly; "there is no need to grieve so; he will soon gladden you again. There cannot be any law that would keep a child from its mother!"

46   Lae Choo dried her tears.

47   "You are right, my husband," she meekly murmured. She arose and stepped about the apartment, setting things to rights. The box of presents she had

brought for her California friends had been opened the evening before; and silks, embroideries, carved ivories, ornamental lacquer-ware, brasses, camphor-wood boxes, fans, and chinaware were scattered around in confused heaps. In the midst of unpacking the thought of her child in the hands of strangers had overpowered her, and she had left everything to crawl into bed and weep.

Having arranged her gifts in order she stepped out on to the deep balcony. 48

The star had faded from view and there were bright streaks in the western 49 sky. Lae Choo looked down the street and around. Beneath the flat occupied by her and her husband were quarters for a number of bachelor Chinamen, and she could hear them from where she stood, taking their early morning breakfast. Below their dining-room was her husband's grocery store. Across the way was a large restaurant. Last night it had been resplendent with gay colored lanterns and the sound of music. The rejoicings over "the completion of the moon," by Quong Sum's firstborn, had been long and loud, and had caused her to tie a handkerchief over her ears. She, a bereaved mother, had it not in her heart to rejoice with other parents. This morning the place was more in accord with her mood. It was still and quiet. The revellers had dispersed or were asleep.

A roly-poly woman in black sateen, with long pendant earrings in her ears, 50 looked up from the street below and waved her a smiling greeting. It was her old neighbor, Kuie Hoe, the wife of the gold embosser, Mark Sing. With her was a little boy in yellow jacket and lavender pantaloons. Lae Choo remembered him as a baby. She used to like to play with him in those days when she had no child of her own. What a long time ago that seemed! She caught her breath in a sigh, and laughed instead.

"Why are you so merry?" called her husband from within. 51

"Because my Little One is coming home," answered Lae Choo. "I am a 52 happy mother—a happy mother."

She pattered into the room with a smile on her face. 53

The noon hour had arrived. The rice was steaming in the bowls and a fragrant 54 dish of chicken and bamboo shoots was awaiting Hom Hing. Not for one moment had Lae Choo paused to rest during the morning hours; her activity had been ceaseless. Every now and again, however, she had raised her eyes to the gilded clock on the curiously carved mantelpiece. Once, she had exclaimed:

"Why so long, oh! why so long?" Then, apostrophizing herself: "Lae Choo, 55 be happy. The Little One is coming! The Little One is coming!" Several times she burst into tears, and several times she laughed aloud.

Hom Hing entered the room; his arms hung down by his side. 56

"The Little One!" shrieked Lae Choo. 57

"They bid me call tomorrow." 58

With a moan the mother sank to the floor. 59

The noon hour passed. The dinner remained on the table. 60

III

61 The winter rains were over: the spring had come to California, flushing the hills with green and causing an ever-changing pageant of flowers to pass over them. But there was no spring in Lae Choo's heart, for the Little One remained away from her arms. He was being kept in a mission. White women were caring for him, and though for one full moon he had pined for his mother and refused to be comforted he was now apparently happy and contented. Five moons or five months had gone by since the day he had passed with Lae Choo through the Golden Gate; but the great Government at Washington still delayed sending the answer which would return him to his parents.

62 Hom Hing was disconsolately rolling up and down the balls in his abacus box when a keen-faced young man stepped into his store.

63 "What news?" asked the Chinese merchant.

64 "This!" The young man brought forth a typewritten letter. Hon Hing read the words:

65 "Re Chinese child, alleged to be the son of Hom Hing, Chinese merchant, doing business at 425 Clay Street, San Francisco.

66 "Same will have attention as soon as possible."

67 Hom Hing returned the letter, and without a word continued his manipulation of the counting machine.

68 "Have you anything to say?" asked the young man.

69 "Nothing. They have sent the same letter fifteen times before. Have you not yourself showed it to me?"

70 "True!" The young man eyed the Chinese merchant furtively. He had a proposition to make and was pondering whether or not the time was opportune.

71 "How is your wife?" he inquired solicitously—and diplomatically.

72 Hom Hing shook his head mournfully.

73 "She seems less every day," he replied. "Her food she takes only when I bid her and her tears fall continuously. She finds no pleasure in dress or flowers and cares not to see her friends. Her eyes stare all night. I think before another moon she will pass into the land of spirits."

74 "No!" exclaimed the young man, genuinely startled.

75 "If the boy not come home I lose my wife sure," continued Hom Hing with bitter sadness.

76 "It's not right," cried the young man indignantly. Then he made his proposition.

77 The Chinese father's eyes brightened exceedingly.

78 "Will I like you to go to Washington and make them give you the paper to restore my son?" cried he. "How can you ask when you know my heart's desire?"

79 "Then," said the young fellow, "I will start next week. I am anxious to see this thing through if only for the sake of your wife's peace of mind."

"I will call her. To hear what you think to do will make her glad," said Hom Hing.   80

He called a message to Lae Choo upstairs through a tube in the wall.   81

In a few moments she appeared, listless, wan, and hollow-eyed; but when her husband told her the young lawyer's suggestion she became electrified; her form straightened, her eyes glistened; the color flushed to her cheeks.   82

"Oh," she cried, turning to James Clancy. "You are a hundred man good!"   83

The young man felt somewhat embarrassed; his eyes shifted a little under the intense gaze of the Chinese mother.   84

"Well, we must get your boy for you," he responded. "Of course"—turning to Hom Hing—"it will cost a little money. You can't get fellows to hurry the Government for you without gold in your pocket."   85

Hom Hing stared blankly for a moment. Then: "How much do you want, Mr. Clancy?" he asked quietly.   86

"Well, I will need at least five hundred to start with."   87

Hom Hing cleared his throat.   88

"I think I told to you the time I last paid you for writing letters for me and seeing the Custom boss here that nearly all I had was gone!"   89

"Oh, well then we won't talk about it, old fellow. It won't harm the boy to stay where he is, and your wife may get over it all right."   90

"What that you say?" quavered Lae Choo.   91

James Clancy looked out of the window.   92

"He says," explained Hom Hing in English, "that to get our boy we have to have much money."   93

"Money! Oh, yes."   94

Lae Choo nodded her head.   95

"I have not got the money to give him."   96

For a moment Lae Choo gazed wonderingly from one face to the other; then, comprehension dawning upon her, with swift anger, pointing to the lawyer, she cried: "You not one hundred man good; you just common white man."   97

"Yes, ma'am," returned James Clancy, bowing and smiling ironically.   98

Hom Hing pushed his wife behind him and addressed the lawyer again: "I might try," said he, "to raise something; but five hundred—it is not possible."   99

"What about four?"   100

"I tell you I have next to nothing left and my friends are not rich."   101

"Very well!"   102

The lawyer moved leisurely toward the door, pausing on its threshold to light a cigarette.   103

"Stop, white man; white man, stop!"   104

Lae Choo, panting and terrified, had started forward and now stood beside him, clutching his sleeve excitedly.   105

"You say you can go to get paper to bring my Little One to me if Hom Hing give you five hundred dollars?"   106

107　　The lawyer nodded carelessly; his eyes were intent upon the cigarette which would not take the fire from the match.

108　　"Then you go get paper. If Hom Hing not can give you five hundred dollars—I give you perhaps what more that much."

109　　She slipped a heavy gold bracelet from her wrist and held it out to the man. Mechanically he took it.

110　　"I go get more!"

111　　She scurried away, disappearing behind the door through which she had come.

112　　"Oh, look here, I can't accept this," said James Clancy, walking back to Hom Hing and laying down the bracelet before him.

113　　"It's all right," said Hom Hing, seriously, "pure China gold. My wife's parent give it to her when we married."

114　　"But I can't take it anyway," protested the young man.

115　　"It is all same as money. And you want money to go to Washington," replied Hom Hing in a matter-of-fact manner.

116　　"See, my jade earrings—my gold buttons—my hairpins—my comb of pearl and my rings—one, two, three, four, five rings; very good—very good—all same much money. I give them all to you. You take and bring me paper for my Little One."

117　　Lae Choo piled up her jewels before the layer.

118　　Hom Hing laid a restraining hand upon her shoulder. "Not all, my wife," he said in Chinese. He selected a ring—his gift to Lae Choo when she dreamed of the tree with the red flower. The rest of the jewels he pushed toward the white man.

119　　"Take them and sell them," said he. "They will pay your fare to Washington and bring you back with the paper."

120　　For one moment James Clancy hesitated. He was not a sentimental man; but something within him arose against accepting such payment for his services.

121　　"They are good, good," pleadingly asserted Lae Choo, seeing his hesitation.

122　　Whereupon he seized the jewels, thrust them into his coat pocket, and walked rapidly away from the store.

IV

123　　Lae Choo followed after the missionary woman through the mission nursery school. Her heart was beating so high with happiness that she could scarcely breathe. The paper had come at last—the precious paper which gave Hom Hing and his wife the right to the possession of their own child. It was ten months now since he had been taken from them—ten months since the sun had ceased to shine for Lae Choo.

124　　The room was filled with children—most of them wee tots, but none so wee as her own. The mission woman talked as she walked. She told Lae Choo that little Kim, as he had been named by the school, was the pet of the place, and that his little tricks and ways amused and delighted every one. He had been rather difficult to manage at first and had cried much for his mother; "but children so soon forget, and after a month he seemed quite at home and played around as bright and happy as a bird."

"Yes," responded Lae Choo. "Oh, yes, yes!" 125

But she did not hear what was said to her. She was walking in a maze of anticipatory joy. 126

"Wait here, please," said the mission woman, placing Lae Choo in a chair. "The very youngest ones are having their breakfast." 127

She withdrew for a moment—it seemed like an hour to the mother—then she reappeared leading by the hand a little boy dressed in blue cotton overalls and white-soled shoes. The little boy's face was round and dimpled and his eyes were very bright. 128

"Little One, ah, my Little One!" cried Lae Choo. 129

She fell on her knees and stretched her hungry arms toward her son. 130

But the Little One shrunk from her and tried to hide himself in the folds of the white woman's skirt. 131

"Go 'way, go 'way!" he bade his mother. ✠ 132

RESPONDING

1. Although the language and writing style of the story is dated, the theme of being caught in the trap of official bureaucracy is current. Rewrite the story with a contemporary setting. Or write a journal entry about a time when you or someone you know had to fight what seemed to be endless red tape.

2. Working individually or in a group, analyze the motivation and behavior of James Clancy. Do you think he is sincerely trying to help Hom Hing? He hesitates before taking the jewels in payment for his services. What do you think is going through his mind at that moment? Why does he accept them as payment? What do you think he should have done? Share your conclusions with the class.

3. In an essay, explain the author's choice for the title. What was she trying to convey to her readers about America? Is the title ironic? Consider the possible response of different readers: readers of the story when it was published, native Americans and immigrants, and modern readers.

4. Write an essay analyzing the way the story illustrates the fears of loss of culture and identity that plague many new immigrants to the United States.

PARDEE LOWE

Pardee Lowe was born in California in 1905 to parents who had emigrated from south China. (They named their son Pardee after the governor of California, George Pardee.) He earned his bachelor's degree from Stanford University and his master's in business from Harvard University. During the 1930s he served as the international secretariat of the Institute for Pacific Relations, a cultural and civic organization. He later assisted in the Chinese War Relief Organization, which supplied food and medicine to Chinese war refugees. He began publishing articles on these efforts in The Yale Review *and other journals during the 1940s.*

In his book Father and Glorious Descendant, *Pardee Lowe uses his father's biography as the focal point from which to examine his own family's and other immigrants' experiences in the United States. The book recounts the early days in San Francisco's Chinatown, the effects of the Great Earthquake of 1906, and the family's resettlement in the Stockton area. Throughout the text Lowe expresses both a faith in the potential for success in the new country and a respect for the ritual and customs that comprise the family's cultural heritage.*

The selection that follows, a chapter from Father and Glorious Descendant, *shows the ways in which the American dream, held out to many immigrants, was often shattered by prejudice.*

FATHER CURES A PRESIDENTIAL FEVER

1 How I CAME TO BE INFECTED with Presidentitis even now I find somewhat difficult to explain. That it was not congenital was amply demonstrated by Father's matter-of-fact superiority over such divine foolishness. And Mother, bless her realistic Chinese soul, never affected awareness of such mundane matters until the political clubs of our neighborhood (we lived in the toughest one in East Belleville) celebrated under her very nose with torchlight parades, drunken sprees, black eyes and cracked skulls the glorious victories of their Men of the People. Whenever this happened she would exclaim, "My, my, what queer people the Americans are!"

2 The first time Father discovered how long the first-born man child of his household had been exposed to the ravages of this dread disease, he was horrified. "Unbelievable!" he stormed. But Mother, who had a strong will of her own, flew right back at him. And when she cried aloud, with Heaven as her witness, that she did not know how I caught it or how she could have prevented

it, Father recognized the justice of her remarks. She couldn't. Kwong Chong, our own neighborhood dry-goods store, household duties, and two new babies kept Mother so harassed that she had no time to chase us about the streets or down the back alleys. Later, to still her flow of tears, Father even grudgingly admitted his full responsibility. By moving our family to an American neighborhood, according to Mother, he had needlessly exposed us all to the malady.

That this was the source of the trouble, probably no one knew better than Father. When the 1906 San Francisco earthquake and fire consumed all his worldly goods and forced him to flee Chinatown with his wife, two babies in arms, and a motley feudal retinue of kinsmen, relatives, and garment-sewing employees, he merely considered it more or less a blessing in disguise. From the ashes of this catastrophe, which represented for Mother the end of her Chinatownian world, Father's thoughts and plans for the future soared like a phoenix.

At long last the visions and dreams for his offspring, present and potential, would be realized. His family would rub shoulders with Americans. They would become good American citizens albeit remaining Chinese. They would inhabit a hyphenated world. By some formula, which he never was able to explain, they would select only the finest attributes of each contributory culture. They would reflect everlasting credit on him and on the name of Lowe.

(Even then, Father's faith passed all human understanding. He expected us somehow to muddle through. We did—but in a manner totally unexpected.)

From Father's point of view, we children were to be raised at home according to the old and strict Chinese ideal. But in that ever-widening circle of American neighborhood life beyond the narrow confines of our home, Father had no control. A daily commuter to his shop in San Francisco's Chinatown, an hour's ride away by steam train and ferry, he was never fully apprised of our actions until too late.

He was ignorant, for instance, of what transpired in the large wooden public school situated some three short blocks from our home. He was confident we were in good hands. If he had only known what was awaiting his son there, he might not have been so eager to have me acquire an American schooling.

When at the age of five I entered the portals of this mid-Victorian architectural firetrap, surrounded by its iron-spiked fence and tall trees, for the first time, I recognized it as an international institution in which I was free to indulge my own most un-Chinese inclinations—and, unintentionally to be sure, to undermine Father's high hopes.

I can still vividly remember the strange excitement of the first morning roll call, which was to be repeated daily for many years to come. Clumsily, the teacher pronounced our names. As we rose, she checked our nationality.

"Louisa Fleishhacker—*Austrian*." She underlined the word *Austrian*. "Elsie Forsythe—*English*. Penelope Lincoln—*American Negro*. Yuri Matsuyama—*Japanese*. Nancy Mullins—*Irish*. Maria Pucinelli—*Italian*. Stella Saceanu—*Rumanian*. Anna Zorich—*Serbian*." Finishing with the girls, she turned the page. "Michael

Castro—*Portuguese*. Heinz Creyer—*German*. Thorvald Ericson—*Swedish*. Philippe Etienne—*French*. Nicholas Katanov—*Russian*. Pardee Lowe—*Chinese*. Robert MacPherson—*Scotch*. And Francisco Trujillo—*Mexican*."

11   There we stood. In the company of fifteen other beginners, no two in the entire group of the same nationality, I was embarking upon a new and glorious adventure, the educational melting pot, which was to make every one of us, beyond peradventure, an American.

12   It pleased Father no end to know that I liked to go to American school. He informed Mother proudly that it denoted a scholarly spirit well-becoming a Chinese. If he had only glimpsed what lay back of my mind as I saw him gaily off on the morning seven-forty commuters' train he might have derived much less satisfaction.

13   No sooner was Father's back turned than I would dash madly to the streetcar line. On my way I would stop and pick a bunch of posies from our neighbors' back yards, praying fervently that I would be the only pupil waiting for Miss McIntyre, our teacher. Disappointment invariably awaited me, for I was not alone. Anna, Nancy, Penelope, and Robert, sharing exactly the same sentiments, always managed to get there ahead of me.

14   As soon as we spotted Miss McIntyre's tall figure alighting from the car, we sprang forward. With a warm smile of affection which enfolded us all, she allowed us to grab her hands, snatch her books from her arms and literally drag her from the rear step of the car to the front steps of the school, happily protesting every step of the way: "Now, children! . . . Now, *children!*"

15   Coming mainly from immigrant homes where parents were too preoccupied with earning a living to devote much time to their children, we transferred our youthful affections to this one person who had both the time and the disposition to mother us. We showered upon our white-haired teacher the blind-whole-hearted loyalty of the young. Our studies we readily absorbed, not because we particularly liked them so much as because it was "she" who taught us. Thus, with the three R's, games, stories, a weekly bath which she personally administered in the school's bathroom—two pupils at a time—and her love, she whom we staunchly enshrined in our hearts laid the rudimentary but firm foundation of our personal brand of American culture.

16   Then, one day it happened. Miss McIntyre, herself the daughter of an Irish immigrant who had come to California during the Gold Rush, read to us with deep emotion the life of George Washington. The virtues displayed by the Father of Our Country, particularly when confessing his act of chopping down the cherry tree, were, she led us to believe, the very ones which would, if faithfully practiced, win us equal fame. Concluding the narrative, she looked in turn at Anna, Penelope, and Robert. She was challenging us to higher things. As her eyes caught mine, she added with conviction, "And every single one of you can be President of the United States someday!"

17   I shall never forget that occasion. To be President in our minds was like

being God, with the difference that everybody knew what the President[1] looked like. His pictures were in every newspaper. Even in the funny sheets, I sometimes saw him. Big as life, with his grinning mouthful of teeth, eyeglasses gleaming, and his mustache bristling in the breeze of the political opposition—he looked the spitting image of Father. The only difference I could detect was that Father preferred the bamboo duster to the "Big Stick," and "*Jun Ho Ah!*" was as near as he ever came to "Bully!"

Everything I did from this moment on served only to strengthen the grandiose dream whose chief interlocking threads included myself, Father, and the Presidency. Much to the disgust of my more active playmates and the envy of my bookworm friends, I became a walking encyclopedia of American history. I could repeat the full names and dates of every President of these United States. And I knew the vivid, gory details, authentic and apocryphal, of every important military engagement in which Americans took part—and always victoriously. 18

I hounded the settlement librarian for books, and more books. Like one famished, I devoured all of James Fenimore Cooper's novels. Lodge and Roosevelt's *Hero Tales from American History* fascinated me. As I read Abbot's *The Story of Our Navy* and Johnston's *Famous Scouts, Including Trappers, Pioneers and Soldiers of the Frontier*, my sense of patriotism quickened. So stirred was I by Tomlinson's narrative that in my childish imagination I followed George Washington as a young scout, or marched resolutely forward to engage the Iroquois and Red Coats. Of all the books, however, Coffin's *Boys of '76* was my favorite. And many were the evenings in which I descended from the New Hampshire hills with sixteen-year-old Elijah Favor to fight at Lexington and Concord and finally to share the fruits of revolutionary victory at Yorktown. 19

However, by the time I could recite with relish and gusto Scott's lines:— 20

> "Breathes there the man, with soul so dead,
> Who never to himself hath said,
> This is my own, my native land! . . ."

the President's picture had changed. In the course of the years, he had become huge, the size of a bear, but he still wore a mustache. He was less like Father now. And while I found it difficult to imagine myself becoming as stout, I felt that even flabby avoirdupois, if associated with the Presidency, had its compensations. No matter what his shape, I told myself, everybody still loved and worshiped the President of the United States.

Of this deadly and insidious fever that racked my chubby frame, Father was totally ignorant. Nor would he have ever divined my secret if it had not been for our journey to the Mother Lode country. 21

It was our first long overnight trip away from home together. The train 22

1. President Theodore Roosevelt.

ride, needless to say, was nothing short of glorious. For two whole days I had all to myself a father whom I seldom saw, but to whom I was thoroughly devoted. Besides, a city boy, I had never seen mountains so tall or sights so strange and fleeting. But the most enjoyable part of all was to bounce on the red-plush train seats and stop the vendor whenever he passed by with his hamper filled with peanuts, candies, and soda pop.

23   After a full day's ride, we arrived at our destination, a small silver-mining town in the Sierra Nevada. At the station platform, Father and I were met by a roly-poly Westerner dressed in baggy clothes, riding boots, and a huge sombrero and mouthing ominously an equally formidable black cigar. After "How-de-doing" us, the stranger offered Father a cigar. A "cheroot" I think he called it. Then followed a ritual that filled me with amazement.

24   While Mr. Brown sized up Father skeptically, Father planted himself firmly on both feet, rolled the unlighted cigar in his hands, stroked it gently, and drew it slowly beneath his nose. With a deep sign of satisfaction, he inhaled deeply.

25   "Havana Perfecto?" inquired Father, more as a statement of fact than a question.

26   "Splendid!" assented Mr. Brown with a vigorous nod. Smiling broadly for the first time, he slapped Father approvingly on the back and swept me up into his arms. As we drove majestically down the dusty street in his creaky cart, our now genial host vouchsafed that Father was one of the few "damned furriners" and certainly the first *Chinaman* to pass this unusual inspection.

27   By the way that Father puffed at his cigar and blew magnificent smoke rings, I could see that he was pleased with Mr. Brown's compliment. But never a word did he mention about his being the proprietor of Sun Loy, the largest tobacco shop in Chinatown. Since he didn't, neither did I.

28   Arriving at a large two-story hotel, resembling in size, shape, and color an old Southern mansion, Mr. Brown, whom we now knew to be the proprietor, roared from his sagging seat: "Hi there, folks! I've picked up my Chinamen!"

29   Out trooped the few American residents of the hotel, glad to witness anything that would break the monotony of a long hot summer's day, followed by six white-clad Chinese domestics who greeted us with an explosion of the Fragrant Mountain dialect. "*Ah Kung Ah!*" (Respected Great-Uncle!) "We hope all is well with you!"

30   It gave me a great thrill to see everybody, even the Americans, so deferential to Father. There was something about him that commanded universal respect. Chinese in Western clothes, especially of the latest cut, were a decided rarity in those days. And Father in his first suit of tailor-mades from a nobby American clothier looked simply grand. Tall, well-built, and sporting a bushy mustache, he looked every inch a distinguished personage. I could well understand why his American business associates persisted in nicknaming him "The Duke."

31   Mr. Brown, having already been informed of the purpose of our visit, drew quietly aside. So did the Americans, no longer interested in a group of jabbering,

gesticulating Orientals. This gave a few of my kinsmen an opportunity to converse with me in our dialect, which I understood, but, much to their chagrin, could not speak. Shocked that a Chinese boy should be ignorant of his own dialect, the eldest exclaimed, "*Chow Mah!*" (Positively disgraceful!) The way he said it made me more than a little ashamed of myself.

However, Father cut short my uncomfortable moment by introducing me to the object of our visit. "This—" indicating a short, slender chap who appeared exceedingly glum—"is your Fourth Paternal Uncle, Precious Fortune." 32

Fourth Uncle, despite his title, was only a distant kinsman and, from his point of view, had every reason for sulkiness. Just as he had conveniently forgotten about his grieving mother and childless wife in China for the pleasures of Chinatown's gambling tables, Father appeared—and Fourth Uncle didn't like it one bit. Father was the personification of outraged Chinese family conscience on the warpath. To him, in place of his own father, Fourth Uncle had to account for his glaring lapses in filial piety. He had to explain, for example, why had not written them in three years; why he never sent them money; and, worst of all, why he persisted in leaving his aging mother grandchildless. 33

As the Clan's Senior Elder, Father took his Greater Family responsibilities very seriously. All through dinner, he informed Mr. Brown spiritedly that Fourth Uncle would have to leave. At first, Mr. Brown replied that he hated to part with an excellent cook, but when we came to dessert he finally agreed that in view of Fourth Uncle's wicked profligacy, it appeared the wisest course. 34

Having disposed of the fried chicken, apple pie, and Fourth Uncle so satisfactorily, Mr. Brown next turned to me. "Son," he inquired, "what are you studying to become? Would you like to stay with me and be my cook, taking your uncle's place?" 35

The last question passed me by completely; I answered the first one. "I want to be President," I said. 36

A sharp silence smote the mellow dining room. Now the secret was out. I was amazed at my own stupidity. Happily absorbed with my second helping of apple pie and fresh rich country milk, I had recklessly given vent to my Presidential aspirations. Now what would Father say? 37

Father, uncertain of the exact nature of the enchantment that had suddenly ensnared his son, looked at me queerly as though he doubted his ears. Mr. Brown laughed long and loud with a strange catch in his voice. "Sure, son, that's right," he added. "Study hard and you'll be President someday." 38

I wondered then why Mr. Brown's laughter sounded so odd, but I never associated this with pity until much, much later. By then, however, I had been thoroughly cured by Father. 39

Homeward bound Father said precious little. Not even to Fourth Uncle, still glum, whom we brought home with us to start life anew. Father's silence was disturbing and he attempted to cloak it, and his thoughts, with liberal benefactions. When we reached Belleville Junction I had no further use for the 40 newspaper vendor and his basket of allurements—and Father no use for silence. In his own mind he had worked out a series of special therapeutic treatments to counteract my desperate malady, Presidentitis.

41 A few days after our return from the Sierra Nevada, Father said gently, "Glorious Descendant, how would you like to go to a private boarding school in China?"

42 I shuddered at the full significance of his suggestion. To be separated from America and from my family? And never to see them again for years and years? "No! No!" I wailed. "I don't want to go!" Rejecting the idea with all the vehemence at my command, I added, "I want to stay in America!"

43 Father dwelt patiently on all the advantages of such a schooling but to no avail. Nothing he said moved me. What about my future, inquired Father, didn't I care? Of course, I replied, but I didn't want to be a mandarin or a Chinese merchant prince at such a terrific sacrifice. Father's questions became more penetrating; they stripped the future of everything but realities. Could I, as a Chinese, ever hope to find a good job in American society? At this, I laughed. Miss McIntyre, I told him, had plainly said that I could even be President.

44 In these sessions, I revealed to Father the seriousness of my infection. I opened the gates to that part of my youthful life he had never known. I told him in no uncertain terms that I loved America, particularly East Belleville, which I considered to be the grandest place in all the world. Besides, I continued, why would I wish to go to China? All the things I had heard from our kinsfolk about the old country were bad, with no redeeming features. After all, I added as my clinching argument, if this were not so, why should our kinsmen wish to come to the United States?

45 Our cousins and uncles, Father tried desperately to explain, really wanted to stay at home with their wives and children, but because times seemed so difficult in China they were compelled, by economic necessity, to come and work in the Golden Mountains. "Don't think you're the only one who loves his family and hates to leave it," concluded Father somewhat angrily.

46 The argument became endless. The more Father pleaded, the more determined I became. America, I swore, was God's own country. It abounded in free public schools, libraries, newspapers, bathtubs, toilets, vaudeville theaters, and railroad trains. On the other hand, I reminded him, China was a place where anything might happen: One might be kidnapped, caught in a revolution, die from the heat, perish from the cold, or even pick up ringworm diseases which left huge bald patches on one's scalp.

47 Finally Father was convinced. Since I did not personally regard his idea with favor, trying to send me to China was hopeless. This by no means exhausted Father's remedial efforts on my behalf. Plan number one having failed, Father put number two into operation. He decided that if I wouldn't go to China I was to spend an extra hour each day on my Chinese studies for Tutor Chun.

48 Now I knew leisure no longer. My American playmates, and endless trips

to the settlement library, were given up—but not forgotten. And I discovered to my painful sorrow that I had only substituted one necessary evil for another. Every evening from five to eight I despondently memorized, recited, and copied endless columns of queer-shaped characters which bore not the slightest resemblance to English. As I went to this school on Saturday mornings and studied my lessons on Sunday, I envied Penelope. Heinz, and Francisco, my poorest foreign playmates, their luxurious freedom. They did not have to learn Chinese.

Unlike my American education, my Chinese one was not crowned with success. It was not that I was entirely unwilling to learn, but simply that my brain was not ambidextrous. Whenever I stood with my back to the teacher, my lips attempted to recite correctly in poetical prose Chinese history, geography, or ethics, while my inner spirit was wrestling victoriously with the details of the Battle of Bunker Hill, Custer's Last Stand, or the tussle between the *Monitor* and *Merrimac*.

When it became apparent to Tutor Chun that, in spite of my extra hour a day, I was unable to balance cultural waters on both shoulders, he mercifully desisted flailing me with the bamboo duster. No amount of chastising, he informed me bitterly, would ever unravel the cultural chop suey I was making of my studies. But, in the long run, even the gentle soul of the Chinese teacher could not tolerate my muddle-headedness. One day after a particularly heart-rending recitation on my part, he telephoned Mother in despair. "Madame," he exclaimed in mortal anguish, "never have I had a pupil the equal of your son. I strain all my efforts but, alas, I profoundly regret that I am unable to teach him anything!"

Father was appalled at this news, but since he was not the kind of man who gave up easily, his determination waxed all the stronger. Subtler methods, bribery, were tried. Perhaps, he reasoned, I might develop a taste for Chinese as well as English literature if it were only made financially worth my while. Each Sunday a shining quarter would be mine, he said, if I would present him with a daily ten-minute verbal Chinese translation of the latest newspaper reports on European war developments.[2]

Lured by this largess, I made my translations. They were, to be sure, crude and swiftly drawn. But then, ten minutes was all too brief a period in which to circumnavigate the globe and report on its current events. I endowed the military movements of von Kluck's, Foch's, and Haig's armies with the élan of Sheridan's sweep down the Shenandoah, unencumbered with the intricate mechanized paraphernalia of modern warfare. And long before Wilson, Clemenceau, and Lloyd George assembled at Versailles, I had made and remade the map of Europe a dozen times.

Father's clever scheme not only worked, but it proved mutually beneficial. During the four years of the war, we kept it up. Thanks to the revolutionary *Young China*, and the *Christian Chinese Western Daily*, he was never entirely in

2. World War I.

the dark as to which armies won which campaign and who finally won the war. Naturally, Father learned a great deal about history that wasn't so, but he did not particularly mind. I was improving my Chinese.

54   During this period my youthful cup of patriotism was filled to overflowing. In the first place our Americanism had finally reached the ears of the White House. The christening of my twin brothers brought two important letters of congratulation from Washington, which Father proudly framed and hung conspicuously in his private office. As might be imagined, they exerted a profound influence on all our lives.

55   When I felt particularly in need of encouragement, I would go to the back wall of Father's office and read aloud Vice President Marshall's letter to Father. It was a human one, glowing with warmth and inspiration. There was one sentence which stood out: "To be a good American citizen, in my judgment, is about the best thing on earth, and while I cannot endow your children with any worldly goods, I can bless them with the hope that they may grow up to be an honor to their parents and a credit to the commonwealth."

56   I recall this Vice-Presidential blessing so vividly because it was the crux of our family problem. It summed up our difficulties as well as our goal. For me, at least, it was difficult to be a filial Chinese son and a good American citizen at one and the same time. For many years I used to wonder why this was so, but I appreciate now it was because I was the eldest son in what was essentially a pioneering family. Father was pioneering with Americanism—and so was I. And more often than not, we blazed entirely different trails.

57   When America finally entered the War, even Father's sturdy common sense softened somewhat under the heat waves of patriotism that constantly beat down upon us. I was in paradise. My youthful fancies appreciated that only strife and turmoil made heroes. When I recalled that practically every great President— Washington, Jackson, Lincoln, Grant, and Roosevelt—had once been a soldier, I bitterly lamented the fact that I was not old enough. I'd show those "Huns" (by this time I had already imbibed freely at the fount of propaganda) a thing or two, I informed Father. But Father only snorted something about waiting until I could shoulder a gun, and studying Chinese.

58   The next summer, my thirteenth, I decided to go to work during vacation. I needed spending money badly for my first term in high school. Father applauded this show of independence until I informed him that I intended, if possible, to become an office boy in an American business firm. Then he was seized with profound misgivings. "Would they hire you?" Father inquired.

59   Why shouldn't they, I replied, with overweening self-confidence. "See!" I pointed to the Sunday editions of the *San Francisco Chronicle*. "I can hold any of these jobs."

60   Father looked at the classified advertisements I had checked. Whether he knew what all the abbreviations meant, I wasn't certain. I didn't, but that was totally immaterial. The world was new, I was young, and for $40 a month I was willing to learn the ins., or exp. bus., work for good opps., be ready to asst. on files, and, for good measure, do gen. off. wk. for perm. adv.

Father remarked that he wasn't so certain that the millennium had arrived, 61
but he was open to conviction. He agreed to let me proceed on one condition:
If I failed to find a job I was to return to Tutor Chun and study my Chinese
lessons faithfully.

Blithely one sunny July morning I went forth job hunting, well-scrubbed, 62
wearing my Sunday suit and totally unaware of the difficulties that confronted
me. In my pocket were ten clipped newspaper advertisements, each one, I
thought, with a job purposely made for me.

I took out the most promising one. It was for seven enterp. boys, between 63
the ages of 12 and 16; and they were wanted at once for a bond house which
offered good opps. as well as $50 per month. The address was on California
Street.

Stopping in front of an imposing marble palace of San Francisco finance, 64
I compared the address with the clipping. It checked. How simply grand it would
be to work for such a firm, I thought, as the elevator majestically pulled us up
to the ninth floor. I trembled with eager anticipation as I pushed open the glass
door of Richards and Mathison, for it seemed as though a new world were
swimming into view.

"Wad-a-ya-wunt?" barked the sharp voice of a young lady. I looked in her 65
direction. There she sat behind a shiny, thin brass cage, just like a bank
teller—or a monkey, for above her head hung a sign. It read INFORMATION.

"Please, ma'am," I asked, "can you tell me where I can find Mr. Royal?" 66

"Humph!" she snorted, as she looked me up and down as if to say I didn't 67
have a chance. "He's busy, you'll have to wait."

After what seemed hours, the girl threw open the office gate and motioned 68
me to enter. I followed her down a long aisle of desks, every one as large as a
kitchen table. At each desk sat a man or a girl shuffling large cards or scribbling
on long sheets of paper. As we passed, they stopped their work and looked at
me queerly. I noticed several boys of my own age putting their heads together.
I knew they were talking about me. And when they snickered, I wanted to punch
their noses.

Opening a door marked PRIVATE, the girl announced: "Mr. Royal, here is 69
another boy." He raised his head.

There it was. On Mr. Royal's lean, smooth-shaven face was the same look 70
of incredulity that I had once noticed on Mr. Brown's. But only for a moment.
For he suddenly reached for a cigarette, lit it, and looked at me quizzically,
while I hopped on one foot and then on the other.

"Young man," he said, "I understand you would like to work for us? Well 71
then, you'd better tell us something of yourself."

"Why, of course," I said, "of course." And impulsively I told everything: all 72
about my graduation from grammar school, my boy-scout training, and my
desire to earn my own keep during the summer.

Mr. Royal seemed visibly impressed. When a faint smile replaced his frown, 73
I stopped fidgeting. I fully expected him to ask me to come to work in the
morning. Therefore, I was appalled when he told me that he was sorry, but all

the jobs were taken. It never occurred to me that our interview would end like this.

74   My face fell. I hadn't expected such an answer. To soften the blow, Mr. Royal added that if I filled out an application he would call me if there were any openings.

75   I filled out the application under the unsympathetic eyes of the information girl, and stumbled miserably out of the office, vaguely sensible of the fact that there would never be any opening.

76   The feeling was intensified as I made the round of the other nine firms. Everywhere I was greeted with perturbation, amusement, pity, or irritation—and always with identically the same answer. "Sorry," they invariably said, "the position has just been filled." My jaunty self-confidence soon wilted. I sensed that something was radically, fundamentally wrong. It just didn't seem possible that overnight all of the positions could have been occupied, particularly not when everybody spoke of a labor shortage. Suspicion began to dawn. What had Father said? "American firms do not customarily employ Chinese." To verify his statement, I looked again in the newspaper the next morning and for the week after and, sure enough, just as I expected, the same ten ads were still in the newspaper.

77   For another week, I tried my luck. By now I was thoroughly shellshocked. What had begun as a glorious adventure had turned into a hideous, long-drawn nightmare.

78   Father during this trying period wisely said nothing. Then, one morning, he dusted off my dog-eared paper-bound Chinese textbooks. When I came to breakfast I found them on my desk, mute but eloquent reminders of my promise. I looked at them disconsolately. A bargain was a bargain.

79   When our clock struck nine, I picked up my bundle of books. Fortunately for me, Father had already commuted to work. Only Mother saw me off. Patting me sympathetically on the shoulder, she regarded me reflectively. It was an invitation for me to unburden my heart. But not even for her would I confess my full recovery from a nearly fatal disease. That moment was reserved for my long walk to language school.

80   I marched out of the house insouciant. When I wasn't whistling I was muttering to myself a Jewish slang phrase I had just picked up. It was "Ish-kabibble" and it meant that I didn't care. And I didn't until I reached the park where all my most vivid daydreaming periods were spent. There, I broke down and wept. For the first time I admitted to myself the cruel truth—I didn't have a "Chinaman's chance" of becoming President of the United States. In this crash of the lofty hopes which Miss McIntyre had raised, it did not occur to me to reflect that the chances of Francisco Trujillo, Yuri Matsuyama, or Penelope Lincoln were actually no better than mine. But after a good cry I felt better—anyway, I could go to an American school again in the fall. ✤

RESPONDING

1. Lowe's father holds certain hopes and aspirations for his son. In a journal entry, compare them with the aspirations Pardee holds for himself.

2. Working individually or in a group, list the roles and responsibilities of the members of the extended Lowe family. Compare the family with other families presented in this book or with your own family.

3. In an essay, explain what happens to Pardee Lowe to change his original optimism about equal opportunity in America and a recognition of his place in San Francisco society at that time. What opportunities would be open to Pardee Lowe today? Could he be elected president of the United States?

4. Pardee Lowe has problems being a "filial Chinese son and a good American citizen at one and the same time" (paragraph 56). Write an essay arguing that it is or is not difficult to be a part of two cultures. In your essay, use the readings as well as your own and your friends' experiences to support your argument.

MAXINE HONG KINGSTON

Maxine Hong Kingston was born in Stockton, California, in 1940, the daughter of Chinese immigrants. Kingston attended the University of California at Berkeley, earning her bachelor's degree in 1962 and later a teaching certificate. After college she taught high school English in California and Hawaii, then college English in Hawaii.

Kingston's first book, The Woman Warrior: Memoirs of a Girlhood Among Ghosts, *was published in 1976. Combining realism and fantasy,* The Woman Warrior *tells Kingston's mother's story, describing her life as a medical student in China and then as an immigrant to the United States. It was awarded the National Book Critics Circle Award in 1976. Kingston has also published the novel* Tripmaster Monkey: His Fake Book *(1989) which is set in Berkeley, California during the 1960s.*

Kingston considers China Men *the companion volume to* Woman Warrior. China Men *relates some of the experiences of the male family members who often immigrated first to make a home for their families in the new land. This volume received the American Book Award in 1981. The following chapter from* China Men *describes Kingston's grandfather's experiences while working in the mines and building the railroads. In fictional and nonfictional episodes, the chapter dramatizes the immigrants' struggles for success. In describing the sacrifice and determination required of these men, it also reflects on the legacy they have left their descendants.*

✥

THE GRANDFATHER OF THE
SIERRA NEVADA MOUNTAINS

1 THE TRAINS USED TO CROSS THE SKY. The house jumped and dust shook down from the attic. Sometimes two trains ran parallel going in opposite directions; the railroad men walked on top of the leaning cars, stepped off one train onto the back of the other, and traveled the opposite way. They headed for the caboose while the train moved against their walk, or they walked toward the engine while the train moved out from under their feet. Hoboes ran alongside, caught the ladders, and swung aboard. I would have to learn to ride like that, choose my boxcar, grab a ladder at a run, and fling myself up and sideways into an open door. Elsewhere I would step smoothly off. Bad runaway boys lost their legs trying for such rides. The train crunched past—pistons stroking like elbows and knees, the coal cars dropping coal, cows looking out between the slats

of the cattlecars, the boxcars almost stringing together sentences—Hydro-Cushion, Georgia Flyer, Route of the Eagle—and suddenly sunlight filled the windows again, the slough wide again and waving with tules, for which the city was once named; red-winged blackbirds and squirrels settled. We children ran to the tracks and found the nails we'd placed on them; the wheels had flattened them into knives that sparked.

Once in a while an adult said, "Your grandfather built the railroad." (Or "Your grandfathers built the railroad." Plural and singular are by context.) We children believed that it was that very railroad, those trains, those tracks running past our house; our own giant grandfather had set those very logs into the ground, poured the iron for those very spikes with the big heads and pounded them until the heads spread like that, mere nails to him. He had built the railroad so that trains would thunder over us, on a street that inclined toward us. We lived on a special spot of the earth, Stockton, the only city on the Pacific coast with three railroads—the Santa Fe, Southern Pacific, and Western Pacific. The three railroads intersecting accounted for the flocks of hoboes. The few times that the train stopped, the cows moaned all night, their hooves stumbling crowdedly and banging against the wood.

Grandfather left a railroad for his message: We had to go somewhere difficult. Ride a train. Go somewhere important. In case of danger, the train was to be ready for us.

The railroad men disconnected the rails and took the steel away. They did not come back. Our family dug up the square logs and rolled them downhill home. We collected the spikes too. We used the logs for benches, edged the yard with them, made bases for fences, embedded them in the ground for walkways. The spikes came in handy too, good for paperweights, levers, wedges, chisels. I am glad to know exactly the weight of ties and the size of nails.

Grandfather's picture hangs in the dining room next to an equally large one of Grandmother, and another one of Guan Goong, God of War and Literature. My grandparents' similarity is in the set of their mouths; they seem to have hauled with their mouths. My mouth also feels the tug and strain of weights in its corners. In the family album, Grandfather wears a greatcoat and Western shoes, but his ankles show. He hasn't shaved either. Maybe he became sloppy after the Japanese soldier bayoneted his head for not giving directions. Or he was born slow and without a sense of direction.

The photographer came to the village regularly and set up a spinet, potted trees, an ornate table stacked with hardbound books of matching size, and a backdrop with a picture of paths curving through gardens into panoramas; he lent his subjects dressy ancient mandarin clothes, Western suits, and hats. An aunt tied the fingers of the lame cousin to a book, the string leading down his sleeve; he looks like he's carrying it. The family hurried from clothes chests to mirrors without explaining to Grandfather, hiding Grandfather. In the family album are group pictures with Grandmother in the middle, the family arranged on either side of her and behind her, second wives at the ends, no Grandfather.

Grandmother's earrings, bracelets, and rings are tinted jade green, everything and everybody else black and white, her little feet together neatly, two knobs at the bottom of her gown. My mother, indignant that nobody had readied Grandfather, threw his greatcoat over his nightclothes, shouted, "Wait! Wait!" and encouraged him into the sunlight. "Hurry," she said, and he ran, coat flapping, to be in the picture. She would have slipped him into the group and had the camera catch him like a peeping ghost, but Grandmother chased him away. "What a waste of film," she said. Grandfather always appears alone with white stubble on his chin. He was a thin man with big eyes that looked straight ahead. When we children talked about overcoat men, exhibitionists, we meant Grandfather, Ah Goong, who must have yanked open that greatcoat—no pants.

7   MaMa was the only person to listen to him, and so he followed her everywhere, and talked and talked. What he liked telling was his journeys to the Gold Mountain. He wasn't smart, yet he traveled there three times. Left to himself, he would have stayed in China to play with babies or stayed in the United States once he got there, but Grandmother forced him to leave both places. "Make money," she said. "Don't stay here eating." "Come home," she said.

8   Ah Goong sat outside her open door when MaMa worked. (In those days a man did not visit a good woman alone unless married to her.) He saw her at her loom and came running with his chair. He told her that he had found a wondrous country, really gold, and he himself had gotten two bags of it, one of which he had had made into a ring. His wife had given that ring to their son for his wedding ring. "That ring on your finger," he told Mother, "proves that the Gold Mountain exists and that I went there."

9   Another of his peculiarities was that he heard the crackles, bangs, gunshots that go off when the world lurches; the gears on its axis snap. Listening to a faraway New Year, he had followed the noise and come upon the blasting in the Sierras. (There is a Buddhist instruction that that which is most elusive must, of course, be the very thing to be pursued; listen to the farthest sound.) The Central Pacific hired him on sight; chinamen had a natural talent for explosions. Also there were not enough workingmen to do all the labor of building a new country. Some of the banging came from the war to decide whether or not black people would continue to work for nothing.

10   Slow as usual, Ah Goong arrived in the spring; the work had begun in January 1863. The demon that hired him pointed up and up, east above the hills of poppies. His first job was to fell a redwood, which was thick enough to divide into three or four beams. His tree's many branches spread out, each limb like a little tree. He circled the tree. How to attack it? No side looked like the side made to be cut, nor did any ground seem the place for it to fall. He axed for almost a day the side he'd decided would hit the ground. Halfway through, imitating the other lumberjacks, he struck the other side of the tree, above the cut, until he had to run away. The tree swayed and slowly dived to earth, creaking and screeching like a green animal. He was so awed, he forgot he was

supposed to yell. Hardly any branches broke; the tree sprang, bounced, pushed at the ground with its arms. The limbs did not wilt and fold; they were a small forest, which he chopped. The trunk lay like a long red torso; sap ran from its cuts like crying blind eyes. At last it stopped fighting. He set the log across sawhorses to be cured over smoke and in the sun.

He joined a team of men who did not ax one another as they took alternate hits. They blew up the stumps with gunpowder. "It was like uprooting a tooth," Ah Goong said. They also packed gunpowder at the roots of a whole tree. Not at the same time as the bang but before that, the tree rose from the ground. It stood, then plunged with a tearing of veins and muscles. It was big enough to carve a house into. The men measured themselves against the upturned white roots, which looked like claws, a sun with claws. A hundred men stood or sat on the trunk. They lifted a wagon on it and took a photograph. The demons also had their photograph taken. 11

Because these mountains were made out of gold. Ah Goong rushed over to the root hole to look for gold veins and ore. He selected the shiniest rocks to be assayed later in San Francisco. When he drank from the streams and saw a flash, he dived in like a duck; only sometimes did it turn out to be the sun or the water. The very dirt winked with specks. 12

He made a dollar a day salary. The lucky men gambled, but he was not good at remembering game rules. The work so far was endurable. "I could take it," he said. 13

The days were sunny and blue, the wind exhilarating, the heights godlike. At night the stars were diamonds, crystals, silver, snow, ice. He had never seen diamonds. He had never seen snow and ice. As spring turned into summer, and he lay under that sky, he saw the order in the stars. He recognized constellations from China. There—not a cloud but the Silver River, and there, on either side of it—Altair and Vega, the Spinning Girl and the Cowboy, far, far apart. He felt his heart breaking of loneliness at so much blue-black space between star and star. The railroad he was building would not lead him to his family. He jumped out of his bedroll. "Look! Look!" Other China Men jumped awake. An accident? An avalanche? Injun demons? "The stars," he said. "The stars are here." "Another China Man gone out of his mind," men grumbled. "A sleep-walker." "Go to sleep, sleepwalker." "There. And there," said Ah Goong, two hands pointing. "The Spinning Girl and the Cowboy. Don't you see them?" "Homesick China Man," said the China Men and pulled their blankets over their heads. "Didn't you know they were here? I could have told you they were here. Same as in China. Same moon. Why not same stars?" "Nah. Those are American stars." 14

Pretending that a little girl was listening, he told himself the story about the Spinning Girl and the Cowboy: A long time ago they had visited earth, where they met, fell in love, and married. Instead of growing used to each other, they remained enchanted their entire lifetimes and beyond. They were too happy. They wanted to be doves or two branches of the same tree. When they 15 returned to live in the sky, they were so engrossed in each other that they neglected their work. The Queen of the Sky scratched a river between them with one stroke of her silver hairpin—the river a galaxy in width. The lovers suffered, but she did devote her time to spinning now, and he herded his cow. The King of the Sky took pity on them and ordered that once each year, they be allowed to meet. On the seventh day of the seventh month (which is not the same as July 7), magpies form a bridge for them to cross to each other. The lovers are together for one night of the year. On their parting, the Spinner cries the heavy summer rains.

16   Ah Goong's discovery of the two stars gave him something to look forward to besides meals and tea breaks. Every night he located Altair and Vega and gauged how much closer they had come since the night before. During the day he watched the magpies, big black and white birds with round bodies like balls with wings; they were a welcome sight, a promise of meetings. He had found two familiars in the wilderness: magpies and stars. On the meeting day, he did not see any magpies nor hear their chattering jaybird cries. Some black and white birds flew overhead, but they may have been American crows or late magpies on their way. Some men laughed at him, but he was not the only China Man to collect water in pots, bottles, and canteens that day. The water would stay fresh forever and cure anything. In ancient days the tutelary gods of the mountains sprinkled corpses with this water and brought them to life. That night, no women to light candles, burn incense, cook special food, Grandfather watched for the convergence and bowed. He saw the two little stars next to Vega—the couple's children. And bridging the Silver River, surely those were black flapping wings of magpies and translucent-winged angels and faeries. Toward morning, he was awakened by rain, and pulled his blankets into his tent.

17   The next day, the fantailed orange-beaked magpies returned. Altair and Vega were beginning their journeys apart, another year of spinning and herding. Ah Goong had to find something else to look forward to. The Spinning Girl and the Cowboy met and parted six times before the railroad was finished.

18   When cliffs, sheer drops under impossible overhangs, ended the road, the workers filled the ravines or built bridges over them. They climbed above the site for tunnel or bridge and lowered one another down in wicker baskets made stronger by the lucky words they had painted on four sides. Ah Goong got to be a basketman because he was thin and light. Some basketmen were fifteen-year-old boys. He rode the basket barefoot, so his boots, the kind to stomp snakes with, would not break through the bottom. The basket swung and twirled, and he saw the world sweep underneath him; it was fun in a way, a cold new feeling of doing what had never been done before. Suspended in the quiet sky, he thought all kinds of crazy thoughts, that if a man didn't want to live any more, he could just cut the ropes or, easier, tilt the basket, dip, and never have to worry again. He could spread his arms and the air would momentarily hold him before he fell past the buzzards, hawks, and eagles, and landed impaled on

the tip of a sequoia. This high and he didn't see any gods, no Cowboy, no Spinner. He knelt in the basket though he was not bumping his head against the sky. Through the wickerwork, slivers of depths darted like needles, nothing between him and air but thin rattan. Gusts of wind spun the light basket. "Aiya," said Ah Goong. Winds came up under the basket, bouncing it. Neighboring baskets swung together and parted. He and the man next to him looked at each other's faces. They laughed. They might as well have gone to Malaysia to collect bird nests. Those who had done high work there said it had been worse; the birds screamed and scratched at them. Swinging near the cliff, Ah Goong stood up and grabbed it by a twig. He dug holes, then inserted gunpowder and fuses. He worked neither too fast nor too slow, keeping even with the others. The basketmen signaled one another to light the fuses. He struck match after match and dropped the burnt matches over the sides. At last his fuse caught; he waved, and the men above pulled hand over hand hauling him up, pulleys creaking. The scaffolds stood like a row of gibbets. Gallows trees along a ridge. "Hurry, hurry," he said. Some impatient men clambered up their ropes. Ah Goong ran up the ledge road they'd cleared and watched the explosions, which banged almost synchronously, echoes booming like war. He moved his scaffold to the next section of cliff and went down in the basket again, with bags of dirt, and set the next charge.

This time two men were blown up. One knocked out or killed by the explosion fell silently, the other screaming, his arms and legs struggling. A desire shot out of Ah Goong for an arm long enough to reach down and catch them. Much time passed as they fell like plummets. The shreds of baskets and a cowboy hat skimmed and tacked. The winds that pushed birds off course and against mountains did not carry men. Ah Goong also wished that the conscious man would fall faster and get it over with. He hands gripped the ropes, and it was difficult to let go and get on with the work. "It can't happen twice in a row," the basketmen said the next trip down. "Our chances are very good. The trip after an accident is probably the safest one." They raced to their favorite basket, checked and double-checked the four ropes, yanked the strands, tested the pulleys, oiled them, reminded the pulleymen about the signals, and entered the sky again. 19

Another time, Ah Goong had been lowered to the bottom of a ravine, which had to be cleared for the base of a trestle, when a man fell, and he saw his face. He had not died of shock before hitting bottom. His hands were grabbing at air. His stomach and groin must have felt the fall all the way down. At night Ah Goong woke up falling, though he slept on the ground, and heard other men call out in their sleep. No warm women tweaked their ears and hugged them. "It was only a falling dream," he reassured himself. 20

Across a valley, a chain of men working on the next mountain, men like ants changing the face of the world, fell, but it was very far away. Godlike, he watched men whose faces he could not see and whose screams he did not hear roll and bounce and slide like a handful of sprinkled gravel. 21

22   After a fall, the buzzards circled the spot and reminded the workers for days that a man was dead down there. The men threw piles of rocks and branches to cover bodies from sight.

23   The mountainface reshaped, they drove supports for a bridge. Since hammering was less dangerous than the blowing up, the men played a little; they rode the baskets swooping in wide arcs; they twisted the ropes and let them unwind like tops. "Look at me," said Ah Goong, pulled open his pants, and pissed overboard, the wind scattering the drops. "I'm a waterfall," he said. He had sent a part of himself hurtling. On rare windless days he watched his piss fall in a continuous stream from himself almost to the bottom of the valley.

24   One beautiful day, dangling in the sun above a new valley, not the desire to urinate but sexual desire clutched him so hard he bent over in the basket. He curled up, overcome by beauty and fear, which shot to his penis. He tried to rub himself calm. Suddenly he stood up tall and squirted out into space. "I am fucking the world," he said. The world's vagina was big, big as the sky, big as a valley. He grew a habit: whenever he was lowered in the basket, his blood rushed to his penis, and he fucked the world.

25   Then it was autumn, and the wind blew so fiercely, the men had to postpone the basketwork. Clouds moved in several directions at once. Men pointed at dust devils, which turned their mouths crooked. There was ceaseless motion; clothes kept moving; hair moved; sleeves puffed out. Nothing stayed still long enough for Ah Goong to figure it out. The wind sucked the breath out of his mouth and blew thoughts from his brains. The food convoys from San Francisco brought tents to replace the ones that whipped away. The baskets from China, which the men saved for high work, carried cowboy jackets, long underwear, Levi pants, boots, earmuffs, leather gloves, flannel shirts, coats. They sewed rabbit fur and deerskin into the linings. They tied the wide brims of their cowboy hats over their ears with mufflers. And still the wind made confusing howls into ears, and it was hard to think.

26   The days became nights when the crews tunneled inside the mountain, which sheltered them from the wind, but also hid the light and sky. Ah Goong pickaxed the mountain, the dirt filling his nostrils through a cowboy bandanna. He shoveled the dirt into a cart and pushed it to a place that was tall enough for the mule, which hauled it the rest of the way out. He looked forward to cart duty to edge closer to the entrance. Eyes darkened, nose plugged, his windy cough worse, he was to mole a thousand feet and meet others digging from the other side. How much he'd pay now to go swinging in a basket. He might as well have gone to work in a tin mine. Coming out of the tunnel at the end of a shift, he forgot whether it was supposed to be day or night. He blew his nose fifteen times before the mucus cleared again.

27   The dirt was the easiest part of tunneling. Beneath the soil, they hit granite. Ah Goong struck it with his pickax, and it jarred his bones, chattered his teeth. He swung his sledgehammer against it, and the impact rang in the dome of his skull. The mountain that was millions of years old was locked against them and

was not to be broken into. The men teased him, "Let's see you fuck the world now." "Let's see you fuck the Gold Mountain now." But he no longer felt like it. "A man ought to be made of tougher material than flesh," he said. "Skin is too soft. Our bones ought to be filled with iron." He lifted the hammer high, careful that it not pull him backward, and let it fall forward of its own weight against the rock. Nothing happened to that gray wall; he had to slam with strength and will. He hit at the same spot over and over again, the same rock. Some chips and flakes broke off. The granite looked everywhere the same. It had no softer or weaker spots anywhere, the same hard gray. He learned to slide his hand up the handle, lift, slide and swing, a circular motion, hammering, hammering, hammering. He would bite like a rat through that mountain. His eyes couldn't see; his nose couldn't smell; and now his ears were filled with the noise of hammering. This rock is what is real, he thought. This rock is what real is, not clouds or mist, which make mysterious promises, and when you go through them are nothing. When the foreman measured at the end of twenty-four hours of pounding, the rock had given a foot. The hammering went on day and night. The men worked eight hours on and eight hours off. They worked on all eighteen tunnels at once. While Ah Goong slept, he could hear the sledgehammers of other men working in the earth. The steady banging reminded him of holidays and harvests; falling asleep, he heard the women chopping mincemeat and the millstones striking.

The demons in boss suits came into the tunnel occasionally, measured with a yardstick and shook their heads. "Faster," they said. "Faster. Chinamen too slow. Too slow." "Tell us we're slow," the China Men grumbled. The ones in top tiers of scaffolding let rocks drop, a hammer drop. Ropes tangled around the demons' heads and feet. The cave China Men muttered and flexed, glared out of the corners of their eyes. But usually there was no diversion—one day the same as the next, one hour no different from another—the beating against the same granite. 28

After tunneling into granite for about three years, Ah Goong understood the immovability of the earth. Men change, men die, weather changes, but a mountain is the same as permanence and time. This mountain would have taken no new shape for centuries, ten thousand centuries, the world a still, still place, time unmoving. He worked in the tunnel so long, he learned to see many colors in black. When he stumbled out, he tried to talk about time. "I felt time," he said. "I saw time. I saw world." He tried again, "I saw what's real. I saw time, and it doesn't move. If we break through the mountain, hollow it, time won't have moved anyway. You translators ought to tell the foreigners that." 29

Summer came again, but after the first summer, he felt less nostalgia at the meeting of the Spinning Girl and the Cowboy. He now knew men who had been in this country for twenty years and thirty years, and the Cowboy's one year away from his lady was no time at all. His own patience was longer. The stars were meeting and would meet again next year, but he would not have seen his family. He joined the others celebrating Souls' Day, the holiday a week later, 30 the fourteenth day of the seventh month. The supply wagons from San Francisco and Sacramento brought watermelon, meat, fish, crab, pressed duck. "There, ghosts, there you are. Come and get it." They displayed the feast complete for a moment before falling to, eating on the dead's behalf.

31   In the third year of pounding granite by hand, a demon invented dynamite. The railroad workers were to test it. They had stopped using gunpowder in the tunnels after avalanches, but the demons said that dynamite was more precise. They watched a scientist demon mix nitrate, sulphate, and glycerine, then flick the yellow oil, which exploded off his fingertips. Sitting in a meadow to watch the dynamite detonated in the open, Ah Goong saw the men in front of him leap impossibly high into the air; then he felt a shove as if from a giant's unseen hand—he fell backward. The boom broke the mountain silence like fear breaking inside stomach and chest and groin. No one had gotten hurt; they stood up laughing and amazed, looking around at how they had fallen, the pattern of the explosion. Dynamite was much more powerful than gunpowder. Ah Goong had felt a nudge, as if something kind were moving him out of harm's way. "All of a sudden I was sitting next to you." "Aiya. If we had been nearer, it would have killed us." "If we were stiff, it would have gone through us." "A fist." "A hand." "We leapt like acrobats." Next time Ah Goong flattened himself on the ground, and the explosion rolled over him.

32   He never got used to the blasting; a blast always surprised him. Even when he himself set the fuse and watched it burn, anticipated the explosion, the bang—*bahng* in Chinese—when it came, always startled. It cleaned the crazy words, the crackling, and bingbangs out of his brain. It was like New Year's, when every problem and thought was knocked clean out of him by firecrackers, and he could begin fresh. He couldn't worry during an explosion, which jerked every head to attention. Hills flew up in rocks and dirt. Boulders turned over and over. Sparks, fires, debris, rocks, smoke burst up, not at the same time as the boom (*bum*) but before that—the sound a separate occurrence, not useful as a signal.

33   The terrain changed immediately. Streams were diverted, rockscapes exposed. Ah Goong found it difficult to remember what land had looked like before an explosion. It was a good thing the dynamite was invented after the Civil War to the east was over.

34   The dynamite added more accidents and ways of dying, but if it were not used, the railroad would take fifty more years to finish. Nitroglycerine exploded when it was jounced on a horse or dropped. A man who fell with it in his pocket blew himself up into red pieces. Sometimes it combusted merely standing. Human bodies skipped through the air like puppets and made Ah Goong laugh crazily as if the arms and legs would come together again. The smell of burned flesh remained in rocks.

35   In the tunnels, the men bored holes fifteen to eighteen inches deep with a power drill, stuffed them with hay and dynamite, and imbedded the fuse in sand. Once, for extra pay, Ah Goong ran back in to see why some dynamite had not

gone off and hurried back out again; it was just a slow fuse. When the explosion settled, he helped carry two-hundred-, three-hundred-, five-hundred-pound boulders out of the tunnel.

As a boy he had visited a Taoist monastery where there were nine rooms, each a replica of one of the nine hells. Lifesize sculptures of men and women were spitted on turning wheels. Eerie candles under the suffering faces emphasized eyes poked out, tongues pulled, red mouths and eyes, and real hair, eyelashes, and eyebrows. Women were split apart and men dismembered. He could have reached out and touched the sufferers and the implements. He had dug and dynamited his way into one of these hells. "Only here there are eighteen tunnels, not nine, plus all the tracks between them," he said.

One day he came out of the tunnel to find the mountains white, the evergreens and bare trees decorated, white tree sculptures and lace bushes everywhere. The men from snow country called the icicles "ice chopsticks." He sat in his basket and slid down the slopes. The snow covered the gouged land, the broken trees, the tracks, the mud, the campfire ashes, the unburied dead. Streams were stilled in mid-run, the water petrified. That winter he thought it was the task of the human race to quicken the world, blast the freeze, fire it, redden it with blood. He had to change the stupid slowness of one sunrise and one sunset per day. He had to enliven the silent world with sound. "The rock," he tried to tell the others. "The ice." "Time."

The dynamiting loosed blizzards on the men. Ears and toes fell off. Fingers stuck to the cold silver rails. Snowblind men stumbled about with bandannas over their eyes. Ah Goong helped build wood tunnels roofing the track route. Falling ice scrabbled on the roofs. The men stayed under the snow for weeks at a time. Snowslides covered the entrances to the tunnels, which they had to dig out to enter and exit, white tunnels and black tunnels. Ah Goong looked at his gang and thought, if there is an avalanche, these are the people I'll be trapped with, and wondered which ones would share food. A party of snowbound barbarians had eaten the dead. Cannibals, thought Ah Goong, and looked around. Food was not scarce; the tea man brought whiskey barrels of hot tea, and he warmed his hands and feet, held the teacup to his nose and ears. Someday, he planned, he would buy a chair with metal doors for putting hot coal inside it. The magpies did not abandon him but stayed all winter and searched the snow for food.

The men who died slowly enough to say last words said, "Don't leave me frozen under the snow. Send my body home. Burn it and put the ashes in a tin can. Take the bone jar when you come down the mountain." "When you ride the fire car back to China, tell my descendants to come for me." "Shut up," scolded the hearty men. "We don't want to hear about bone jars and dying." "You're lucky to have a body to bury, not blown to smithereens." "Stupid man to hurt yourself," they bawled out the sick and wounded. How their wives would scold if they brought back deadmen's bones. "Aiya. To be buried here, nowhere." "But this is somewhere," Ah Goong promised. "This is the Gold

Mountain. We're marking the land now. The track sections are numbered, and your family will know where we leave you." But he was a crazy man, and they didn't listen to him.

40 Spring did come, and when the snow melted, it revealed the past year, what had happened, what they had done, where they had worked, the lost tools, the thawing bodies, some standing with tools in hand, the bright rails. "Remember Uncle Long Winded Leong?" "Remember Strong Back Wong?" "Remember Lee Brother?" "And Fong Uncle?" They lost count of the number dead; there is no record of how many died building the railroad. Or maybe it was demons doing the counting and chinamen not worth counting. Whether it was good luck or bad luck, the dead were buried or cairned next to the last section of track they had worked on. "May his ghost not have to toil," they said over graves. (In China a woodcutter ghost chops eternally; people have heard chopping in the snow and in the heat.) "Maybe his ghost will ride the train home." The scientific demons said the transcontinental railroad would connect the West to Cathay. "What if he rides back and forth from Sacramento to New York forever?" "That wouldn't be so bad. I hear the cars will be like houses on wheels." The funerals were short. "No time. No time," said both China Men and demons. The railroad was as straight as they could build it, but no ghosts sat on the tracks; no strange presences haunted the tunnels. The blasts scared ghosts away.

41 When the Big Dipper pointed east and the China Men detonated nitroglycerine and shot off guns for the New Year, which comes with the spring, these special bangs were not as loud as the daily bangs, not as numerous as the bangs all year. Shouldn't the New Year be the loudest day of all to obliterate the noises of the old year? But to make a bang of that magnitude, they would have to blow up at least a year's supply of dynamite in one blast. They arranged strings in chain reactions in circles and long lines, banging faster and louder to culminate in a big bang. And most importantly, there were random explosions— surprise. Surprise. SURPRISE. They had no dragon, the railroad their dragon.

42 The demons invented games for working faster, gold coins for miles of track laid, for the heaviest rock, a grand prize for the first team to break through a tunnel. Day shifts raced against night shifts, China Men against Welshmen, China Men against Irishmen, China Men against Injuns and black demons. The fastest races were China Men against China Men, who bet on their own teams. China Men always won because of good teamwork, smart thinking, and the need for the money. Also, they had the most workers to choose teams from. Whenever his team won anything, Ah Goong added to his gold stash. The Central Pacific or Union Pacific won the land on either side of the tracks it built.

43 One summer day, demon officials and China Man translators went from group to group and announced, "We're raising the pay—thirty-five dollars a month. Because of your excellent work, the Central Pacific Railroad is giving you a four-dollar raise per month." The workers who didn't know better cheered. "What's the catch?" said the smarter men. "You'll have the opportunity

to put in more time," said the railroad demons. "Two more hours per shift." Ten-hour shifts inside the tunnels. "It's not ten hours straight," said the demons. "You have time off for tea and meals. Now that you have dynamite, the work isn't so hard." They had been working for three and a half years already, and the track through the Donner Summit was still not done.

The workers discussed the ten-hour shift, swearing their China Man obscenities. "Two extra hours a day—sixty hours a month for four dollars." "Pig catcher demons." "Snakes." "Turtles." "Dead demons." "A human body can't work like that." "The demons don't believe this is a human body. This is a chinaman's body." To bargain, they sent a delegation of English speakers, who were summarily noted as troublemakers, turned away, docked.

The China Men, then, decided to go on strike and demand forty-five dollars a month and the eight-hour shift. They risked going to jail and the Central Pacific keeping the pay it was banking for them. Ah Goong memorized the English, "Forty-five dollars a month—eight-hour shift." He practiced the strike slogan: "Eight hours a day good for white man, all the same good for China Man."

The men wrapped barley and beans in ti leaves, which came from Hawai'i via San Francisco, for celebrating the fifth day of the fifth month (not May but mid-June, the summer solstice). Usually the way the red string is wound and knotted tells what flavors are inside—the salty barley with pickled egg, or beans and pork, or the gelatin pudding. Ah Goong folded ti leaves into a cup and packed it with food. One of the literate men slipped in a piece of paper with the strike plan, and Ah Goong tied the bundle with a special pattern of red string. The time and place for the revolution against Kublai Khan had been hidden inside autumn mooncakes. Ah Goong looked from one face to another in admiration. Of course, of course. No China Men, no railroad. They were indispensable labor. Throughout these mountains were brothers and uncles with a common idea, free men, not coolies, calling for fair working conditions. The demons were not suspicious as the China Men went gandying up and down the tracks delivering the bundles tied together like lines of fish. They had exchanged these gifts every year. When the summer solstice cakes came from other camps, the recipients cut them into neat slices by drawing the string through them. The orange jellies, which had a red dye stick inside soaked in lye, fell into a series of sunrises and sunsets. The aged yolks and the barley also looked like suns. The notes gave a Yes strike vote. The yellow flags to ward off the five evils—centipedes, scorpions, snakes, poisonous lizards, and toads—now flew as banners.

The strike began on Tuesday morning, June 25, 1867. The men who were working at that hour walked out of the tunnels and away from the tracks. The ones who were sleeping slept on and rose as late as they pleased. They bathed in streams and shaved their moustaches and wild beards. Some went fishing and hunting. The violinists tuned and played their instruments. The drummers beat theirs at the punchlines of jokes. The gamblers shuffled and played their cards and tiles. The smokers passed their pipes, and the drinkers bet for drinks by making figures with their hands. The cooks made party food. The opera singers' falsettos almost perforated the mountains. The men sang new songs about the railroad. They made up verses and shouted Ho at the good ones, and laughed at the rhymes. Oh, they were madly singing in the mountains. The storytellers told about the rise of new kings. The opium smokers when they roused themselves told their florid images. Ah Goong sifted for gold. All the while the English-speaking China Men, who were being advised by the shrewdest bargainers, were at the demons' headquarters repeating the demand: "Eight hours a day good for white man, all the same good for China Man." They had probably negotiated the demons down to nine-hour shifts by now.

48   The sounds of hammering continued along the tracks and occasionally there were blasts from the tunnels. The scabby white demons had refused to join the strike. "Eight hours a day good for white man, all the same good for China Man," the China Men explained to them. "Cheap John Chinaman," said the demons, many of whom had red hair. The China Men scowled out of the corners of their eyes.

49   On the second day, artist demons climbed the mountains to draw the China Men for the newspapers. The men posed bare-chested, their fists clenched, showing off their arms and backs. The artists sketched them as perfect young gods reclining against rocks, wise expressions on their handsome noble-nosed faces, long torsos with lean stomachs, a strong arm extended over a bent knee, long fingers holding a pipe, a rope of hair over a wide shoulder. Other artists drew faeries with antennae for eyebrows and brownies with elfish pigtails; they danced in white socks and black slippers among mushroom rings by moonlight.

50   Ah Goong acquired another idea that added to his reputation for craziness: The pale, thin Chinese scholars and the rich men fat like Buddhas were less beautiful, less manly than these brown muscular railroad men, of whom he was one. One of ten thousand heroes.

51   On the third day, in a woods—he would be looking at a deer or a rabbit or an Injun watching him before he knew what he was seeing—a demon dressed in a white suit and tall hat beckoned him. They talked privately in the wilderness. The demon said, "I Citizenship Judge invite you to be U.S. citizen. Only one bag gold." Ah Goong was thrilled. What an honor. He would accept this invitation. Also what advantages, he calculated shrewdly; if he were going to be jailed for this strike, an American would have a trial. The Citizenship Judge unfurled a parchment sealed with gold and ribbon. Ah Goong bought it with one bag of gold. "You vote," said the Citizenship Judge. "You talk in court, buy land, no more chinaman tax." Ah Goong hid the paper on his person so that it would protect him from arrest and lynching. He was already a part of this new country, but now he had it in writing.

52   The fourth day, the strikers heard that the U.S. Cavalry was riding single file up the tracks to shoot them. They argued whether to engage the Army with dynamite. But the troops did not come. Instead the cowardly demons blockaded

the food wagons. No food. Ah Goong listened to the optimistic China Men, who said, "Don't panic. We'll hold out forever. We can hunt. We can last fifty days on water." The complainers said, "Aiya. Only saints can do that. Only magic men and monks who've practiced." The China Men refused to declare a last day for the strike.

The foresighted China Men had cured jerky, fermented wine, dried and strung orange and grapefruit peels, pickled and preserved leftovers. Ah Goong, one of the best hoarders, had set aside extra helpings from each meal. This same quandary, whether to give away food or to appear selfish, had occurred during each of the six famines he had lived through. The foodless men identified themselves. Sure enough, they were the shiftless, piggy, arrogant type who didn't worry enough. The donors scolded them and shamed them the whole while they were handing them food: "So you lived like a grasshopper at our expense." "Fleaman." "You'll be the cause of our not holding out long enough." "Rich man's kid. Too good to hoard." Ah Goong contributed some rice crusts from the bottoms of pans. He kept how much more food he owned a secret, as he kept the secret of his gold. In apology for not contributing richer food, he repeated a Mohist saying that had guided him in China: "'The superior man does not push humaneness to the point of stupidity.'" He could hear his wife scolding him for feeding strangers. The opium men offered shit and said that it calmed the appetite.

On the fifth and sixth days, Ah Goong organized his possessions and patched his clothes and tent. He forebore repairing carts, picks, ropes, baskets. His work-habituated hands arranged rocks and twigs in designs. He asked a reader to read again his family's letters. His wife sounded like herself except for the polite phrases added professionally at the beginnings and the ends. "Idiot," she said, "why are you taking so long? Are you wasting the money? Are you spending it on girls and gambling and whiskey? Here's my advice to you: Be a little more frugal. Remember how it felt to go hungry. Work hard." He had been an idle man for almost a week. "I need a new dress to wear to weddings. I refuse to go to another banquet in the same old dress. If you weren't such a spendthrift, we could be building the new courtyard where we'll drink wine among the flowers and sit about in silk gowns all day. We'll hire peasants to till the fields. Or lease them to tenants, and buy all our food at market. We'll have clean fingernails and toenails." Other relatives said, "I need a gold watch. Send me the money. Your wife gambles it away and throws parties and doesn't disburse it fairly among us. You might as well come home." It was after one of these letters that he had made a bonus checking on some dud dynamite.

Ah Goong did not spend his money on women. The strikers passed the word that a woman was traveling up the railroad and would be at his camp on the seventh and eighth day of the strike. Some said she was a demoness and some that she was a Chinese and her master a China Man. He pictured a nurse coming to bandage wounds and touch foreheads or a princess surveying her subjects; or perhaps she was a merciful Jesus demoness. But she was a pitiful woman, led on a leash around her waist, not entirely alive. Her owner sold lottery tickets for the use of her. Ah Goong did not buy one. He took out his penis under his blanket or bared it in the woods and thought about nurses and princesses. He also just looked at it, wondering what it was that it was for, what a man was for, what he had to have a penis for.

There was a rumor also of an Injun woman called Woman Chief, who led a nomadic fighting tribe from the eastern plains as far as these mountains. She was so powerful that she had four wives and many horses. He never saw her though.

The strike ended on the ninth day. The Central Pacific announced that in its benevolence it was giving the workers a four-dollar raise, not the fourteen dollars they had asked for. And that the shifts in the tunnels would remain eight hours long. "We were planning to give you the four-dollar raise all along," the demons said to diminish the victory. So they got thirty-five dollars a month and the eight-hour shift. They would have won forty-five dollars if the thousand demon workers had joined the strike. Demons would have listened to demons. The China Men went back to work quietly. No use singing and shouting over a compromise and losing nine days' work.

There were two days that Ah Goong did cheer and throw his hat in the air, jumping up and down and screaming Yippee like a cowboy. One: the day his team broke through the tunnel at last. Toward the end they did not dynamite but again used picks and sledgehammers. Through the granite, they heard answering poundings, and answers to their shouts. It was not a mountain before them any more but only a wall with people breaking through from the other side. They worked faster. Forward. Into day. They stuck their arms through the holes and shook hands with men on the other side. Ah Goong saw dirty faces as wondrous as if he were seeing Nu Wo, the creator goddess who repairs cracks in the sky with stone slabs; sometimes she peeks through and human beings see her face. The wall broke. Each team gave the other a gift of half a tunnel, dug. They stepped back and forth where the wall had been. Ah Goong ran and ran, his boots thudding to the very end of the tunnel, looked at the other side of the mountain, and ran back, clear through the entire tunnel. All the way through.

He spent the rest of his time on the railroad laying and bending and hammering the ties and rails. The second day the China Men cheered was when the engine from the West and the one from the East rolled toward one another and touched. The transcontinental railroad was finished. They Yippee'd like madmen. The white demon officials gave speeches. "The Greatest Feat of the Nineteenth Century," they said. "The Greatest Feat in the History of Mankind," they said. "Only Americans could have done it," they said, which is true. Even if Ah Goong had not spent half his gold on Citizenship Papers, he was an American for having built the railroad. A white demon in top hat tap-tapped on the gold spike, and pulled it back out. Then one China Man held the real spike, the steel one, and another hammered it in.

While the demons posed for photographs, the China Men dispersed. It was dangerous to stay. The Driving Out had begun. Ah Goong does not appear in railroad photographs. Scattering, some China Men followed the north star in the constellation Tortoise the Black Warrior to Canada, or they kept the constellation Phoenix ahead of them to South America or the White Tiger west or the Wolf east. Seventy lucky men rode the Union Pacific to Massachusetts for jobs at a shoe factory. Fifteen hundred went to Fou Loy Company in New Orleans and San Francisco, several hundred to plantations in Mississippi, Georgia, and Arkansas, and sugarcane plantations in Louisiana and Cuba. (From the South, they sent word that it was a custom to step off the sidewalk along with the black demons when a white demon walked by.) Seventy went to New Orleans to grade a route for a railroad, then to Pennsylvania to work in a knife factory. The Colorado State Legislature passed a resolution welcoming the railroad China Men to come build the new state. They built railroads in every part of the country—the Alabama and Chattanooga Railroad, the Houston and Texas Railroad, the Southern Pacific, the railroads in Louisiana and Boston, the Pacific Northwest, and Alaska. After the Civil War, China Men banded the nation North and South, East and West, with crisscrossing steel. They were the binding and building ancestors of this place.

Ah Goong would have liked a leisurely walk along the tracks to review his finished handiwork, or to walk east to see the rest of his new country. But instead, Driven Out, he slid down mountains, leapt across valleys and streams, crossed plains, hid sometimes with companions and often alone, and eluded bandits who would hold him up for his railroad pay and shoot him for practice as they shot Injuns and jackrabbits. Detouring and backtracking, his path wound back and forth to his railroad, a familiar silver road in the wilderness. When a train came, he hid against the shaking ground in case a demon with a shotgun was hunting from it. He picked over camps where he had once lived. He was careful to find hidden places to sleep. In China bandits did not normally kill people, the booty the main thing, but here the demons killed for fun and hate. They tied pigtails to horses and dragged chinamen. He decided that he had better head for San Francisco, where he would catch a ship to China.

Perched on hillsides, he watched many sunsets, the place it was setting, the direction he was going. There were fields of grass that he tunneled through, hid in, rolled in, dived and swam in, suddenly jumped up laughing, suddenly stopped. He needed to find a town and human company. The spooky tumbleweeds caught in barbed wire were peering at him, waiting for him; he had to find a town. Towns grew along the tracks as they did along rivers. He sat looking at a town all day, then ducked into it by night.

At the familiar sight of a garden laid out in a Chinese scheme—vegetables in beds, white cabbages, red plants, chives, and coriander for immortality, herbs boxed with boards—he knocked on the back door. The China Man who answered gave him food, the appropriate food for the nearest holiday, talked story, exclaimed at how close their ancestral villages were to each other. They exchanged information on how many others lived how near, which towns had

Chinatowns, what size, two or three stores or a block, which towns to avoid. "Do you have a wife?" they asked one another. "Yes. She lives in China. I have been sending money for twenty years now." They exchanged vegetable seeds, slips, and cuttings, and Ah Goong carried letters to another town or China.

64   Some demons who had never seen the likes of him gave him things and touched him. He also came across lone China Men who were alarmed to have him appear, and, unwelcome, he left quickly; they must have wanted to be the only China Man of that area, the special China Man.

65   He met miraculous China Men who had produced families out of no-where—a wife and children, both boys and girls. "Uncle," the children called him, and he wanted to stay to be the uncle of the family. The wife washed his clothes, and he went on his way when they were dry.

66   On a farm road, he came across an imp child playing in the dirt. It looked at him, and he looked at it. He held out a piece of sugar; he cupped a grassblade between his thumbs and whistled. He sat on the ground with his legs crossed, and the child climbed into the hollow of his arms and legs. "I wish you were my baby," he told it. "My baby." He was very satisfied sitting there under the humming sun with the baby, who was satisfied too, no squirming. "My daughter," he said. "My son." He couldn't tell whether it was a boy or a girl. He touched the baby's fat arm and cheeks, its gold hair, and looked into its blue eyes. He made a wish that it not have to carry a sledgehammer and crawl into the dark. But he would not feel sorry for it; other people must not suffer any more than he did, and he could endure anything. Its mother came walking out into the road. She had her hands above her like a salute. She walked tentatively towards them, held out her hand, smiled, spoke. He did not understand what she said except "Bye-bye." The child waved and said, "Bye-bye," crawled over his legs, and toddled to her. Ah Goong continued on his way in a direction she could not point out to a posse looking for a kidnapper chinaman.

67   Explosions followed him. He heard screams and went on, saw flames outlining black windows and doors, and went on. He ran in the opposite direction from gunshots and the yell—*eeha awha*—the cowboys made when they herded cattle and sang their savage songs.

68   Good at hiding, disappearing—decades unaccounted for—he was not working in a mine when forty thousand chinamen were Driven Out of mining. He was not killed or kidnapped in the Los Angeles Massacre, though he gave money toward ransoming those whose toes and fingers, a digit per week, and ears grotesquely rotting or pickled, and scalped queues, were displayed in China-towns. Demons believed that the poorer a chinaman looked, the more gold he had buried somewhere, that chinamen stuck together and would always ransom one another. If he got kidnapped, Ah Goong planned, he would whip out his Citizenship Paper and show that he was an American. He was lucky not to be in Colorado when the Denver demons burned all chinamen homes and busi-nesses, nor in Rock Springs, Wyoming, when the miner demons killed twenty-

eight or fifty chinamen. The Rock Springs Massacre began in a large coal mine owned by the Union Pacific; the outnumbered chinamen were shot in the back as they ran to Chinatown, which the demons burned. They forced chinamen out into the open and shot them; demon women and children threw the wounded back in the flames. (There was a rumor of a good white lady in Green Springs who hid China Men in the Pacific Hotel and shamed the demons away.) The hunt went on for a month before federal troops came. The count of the dead was inexact because bodies were mutilated and pieces scattered all over the Wyoming Territory. No white miners were indicted, but the government paid $150,000 in reparations to victims' families. There were many family men, then. There were settlers—abiding China Men. And China Women. Ah Goong was running elsewhere during the Drivings Out of Tacoma, Seattle, Oregon City, Albania, and Marysville. The demons of Tacoma packed all its chinamen into boxcars and sent them to Portland, where they were run out of town. China Men returned to Seattle, though, and refused to sell their land and stores but fought until the army came; the demon rioters were tried and acquitted. And when the Boston police imprisoned and beat 234 chinamen, it was 1902, and Ah Goong had already reached San Francisco or China, and perhaps San Francisco again.

In Second City (Sacramento), he spent some of his railroad money at the theater. The main actor's face was painted red with thick black eyebrows and long black beard, and when he strode onto the stage, Ah Goong recognized the hero, Guan Goong; his puppet horse had red nostrils and rolling eyes. Ah Goong's heart leapt to recognize hero and horse in the wilds of America. Guan Goong murdered his enemy—crash! bang! of cymbals and drum—and left his home village—sad, sad flute music. But to the glad clamor of cymbals entered his friends—Liu Pei (pronounced the same as Running Nose) and Chang Fei. In a joyful burst of pink flowers, the three men swore the Peach Garden Oath. Each friend sang an aria to friendship; together they would fight side by side and live and die one for all and all for one. Ah Goong felt as warm as if he were with friends at a party. Then Guan Goong's archenemy, the sly Ts'ao Ts'ao, captured him and two of Liu Pei's wives, the Lady Kan and the Lady Mi. Though Ah Goong knew they were boy actors, he basked in the presence of Chinese ladies. The prisoners traveled to the capital, the soldiers waving horse-hair whisks, signifying horses, the ladies walking between horizontal banners, signifying palanquins. All the prisoners were put in one bedroom, but Guan Goong stood all night outside the door with a lighted candle in his hand, singing an aria about faithfulness. When the capital was attacked by a common enemy, Guan Goong fought the biggest man in one-to-one combat, a twirling, jumping sword dance that strengthened the China Men who watched it. From afar Guan Goong's two partners heard about the feats of the man with the red face and intelligent horse. The three friends were reunited and fought until they secured their rightful kingdom.

70   Ah Goong felt refreshed and inspired. He called out Bravo like the demons in the audience, who had not seen theater before. Guan Goong, the God of War, also God of War and Literature, had come to America—Guan Goong, Grandfather Guan, our own ancestor of writers and fighters, of actors and gamblers, and avenging executioners who mete out justice. Our own kin. Not a distant ancestor but Grandfather.

71   In the Big City (San Francisco), a goldsmith convinced Ah Goong to have his gold made into jewelry, which would organize it into one piece and also delight his wife. So he handed over a second bag of gold. He got it back as a small ring in a design he thought up himself, two hands clasping in a handshake. "So small?" he said, but the goldsmith said that only some of the ore had been true gold.

72   He got a ship out of San Francisco without being captured near the docks, where there was a stockade full of jailed chinamen; the demonesses came down from Nob Hill and took them home to be servants, cooks, and baby-sitters.

73   Grandmother liked the gold ring very much. The gold was so pure, it squished to fit her finger. She never washed dishes, so the gold did not wear away. She quickly spent the railroad money, and Ah Goong said he would go to America again. He had a Certificate of Return and his Citizenship Paper.

74   But this time, there was no railroad to sell his strength to. He lived in a basement that was rumored to connect with tunnels beneath Chinatown. In an underground arsenal, he held a pistol and said, "I feel the death in it." "The holes for the bullets were like chambers in a beehive or wasp nest," he said. He was inside the earth when the San Francisco Earthquake and Fire began. Thunder rumbled from the ground. Some say he died falling into the cracking earth. It was a miraculous earthquake and fire. The Hall of Records burned completely. Citizenship Papers burned, Certificates of Return, Birth Certificates, Residency Certificates, passenger lists, Marriage Certificates—every paper a China Man wanted for citizenship and legality burned in that fire. An authentic citizen, then, had no more papers than an alien. Any paper a China Man could not produce had been "burned up in the Fire of 1906." Every China Man was reborn out of that fire a citizen.

75   Some say the family went into debt and sent for Ah Goong, who was not making money; he was a homeless wanderer, a shiftless, dirty, jobless man with matted hair, ragged clothes, and fleas all over his body. He ate out of garbage cans. He was a louse eaten by lice. A fleaman. It cost two thousand dollars to bring him back to China, his oldest sons signing promissory notes for one thousand, his youngest to repay four hundred to one neighbor and six hundred to another. Maybe he hadn't died in San Francisco, it was just his papers that burned; it was just that his existence was outlawed by Chinese Exclusion Acts. The family called him Fleaman. They did not understand his accomplishments as an American ancestor, a holding, homing ancestor of this place. He'd gotten the legal or illegal papers burned in the San Francisco Earthquake and Fire; he

appeared in America in time to be a citizen and to father citizens. He had also been seen carrying a child out of the fire, a child of his own in spite of the laws against marrying. He had built a railroad out of sweat, why not have an American child out of longing? ✣

RESPONDING

1. Maxine Hong Kingston calls her grandfather "an American ancestor, a holding, homing ancestor of this place" (paragraph 75), even though he was never legally an American citizen. Explain his contribution to this country in a journal entry.

2. Working in a group, discuss the ways in which Kingston's grandfather's life was shaped by the place where he was living and the opportunities available to him. Write a journal entry or an essay about the ways in which you or any of your relatives have been directly affected by the period or place in which you happen to be born or live.

3. Imagine that you are a reporter for a San Francisco newspaper in the late 1800s. You have just returned from interviewing Chinese railroad workers. Write a feature story for your newspaper arguing that they are being exploited and mistreated by the "demon" bosses. Or write a story from the bosses' point of view about working conditions on the railroad.

4. Choose one of the atrocities Kingston writes about and expand your knowledge of the circumstances by researching the incident in your school library. Write your own version and share it with the class.

CONNIE YOUNG YU

Connie Young Yu is a specialist in Asian American immigration history and culture. One of the founders of the Angel Island Immigration Station Historical Advisory Committee, Young Yu has also played active roles in the Santa Clara County Asian Health Needs Assessment Study and the Chinatown Housing and Health Resource Project of San Francisco. Her research has appeared in such publications as The Civil Rights Digest, Amerasia, *and the anthology* Working It Out. *More recently, she has published* Profiles in Excellence, *a series of biographies of Asian American women.*

In the essay that follows Young Yu examines how the experiences of her grandmother provide a special perspective on the history of her family and the larger community.

✥

THE WORLD OF OUR GRANDMOTHERS

1   IN ASIAN AMERICA there are two kinds of history. The first is what is written about us in various old volumes on immigrants and echoed in textbooks, and the second is our own oral history, what we learn in the family chain of generations. We are writing this oral history ourselves. But as we research the factual background of our story, we face the dilemma of finding sources. Worse than burning the books is not being included in the record at all, and in American history—traditionally viewed from the white male perspective—minority women have been virtually ignored. Certainly the accomplishments and struggles of early Chinese immigrants, men as well as women, have been obscured.

2   Yet for a period in the development of the West, Chinese immigration was a focus of prolonged political and social debate and a subject of daily news. When I first began searching into the background of my people, I read this nineteenth-century material with curious excitement, grateful for any information on Chinese immigration.

3   Looking for the history of Chinese pioneer women, I began with the first glimpses of Chinese in America—newspaper accounts found in bound volumes of the *Alta California* in the basement of a university library. For Chinese workers, survival in the hostile and chaotic world of Gum San, or Gold Mountain, as California was called by Chinese immigrants, was perilous and a constant struggle, leaving little time or inclination for reflection or diary writing. So for a look into the everyday life of early arrivals from China, we have only the impressions of white reporters on which to depend.

The newspapers told of the comings and goings of "Chinamen," their 4
mining activities, new Chinese settlements, their murders by claim-jumpers, and
assaults by whites in the city. An item from 17 August 1855, reported a
"disgraceful outrage": Mr. Ho Alum was setting his watch under a street clock
when a man called Thomas Field walked up and deliberately dashed the time-
piece to the pavement. "Such unprovoked assaults upon unoffending Chinamen
are not of rare occurrence. . . ." On the same day the paper also reported the
suicide of a Chinese prostitute. In this item no name, details, or commentary
were given, only a stark announcement. We can imagine the tragic story behind
it: the short miserable life of a young girl sold into slavery by her impoverished
parents and taken to Gum San to be a prostitute in a society of single men.

An early history of this period, *Lights and Shades in San Francisco* by B. E. 5
Lloyd (1878), devoted ten chapters to the life of California Chinese, describing
in detail "the subjects of the Celestial Kingdom." Chinese women, however, are
relegated to a single paragraph:

> Females are little better than slaves. They are looked upon as merchantable
> property, and are bought and sold like any other article of traffic, though their
> value is not generally great. A Chinese woman never gains any distinction until
> after death. . . . Considering the humble position the women occupy in China,
> and the hard life they therefore lead, it would perhaps be better (certainly
> more merciful) were they all slain in infancy, and better still, were they never
> born.[1]

Public opinion, inflamed by lurid stories of Chinese slave girls, agreed with 6
this odious commentary. The only Chinese women whose existence American
society acknowledged were the prostitutes who lived miserable and usually short
lives. Senate hearings on Chinese immigration in 1876 resounded with ha-
rangues about prostitutes and slave girls corrupting the morals of young white
boys. "The Chinese race is debauched," claimed one lawyer arguing for the
passage of the Chinese Exclusion Law: "They bring no decent women with
them." This stigma on the Chinese immigrant woman remained for many
decades, causing unnecessary hardships for countless wives, daughters, and slave
girls.

Chinese American society finally established itself as families appeared, just 7
as they did in the white society of the forty-niners who arrived from the East
Coast without bringing "decent women" with them. Despite American laws
intended to prevent the "settlement" of Chinese, Chinese women did make the
journey and endured the isolation and hostility, braving it for future generations
here.

Even though Chinese working men were excluded from most facets of 8

1. B. E. Lloyd, *Lights and Shades in San Francisco* (San Francisco: San Francisco Press, 1878).

American society and their lives were left unrecorded, their labors bespoke their existence—completed railroads, reclaimed lands, and a myriad of new industries. The evidence of women's lives seems less tangible. Perhaps the record of their struggles to immigrate and overcome discriminatory barriers is their greatest legacy. Tracing that record therefore becomes a means of recovering our history.

9 Our grandmothers are our historical links. As a fourth-generation Chinese American on my mother's side, and a third-generation on my father's, I grew up hearing stories about ancestors coming from China and going back and returning again. Both of my grandmothers, like so many others, spent a lot of time waiting in China.

10 My father's parents lived with us when I was growing up, and through them I absorbed a village culture and the heritage of my pioneer Chinese family. In the kitchen my grandmother told repeated stories of coming to America after waiting for her husband to send for her. (It took sixteen years before Grandfather could attain the status of merchant and only then arrange for her passage to this country.)[2] She also told stories from the village about bandits, festivals, and incidents showing the tyranny of tradition. For example, Grandma was forbidden by her mother-in-law to return to her own village to visit her mother: A married woman belonged solely within the boundaries of her husband's world.

11 Sometimes I was too young to understand or didn't listen, so my mother—who knew all the stories by heart—told me those stories again later. We heard over and over how lucky Grandpa was to have come to America when he was eleven—just one year before the gate was shut by the exclusion law banning Chinese laborers. Grandpa told of his many jobs washing dishes, making bricks, and working on a strawberry farm. Once, while walking outside Chinatown, he was stoned by a group of whites and ran so fast he lost his cap. Grandma had this story to tell of her anger and frustration: "While I was waiting in the immigration shed,[3] Grandpa sent in a box of *dim sum*.[4] I was still waiting to be released. I would have jumped in the ocean if they decided to deport me." A woman in her position was quite helpless, but she still had her pride and was not easily pacified. "I threw the box of *dim sum* out the window."

12 Such was the kind of history I absorbed. I regret deeply that I was too young to have asked the questions about the past that I now want answered; all my grandparents are now gone. But I have another chance to recover some history from my mother's side. Family papers, photographs, old trunks that have

2. Under the Chinese Exclusion Act of 1882, Chinese laborers could no longer immigrate to America. Until the act was repealed in 1943, only merchants, diplomats, students, and visitors were allowed to enter.
3. Between 1910 and 1940 Chinese immigrants arriving in the port of San Francisco were detained at the Angel Island Immigration Station to await physical examinations and interrogation to determine their right to enter this country. Prior to 1910 immigrants were detained in a building on the wharf known as "the shed."
4. Chinese pastries

traveled across the ocean several times filled with clothes, letters, and mementos provide a documentary on our immigration. My mother—and some of my grandmother's younger contemporaries—fill in the narrative.

A year before the Joint Special Committee of Congress to investigate [13] Chinese immigration met in San Francisco in 1876, my great-grandmother, Chin Shee, arrived to join her husband, Lee Wong Sang, who had come to America a decade earlier to work on the transcontinental railroad. Chin Shee arrived with two brides who had never seen their husbands. Like her own, their marriages had been arranged by their families. The voyage on the clipper ship was rough and long. Seasick for weeks, rolling back and forth as she lay in the bunk, Chin Shee lost most of her hair. The two other women laughed, "Some newlywed you'll make!" But the joke was on them as they mistakenly set off with the wrong husbands, the situation realized only when one man looked at his bride's normal-sized feet and exclaimed, "But the letter described my bride as having bound feet!" Chin Shee did not have her feet bound because she came from a peasant family. But her husband did not seem to care about that nor that the back of her head was practically bald. He felt himself fortunate just to be able to bring his wife to Gum San.

Chin Shee bore six children in San Francisco, where her husband assisted [14] in the deliveries. They all lived in the rear of their grocery store, which also exported dried shrimp and seaweed to China. Great-Grandma seldom left home; she could count the number of times she went out. She and other Chinese wives did not appear in the streets even for holidays, lest they be looked upon as prostitutes. She took care of the children, made special cakes to sell on feast days, and helped with her husband's work. A photograph of her shows a middle-aged woman with a kindly, but careworn face, wearing a very regal brocade gown and a long, beaded necklace. As a respectable, well-to-do Chinese wife in America, married to a successful Chinatown merchant, with children who were by birthright American citizens, she was a rarity in her day. (In contrast, in 1884 Mrs. Jew Lim, the wife of a laborer, sued in federal court to be allowed to join her husband, but was denied and deported.)

In 1890 there were only 3,868 Chinese women among 103,620 Chinese [15] males in America. Men such as Lee Yoke Suey, my mother's father, went to China to marry. He was one of Chin Shee's sons born in the rear of the grocery store, and he grew up learning the import and export trade. As a Gum San merchant, he had money and status and was able to build a fine house in Toishan. Not only did he acquire a wife but also two concubines. When his wife became very ill after giving birth to an infant who soon died, Yoke Suey was warned by his father that she was too weak to return to America with him. Reminding Yoke Suey of the harsh life in Gum San, he advised his son to get a new wife.

In the town of Foshan, not far from my grandfather's village, lived a girl [16] who was recommended to him by his father's friend. Extremely capable, bright, and with some education, she was from a once prosperous family that had fallen on hard times. A plague had killed her two older brothers, and her heartbroken mother died soon afterwards. She was an excellent cook and took good care of her father, an herb doctor. Her name was Jeong Hing Tong, and she was pretty, with bound feet only three and a half inches long. Her father rejected the offer of the Lee family at first; he did not want his daughter to be a concubine, even to a wealthy Gum San merchant. But the elder Lee assured him this girl would be the wife, the one who would go to America with her husband.

17   So my maternal grandmother, bride of sixteen, went with my grandfather, then twenty-six, to live in America. Once in San Francisco, Grandmother lived a life of confinement, as did her mother-in-law before her. When she went out, even in Chinatown, she was ridiculed for her bound feet. People called out mockingly to her, "*Jhat!*" meaning bound. She tried to unbind her feet by soaking them every night and putting a heavy weight on each foot. But she was already a grown woman, and her feet were permanently stunted, the arches bent and the toes crippled. It was hard for her to stand for long periods of time, and she frequently had to sit on the floor to do her chores. My mother comments: "Tradition makes life so hard. My father traveled all over the world. There were stamps all over his passport—London, Paris—and stickers all over his suitcases, but his wife could not go into the street by herself."

18   Their first child was a girl, and on the morning of her month-old "red eggs and ginger party" the earth shook 8.3 on the Richter scale. Everyone in San Francisco, even Chinese women, poured out into the streets. My grandmother, babe in arms, managed to get a ride to Golden Gate Park on a horse-drawn wagon. Two other Chinese women who survived the earthquake recall the shock of suddenly being out in the street milling with thousands of people. The elderly goldsmith in a dimly lit Chinatown store had a twinkle in his eye when I asked him about the scene after the quake. "We all stared at the women because we so seldom saw them in the streets." The city was soon in flames. "We could feel the fire on our faces," recalls Lily Sung, who was seven at the time, "but my sister and I couldn't walk very fast because we had to escort this lady, our neighbor, who had bound feet." The poor woman kept stumbling and falling on the rubble and debris during their long walk to the Oakland-bound ferry.

19   That devastating natural disaster forced some modernity on the San Francisco Chinese community. Women had to adjust to the emergency and makeshift living conditions and had to work right alongside the men. Life in America, my grandmother found, was indeed rugged and unpredictable.

20   As the city began to rebuild itself, she proceeded to raise a large family, bearing four more children. The only school in San Francisco admitting Chinese was the Oriental school in Chinatown. But her husband felt, as did most men of his class, that the only way his children could get a good education was for the family to return to China. So they lived in China and my grandfather traveled back and forth to the United States for his trade business. Then suddenly, at the age of forty-three, he died of an illness on board a ship returning

to China. After a long and painful mourning, Grandmother decided to return to America with her brood of now seven children. That decision eventually affected immigration history.

At the Angel Island immigration station in San Francisco Bay, Grandmother 21
went through a physical examination so thorough that even her teeth were checked to determine whether she was the age stated on her passport. The health inspector said she had filariasis, liver fluke, a common ailment of Asian immigrants which caused their deportation by countless numbers. The authorities thereby ordered Grandmother to be deported as well.

While her distraught children had to fend for themselves in San Francisco 22
(my mother, then fifteen, and her older sister had found work in a sewing factory), a lawyer was hired to fight for Grandmother's release from the detention barracks. A letter addressed to her on Angel Island from her attorney, C. M. Fickert, dated 24 March 1924, reads: "Everything I can legitimately do will be done on your behalf. As you say, it seems most inhuman for you to be separated from your children who need your care. I am sorry that the immigration officers will not look at the human side of your case."

Times were tough for Chinese immigrants in 1924. Two years before, the 23
federal government had passed the Cable Act, which provided that any woman born in the United States who married a man "ineligible for citizenship" (including the Chinese, whose naturalization rights had been eliminated by the Chinese Exclusion Act) would lose her own citizenship. So, for example, when American-born Lily Sung, whom I also interviewed, married a Chinese citizen she forfeited her birthright. When she and her four daughters tried to re-enter the United States after a stay in China, they were denied permission. The immigration inspector accused her of "smuggling little girls to sell." The Cable Act was not repealed until 1930.

The year my grandmother was detained on Angel Island, a law had just 24
taken effect that forbade all aliens ineligible for citizenship from landing in America.[5] This constituted a virtual ban on the immigration of all Chinese, including Chinese wives of U.S. citizens.

Waiting month after month in the bleak barracks, Grandmother heard 25
many heart-rending stories from women awaiting deportation. They spoke of the suicides of several despondent women who hanged themselves in the shower stalls. Grandmother could see the calligraphy carved on the walls by other detained immigrants, eloquent poems expressing homesickness, sorrow, and a sense of injustice.

Meanwhile, Fickert was sending telegrams to Washington (a total of ten 26
the bill stated) and building up a case for the circuit court. Mrs. Lee, after all,

5. The Immigration Act of 1924 affected all Asians who sought to immigrate to the United States. Congress repealed the law as to Chinese in 1943, and then in 1952 through the McCarran-Walter Act as to other Asian ethnic groups.

was the wife of a citizen who was a respected San Francisco merchant, and her children were American citizens. He also consulted a medical authority to see about a cure for liver fluke.

27   My mother took the ferry from San Francisco twice a week to visit Grandmother and take her Chinese dishes such as salted eggs and steamed pork because Grandmother could not eat the beef stew served in the mess hall. Mother and daughter could not help crying frequently during their short visits in the administration building. They were under close watch of both a guard and an interpreter.

28   After fifteen months the case was finally won. Grandmother was easily cured of filariasis and was allowed—with nine months probation—to join her children in San Francisco. The legal fees amounted to $782.50, a fortune in those days.

29   In 1927 Dr. Frederick Lam in Hawaii, moved by the plight of Chinese families deported from the islands because of the liver fluke disease, worked to convince federal health officials that the disease was noncommunicable. He used the case of Mrs. Lee Yoke Suey, my grandmother, as a precedent for allowing an immigrant to land with such an ailment and thus succeeded in breaking down a major barrier to Asian immigration.

30   My most vivid memory of Grandmother Lee is when she was in her seventies and studying for her citizenship. She had asked me to test her on the three branches of government and how to pronounce them correctly. I was a sophomore in high school and had entered the "What American Democracy Means To Me" speech contest of the Chinese American Citizens Alliance. When I said the words "judicial, executive, and legislative," I looked directly at my grandmother in the audience. She didn't smile, and afterwards, didn't comment much on my patriotic words. She had never told me about being on Angel Island or about her friends losing their citizenship. It wasn't in my textbooks either. I may have thought she wanted to be a citizen because her sons and sons-in-law had fought for this country, and we lived in a land of freedom and opportunity, but my guess now is that she wanted to avoid any possible confrontation—even at her age—with immigration authorities. The bad laws had been repealed, but she wasn't taking any chances.

31   I think a lot about my grandmother now and can understand why, despite her quiet, elegant dignity, an aura of sadness always surrounded her. She suffered from racism in the new country, as well as from traditional cruelties in the old. We, her grandchildren, remember walking very slowly with her, escorting her to a family banquet in Chinatown, hating the stares of tourists at her tiny feet. Did she, I wonder, ever feel like the victim of a terrible hoax, told as a small weeping girl that if she tried to untie the bandages tightly binding her feet she would grow up ugly, unwanted, and without the comforts and privileges of the wife of a wealthy man?

32   We seemed so huge and clumsy around her—a small, slim figure always dressed in black. She exclaimed once that the size of my growing feet were "like

boats." But she lived to see some of her granddaughters graduate from college and pursue careers and feel that the world she once knew with its feudal customs had begun to crumble. I wonder what she would have said of my own daughter who is now attending a university on an athletic scholarship. Feet like boats travel far?

I keep looking at the artifacts of the past: the photograph of my grandmother when she was an innocent young bride and the sad face in the news photo taken on Angel Island. I visit the immigration barracks from time to time, a weather-beaten wooden building with its walls marked by calligraphy bespeaking the struggles of our history. I see the view of sky and water from the window out of which my grandmother gazed. My mother told me how, after visiting hours, she would walk to the ferry and turn back to see her mother waving to her from this window. This image has been passed on to me like an heirloom of pain and of love. When I leave the building, emerging from the darkness into the glaring sunlight of the island, I too turn back to look at my grandmother's window. �֎

33

RESPONDING

1. Connie Young Yu expresses the wish that she had asked her grandmother more about her history. Write a journal entry either presenting the history of your own grandparents or formulating the questions you would like to ask your parents or grandparents.

2. Working individually or in a group, list the immigration laws to which Young Yu refers. Do you think those laws were appropriate and necessary? Compare them to our current immigration policies, reviewing these first in the library if necessary. Share your conclusions with the class or organize a class debate.

3. Explain in an essay why Young Yu's mother believes that "tradition makes life so hard" (paragraph 17). Do you agree or disagree? Support your point of view with evidence from the reading and other sources, as well as your own knowledge.

4. Imagine that you are the attorney representing Mrs. Lee. Write the appeal you will present to the circuit court arguing that she should be admitted to the country.

✜

CONNECTING

Critical Thinking and Writing

1. Write an essay speculating on the possible social, psychological, and economic effects of the Exclusion Act on Chinese already in the United States when it was passed. Use examples from the readings to support your opinions.

2. Using the readings as a resource, compile a list of the customs and folklore that were a part of Chinese culture in the late 1800s. Write an essay discussing the folklore of your family or culture or of another culture with which you are familiar.

3. Discuss the lives of the women portrayed in this section. What opportunities were available for Chinese women of the period? What obligations did they have to fulfill? In an essay compare their situation to the situation of Chinese men.

4. The year is 1882. Choose an identity for yourself. Perhaps you are a worker, a merchant, a factory owner, a wife and mother. Take a position for or against the importation of Chinese workers, and write a letter to the editor of a San Francisco newspaper presenting your position. Support your ideas with examples from the readings, material from other sources, or your own knowledge.

5. The author of the Gold Mountain poems in this section is a man. Compare his experience at Angel Island with the experience of Young Yu's grandmother, Mrs. Lee. What might Mrs. Lee have written in a poem?

6. Consider the similar ways in which Sui Sin Far uses the phrase "the land of the free" and Connie Young Yu uses the phrase "a land of freedom." Write an essay arguing that Young Yu's essay does or does not validate the events presented in Sin Far's short story.

7. According to the reading, what aspects of Chinese culture and character helped the Chinese become successful in America? After isolating those characteristics, list the values that seemed to be important to Chinese culture. Compare these values to your own. Are these values important to you, to contemporary American society?

8. Using information from these readings, describe the role of women in traditional Chinese culture. Compare the Chinese woman immigrant of the late

1800s to women from other immigrant groups of the same period, such as those from Europe.

9.   Many Chinese came to the United States in the late 1800s. Using evidence from the readings, write an essay comparing their reasons for immigrating with those of other groups who came during the same period.

10. Compare the working conditions of the Chinese on the railway as described by Kingston to the working conditions of other groups described in readings by Panunzio in Chapter 1 and Chavez in Chapter 7, among others. How was each group treated? You may compare the treatment of a group or the experiences of individuals.

11. Discuss the causes and effects of organized resistance among the Chinese railroad workers that Kingston reports and compare those to Chavez's description of Chicano efforts to organize almost one hundred years later.

12. The issue of parents wishing to maintain a native culture while raising their children in an alien culture is a recurrent theme in these readings. Some parents find it easier to accept the assimilation of their children than others. Compare the reactions of any two families in this or other chapters when their children begin to become Americanized.

13. Trace the struggles for civil rights and acceptance that faced the immigrant Chinese in America. Using information from this chapter and Chapter 5 about Japanese-American experiences during World War II, compare the problems facing the Chinese during the late 1800s with those of the Japanese during the 1940s.

14. Discuss the influence of the American school system on the children of immigrants. Is education a force that melds society? Is it a force that separates parents and children?

15. Discuss the relationship between parents and children portrayed in this chapter. What duties did a Chinese child of the late 1800s and early 1900s owe to parents and to the rest of the family?

For Further Research

1.   Angel Island has been called the Ellis Island of the West Coast. Research and compare the situation at the two ports of entry to the United States.

2.   Research the changes in family life that have taken place in Chinese families living in America over the last sixty years.

REFERENCES AND ADDITIONAL SOURCES

Barth, Gunther. *Bitter Strength: A History of the Chinese in the United States, 1850–1870.* Cambridge, Mass.: Harvard University Press, 1964.

Chan, Sucheng, ed. *Entry Denied: Exclusion and the Chinese Community in America, 1882–1943.* Philadelphia: Temple University Press, 1991.

——. *This Bittersweet Soil: The Chinese in California Agriculture, 1860–1910.* Berkeley: University of California Press, 1986.

Char, Tin Yuke. *The Sandalwood Mountains: Readings and Stories of the Early Chinese in Hawaii.* Honolulu: The University Press of Hawaii, 1975.

Chinn, Thomas, et al. *A History of the Chinese in California: A Syllabus.* San Francisco, Ca.: Chinese Historical Society of America, 1969, 1973.

Genthe, Arnold, and John K. Tchen. *Genthe's Photographs of San Francisco's Old Chinatown.* New York: Dover, 1984.

Hom, Marlon K. *Songs of the Gold Mountain: Cantonese Rhymes from San Francisco Chinatown.* Berkeley and Los Angeles: University of California Press, 1987.

Hwang, David Henry. *The Dance and the Railroad and Family Devotions: Two Plays by David Henry Hwang.* New York: Dramatists Play Service Inc., 1983.

Kim, Elaine. *Asian American Literature: An Introduction to Their Writings and Their Social Context.* Philadelphia: Temple University Press, 1982.

Kim, Hyung-Chan, ed. *Dictionary of Asian American History.* Westwood, Conn.: Greenwood, 1986.

Lai, Him Mark, et al. *Island: Poetry and History of Chinese Immigrants on Angel Island, 1910–1940.* San Francisco: HOC DOI Project, 1980. Seattle: University of Washington Press, 1991.

Lim, Genny. *The Chinese American Experience: Papers for the Second National Conference on Chinese American Studies (1980).* San Francisco: The Chinese Historical Society of America and the Chinese Culture Foundation of San Francisco, 1984.

Ling, Amy. *Between Worlds: Women Writers of Chinese Ancestry.* New York: Pergamon Press, 1990.

Mark, Diane Mei Lin, and Ginger Chih. *A Place Called Chinese America.* Dubuque, Iowa, 1982.

Miller, Stuart C. *The Unwelcome Immigrant: The American Image of the Chinese, 1785–1882.* Berkeley: University of California Press, 1969.

Saxton, Alexander. *The Indispensable Enemy: Labor and the Anti-Chinese Movement in California.* Berkeley: University of California Press, 1971.

Solberg, S. E. "Sui, Storyteller: Sui Sin Far," in *Turning Shadows into Light: Art and Culture of the Northwest's Early Asian/Pacific Community*, Muyami Tsutakawa and Alan Chong Lau, eds. Seattle: Young Pine Press, Asian Multi-Media Center, 1982.

——. "Sui Sin Far/Edith Eaton: First Chinese American Fictionalist," in *Melus* 8:1 (1981), 27–39.

Takaki, Ronald. *Strangers from a Different Shore: A History of Asian Americans.* Boston: Little, Brown, 1989. Penguin, 1990.

Tsai, Shih Shan Henry. *The Chinese Experience in America.* Bloomington: Indiana University Press, 1986.

Tung, William L. *The Chinese in America 1820–1973: A Chronology and Fact Book.* Dobbs Ferry, N.Y.: Oceana, 1974.

Yung, Judy. *Chinese Women of America: A Pictoral History.* Seattle: University of Washington Press, 1986.

3

AFRICAN AMERICANS

The Migration North and the Harlem Renaissance

Above: From Jacob Lawrence *The migrants arrived in great numbers,* plate 40 from *The Migration of the Negro. (Courtesy the artist and Francine Seders Gallery)*

Opposite: Invitation to awards dinner for first literary contest, May 1, 1925. "Opportunity, Journal of Negro Life" was published by the National Urban League. *(Moorland-Spingarn Research Center, Mary O'H. Williamson Collection/Howard University)*

SETTING THE HISTORICAL AND CULTURAL CONTEXT

IN HIS POEM "Afro American Fragment," Langston Hughes writes of the importance of recovering a sense of history, a past that had been lost for too long:

> . . . Subdued and time-lost
> Are the drums—and yet
> Through some vast mist of race
> There comes this song
> I do not understand
> This song of atavistic land . . .

The images of awakening, recovery, and rebirth reflect several themes important during the Harlem Renaissance, a period when African Americans used the arts to express pride in their traditions and their communities. Like other renaissances, the cultural movement in Harlem sought renewal through a recovery of history. Just as the poets and artists of the Italian Renaissance turned away from the Middle Ages and toward classical traditions, African American writers during the 1920s turned away from the years of slavery and toward the African homeland left behind.

The Harlem Renaissance was both a cultural and a political movement. Occurring in the wake of the Great Migration of African Americans during the first two decades of the twentieth century, the movement stressed what the critic Alain Locke called a corresponding "migration of the spirit." This cultural and political awakening resulted in part from the new urban concentration and some accumulation of capital among African Americans. During this time the debate about the best ways to obtain equality and social justice began to include larger segments of society, both within and outside the African American community.

The great migration of African Americans from the southern states began in the 1880s, as a reaction to the poor economic and sociopolitical conditions they experienced in the South. Years of poor weather and insect infestation had depressed the South's agricultural economy; many African American southerners, seeing little future in these rural areas, headed to the industrialized centers of the North. As important, the migration was a reaction to and a protest against the increasingly segregated South, where state legislatures routinely allowed racial considerations to take precedence over constitutional guarantees.

The Reconstruction Act of 1867 and the subsequent Fourteenth and Fifteenth amendments to the Constitution had been intended to guarantee African Americans full citizenship and participation in the electoral process—to enable African Americans to vote, hold office, participate in state constitutional conventions, and establish schools. But Reconstruction was of only limited help in overcoming the liabilities of years of slavery. Without federal resettlement or land-redistribution programs, African Americans remained economically subservient to landowning Caucasians. Moreover, they had to endure the persecution, harassment, and terror of such racist organizations as the Ku Klux Klan, which was determined to limit the rights of African Americans at all costs.

The period after Reconstruction (1877–1896) saw a dramatic erosion in the federal government's commitment to the rights of African Americans. Federal laws were less strenuously enforced, and the federal government provided fewer obstacles to those states intent upon limiting the rights of African Americans. A low point was reached in the Supreme Court's 1896 decision in *Plessy* v. *Ferguson*, which upheld segregation by establishing the "separate but equal" doctrine in the nation's public schools.

Throughout the 1880s, when civic leaders in the North were celebrating the United States as a land of opportunity and a refuge for the world's oppressed peoples, southern legislatures were drafting measures that would limit African Americans' access to such public facilities as streetcars, waiting rooms, water fountains, and restrooms. Vital institutions such as schools and hospitals were now to be run on a segregated basis as well. One state after another altered its constitution in order to segregate and exclude African Americans. By 1907 all the southern states had adopted segregation measures.

Southern states were able to institute and maintain segregation by eliminating the voting rights of many African Americans. This process, known as disfranchisement, began in the early 1890s; it required people to pay poll taxes, pass literacy tests, or prove that they owned property before they would be allowed to vote. Often applicants were also required to read and be examined on whatever sections of the state constitution the examiner deemed appropriate. When legislators discovered that some Caucasians were also having difficulty passing these tests, they found another way in which to give them preferential treatment: they instituted so-called grandfather clauses, which exempted from testing and property requirements any man whose father or grandfather had been eligible to vote in the state on a given date, usually the early 1860s. Because African Americans had not been allowed to vote during the years of slavery, their descendants were effectively prevented from voting as well.

African Americans were also excluded from many educational and employment opportunities. Despite the state governments' assertion that African American and Caucasian schools were "separate but equal," the facilities for African Americans were clearly inferior to those for Caucasians. Not only were their schools inferior, but even those who were able to obtain an education were routinely barred from membership in unions and other professional organizations.

During the late nineteenth and early twentieth centuries, African Americans protested against racial injustice in several ways. They established and supported African American newspapers such as the *Chicago Defender*, where their opinions could be expressed. They also devised strategies such as economic boycotts that would be put to good use again during the civil rights period of the 1960s. Despite occasional successes, however, segregation and discrimination were not addressed in a substantial way until the Civil Rights Acts of 1964 and 1968 and the Voting Rights Act of 1965. Driven from the South by poverty, oppression, and prejudice, and responding to the assurances of greater economic and political opportunity in the North, African Americans migrated—in small numbers to the West and in large numbers to the urban centers of the North.

With the increased concentration of African Americans in cities, there were greater opportunities for political dialogue and debate. The "New Negro" movement of the 1920s rejected an earlier attitude toward racial advancement popularized by educator Booker T. Washington during the late nineteenth century. Washington exhorted African Americans to earn the respect of Caucasians by pursuing moral, educational, and occupational self-improvement; the last could be gained, for example, by mastering skills that would lead to better-paying jobs in existing industries and therefore to a better place in American society. The historian and scholar W. E. B. Du Bois challenged Washington's beliefs, maintaining that his accommodationist position would only perpetuate the status of African Americans as second-class citizens. At the Niagara Conference for equality held in Niagara Falls, Canada, in 1905, Du Bois asserted that African Americans should instead develop their own society and culture as they pressed for full rights as American citizens. Du Bois soon became one of the founders of the National Association for the Advancement of Colored People (NAACP) and the editor of *Crisis*, a periodical that remained influential well beyond the Harlem Renaissance period.

Other leaders also worked within the African American community to achieve social justice. A. Philip Randolph organized and unionized the Brotherhood of Sleeping Car Porters; his organization published *The Messenger*, a magazine critical of both Washington and Du Bois. Marcus Garvey, born in Jamaica, founded the Universal Negro Improvement Association in 1911, before emigrating to the United States in 1916. The UNIA sought equality for blacks through their social, political, and economic independence from whites. In the United States, Garvey advocated separatism and called on African Americans to unite to promote the liberation and development of the African homeland. Garvey received some support from African Americans and Caucasians before being imprisoned for mail fraud and deported. Garvey's advocacy of separatism continues to influence some African American leaders today.

In the words of Alain Locke, the Harlem Renaissance movement attempted to address "the discrepancy between the American social creed and

American social practice." Although the American social creed supposedly advocated freedom and justice for all, its social practice still involved prejudice and discrimination; far worse offenses, such as lynchings, persisted. The status of the African Americans in their own country, then, led to conflicts within the African American community about its proper role in World War I. Although African Americans were at first hesitant, many community leaders, Du Bois among them, encouraged them to support the war effort as a means of improving their status at home. Despite their distinguished service, however, African American soldiers returning from World War I found that conditions had improved little; in some places, they had worsened. Even before the end of the war, the Wilson administration, in an effort to appease southerners, had begun to segregate all public facilities within the District of Columbia. African Americans in other urban centers continued to face restrictive housing covenants and discriminatory employment practices. There was also a dramatic increase in racially motivated violence: eighty people were killed during the East St. Louis, Illinois riots of 1917, and twenty-five other cities and towns had violent confrontations over race.

Leading periodicals such as *Crisis* and *Opportunity* addressed the rising violence by printing monthly reports of the number of African Americans who had been lynched. These periodicals also provided a forum for work that voiced the anger of the period. One of the earliest poems of the Harlem Renaissance, Claude McKay's "If We Must Die," protests the dehumanizing way in which African Americans were still being treated:

If we must die—let it not be like hogs
Hunted and penned in an inglorious spot,
While round us bark the mad and hungry dogs,
Making their mock at our accursed lot.
If we must die—O let us nobly die,
So that our precious blood may not be shed
In vain; then even the monsters we defy
Shall be constrained to honor us though dead!
O kinsmen! we must meet the common foe!
Though far outnumbered let us show brave,
And for their thousand blows deal one deathblow!
What though before us lies the open grave?
Like men we'll face the murderous, cowardly pack,
Pressed to the wall, dying, but fighting back!

Amidst these voices of protest, however, there were also voices of rebirth. Art was used not only to reflect on current social realities, but also to transcend those conditions. In its essays, poetry, and art the movement proclaimed, in the language of the time, the emergence of the "New Negro," the African American who was no longer willing to accept secondary status in the society. While some of the writings called for equality and brotherhood, other works called on African Americans not to look to a Caucasian aesthetic or value system for their inspiration.

New York City attracted artists from all over the country, and Harlem became a kind of cultural and intellectual Mecca for African Americans. Indeed, few of the Harlem Renaissance writers were actually from the northeast. Although Countee Cullen was born in Harlem, Jean Toomer, Jessie Fauset, and Zora Neale Hurston were from the South, Langston Hughes was from the Midwest, and Claude McKay was from the Caribbean. And much of the art that was produced in Harlem found its inspiration in other, often rural, settings. In some of Langston Hughes's poems, such as "Afro-American Fragment," the landscape evokes a sense of the collective memory. While the background for such work is often an African setting, the exploration of heritage sometimes uses as its backdrop rural areas in the American South. In Hurston's "The Gilded Six-Bits," for example, the reader can sense the importance of community customs as well as the presence of folk traditions. In works such as "Theater" from Jean Toomer's *Cane*, which include elements of jazz, personal experience is filtered through cultural traditions and the sense of community is something still in the making. The vitality of that age, as well as the excitement of what the city held for many migrants, is represented as well in the selection from Toni Morrison's *Jazz*, whose language could be said to recall that of Toomer in the richness of its cadences.

While essays such as Locke's "The New Negro" convey an optimistic attitude toward the ability of the African American to confront his circumstances, other works are less sanguine in their attitudes toward the individual's fate in a society that condones racial prejudice. The selection from Wallace Thurman's novel *The Blacker the Berry* suggests that members of the African American community were not immune to another form of prejudice, known as colorism. The attitudes of Locke, Thurman, and other writers are evaluated from a historical perspective in the chapter's final essay by Darwin Turner.

The Harlem Renaissance period ended abruptly with the stock market crash of 1929 and the Depression that followed. Many of the writers and artists, no longer finding an audience for their work, emigrated to Europe, to such a degree that it is often said that the Harlem Renaissance was transferred to Paris. Others, such as Zora Neale Hurston and Arna Bontemps, returned to the South and led obscure lives.

A short-lived artistic movement, the Harlem Renaissance was in many ways full of contradictions. While the community asserted its "otherness"—its reliance not on an American aesthetic but on an African one—many of the artists found financial and critical support for their ideas within the Greenwich Village avant-garde of the Caucasian community. While the Harlem Renaissance existed to proclaim the black community's rebirth as a cultural center, that sense of rebirth was too often missing from the lives of the everyday people of that community, who had to endure the frustration of living in a discriminatory system. Although founded in political activism, the Harlem Renaissance moved more toward personal experience and expression. Yet there is no controversy about the achievements of the Harlem Renaissance, a period when African Americans asserted a new political voice and restored and refashioned cultural traditions in a way that was recognized throughout the world.

BEGINNING: Pre-reading/Writing

What's in a name? A great deal, especially if it's the name of a group you belong to. Discuss why the name of an ethnic group is a particularly sensitive issue for people within that group. Consider the ways in which ethnic group names are chosen. Who does the naming, and who uses the name? Why do groups sometimes decide that they prefer to be called by a new name? For example, why was the name "Negro" rejected by the African American community? What are the psychological effects of names with positive and names with negative connotations? Why are some names appropriate when used by group members but not by outsiders?

The Constitution of South Carolina (1895) illustrates a trend that began in southern states in the 1880s and 1890s. In a process known as disfranchisement, the state legislature set limits on voting rights, based on such criteria as the applicant's ownership of property, payment of a poll tax, and ability to pass a literacy test. Such laws effectively excluded most African Americans from the voting process. It was not until the 1960s that these laws were repealed. Disfranchisement is considered one of the primary causes of the great migration of African Americans from the South.

⁜

From THE CONSTITUTION OF SOUTH CAROLINA

Article II: Right of Suffrage

1   SECTION 1. All elections by the people shall be by ballot, and elections shall never be held or the ballots counted in secret.

2   SEC. 2. Every qualified elector shall be eligible to any office to be voted for, unless disqualified by age, as prescribed in this Constitution. But no person shall hold two offices of honor or profit at the same time: *Provided*, That any person holding another office may at the same time be an officer in the militia or a Notary Public.

3   SEC. 3. Every male citizen of this State and of the United States twenty-one years of age and upwards, not laboring under the disabilities named in this Constitution and possessing the qualifications required by it, shall be an elector.

4   SEC. 4. The qualifications for suffrage shall be as follows:

5   (*a*) Residence in the State for two years, in the County one year, in the polling precinct in which the elector offers to vote four months, and the payment six months before any election of any poll tax then due and payable: *Provided*, That ministers in charge of an organized church and teachers of public schools shall be entitled to vote after six months' residence in the State, otherwise qualified.

6   (*b*) Registration, which shall provide for the enrollment of every elector once in ten years, and also an enrollment during each and every year of every elector not previously registered under the provisions of this Article.

7   (*c*) Up to January 1st 1898, all male persons of voting age applying for registration who can read any Section in this Constitution submitted to them by the registration officer, or understand and explain it when read to them by the registration officer, shall be entitled to register and become electors. A separate record of all persons registered before January 1st, 1898, sworn to by the registration officer, shall be filed, one copy with the Clerk of Court and one

in the office of the Secretary of State, on or before February 1st, 1898, and such persons shall remain during life qualified electors unless disqualified by the other provisions of this Article. The certificate of the Clerk of Court or Secretary of State shall be sufficient evidence to establish the right of said citizens to any subsequent registration and the franchise under the limitations herein imposed.

(*d*) Any person who shall apply for registration after January 1st, 1898, if otherwise qualified, shall be registered: *Provided*, That he can both read and write any Section of this Constitution submitted to him by the registration officer or can show that he owns, and has paid all taxes collectible during the previous year on property in this State assessed at three hundred dollars ($300) or more.

(*e*) Managers of election shall require of every elector offering to vote at any election, before allowing him to vote, proof of the payment of all taxes, including poll tax, assessed against him and collectible during the previous year. The production of a certificate or of the receipt of the officer authorized to collect such taxes shall be conclusive proof of the payment thereof.

(*f*) The General Assembly shall provide for issuing to each duly registered elector a certificate of registration, and shall provide for the renewal of such certificate when lost, mutilated or destroyed, if the applicant is still a qualified elector under the provisions of this Constitution, or if he has been registered as provided in subsection (*c*). ✤

RESPONDING

1. Find the provisions in the section of the Constitution of South Carolina that could be used to keep someone from voting. In a journal entry, discuss who has the discretion to grant someone the right to vote and the implications of that power.

2. Working in a group, discuss the ways in which the power structure in a society can work to disfranchise certain citizens.

3. Are you surprised that such laws were not challenged in the courts? Write an essay comparing these provisions with the guarantees in the Bill of Rights. Argue that they do or do not violate the rights guaranteed in the United States Constitution.

ALAIN LOCKE

Alain Locke was born in Philadelphia in 1886. After earning a bachelor's degree and a doctorate in philosophy from Harvard University, he later became the first African American Rhodes Scholar. He taught philosophy at Howard University and several other colleges, wrote more than half a dozen books, and served as literary editor of Opportunity *and* Phylon, *two important journals of the Harlem Renaissance. Throughout his life he also served as a patron and mentor for many writers and artists within the African American community. Alain Locke died in 1954.*

Credited with being the intellectual leader of the Harlem Renaissance, Locke oversaw the editing of The New Negro *anthology (1925). His classic essay, "The New Negro," which introduces the anthology, announces the goals of the movement and celebrates the talents of those given voice in the collection.*

✥

THE NEW NEGRO

1   IN THE LAST DECADE something beyond the watch and guard of statistics has happened in the life of the American Negro and the three norns who have traditionally presided over the Negro problem have a changeling in their laps. The Sociologist, the Philanthropist, the Race-leader are not unaware of the New Negro, but they are at a loss to account for him. He simply cannot be swathed in their formulæ. For the younger generation is vibrant with a new psychology; the new spirit is awake in the masses, and under the very eyes of the professional observers is transforming what has been a perennial problem into the progressive phases of contemporary Negro life.

2   Could such a metamorphosis have taken place as suddenly as it has appeared to? The answer is no; not because the New Negro is not here, but because the Old Negro had long become more of a myth than a man. The Old Negro, we must remember, was a creature of moral debate and historical controversy. His has been a stock figure perpetuated as an historical fiction partly in innocent sentimentalism, partly in deliberate reactionism. The Negro himself has contributed his share to this through a sort of protective social mimicry forced upon him by the adverse circumstances of dependence. So for generations in the mind of America, the Negro has been more of a formula than a human being—a something to be argued about, condemned or defended, to be "kept down," or "in his place," or "helped up," to be worried with or worried over, harassed or patronized, a social bogey or a social burden. The thinking Negro even has been induced to share this same general attitude, to focus his attention on controversial issues, to see himself in the distorted perspective of a social problem. His shadow, so to speak, has been more real to him than his person-

ality. Through having had to appeal from the unjust stereotypes of his oppres-
sors and traducers to those of his liberators, friends and benefactors he has had
to subscribe to the traditional positions from which his case has been viewed.
Little true social or self-understanding has or could come from such a situation.

But while the minds of most of us, black and white, have thus burrowed in   3
the trenches of the Civil War and Reconstruction, the actual march of development has simply flanked these positions, necessitating a sudden reorientation
of view. We have not been watching in the right direction; set North and South
on a sectional axis, we have not noticed the East till the sun has us blinking.

Recall how suddenly the Negro spirituals revealed themselves; suppressed   4
for generations under the stereotypes of Wesleyan hymn harmony, secretive,
half-ashamed, until the courage of being natural brought them out—and behold,
there was folk-music. Similarly the mind of the Negro seems suddenly to have
slipped from under the tyranny of social intimidation and to be shaking off the
psychology of imitation and implied inferiority. By shedding the old chrysalis
of the Negro problem we are achieving something like a spiritual emancipation.
Until recently, lacking self-understanding, we have been almost as much of a
problem to ourselves as we still are to others. But the decade that found us with
a problem has left us with only a task. The multitude perhaps feels as yet only
a strange relief and a new vague urge, but the thinking few know that in the
reaction the vital inner grip of prejudice has been broken.

With this renewed self-respect and self-dependence, the life of the Negro   5
community is bound to enter a new dynamic phase, the buoyancy from within
compensating for whatever pressure there may be of conditions from without.
The migrant masses, shifting from countryside to city, hurdle several generations of experience at a leap, but more important, the same thing happens
spiritually in the life-attitudes and self-expression of the Young Negro, in his
poetry, his art, his education and his new outlook, with the additional advantage,
of course, of the poise and greater certainty of knowing what it is all about.
From this comes the promise and warrant of a new leadership. As one of them
has discerningly put it:

> We have tomorrow
> Bright before us
> Like a flame.
>
> Yesterday, a night-gone thing
> A sun-down name.
>
> And dawn today
> Broach arch above the road we came.
> We march!

This is what, even more than any "most creditable record of fifty years of   6
freedom," requires that the Negro of to-day be seen through other than the

dusty spectacles of past controversy. The day of "aunties," "uncles" and "mammies" is equally gone. Uncle Tom and Sambo have passed on, and even the "Colonel" and "George" play barnstorm rôles from which they escape with relief when the public spotlight is off. The popular melodrama has about played itself out, and it is time to scrap the fictions, garret the bogeys and settle down to a realistic facing of facts.

7   First we must observe some of the changes which since the traditional lines of opinion were drawn have rendered these quite obsolete. A main change has been, of course, that shifting of the Negro population which has made the Negro problem no longer exclusively or even predominantly Southern. Why should our minds remain sectionalized, when the problem itself no longer is? Then the trend of migration has not only been toward the North and the Central Midwest, but city-ward and to the great centers of industry—the problems of adjustment are new, practical, local and not peculiarly racial. Rather they are an integral part of the large industrial and social problems of our present-day democracy. And finally, with the Negro rapidly in process of class differentiation, if it ever was warrantable to regard and treat the Negro *en masse* it is becoming with every day less possible, more unjust and more ridiculous.

8   In the very process of being transplanted, the Negro is becoming transformed.

9   The tide of Negro migration, northward and city-ward, is not to be fully explained as a blind flood started by the demands of war industry coupled with the shutting off of foreign migration, or by the pressure of poor crops coupled with increased social terrorism in certain sections of the South and Southwest. Neither labor demand, the boll-weevil nor the Ku Klux Klan is a basic factor, however contributory any or all of them may have been. The wash and rush of this human tide on the beach line of the northern city centers is to be explained primarily in terms of a new vision of opportunity, of social and economic freedom, of a spirit to seize, even in the face of an extortionate and heavy toll, a chance for the improvement of conditions. With each successive wave of it, the movement of the Negro becomes more and more a mass movement toward the larger and the more democratic chance—in the Negro's case a deliberate flight not only from countryside to city, but from medieval America to modern.

10   Take Harlem as an instance of this. Here in Manhattan is not merely the largest Negro community in the world, but the first concentration in history of so many diverse elements of Negro life. It has attracted the African, the West Indian, the Negro American; has brought together the Negro of the North and the Negro of the South; the man from the city and the man from the town and village; the peasant, the student, the business man, the professional man, artist, poet, musician, adventurer and worker, preacher and criminal, exploiter and social outcast. Each group has come with its own separate motives and for its own special ends, but their greatest experience has been the finding of one another. Proscription and prejudice have thrown these dissimilar elements into a common area of contact and interaction. Within this area, race sympathy and

unity have determined a further fusing of sentiment and experience. So what
began in terms of segregation becomes more and more, as its elements mix and
react, the laboratory of a great race-welding. Hitherto, it must be admitted that
American Negroes have been a race more in name than in fact, or to be exact,
more in sentiment than in experience. The chief bond between them has been
that of a common condition rather than a common consciousness; a problem
in common rather than a life in common. In Harlem, Negro life is seizing upon
its first chances for group expression and self-determination. It is—or promises
at least to be—a race capital. That is why our comparison is taken with those
nascent centers of folk-expression and self-determination which are playing a
creative part in the world to-day. Without pretense to their political significance,
Harlem has the same rôle to play for the New Negro as Dublin has had for the
New Ireland or Prague for the New Czechoslovakia.

Harlem, I grant you, isn't typical—but it is significant, it is prophetic. No   11
sane observer, however sympathetic to the new trend, would contend that the
great masses are articulate as yet, but they stir, they move, they are more than
physically restless. The challenge of the new intellectuals among them is clear
enough—the "race radicals" and realists who have broken with the old epoch
of philanthropic guidance, sentimental appeal and protest. But are we after all
only reading into the stirrings of a sleeping giant the dreams of an agitator?
The answer is in the migrating peasant. It is the "man farthest down" who is
most active in getting up. One of the most characteristic symptoms of this is
the professional man, himself migrating to recapture his constituency after a
vain effort to maintain in some Southern corner what for years back seemed an
established living and clientele. The clergyman following his errant flock, the
physician or lawyer trailing his clients, supply the true clues. In a real sense it
is the rank and file who are leading, and the leaders who are following. A
transformed and transforming psychology permeates the masses.

When the racial leaders of twenty years ago spoke of developing race-pride   12
and stimulating race-consciousness, and of the desirability of race solidarity,
they could not in any accurate degree have anticipated the abrupt feeling that
has surged up and now pervades the awakened centers. Some of the recognized
Negro leaders and a powerful section of white opinion identified with "race
work" of the older order have indeed attempted to discount this feeling as a
"passing phase," an attack of "race nerves" so to speak, an "aftermath of the
war," and the like. It has not abated, however, if we are to gauge by the present
tone and temper of the Negro press, or by the shift in popular support from
the officially recognized and orthodox spokesman to those of the independent,
popular, and often radical type who are unmistakable symptoms of a new order.
It is a social disservice to blunt the fact that the Negro of the Northern centers
has reached a stage where tutelage, even of the most interested and well-inten-
tioned sort, must give place to new relationships, where positive self-direction
must be reckoned with in ever increasing measure. The American mind must
reckon with a fundamentally changed Negro.

13   The Negro too, for his part, has idols of the tribe to smash. If on the one hand the white man has erred in making the Negro appear to be that which would excuse or extenuate his treatment of him, the Negro, in turn, has too often unnecessarily excused himself because of the way he has been treated. The intelligent Negro of to-day is resolved not to make discrimination an extenuation for his shortcomings in performance, individual or collective; he is trying to hold himself at par, neither inflated by sentimental allowances nor depreciated by current social discounts. For this he must know himself and be known for precisely what he is, and for that reason he welcomes the new scientific rather than the old sentimental interest. Sentimental interest in the Negro has ebbed. We used to lament this as the falling off of our friends; now we rejoice and pray to be delivered both from self-pity and condescension. The mind of each racial group has had a bitter weaning, apathy or hatred on one side matching disillusionment or resentment on the other; but they face each other to-day with the possibility at least of entirely new mutual attitudes.

14   It does not follow that if the Negro were better known, he would be better liked or better treated. But mutual understanding is basic for any subsequent coöperation and adjustment. The effort toward this will at least have the effect of remedying in large part what has been the most unsatisfactory feature of our present stage of race relationships in America, namely the fact that the more intelligent and representative elements of the two race groups have at so many points got quite out of vital touch with one another.

15   The fiction is that the life of the races is separate, and increasingly so. The fact is that they have touched too closely at the unfavorable and too lightly at the favorable levels.

16   While inter-racial councils have sprung up in the South, drawing on forward elements of both races, in the Northern cities manual laborers may brush elbows in their everyday work, but the community and business leaders have experienced no such interplay or far too little of it. These segments must achieve contact or the race situation in America becomes desperate. Fortunately this is happening. There is a growing realization that in social effort the cooperative basis must supplant long-distance philanthropy, and that the only safeguard for mass relations in the future must be provided in the carefully maintained contacts of the enlightened minorities of both race groups. In the intellectual realm a renewed and keen curiosity is replacing the recent apathy; the Negro is being carefully studied, not just talked about and discussed. In art and letters, instead of being wholly caricatured, he is being seriously portrayed and painted.

17   To all of this the New Negro is keenly responsive as an augury of a new democracy in American culture. He is contributing his share to the new social understanding. But the desire to be understood would never in itself have been sufficient to have opened so completely the protectively closed portals of the thinking Negro's mind. There is still too much possibility of being snubbed or patronized for that. It was rather the necessity for fuller, truer self-expression, the realization of the unwisdom of allowing social discrimination to segregate

him mentally, and a counter-attitude to cramp and fetter his own living—and so the "spite-wall" that the intellectuals built over the "color-line" has happily been taken down. Much of this reopening of intellectual contacts has centered in New York and has been richly fruitful not merely in the enlarging of personal experience, but in the definite enrichment of American art and letters and in the clarifying of our common vision of the social tasks ahead.

The particular significance in the re-establishment of contact between the more advanced and representative classes is that it promises to offset some of the unfavorable reactions of the past, or at least to re-surface race contacts somewhat for the future. Subtly the conditions that are molding a New Negro are molding a new American attitude. 18

However, this new phase of things is delicate; it will call for less charity but more justice; less help, but infinitely closer understanding. This is indeed a critical stage of race relationships because of the likelihood, if the new temper is not understood, of engendering sharp group antagonism and a second crop of more calculated prejudice. In some quarters, it has already done so. Having weaned the Negro, public opinion cannot continue to paternalize. The Negro to-day is inevitably moving forward under the control largely of his own objectives. What are these objectives? Those of his outer life are happily already well and finally formulated, for they are none other than the ideals of American institutions and democracy. Those of his inner life are yet in process of formation, for the new psychology at present is more of a consensus of feeling than of opinion, of attitude rather than of program. Still some points seem to have crystallized. 19

Up to the present one may adequately describe the Negro's "inner objectives" as an attempt to repair a damaged group psychology and reshape a warped social perspective. Their realization has required a new mentality for the American Negro. And as it matures we begin to see its effects; at first, negative, iconoclastic, and then positive and constructive. In this new group psychology we note the lapse of sentimental appeal, then the development of a more positive self-respect and self-reliance; the repudiation of social dependence, and then the gradual recovery from hyper-sensitiveness and "touchy" nerves, the repudiation of the double standard of judgment with its special philanthropic allowances and then the sturdier desire for objective and scientific appraisal, and finally the rise from social disillusionment to race pride, from the sense of social debt to the responsibilities of social contribution, and offsetting the necessary working and commonsense acceptance of restricted conditions, the belief in ultimate esteem and recognition. Therefore the Negro to-day wishes to be known for what he is, even in his faults and shortcomings, and scorns a craven and precarious survival at the price of seeming to be what he is not. He resents being spoken of as a social ward or minor, even by his own, and to being regarded a chronic patient for the sociological clinic, the sick man of American Democracy. For the same reasons, he himself is through with those social nostrums and panaceas, the so-called "solutions" of his "problem," with which 20 he and the country have been so liberally dosed in the past. Religion, freedom, education, money—in turn, he has ardently hoped for and peculiarly trusted these things; he still believes in them, but not in blind trust that they alone will solve his life-problem.

21   Each generation, however, will have its creed, and that of the present is the belief in the efficacy of collective effort, in race co-operation. This deep feeling of race is at present the mainspring of Negro life. It seems to be the outcome of the reaction to proscription and prejudice; an attempt, fairly successful on the whole, to convert a defensive into an offensive position, a handicap into an incentive. It is radical in tone, but not in purpose and only the most stupid forms of opposition, misunderstanding or persecution could make it otherwise. Of course, the thinking Negro has shifted a little toward the left with the world-trend, and there is an increasing group who affiliate with radical and liberal movements. But fundamentally for the present the Negro is radical on race matters, conservative on others, in other words, a "forced radical," a social protestant rather than a genuine radical. Yet under further pressure and injustice iconoclastic thought and motives will inevitably increase. Harlem's quixotic radicalisms call for their ounce of democracy to-day lest to-morrow they be beyond cure.

22   The Negro mind reaches out as yet to nothing but American wants, American ideas. But this forced attempt to build his Americanism on race values is a unique social experiment, and its ultimate success is impossible except through the fullest sharing of American culture and institutions. There should be no delusion about this. American nerves in sections unstrung with race hysteria are often fed the opiate that the trend of Negro advance is wholly separatist, and that the effect of its operation will be to encyst the Negro as a benign foreign body in the body politic. This cannot be—even if it were desirable. The radicalism of the Negro is no limitation or reservation with respect to American life; it is only a constructive effort to build the obstructions in the stream of his progress into an efficient dam of social energy and power. Democracy itself is obstructed and stagnated to the extent that any of its channels are closed. Indeed they cannot be selectively closed. So the choice is not between one way for the Negro and another way for the rest, but between American institutions frustrated on the one hand and American ideals progressively fulfilled and realized on the other.

23   There is, of course, a warrantably comfortable feeling in being on the right side of the country's professed ideals. We realize that we cannot be undone without America's undoing. It is within the gamut of this attitude that the thinking Negro faces America, but with variations of mood that are if anything more significant than the attitude itself. Sometimes we have it taken with the defiant ironic challenge of McKay:[1]

---

1. Claude McKay (1889–1948) Jamaican-born poet and novelist who figured prominently in the Harlem Renaissance.

Mine is the future grinding down to-day
Like a great landslip moving to the sea,
Bearing its freight of débris far away
Where the green hungry waters restlessly
Heave mammoth pyramids, and break and roar
Their eerie challenge to the crumbling shore.

Sometimes, perhaps more frequently as yet, it is taken in the fervent and almost filial appeal and counsel of Weldon Johnson's:[2]

O Southland, dear Southland!
Then why do you still cling
To an idle age and a musty page,
To a dead and useless thing?

But between defiance and appeal, midway almost between cynicism and hope, the prevailing mind stands in the mood of the same author's *To America*, an attitude of sober query and stoical challenge:

How would you have us, as we are?
    Or sinking 'neath the load we bear,
Our eyes fixed forward on a star,
    Or gazing empty at despair?

Rising or falling? Men or things?
    With dragging pace or footsteps fleet?
Strong, willing sinews in your wings,
    Or tightening chains about your feet?

More and more, however, an intelligent realization of the great discrepancy between the American social creed and the American social practice forces upon the Negro the taking of the moral advantage that is his. Only the steadying and sobering effect of a truly characteristic gentleness of spirit prevents the rapid rise of a definite cynicism and counter-hate and a defiant superiority feeling. Human as this reaction would be, the majority still deprecate its advent, and would gladly see it forestalled by the speedy amelioration of its causes. We wish our race pride to be a healthier, more positive achievement than a feeling based upon a realization of the shortcomings of others. But all paths toward the attainment of a sound social attitude have been difficult; only a relatively few, enlightened minds have been able as the phrase puts it "to rise above" prejudice. The ordinary man has had until recently only a hard choice between the

24

2. James Weldon Johnson (1871–1938), social reformer, educator, poet, essayist, song writer, and lawyer.

alternatives of supine and humiliating submission and stimulating but hurtful counter-prejudice. Fortunately from some inner, desperate resourcefulness has recently sprung up the simple expedient of fighting prejudice by mental passive resistance, in other words by trying to ignore it. For the few, this manna may perhaps be effective, but the masses cannot thrive upon it.

25   Fortunately there are constructive channels opening out into which the balked social feelings of the American Negro can flow freely.

26   Without them there would be much more pressure and danger than there is. These compensating interests are racial but in a new and enlarged way. One is the consciousness of acting as the advance-guard of the African peoples in their contact with Twentieth Century civilization; the other, the sense of a mission of rehabilitating the race in world esteem from that loss of prestige for which the fate and conditions of slavery have so largely been responsible. Harlem, as we shall see, is the center of both these movements; she is the home of the Negro's "Zionism." The pulse of the Negro world has begun to beat in Harlem. A Negro newspaper carrying news material in English, French and Spanish, gathered from all quarters of America, the West Indies and Africa has maintained itself in Harlem for over five years. Two important magazines, both edited from New York, maintain their news and circulation consistently on a cosmopolitan scale. Under American auspices and backing, three pan-African congresses have been held abroad for the discussion of common interests, colonial questions and the future co-operative development of Africa. In terms of the race question as a world problem, the Negro mind has leapt, so to speak, upon the parapets of prejudice and extended its cramped horizons. In so doing it has linked up with the growing group consciousness of the dark-peoples and is gradually learning their common interests. As one of our writers has recently put it: "It is imperative that we understand the white world in its relations to the non-white world." As with the Jew, persecution is making the Negro international.

27   As a world phenomenon this wider race consciousness is a different thing from the much asserted rising tide of color. Its inevitable causes are not of our making. The consequences are not necessarily damaging to the best interests of civilization. Whether it actually brings into being new Armadas of conflict or argosies of cultural exchange and enlightenment can only be decided by the attitude of the dominant races in an era of critical change. With the American Negro, his new internationalism is primarily an effort to recapture contact with the scattered peoples of African derivation. Garveyism[3] may be a transient, if spectacular, phenomenon, but the possible role of the American Negro in the future development of Africa is one of the most constructive and universally helpful missions that any modern people can lay claim to.

28   Constructive participation in such causes cannot help giving the Negro

3. Movement named after Black Nationalist leader Marcus Garvey (1887–1940) which promoted separatism and encouraged liberation and development for the African homeland.

valuable group incentives, as well as increased prestige at home and abroad. Our greatest rehabilitation may possibly come through such channels, but for the present, more immediate hope rests in the revaluation by white and black alike of the Negro in terms of his artistic endowments and cultural contributions, past and prospective. It must be increasingly recognized that the Negro has already made very substantial contributions, not only in his folk-art, music especially, which has always found appreciation, but in larger, though humbler and less acknowledged ways. For generations the Negro has been the peasant matrix of that section of America which has most undervalued him, and here he has contributed not only materially in labor and in social patience, but spiritually as well. The South has unconsciously absorbed the gift of his folk-temperament. In less than half a generation it will be easier to recognize this, but the fact remains that a leaven of humor, sentiment, imagination and tropic nonchalance has gone into the making of the South from a humble, unacknowledged source. A second crop of the Negro's gifts promises still more largely. He now becomes a conscious contributor and lays aside the status of a beneficiary and ward for that of a collaborator and participant in American civilization. The great social gain in this is the releasing of our talented group from the arid fields of controversy and debate to the productive fields of creative expression. The especially cultural recognition they win should in turn prove the key to that revaluation of the Negro which must precede or accompany any considerable further betterment of race relationships. But whatever the general effect, the present generation will have added the motives of self-expression and spiritual development to the old and still unfinished task of making material headway and progress. No one who understandingly faces the situation with its substantial accomplishment or views the new scene with its still more abundant promise can be entirely without hope. And certainly, if in our lifetime the Negro should not be able to celebrate its full initiation into American democracy, he can at least, on the warrant of these things, celebrate the attainment of a significant and satisfying new phase of group development, and with it a spiritual Coming of Age.

RESPONDING

1. In a journal entry, define what Locke means by the old and new images of the Negro. What diverse elements comprised the "largest Negro community in the world" (paragraph 10) in Harlem in the 1920s?

2. Working individually or in a group, list the changes Locke describes as taking place in race relations during the 1920s. Are some of these changes now outdated by other changes in society? Describe the "contact and cooperation" today between diverse groups of people in your community.

3. Write an essay that discusses the purpose of Locke's essay and defines his intended audience. Do you think he was primarily writing for a Caucasian or African American audience? Support your conclusions with specific examples from the essay.

4. Locke explains the movement of African Americans from the South to the North "primarily in terms of a new vision of opportunity, of social and economic freedom, of a spirit to seize, even in the face of an extortionate and heavy toll, a chance for the improvement of conditions" (paragraph 9). Using information from the reading and from your own knowledge, write an essay agreeing or disagreeing that movement to the North improved conditions for southern African Americans in the 1920s.

Zora Neale Hurston

Zora Neale Hurston was born in Eatonville, Florida, in 1903. She studied anthropology at Howard University and Barnard College, later publishing several works based on the folklore of the African American community. During the Harlem Renaissance, Hurston worked with Langston Hughes and Wallace Thurman on editorial projects such as the literary journal Fire!!!. *Although she wrote some short stories during this period, much of Hurston's writing was not published until after the Harlem Renaissance. Her major works include* Jonah's Gourd Vine *(1934),* Their Eyes Were Watching God *(1937),* Moses, Man of the Mountain *(1939),* Seraph on the Suwanee *(1948), and her autobiography,* Dust Tracks on a Road *(1942). In her later years she had less success having her works published. She died in poverty in Florida in 1960. In more recent years, because of the efforts of Alice Walker and other African American writers, Hurston's work has found a wider audience.*

The short story that follows, like many other texts from the Harlem Renaissance, is set in the South. It uses a rural setting and folk themes to explore fidelity and forgiveness.

❖

THE GILDED SIX-BITS

IT WAS A NEGRO YARD around a Negro house in a Negro settlement that looked to the payroll of the G and G Fertilizer works for its support.

But there was something happy about the place. The front yard was parted in the middle by a sidewalk from gate to door-step, a sidewalk edged on either side by quart bottles driven neck down to the ground on a slant. A mess of homey flowers planted without a plan but blooming cheerily from their helter-skelter places. The fence and house were whitewashed. The porch and steps scrubbed white.

The front door stood open to the sunshine so that the floor of the front room could finish drying after its weekly scouring. It was Saturday. Everything clean from the front gate to the privy house. Yard raked so that the strokes of the rake would make a pattern. Fresh newspaper cut in fancy-edge on the kitchen shelves.

Missie May was bathing herself in the galvanized washtub in the bedroom. Her dark-brown skin glistened under the soapsuds that skittered down from her wash rag. Her stiff young breasts thrust forward aggressively like broad-based cones with the tips lacquered in black.

5   She heard men's voices in the distance and glanced at the dollar clock on the dresser.

6   "Humph! Ah'm way behind time t'day! Joe gointer be heah 'fore Ah git mah clothes on if Ah don't make haste."

7   She grabbed the clean meal sack at hand and dried herself hurriedly and began to dress. But before she could tie her slippers, there came the ring of singing metal on wood. Nine times.

8   Missie May grinned with delight. She had not seen the big tall man come stealing in the gate and creep up the walk grinning happily at the joyful mischief he was about to commit. But she knew that it was her husband throwing silver dollars in the door for her to pick up and pile beside her plate at dinner. It was this way every Saturday afternoon. The nine dollars hurled into the open door, he scurried to a hiding place behind the cape jasmine bush and waited.

9   Missie May promptly appeared at the door in mock alarm.

10   "Who dat chunkin' money in mah do'way?" she demanded. No answer from the yard. She leaped off the porch and began to search the shrubbery. She peeped under the porch and hung over the gate to look up and down the road. While she did this, the man behind the jasmine darted to the chinaberry tree. She spied him and gave chase.

11   "Nobody ain't gointer be chunkin' money at me and Ah not do'em nothin'," she shouted in mock anger. He ran around the house with Missie May at his heels. She overtook him at the kitchen door. He ran inside but could not close it after him before she crowded in and locked with him in a rough and tumble. For several minutes the two were a furious mass of male and female energy. Shouting, laughing, twisting, turning, and Joe trying, but not too hard, to get away.

12   "Missie May, take yo' hand out mah pocket!" Joe shouted out between laughs.

13   "Ah ain't, Joe, not lessen you gwine gimme whateve' it is good you got in yo' pocket. Turn it go Joe, do Ah'll tear yo' clothes."

14   "Go on tear 'em. You de one dat pushes de needles round heah. Move yo' hand Missie May."

15   "Lemme git dat paper sack out yo' pocket. Ah bet its candy kisses."

16   "Tain't. Move yo' hand. Woman ain't got no business in a man's clothes nohow. Go 'way."

17   Missie May gouged way down and gave an upward jerk and triumphed.

18   "Unhhunh! Ah got it. It 'tis so candy kisses. Ah knowed you had somethin' for me in yo' clothes. Now Ah got to see whut's in every pocket you got."

19   Joe smiled indulgently and let his wife go through all of his pockets and take out the things that he had hidden there for her to find. She bore off the chewing gum, the cake of sweet soap, the pocket handkerchief as if she had wrested them from him, as if they had not been bought for the sake of this friendly battle.

"Whew! dat play-fight done got me all warmed up," Joe exclaimed. "Got   20
me some water in de kittle?"

"Yo' water is on de fire and yo' clean things is cross de bed. Hurry up and   21
wash yo'self and git changed so we kin eat. Ah'm hongry." As Missie said this,
she bore the steaming kettle into the bedroom.

"You ain't hongry, sugar," Joe contradicted her. "Youse jes's little empty.   22
Ah'm de one whut's hongry. Ah could eat up camp meetin,' back off 'ssociation,
and drink Jurdan dry. Have it on de table when Ah git out de tub."

"Don't you mess wid mah business, man. You git in yo' clothes. Ah'm a   23
real wife, not no dress and breath. Ah might not look lak one, but if you burn
me, you won't git a thing but wife ashes."

Joe splashed in the bedroom and Missie May fanned around in the kitchen.   24
A fresh red and white checked cloth on the table. Big pitcher of buttermilk
beaded with pale drops of butter from the churn. Hot fried mullet, crackling
bread, ham hocks atop a mound of string beans and new potatoes, and perched
on the window-sill a pone of spicy potato pudding.

Very little talk during the meal but that little consisted of banter that   25
pretended to deny affection but in reality flaunted it. Like when Missie May
reached for a second helping of the tater pone. Joe snatched it out of her reach.
After Missie May had made two or three unsuccessful grabs at the pan, she
begged, "Aw, Joe gimme some mo' dat tater pone."

"Nope, sweetenin' is for us men-folks. Y'all pritty li'l frail eels don't need   26
nothin' lak dis. You too sweet already."

"Please, Joe."   27

"Naw, naw. Ah don't want you to git no sweeter than whut you is already.   28
We goin' down de road al li'l piece t'night so you go put on yo' Sunday-go-to-
meetin' things."

Missie May looked at her husband to see if he was playing some prank.   29
"Sho' nuff, Joe?"

"Yeah. We goin' to de ice cream parlor."   30

"Where de ice cream parlor at, Joe?"   31

"A new man done come heah from Chicago and he done got a place and   32
took and opened it up for a ice cream parlor, and bein' as it's real swell, Ah
wants you to be one de first ladies to walk in dere and have some set down."

"Do Jesus, Ah ain't knowed nothin' 'bout it. Who de man done it?"   33

"Mister Otis D. Slemmons, of spots and places—Memphis, Chicago, Jack-   34
sonville, Philadelphia and so on."

"Dat heavy-set man wid his mouth full of gold teethes?"   35

"Yeah. Where did you see 'im at?"   36

"Ah went down to de sto' tuh git a box of lye and Ah seen 'im standin' on   37
de corner talkin' to some of de mens, and Ah come on back and went to
scrubbin' de floor, and he passed and tipped his hat whilst Ah was scourin' de
steps. Ah thought never Ah seen *him* befo'."

38   Joe smiled pleasantly. "Yeah, he's up to date. He got de finest clothes Ah ever seen on a colored man's back."

39   "Aw, he don't look no better in his clothes than you do in yourn. He got a puzzlegut on 'im and he so chuckle-headed, he got a pone behind his neck."

40   Joe looked down at his own abdomen and said wistfully, "Wisht Ah had a build on me lak he got. He ain't puzzle-gutted, honey. He jes' got a corperation. Dat make 'm look lak a rich white man. All rich mens is got some belly on 'em."

41   "Ah seen de pitchers of Henry Ford and he's a spare-built man and Rockefeller look lak he ain't got but one gut. But Ford and Rockefeller and dis Slemmons and all de rest kin be as many-gutted as dey please, ah'm satisfied wid you jes' lak you is, baby. God took pattern after a pine tree and built you noble. Youse a pretty still man, and if Ah knowed any way to make you mo' pritty still Ah'd take and do it."

42   Joe reached over gently and toyed with Missie May's ear. "You jes' say dat cause you love me, but Ah know Ah can't hold no light to Otis D. Slemmons. Ah ain't never been nowhere and Ah ain't got nothin' but you."

43   "How you know dat, Joe."

44   "He tole us so hisself."

45   "Dat don't make it so. His mouf is cut cross-ways, ain't it? Well, he kin lie jes' lak anybody els."

46   "Good Lawd, Missie! You womens sho' is hard to sense into things. He's got a five-dollar gold piece for a stick-pin and he got a ten-dollar gold piece on his watch chain and his mouf is jes' crammed full of gold teethes. Sho' wisht it wuz mine. And whut make it so cool, he got money 'cumulated. And womens give it all to 'im."

47   "Ah don't see whut de womens see on 'im. Ah wouldn't give 'im a wind if de sherff wuz after 'im."

48   "Well, he tole us how de white womens in Chicago give 'im all dat gold money. So he don't 'low nobody to touch it at all. Not even put dey finger on it. Dey tole 'im not to. You kin make 'miration at it, but don't tetch it."

49   "Whyn't he stay up dere where dey so crazy 'bout 'im?"

50   "Ah reckon dey done made 'im vast-rich and he wants to travel some. He say dey wouldn't leave 'im hit a lick of work. He got mo' lady people crazy 'bout him than he kin shake a stick at."

51   "Joe, Ah hates to see you so dumb. Dat stray nigger jes' tell y'all anything and y'all b'lieve it."

52   "Go 'head on now, honey and put on yo' clothes. He talkin' 'bout his pritty womens—Ah want 'im to see *mine*."

53   Missie May went off to dress and Joe spent the time trying to make his stomach punch out like Slemmons' middle. He tried the rolling swagger of the stranger, but found that his tall bone-and-muscle stride fitted ill with it. He just had time to drop back into his seat before Missie May came in dressed to go.

54   On the way home that night Joe was exultant. "Didn't Ah say old Otis was swell? Can't he talk Chicago talk? Wuzn't dat funny whut he said when great

big fat old Ida Armstrong come in? He asted me, "'Who is dat broad wid de forty shake?' Dat's a new word. Us always thought forty was a set of figgers but he showed us where it means a whole heap of things. Sometimes he don't say forty, he jes' say thirty-eight and two and dat mean de same thing. Know whut he tole me when Ah was payin' for our ice cream? He say, 'Ah have to hand it to you, Joe. Dat wife of yours is jes' thirty-eight and two. Yessuh, she's forty!' Ain't he killin'?"

"He'll do in case of a rush. But he sho' is got uh heap uh gold on 'im. Dat's   55
de first time Ah ever seed gold money. It lookted good on him sho' nuff, but it'd look a whole heap better on you."

"Who, me? Missie May was youse crazy! Where would a po' man lak me   56
git gold money from?"

Missie May was silent for a minute, then she said, "Us might find some   57
goin' long de road some time. Us could."

"Who would be losin' gold money 'round heah? We ain't even seen none   58
dese white folks wearin' no gold money on dey watch chain. You must be figgeren' Mister Packard or Mister Cadillac goin' pass through heah . . ."

"You don't know whut been lost 'round heah. Maybe somebody way back   59
in memorial times lost they gold money and went on off and it ain't never been found. And then if we wuz to find it, you could wear some 'thout havin' no gang of womens lak dat Slemmons say he got."

Joe laughed and hugged her. "Don't be so wishful 'bout me. Ah'm satisfied   60
de way Ah is. So long as Ah be yo' husband, ah don't keer 'bout nothin' else. Ah'd ruther all de other womens in de world to be dead than for you to have de toothache. Less we go to bed and git our night rest."

It was Saturday night once more before Joe could parade his wife in   61
Slemmons' ice cream parlor again. He worked the night shift and Saturday was his only night off. Every other evening around six o'clock he left home, and dying dawn saw him hustling home around the lake where the challenging sun flung a flaming sword from east to west across the trembling water.

That was the best part of life—going home to Missie May. Their white-   62
washed house, the mock battle on Saturday, the dinner and ice cream parlor afterwards, church on Sunday nights when Missie outdressed any woman in town—all, everything was right.

One night around eleven the acid ran out at the G and G. The foreman   63
knocked off the crew and let the steam die down. As Joe rounded the lake on his way home, a lean moon rode the lake in a silver boat. If anybody had asked Joe about the moon on the lake, he would have said he hadn't paid it any attention. But he saw it with his feelings. It made him yearn painfully for Missie. Creation obsessed him. He thought about children. They had been married for more than a year now. They had money put away. They ought to be making little feet for shoes. A little boy child would be about right.

He saw a dim light in the bedroom and decided to come in through the   64
kitchen door. He could wash the fertilizer dust off himself before presenting

himself to Missie May. It would be nice for her not to know that he was there until he slipped into his place in bed and hugged her back. She always liked that.

65   He eased the kitchen door open slowly and silently, but when he went to set his dinner bucket on the table he bumped it into a pile of dishes, and something crashed to the floor. He heard his wife gasp in fright and hurried to reassure her.

66   "Iss me, honey. Don't get skeered."

67   There was a quick, large movement in the bedroom. A rustle, a thud, and a stealthy silence. The light went out.

68   What? Robbers? Murderers? Some varmint attacking his helpless wife, perhaps. He struck a match, threw himself on guard and stepped over the door-sill into the bedroom.

69   The great belt on the wheel of Time slipped and eternity stood still. By the match light he could see the man's legs fighting with his breeches in his frantic desire to get them on. He had both chance and time to kill the intruder in his helpless condition—half-in and half-out of his pants—but he was too weak to take action. The shapeless enemies of humanity that live in the hours of Time had waylaid Joe. He was assaulted in his weakness. Like Samson awakening after his haircut. So he just opened his mouth and laughed.

70   The match went out and he struck another and lit the lamp. A howling wind raced across his heart, but underneath its fury he heard his wife sobbing and Slemmons pleading for his life. Offering to buy it with all that he had. "Please, suh, don't kill me. Sixty-two dollars at de sto' gold money."

71   Joe just stood. Slemmons looked at the window, but it was screened. Joe stood out like a rough-backed mountain between him and the door. Barring him from escape, from sunrise, from life.

72   He considered a surprise attack upon the big clown that stood there laughing like a chessy cat. But before his fist could travel an inch, Joe's own rushed out to crush him like a battering ram. Then Joe stood over him.

73   "Git into yo' damn rags, Slemmons, and dat quick."

74   Slemmons scrambled to his feet and into his vest and coat. As he grabbed his hat, Joe's fury overrode his intentions and he grabbed at Slemmons with his left hand and struck at him with his right. The right landed. The left grazed the front of his vest. Slemmons was knocked a somersault into the kitchen and fled through the open door. Joe found himself alone with Missie May, with the golden watch charm clutched in his left fist. A short bit of broken chain dangled between his fingers.

75   Missie May was sobbing. Wails of weeping without words. Joe stood, and after awhile she found out that he had something in his hand. And then he stood and felt without thinking and without seeing with his natural eyes. Missie May kept on crying and Joe kept on feeling so much and not knowing what to do with all his feelings, he put Slemmons' watch charm in his pants pocket and took a good laugh and went to bed.

76   "Missie May, whut you crying for?"

"Cause Ah love you so hard and Ah know you don't love *me* no mo'."   77

Joe sank his face into the pillow for a spell then he said huskily, "You don't   78
know de feelings of dat yet, Missie May."

"Oh Joe, honey, he said he wuz gointer gimme dat gold money and he jes'   79
kept on after me—"

Joe was very still and silent for a long time. Then he said, "Well, don't cry   80
no mo', Missie May. Ah got yo' gold piece for you."

The hours went past on their rusty ankles. Joe still and quiet on one bed-rail   81
and Missie May wrung dry of sobs on the other. Finally the sun's tide crept
upon the shore of night and drowned all its hours. Missie May with her face
stiff and streaked towards the window saw the dawn come into her yard. It was
day. Nothing more. Joe wouldn't be coming home as usual. No need to fling
open the front door and sweep off the porch, making it nice for Joe. Never no
more breakfast to cook; no more washing and starching of Joe's jumper-jackets
and pants. No more nothing. So why get up?

With this strange man in her bed, she felt embarrassed to get up and dress.   82
She decided to wait till he had dressed and gone. Then she would get up, dress
quickly and be gone forever beyond reach of Joe's looks and laughs. But he
never moved. Red light turned to yellow, then white.

From beyond the no-man's land between them came a voice. A strange   83
voice that yesterday had been Joe's.

"Missie May, ain't you gonna fix me no breakfus'?"   84

She sprang out of bed. "Yeah, Joe. Ah didn't reckon you wuz hongry."   85

No need to die today. Joe needed her for a few more minutes anyhow.   86

Soon there was a roaring fire in the cook stove. Water bucket full and two   87
chickens killed. Joe loved fried chicken and rice. She didn't deserve a thing and
good Joe was letting her cook him some breakfast. She rushed hot biscuits to
the table as Joe took his seat.

He ate with his eyes on his plate. No laughter, no banter.   88

"Missie May, you ain't eatin' yo' breakfus'."   89

"Ah don't choose none, Ah thank yuh."   90

His coffee cup was empty. She sprang to refill it. When she turned from   91
the stove and bent to set the cup beside Joe's plate, she saw the yellow coin on
the table between them.

She slumped into her seat and wept into her arms.   92

Presently Joe said calmly, "Missie May, you cry too much. Don't look back   93
lak Lot's wife and turn to salt."

The sun, the hero of every day, the impersonal old man that beams as   94
brightly on death as on birth, came up every morning and raced across the blue
dome and dipped into the sea of fire every evening. Water ran down hill and
birds nested.

Missie knew why she didn't leave Joe. She couldn't. She loved him too   95
much. But she couldn't understand why Joe didn't leave her. He was polite,
even kind at times, but aloof.

There were no more Saturday romps. No ringing silver dollars to stack   96 beside her plate. No pockets to rifle. In fact the yellow coin in his trousers was like a monster hiding in the cave of his pockets to destroy her.

97   She often wondered if he still had it, but nothing could have induced her to ask nor yet to explore his pockets to see for herself. Its shadow was in the house whether or no.

98   One night Joe came home around midnight and complained of pains in the back. He asked Missie to rub him down with liniment. It had been three months since Missie had touched his body and it all seemed strange. But she rubbed him. Grateful for the chance. Before morning, youth triumphed and Missie exulted. But the next day, as she joyfully made up their bed, beneath her pillow she found the piece of money with the bit of chain attached.

99   Alone to herself, she looked at the thing with loathing, but look she must. She took it into her hands with trembling and saw first thing that it was no gold piece. It was a gilded half-dollar. Then she knew why Slemmons had forbidden anyone to touch his gold. He trusted village eyes at a distance not to recognize his stick-pin as a gilded quarter, and his watch charm as a four-bit piece.

100   She was glad at first that Joe had left it there. Perhaps he was through with her punishment. They were man and wife again. Then another thought came clawing at her. He had come home to buy from her as if she were any woman in the long house. Fifty cents for her love. As if to say that he could pay as well as Slemmons. She slid the coin into his Sunday pants pocket and dressed herself and left his house.

101   Halfway between her house and the quarters she met her husband's mother, and after a short talk she turned and went back home. If she had not the substance of marriage, she had the outside show. Joe must leave *her*. She let him see she didn't want his old gold four-bits too.

102   She saw no more of the coin for some time though she knew that Joe could not help finding it in his pocket. But his health kept poor, and he came home at least every ten days to be rubbed.

103   The sun swept around the horizon, trailing its robes of weeks and days. One morning as Joe came in from work, he found Missie May chopping wood. Without a word he took the ax and chopped a huge pile before he stopped.

104   "You ain't got no business choppin' wood, and you know it."

105   "How come? Ah been choppin' it for de last longest."

106   "Ah ain't blind. You makin' feet for shoes."

107   "Won't you be glad to have a li'l baby chile, Joe?"

108   "You know dat 'thout astin' me."

109   "Iss gointer be a boy chile and de very spit of you."

110   "You reckon, Missie May?"

111   "Who else could it look lak?"

112   Joe said nothing, but he thrust his hand deep into his pocket and fingered something there.

113   It was almost six months later Missie May took to bed and Joe went and got his mother to come wait on the house.

Missie May delivered a fine boy. Her travail was over when Joe came in   114
from work one morning. His mother and the old women were drinking great
bowls of coffee around the fire in the kitchen.

The minute Joe came into the room his mother called him aside.   115

"How did Missie May make out?" he asked quickly.   116

"Who, dat gal? She strong as a ox. She gointer have plenty mo'. We done   117
fixed her wid de sugar and lard to sweeten her for de nex' one."

Joe stood silent awhile.   118

"You ain't ast 'bout de baby, Joe. You oughter be mighty proud cause he   119
sho' is de spittin' image of yuh, son. Dat's yourn all right, if you never git
another one, dat un is yourn. And you know Ah'm mighty proud too, son, cause
Ah never thought well of you marryin' Missie May cause her ma used tuh fan
her foot 'round right smart and Ah been mighty skeered dat Missie May wuz
gointer git misput on her road."

Joe said nothing. He fooled around the house till late in the day then just 120
before he went to work, he went and stood at the foot of the bed and asked his
wife how she felt. He did this every day during the week.

On Saturday he went to Orlando to make his market. It had been a long   121
time since he had done that.

Meat and lard, meal and flour, soap and starch. Cans of corn and tomatoes. 122
All the staples. He fooled around town for awhile and bought bananas and
apples. Way after while he went around to the candy store.

"Hellow, Joe," the clerk greeted him. "Ain't seen you in a long time."   123

"Nope, Ah ain't been heah. Been 'round spots and places."   124

"Want some of them molasses kisses you always buy?"   125

"Yessuh." He threw the gilded half-dollar on the counter. "Will dat spend?" 126

"Whut is it, Joe? Well, I'll be doggone! A gold-plated four-bit piece.   127
Where'd you git it, Joe?"

"Offen a stray nigger dat come through Eatonville. He had it on his watch   128
chain for a charm—goin' 'round making out iss gold money. Ha ha! He had a
quarter on his tie pin and it wuz all golded up too. Tryin' to fool people. Makin'
out he so rich and everything. Ha! Ha! Tryin' to tole off folkses wives from
home."

"How did you git it, Joe? Did he fool you, too?"   129

"Who, me? Naw suh! He ain't fooled me none. Know whut Ah done? He   130
come 'round me wid his smart talk. Ah hauled off and knocked 'im down and
took his old four-bits 'way from 'im. Gointer buy my wife some good ole 'lasses
kisses wid it. Gimme fifty cents worth of dem candy kisses."

"Fifty cents buys a mightly lot of candy kisses, Joe. Why don't you split it 131
up and take some chocolate bars, too. They eat good, too."

"Yessuh, dey do, but Ah wants all dat in kisses. Ah got a li'l boy chile home 132
now. Tain't a week old yet, but he kin suck a sugar tit and maybe eat one them
kisses hisself."

Joe got his candy and left the store. The clerk turned to the next customer. 133

"Wisht I could be like these darkies. Laughin' all the time. Nothin' worries 'em."

134 Back in Eatonville, Joe reached his own front door. There was the ring of singing metal on wood. Fifteen times. Missie May couldn't run to the door, but she crept there as quickly as she could.

135 "Joe Banks, Ah hear you chunkin' money in mah do'way. You wait till Ah got mah strength back and Ah'm gointer fix you for dat." ✠

RESPONDING

1. Write a journal entry about a time when you or someone you know were fooled by appearances. How did you feel when your eyes were opened? How do you think Missie May felt?

2. Underline any part of the dialogue you might not have understood because it is written in a dialect that is unfamiliar to you. Working individually or in a group, try to put those phrases into other words.

3. Write an essay examining the clerk's comment "Wisht I could be like these darkies. Laughin' all the time. Nothin' worries 'em" (paragraph 133). What does it reveal about the attitudes of Caucasians toward African Americans at that time and place?

4. Consider the responses of Joe and Missie May to their estrangement. How might you have reacted in their place? Would you have been as forgiving as Joe? Write an essay agreeing or disagreeing with either character's response to the situation. Evaluate their solution to the problem or present your own solution. You might want to rewrite the ending of the story.

LANGSTON HUGHES

Langston Hughes, who was born in Joplin, Missouri, in 1902, studied at Columbia University and Lincoln University. During a literary career of over forty years, he wrote poetry, fiction, drama, and a two-volume autobiography, The Big Sea *(1940) and* I Wonder as I Wander *(1956). His work has been praised for its simplicity and its wit. During the 1920s, Hughes participated in many of the editorial activities and the lively debates of the Harlem Renaissance. He died in 1967.*

The two poems that follow explore the issues of heritage, identity, and ambition. They invite us to consider the relationships between individuals and groups and the power that each of us has to make others feel accepted or rejected.

MOTHER TO SON

WELL, SON, I'll tell you:
Life for me ain't been no crystal stair.
It's had tacks in it,
And splinters,
And boards torn up,
And places with no carpet on the floor—
Bare.
But all the time
I'se been a-climbin' on,
And reachin' landin's,
And turnin' corners,
And sometimes goin' in the dark
Where there ain't been no light.
So boy, don't you turn back.
Don't you set down on the steps
'Cause you finds it's kinder hard.
Don't you fall now—
For I'se still goin', honey,
I'se still climbin',
And life for me ain't been no crystal stair.

RESPONDING

1. In a journal entry, write a letter or a poem that the son might write in response to his mother.

2. We don't know many details about the speaker's life. Working individually or in a group, flesh out the character of the speaker by adding some of the specifics that you imagine have made her life "no crystal stair."

3. Using your own knowledge and experience, describe some of the problems that the boy might encounter in growing up that would make him "set down on the steps."

4. Critics have called this a poem of racial affirmation. In an essay, explain why you agree or disagree.

✣

THEME FOR ENGLISH B

THE INSTRUCTOR SAID,

> *Go home and write*
> *a page tonight.*
> *And let that page come out of you—*
> *Then, it will be true.*

I wonder if it's that simple?

I am twenty-two, colored, born in Winston-Salem.
I went to school there, then Durham, then here
to this college on the hill above Harlem.
I am the only colored student in my class.
The steps from the hill lead down into Harlem,
through a park, then I cross St. Nicholas,
Eighth Avenue, Seventh, and I come to the Y,
the Harlem Branch Y, where I take the elevator
up to my room, sit down, and write this page:

It's not easy to know what is true for you or me
at twenty-two, my age. But I guess I'm what
I feel and see and hear. Harlem, I hear you:
hear you, hear me—we two—you, me, talk on this page.
(I hear New York, too.) Me—who?

Well, I like to eat, sleep, drink, and be in love.
I like to work, read, learn, and understand life.
I like a pipe for a Christmas present,
or records—Bessie, bop, or Bach.
I guess being colored doesn't make me *not* like
the same things other folks like who are other races.

So will my page be colored that I write?
Being me, it will not be white.
But it will be
a part of you, instructor.
You are white—
yet a part of me, as I am a part of you.
That's American.
Sometimes perhaps you don't want to be a part of me.
Nor do I often want to be a part of you.
But we are, that's true!
As I learn from you,
I guess you learn from me—
although you're older—and white—
and somewhat more free.

This is my page for English B. ✤

RESPONDING

1. The speaker is the only "colored student" in his university class. How do
   you think he feels about that situation? Write a journal entry about a time
   when you or a relative or friend were the only representative of a group,
   for example, the only woman or man, the only American, the only north-
   erner, among a group of "others." How did you respond in that situation?
   How did the "others" treat you?

2. Working individually or in a group, list the ways in which the speaker sees
   himself as similar to everyone else in his class and the ways in which he
   sees himself as different.

3. Write an essay explaining what the speaker means when he says, "you are
   . . . a part of me, as I am a part of you. That's American." You might want
   to include your own prose version of the lines.

JEAN TOOMER

Jean Toomer was born in Washington, D.C., in 1894. He studied at several universities, including the University of Wisconsin, New York University, and the City University of New York, before deciding to become a writer. In the 1920s he settled in Harlem and became a part of the literary circle there. His first book, Cane *(1925) received great critical acclaim. In his later years he spent time in Europe, where he studied philosophy and served on the faculty of the George Gurdjieff Institute in Fontainebleau, France. His later writing—including short stories, poetry, and a play—did not enjoy the critical success of* Cane. *Toomer died in poverty in 1967.*

Cane, from which this excerpt is taken, was celebrated during its time as one of the preeminent works of the Harlem Renaissance. Its combination of prose and verse as well as its use of dialect, drama, and narrative was considered especially innovative.

❖

THEATER

1   LIFE OF NIGGER ALLEYS, of pool rooms and restaurants and near-beer saloons soaks into the walls of Howard Theater[1] and sets them throbbing jazz songs. Black-skinned, they dance and shout above the tick and trill of white-walled buildings. At night, they open doors to people who come in to stamp their feet and shout. At night, road-shows volley songs into the mass-heart of black people. Songs soak the walls and seep out to the nigger life of alleys and near-beer saloons, of the Poodle Dog and Black Bear cabarets. Afternoons, the house is dark, and the walls are sleeping singers until rehearsal begins. Or until John comes within them. Then they start throbbing to a subtle syncopation. And the space-dark air grows softly luminous.

2   John is the manager's brother. He is seated at the center of the theater, just before rehearsal. Light streaks down upon him from a window high above. One half his face is orange in it. One half his face is in shadow. The soft glow of the house rushes to, and compacts about, the shaft of light. John's mind coincides with the shaft of light. Thoughts rush to, and compact about it. Life of the house and of the slowly awakening stage swirls to the body of John, and thrills it. John's body is separate from the thoughts that pack his mind.

3   Stage-lights, soft, as if they shine through clear pink fingers. Beneath them,

---

1. A theater in the Afro-American section of Washington, D.C.: the audiences and the performers were also Afro-American. [Author's note]

hid by the shadow of a set, Dorris. Other chorus girls drift in. John feels them in the mass. And as if his own body were the mass-heart of a black audience listening to them singing, he wants to stamp his feet and shout. His mind, contained above desires of his body, singles the girls out, and tries to trace origins and plot destinies.

A pianist slips into the pit and improvises jazz. The walls awake. Arms of   4
the girls, and their limbs, which . . . jazz, jazz . . . by lifting up their tight street skirts they set free, jab the air and clog the floor in rhythm to the music. (Lift your skirts, Baby, and talk t papa!) Crude, individualized, and yet . . . monotonous . . .

John: Soon the director will herd you, my full-lipped, distant beauties, and   5
tame you, and blunt your sharp thrusts in loosely suggestive movements, appropriate to Broadway. (O dance!) Soon the audience will paint your dusk faces white, and call you beautiful. (O dance!) Soon I . . . (O dance!) I'd like . . .

Girls laugh and shout. Sing discordant snatches of other jazz songs. Whirl   6
with loose passion into the arms of passing show-men.

John: Too thick. Too easy. Too monotonous. Her whom I'd love I'd leave   7
before she knew that I was with her. Her? Which? (O dance!) I'd like to . . .

Girls dance and sing. Men clap. The walls sing and press inward. They   8
press the men and girls, they press John towards a center of physical ecstasy. Go to it, Baby! Fan yourself, and feed your papa! Put . . . nobody lied . . . and take . . . when they said I cried over you. No lie! The glitter and color of stacked scenes, the gilt and brass and crimson of the house, converge towards a center of physical ecstasy. John's feet and torso and his blood press in. He wills thought to rid his mind of passion.

"All right, girls. Alaska. Miss Reynolds, please."   9
The director wants to get the rehearsal through with.   10

The girls line up. John sees the front row: dancing ponies. The rest are in   11
shadow. The leading lady fits loosely in the front. Lack-life, monotonous. "One, two, three—" Music starts. The song is somewhere where it will not strain the leading lady's throat. The dance is somewhere where it will not strain the girls. Above the staleness, one dancer throws herself into it. Dorris. John sees her. Her hair, crisp-curled, is bobbed. Bushy, black hair bobbing about her lemon-colored face. Her lips are curiously full, and very red. Her limbs in silk purple stockings are lovely. John feels them. Desires her. Holds off.

John: Stage-door johnny;[2] chorus-girl. No, that would be all right. Dictie,[3]   12
educated, stuck-up; show-girl. Yep. Her suspicion would be stronger than her passion. It wouldn't work. Keep her loveliness. Let her go.

---

2. Slang term referring to men who dated actresses, singers, and dancers and who, after performances, waited for them at the stage door. [Author's note]
3. Slang term referring to educated, middle-class Afro-Americans who behave as though they consider themselves socially superior to other Afro-Americans—similar to "stuck-up," "snobbish." [Author's note]

13   Dorris sees John and knows that he is looking at her. Her own glowing is too rich a thing to let her feel the slimness of his diluted passion.

14   "Who's that?" she asks her dancing partner.

15   "Th manager's brother. Dictie. Nothin doin, hon."

16   Dorris tosses her head and dances for him until she feels she has him. Then, withdrawing disdainfully, she flirts with the director.

17   Dorris: Nothin doin? How come? Aint I as good as him? Couldnt I have got an education if I'd wanted one? Dont I know respectable folks, lots of em, in Philadelphia and New York and Chicago? Aint I had men as good as him? Better. Doctors an lawyers. Whats a manager's brother, anyhow?

18   Two steps back, and two steps front.

19   "Say, Mame, where do you get that stuff?"

20   "Whatshmean, Dorris?"

21   "If you two girls cant listen to what I'm telling you, I know where I can get some who can. Now Listen."

22   Mame: Go to hell, you black bastard.

23   Dorris: Whats eatin at him, anyway?

24   "Now follow me in this, you girls. Its three counts to the right, three counts to the left, and then you shimmy—"

25   John: —and then you shimmy. I'll bet she can. Some good cabaret, with rooms upstairs. And what in hell do you think you'd get from it? Youre going wrong. Here's right: get her to herself—(Christ, but how she'd bore you after the first five minutes)—not if you get her right she wouldnt. Touch her, I mean. To herself—in some room perhaps. Some cheap, dingy bedroom. Hell no. Cant be done. But the point is, brother John, it can be done. Get her to herself somewhere, anywhere. Go down in yourself—and she'd be calling you all sorts of asses while you were in the process of going down. Hold em, bud. Cant be done. Let her go. (Dance and I'll love you!) And keep her loveliness.

26   "All right now, Chicken Chaser.[4] Dorris and girls. Where's Dorris? I told you to stay on the stage, didnt I? Well? Now thats enough. All right. All right there, Professor? All right. One, two, three—"

27   Dorris swings to the front. The line of girls, four deep, blurs within the shadow of suspended scenes. Dorris wants to dance. The director feels that and steps to one side. He smiles, and picks her for a leading lady, one of these days. Odd ends of stage-men emerge from the wings, and stare and clap. A crap game in the alley suddenly ends. Black faces crowd the rear stage doors. The girls, catching joy from Dorris, whip up within the footlights' glow. They forget set steps; they find their own. The director forgets to bawl them out. Dorris dances.

28   John: Her head bobs to Broadway. Dance from yourself. Dance! O just a little more.

29   Dorris' eyes burn across the space of seats to him.

30   Dorris: I bet he can love. Hell, he cant love. He's too skinny. His lips are

---

4. A dance.

too skinny. He wouldnt love me anyway, only for that. But I'd get a pair of silk stockings out of it. Red silk. I got purple. Cut it, kid. You cant win him to respect you that away. He wouldnt anyway. Maybe he would. Maybe he'd love. I've heard em say that men who look like him (what does he look like?) will marry if they love. O will you love me? And give me kids, and a home, and everything? (I'd like to make your nest, and honest, hon, I wouldnt run out on you.) You will if I make you. Just watch me.

    Dorris dances. She forgets her tricks.[5] She dances.   31

    Glorious songs are the muscles of her limbs.   32

    And her singing is of canebrake loves and mangrove feastings.   33

    The walls press in, singing. Flesh of a throbbing body, they press close to   34
John and Dorris. They close them in. John's heart beats tensely against her dancing body. Walls press his mind within his heart. And then, the shaft of light goes out the window high above him. John's mind sweeps up to follow it. Mind pulls him upward into dream.   Dorris dances . . .
John dreams:

Dorris is dressed in a loose black gown splashed with lemon ribbons. Her feet taper long and slip from trim ankles. She waits for him just inside the stage door. John, collar and tie colorful and flaring, walks towards the stage door. There are no trees in the alley. But his feet feel as though they step on autumn leaves whose rustle has been pressed out of them by the passing of a million satin slippers. The air is sweet with roasting chestnuts, sweet with bonfires of old leaves. John's melancholy is a deep thing that seals all senses but his eyes, and makes him whole.

    Dorris knows that he is coming. Just at the right moment she steps from the door, as if there were no door. Her face is tinted like the autumn alley. Of old flowers, or of a southern canefield, her perfume. "Glorious Dorris." So his eyes speak. And their sadness is too deep for sweet untruth. She barely touches his arm. They glide off with footfalls softened on the leaves, the old leaves powdered by a million satin slippers.

    They are in a room. John knows nothing of it. Only, that the flesh and blood of Dorris are its walls. Singing walls. Lights, soft, as if they shine through clear pink fingers. Soft lights, and warm.

    John reaches for a manuscript of his, and reads. Dorris, who has no eyes, has eyes to understand him. He comes to a dancing scene. The scene is Dorris. She dances. Dorris dances. Glorious Dorris. Dorris whirls, whirls, dances . . .

                                   Dorris dances.
The pianist crashes a bumper chord. The whole stage claps. Dorris, flushed, looks quick at John. His whole face is in shadow. She seeks for her dance in it.

---

5. Her practiced or stylized dance routine. [Author's note]

She finds it a dead thing in the shadow which is his dream. She rushes from the stage. Falls down the steps into her dressing-room. Pulls her hair. Her eyes, over a floor of tears, stare at the whitewashed ceiling. (Smell of dry paste, and paint, and soiled clothing.) Her pal comes in. Dorris flings herself into the old safe arms, and cries bitterly.

35   "I told you nothin doin," is what Mame says to comfort her. ❖

RESPONDING

1. In a journal entry, describe a situation where you have wanted to do something but your anxiety, shyness, or fear of embarrassment kept you from taking risks.

2. Working in a group, list the arguments for and against John approaching Dorris or the arguments for and against Dorris approaching John. Combine groups and compare lists. What did each character stand to gain or lose by approaching the other?

3. Write an essay that discusses Toomer's use of the word "nigger." In what ways does its use offend contemporary readers? Do you think it offended readers when the story was written? Why might the fact that Toomer was black enable him to use a word such as nigger without offending a black audience?

4. Read a section of the text aloud. What do you notice about Toomer's language and writing style? Do the sounds of the words and the length of sentences particularly fit the subject matter? Write an essay exploring the relationship of language choices and the effect the author is trying to achieve. Be sure you support your points with specific examples from the reading.

WALLACE THURMAN

Wallace Thurman was born in Salt Lake City in 1902. After studying at the University of Southern California, he settled in Harlem, where he worked on several of the important periodicals of the Harlem Renaissance period, including The Messenger. *He collaborated with many of the foremost writers of the movement: with W. J. Rapp he wrote the play* Harlem, *and with Zora Neale Hurston and Langston Hughes he edited the literary publication* Fire!!!. *Thurman also wrote two novels,* The Blacker the Berry *(1929) and* Infants of the Spring *(1932). The second novel satirized some of the pretensions of the Harlem Renaissance itself. Thurman died of tuberculosis at the age of thirty-two.*

The following excerpt, from The Blacker the Berry, *examines the influence of unconscious prejudices on first impressions.*

⊞

From THE BLACKER THE BERRY

SUMMER VACATION was nearly over and it had not yet been decided what to do with Emma Lou now that she had graduated from high school. She herself gave no help nor offered any suggestions. As it was, she really did not care what became of her. After all it didn't seem to matter. There was no place in the world for a girl as black as she anyway. Her grandmother had assured her that she would never find a husband worth a dime, and her mother had said again and again, "Oh, if you had only been a boy!" until Emma Lou had often wondered why it was that people were not able to effect a change of sex or at least a change of complexion. 1

It was her Uncle Joe who finally prevailed upon her mother to send her to the University of Southern California in Los Angeles. There, he reasoned, she would find a larger and more intelligent social circle. In a city the size of Los Angeles there were Negroes of every class, color, and social position. Let Emma Lou go there where she would not be as far away from home as if she were to go to some eastern college. 2

Jane and Maria, while not agreeing entirely with what Joe said, were nevertheless glad that at last something which seemed adequate and sensible could be done for Emma Lou. She was to take the four year college course, receive a bachelor degree in education, then go South to teach. That, they thought, was a promising future, and for once in the eighteen years of Emma Lou's life every one was satisfied in some measure. Even Emma Lou grew elated over the prospects of the trip. Her Uncle Joe's insistence upon the differences 3 of social contacts in larger cities intrigued her. Perhaps he was right after all in continually reasserting to them that as long as one was a Negro, one's specific color had little to do with one's life. Salvation depended upon the individual. And he also told Emma Lou, during one of their usual private talks, that it was only in small cities one encountered stupid color prejudice such as she had encountered among the blue vein circle in her home town.

4   "People in large cities," he had said, "are broad. They do not have time to think of petty things. The people in Boise are fifty years behind the times, but you will find that Los Angeles is one of the world's greatest and most modern cities, and you will be happy there."

5   On arriving in Los Angeles, Emma Lou was so busy observing the colored inhabitants that she had little time to pay attention to other things. Palm trees and wild geraniums were pleasant to behold, and such strange phenomena as pepper trees and century plants had to be admired. They were very obvious and they were also strange and beautiful, but they impinged upon only a small corner of Emma Lou's consciousness. She was minutely aware of them, necessarily took them in while passing, viewing the totality without pondering over or lingering to praise their stylistic details. They were, in this instance, exquisite theatrical props, rendered insignificant by a more strange and a more beautiful human pageant. For Emma Lou, who, in all her life, had never seen over five hundred Negroes, the spectacle presented by a community containing over fifty thousand, was sufficient to make relatively commonplace many more important and charming things than the far famed natural scenery of Southern California.

6   She had arrived in Los Angeles a week before registration day at the university, and had spent her time in being shown and seeing the city. But whenever these sightseeing excursions took her away from the sections where Negroes lived, she immediately lost all interest in what she was being shown. The Pacific Ocean in itself did not cause her heart beat to quicken, nor did the roaring of its waves find an emotional echo within her. But on coming upon Bruce's Beach for colored people near Redondo, or the little strip of sandied shore they had appropriated for themselves at Santa Monica, the Pacific Ocean became an intriguing something to contemplate as a background for their activities. Everything was interesting as it was patronized, reflected through, or acquired by Negroes.

7   Her Uncle Joe had been right. Here, in the colored social circles of Los Angeles, Emma Lou was certain that she would find many suitable companions, intelligent, broad-minded people of all complexions, intermixing and being too occupied otherwise to worry about either their own skin color or the skin color of those around them. Her Uncle Joe had said that Negroes were Negroes whether they happened to be yellow, brown, or black, and a conscious effort to eliminate the darker elements would neither prove nor solve anything. There was nothing quite so silly as the creed of the blue veins: "Whiter and whiter, every generation. The nearer white you are the more white people will respect you. Therefore all light Negroes marry light Negroes. Continue to do so

generation after generation, and eventually white people will accept this racially bastard aristocracy, thus enabling those Negroes who really matter to escape the social and economic inferiority of the American Negro."

Such had been the credo of her grandmother and of her mother and of their small circle of friends in Boise. But Boise was a provincial town, given to the molding of provincial people with provincial minds. Boise was a backward town out of the mainstream of modern thought and progress. Its people were cramped and narrow, their intellectual concepts stereotyped and static. Los Angeles was a happy contrast in all respects.

On registration day, Emma Lou rushed out to the campus of the University of Southern California one hour before the registrar's office was scheduled to open. She spent the time roaming around, familiarizing herself with the layout of the campus and learning the names of the various buildings, some old and vineclad, others new and shiny in the sun, and watching the crowds of laughing students, rushing to and fro, greeting one another and talking over their plans for the coming school year. But her main reason for such an early arrival on the campus had been to find some of her fellow Negro students. She had heard that there were to be quite a number enrolled, but in all her hour's stroll she saw not one, and finally somewhat disheartened she got into the line stretched out in front of the registrar's office, and, for the moment, became engrossed in becoming a college freshman.

All the while, though, she kept searching for a colored face, but it was not until she had been duly signed up as a student and sent in search of her advisor that she saw one. Then three colored girls had sauntered into the room where she was having a conference with her advisor, sauntered in, arms interlocked, greeted her advisor, then sauntered out again. Emma Lou had wanted to rush after them—to introduce herself, but of course it had been impossible under the circumstances. She had immediately taken a liking to all three, each of whom was what is known in the parlance of the black belt as high brown, with modishly-shingled bobbed hair and well formed bodies, fashionably attired in flashy sport garments. From then on Emma Lou paid little attention to the business of choosing subjects and class hours, so little attention in fact that the advisor thought her exceptionally tractable and somewhat dumb. But she liked students to come that way. It made the task of being advisor easy. One just made out the program to suit oneself, and had no tedious explanations to make as to why the student could not have such and such a subject at such and such an hour, and why such and such a professor's class was already full.

After her program had been made out, Emma Lou was directed to the bursar's office to pay her fees. While going down the stairs she almost bumped into two dark-brown-skinned boys, obviously brothers if not twins, arguing as to where they should go next. One insisted that they should go back to the registrar's office. The other was being equally insistent that they should go to the gymnasium and make an appointment for their required physical examination. Emma Lou boldly stopped when she saw them, hoping they would speak, but they merely glanced up at her and continued their argument, bringing cards and pamphlets out of their pockets for reference and guidance. Emma Lou wanted to introduce herself to them, but she was too bashful to do so. She wasn't yet used to going to school with other Negro students, and she wasn't exactly certain how one went about becoming acquainted. But she finally decided that she had better let the advances come from the others, especially if they were men. There was nothing forward about her, and since she was a stranger it was no more than right that the old-timers should make her welcome. Still, if these had been girls . . . , but they weren't, so she continued her way down the stairs.

12   In the bursar's office, she was somewhat overjoyed at first to find that she had fallen into line behind another colored girl who had turned around immediately, and, after saying hello, announced in a loud, harsh voice:

13   "My feet are sure some tired!"

14   Emma Lou was so taken aback that she couldn't answer. People in college didn't talk that way. But meanwhile the girl was continuing:

15   "Ain't this registration a mess?"

16   Two white girls who had fallen into line behind Emma Lou snickered. Emma Lou answered by shaking her head. The girl continued:

17   "I've been standin' in line and climbin' stairs and talkin' and a-signin' till I'm just 'bout done for."

18   "It is tiresome," Emma Lou returned softly, hoping the girl would take a hint and lower her own strident voice. But she didn't.

19   "Tiresome ain't no name for it," she declared more loudly than ever before, then, "Is you a new student?"

20   "I am," answered Emma Lou, putting much emphasis on the "I am."

21   She wanted the white people who were listening to know that she knew her grammar if this other person didn't. "Is you," indeed! If this girl was a specimen of the Negro students with whom she was to associate, she most certainly did not want to meet another one. But it couldn't be possible that all of them—those three girls and those two boys for instance—were like this girl. Emma Lou was unable to imagine how such a person had ever gotten out of high school. Where on earth could she have gone to high school? Surely not in the North. Then she must be a southerner. That's what she was, a southerner—Emma Lou curled her lips a little—no wonder the colored people in Boise spoke as they did about southern Negroes and wished that they would stay South. Imagine anyone preparing to enter college saying "Is you," and, to make it worse, right before all these white people, these staring white people, so eager and ready to laugh. Emma Lou's face burned.

22   "Two mo', then I goes in my sock."

23   Emma Lou was almost at the place where she was ready to take even this statement literally, and was on the verge of leaving the line. Supposing this creature did "go in her sock"! God forbid!

"Wonder where all the spades keep themselves? I ain't seen but two 'sides you." 24

"I really do not know," Emma Lou returned precisely and chillily. She had 25 no intentions of becoming friendly with this sort of person. Why she would be ashamed even to be seen on the street with her, dressed as she was in a red-striped sport suit, a white hat, and white shoes and stockings. Didn't she know that black people had to be careful about the colors they affected?

The girl had finally reached the bursar's window and was paying her fees, 26 and loudly differing with the cashier about the total amount due.

"I tell you it ain't that much," she shouted through the window bars. "I 27 figured it up myself before I left home."

The cashier obligingly turned to her adding machine and once more 28 obtained the same total. When shown this, the girl merely grinned, examined the list closely, and said:

"I'm gonna' pay it; but I still think you're wrong." 29

Finally she moved away from the window, but not before she had turned 30 to Emma Lou and said,

"You're next," and then proceeded to wait until Emma Lou had finished. 31

Emma Lou vainly sought some way to escape, but was unable to do so, and 32 had no choice but to walk with the girl to the registrar's office where they had their cards stamped in return for the bursar's receipt. This done, they went onto the campus together. Hazel Mason was the girl's name. Emma Lou had fully expected it to be either Hyacinth or Geranium. Hazel was from Texas, Prairie Valley, Texas, and she told Emma Lou that her father, having become quite wealthy when oil had been found on his farm lands, had been enabled to realize two life ambitions—obtain a Packard touring car and send his only daughter to a "fust-class" white school.

Emma Lou had planned to loiter around the campus. She was still eager to 33 become acquainted with the colored members of the student body, and this encounter with the crass and vulgar Hazel Mason had only made her the more eager. She resented being approached by any one so flagrantly inferior, any one so noticeably a typical southern darky, who had no business obtruding into the more refined scheme of things. Emma Lou planned to lose her unwelcome companion somewhere on the campus so that she could continue unhindered her quest for agreeable acquaintances.

But Hazel was as anxious to meet one as was Emma Lou, and having found 34 her was not going to let her get away without a struggle. She, too, was new to this environment and in a way was more lonely and eager for the companionship of her own kind than Emma Lou, for never before had she come into such close contact with so many whites. Her life had been spent only among Negroes. Her fellow pupils and teachers in school had always been colored, and as she confessed to Emma Lou, she couldn't get used "to all these white folks."

"Honey, I was just achin' to see a black face," she had said, and, though 35 Emma Lou was experiencing the same ache, she found herself unable to sympathize with the other girl, for Emma Lou classified Hazel as a barbarian who had most certainly not come from a family of best people. No doubt her mother had been a washerwoman. No doubt she had innumerable relatives and friends all as ignorant and as ugly as she. There was no sense in any one having a face as ugly as Hazel's, and Emma Lou thanked her stars that though she was black, her skin was not rough and pimply, nor was her hair kinky, nor were her nostrils completely flattened out until they seemed to spread all over her face. No wonder people were prejudiced against dark skin people when they were so ugly, so haphazard in their dress, and so boisterously mannered as was this present specimen. She herself was black, but nevertheless she had come from a good family, and she could easily take her place in a society of the right sort of people.

36   The two strolled along the lawn-bordered gravel path which led to a vine-covered building at the end of the campus. Hazel never ceased talking. She kept shouting at Emma Lou, shouting all sorts of personal intimacies as if she were desirous of the whole world hearing them. There was no necessity for her to talk so loudly, no necessity for her to afford every one on the crowded campus the chance to stare and laugh at them as they passed. Emma Lou had never before been so humiliated and so embarrassed. She felt that she must get away from her offensive companion. What did she care if she had to hurt her feelings to do so? The more insulting she could be now, the less friendly she would have to be in the future.

37   "Good-bye," she said abruptly, "I must go home." With which she turned away and walked rapidly in the opposite direction. She had only gone a few steps when she was aware of the fact that the girl was following her. She quickened her pace, but the girl caught up with her and grabbing hold of Emma Lou's arm, shouted,

38   "Whoa there, Sally."

39   It seemed to Emma Lou as if every one on the campus was viewing and enjoying this minstrel-like performance. Angrily she tried to jerk away, but the girl held fast.

40   "Gal, you sure walk fast. I'm going your way. Come on, let me drive you home in my buggy."

41   And still holding on the Emma Lou's arm, she led the way to the side street where the students parked their cars. Emma Lou was powerless to resist. The girl didn't give her a chance, for she held tight, then immediately resumed the monologue which Emma Lou's attempted leave-taking had interrupted. They reached the street, Hazel still talking loudly, and making elaborate gestures with her free hand.

42   "Here we are," she shouted, and releasing Emma Lou's arm, salaamed before a sport model Stutz roadster. "Oscar," she continued, "meet the new girl friend. Pleased to meetcha, says he. Climb aboard."

43   And Emma Lou had climbed aboard, perplexed, chagrined, thoroughly angry, and disgusted. What was this little black fool doing with a Stutz roadster? And of course, it would be painted red—Negroes always bedecked themselves and their belongings in ridiculously unbecoming colors and ornaments. It

seemed to be a part of their primitive heritage which they did not seem to have sense enough to forget and deny. Black girl—white hat—red and white striped sport suit—white shoes and stockings—red roadster. The picture was complete. All Hazel needed to complete her circus-like appearance, thought Emma Lou, was to have some purple feathers stuck in her hat.

Still talking, the girl unlocked and proceeded to start the car. As she was backing it out of the narrow parking space, Emma Lou heard a chorus of semi-suppressed giggles from a neighboring automobile. In her anger she had failed to notice that there were people in the car parked next to the Stutz. But as Hazel expertly swung her machine around, Emma Lou caught a glimpse of them. They were all colored and they were all staring at her and at Hazel. She thought she recognized one of the girls as being one of the group she had seen earlier that morning, and she did recognize the two brothers she had passed on the stairs. And as the roadster sped away, their laugher echoed in her ears, although she hadn't actually heard it. But she had seen the strain in their faces, and she knew that as soon as she and Hazel were out of sight, they would give free rein to their suppressed mirth. 44

Although Emma Lou had finished registering, she returned to the university campus on the following morning in order to continue her quest for collegiate companions without the alarming and unwelcome presence of Hazel Mason. She didn't know whether to be sorry for that girl and try to help her or to be disgusted and avoid her. She didn't want to be intimately associated with any such vulgar person. It would damage her own position, cause her to be classified with some one who was in a class by herself, for Emma Lou was certain that there was not, and could not be, any one else in the university just like Hazel. But despite her vulgarity, the girl was not all bad. Her good nature was infectious, and Emma Lou had surmised from her monologue on the day before how utterly unselfish a person she could be and was. All of her store of the world's goods were at hand to be used and enjoyed by her friends. There was not, as she had said "a selfish bone in her body." But even that did not alter the disgusting fact that she was not one who would be welcome by the "right sort of people." Her flamboyant style of dress, her loud voice, her raucous laughter, and her flagrant disregard or ignorance of English grammar seemed inexcusable to Emma Lou, who was unable to understand how such a person could stray so far from the environment in which she rightfully belonged to enter a first-class university. Now Hazel, according to Emma Lou, was the type of Negro who should go to a Negro college. There were plenty of them in the South whose standard of scholarship was not beyond her ability. And, then, in one of those schools, her darky-like clownishness would not have to be paraded in front of white people, thereby causing discomfort and embarrassment to others of her race, more civilized and circumspect than she. 45

The problem irritated Emma Lou. She didn't see why it had to be. She had looked forward so anxiously, and so happily to her introductory days on the campus, and now her first experience with one of her fellow colored students had been an unpleasant one. But she didn't intend to let that make her unhappy. 46

She was determined to return to the campus alone, seek out other companions, see whether they accepted or ignored the offending Hazel, and govern herself accordingly.

47   It was early and there were few people on the campus. The grass was still wet from a heavy overnight dew, and the sun had not yet dispelled the coolness of the early morning. Emma Lou's dress was of thin material and she shivered as she walked or stood in the shade. She had no school business to attend to; there was nothing for her to do but to walk aimlessly about the campus.

48   In another hour, Emma Lou was pleased to see that the campus walks were becoming crowded, and that the side streets surrounding the campus were now heavy with student traffic. Things were beginning to awaken. Emma Lou became jubilant and walked with jaunty step from path to path, from building to building. It then occurred to her that she had been told that there were more Negro students enrolled in the School of Pharmacy than in any other department of the university, so finding the Pharmacy building she began to wander through its crowded hallways.

49   Almost immediately, she saw a group of five Negro students, three boys and two girls, standing near a water fountain. She was both excited and perplexed, excited over the fact that she was so close to those she wished to find, and perplexed because she did not know how to approach them. Had there been only one person standing there, the matter would have been comparatively easy. She could have approached with a smile and said, "Good morning." The person would have returned her greeting, and it would then have been a simple matter to get acquainted.

50   But five people in one bunch all known to one another and all chatting intimately together!—it would seem too much like an intrusion to go bursting into their gathering—too forward and too vulgar. Then, there was nothing she could say after having said "good morning." One just didn't break into a group of five and say, "I'm Emma Lou Morgan, a new student, and I want to make friends with you." No, she couldn't do that. She would just smile as she passed, smile graciously and friendly. They would know that she was a stranger, and her smile would assure them that she was anxious to make friends, anxious to become a welcome addition to their group.

51   One of the group of five had sighted Emma Lou as soon as she had sighted them:

52   "Who's this?" queried Helen Wheaton, a senior in the College of Law.

53   "Some new 'pick,' I guess," answered Bob Armstrong, who was Helen's fiance and a senior in the School of Architecture.

54   "I bet she's going to take Pharmacy," whispered Amos Blaine.

55   "She's hottentot enough to take something," mumbled Tommy Brown. "Thank God, she won't be in any of our classes, eh Amos?" ✠

RESPONDING

1. Emma Lou is a victim of prejudice within her family. Yet when she goes to college, she is prejudiced against Hazel Mason. Why is Emma Lou's family biased against her, and why is she biased against Hazel? She is aware of her victimization but unaware of her victimizing. In contemporary terms, Emma Lou needs her consciousness raised. Write her a letter making her aware of what she is doing.

2. Working individually or in a group, list all of Hazel Mason's good and bad qualities according to Emma Lou's assessment. From Emma Lou's point of view, consider whether she should befriend Hazel. Do you think the two young women will become friends? Share your reasons with the class.

3. Thurman takes his title *The Blacker the Berry* from the folk saying "The blacker the berry, the sweeter the juice." In an essay, explain what this title reveals about Thurman's attitudes toward racial characteristics. Speculate about what he will have Emma Lou come to realize by the end of the novel.

4. Emma Lou is rejected by the students she wishes to befriend. Why are they laughing at her? Whose criteria are the group members using as their model? Using examples from the selection, your own experience, or sources such as Spike Lee's film *School Daze*, write an essay explaining the ways in which prejudice within a racial group can distort relationships and under-mine the members of the group.

TONI MORRISON

The novelist, poet, and essayist Toni Morrison was born in Lorain, Ohio, in 1931. She received a bachelor's degree from Howard University in 1953 and a master's from Cornell University in 1955. She has lectured and held faculty positions at Howard University, the State University of New York, Bard College, Yale University, and Rutgers University. She currently teaches at Princeton University

*In addition to writing fiction, Morrison has contributed essays and reviews to such journals a*s The New York Times Book Review, The New Yorker, The Times Literary Supplement, The New Republic, *and the* Chicago Tribune. *Her novels, recognized generally for their richness in voice, metaphor, and verbal nuance, include* The Bluest Eye *(1970),* Sula *(1973),* Song of Solomon *(1977), for which she received the National Book Critics Circle Award,* Tar Baby *(1981), and the Pulitzer Prize–winning* Beloved *(1987). Toni Morrison was awarded the Nobel Prize for Literature in 1993.*

The selection from Jazz *that follows is set during the Harlem Renaissance; its prose evokes the cadences of the prose of that period. The passage, which vividly describes the excitement of the trip from the rural South to "the city," illustrates how the Harlem Renaissance has remained a rich source of imagery and themes for modern writers.*

⚏

From JAZZ

1   THEY MET IN VESPER COUNTY, Virginia, under a walnut tree. She had been working in the fields like everybody else, and stayed past picking time to live with a family twenty miles away from her own. They knew people in common; and suspected they had at least one relative in common. They were drawn together because they had been put together, and all they decided for themselves was when and where to meet at night.

2   Violet and Joe left Tyrell, a railway stop through Vesper County, in 1906, and boarded the colored section of the Southern Sky. When the train trembled approaching the water surrounding the City, they thought it was like them: nervous at having gotten there at last, but terrified of what was on the other side. Eager, a little scared, they did not even nap during the fourteen hours of a ride smoother than a rocking cradle. The quick darkness in the carriage cars when they shot through a tunnel made them wonder if maybe there was a wall ahead to crash into or a cliff hanging over nothing. The train shivered with them at the thought but went on and sure enough there was ground up ahead

and the trembling became the dancing under their feet. Joe stood up, his fingers clutching the baggage rack above his head. He felt the dancing better that way, and told Violet to do the same.

They were hanging there, a young country couple, laughing and tapping back at the tracks, when the attendant came through, pleasant but unsmiling now that he didn't have to smile in this car full of colored people.

"Breakfast in the dining car. Breakfast in the dining car. Good morning. Full breakfast in the dining car." He held a carriage blanket over his arm and from underneath it drew a pint bottle of milk, which he placed in the hands of a young woman with a baby asleep across her knees. "Full breakfast."

He never got his way, this attendant. He wanted the whole coach to file into the dining car, now that they could. Immediately, now that they were out of Delaware and a long way from Maryland there would be no green-as-poison curtain separating the colored people eating from the rest of the diners. The cooks would not feel obliged to pile extra helpings on the plates headed for the curtain; three lemon slices in the iced tea, two pieces of coconut cake arranged to look like one—to take the sting out of the curtain; homey it up with a little extra on the plate. Now, skirting the City, there were no green curtains; the whole car could be full of colored people and everybody on a first-come first-serve basis. If only they would. If only they would tuck those little boxes and baskets underneath the seat; close those paper bags, for once, put the bacon-stuffed biscuits back into the cloth they were wrapped in, and troop single file through the five cars ahead on into the dining car, where the table linen was at least as white as the sheets they dried on juniper bushes; where the napkins were folded with a crease as stiff as the ones they ironed for Sunday dinner; where the gravy was as smooth as their own, and the biscuits did not take second place to the bacon-stuffed ones they wrapped in cloth. Once in a while it happened. Some well-shod woman with two young girls, a preacherly kind of man with a watch chain and a rolled-brim hat might stand up, adjust their clothes and weave through the coaches toward the tables, foamy white with heavy silvery knives and forks. Presided over and waited upon by a black man who did not have to lace his dignity with a smile.

Joe and Violet wouldn't think of it—paying money for a meal they had not missed and that required them to sit still at, or worse, separated by, a table. Not now. Not entering the lip of the City dancing all the way. Her hip bones rubbed his thigh as they stood in the aisle unable to stop smiling. They weren't even there yet and already the City was speaking to them. They were dancing. And like a million others, chests pounding, tracks controlling their feet, they stared out the windows for first sight of the City that danced with them, proving already how much it loved them. Like a million more they could hardly wait to get there and love it back.

Some were slow about it and traveled from Georgia to Illinois, to the City, back to Georgia, out to San Diego and finally, shaking their heads, surrendered themselves to the City. Others knew right away that it was for them, this City and no other. They came on a whim because there it was and why not? They came after much planning, many letters written to and from, to make sure and know how and how much and where. They came for a visit and forgot to go back to tall cotton or short. Discharged with or without honor, fired with or without severance, dispossessed with or without notice, they hung around for a while and then could not imagine themselves anywhere else. Others came because a relative or hometown buddy said, Man, you best see this place before you die; or, We got room now, so pack your suitcase and don't bring no high-top shoes.

8   However they came, when or why, the minute the leather of their soles hit the pavement—there was no turning around. Even if the room they rented was smaller than the heifer's stall and darker than a morning privy, they stayed to look at their number, hear themselves in an audience, feel themselves moving down the street among hundreds of others who moved the way they did, and who, when they spoke, regardless of the accent, treated language like the same intricate, malleable toy designed for their play. Part of why they loved it was the specter they left behind. The slumped spines of the veterans of the 27th Battalion betrayed by the commander for whom they had fought like lunatics. The eyes of thousands, stupefied with disgust at having been imported by Mr. Armour, Mr. Swift, Mr. Montgomery Ward to break strikes then dismissed for having done so. The broken shoes of two thousand Galveston longshoremen that Mr. Mallory would never pay fifty cents an hour like the white ones. The praying palms, the raspy breathing, the quiet children of the ones who had escaped from Springfield Ohio, Springfield Indiana, Greensburg Indiana, Wilmington Delaware, New Orleans Louisiana, after raving whites had foamed all over the lanes and yards of home.

9   The wave of black people running from want and violence crested in the 1870s; the '80s; the '90s but was a steady stream in 1906 when Joe and Violet joined it. Like the others, they were country people, but how soon country people forget. When they fall in love with a city, it is for forever, and it is like forever. As though there never was a time when they didn't love it. The minute they arrive at the train station or get off the ferry and glimpse the wide streets and the wasteful lamps lighting them, they know they are born for it. There, in a city, they are not so much new as themselves: their stronger, riskier selves. And in the beginning when they first arrive, and twenty years later when they and the City have grown up, they love that part of themselves so much they forget what loving other people was like—if they ever knew, that is. I don't mean they hate them, no, just that what they start to love is the way a person is in the City; the way a schoolgirl never pauses at a stoplight but looks up and down the street before stepping off the curb; how men accommodate themselves to tall buildings and wee porches, what a woman looks like moving in a crowd, or how shocking her profile is against the backdrop of the East River. The restfulness in kitchen chores when she knows the lamp oil or the staple is just

around the corner and not seven miles away; the amazement of throwing open the window and being hypnotized for hours by people on the street below.

Little of that makes for love, but it does pump desire. The woman who churned a man's blood as she leaned all alone on a fence by a country road might not expect even to catch his eye in the City. But if she is clipping quickly down the big-city street in heels, swinging her purse, or sitting on a stoop with a cool beer in her hand, dangling her shoe from the toes of her foot, the man, reacting to her posture, to soft skin on stone, the weight of the building stressing the delicate, dangling shoe, is captured. And he'd think it was the woman he wanted, and not some combination of curved stone, and a swinging, high-heeled shoe moving in and out of sunlight. He would know right away the deception, the trick of shapes and light and movement, but it wouldn't matter at all because the deception was part of it too. Anyway, he could feel his lungs going in and out. There is no air in the City but there is breath, and every morning it races through him like laughing gas brightening his eyes, his talk, and his expectations. In no time at all he forgets little pebbly creeks and apple trees so old they lay their branches along the ground and you have to reach down or stoop to pick the fruit. He forgets a sun that used to slide up like the yolk of a good country egg, thick and red-orange at the bottom of the sky, and he doesn't mind it, doesn't look up to see what happened to it or to stars made irrelevant by the light of thrilling, wasteful street lamps. 10

That kind of fascination, permanent and out of control, seizes children, young girls, men of every description, mothers, brides, and barfly women, and if they have their way and get to the City, they feel more like themselves, more like the people they always believed they were. Nothing can pry them away from that; the City is what they want it to be: thriftless, warm, scary and full of amiable strangers. No wonder they forget pebbly creeks and when they do not forget the sky completely think of it as a tiny piece of information about the time of day or night. 11

But I have seen the City do an unbelievable sky. Redcaps and dining-car attendants who wouldn't think of moving out of the City sometimes go on at great length about country skies they have seen from the windows of trains. But there is nothing to beat what the City can make of a nightsky. It can empty itself of surface, and more like the ocean than the ocean itself, go deep, starless. Close up on the tops of buildings, near, nearer than the cap you are wearing, such a citysky presses and retreats, presses and retreats, making me think of the free but illegal love of sweethearts before they are discovered. Looking at it, this nightsky booming over a glittering city, it's possible for me to avoid dreaming of what I know is in the ocean, and the bays and tributaries it feeds: the two-seat aeroplanes, nose down in the muck, pilot and passenger staring at schools of passing bluefish; money, soaked and salty in canvas bags, or waving their edges gently from metal bands made to hold them forever. They are down there, along with yellow flowers that eat water beetles and eggs floating away 12 from thrashing fins; along with the children who made a mistake in the parents they chose; along with slabs of Carrara pried from unfashionable buildings. There are bottles too, made of glass beautiful enough to rival stars I cannot see above me because the citysky has hidden them. Otherwise, if it wanted to, it could show me stars cut from the lamé gowns of chorus girls, or mirrored in the eyes of sweethearts furtive and happy under the pressure of a deep, touchable sky.

13   But that's not all a citysky can do. It can go purple and keep an orange heart so the clothes of the people on the streets glow like dance-hall costumes. I have seen women stir shirts into boiled starch or put the tiniest stitches into their hose while a girl straightens the hair of her sister at the stove, and all the while heaven, unnoticed and as beautiful as an Iroquois, drifts past their windows. As well as the windows where sweethearts, free and illegal, tell each other things.

14   Twenty years after Joe and Violet train-danced on into the City, they were still a couple but barely speaking to each other, let alone laughing together or acting like the ground was a dance-hall floor. Convinced that he alone remembers those days, and wants them back, aware of what it looked like but not at all of what it felt like, he coupled himself elsewhere. He rented a room from a neighbor who knows the exact cost of her discretion. Six hours a week he has purchased. Time for the citysky to move from a thin ice blue to purple with a heart of gold. And time enough, when the sun sinks, to tell his new love things he never told his wife. ✛

RESPONDING

1. In a journal entry, write about a time you looked forward to going somewhere or doing something special. How did the reality compare with the expectation?

2. Working individually or in a group, list the pros and cons of moving to a northern city for African Americans in the early 1900s.

3. Imagine that you are Violet or Joe. Write a letter home to relatives either encouraging or discouraging them from coming north.

4. In an essay, agree or disagree that the city lived up to its promise for African Americans who moved there. Use information from the readings in this section or outside knowledge.

DARWIN TURNER

Darwin Turner was born in Cincinnati in 1931. He earned his bachelor's and master's degrees at the University of Cincinnati in 1947 and 1949, respectively, and his doctorate at the University of Chicago in 1956. He taught English at several universities, including the University of Indiana, the University of Michigan, and the University of Iowa. Turner wrote extensively on the African American literary experience. His own writings include In a Minor Chord: Three Afro-American Writers and Their Search for Identity *(1971). He edited* The Wayward and the Seeking: A Collection of Writings by Jean Toomer *(1980) and the critical edition of Toomer's* Cane *(1975). Darwin Turner died in 1991.*

In the essay that follows, Turner evaluates the contribution of Harlem Renaissance writers from a contemporary perspective. In contrast to earlier critics, who stressed the elitism or excessiveness of the movement, he explores the Harlem Renaissance as a "serious way of examining the problems of living."

⊞

THE HARLEM RENAISSANCE: ONE FACET OF AN UNTURNED KALEIDOSCOPE

GERALDINE'S BRASH CRY, "What you see is what you get," is appropriate com-   1
ment on the tendency of many Americans to fix their attention on only a particular aspect of Black life in America—usually the most spectacular aspect. If they would twist the base of the kaleidoscope of Black life, the multicolored fragments would rearrange themselves into different patterns, some of them startlingly different. But few viewers choose to adjust the kaleidoscope.

As a result, out of the many patterns of Black life during the 1920's, the   2
dominant image emblazoned on the vision of America is the Harlem Renaissance. By the same process, from the Harlem Renaissance itself, a Jazzed Abandon has become the most memorable spectacle. James Weldon Johnson's description of reactions to Harlem summarizes the legend of the Harlem Renaissance:

It is known in Europe and the Orient, and it is talked about by natives in the interior of Africa. It is farthest known as being exotic, colourful [*sic*], and sensuous; a place of laughing, singing, and dancing; a place where life wakes up at night. This phase of Harlem's fame is most widely known because, in addition to being spread by ordinary agencies, it has been proclaimed in story and song. And certainly this is Harlem's most striking and fascinating aspect. New Yorkers and people visiting New York from the world over go to the night-clubs of Harlem and dance to such jazz music as can be heard nowhere else; and they get an exhilaration impossible to duplicate. Some of these seekers after new sensations go beyond the gay night-clubs; they peep in under the more seamy side of things; they nose down into lower strata of life. A visit to Harlem at night—the principal streets never deserted, gay crowds skipping from one place of amusement to another, lines of taxicabs and limousines standing under the sparkling lights of the entrances to the famous night-clubs, the subways kiosks swallowing and disgorging crowds all night long—gives the impression that Harlem never sleeps and that the inhabitants thereof jazz through existence.[1]

3 Johnson continued, "But, of course, no one can seriously think that the two hundred thousand and more Negroes in Harlem spend their nights on any such pleasance."[2] So we can say, "Surely, no one seriously thinks that this picture or even the entire 'Renaissance' constitutes the totality of the patterns housed in the kaleidoscope of Black life during the 1920's, the decade of the 'New Negro.'"

4 Even if one examines only the literary portraiture of the decade, one discerns more than a single image as the minute, tinted mirrors arrange and rearrange themselves into diverse patterns reflecting the actuality of Black life or reflecting the psyches of the Black and white artists who depicted that life. A knowledgeable individual twists the instrument to view the primitivism depicted by such white authors as Julia Peterkin, Eugene O'Neill, Sherwood Anderson, Dubose Heyward, Mary Wiborg, and William Faulkner, or the exotic abandon simulated by Carl Van Vechten. But a slight adjustment reshapes those images into the cultural elitism revealed by Van Vechten and cherished by W. E. B. DuBois. Another adjustment reveals the integrationist optimism of Langston Hughes, or the pan-Africanism of W. E. B. Dubois, or the Black nationalism of Marcus Garvey. Examine rural southern Blacks from the perspectives of Peterkin, Heyward, Faulkner, and Jean Toomer; or scrutinize the urban northerners of Toomer, Claude McKay, Rudolph Fisher, Langston Hughes, and Countee Cullen. Smile at the enthusiastic and naive Carl Van Vechtens, Mabel Dodges, and other white patrons as they prance about with their trophies collected on safaris into the Black jungles; then scowl at the lynchers painted by Claude McKay and photographed by Walter White. Admire the "patient endurance," with which William Faulkner colored his Dilsey; but do not overlook the militant impatience that inflames McKay's poetic voice. Consider the African nationalism vaguely sketched by Cullen, Hughes, and

---

1. James W. Johnson, *Black Manhattan* (New York, 1968; originally published, 1930), pp. 160–161. [Author's note]
2. Ibid., p. 161. [Author's note]

McKay; but compare it with Hughes' poetic demands for American integration and McKay's impressionistic sketches of the damnable siren, America, that fascinates, challenges, and captivates Blacks. Excite yourself with sexual abandon garishly painted by Van Vechten, Anderson, McKay, and Toomer; but study also the conservative, often frustrated Blacks portrayed by Jessie Fauset and Toomer. Weep for the impotent failures depicted by O'Neill and Paul Green; but rejoice with the bold, determined aspirants of Fauset and Fisher.

Beyond the literary spectrum, the images are equally diverse. The decade 5 of the 1920's was ushered in by the triumphant return in 1919 of the highly decorated Black 369th Infantry, which marched from the docks, down Broadway, and through Harlem, led every step of the way by James Europe's jazz band. But the decade was ushered in also by the "Red Summer" of 1919. In that year alone, according to historian John Hope Franklin, approximately twenty-five race riots throughout the nation spilled blood on the streets of the democratic land that, less than a year earlier, had won the war (so Americans said) that, President Wilson boasted, would end all wars and would safeguard democracy. Jazz was in vogue: such Black musicians as Duke Ellington and Fletcher Henderson attracted thousands of excited people to hear their bands, and Louis Armstrong gained new fans with each performance. But poverty was in vogue also: Black migrants who could not find jobs and older residents who had lost theirs to a new influx of whites gave rent parties, which remained joyous as long as no one remembered that the only reason for the party was the inability to pay the rent. Occupants of Harlem for less than a decade, Blacks were buying homes for residence and for profit on a scale rivaling the stock market speculations of their white contemporaries; but hard times had already established residence in the South, as Waring Cuney revealed in "Hard Times Blues":

> I went down home
> About a year ago
> Things looked so bad
> My heart was sore.
> People had nothing
> It was a sinning shame,
> Everybody said
> Hard times was to blame.
>
> Great-God-A-Mighty
> Folks feeling bad,
> Lost all they ever had.

Sun was shining fourteen
Days and no rain,
Hoeing and planting
Was all in vain.
It was hard times, Lawd,
All around,
Meal barrels empty,
Crops burnt to the ground.

Great-God-A-Mighty
Folks feeling bad,
Lost all they ever had.

Skinny looking children
Bellies poking out,
Old pellagra
Without a doubt,
Old folks hanging 'round
The cabin door
Aint seen things
This bad before.

Great-God-A-Mighty
Folks feeling bad,
Lost all they ever had.

Went to the Boss
At the Commissary Store,
Folks all hungry
Please don't close the
door,
Want more food, little
time to pay.
Boss man laughed
And walked away.

Great-God-A-Mighty
Folks feeling bad,
Lost all they ever had.

Landlord coming 'round
When the rent's due,
Aint got the money
Take your home from you.
Takes your mule and horse
Even take your cow,
Says get off this land
You no good no how.

Great-God-A-Mighty
Folks feeling bad,
Lost all they ever had.

For Black folks, and many rural whites, times were bad—at the very height 6
of the Jazz Age when Scott Fitzgerald's sheiks, flappers, and Gatsbys were
staging their most lavish parties. Blacks were not naive about the times. With
the assistance of Walter White, a Caucasian-looking Black, the N.A.A.C.P.
launched its three-decades-long campaign against lynching. The *Messenger*, a
Black newspaper, advocated socialism as the only solution to the economic
problems of Black Americans; and *The Crusader*, another Black newspaper,
denounced American bigotry in tones that a subsequent generation would
believe originated in the 1960's. Recognizing the inability of nonunionized
workers to withstand the arbitrary practices of the bosses, Black workers struggled to enter or establish unions: in the Brotherhood of Sleeping Car Porters,
A. Philip Randolph created the most enduring of them all. Scorning any hope
for Black economic or political power in the United States, Marcus Garvey, a
West Indian, enlisted thousands of new followers who wished to sail the Black
Star Line back to Africa. Ironically, Garvey, an actual Black from an island, won
more power and financial support in America than Eugene O'Neill ever envis-
aged for his Emperor Jones, a fictional Black American who seizes control of a
Black island.

Such awareness of the multiplicity of patterns of Black life during the 7
1920's justifies a reexamination, necessarily brief and somewhat superficial,
of the Harlem Renaissance, particularly the literary Renaissance—to determine the reasons for its image as Jazzed Abandon, to trace more closely the
more serious themes of the literature, and to reassess the significance of the
Renaissance.

If we of the 1970's picture Black life in the 1920's as a riotous night-club 8
tour, we cannot blame the best-known white writers for our misconception.
Ironically, although Blacks became so popular as a subject that almost every
prominent American author of the decade featured them in at least one major
work, most of these authors ignored the Harlem scene in their literature. Such
obvious neglect prompts speculation about the reasons: Were the authors de-

scribing the Afro-Americans they knew best? Or were they deliberately creating Black characters who would contrast with, and perhaps obscure, the image of the proud Renaissance Blacks?

9   Of course, in 1920, when O'Neill's *Emperor Jones* appeared, the Harlem Renaissance was less than a flutter in the heart of Alain Locke, the Black philosopher and cultural historian who named that era. O'Neill cannot be accused of ignoring what he could not have been expected to see. Situating his Black on a Caribbean island, O'Neill showed how fear, stripping away civilized veneer, reduces a man—in this instance, a southern Black—to a primitive.

10   The contrast between the Renaissance and O'Neill's work, however, appears in *All God's Chillun Got Wings* (1924). This drama, necessarily set in the North, describes the pathetic relationship between a Black man, who aspires to be a lawyer, and the "fallen" white woman whom he marries. The woman, betrayed and deserted by a white lover, marries the Black but becomes insane—or more insane, according to your view. The Black fails to become a lawyer partly because his wife, not wanting him to succeed, interferes with his study. The more crucial reason for his failure, however, is that whenever he is examined by whites, he forgets whatever he knows. In 1924, the year the play appeared, Jessie Fauset and Walter White published the first Black novels of the decade: *There Is Confusion*, which centers on the lives of middle-class Blacks in Philadelphia, among them a Black graduate of a white medical school, and *The Fire in the Flint*, a protest against lynching. For three years, Black musicals had been the rage of Broadway theater. BLACK was in, by 1924. The next year *Survey Graphic* would focus an entire issue on the "New Negro," James Weldon Johnson would hail Harlem as the capital of Black America, others would call it "mecca." Despite these events, O'Neill provided New York theatergoers with a Black protagonist whose aspirations exceed his ability. Whatever O'Neill's reasons for the theme, the choice of an actor to portray the protagonist could not have been more ironic. The Black who panics when examined by whites was played by Paul Robeson, all-American football player (I believe that he was the first Black selected by Walter Camp as an All-American), a twelve-letter man in athletics, and a Phi Betta Kappa graduate, who earned one of the highest academic averages in the history of Rutgers University.

11   The spectacle of Black failure was continued by Paul Green, a North Carolinian who wrote more plays about Blacks than any other white person during the decade. In 1926 Green won the Pulitzer Prize for *In Abraham's Bosom*, a drama in which Black Abe McCrannie, during Reconstruction, tries futilely to establish a school for Blacks. In the same year, 1926, W. E. B. DuBois, editor of *The Crisis*, the voice of the N.A.A.C.P., continuing a practice intended to encourage Black scholarship, published the pictures of the year's Black college graduates. Within a few years, DuBois would proudly announce that the large number of graduates prohibited his publishing the pictures of all.

12   Another memorable drama of the decade was Dubose Heyward's *Porgy*, now an American "classic," a story of a Black and crippled junk dealer, who

strives to win Bess, a fallen woman, from Crown, a bad, bad man. Perhaps the most appropriate evaluation of the drama comes from W. E. B. DuBois, who insisted that he did not object to the play. Then, sniffing delicately from the rarified atmosphere surrounding a New England Brahmin who was a Ph.D. graduate from Harvard and had been a graduate student at Heidelberg, DuBois explained that, although he did not doubt that Heyward's Blacks existed in Charleston, South Carolina, he regretted Heyward's failure to portray the educated Blacks DuBois associated with when he visited that city.

During the 1920's William Faulkner foreshadowed his future with *The Sound and the Fury*, located primarily in Mississippi, with a glance at Cambridge, Massachusetts. Faulkner's major Black character in this novel is Dilsey, prototype of "the Black who endures." Like Green and O'Neill, Faulkner probably had not read Alain Locke's introduction to *The New Negro* (1925). Locke asserted: "Sentimental interest in the Negro has ebbed. We used to lament this as the falling off of our friends; now we rejoice and pray to be delivered both from self-pity and condescension. The mind of each racial group has had a better weaning, apathy or hatred on one side matching disillusionment or resentment on the other; but they face each other today with the possibility at least of entirely new mutual attitudes."[3]

The decade ended with a production of the extraordinarily popular *Green Pastures* (1930) by Marc Connelly. Based on Roark Bradford's *Ol' Man Adam and His Chillun*, the drama seems to retell the Old Testament from the perspective of a Black child at a church fish-fry. The narrator is not a child, however; he is an adult.

However distorted their vision of Blacks may have been, well-known white American authors of the 1920's cannot be blamed for the exotic image of the nightclub Black. That image comes from Blacks themselves and from a few whites who identified themselves as promoters of Blacks or as sympathizers.

The image may have begun with *Shuffle Along* (1921), a brilliant and popular musical, written and directed by four Blacks—Flournoy Miller, Eubie Blake, Noble Sissel, and Aubrey Lyles. In the same year, *Shuffle Along* was succeeded by *Put and Take*, another musical by a Black—Irving C. Miller, who also produced *Liza* (1923), which was followed in the same year by *Runnin' Wild* by Miller and Lyles. The beauty of Afro-American chorus girls such as Florence Mills and Josephine Baker, the exotic foreign settings, the gaiety and the frenzy of these musicals and their successors may have cultivated in Broadway audiences a taste for particular depictions of Black life. Furthermore, these musicals may have created an image difficult to change.

Although it is located in the South, Sherwood Anderson's *Dark Laughter* (1925) conjures up the image of a joyful, untroubled people who, themselves freed from the need to read Freud, laugh gently at frustrated whites, who repress their own sexual desires. The image of joy continues in Carl Van Vechten's

3. Locke, "The New Negro," *The New Negro* (New York, 1968), p. 8. [Author's note]

novel, *Nigger Heaven* (1926), set in Harlem. Although Van Vechten later proclaimed his desire to familiarize white readers with a cultural Black society which
gives soirées and speaks French, he glamorized the Scarlet Creeper, a "sweet-
man" (gigolo), and he depicted Black night life with an excitement certain to
allure readers.

18   The exoticism and gaiety appear in the words of Black writers themselves.
Even Countee Cullen, known to subsequent generations as a somewhat
prim purveyor of high art, contrasted the warmth of Blacks with the coldness
of whites, wrote atavistically of the African rhythm inherent in the walk of a
Black waiter (in *Color*, 1925), and rhapsodized the wildness of the African
heritage.

19   In his first collection, *The Weary Blues* (1926), Langston Hughes not only
created jazz/blues poems but also wrote with an exuberance tending to promote
the image of an uninhibited people:

Dream Variation

To fling my arms wide
In some place of the sun,
To whirl and to dance
Till the white day is done.
Then rest at cool evening
Beneath a tall tree
While night comes on gently,
      Dark like me,—
That is my dream!

To fling my arms wide
In the face of the sun,
Dance! whirl! whirl!
Till the quick day is done.
Rest at pale evening. . . .
A tall, slim tree. . . .
Night coming tenderly
      Black like me.[4]

Black novelists also contributed to the image of an uninhibited people whose
lives are exotic whirls. In *Home to Harlem* (1928), Claude McKay, a Black West
Indian, drowned social protest in a flood of night life—prostitutes, sweetmen,
jazz, nightclub fights—as he told the story of a Black deserter from the armed
services who searches through Harlem for the prostitute whom he loves. Suc-

---

[4]Hughes, *The Weary Blues* (New York, 1926). [Author's note]

ceeding novelists, such as Rudolph Fisher (*The Walls of Jericho*, 1928) and Wallace Thurman (*The Blacker the Berry*, 1929), seemed almost compelled to include irrelevant nightclub scenes as though they had become clichés of Black life.

It should not be wondered then that W. E. B. DuBois, editor of *The Crisis*, [20] reserved sections of several issues to question whether writers and publishers shared his fear that Black writers were being encouraged to create derogatory pictures of Blacks. Seriously concerned about respectable images of Blacks, DuBois, more than two decades earlier, had rationalized their enthusiasm as a primitivism promoted by the experience of slavery, a primitivism which would be modified when Black Americans matured into the sophistication of Euro-American society. Now that his "Talented Tenth" seemed to promote spectacles of frenzy, however, DuBois suspected that their desire to publish persuaded them to ignore the truth of Black life and to pander to whites by creating images designed to titillate.

Beneath the surfaces of gay abandon during the 1920's, however, are more [21] somber issues, more somber themes which should be examined more closely. The same writers who seem to rejoice in the enthusiasm of Black life also sounded what Langston Hughes described as "the sob of the jazz band"—the melancholy undertone of Black life, ever present but sometimes unheard by those who fail to listen carefully.

Claude McKay pictured a Harlem dancer who guards her soul from the [22] lascivious image suggested by her dance (*Harlem Shadows*, 1922), and Langston Hughes described the weariness of a jazz pianist (*The Weary Blues*, 1926). In *The Walls of Jericho* (1928) Fisher overshadowed the scenes of night life with a quieter depiction of the romance of two working people of Harlem. Thurman tempered his scenes of night life and dances in *The Blacker the Berry* by revealing that some Blacks visited dance halls not to gorge themselves with gaiety but to discover companionship to ease their loneliness. In the same novel a white Chicagoan confirms his impression that the exotic savagery of Harlemites is grossly exaggerated by their white press agents. While his actress-sister revels in what she considers the barbaric splendor of the Black club they visit, the Chicagoan sees a generally decorous behavior which assures him that Harlemites are no wilder than the Blacks he has known in Chicago (and perhaps not as wild as the whites in either city). Countee Cullen asserted that he wrote *One Way to Heaven* (1932) to counter Carl Van Vechten's *Nigger Heaven* by showing the humanity of Black life in Harlem. In scene after scene, Cullen balances superficial exuberance with sober explanation: The enthusiasm of a religious revival does not obscure the fact that in attendance also are some morally respectable Blacks who are not swept away by the emotion. The heroine, a morally circumspect, hard-working woman, has attended several revivals to which she has been indifferent. A male's illicit love affair is ascribed partly to the nature of the wandering male and partly to a desire to find companionship because his wife, who has become a religious fanatic, is engaged in an affair with Jesus.

23   These more serious vestiges of Black life in America should not be ignored when one considers the literature of the Renaissance; for, far from being mere entertainers, many Black writers regarded literature as a means of seriously examining problems of living. Moreover, they did not restrict their examinations to problems of Blacks in an adversary relationship with white society. Almost from the first they were concerned with issues which might be considered universal if American critics were more willing to discover universality in the lives of Black people.

24   The interest in human conditions appears in Jean Toomer's *Cane* (1923), the work of the Renaissance which is the best known and the most highly respected in academic circles. Toomer delineates many protagonists whose difficulties do not depend primarily upon their ancestry: Karintha has matured too soon sexually; Carma lives in a society which pretends that a woman should become sexless if her husband does not live with her; Esther cannot reconcile her sexual urges with the education by a society which has taught her that "good" girls do not feel such urges; John, in "Theater," cannot adapt his idealized romanticizing into a satisfactory relationship with an actual woman; Dorris, in "Theater," dreams of a companionship that will provide a real substitute for the artificiality of the theater; Muriel, in "Box Seat," fears to defy the little-minded, social regulators of the world; Avery finds it more pleasurable to be supported by men than to labor as a teacher in a normal school. The problems of these individuals may be complicated or intensified by their condition as Blacks in America, but the problems would exist regardless of their race.

25   Jessie Fauset, the too little-known author of *There Is Confusion* (1924), *Plum Bun* (1929), *The Chinaberry Tree* (1933), and *Comedy: American Style* (1933), contrived her novels to focus on the problems of Blacks whose lives are not continuously affected by their interrelationships with whites. Most often their problems derive from their ambition or from a society excessively willing to evaluate individuals according to false criteria. In *There Is Confusion*, for example, an ambitious young Black protagonist disrupts and nearly destroys the people around her because she tries to regulate their lives according to her delusions. Because she believes that people should not marry outside their class, she interferes with her brother's romance with a young woman whose family background is different. Doing "the right thing," by withdrawing from the relationship, the second young woman then rushes into an unfortunate marriage. Because the protagonist believes that suitors must be trained into suitably devoted servants, she refuses to apologize to the man she loves even though she is wrong. After he apologizes in order to effect a reconciliation, she delays a response with the deliberate intention of causing him to learn that he cannot win her too easily. She begins to realize her error only when he, jolted

by her rebuff, proposes to a woman who offers him affection without reservation.

In stories which she published during the 1920's, Zora Neale Hurston of Florida explores such an "in-group" issue as the manner in which townspeople affect individuals by forcing them to act out of character in order to maintain the respect of the mob ("Spunk"). In addition, she vividly revealed the problems which disturb male-female relationships: the alienation which develops when a naive wife is seduced by a traveling salesman ("The Gilded Six-Bits"); the tragic consequences when a self-centered husband who has exploited his wife tries to replace her ("Sweat"). 26

Black dramatists, such as Willis Richardson and Georgia D. Johnson, prepared domestic dramas for the Black community: the tensions between a man and his improvident brothers-in-law ("The Broken Banjo"); the pathos of a situation in which a child is permitted to die because the mother favors the healing power of faith above that of man's medicine. 27

In such ways as these, Black people of the Renaissance explored serious issues involving Black people but not deriving primarily from the racial ancestry or from their relationship with whites. This statement, however, should not encourage a fallacious assumption that the Black writers evaded their racial identity or ignored problems which do derive from interracial conflict. To the contrary, Black Renaissance writers frequently expressed concerns which strikingly anticipate major themes identified with the revolutionary Black Arts writers of the 1960's: a search for and affirmation of ancestral heritage, a feeling of alienation from the white Euro-American world; a presentation of and protest against oppression; and even militant defiance of oppression. 28

Just as Black Arts writers of today affirm their African heritage, so many Renaissance writers sought identity through identification with an ancestral past. Jean Toomer sought identity derived in part from the consciousness of the slave South and Africa (*Cane*, 1923, and "Natalie Mann"). As I have pointed out earlier, Countee Cullen proclaimed that the sober teachings of Christian civilization could not curb the memories and the urges which linked him with Africa ("Heritage"). Langston Hughes found pride in identification with a race so old in human history that it had lived when rivers were young ("The Negro Speaks of Rivers"). Although some of these ancestral searches may seem rhetorical rather than actual, although some of the thoughts of Africa are sufficiently atavistic to promote a concept of exotic primitivism, the quests respond partly at least to Alain Locke's urgings that Black artists search for subject and style in an African tradition. 29

For the Black American writer of the 1920's, however, the search for ancestry proved more difficult than for white Americans. Some Blacks, ashamed of their ancestry as slaves and as descendants of Africans whom they judged to have been savages, attempted to evolve more respectable ancestry from identification with former masters. In *There Is Confusion* (1924) Jessie Fauset sug- 30 gested the problems sometimes posed by the quest for European ancestry. Moreover, Blacks who wished to affirm a Black heritage were forced to identify with a continent rather than with a particular tribe or nation. Hence, the identification sometimes became intellectual and abstract rather than personal. The problem is suggested by Hughes:

Afro-American Fragment

So long,
So far away
Is Africa.
Not even memories alive
Save those that history books create,
Save those that songs
Beat back into the blood—
Beat out of blood with words sad-sung
In strange un-Negro tongue—
So long
So far away.

Subdued and time-lost
Are the drums—and yet
Through some vast mist of race
There comes this song
I do not understand,
This song of atavistic land,
Of bitter yearning lost
Without a place—
So long,
So far away
Is Africa's
Dark face.

31   Failure to establish psychological identity with the Black heritage and corresponding awareness of exclusion from the European heritage sometimes produced a sense of alienation comparable to that expressed by Black Arts writers today. The feeling resounds vividly from McKay's "Outcast."

For the dim regions whence my fathers came
My spirit, bondaged by the body, longs.
Words felt, but never heard, my lips would frame:
My soul would sing forgotten jungle songs.
I would go back to darkness and to peace,
But the great western world holds me in fee,
And I may never hope for full release,
While to its alien gods I bend my knee.
Something in me is lost, forever lost,
Some vital thing has gone out of my heart,
And I must walk the way of life a ghost
Among the sons of earth, a thing apart;
For I was born, far from my native clime,
Under the white man's menace, out of time.

The serious themes that Renaissance writers explored most frequently, as might be expected, are protests against oppression. The presence of such themes has been obscured by three facts: (1) many readers remember the glamorous gaiety and forget the serious comments; (2) some protests appear as brief asides rather than fully developed explanations; (3) some protests seem mild because, rather than directly assaulting whites, they adumbrate the manner in which external oppression causes Blacks to oppress themselves. The way that serious protest can be ignored is evidenced by the customary reactions of casual readers to McKay's *Home to Harlem* (1928), which appears, even in this paper, as a prototype of a Black work that promotes exoticism. The vividly exotic spectacles blind many readers to McKay's presentation of such facts as the following: During World War I many Black soldiers who enlisted to fight for democracy were restricted to service as laborers; during the 1920's some Harlem clubs, whether owned by whites or Blacks, discriminated against Blacks by refusing them admission—except as entertainers or waiters; in many occupations Black workers surrendered their dignity to the caprice of white supervisors. [32]

It is true that no *Native Son* burst from the Renaissance to denounce American oppression. But Walter White's novel *The Fire in the Flint* (1924) decries the brutality of lynchings, as does Claude McKay's "The Lynching." Toomer's "Blood-Burning Moon" and "Kabnis" (*Cane*) reveal the powerlessness of Blacks to protect themselves from white brutality: a successful self-defense summons the lynch mob as quickly as a murder would. [33]

Much more prevalent is the Renaissance writers' tendency to attack oppression indirectly by showing how it causes Blacks to turn against themselves. Because color, as an evidence of African ancestry, was a shibboleth of whites against Blacks, many Blacks used color as a criterion of intra-group evaluation. In *The Blacker the Berry* the protagonist, because of her dark skin, suffers within her family, in school and college, and in efforts to secure employment. Yet [34] pathetically, as Thurman shows, the heroine cherishes the same criteria which have victimized her. She desires only men who are of lighter complexion and Caucasian appearance; and she undervalues herself, believing for a time at least that her Blackness is an ineradicable blot upon her record. In *Comedy: American Style* (1933), Fauset censured a Negro mother who values her children according to the degree of their approximation to Caucasian appearance. Walter White's *Flight* (1928) and Nella Larsen's *Passing* (1929) show the dilemmas of heroines who, repressed by the conditions of life as Blacks, attempt to improve their lot by passing for white.

35   In ironic repudiation of the images of Blacks as amoral beings, Jean Toomer repeatedly stressed the necessity for middle-class Negroes to liberate themselves from conscious imitation of the restrictive morality of Anglo-Saxons. "Esther," "Theater," and "Box-Seat" all reveal the frustrations of Black people who, desiring social approval, repress their emotion, their humanness. In "Kabnis" Carrie K., fearing censure by others, represses her instinctual attraction to Lewis. Paul ("Rona and Paul," *Cane*) loses a female companion because of his self-conscious desire to explain to a bystander that the relationship is not lustful. Toomer's most fully developed attack on middle-class morality appears in the unpublished drama "Natalie Mann." Mert, a school teacher, dies because she perceives too late that she must enjoy passion fully without concern for society's censure. Natalie, the protagonist, develops to this awareness only through the assistance of a Christ-like male who himself has experienced the rebukes of the middle class.

36   Toomer was not the only writer to question the excessive effort of Blacks to conform to the standards presumed to be those of whites. The protagonist in Walter White's *Flight* is forced to leave town and, temporarily, to deny her race because Blacks will not permit her to forget that she has had a child out of wedlock: her lover's proposal of abortion so diminished him in her esteem that she refused his subsequent efforts to marry her.

37   During the 1920's few writers reacted militantly to oppression with the kind of rhetoric for which Black revolutionary literature became notorious during the 1960's. There are several reasons. A generally optimistic faith that talented Blacks soon would emerge with the mainstream muted rhetorical violence and violent rhetoric. Furthermore, publishers during the 1920's did not permit the kind of language and the explicit description of violent action which became almost commonplace in later decades. Third, the publishing houses were controlled by whites. It should be remembered that much of the Black revolutionary literature of the 1960's issued from Black publishers of poetry and in Black community drama.

38   Under the circumstances it is not surprising that the militant reaction often was expressed as self-defense, as in Claude McKay's well-known "If We Must Die" (*Harlem Shadows*). Less frequently came prayers for destruction, as in McKay's "Enslaved" (*Harlem Shadows*). Most often the militancy is a proud hostility toward whites. At the end of *Flight* the male protagonist learns why his

father abhorred whites: they had deprived him of inheritance by refusing to recognize him as their offspring. In turn he refuses to permit an elderly white to ease his own conscience by making a monetary donation while continuing to ignore the blood relationship.

I cannot conclude without reassessing the significance of the literary Harlem Renaissance. If it is remembered for expression of gaiety rather than for the serious concerns of the Black authors; if it was a movement which involved only talented artists in one segment of the Black American population; if it reflects primarily the life of only one part of one city inhabited by Blacks; if it evidences little awareness of such a significant issue for Blacks as DuBois' dreams and promotions of Pan-Africanism and even less awareness of or respect for Marcus Garvey's Back-to-Africa movement—if the literary Renaissance is so limited, does it merit serious study? Was it, as Harold Cruse has suggested, an era to be examined only as a pathetic example of a time when Black artists might have established criteria for their art but failed to do so? Was it, as W. E. B. DuBois stated and as LeRoi Jones insisted more forcefully later, a movement that lost validity as it became a plaything of white culture? In fact, is the very attention given to it by historians of Black culture evidence of the willingness of Blacks and whites to glorify, or permit glorification of, inferior art by Blacks? [39]

Each of these allegations has partial validity. But such objections based on idealistic absolutes fail to consider the actual significances of the literary Renaissance. First, in no other decade had Black novelists been afforded such opportunity for publication. If fewer than twenty original, non-vanity-press novels appeared between 1924 and 1933, that figure nevertheless exceeded the number published by American commercial houses in all the years since the publication of the first Black American novel, Williams Wells Brown's *Clotel* (1853). Even the Depression and the closing of some outlets could not dispel the new awareness that possibilities existed for Blacks who wished to write novels. The field was open to many writers, not merely to the individual geniuses—the Paul Dunbar or the Charles Chestnutt of an earlier decade. This productivity, as well as the later success of Richard Wright, undoubtedly encouraged such novelists as Chester Hines, Ann Petry, Frank Yerby, and William G. Smith, who developed during the late 1930's and early 1940's. [40]

The literary examples and inspirations were not limited to the novel. Only a few serious Black dramas reached Broadway, but the enthusiastic establishment of Black community theaters during the 1920's furthered the creation of a Black audience for drama and promoted awareness of the need for writers to create material for that audience. [41]

Perhaps the productivity in poetry had less significant influence because Blacks previously had found outlets for poetry—the national reputation of Paul Laurence Dunbar was known by Blacks. Moreover, poetry was still to be considered an avocation which one supported by revenue derived from a stable vocation. But there was hope that Black writers might be able to sustain themselves partly through grants, for Countée Cullen had established a precedent [42] by winning a Guggenheim fellowship for his proposal of a poetry-writing project.

43   Of final benefit to future writers was the mere fact that entrées had been established. A Langston Hughes or Wallace Thurman or Countee Cullen or, later, an Arna Bontemps knew publishers and knew other people who might be able to assist prospective authors. In all these senses, the Renaissance was not a rebirth but, in very significant ways, a first birth for Black Americans in literature.

44   A second significance of the literary Renaissance is its inspiration for African and Caribbean poets such as Léopold Senghor, Aimé Césaire, and Léon Damas who, a generation later in the 1930's and 1940's, promoted Negritude, a literary-cultural movement which emphasized consciousness of African identity and pride in the Black heritage. More than a decade after the Negritude writers, newer Black American writers of the 1960's looked to African Negritude for inspiration. Thus, both directly and circuitously, the Renaissance promoted Black American literature and Black consciousness of future decades.

45   Finally, the Renaissance has importance as a symbol. In many respects, the actuality of a culture is less important than the myth which envelops and extends from that culture. The memory that Black Americans had been recognized and respected for literary achievements, as well as other artistic achievements, established awareness that there could be a literary culture among Blacks. If the memory faded rapidly from the consciousness of white America, it did not fade from the minds of Blacks responsible for continuing the culture among their people. Marcus Garvey did not succeed in restoring Black Americans to Africa; consequently, he is remembered as a dream that faded. But the Renaissance, for Black Americans and others, has gained strength as the mythic memory of a time when Blacks first burst into national consciousness as a talented group that was young, rebellious, proud, and beautiful. ⬛

RESPONDING

1. In a journal entry, explain why Turner wants us to twist the kaleidoscope of African American life for a different view of the Harlem Renaissance.

2. Working individually or in a group, use examples from the selections in this chapter to illustrate the serious themes African American writers dealt with during the Harlem Renaissance. Discuss the reasons Turner gives to explain why the importance of this serious work has been obscured.

3. In an essay, contrast the "spectacle" of African American failure presented by many Caucasian writers of the 1920s with some of the successes Turner mentions. What reasons does he present to explain the distorted picture of African Americans in the literature and theater of the time?

4. W. E. B. Du Bois and LeRoi Jones criticized the Harlem Renaissance as "a movement that lost validity as it became a plaything of white culture." Review Turner's response to that criticism (paragraphs 40–45). Write an essay that considers whether the same criticism could be applied to contemporary African American art. Have rap music or the films of Spike Lee lost their validity because they are so popular with white audiences?

✛

CONNECTING

Critical Thinking and Writing

1. Compare the situation for people of color in universities today with the situation for the speaker in "Theme for English B" or for Emma Lou in *The Blacker the Berry*. In what ways has your university tried to welcome and encourage students who are people of color? How successful have these attempts been?

2. Locke says, "Each generation . . . will have its creed" (paragraph 21). Using evidence from the readings, identify the creed of the Harlem Renaissance. Write an essay explaining how this creed influenced the writing of the period. Use specific examples from the readings in this chapter to support your points.

3. Review Turner's comments about one of the selections in this chapter. Write an essay supporting his statements with fully developed examples from the reading.

4. Define "renaissance" as used by Locke and illustrated in this chapter. Compare this movement to other renaissances for people of color in this country. Discuss the similarities and differences between the impetus that sparked the rebirth and the artistic production that resulted.

5. Locke speaks of "the racial leaders of twenty years ago [who] spoke of developing race-pride and stimulating race consciousness, and the desirability of race solidarity" (paragraph 12). These were also the goals of the Harlem Renaissance. Compare these goals to those of later movements such as the civil rights movement, which is the subject of Chapter 6. What would various leaders of the movement such as Martin Luther King, Jr., or Malcolm X say about these goals?

6. Choose an issue that emerges from these readings and design your own essay question.

7. Characters such as Emma Lou in *The Blacker the Berry* and Hanneh Breineh in "The Fat of the Land" in Chapter 1 are rejected by their own families. Compare their situations. Analyze what such a rejection reveals about the families themselves.

8. Write an essay comparing the relationship between Missie May and Joe in "The Gilded Six-Bits" and another husband and wife in one of the readings, such as Grandma and Grandpa Kashpaw in the excerpt from *Love Medicine* in Chapter 8 or Vinita and her husband in "Visitors" in Chapter 9.

9. Emma Lou has a problem in *The Blacker the Berry* because she is perceived by some as "too" dark. Compare her situation with the one Greg Sarris describes in "Battling Illegitimacy" in Chapter 8.

10. Both the Harlem Renaissance and the Native American Renaissance of the 1960s celebrate pride and cultural heritage. Compare a reading from this chapter with one from Chapter 8 to show the different ways each group uses cultural materials as the basis for creating new works of art.

11. Compare the Native American Renaissance with the Harlem Renaissance as it is described in the readings. What do the two periods have in common? Does each deserve to be called a renaissance?

For Further Research

1. In the 1920s, Harlem was a flourishing community for artists, writers, and entertainers. Research the rise and decline of that community and compare the Harlem of the 1920s to Harlem today.

2. Trace the development of African Americans' interest in African language and culture from the 1920s to the present.

3. Research Marcus Garvey and his "Back to Africa Movement." Discuss the history of the movement and its status today.

REFERENCES AND ADDITIONAL SOURCES

Baker, Houston A., Jr. *Afro-American Poetics: Revisions of Harlem and the Black Aesthetic.* Madison, Wis.: University of Wisconsin Press, 1987.

——. *Modernism and the Harlem Renaissance.* Chicago: University of Chicago Press, 1989.

Bell, Bernard W. *The Afro-American Novel and Its Tradition*. Amherst: University of Massachusetts Press, 1987.

Berghahn, Marion. *Images of Africa in Black American Literature*. Totowa, N.J.: Rowman and Littlefield, 1977.

Bontemps, Arna, ed. *The Harlem Renaissance Remembered: Essays Edited with a Memoir by Arna Bontemps*. New York: Dodd, 1984.

Brown, Sterling. *Negro Poetry and Drama*. New York: Arno, 1969.

Cruse, Harold. *The Crisis of the Negro Intellectual: A Historical Analysis of the Failure of Black Leadership*. New York: Morrow, 1967. New York: Quill, 1984.

Davis, Arthur P., and Michael Peplow, eds. *The New Negro Renaissance: An Anthology*. New York: Holt, Rinehart, and Winston, 1975.

De Jongh, James. *Vicious Modernism: Black Harlem and the Literary Imagination*. Cambridge, Eng.: Cambridge University Press, 1990.

Goldfield, David R. *Black, White and Southern*. Baton Rouge, La.: Louisiana State University Press, 1990.

Huggins, Nathan I. *Harlem Renaissance*. London: Oxford University Press, 1971, 1973.

Hull, Gloria T., ed. *Color, Sex & Poetry: Three Women Writers of the Harlem Renaissance*. Bloomington: Indiana University Press, 1987.

Ikonné, Chidi. *From Du Bois to Van Vechten: The Early New Negro Literature, 1903–1926*. Westport, Conn.: Greenwood Press, 1981.

Johnson, James Weldon. *Black Manhattan*. New York: A. A. Knopf, 1930. New York: De Capo, 1991.

Jones, Jacklyn. *Labor of Love, Labor of Sorrow*. New York: Basic Books, 1985.

Lehman, Nicholas. *The Promised Land*. New York: Knopf, 1991.

Locke, Alain. *The New Negro*. New York: A and C Boni, 1925. New York: Maxwell Macmillan International (Introduction by Arnold Rampersad), 1992.

Martin, Tony. *Literary Garveyism: Garvey, Black Arts, and the Harlem Renaissance*. Dover, Mass.: Majority Press, 1983.

Perry, Margaret. *Silence to the Drums: A Survey of the Literature of the Renaissance* Westport, CT: Greenwood, 1976. New York: Garland, 1982.

Roses, Lorraine Elena, and Ruth Elizabeth Randolph. *Harlem Renaissance and Beyond: Literary Biographies of 100 Black Women Writers, 1900–1945*. Boston: G. K. Hall, 1990.

Wagner, Jean. *Black Poets of the United States: From Paul Laurence Dunbar to Langston Hughes*. Trans. by Kenneth Douglas. Champaign-Urbana: University of Illinois Press, 1973.

4

PUERTO RICANS

The View from the Mainland

✠

Above: Puerto Rican immigrants arriving in the U.S., 1945. First immigrants to arrive by air to the U.S. (Culver Pictures, Inc.)
Opposite: (© Cliff Garboden/Stock Boston)

SETTING THE HISTORICAL AND CULTURAL CONTEXT

IN HIS POEM "Puerto Rican Obituary," Pedro Pietro describes the feelings of many persons from Puerto Rico who migrated to the United States mainland expecting a better life for their families:

> All died yesterday today
> And will die tomorrow . . .
> Waiting for the Garden of Eden
> To open up again,
> All died
> Dreaming about america.

In one sense the disappointment expressed here can be compared to the experiences of other immigrants. In another, more important, sense, the Puerto Rican experience is unique. All citizens of Puerto Rico, whether they live on the island or the mainland, are American citizens.

The island of Puerto Rico is referred to as a "free state associated" with the United States. Attracted to the United States by promises of employment or driven from the island by the pressures of a large population and high unemployment, Puerto Ricans have become a significant presence in United States cities, especially since World War II. Indeed, 40 percent of the Puerto Rican population now lives on the mainland. Despite their status as citizens, however, they have met barriers to economic success. They have had to contend with prejudice and discrimination over differences in race, culture, and language as they retain roots in their home island and a stake in its centuries-old debate over cultural and political identity.

In 1493 Columbus claimed the island, then inhabited by peaceful Arawaks, for Spain. As a Spanish colony, Puerto Rico was eventually put under the *encomienda* system, a type of forced labor practiced until the nineteenth century. Exploited for its agricultural production and strategic importance, the island remained under Spanish control until it was ceded to the United States in 1898, after the Spanish-American War. Liberal forces had campaigned throughout the nineteenth century for reform of the colonial government, achieving two major goals: the abolition of slavery and the institution of an autonomous island government. The second of these major reforms, however, was swept away when the United States established military control.

Several factors influenced the United States's interest in Puerto Rico, among them the island's economic potential and strategic importance. American corporations noted its potential for agrarian production, specifically coffee and sugar-cane crops. Strategically, Puerto Rico was considered important because of its proximity to the proposed canal connecting the Atlantic and Pacific oceans. The Treaty of Paris, which ended the Spanish-American War, made Puerto Rico—along with Cuba, Guam, and the Philippines—a territory of the United States.

Puerto Rico became a United States territory, now subject to the United States Congress, which shaped policy through a series of legislative acts. The Foraker Act (1900) replaced the interim military government with a civil administration under a presidentially appointed governor. The Jones Act (1917), passed in response to the demands of the Puerto Rican people for self-government, made the island a United States territory and granted citizenship to its residents. The benefits of the act were, however, extremely limited. Puerto Ricans gained a representative in Congress, but that member was permitted neither to speak nor vote. Although the island would now have a civilian rather than a military governor, that person would continue to be an appointed official; Puerto Ricans would have no say in selecting him.

Despite the fact that Puerto Ricans were not given all the rights of American citizenship, they were expected to meet many of the obligations of citizenship. Indeed, the Jones Act made all eligible citizens subject to the American military draft during the final months of World War I. Not until 1948 did Congress permit Puerto Ricans to elect their governor by popular vote, and not until 1952 did it permit them to adopt a constitution. Under this document, the island became fully self-governing as the Commonwealth of Puerto Rico while remaining in voluntary association with the United States.

United States government attempts at agrarian reform and industrialization were controversial. Generally, the policy has been to consolidate land and the means of production of food and other commodities—changes usually designed to benefit mainland investors. The most famous of these, Operation Bootstrap, was begun during the 1940s, under Franklin Delano Roosevelt's New Deal. Under this program, agricultural land was cleared for the development of industrial sites; the government gave investors tax reductions and helped with the construction of hotels, factories, and other businesses. Many of the substandard housing units were replaced by concrete buildings; roads were paved throughout the countryside. Proponents of Operation Bootstrap point to the increase in literacy, the decrease in infant mortality, and the increased employment brought about by the introduction of technology and industrialization. Critics have charged that such controlled economic programs interfere with, rather than promote, local development and that they displace agricultural workers without creating new employment for them. Pointing out these effects of absentee ownership of land and the urban congestion caused by the necessary migrations from rural areas, critics contend that those who profited most by the rapid industrialization were the American corporations themselves.

Migration from Puerto Rico to the mainland of the United States began in the mid-nineteenth century. It has sometimes been for political reasons, as when Puerto Ricans involved in the unsuccessful rebellion against Spain in the 1870s sought refuge in New York. More often, however, socioeconomic factors have taken precedence. Because of the increased prosperity brought about by mainland investment, migration has helped to reduce the pressure of overcrowding resulting from a high birthrate and improved public health. In fact, migration has been so important to the island's economic stability that the Puerto Rican government has long maintained an office in New York City to facilitate it. By 1930 a large majority of Puerto Rican migrants had settled in East Harlem (now called Spanish Harlem) and in parts of Brooklyn and the Bronx, often working in the garment and tobacco industries. The readings by Bernardo Vega and Jesús Colón illustrate the struggles of the new arrivals not only to survive in the new surroundings, but also to educate themselves and to prosper; in both works newcomers rely on communities of earlier migrants for the support they require.

The migration has also served American commercial interests. In the 1950s New York mayor Robert Wagner visited Puerto Rico to recruit workers and American corporations routinely sent recruiters there. The most significant period of immigration to the mainland, however, occurred during the late 1940s, just after World War II, when the postwar economic boom caused a demand for labor. This factor, combined with the introduction of cheap airfares, led to a dramatic increase in the number of persons leaving for the mainland. Although some migrants were recruited for work in the western States and Hawaii, the great majority settled in the northeastern United States, especially in New York City.

At first, the social and cultural cohesiveness of their communities helped Puerto Ricans endure the changes in climate and culture. While the chapter from Piri Thomas's book describes some of this cohesiveness on a familial level, the essay by Virginia Sánchez Korrol investigates the cultural factors that helped strengthen the *colonia*. Korrol's essay, entitled "Latinismo among Early Puerto Rican Migrants in New York City," traces the role of newspapers, music shops, and political and social organizations in providing the *colonia* with a strong sense of cultural identity despite its many socioeconomic problems. The issues of identity, dignity, and affiliation emerge in a different way in the poem by Martín Espada, which is set in a deteriorating urban environment.

Although Puerto Ricans' social status was generally lower than it would have been in Puerto Rico, those living on the mainland were compensated by health and educational opportunities, increased wages, and a higher standard of living. But their increasing separation from Puerto Rican family, religious, and cultural values has begun to weaken these communities. This conflict is explored in selections by Judith Ortiz Cofer and Nicholasa Mohr. In the chapter from Cofer's *The Line of the Sun*, characters must renegotiate their social roles in order to survive and to prosper. In Mohr's "A Thanksgiving Celebration," a family in crisis depends on a female head of household to refashion not only a ritual celebration but a new life for them.

The erosion of the mainland economy of the 1970s further undermined Puerto Ricans' social and economic position. As the industries that used their semiskilled labor began to close, automate, or relocate, many migrants turned to the service economy, filling positions as maids, waiters, dishwashers, and busboys; they were often required to work long hours and at low wages. Even highly educated professionals found that the licenses they had held in Puerto Rico were not honored in the United States; as a result, many had to accept positions below their qualifications in order to remain employed.

Education, which has traditionally been considered a means for immigrant populations to improve their position in society, began to fail the Puerto Rican communities. Access to free university education and other social services was reduced as the economy deteriorated; moreover, the needs of Puerto Rican elementary and high school students were often neglected. The *1976 Report of the United States Civil Rights Commission* concluded that the conditions in public schools were substandard; opportunities for higher education were rare. The Civil Rights Commission also found that Puerto Rican children were often treated unfairly; because their first language was Spanish, they were misidentified as slow learners and kept back in school. Students also complained of being pressured to select basic studies or vocational, rather than college preparatory, tracks. Although federal programs were started in the late 1960s to combat discrimination in education and employment, many were later abandoned because of funding and administrative problems.

In the early part of the century, Puerto Ricans attempted to address such socioeconomic problems by establishing and participating in political and labor organizations that worked for social change. Especially after gaining citizenship in 1917, Puerto Ricans became more involved in local government. In the 1940s and 1950s social and cultural organizations were founded to help ease the tensions between those already settled on the mainland and the large numbers of new arrivals. In the 1960s organizations such as the Puerto Rican Community Development Project were founded to unify old and new members of the community and to take advantage of federal programs and other opportunities for improvement and advancement.

Since the 1960s, there has been an increasing integration of Puerto Ricans into the political mainstream. One example of this is the Democratic official Herman Badillo of New York, who, after serving in the United States Congress for eight years, held several offices in New York city and state government, including deputy mayor of the city. At the same time, the last thirty years have witnessed an increased militancy on the part of some younger Puerto Ricans, especially college students, who are restless with what they perceive as the community's continued dependence on federal money and political alliances with other groups.

In November 1993 Puerto Ricans on the island voted to retain their status as a commonwealth, just as they had in 1967. In voting this way island residents rejected both independence, with its attendant cultural autonomy, and statehood, which would mean increased economic, political, and cultural affiliation with the United States.

As we will see from several of the readings, migrants came to the United States anticipating new political and economic opportunities. For the vast majority, the dream of prosperity and a better life in the United States has not yet been realized.

BEGINNING: Pre-reading/Writing

In a class discussion, speculate about the political, economic, and personal reasons why Puerto Ricans emigrate to the United States. Consider whether the political relationship between Puerto Rico and the United States creates circumstances for Puerto Ricans that are different from those of immigrants from other countries.

The Foraker Act, which was passed in 1900, instituted a civil government for Puerto Rico, under the jurisdiction of an American military governor and an eleven-member executive council with an American majority. The act also designated English as the Island's official language. It remained in effect until 1917, when the Jones Act granted Island residents American citizenship. Puerto Ricans were not allowed to elect their own governor, however, until 1948; they could not write their own constitution until 1950.

⁑

From THE FORAKER ACT

The Governor

Sec. 17. That the official title of the chief executive officer shall be "The Governor of Porto Rico." He shall be appointed by the President, by and with the advice and consent of the Senate; he shall hold his office for a term of four years and until his successor is chosen and qualified unless sooner removed by the President; he shall reside in Porto Rico during his official incumbency, and shall maintain his office at the seat of government; he may grant pardons and reprieves, and remit fines and forfeitures for offenses against the laws of Porto Rico, and respites for offenses against the laws of the United States, until the decision of the President can be ascertained; he shall commission all officers that he may be authorized to appoint, and may veto any legislation enacted, as hereinafter provided; he shall be the commander in chief of the militia, and shall at all times faithfully execute the laws, and he shall in that behalf have all the powers of governors of the Territories of the United States that are not locally inapplicable; and he shall annually, and at such other times as he may be required, make official report of the transactions of the government in Porto Rico, through the Secretary of State, to the President of the United States: *Provided,* That the President may, in his discretion, delegate and assign to him such executive duties and functions as may in pursuance with law be so delegated and assigned.

The Executive Council

Sec. 18. That there shall be appointed by the President, by and with the advice and consent of the Senate, for the period of four years, unless sooner removed by the President, a secretary, an attorney-general, a treasurer, an auditor, a commissioner of the interior, and a commissioner of education, each of whom shall reside in Porto Rico during his official incumbency and have the powers and duties hereinafter provided for them, respectively, and who, together with five other persons of good repute, to be also appointed by the President for a like term of four years, by and with the advice and consent of the Senate, shall constitute an executive council, at least five of whom shall be native inhabitants of Porto Rico, and, in addition to the legislative duties hereinafter imposed upon them as a body, shall exercise such powers and perform such duties as are hereinafter provided for them, respectively, and who shall have power to employ all necessary deputies and assistants for the proper discharge of their duties as such officials and as such executive council. ✠

RESPONDING

1. In a journal entry, summarize these provisions of the Foraker Act in your own words. What duties and responsibilities are given to the governor?

2. Working individually or in a group, discuss the way officials were chosen to govern Puerto Rico before 1948. Who made these appointments? What role did local Puerto Ricans play? Speculate on the reaction of local people to this situation.

3. Imagine that the year is 1947. You are a resident of Puerto Rico. Write a letter to the United States Congress detailing your opinion of the Foraker Act. Or write a letter arguing that Puerto Ricans do or do not deserve the rights and privileges of citizenship.

BERNARDO VEGA

Bernardo Vega was born in Farallon, Puerto Rico, in 1885. During his early years as a tabaquero, *or tobacco worker, Vega participated in the island's first labor union. After leaving Puerto Rico for New York in 1916, he worked for many years as a cigar maker, once again actively participating in the organized labor movement. His involvement in New York's political and social organizations also put him into contact with some of the leading members of the Latino intellectual community in exile, such as the Cuban poet José Martí. Vega spent his final years working for the proindependence movement in Puerto Rico, where he died in 1965.*

Vega's Memoirs *provide a vivid account of the experiences of Puerto Rican workers who settled in New York during the early 1900s. Although he wrote them in the 1940s, the memoirs were not published until after his death. The manuscript version was edited by César Andreu Iglesias, who altered the third-person account to the first person. Juan Flores translated the book into English.*

❖

THE CUSTOMS AND TRADITIONS OF THE *TABAQUEROS* AND WHAT IT WAS LIKE TO WORK IN A CIGAR FACTORY IN NEW YORK CITY

SINCE THE DAY WE HAD OUR STREET CLOTHES STOLEN and had to come home 1
from work in rags, Pepe and I started thinking of quitting work at the munitions plant. But we had no other job in mind, or time to look for one. One day I found Pepe gloomier than a rooster after a cockfight. I tried to console him, but he just broke down, crying his heart out. The job was even more unbearable for him than it was for me. He got sick and gave up.

I kept up that fierce daily battle for another few weeks. But one morning I 2
caught sight of a bunch of rags on fire alongside a powder keg and, had I not grabbed an extinguisher and put out the fire just in time, right there and then I might have taken leave of the world of the living.

For fear of losing my skin, time had come to give notice. Payday was every 3
two weeks, and I had worked only half that. I decided to leave that day no matter what, though I wanted to be sure of collecting what was due me. The only way I would see was to pick a fight with someone and force them to fire me. I chose as my victim the first co-worker who showed up. The foreman pulled us apart

and took us to the office to fire us both. Once I got my pay, I assured the foreman that it was I who had started the trouble and that the other guy was innocent. The foreman shouted, "You son of a bitch!" That was the first time, though certainly not the last, that I was called by that name in the United States.

4   One day a few weeks later I picked up the morning newspaper and felt my heart skip a beat—that same plant had been blown to bits in an explosion!

5   With what savings I had I bought myself some clothes for winter. Having no notion yet what that season would demand, I made the sinful mistake of buying two loud colored suits and an equally flashy overcoat. Friends who had already spent a few winters in New York made fun of my new purchases. So there I was, after all that hardship, in the same old straits—flat broke and without the clothes I needed for winter.

6   It took "El Salvaje," as Ramón Quiñones—another fellow townsman from Cayey and a first-rate *tabaquero*[1]—was called, to get me out of my predicament. Though gentle and good-hearted, he would resort to his fists at the slightest provocation, and was always quick to seize the limelight. He never carried firearms, but tried to solve all his problems with his bare hands. That's how he got the nickname "Wild Man."

7   One day my friend "El Salvaje" took me down to Fuentes & Co., a cigar factory located on Pearl Street, near Fulton Street, in lower Manhattan. I started work immediately, but within a week they had marked down the price of my make of cigar, and I quit.[2] When "El Salvaje" found out, he went down to the shop in person and, as was his custom, had it out with the foreman with his bare fists. He had to pay a fine to stop them from locking him up.

8   As for me, I was actually lucky to leave that job. A few days later I found work at another cigar factory, "El Morito" ("The Little Moor"), on 86th Street off Third Avenue, a few steps from where I was living. At that wonderful place I struck up friendships with a lot of Cubans, Spaniards, and some fellow countrymen, all of whom awakened in me an eagerness to study. Among them, two Cubans remain prominently in my mind. One of them, Juan Bonilla, had been a close friend of José Martí. He was a noted orator and one of the editors of *Patria*, the newspaper founded in New York by the Apostle of the Cuban Revolution himself. The other was T. de Castro Palomino, a man of vast erudition, who had also gained renown for his role in the liberation struggles of the Antilles.

9   Of the Spaniards I remember fondly Maximiliano Olay, still hardly more

---

1. Cigarmaker.
2. Cigar prices varied according to the "make" or *vitola*—the quality of the tobacco and the cigarmakers' reputation. The *vitola* was indicated by the cigar ring.

Cigar factories ranged in size from the *chinchal* (workshop), which might include no more than the master cigarmaker and two or three apprentices, to *fábricas* (factories), which employed from fifty to four hundred workers. Some *fábricas* engaged in all phases of cigar production; in others, called *despalillados*, most of the workers were women, who separated the tobacco leaves from the stems. [Author's note] than a boy in those years, who had had to flee Spain to escape charges of complicity in an anarchist assassination of a leading political figure. He was a loyal friend of many Puerto Rican migrants; more than once I heard him claim that destiny had made him a brother of the Puerto Ricans, for one of them had once saved his life.

Maximiliano was born in Collota, a village in the Asturian mountains of Spain. Two of the Guardia Civil on duty in his town were from Puerto Rico. They were friends of his family, who had watched him grow up from early childhood. As a young man he got himself into serious trouble for political activities. He was arrested and the charges against him would have cost him his head. But one of the Guardia Civil hid him and arranged for his escape. He crossed the border into France and managed to get away to New York. "Now you see why all Puerto Ricans are my brothers," Maximiliano would say.

Another good Spaniard and dear friend of Puerto Ricans was Rufino Alonso, whom they used to call "Primo Bruto" ("Dumb Cousin"). Another of the Puerto Ricans I got to know there and still remember was Juan Hernández, the director of the workers' paper *El Internacional.* There was also the fine writer Enrique Rosario Ortiz, and J. Navas, Tomás Flores, Francisco Guevara, Ramón Rodríguez, Matías Nieves—known as "El Cojo Ravelo" ("Limping Ravelo")— all of whom were active in the cigarworkers' struggle and in the Hispanic community in general.

With workers of this caliber, "El Morito" seemed like a university. At the time the official "reader" was Fernando García. He would read to us for one hour in the morning and one in the afternoon. He dedicated the morning session to current news and events of the day, which he received from the latest wireless information bulletins. The afternoon sessions were devoted to more substantial readings of a political and literary nature. A Committee on Reading suggested the books to be read, and their recommendations were voted on by all the workers in the shop. The readings alternated between works of philosophical, political, or scientific interest, and novels, chosen from the writings of Zola, Dumas, Victor Hugo, Flaubert, Jules Verne, Pierre Loti, Vargas Vila, Pérez Galdós, Palacio Valdés, Dostoyevsky, Gogol, Gorky, or Tolstoy.[3] All these authors were well known to the cigarworkers at the time.

It used to be that a factory reader would choose the texts himself, and they were mostly light reading, like the novels of Pérez Escrich, Luis Val, and the like. But as they developed politically, the workers had more and more to say in the selection. Their preference for works of social theory won out. From then on the readings were most often from books by Gustave LeBon, Ludwig Buchner, Darwin, Marx, Engels, Bakunin.[4] . . . And let me tell you, I never knew a single *tabaquero* who fell asleep.

3. Popular French, Spanish, and Russian novelists of the nineteenth century.
4. Prominent scientists and theorists of the nineteenth century, several of whom—Marx, Engels, and Bakunin—were instrumental in the development of modern socialism.

14 The institution of factory readings made the *tabaqueros* into the most enlightened sector of the working class. The practice began in the factories of Viñas & Co., in Bejucal, Cuba, around 1864. Of course there were readings before then, but they weren't daily. Emigrants to Key West and Tampa introduced the practice into the United States around 1869—at least, I was told that in that year the shop owned by Martínez Ibor in Key West had an official reader.

15 In Puerto Rico the practice spread with the development of cigar production, and it was Cubans and Puerto Ricans who brought it to New York. It is safe to say that there were no factories with Hispanic cigarworkers without a reader. Things were different in English-speaking shops where, as far as I know, no such readings took place.

16 During the readings at "El Morito" and other factories, silence reigned supreme—it was almost like being in church. Whenever we got excited about a certain passage we showed our appreciation by tapping our tobacco cutters on the worktables. Our applause resounded from one end of the shop to the other. Especially when it came to polemical matters no one wanted to miss a word. Whenever someone on the other side of the room had trouble hearing, he would let it be known and the reader would raise his voice and repeat the whole passage in question.

17 At the end of each session there would be a discussion of what had been read. Conversation went from one table to another without our interrupting our work. Though nobody was formally leading the discussion, everyone took turns speaking. When some controversy remained unresolved and each side would stick to a point of view, one of the more educated workers would act as arbiter. And should dates or questions of fact provoke discussion, there was always someone who insisted on going to the *mataburros* or "donkey-slayers"— that's what we called reference books.

18 It was not uncommon for one of the workers to have an encyclopedia right there on his worktable. That's how it was at "El Morito," where Juan Hernández, Palomino, Bonilla, Rosario, and young Olay stood out as the arbiters of discussion. And when a point of contention escaped even their knowledge, the dogfight, as we used to call it, was laid to rest by appealing to the authority of the *mataburro*.

19 I remember times when a *tabaquero* would get so worked up defending his position that he didn't mind losing an hour's work—it was piecework—trying to prove his point. He would quote from the books at hand, and if there weren't any in the shop he'd come back the next day with books from home, or from the public library. The main issues in these discussions centered around different trends in the socialist and anarchist movements.

20 In those years of World War I, a central topic was imperialism and its relation to pacifism. In "El Morito" we had just been reading Henri Barbusse's *Le feu* (*Under Fire*). The hair-raising depiction of life in the trenches gave rise to an endless discussion among the socialists, anarchists, and the handful of Germanophiles in the factory. Earlier we had read *La Hyene Enragée* (*The Trial*

of the Barbarians) by Pierre Loti, one of the writers often read to pass the time. But this particular book did a great deal to disarm the pacifists. The forceful description of the ruins of Rheims and Arras, the destructive avalanche of the Kaiser's soldiers, so graphically depicted, stirred us to thoughts of revenge and gained our deepest sympathy for the Allies. Just like so many of our comrades in both France and Germany, we fell prey to the call to "defend the fatherland," losing sight of the proletarian internationalism on which socialism is founded. Needless to say, Lenin and Bolshevism were still totally unknown in New York at the time.

When the Catholic newspapers in France took up their campaign against [21] Marx and Marxism, we read the rigorous defense made by the socialist Jean Longuet. His articles kindled lively debates among the *tabaqueros*. For a while the sentiment in defense of France, inspired by Barbusse and Loti, began to lose support. The most militant pacifists among us struck back by arguing: "The French and the Germans both represent imperialist capitalism. We workers should not favor either one of them!" But this revolutionary position was again undermined by the reading of the Manifesto of March 1916, signed by the leaders of pacifist internationalism—Jean Grave, Carlo Malato, Paul Reclus, and Peter Kropotkin. This declaration struck a mortal blow to the worldwide anti-imperialist movement. "To talk of peace," it read, "is to play into the hands of the German government. . . . Teutonic aggression is a threat not only to our hopes for social emancipation but to human progress in general. For that reason we, who are antimilitarists, archenemies of war, and ardent partisans of peace and brotherhood among all nations, stand alongside of those who resist."

"Those who resist," of course, were the French. As a result, a growing [22] current of Francophilia spread among socialists. A great majority of *tabaqueros* saw France as the standardbearer of democracy and progress, if not of socialism.

The dominant trend among North American socialists, however, and per- [23] haps among the people of the United States in general, was neutrality. The leading pacifist and anarchist among the Spanish-speaking workers in New York was Pedro Esteves, who put out the paper *Cultura Proletaria*. As I mentioned before, most of the *tabaqueros* believed that the Germans had to be defeated. Many of them enlisted in the French army. Outstanding among them were Juan Sanz and Mario César Miranda, two leaders of the workers' movement who left Puerto Rico and were killed in combat in the first battle of Verdun. Florencio Lumbano, a Puerto Rican cigarworker in New York, also fell on the battlefields of France. Another *tabaquero* to take up arms was Justo Baerga. Years later I was told that he had been seen, old and sickly, in Marseilles.

Many, in fact, are the Puerto Ricans who have fought in defense of other [24] countries. Perhaps for that reason, they have found themselves so alone in their own land. It was right there in "El Morito" that I first heard of the role of the *tabaqueros* in the Cuban wars of independence. There, too, I began to learn of the distinguished contribution our countrymen made to the Cuban revolution. I heard many true stories from the lips of Juan Bonilla and Castro Palomino, who had experienced them first hand. From then on, I was determined to write an account of the participation of Puerto Ricans in the Cuban independence struggle, which after all was a struggle for the independence of Puerto Rico as well.

25 But life among the *tabaqueros* was not all serious and sober. There was a lot of fun, too, especially on the part of the Cuban comrades. Many were the times that, after a stormy discussion, someone would take his turn by telling a hilarious joke. Right away tempers would cool down and the whole shop would burst out laughing.

26 None of the factories was without its happy-go-lucky fellow who would spend the whole time cracking jokes. In "El Morito" our man of good cheer was a Cuban named Angelito, who was known for how little work he did. He would get to the shop in the morning, take his place at his worktable, roll a cigar, light it, and then go change his clothes. When he returned to his table he would take the cigar from his mouth and tell his first joke. The co-workers nearest him would laugh, and after every cigar he'd tell another joke. He would announce when he had made enough cigars to cover that day's rent. Then he'd set out to roll enough to take care of his expenses. Once this goal was reached, he wouldn't make one more cigar, but would leave his workplace, wash up, get dressed, and head for the Broadway theaters.

27 A good-looking man, Angelito was tall and slender. He had a charming face and was an elegant dresser. He had arrived in the United States with a single, fixed idea in mind, which he admitted openly to anyone who would listen: he wanted to hook up with a rich woman. Pursuing his prey, he would walk up and down the streets, looking, as he himself would say, for his lottery prize. And the truth is that it didn't take him long to find it. A few months after I started at "El Morito" he landed a rich girl, who was beautiful and a violinist to boot. He married her and lived—in his own words—like a prince. But he never forgot us: time and again he would show up the shop to tell us of his exploits and bless us with the latest addition to his vast repertoire of jokes.

28 Around that time news reached us at "El Morito" of a major strike in the sugar industry in Puerto Rico. A call went out for a rally in solidarity with the strikers. It took place on 85th Street near Lexington Avenue, and was attended by over a hundred *tabaqueros*, mostly Puerto Ricans. Santiago Rodríguez presided, and Juan Fonseca served as secretary. Many of those attending stood up to speak, including Ventura Mijón, Herminio Colón, Angel María Dieppa, Enrique Plaza, Pedro San Miguel, Miguel Rivera, Alfonso Dieppa, Rafael Correa, and Antonio Vega. The last mentioned immediately attracted my attention because of the way he spoke, and even more because of his appearance.

29 While I was listening to Antonio Vega I recalled how my father used to talk all the time about his lost brother, who had never been seen or heard from since he was very young. I'm not sure if it was the memory that did it, but I know I felt deeply moved by the man who bore my last name. He was a tall fellow, with a broad forehead, a full head of gray hair, a big handle-bar mustache,

green eyes, and an oval-shaped face. . . . When I went up to him he jumped to his feet with the ease of an ex-soldier and responded very courteously when I congratulated him for his speech. We then struck up a conversation, at the end of which we hugged each other emotionally. He was none other than my father's long lost brother. ✤

RESPONDING

1. In a journal entry, describe the education Vega received in the factory. How did it compare to your own, more traditional education? What are the strengths and weaknesses of each?

2. Working individually or in a group, design your own curriculum for an adult literacy class at your local library. Choose readings and discussion topics. Compare your choices with those of the *tabaqueros.*

3. Vega says, "I remember times when a *tabaquero* would get so worked up defending his position that he didn't mind losing an hour's work—it was piecework—trying to prove his point. He would quote from the books at hand, and if there weren't any in the shop he'd come back the next day with books from home, or from the public library" (paragraph 19). Why did the workers become so engaged in these issues? In an essay, explore the lessons we can learn from this example to promote literacy and improve our educational system.

4. Think about the image of blue-collar workers that you have formed from your own experience and from their portrayal in books and in the media. Compare that image to Vega and his fellow workers in the cigar factory at the turn of the century. Why did he call the *tabaqueros* "the most enlightened sector of the working class" (paragraph 14)? In an essay explain why education and political ideas were so important to these particular people.

JESUS COLON

*Jesús Colón, born in Puerto Rico, immigrated to the United States around
1916, as a stowaway aboard ship. He spent his early years working at odd
jobs in order to support himself, and later drew on these experiences for a
column for the* Daily Worker. *His column became the source of many of the
essays in* A Puerto Rican in New York.*

*Throughout this collection, Colón explores the tension between what he
expected to find in the United States and what he actually discovered. As a
black Puerto Rican emigré, Colón had to confront American society's prejudices
against his language and his race. In the following selection he describes his
reaction to being judged not by the quality of his work but by the color of his
skin.*

⁂

KIPLING AND I

1   SOMETIMES I PASS DEBEVOISE PLACE at the corner of Willoughby Street. . . . I
look at the old wooden house, gray and ancient, the house where I used to live
some forty years ago. . . .

2   My room was on the second floor at the corner. On hot summer nights I
would sit at the window reading by the electric light from the street lamp which
was almost at a level with the window sill.

3   It was nice to come home late during the winter, look for some scrap of
old newspaper, some bits of wood and a few chunks of coal and start a sparkling
fire in the chunky fourlegged coal stove. I would be rewarded with an intimate
warmth as little by little the pigmy stove became alive, puffing out its sides, hot
and red, like the crimson cheeks of a Santa Claus.

4   My few books were in a soap box nailed to the wall. But my most prized
possession in those days was a poem I had bought in a five and ten cent store
on Fulton Street. (I wonder what has become of these poems, maxims and
sayings of wise men that they used to sell at the five and ten cent stores?) The
poem was printed on gold paper and mounted on a gilded frame ready to be
hung in a conspicuous place in the house. I bought one of those fancy silken
picture cords finishing in a rosette to match the color of the frame.

5   I was seventeen. This poem to me then seemed to summarize the wisdom
of all the sages that ever lived in one poetical nutshell. It was what I was looking
for, something to guide myself by, a way of life, a compendium of the wise, the
true and the beautiful. All I had to do was to live according to the counsel of
the poem and follow its instructions and I would be a perfect man—the useful,
the good, the true human being. I was very happy that day, forty years ago.

The poem had to have the most prominent place in the room. Where could   6
I hang it? I decided that the best place for the poem was on the wall right by
the entrance to the room. No one coming in and out would miss it. Perhaps
someone would be interested enough to read it and drink the profound waters
of its message. . . .

Every morning as I prepared to leave, I stood in front of the poem and read   7
it over and over again, sometimes half a dozen times. I let the sonorous music
of the verse carry me away. I brought with me a handwritten copy as I stepped
out every morning looking for work, repeating verses and stanzas from memory
until the whole poem came to be part of me. Other days my lips kept repeating
a single verse of the poem at intervals throughout the day.

In the subways I loved to compete with the shrill noises of the many wheels   8
below by chanting the lines of the poem. People stared at me moving my lips
as though I were in a trance. I looked back with pity. They were not so fortunate
as I who had as a guide to direct my life a great poem to make me wise, useful
and happy.

And I chanted: 9

> If you can keep your head when all about you
> Are losing theirs and blaming it on you . . .
>
> If you can wait and not be tired by waiting
> Or being hated don't give way to hating . . .
>
> If you can make one heap of all your winnings
> And risk it on a turn of pitch and toss . . .
> And lose and start again at your beginnings . . .

"If," by Kipling, was the poem. At seventeen, my evening prayer and my   10
first morning thought. I repeated it every day with the resolution to live up to
the very last line of that poem.

I would visit the government employment office on Jay Street. The con-   11
versations among the Puerto Ricans on the large wooden benches in the
employment office were always on the same subject. How to find a decent place
to live. How they would not rent to Negroes or Puerto Ricans. How Negroes
and Puerto Ricans were given the pink slips first at work.

From the employment office I would call door to door at the piers, factories   12
and storage houses in the streets under the Brooklyn and Manhattan bridges.
"Sorry, nothing today." It seemed to me that "today" was a continuation and
combination of all the yesterdays, todays and tomorrows.

From the factories I would go to the restaurants looking for a job as a porter   13
or dishwasher. At least I would eat and be warm in a kitchen.

"Sorry" . . . "Sorry" . . .   14

Sometimes I was hired at ten dollars a week, ten hours a day including   15
Sundays and holidays. One day off during the week. My work was that of three

men: dishwasher, porter, busboy. And to clear the sidewalk of snow and slush "when you have nothing else to do." I was to be appropriately humble and grateful not only to the owner but to everybody else in the place.

16   If I rebelled at insults or at a pointed innuendo or just the inhuman amount of work, I was unceremoniously thrown out and told to come "next week for your pay." "Next week" meant weeks of calling for the paltry dollars owed me. The owners relished this "next week."

17   I clung to my poem as to a faith. Like a potent amulet, my precious poem was clenched in the fist of my right hand inside my second-hand overcoat. Again and again I declaimed aloud a few precious lines when discouragement and disillusionment threatened to overwhelm me.

> If you can force your heart and nerve and sinew
> To serve your turn long after you are gone . . .

18   The weeks of unemployment and hard knocks turned into months. I continued to find two or three days of work here and there. And I continued to be thrown out when I rebelled at the ill treatment, overwork and insults. I kept pounding the streets looking for a place where they would treat me half decently, where my devotion to work and faith in Kipling's poem would be appreciated. I remember the worn out shoes I bought in a second-hand store on Myrtle Avenue at the corner of Adams Street. The round holes in the soles that I tried to cover with pieces of carton were no match for the frigid knives of the unrelenting snow.

19   One night I returned late after a long day of working for work. I was hungry. My room was dark and cold. I wanted to warm my numb body. I lit a match and began looking for some scraps of wood and a piece of paper to start a fire. I searched all over the floor. No wood, no paper. As I stood up, the glimmering flicker of the dying match was reflected in the glass surface of the framed poem. I unhooked the poem from the wall. I reflected for a minute, a minute that felt like an eternity. I took the frame apart, placing the square glass upon the small table. I tore the gold paper on which the poem was printed, threw its pieces inside the stove and placing the small bits of wood from the frame on top of the paper I lit it, adding soft and hard coal as the fire began to gain strength and brightness.

20   I watched how the lines of the poem withered into ashes inside the small stove. ✤

RESPONDING

1. Read the entire poem "If—," which appears below. In a journal entry, discuss how realistic you find its premise. Do you believe what the poem promises? Give examples to support your opinion.

IF—

If you can keep your head when all about you
    Are losing theirs and blaming it on you;
If you can trust yourself when all men doubt you,
    But make allowance for their doubting too:
If you can wait and not be tired by waiting,
    Or being lied about, don't deal in lies,
Or being hated, don't give way to hating,
    And yet don't look too good, nor talk too wise;

If you can dream—and not make dreams your master;
    If you can think—and not make thoughts your aim,
If you can meet with Triumph and Disaster
    And treat those two impostors just the same:
If you can bear to hear the truth you've spoken
    Twisted by knaves to make a trap for fools,
Or watch the things you gave your life to, broken,
    And stoop and build 'em up with worn-out tools;

IF—

If you can make one heap of all your winnings
    And risk it on one turn of pitch-and-toss,
And lose, and start again at your beginnings
    And never breathe a word about your loss:
If you can force your heart and nerve and sinew
    To serve your turn long after they are gone,
And so hold on when there is nothing in you
    Except the Will which says to them: "Hold on!"

If you can talk with crowds and keep your virtue,
　　Or walk with Kings—nor lose the common touch,
If neither foes nor loving friends can hurt you,
　　If all men count with you, but none too much:
If you can fill the unforgiving minute
　　With sixty seconds' worth of distance run,
Yours is the Earth and everything that's in it,
　　And—which is more—you'll be a Man, my son!

2.　Colón has many problems earning a living in New York City. Working individually or in a group, list Colón's difficulties living and working in New York. Use evidence from the reading to discuss the reasons for his problems. Share your conclusions with the class.

3.　After reading Colón's work, one could argue that he must confront a system where material things are more important than human suffering. Write an essay agreeing or disagreeing with this view of American society. You may consider his experience and the historical period he wrote about or deal with the issue in relation to contemporary society.

4.　Why does Colón burn the poem at the end of the selection? Write an essay explaining why a reader might claim that it is a symbolic as well as an actual act.

PIRI THOMAS

*Piri Thomas, born in Spanish Harlem in 1928, began writing while in prison
for armed robbery. His books include* Down These Mean Streets *(1967);*
Savior, Savior Hold My Hand *(1972);* Seven Times Long *(1974); and*
The View from El Barrio *(1978).*

The excerpt that follows is from Down These Mean Streets. *The stories
in this book, describing Thomas's involvement with street gangs and drug
addiction, are often raw in their use of language, sexually explicit and violent.
However, in this story Thomas uses a more nostalgic, more pensive tone to
describe gatherings in the small New York apartment that his family shared.
The passage has as its focus the author's mother and her memories of the Island
she left behind.*

⌗

PUERTO RICAN PARADISE

POPPA DIDN'T TALK TO ME the next day. Soon he didn't talk much to anyone. 1
He lost his night job—I forget why, and probably it was worth forgetting—and
went back on home relief. It was 1941, and the Great Hunger called Depression
was still down on Harlem.

But there was still the good old WPA. If a man was poor enough, he could 2
dig a ditch for the government. Now Poppa was poor enough again.

The weather turned cold one more time, and so did our apartment. In the 3
summer the cooped-up apartments in Harlem seem to catch all the heat and
improve on it. It's the same in the winter. The cold, plastered walls embrace
that cold from outside and make it a part of the apartment, till you don't know
whether it's better to freeze out in the snow or by the stove, where four jets,
wide open, spout futile, blue-yellow flames. It's hard on the rats, too.

Snow was falling. "My *Cristo*," Momma said, "*qué frío*. Doesn't that landlord 4
have any *corazón*?[1] Why don't he give more heat?" I wondered how Pops was
making out working a pick and shovel in that falling snow.

Momma picked up a hammer and began to beat the beat-up radiator that's 5
copped a plea from so many beatings. Poor steam radiator, how could it give
out heat when it was freezing itself? The hollow sounds Momma beat out of it
brought echoes from other freezing people in the building. Everybody picked

1. heart

up the beat and it seemed a crazy, good idea. If everybody took turns beating on the radiators, everybody could keep warm from the exercise.

6   We drank hot cocoa and talked about summertime. Momma talked about Puerto Rico and how great it was, and how she'd like to go back one day, and how it was warm all the time there and no matter how poor you were over there, you could always live on green bananas, *bacalao*,[2] and rice and beans. "*Dios mío*," she said, "I don't think I'll ever see my island again."

7   "Sure you will, Mommie," said Miriam, my kid sister. She was eleven. "Tell us, tell us all about Porto Rico."

8   "It's not Porto Rico, it's Puerto Rico," said Momma.

9   "Tell us, Moms," said nine-year-old James, "about Puerto Rico."

10   "Yeah, Mommie," said six-year-old José.

11   Even the baby, Paulie, smiled.

12   Moms copped that wet-eyed look and began to dream-talk about her *isla verde*,[3] Moses' land of milk and honey.

13   "When I was a little girl," she said, "I remember the getting up in the morning and getting the water from the river and getting the wood for the fire and the quiet of the greenlands and the golden color of the morning sky, the grass wet from the *lluvia*[4] . . . *Ai, Dios*, the *coquís*[5] and the *pajaritos*[6] making all the *música* . . ."

14   "Mommie, were you poor?" asked Miriam.

15   "*Sí, muy pobre*, but very happy. I remember the hard work and the very little bit we had, but it was a good little bit. It counted very much. Sometimes when you have too much, the good gets lost within and you have to look very hard. But when you have a little, then the good does not have to be looked for so hard."

16   "Moms," I asked, "did everybody love each other—I mean, like if everybody was worth something, not like if some weren't important because they were poor—you know what I mean?"

17   "*Bueno hijo*, you have people everywhere who, because they have more, don't remember those who have very little. But in Puerto Rico those around you share *la pobreza*[7] with you and they love you, because only poor people can understand poor people. I like *los Estados Unidos*, but it's sometimes a cold place to live—not because of the winter and the landlord not giving heat but because of the snow in the hearts of the people."

18   "Moms, didn't our people have any money or land?" I leaned forward, hoping to hear that my ancestors were noble princes born in Spain.

19   "Your grandmother and grandfather had a lot of land, but they lost that."

20   "How come, Moms?"

2. codfish
3. green island
4. rain

5. small treetoads
6. little birds
7. poverty

"Well, in those days there was nothing of what you call *contratos*,[8] and when   21
you bought or sold something, it was on your word and a handshake, and that's
the way your *abuelos*[9] bought their land and then lost it."

"Is that why we ain't got nuttin' now?" James asked pointedly.   22

"Oh, it—"   23

The door opened and put an end to the kitchen yak. It was Poppa coming   24
home from work. He came into the kitchen and brought all the cold with him.
Poor Poppa, he looked so lost in the clothes he had on. A jacket and coat,
sweaters on top of sweaters, two pairs of long johns, two pairs of pants, two
pairs of socks, and a woolen cap. And under all that he was cold. His eyes were
cold; his ears were red with pain. He took off his gloves and his fingers were
stiff with cold.

"*Cómo está?*"[10] said Momma. "I will make you coffee."   25

Poppa said nothing. His eyes were running hot frozen tears. He worked his   26
fingers and rubbed his ears, and the pain made him make faces. "Get me some
snow, Piri," he said finally.

I ran to the window, opened it, and scraped all the snow on the sill into   27
one big snowball and brought it to him. We all watched in frozen wonder as
Poppa took that snow and rubbed it on his ears and hands.

"Gee, Pops, don't it hurt?" I asked.   28

"*Sí*, but it's good for it. It hurts a little first, but it's good for the frozen   29
parts."

I wondered why.   30

"How was it today?" Momma asked.   31

"Cold. My God, ice cold."   32

Gee, I thought, *I'm sorry for you, Pops. You gotta suffer like this.*   33

"It was not always like this," my father said to the cold walls. "It's all the   34
fault of the damn depression."

"Don't say 'damn,'" Momma said.   35

"Lola, I say 'damn' because that's what it is—*damn.*"   36

And Momma kept quiet. She knew it was "damn."   37

My father kept talking to the walls. Some of the words came out loud,   38
others stayed inside. I caught the inside ones—the damn WPA, the damn
depression, the damn home relief, the damn poorness, the damn cold, the damn
crummy apartments, the damn look on his damn kids, living so damn damned
and his not being able to do a damn thing about it.

And Momma looked at Poppa and at us and thought about her Puerto Rico   39
and maybe being there where you didn't have to wear a lot of extra clothes and

---

8. contracts
9. grandparents
10. How are you?

feel so full of damns, and how when she was a little girl all the green was wet from the *lluvias.*

40   And Poppa looking at Momma and us, thinking how did he get trapped and why did he love us so much that he dug in damn snow to give us a piece of chance? And why couldn't he make it from home, maybe, and keep running?

41   And Miriam, James, José, Paulie, and me just looking and thinking about snowballs and Puerto Rico and summertime in the street and whether we were gonna live like this forever and not know enough to be sorry for ourselves.

42   The kitchen all of a sudden felt warmer to me, like being all together made it like we wanted it to be. Poppa made it into the toilet and we could hear everything he did, and when he finished, the horsey gurgling of the flushed toilet told us he'd soon be out. I looked at the clock and it was time for "Jack Armstrong, the All-American Boy."

43   José, James, and I got some blankets and, like Indians, huddled around the radio digging the All-American Jack and his adventures, while Poppa ate dinner quietly. Poppa was funny about eating—like when he ate, nobody better bother him. When Poppa finished, he came into the living room and stood there looking at us. We smiled at him, and he stood there looking at us.

44   All of a sudden he yelled, "How many wanna play 'Major Bowes' Amateur Hour'?"

45   "Hoo-ray! Yeah, we wanna play," said José.

46   "Okay, first I'll make some taffy outta molasses, and the one who wins first prize gets first choice at the biggest piece, okay?"

47   "Yeah, hoo-ray, *chevere.*"

48   *Gee, Pops, you're great,* I thought, *you're the swellest, the bestest Pops in the whole world, even though you don't understand us too good.*

49   When the candy was all ready, everybody went into the living room. Poppa came in with a broom and put an empty can over the stick. It became a microphone, just like on the radio.

50   "Pops, can I be Major Bowes?" I asked.

51   "Sure, Piri," and the floor was mine.

52   "Ladies and gentlemen," I announced, "tonight we present 'Major Bowes' Amateur Hour,' and for our first number—"

53   "Wait a minute, son, let me get my ukulele," said Poppa. "We need music."

54   Everybody clapped their hands and Pops came back with his ukulele.

55   "The first con-tes-tant we got is Miss Miriam Thomas."

56   "Oh no, not me first, somebody else goes first," said Miriam, and she hid behind Momma.

57   "Let me! Let me!" said José.

58   Everybody clapped.

59   "What are you gonna sing, sir?" I asked.

60   "Tell the people his name," said Poppa.

61   "Oh yeah. Presenting Mr. José Thomas. And what are you gonna sing, sir?"

I handed José the broom with the can on top and sat back. He sang well   62
and everybody clapped.

Everyone took a turn, and we all agreed that two-year-old Paulie's "gurgle,   63
gurgle" was the best song, and Paulie got first choice at the candy. Everybody
got candy and eats and thought how good it was to be together, and Moms
thought that it was wonderful to have such a good time even if she wasn't in
Puerto Rico where the grass was wet with *lluvia*. Poppa thought about how cold
it was gonna be tomorrow, but then he remembered tomorrow was Sunday and
he wouldn't have to work, and he said so and Momma said "*Sí*," and the talk
got around to Christmas and how maybe things would get better.

The next day the Japanese bombed Pearl Harbor.   64

"My God," said Poppa. "We're at war."   65

"*Dios Mío*," said Momma.   66

I turned to James. "Can you beat that," I said.   67

"Yeah," he nodded. "What's it mean?"   68

"What's it mean?" I said. "You gotta ask, dopey? It means a rumble is on,   69
and a big one, too."

I wondered if the war was gonna make things worse than they were for us.   70
But it didn't. A few weeks later Poppa got a job in an airplane factory. "How
about that?" he said happily. "Things are looking up for us."

Things *were* looking up for us, but it had taken a damn war to do it. A lousy   71
rumble had to get called so we could start to live better. I thought, *How do you
figure this crap out?*

I couldn't figure it out, and after a while I stopped thinking about it. Life   72
in the streets didn't change much. The bitter cold was followed by the sticky
heat; I played stickball, marbles, and Johnny-on-the-Pony, copped girls' drawers
and blew pot. War or peace—what difference did it really make? ✤

RESPONDING

1. Sometimes when we are unhappy with our present circumstances we like
   to think about a time when we were happier. In a journal entry, describe a
   time when you compared your situation in the present to a happier time in
   the past. Were your memories accurate or did you idealize the past? Did
   your memories help you or hinder you in accepting conditions in the
   present? What role do such memories play in the Thomas family?

2. The Thomas family has few material comforts, but family members contribute to each other's comfort. Working individually or in a group, list the
   family's activities. Discuss how these compensate or fail to compensate for
   some of the difficulties of their living conditions. How does your family or

the family of someone you know provide financial and emotional support for its members?

3. Using examples from the reading, write an essay describing Thomas's mother's life in Puerto Rico and contrast it with the situation she finds herself in in Harlem. Consider whether Thomas's mother's memories of Puerto Rico are realistic. He calls the chapter "Puerto Rican Paradise." Do you think this title descriptive or ironic?

4. Mrs. Thomas said, "only poor people can understand poor people" (paragraph 17). Does this mean that only by being a member of a group can you understand the experience of someone in that group? In an essay, argue for or against this position.

NICHOLASA MOHR

*Nicholasa Mohr, who was born in New York in 1935, studied at the Brooklyn
Museum Art School and the Pratt School. Between 1952 and 1967 she worked
as a painter and printmaker and taught in the New York public schools. Since
1972 she has held lectureships and visiting appointments in creative writing,
Puerto Rican studies, and art at several universities, including the State
University of New York at Stony Brook, the University of Illinois, and the
University of Wisconsin.* Mohr's publications include Nilda *(1973)*, El Bronx
Remembered: A Novella and Stories *(1975)*, In Nueva York *(1977)*,
Rituals of Survival: A Women's Portfolio *(1985), and* Going Home
1986).

"A Thanksgiving Celebration," a part of Mohr's collection Rituals of
Survival, *explores the way in which one woman relies on her creativity and
strength of will to gain a sense of control over her decaying environment.*

⸭

A THANKSGIVING CELEBRATION
(AMY)

AMY SAT ON HER BED THINKING. Gary napped soundly in his crib, which was
placed right next to her bed. The sucking sound he made as he chewed on his
thumb interrupted her thoughts from time to time. Amy glanced at Gary and
smiled. He was her constant companion now; he shared her bedroom and was
with her during those frightening moments when, late into the night and early
morning, she wondered if she could face another day just like the one she had
safely survived. Amy looked at the small alarm clock on the bedside table. In
another hour or so it would be time to wake Gary and give him his milk, then
she had just enough time to shop and pick up the others, after school.

She heard the plopping sound of water dropping into a full pail. Amy
hurried into the bathroom, emptied the pail into the toilet, then replaced it so
that the floor remained dry. Last week she had forgotten, and the water had
overflowed out of the pail and onto the floor, leaking down into Mrs. Wynn's
bathroom. Now, Mrs. Wynn was threatening to take her to small claims court,
if the landlord refused to fix the damage done to her bathroom ceiling and
wallpaper. All right, Amy shrugged, she would try calling the landlord once
more. She was tired of the countless phone calls to plead with them to come
and fix the leak in the roof.

"Yes, Mrs. Guzman, we got your message and we'll send somebody over.
Yes, just as soon as we can . . . we got other tenants with bigger problems,

you know. We are doing our best, we'll get somebody over; you gotta be patient . . ."

4   Time and again they had promised, but no one had ever showed up. And it was now more than four mouths that she had been forced to live like this. Damn, Amy walked into her kitchen, they never refuse the rent for that, there's somebody ready any time! Right now, this was the best she could do. The building was still under rent control and she had enough room. Where else could she go? No one in a better neighborhood would rent to her, not the way things were.

5   She stood by the window, leaning her side against the molding, and looked out. It was a crisp sunny autumn day, mild for the end of November. She remembered it was the eve of Thanksgiving and felt a tightness in her chest. Amy took a deep breath, deciding not to worry about that right now.

6   Rows and rows of endless streets scattered with abandoned buildings and small houses stretched out for miles. Some of the blocks were almost entirely leveled, except for clumps of partial structures charred and blackened by fire. From a distance they looked like organic masses pushing their way out of the earth. Garbage, debris, shattered glass, bricks and broken, discarded furniture covered the ground. Rusting carcasses of cars that had been stripped down to the shell shone and glistened a bright orange under the afternoon sun.

7   There were no people to be seen nor traffic, save for a group of children jumping on an old filthy mattress that had been ripped open. They were busy pulling the stuffing out of the mattress and tossing it about playfully. Nearby, several stray dogs searched the garbage for food. One of the boys picked up a brick, then threw it at the dogs, barely missing them. Reluctantly, the dogs moved on.

8   Amy signed and swallowed, it was all getting closer and closer. It seemed as if only last month, when she had looked out of this very window, all of that was much further away; in fact, she recalled feeling somewhat removed and safe. Now the decay was creeping up to this area. The fire engine sirens screeching and screaming in the night reminded her that the devastation was constant, never stopping even for a night's rest. Amy was fearful of living on the top floor. Going down four flights to safety with the kids in case of a fire was another source of worry for her. She remembered how she had argued with Charlie when they had first moved in.

9   "All them steps to climb with Michele and Carlito, plus carrying the carriage for Carlito, is too much."

10   "Come on baby," Charlie had insisted "it's only temporary. The rent's cheaper and we can save something towards buying our own place. Come on . . ."

11   That was seven years ago. There were two more children now, Lisabeth and Gary; and she was still here, without Charlie.

12   "Soon it'll come right to this street and to my doorstep. God Almighty!" Amy whispered. It was like a plague: a disease for which there seemed to be no

cure, no prevention. Gangs of youngsters occupied empty store fronts and basements; derelicts, drunk or wasted on drugs, positioned themselves on street corners and in empty doorways. Every day she saw more abandoned and burned-out sections.

As Amy continued to look out, a feeling that she had been in this same 13 situation before, a long time ago, startled her. The feeling of déjà vu, so real to her, reminded Amy quite vividly of the dream she had last night. In that dream, she had been standing in the center of a circle of little girls. She herself was very young and they were all singing a rhyme. In a soft whisper, Amy sang the rhyme: "London Bridge is falling down, falling down, falling down, London Bridge is falling down, my fair lady. . . ." She stopped and saw herself once again in her dream, picking up her arms and chanting, "Wave your arms and fly away, fly away, fly away . . ."

She stood in the middle of the circle waving her arms, first gently, then 14 more forcefully, until she was flapping them. The other girls stared silently at her. Slowly, Amy had felt herself elevated above the circle, higher and higher until she could barely make out the human figures below. Waving her arms like the wings of a bird, she began to fly. A pleasant breeze pushed her gently, and she glided along, passing through soft white clouds into an intense silence. Then she saw it. Beneath her, huge areas were filled with crumbling buildings and large caverns; miles of destruction spread out in every direction. Amy had felt herself suspended in this silence for a moment and then she began to fall. She flapped her arms and legs furiously, trying to clutch at the air, hoping for a breeze, something to get her going again, but there was nothing. Quickly she fell, faster and faster, as the ground below her swirled and turned, coming closer and closer, revealing destroyed, burned buildings, rubble and a huge dark cavern. In a state of hysteria, Amy had fought against the loss of control and helplessness, as her body descended into the large black hole and had woken up with a start just before she hit bottom.

Amy stepped away from the window for a moment, almost out of breath 15 as she recollected the fear she had felt in her dream. She walked over to the sink and poured herself a glass of water.

"That's it, Europe and the war," she said aloud. "In the movies, just like 16 my dream."

Amy clearly remembered how she had sat as a very little girl in a local 17 movie theatre with her mother and watched horrified at the scenes on the screen. Newsreels showed entire cities almost totally devastated. Exactly as it had been in her dream, she recalled seeing all the destruction caused by warfare. Names like "Munich, Nuremburg, Berlin" and "the German people" identified the areas. Most of the streets were empty, except for the occasional small groups of people who rummaged about, searching among the ruins and huge piles of debris, sharing the spoils with packs of rats who scavenged at a safe distance. Some people pulled wagons and baby carriages loaded with bundles and household goods. Others carried what they owned on their backs.

18   Amy remembered turning to her mother, asking, "What was going on? Mami, who did this? Why did they do it? Who are those people living there?"

19   "The enemy, that's who," her mother had whispered emphatically. "Bad people who started the war against our country and did terrible things to other people and to us. That's where your papa was for so long, fighting in the army. Don't you remember, Amy?"

20   "What kinds of things, Mami? Who were the other people they did bad things to?"

21   "Don't worry about them things. These people got what they deserved. Besides, they are getting help from us, now that we won the war. There's a plan to help them, even though they don't deserve no help from us."

22   Amy had persisted. "Are there any little kids there? Do they go to school? Do they live in them holes?"

23   "Shh . . . let me hear the rest of the news . . ." her mother had responded, annoyed. Amy had sat during the remainder of the double feature, wondering where those people lived and all about the kids there. And she continued to wonder and worry for several days, until one day she forgot all about it.

24   Amy sipped from the glass she held, then emptied most of the water back into the sink. She sat and looked around at her small kitchen. The ceiling was peeling and flakes of paint had fallen on the kitchen table. The entire apartment was in urgent need of a thorough plastering and paint job. She blinked and shook her head, and now? Who are we now? What have I done? Who is the enemy? Is there a war? Are we at war? Amy suppressed a loud chuckle.

25   "Nobody answered my questions then, and nobody's gonna answer them now," she spoke out loud.

26   Amy still wondered and groped for answers about Charlie. No one could tell her what really happened . . . how he had felt and what he was thinking before he died. Almost two years had gone by, but she was still filled with an overwhelming sense of loneliness. That day was just like so many other days; they were together, planning about the kids, living from one crisis to the next, fighting, barely finding the time to make love without being exhausted; then late that night, it was all over. Charlie's late again, Amy had thought, and didn't even call me. She was angry when she heard the doorbell. He forgot the key again. Dammit, Charlie! You would forget your head if it weren't attached to you!

27   They had stood there before her; both had shown her their badges, but only one had spoken.

28   "Come in . . . sit down, won't you."

29   "You better sit down, miss." The stranger told her very calmly and soberly that Charlie was dead.

30   "On the Bruckner Boulevard Expressway . . . head on collision . . . dead on arrival . . . didn't suffer too long . . . nobody was with him, but we found his wallet."

31   Amy had protested and argued—No way! They were lying to her. But

after a while she knew they brought the truth to her, and Charlie wasn't coming back.

Tomorrow would be the second Thanksgiving without him and one she could not celebrate. Celebrate with what? Amy stood and walked over and opened the refrigerator door. She had enough bread, a large pitcher of powdered milk which she had flavored with Hershey's cocoa and powdered sugar. There was plenty of peanut butter and some graham crackers she had kept fresh by sealing them in a plastic bag. For tonight she had enough chopped meat and macaroni. But tomorrow? What could she buy for tomorrow? 32

Amy shut the refrigerator door and reached over to the money tin set way back on one of the shelves. Carefully she took out the money and counted every cent. There was no way she could buy a turkey, even a small one. She still had to manage until the first; she needed every penny just to make it to the next check. Things were bad, worse than they had ever been. In the past, when things were rough, she had turned to Charlie and sharing had made it all easier. Now there was no one. She resealed the money tin and put it away. 33

Amy had thought of calling the lawyers once more. What good would that do? What can they do for me? Right now . . . today! 34

"These cases take time before we get to trial. We don't want to take the first settlement they offer. That wouldn't do you or the children any good. You have a good case, the other driver was at fault. He didn't have his license or the registration, and we have proof he was drinking. His father is a prominent judge who doesn't want that kind of publicity. I know . . . yes, things are rough, but just hold on a little longer. We don't want to accept a poor settlement and risk your future and the future of your children, do we?" Mr. Silverman of Silverman, Knapp and Ullman was handling the case personally. "By early Spring we should be making a date for trial . . . just hang in there a bit longer . . ." And so it went every time she called: the promise that in just a few more months she could hope for relief, some money, enough to live like people. 35

Survivor benefits had not been sufficient, and since they had not kept up premium payments on Charlie's G.I. insurance policy, she had no other income. Amy was given a little more assistance from the Aid to Dependent Children agency. Somehow she had managed so far. 36

The two food stores that extended her credit were still waiting for Amy to settle overdue accounts. In an emergency she could count on a few friends; they would lend her something, but not for this, not for Thanksgiving dinner. 37

She didn't want to go to Papo and Mary's again. She knew her brother meant well, and that she always had an open invitation. They're good people, but we are five more mouths to feed, plus they've been taking care of Papa all these years, ever since Mami died. Enough is enough. Amy shut her eyes. I want my own dinner this year, just for my family, for me and the kids. 38

If I had the money, I'd make a dinner tomorrow and invite Papa and Lou Ann from downstairs and her kids. She's been such a good friend to us. I'd get a gallon of cider and a bottle of wine . . . a large cake at the bakery by 39

Alexander's, some dried fruits and nuts . . . even a holiday centerpiece for the table. Yes, it would be my dinner for us and my friends. I might even invite Jimmy. She hadn't seen Jimmy for a long time. Must be over six months . . . almost a year? He worked with Charlie at the plant. After Charlie's death, Jimmy had come by often, but Amy was not ready to see another man, not just then, so she discouraged him. From time to time, she thought of Jimmy and hoped he would visit her again.

40   Amy opened her eyes and a sinking feeling flowed through her, as she looked down at the chips of paint spread out on the kitchen table. Slowly, Amy brushed them with her hand, making a neat pile.

41   These past few months, she had seriously thought of going out to work. Before she had Michele, she had worked as a clerk-typist for a large insurance company, but that was almost ten years ago. She would have to brush up on her typing and math. Besides, she didn't know if she could earn enough to pay for a sitter. She couldn't leave the kids alone; Gary wasn't even three and Michele had just turned nine. Amy had applied for part-time work as a teacher's aide, but when she learned that her check from Aid to Dependent Children could be discontinued, she withdrew her application. Better to go on like this until the case comes to trial.

42   Amy choked back the tears. I can't let myself get like this. I just can't! Lately, she had begun to find comfort at the thought of never waking up again. What about my kids, then? I must do something. I have to. Tomorrow is going to be for us, just us, our day.

43   Her thoughts went back to her own childhood and the holiday dinners with her family. They had been poor, but there was always food. We used to have such good times. Amy remembered the many stories her grandmother used to tell them. She spoke about her own childhood on a farm in a rural area of Puerto Rico. Her grandmother's stories were about the animals, whom she claimed to know personally and very well. Amy laughed, recalling that most of the stories her grandmother related were too impossible to be true, such as a talking goat who saved the town from a flood, and the handsome mouse and beautiful lady beetle who fell in love, got married and had the biggest and fanciest wedding her grandmother had ever attended. Her grandmother was very old and had died before Amy was ten. Amy had loved her best, more than her own parents, and she still remembered the old woman quite clearly.

44   "Abuelita, did them things really happen? How come them animals talked? Animals don't talk. Everybody knows that."

45   "Oh, but they do talk! And yes, everything I tell you is absolutely the truth. I believe it and you must believe it too." The old woman had been completely convincing. And for many years Amy had secretly believed that when her grandmother was a little girl, somewhere in a special place, animals talked, got married and were heroes.

46   "Abuelita," Amy whispered, "I wish you were here and could help me now." And then she thought of it. Something special for tomorrow. Quickly, Amy took

out the money tin, counting out just the right amount of money she needed. She hesitated for a moment. What if it won't work and I can't convince them? Amy took a deep breath. Never mind, I have to try, I must. She counted out a few more dollars. I'll work it all out somehow. Then she warmed up Gary's milk and got ready to leave.

Amy heard the voices of her children with delight. Shouts and squeals of laughter bounced into the kitchen as they played in the living room. Today they were all happy, anticipating their mother's promise of a celebration. Recently, her frequent moods of depression and short temper had frightened them. Privately, the children had blamed themselves for their mother's unhappiness, fighting with each other in helpless confusion. The children welcomed their mother's energy and good mood with relief. 47

Lately Amy had begun to realize that Michele and Carlito were constantly fighting. Carlito was always angry and would pick on Lisabeth. Poor Lisabeth, she's always so sad. I never have time for her and she's not really much older than Gary. This way of life has been affecting us all . . . but not today. Amy worked quickly. The apartment was filled with an air of festivity. She had set the table with a paper tablecloth, napkins and paper cups to match. These were decorated with turkeys, pilgrims, Indian corn and all the symbols of the Thanksgiving holiday. Amy had also bought a roll of orange paper streamers and decorated the kitchen chairs. Each setting had a name-card printed with bright magic markers. She had even managed to purchase a small holiday cake for dessert. 48

As she worked, Amy fought moments of anxiety and fear that threatened to weaken her sense of self-confidence. What if they laugh at me? Dear God in heaven, will my children think I'm a fool? But she had already spent the money, cooked and arranged everything; she had to go ahead. If I make it through this day, Amy nodded, I'll be all right. 49

She set the food platter in the center of the table and stepped back. A mound of bright yellow rice, flavored with a few spices and bits of fatback, was surrounded by a dozen hardboiled eggs that had been colored a bright orange. Smiling, Amy felt it was all truly beautiful; she was ready for the party. 50

"All right." Amy walked into the living room. "We're ready!" The children quickly followed her into the kitchen. 51

"Oooh, Mommy," Lisabeth shouted, "everything looks so pretty." 52

"Each place has got a card with your own name, so find the right seat." Amy took Gary and sat him down on his special chair next to her. 53

"Mommy," Michele spoke, "is this the whole surprise?" 54

"Yes," Amy answered, "just a minute, we also have some cider." Amy brought a small bottle of cider to the table. 55

"Easter eggs for Thanksgiving?" Carlito asked. 56

"Is that what you think they are, Carlito?" Amy asked. "Because they are not Easter eggs." 57

The children silently turned to one another, exchanging bewildered looks. 58

59   "What are they?" Lisabeth asked.

60   "Well," Amy said, "these are . . . turkey eggs, that's what. What's better than a turkey on Thanksgiving day? Her eggs, right?" Amy continued as all of them watched her. "You see, it's not easy to get these eggs. They're what you call a delicacy. But I found a special store that sells them, and they agreed to sell me a whole dozen for today."

61   "What store is that, Mommy?" Michele asked. "Is it around here?"

62   "No. They don't have stores like that here. It's special, way downtown."

63   "Did the turkey lay them eggs like that? That color?" Carlito asked.

64   "I want an egg," Gary said, pointing to the platter.

65   "No, no . . . I just colored them that way for today, so everything goes together nicely, you know . . ." Amy began to serve the food. "All right, you can start eating."

66   "Well then, what's so special about these eggs? What's the difference between a turkey egg and an egg from a chicken?" Carlito asked.

67   "Ah, the taste, Carlito, just wait until you have some." Amy quickly finished serving everyone. "You see, these eggs are hard to find because they taste so fantastic." She chewed a mouthful of egg. "Ummm . . . fantastic, isn't it?" She nodded at them.

68   "Wonderful, Mommy," said Lisabeth. "It tastes real different."

69   "Oh yeah," Carlito said, "you can taste it right away. Really good."

70   Everyone was busy eating and commenting on how special the eggs tasted. As Amy watched her children, a sense of joy filled her, and she knew it had been a very long time since they had been together like this, close and loving.

71   "Mommy, did you ever eat these kinds of eggs before?" asked Michele.

72   "Yes, when I was little," she answered. "My grandmother got them for me. You know, I talked about my abuelita before. When I first ate them, I couldn't get over how good they tasted, just like you." Amy spoke with assurance, as they listened to every word she said. "Abuelita lived on a farm when she was very little. That's how come she knew all about turkey eggs. She used to tell me the most wonderful stories about her life there."

73   "Tell us!"

74   "Yeah, please Mommy, please tell us."

75   "All right, I'll tell you one about a hero who saved her whole village from a big flood. He was . . . a billy goat."

76   "Mommy," Michele interrupted, "a billy goat?"

77   "That's right, and you have to believe what I'm going to tell you. All of you have to believe me. Because everything I'm going to say is absolutely the truth. Promise? All right, then, in the olden days, when my grandmother was very little, far away in a small town in Puerto Rico . . ."

78   Amy continued, remembering stories that she had long since forgotten. The children listened, intrigued by what their mother had to say. She felt a calmness within. Yes, Amy told herself, today's for us, for me and the kids. ✣

RESPONDING

1. In a journal entry, discuss the role of stories in your family and record a family story that is important to you.

2. Working individually or in a group, examine why Amy lies to her children about the eggs. What is the reason for the lie? If she had asked, what would you have advised her to tell her children? Share your suggestions with the class.

3. The family stories represent more than just pleasant memories. In an essay, discuss their importance to Amy and why she chooses this time to tell them to her children. Explain why this Thanksgiving was so important to her.

4. At the beginning of the story we find Amy, a widow with four children, living on welfare in a run-down apartment in a poor neighborhood. Given this situation, explain why you might have expected an optimistic or a pessimistic resolution. What do you think Mohr is saying about Amy by choosing an optimistic ending? Write an alternate ending for the story. Which ending seems more appropriate to the way Amy thinks and behaves in this story? What changes, if any, would need to be made in the story and Amy's characterization to make your ending fit?

JUDITH ORTIZ COFER

Born in Puerto Rico in 1952, Judith Ortiz Cofer immigrated to the United States with her family in 1956. After earning her bachelor's degree from Augusta College and her master's degree from Florida Atlantic University, she spent a year at Oxford University in 1977. Since then she has taught English and Spanish at several universities, including the University of Miami and the University of Georgia. Cofer's publications include the novel The Line of the Sun *(1985), the essay collection* Silent Dancing *(1990), and five volumes of poetry.*

The following excerpt from The Line of the Sun *explores some of the contrasts between what the narrator calls life in "the tropical paradise" and life on the streets of Paterson, New Jersey. The narrator speculates on how her life would have been different if her family had remained in Puerto Rico. In so doing, the narrative suggests the importance of the imagination in fashioning one's view of both the present and the past.*

⊞

From THE LINE OF THE SUN

1   IT WAS A BITTER WINTER in Paterson. The snow fell white and dry as coconut shavings, but as soon as it touched the dirty pavement it turned into a muddy soup. Though we wore rubber boots, our feet stayed wet and cold all day. The bitter wind brought hot tears to our eyes, but it was so cold that we never felt them streaking our cheeks.

2   During Lent the nuns counted attendance at the seven o'clock mass and gave demerits if we did not take into our dry mouths Christ's warm body in the form of a wafer the priest held in his palm. The church was dark at that hour of the morning, and thick with the steaming garments of children dropped off by anxious mothers or, like us, numb from a seven-block walk.

3   In the hour of the mass, I thawed in the sweet unctuousness of the young Italian priest's voice chanting his prayers for the souls of these young children and their teachers, for their parents, for the dead and the living, for our deprived brothers and sisters, some of whom had not found comfort in Christ and were now in mortal danger of damning their souls to the raging fire of hell. He didn't really say hell, a word carefully avoided in our liturgy: it was all innuendo and Latin words that sounded like expletives. *Kyrie Eleison*, he would challenge; *Christe Eleison*, we would respond heartily, led by the strong voice of Sister Mary Beata, our beautiful homeroom teacher, whose slender body and perfect features were evident in spite of the layers of clothing she wore and the coif that

surrounded her face. She was the envy of our freshman-class girls. In the classroom I sat in the back watching her graceful movements, admiring the translucent quality of her unblemished skin, wondering whether both her calm and her beauty were a gift from God, imagining myself in the medieval clothes of her nun's habit.

I sat in the last desk of the last row of the girl's side of the room, the 4 smallest, darkest member of a class full of the strapping offspring of Irish immigrants with a few upstart Italians recently added to the roll. The blazing red hair of Jackie O'Connell drew my eyes like a flame to the center of the room, and the pattern of freckles on her nose fascinated me. She was a popular girl with the sisters; her father was a big-shot lawyer with political ambitions. Donna Finney was well developed for her age, her woman's body restrained within the angular lines of the green-and-white plaid uniform we would wear until our junior year, when we would be allowed to dress like young ladies in a pleated green skirt and white blouse. Donna sat in the row closest to the boys' side of the room.

The boys were taller and heavier than my friends at El Building; they wore 5 their blue ties and opened doors for girls naturally, as if they did it at home too. At school we were segregated by sex: every classroom was divided into girlside and boyside, and even the playground had an imaginary line right down the middle, where the assigned nun of the day would stand guard at recess and lunchtime. There were some couples in the school, of course. Everyone knew Donna went with a junior boy, a basketball player named Mickey Salvatore, an Italian playing on our Fighting Irish team—and it was a known fact that they went out in his car. After school some girls met their boyfriends at Schulze's drugstore for a soda. I saw them go in on my way home. My mother, following Rafael's instructions, gave us thirty minutes to get home before she put on her coat and high heels and came looking for us. I had just enough time to round up my brother at the grammar-school building across the street and walk briskly the seven blocks home. No soda for me with friends at Schulze's.

Ramona had come looking for us one day when an afternoon assembly had 6 held me up, and that episode had taught me a lesson. Her long black hair loose and wild from the wind, she was wearing black spiked shoes and was wrapped in a red coat and black shawl when she showed up outside the school building. The kids stared at her as if she were a circus freak, and the nuns looked doubtful, thinking perhaps they should ask the gypsy to leave the school grounds. One boy said something about her that made a hot blush of shame creep up my neck and burn my cheeks. They didn't know—couldn't know—that she was my mother, since Rafael made all our school arrangements every year, explaining that his wife could not speak English and therefore would not be attending PTA meetings and so forth. My mother looked like no other mother at the school, and I was glad she did not participate in school activities. Even on Sunday she went to the Spanish mass while we attended our separate service for children. My gypsy mother embarrassed me with her wild beauty. I wanted her to cut and spray her hair into a sculptured hairdo like the other ladies; I wanted her to wear tailored skirts and jackets like Jackie Kennedy; I even resented her youth, which made her look like my older sister. She was what I would have looked like if I hadn't worn my hair in a tight braid, if I had allowed myself to sway when I walked, and if I had worn loud colors and had spoken only Spanish.

7   I was beginning to understand why Rafael wanted to move us away from El Building. The older I got, the more embarrassed I felt about living in this crowded, noisy tenement, which the residents seemed intent on turning into a bizarre facsimile of an Island barrio. But for a while my fascination with Guzmán overpowered all other feelings, and when I came home from the organized, sanitized world of school, I felt drawn into his sickroom like an opium addict. I looked forward to the air thick with the smells of many cigarettes and of alcohol. More and more I took over the nursing duties which Ramona, with her impatient hands, relished little. She was used to fast-healing children and an absent husband. Guzmán's bleeding wound and his careful movements tried her patience.

8   And so it happened that my uncle and I began talking. Guzmán told me about his childhood on the Island in general terms, leaving out things he did not think I would understand, but his silences and omissions were fuel to my imagination and I filled in the details. I questioned him about his friend Rosa, whose name came up whenever he began to describe the Island. It was as if she were the embodiment of all that was beautiful, strange, and tempting about his homeland. He told me about her amazing knowledge of plants and herbs, how she knew what people needed just by talking to them. Once I asked him to describe her to me. His eyes had been closed as he spoke, seeing her, I suppose; but he opened them like one who slowly rises from a dream and looked at me, sitting by the side of his bed in my blue-and-white first Friday uniform, my hair pulled back in a tightly wound bun.

9   "Let your hair down," he said.

10   I reached back and pulled the long black pins out of my thick hair, letting it fall over my shoulders. It was quite long, and I never wore it loose.

11   "She had long black hair like yours," he said rising on his elbows to look intently into my face as if seeing me for the first time. I noticed his knuckles going white from the effort. "And she was light-complexioned like you." He fell back on the pillow, groaning a little. Ramona came in at that moment with fresh bandages and looked strangely at me sitting there with my hair undone, but did not say anything. Ordering Guzmán to shift to his side, she changed his bandage briskly.

12   "I need you to go to the bodega for me, Marisol," she said, not looking at me. I hated going into the gloomy little Spanish grocery store with its fishy smell and loiterers who always had something smart to say to women.

13   "Why can't you send Gabriel?" I asked petulantly, feeling once again that strain developing between my mother and me which kept getting more in the

way of all our attempts at communication. She refused to acknowledge the fact that I was fast becoming too old to order around.

"He is doing his homework." Tucking the sheet around her brother as if he were another child, she turned to me. "Just do what I tell you, niña, without arguments or back talk. It looks like we are going to have a serious discussion with your father when he comes home." She looked at me meaningfully. 14

When she left the room I braided my hair slowly. It was the new impasse we had reached. I would obey her but I would take my time doing so, pushing her to a steady burning anger which could no longer be relieved by the familiar routine of spanking, tears, reconciliation. It was a contest of wills that I knew no one could win, but Ramona was still hoping Rafael would know how to mediate. He was the absent disciplinarian—Solomon, the wise judge, the threat and the promise that hung over us day after day in her constant "when your father comes home." 15

I couldn't understand how she continued to treat me like a child when she had not been much older than I when she married Rafael. If I were on the Island I would be respected as a young woman of marriageable age. I had heard Ramona talking with her friends about a girl's fifteenth year, the *Quinceañera*, when everything changes for her. She no longer plays with children; she dresses like a woman and joins the women at coffee in the afternoon; she is no longer required to attend school if there is more pressing need for her at home, or if she is engaged. I was almost fifteen now—still in my silly uniform, bobby socks and all; still not allowed to socialize with my friends, living in a state of limbo, halfway between cultures. No one at school asked why I didn't participate in the myriad parish activities. They all understood that Marisol was *different*. 16

Talking with my uncle, listening to stories about his life on the Island, and hearing Ramona's constant rhapsodizing about that tropical paradise—all conspired to make me feel deprived. I should have grown up there. I should have been able to play in emerald-green pastures, to eat sweet bananas right off the trees, to learn about life from the women who were strong and wise like the fabled Mamá Cielo. How could she be Ramona's mother? Ramona, who could not make a decision without invoking the name of our father, whose judgment we awaited like the Second Coming. 17

As I reached for the door to leave Guzmán's room, he stirred. 18

"Rosa," he said, groggy from medication. 19

"Do you need anything?" I was trembling. 20

Alert now, he pointed to the dresser against the wall. "Take my wallet from the top drawer and get me a carton of L&M's when you go to the bodega." He closed his eyes again, whispering, "Thanks, niña." 21

I took his wallet, unwilling to make more noise by looking through it for money. In the kitchen Ramona was washing dishes at the sink, her back to me, but she was aware of my presence, and her anger showed in the set of her shoulders. I suddenly remembered how much she used to laugh, and still did when she was around her women friends. 22

23   "The list and the money are on the table, Marisol. Don't take long. I need to start dinner soon."

24   I put my coat on and left the apartment. The smells of beans boiling in a dozen kitchens assailed my nostrils. Rice and beans, the unimaginative staple food of all these people who re-created every day the same routines they had followed in their mamá's houses so long ago. Except that here in Paterson, in the cold rooms stories about the frozen ground, the smells and sounds of a lost way of life could only be a parody.

25   Instead of heading out the front door and to the street, an impulse carried my feet down an extra flight of stairs to El Basement. It was usually deserted at this hour when everyone was preparing to eat. I sat on the bottom step and looked around me at the cavernous room. A yellow light hung over my head. I took Guzmán's wallet from my coat pocket. Bringing it close to my face, I smelled the old leather. Carefully I unfolded it flat on my lap. There were several photos in the plastic. On top was a dark Indian-looking woman whose features looked familiar. Her dark, almond-shaped eyes were just like Ramona's, but her dark skin and high cheekbones were Guzmán's. I guessed this was an early picture of my grandmother, Mamá Cielo. Behind that there was one of two teenage boys, one dark, one blond. They were smiling broadly, arms on each other's shoulders. There was a fake moon in the background like the ones they use in carnival photo booths. Though the picture was bent, cutting the boys at the neck, and of poor quality, I recognized them: it was Guzmán and Rafael. I looked at it for a long time, especially at my father's face, almost unrecognizable to me with its unfamiliar look of innocent joy. Perhaps they had been drinking that night. I had often heard Ramona talking about the festivals dedicated to Our Lady of Salud, the famous smiling Virgin. Maybe they had the photo taken then. Was this the night that Guzmán had seen Rosa dressed like a gypsy at the fair? I had heard that story told late at night in my mother's kitchen, eavesdropping while I pretended to sleep. Did Rafael know Ramona then—was he happy because he was in love with the beautiful fourteen-year-old sister of his best friend?

26   In one of the plastic windows there was a newspaper clipping, yellow and torn, of a Spanish actress, wild black hair falling like a violent storm around a face made up to look glamorous, eyelashes thickened black, glossy lips parted in an open invitation. She was beautiful. I had seen her face often in the magazines my mother bought at the bodega, but why did Guzmán carry this woman's picture around? Was this what Rosa had looked like, or was she just his fantasy?

27   Deeply engrossed in my secret activity of going through my uncle's wallet, I was startled to hear men's voices approaching the top of the landing. I sat still waiting for them to go up the stairs, but they came down instead. There were four or five whose faces I recognized in the dim light as the working men of El Building, young husbands whose wives were Ramona's friends. I was not afraid, but I hid the wallet in my coat pocket and quickly got to my feet. My mind

raced to come up with an excuse, though it was *their* presence in El Basement that was odd. The laundry room was used legitimately by women and otherwise by kids. The only other users, as I very well knew from my encounter with José and the woman, were people who wanted to hide what they were doing.

The voice I heard most clearly was that of Santiago, the only man from El 28 Building ever to have been invited by Rafael into our apartment. After a severe winter week several years before, we had been left without heat until this man went down to city hall and got a judge to force the building superintendent to do something about the frozen heater pipes. Rafael had been in Europe at the time, but he obviously respected Santiago.

Coming down the steps, Santiago's voice directed the others. One man was 29 to stand at the top and wait for the others, the rest were to follow him into the basement. He nearly stumbled over me in the dim light, not seeing me wrapped in my gray coat.

"Niña, *por Dios*, what are you doing here at this hour?" His voice was gentle 30 but I detected irritation.

"My mother lost something here earlier and sent me down to try to find 31 it." I explained rather rapidly in my awkward formal Spanish.

He took my elbow in a fatherly way: "Marisol, I don't believe your mother 32 would be so careless as to send you down here to this dark place at the dinner hour alone. But I won't mention that I saw you here, and you must do the same for me, for us. These men and I want to have a private conversation. Do you understand?

"Yes," I said quickly, wanting to be released from his firm grasp, "I won't 33 say anything." He let go of my arm and I ran up the stairs. Several other men had arrived and were talking in hushed tones at the top of the steps. I managed to catch a few sentences as I slipped by their surprised faces and into the streets. It was the factory they were discussing. Someone had said *huelga*, a strike. They were planning a strike.

Outside it was cold, but not bitter; a hint of spring in the breeze cooled 34 my cheeks without biting into my skin. For once I felt a sense of pride in my father, who had managed to escape the horrible trap of factory work, though he was paying a high price for it. Tonight I'd have something to talk about with Guzmán. He would be interested in the secret basement meeting and the strike. ✤

RESPONDING

1. Discuss Marisol's reaction to her mother's visit to her school. What ideal image does she have in mind for her mother? In a journal entry, talk about a time when you (or someone you know) were in a situation where you felt out of place and wanted to fit in.

2. Working individually or in a group, discuss the conflict of wills between mother and daughter. List examples of their encounters and the reactions of each participant. How much of Marisol's behavior do you think is adolescent rebellion, and how much is a response to her mother's personality?

3. Describe Puerto Rico as Marisol pictures it. In what ways do you think Marisol might have idealized the island? In an essay, discuss the role of Puerto Rico in helping Marisol deal with her everyday life.

4. Marisol describes herself as "halfway between cultures" (paragraph 16). Using information from this and other readings in this section and outside information, write an essay comparing her lifestyle at fifteen in Paterson, New Jersey, with what her life would have been like if she had been born and raised in Puerto Rico.

MARTIN ESPADA

The poet and lawyer Martín Espada was born in Brooklyn, New York, in 1957. He earned a bachelor's degree in history from the University of Wisconsin-Madison and a law degree from Northeastern University. Espada's poems, which have been published in many journals, are collected in his books The Immigrant Iceboy's Bolero *(1982),* Trumpets from the Islands of Their Eviction *(1987),* Rebellion Is the Circle of a Lover's Hands *(1990), and* City of Coughing and Dead Radiators *(1993). Espada has received the P.E.N./Revsen Prize and the Paterson Poetry Prize as well as fellowships from the Massachusetts Artists' Foundation and the National Endowment for the Arts, among other awards. In addition to addressing the Neorican experience, Espada has traveled extensively in Puerto Rico and Nicaragua, writing about political issues there as well. Espada teaches literature and creative writing at the University of Massachusetts, Amherst.*

The poem that follows, from Espada's first collection, addresses the ways in which people forced to live amidst urban decay and deterioration are robbed of their dignity. The poet has stressed the special role of language (what he has called "la fuerza moral de la palabra") for the poor, the oppressed, and the powerless.[1]

❖

MRS. BAEZ SERVES COFFEE ON THE THIRD FLOOR

It hunches
with a brittle black spine
where they poured
gasoline on the stairs
and the bannister
and burnt it.

The fire went running
down the steps,
a naked lunatic,
calling the names
of the neighbors,
cackling in the hall.

---

1. Quotation from *Papiros de Babel: Antología de la poesía puertorriqueña en Nueva York.*

The immigrants
ate terror with their hands
and prayed to Catholic statues
as the fire company
pumped a million gallons in
and burst the roof,
as an old man
on the top floor
with no name known
to authorities
strangled on the smoke
and stopped breathing.

Some of the people left.
There's a room
on the third floor:
high-heeled shoes kicked off,
a broken dresser,
the saint's portrait
hanging where it looked on
shrugging shoulders for years,
soot, trash, burnt tile,
a perfect black light bulb
to remember everything.

And some stayed. The old men
barechested, squatting
on the milk crates to play dominoes
in the front-stoop sun;
the younger ones, the tigres,
watching the block with unemployed faces
bitter as bad liquor;
Mrs. Baez, who serves coffee
on the third floor
from tiny porcelain cups,
insisting that we stay;
the children who live
between narrow kitchens
and charred metal doors
and laugh anyway;
the skinny man, the one
just arrived from Santo Domingo,
who cannot read or write,
with no hot water
for six weeks,
telling us in the hallway
that the landlord set the fire
and everyone knows it,
the building's worth more empty.

The street organizer said it:
burn the building out,
blacken an old Dominicano's lungs
and sell
so that the money-people
can renovate
and live here
where an old Dominicano died,
over the objections
of his choking spirit.

But some have stayed.
Stayed for the malicious winter,
stayed frightened
of the white man who comes
to collect rent
and borrowing from cousins
to pay it,
stayed waiting for the next fire,
and the siren,
hysterical and late.

Someone poured gasoline
on the steps outside her door,
but Mrs. Baez
still servies coffee
in porcelain cups
to strangers,
coffee the color
of a young girl's skin
in Santo Domingo. ✠

RESPONDING

1. In your journal, work through the poem and explain what is happening in prose.

2. Working individually or in a group, list the images (sensory description of places, people, and things) that give this poem its power. Divide your list into images you consider negative and those you consider positive. What is the overall emotional effect this poem has on you, and how do these images help create that effect?

3. The poem says, "everyone knows it, the building's worth more empty." Adopt the point of view of the landlord or one of the tenants and write a letter to your newspaper explaining your reaction to that statement.

4. Imagine that you are one of the residents of the building. Write a story about what your home means to you. Why would you stay in this building after the fire? What might your options be?

VIRGINIA SANCHEZ KORROL

Virginia Sánchez Korrol is an associate professor of Puerto Rican Studies and codirector of the Center for Latino Studies at Brooklyn College. She earned her doctorate from the State University of New York at Stony Brook. Her scholarly works include From Colonia to Community: A History of Puerto Ricans in New York City, 1917–1948 *(1983) and* The Puerto Rican Struggle: Essays on Survival in the United States *(1984), which she coedited.*

The essay that follows explores the Puerto Rican colonia from a sociohistorical perspective. Taking issue with earlier studies, the work asserts that latinismo—*a sense of ethnic and community identity—was present in the Puerto Rican colonia almost from its founding. Sánchez Korrol traces this emergence in the publications and the films of the time, and she goes on to explore the sense of extended community among Latinos living in New York during the period between the world wars.*

❖

LATINISMO AMONG EARLY PUERTO RICAN MIGRANTS IN NEW YORK CITY: A SOCIOHISTORIC INTERPRETATION

SINCE THE TURN OF THE CENTURY, Puerto Ricans residing in New York City have identified themselves as *latinos* or *hispanos*, sharing this preference with other Spanish-speaking inhabitants of their community. This sense of ethnic consciousness, based on common cultural traditions, heritage, language, and a colonial past, has resulted in feelings of solidarity basic to the cultural survival of all the groups. In 1950 Mills et al. pointed to a growth of Spanish consciousness among Puerto Ricans that could evolve into "the adoption of lifeways and social values somewhat different . . . from those of the generalized (middle-class) American."[1] This projection of a *latino* identity, *latinismo*, rested firmly on a common language and manifestations of Spanish culture in the development of the community. The same phenomenon was noted by Elena Padilla. In her study of "Eastville," the word *hispanos* was cited as the preferred manner by which Puerto Ricans addressed themselves. They lived in the *barrio latino* and identified with other Spanish-speaking individuals as *hispanos.*[2]

1. C. Wright Mills, Clarence Senior, and Rose K. Goldsen, *The Puerto Rican Journey* (New York: Harper and Bros., 1950).
2. Elena Padilla, *Up from Puerto Rico* (New York: Columbia University Press, 1958).

2   Yet the issue of ethnic identity among Puerto Ricans has also been controversial. While scholars like Mills, Padilla, and more recently Felix Padilla in his
study of Puerto Ricans in Chicago, have identified a collective Latino image,
others have discounted its existence.[3] The latter support the theory that during
the late 1940s, Puerto Ricans were provincial and that the inability to achieve
socioeconomic stability today stems from the ethnic divisions among Hispanics.[4]
Given the historical limitations of many of the studies on Puerto Ricans in the
United States, the specific factors that led Mills, Padilla, and others to their
conclusions are unclear. However, current research on the Puerto Rican experience, before and immediately after World War II, confirms the presence of a
collective ethnic image and suggests its roots were far more extensive than
previously imagined.

The Early Puerto Rican Community in New York City

3   The Puerto Rican community that existed in New York prior to World
War II was conditioned to cushion the impact of the migration experience and
to perpetuate essential characteristics designed to maintain intact settlements
similar to those the migrants had known in Puerto Rico.[5] Overwhelmingly
working-class, survival for the majority of the migrant population was subject
to the fluctuations of the mainland economy. Despite their basic struggles, many
articulated support for a Puerto Rican life-style, customs, and traditions, coupled
with a sense of affiliation to a broader, equally oppressed Spanish-speaking
community. For some, these formed priorities in more ways than one. Efforts
were especially focused on the preservation of Spanish as the preferred language
of communication and the institutionalization of organizations prepared to
nurture, insulate, isolate, and advocate for the nascent community. One migrant
aptly identified the locus of this activity: "In New York City, the *colonia hispana*
was called Harlem and is still Harlem today . . . the Puerto Rican colony . . .
Harlem . . . was composed predominantly of Puerto Ricans and it has grown
enormously throughout the decades." Puerto Ricans indeed formed the bulk of
the city's Spanish-speaking population, according to the calculations of the New

3. Félix M. Padilla, "The Theoretical and Practical Sides of Latino Ethnic Conscious Behavior in
Chicago, 1970–1974" (De Kalb, Ill: Northern Illinois University, Latin American Studies Program,
1985). Unpublished manuscript.
4. Included among these are Sidney W. Mintz, *Worker in the Cane* (New Haven: Yale University
Press, 1967); and Julian Steward et al., *The People of Puerto Rico: A Study in Social Anthropology*
(Urbana: University of Illinois, 1956).
5. Several studies have focused on the history and development of the Puerto Rican community in
New York. Among the most recent is César Andreu Iglesias (ed.), *Memorias de Bernardo Vega* (Río
Piedras, P.R.: Ediciones Huracán, 1977), translated by Juan Flores as *Memoirs of Bernardo Vega* (New
York: Monthly Review Press, 1984). See also Virginia Sánchez-Korrol, *From Colonia to Community:
The History of Puerto Ricans in New York City, 1917–1948* (Westport, Conn.: Greenwood Press, 1983);
and Centro de Estudios Puertorriqueños, Oral History Task Force, *Labor Migration Under Capitalism*
(New York: Monthly Review Press, 1979).

York Mission Society and community estimates, but Cubans, Venezuelans, Colombians, Mexicans, Dominicans, and Spaniards were also represented.[6]

The use of Spanish as the language of communication served as a bond that not only welded intercommunity relationships but also secured connections with the island and Spanish America. New York *hispanos* read Spanish-language newspapers, saw Mexican and Argentine films, listened to Spanish-language radio stations, formed associations that promoted language, culture, and civic concerns, and danced and listened to Latin music. To a lesser extent, Spanish was the language for worship and Christian ritual.[7] Puerto Ricans readily identified with the ideas, life-cycle events, and circumstances experienced by other Spanish-speaking groups, accepting without question their unique position within this network. More specifically, although they had been American citizens since 1917, many Puerto Ricans in New York viewed themselves as part and parcel of the collective Latino experience. Less provincial in attitudes and background, community leaders like Jesús Colón, Bernardo Vega, and Carlos Tapia articulated the importance of a unified Puerto Rican/Latino identity in the local presses and in the associations of the day.[8] Above all others, it was precisely in the arena of communications and mass media that a Latino/Hispano alliance was forged and sustained.

An abundant supply of foreign or domestically published newspapers and periodicals inundated the Hispanic *colonia* on a daily basis. Among them were *El Buscapié* (founded in 1877); *El Avisador Cubano* (1888); *El Economista Americano* (1887); *Revista de Literatura, Ciencias y Artes* (1887); *América* (1883); *El Latino-Americano* (1885); *Las Novedades* (1887); and *La Juventud* (1889). They were augmented in the twentieth century by *Cultura Proletaria*; *El Heraldo*, a bilingual publication published by Muñoz Rivera; and *La Prensa*.[9] The latter began publishing in 1913 on a weekly basis, appearing as a daily by 1918. This

6. A report issued by the New York Mission Society in 1927 estimated a Hispanic count of between 100,000 and 150,000 individuals. Approximately 85,000 were believed to be Puerto Ricans. In 1926, the annual report of the Porto Rican Brotherhood of America, a fraternal organization based in New York City, estimated Puerto Ricans numbered about 100,000. These figures are not substantiated by census and other indicators, which estimate Puerto Ricans numbered about 45,000 during the 1930s. Undercounting was probably as problematic then as it is today.

7. The Catholic Church was not overly responsive to Puerto Ricans as a group and established few programs for the Spanish-speaking before midcentury. By contrast, Protestant churches, especially the Pentecostal, were highly visible and receptive. See Virginia Sánchez Korrol, "In Search of Non-traditional Puerto Rican Women: Histories of Preachers in N.Y. Before Mid-century," paper presented at the American Historical Association Conference, New York City, December 1985. See also Ana María Díaz Ramírez, "The Roman Catholic Archdiocese of New York and the Puerto Rican Migration, 1950–1973: A Sociological and Historical Analysis" (Ph.D. diss., Fordham University, 1983). A classic analysis of religion and the Puerto Ricans is still Joseph P. Fitzpatrick, *Puerto Rican-Americans: The Meaning of Migration to the Mainland* (Englewood Cliffs, N.J.: Prentice-Hall, 1971, 2nd ed., 1987).

8. Jesús Colón, *A Puerto Rican in New York and Other Sketches* (New York: International Publishers, 1982). See also Ramón Colón, *Carlos Tapia: A Puerto Rican Hero in New York* (New York: Vantage Press, 1976); and Andreu Iglesias, ed., *Memorias de Bernardo Vega*.

9. Sánchez Korrol, *From Colonia to Community*, Ch. 2. See also Iris Zavala and Rafael Rodríguez, eds., *Intellectual Roots of Independence* (New York: Monthly Review Press, 1980), Introduction.

newspaper was destined to become one of the most significant journalistic enterprises of the community. Responsive to the concerns of the city's Hispanics, its motto was "Unico diario español e hispanoamericano en los E.E.U.U." (the only Spanish and Hispano-American newspaper in the United States).

6   Direct community involvement centered on the sponsorship of projects or activities appealing to a diverse Spanish-speaking public. In 1919, for example, *La Prensa* cosponsored a gala ball in conjunction with several community groups, the proceeds of which were slated for building a Hispanic sanitorium. Another example was the participation of the paper's director, José Camprubi, in the inauguration of a newly federated association composed of representatives of numerous neighborhood groups. Finally, *La Prensa* frequently collaborated in fund raising for important community projects, concerts, contests, beauty pageants, and *juegos florales*, which consisted of competitive poetry recitations. The latter was significant because it was one of the many cultural activities that perpetuated Spanish traditions in the New York *colonias*.[10]

7   Journals and magazines also appealed to a collective Hispanic image. One example was *Gráfico*. Its motto was "Semanario defensor de la raza hispana" (weekly defender of the Hispanic race). While it focused predominantly on the concerns of the Puerto Rican working class, it viewed its subject through the lens of an all-encompassing Latino community. *Gráfico* printed announcements, an advice column, organizational news, literary reviews and essays, fiction, and editorials. One representative issue contained an editorial, a novella, a brief biography of the educator-philosopher José Vasconcelos, an autobiographical article by the historian Cayetano Coll y Toste, an article on sports, a movie review of *The Jazz Singer*, and social and cultural news of Puerto Rico, Spanish America, and the New York *colonias*.[11]

8   The editorial, in particular, was the vehicle for grappling with pivotal concerns such as the relative status of Puerto Ricans in the city. One specifically compared Puerto Ricans with other Hispanics in the United States, underscoring the precarious position in which they found themselves:

> The most vulnerable group of those who comprise the large family of Ibero-Americans in New York City is the Puerto Ricans. Truly it seems a paradox that, being American citizens, they should be the most defenseless. . . . For these reasons it is here that Puerto Ricans require a knowledgeable individual authorized to represent and advise them in those relationships which, by virtue of the environment in which we, as aliens, find ourselves, must be maintained with other social groups.[12]

10. *La Prensa*, July 21, 1919, p. 2. Also Sánchez Korrol, *From Colonia to Community*, p. 71.
11. *Gráfico*, July 1, 1928.
12. *Gráfico*, March 27, 1927.

Undoubtedly, those involved with this publication were sensitive to Puerto   9
Rican issues and aware of social relationships among Latinos and non-Hispanics
in the city. Their choice of words was quite deliberate. Puerto Ricans could
perceive themselves as "aliens" because, in spite of their American citizenship,
they failed to enjoy the more obvious protection afforded other Latinos through
the intercession of their embassies. On numerous occasions Puerto Rican civil
rights were put to a test when individuals were forced to "prove" their citizenship. From time to time the local press reported incidents of harassment and
confinement on Ellis Island for failure to show such proof. In these cases, Puerto
Ricans could not seek redress through a consulate.

On yet another occasion, *Gráfico* denounced discrimination and injustice   10
inflicted upon the "large Hispano-American family" by the dominant society:
"Not a day goes by that we do not hear of some maltreatment directed against
individuals of our race."[13] The editorial repudiated the physical and mental
abuse suffered by "yesterday, a Venezuelan, today, a Mexican, tomorrow, a
Cuban, and later on, a Puerto Rican." The solution proposed by the editor,
Ramón del Valle, was to intensify Hispanic political representation in the city,
utilize diplomatic channels, and educate Hispanics on their basic civil rights.

From 1933 to 1945, a less militant publication that continued to focus on   11
issues of *hispanidad* was *Revista de Artes y Letras*. Founded and edited by a Puerto
Rican woman, Josefina Silva de Cintrón, it staunchly supported the preservation
of the Spanish language, and the continuous development and dissemination of
Hispanic culture.[14] Like its predecessors, it centered on matters affecting the
city's Spanish-speaking inhabitants and printed the news and cultural events of
their countries of origin as well. In addition, editorials highlighted the federal,
state, or municipal policies that most affected the Hispanic community.

The unique structure of the journal's editorial board ensured both feminine   12
input and international representation. The board consisted of eleven members,
six of whom were female, each from a different Latin country. The majority of
these individuals were well-educated and accomplished, and related easily to
their peer groups in the United States as well as in their native countries.

The journal's preoccupation with the language issue was clearly demon-   13
strated in the March 1936 issue. In its editorial, *Artes y Letras* launched a crusade
against the testing of Harlem school children, many of whom were Puerto
Rican, by the city's Chamber of Commerce. Denouncing the Chamber's
findings as inconclusive, the journal alerted the community to the situation and
organized a mass meeting to plan its response. Significantly, while the children
involved were mostly Puerto Rican, the plea for justice was not limited to this

---

13. Ibid.
14. For an interesting overview of these early pioneers and their community activity, see Rosa
Estades, "Patterns of Political Participation of Puerto Ricans in New York City" (Ph.D. diss., New
School for Social Research, 1974). Much of this information on Josefina Silva de Cintrón is taken
from a telephone interview conducted by Sánchez Korrol in 1977.

group. All Hispanics were critically affected, and the journal's response reflected community solidarity on a highly sensitive issue.[15]

14   While some of the reading material of the interwar *colonia* molded, refined, and underscored a Hispanic consciousness and a Latino ethnic image, the bonding inherent in a common language became apparent in other ways as well. One was in the area of entertainment; another, through musical and artistic expression. Movies and screen stars generated a subculture that offered escapism in a pre-television era. During the golden age of the Spanish cinema, Argentina and Mexico were the chief exporters of comedies, melodramas, tragedies, musicals, and westerns.

15   Latin filmgoers responded to live and celluloid entertainment, enthusiastically promoting the popularity of such multinational personalities as María Félix, Mapi Cortés, Libertad Lamarque, Carlos Gardel, and Pedro Infante. Thrilled by the exploits of superheroes like Jorge Negrete and Pedro Armendáriz in Mexican westerns or historical melodramas, audiences also applauded the comic antics of Cantinflas and Tin Tan. Viewed by Hispanic audiences of various national origins throughout the country, the films set forth a collective life-style, value system, and historical legacy that stressed the similarities and respected the differences among Latinos, and at the same time inculcated a common experience not shared by non-Hispanics.

16   In addition to films, vaudeville appealed greatly to the Puerto Rican audiences of the 1930s and 1940s. Stand-up comedians, singers, dancers, and musical groups alternated their performances with the films projected on the screens in theaters across the country. Individually or in groups, Puerto Ricans shared directly in the creative process by staging or acting in neighborhood pageants, contests, and other extravaganzas. Community sentiments regarding the entertainment world were expressed in the local press as well as at the box office. On one occasion the inauguration of a new theater on Forty-second Street between Seventh and Eighth Avenues elicited the good wishes of the public, while on another the increasing numbers of English-speaking actors in movies billed as Spanish were severely criticized.[16]

17   Music also played a vital role in uniting Hispanics in New York and in the United States. Two decades into the twentieth century, *danzas, danzones, plenas,* and *aguinaldos* had already been recorded by Columbia and RCA Victor Record companies, finding a lucrative market in the city.[17] By the 1930s, Latin bands played to packed houses in the Teatro Hispano and the Compoamor in the heart of the *barrio latino*. Dance halls like Hunts Point Palace, Tropicana, Park

15. *Revista de Artes y Letras,* March 1936.

16. *Nuestro,* May 1980, pp. 26–27; *Gráfico,* July 8, 1928; *Revista de Artes y Letras,* January 1936; *Gráfico,* April 12, 1930, p. 10.

17. Max Salazar, "Latin Music: The Perseverance of a Culture," in Clara E. Rodríguez, Virginia Sánchez Korrol, and José Oscar Alers, eds., *The Puerto Rican Struggle: Essays on Survival in the U.S.* (Maplewood, N.J.: Waterfront Press, 1985).

Palace, and the Audubon Ballroom hired popular Latin bands to attract ethnically mixed audiences. Neighborhood music stores blared the latest hits and filled the melodic void for those unable to attend public dance halls. Organizations raised funds, celebrated holidays, and rewarded their members with dances held at local halls and hotels.[18]

The small music stores spread quickly throughout the *colonia hispana* and grew to symbolize the Latino settlements in much the same way that "Mom and Pop" candy stores characterized previous immigrant neighborhoods. But while the family businesses served primarily as local hangouts for social exchange, the music store's role was more emphatic. By playing the popular tunes of Spanish America, the Caribbean, and the New York settlements, migrant feelings and attitudes, particularly toward the new environment and the absent homeland, were communicated. Songs were nostalgic, focusing on country, unrequited love, or the impoverished conditions of the migrants. They expressed feelings of patriotism, protest, and alienation. Day and night, the rhythms of *el son* and the *guaracha* combined with the more romantic *boleros* and *danzas* to serenade the streets of Harlem, Brooklyn, or the South Bronx, nurturing a wide range of vital cultural expressions.

The preservation of a shared language and heritage represented one process in defining a Hispanic or Latino ethnic image; the formation of neighborhood organizations was another. Groups based on common goals and interests appeared and disappeared in accordance with the developmental agenda of the community. Some cultivated social, cultural, or educational concerns, while others dealt with the labor issues or political aspirations of the day. Still others served as buffers between the Spanish-speaking groups and the larger-non-Hispanic society.

The earliest Puerto Rican organizations to appear in New York were mutual-aid societies patterned on island counterparts.[19] These were followed by regional or hometown clubs and social/cultural units that incorporated some of the practices and operational modes of the earlier associations. In time, the dispersal of Spanish-speaking individuals throughout the city spurred the growth of more organizations, especially in response to urgent conditions and the changing concerns of their constituents. These included social clubs pledged to provide the migrants with the music, language, and socialization necessary for survival or, more significantly, the insulation for resisting the hostile environment. Others catered to more collective national interests. La Liga Puertorriqueña e Hispana, as a case in point, was a group whose officers and founding members were active in other community organizations.[20] This federation

18. Sánchez Korrol, *From Colonia to Community*, pp. 80–81.
19. Andreu Iglesias, ed., *Memorias de Bernardo Vega*, p. 123.
20. Liga Puertorriqueña e Hispana, certificate of incorporation, File no. 056-59-27C (March 1928), County Clerk's Office, Municipal Building, New York City.

labored to protect the civil rights of all Hispanics, fostered educational goals, and in general spoke for the entire community.

21   Political clubs, in particular, encompassed a wider Hispanic image for two reasons. First, membership in organizations that became political was not limited to Puerto Rican Latinos.[21] Other Hispanics were welcome as well. Second, the issues central to the clubs' membership ranged from concern for the immediate community to the nation and to the country of origin. For example, although the turn-of-the-century Puerto Rican political associations were formed primarily in support of Antillean independence, by the late 1920s and early 1930s, such organizations were broadening their bases and aligning themselves with the Democratic, Republican, or Socialist Party. For the most part, these clubs were formed independently of the regular assembly district units, but often sought and received the recognition of the county, borough, and local bosses. Nationality clubs, as they were known, were not technically part of the regular party organization, but they participated in general electoral activities, especially when votes were needed.[22]

22   These groups combined many of the features of both the regional or hometown clubs and the mutual-aid societies. They sponsored baseball teams, provided jobs and entertainment for their followers, celebrated Puerto Rican holidays, and observed patriotic events.

23   Evidence suggests the Puerto Ricans of the interwar years were far more politicized than previously assumed. One estimate is that over 7000 registered Puerto Rican voters participated in the 1918 election of Governor Alfred E. Smith. By 1926, one community organization calculated that "two thousand Porto Rican voters were credited to the 19th Congressional District while the entire registration for the city was over five thousand."[23]

24   Latin American politics and issues were of equal interest and importance to these organizations. In New York, Puerto Ricans and other Caribbean Hispanics took a stand opposing the dictatorships of Gerardo Machado in Cuba and Juan Vicente Gómez in Venezuela. They protested the rise of fascism in Spain and denounced the Puerto Rican Ponce Massacre by taking to the streets of *el barrio latino* by the thousands, under the banners of community associations. They closely observed political changes in Puerto Rico and in the rest of the hemisphere. Through the creation of neighborhood relief and emergency units, they actively supported the Sandinistas in Nicaragua.

21. For an excellent account of Puerto Rican politics in New York, see James Jennings, *Puerto Rican Politics in New York City* (Washington, D.C.: University Press of America, 1977). See also Andreu Iglesias, ed., *Memorias de Bernardo Vega*.
22. Reference to Puerto Rican nationality clubs appears in Roy V. Peel, *The Political Clubs of New York City* (New York: G. P. Putnam & Sons, 1935). See also Sánchez Korrol, *From Colonia to Community*, Ch. 6.
23. Adalberto López, "Vito Marcantonio," in *Caribbean Review* 8, no. 1 (January–March 1979): 16–21.

Latino Consciousness Outside New York

Did the size and political, economic, and cultural vulnerability of the   *25*
interwar settlements necessitate the formation and continuous renewal of a
Latino ethnic consciousness? Was it, as Mills stated, the "core of resistance to
assimilation"? Apparently the juxtaposition of the Spanish-speaking community
and the numerically larger, more discriminating, and impenetrable non-His-
panic society did motivate alliances across national boundaries, but this factor
was merely one of many. According to some of the early leaders of the Puerto
Rican community, a sense of *latinismo* already existed among the migrants during
the first decades of the migration. In part, this stemmed from an acute awareness
of their historical place within the Ibero-American family.[24]

Throughout Latin America and the Spanish Caribbean, the early decades   *26*
of this century witnessed a reaction against U.S. policies that resulted, among
other things, in a renewed commitment to Pan Americanism, coupled with a
rise in nationalism. Cultural and literary movements fanned the fires of solidarity
by stressing national consciousness, heritage, and the colonial past. By the 1930s,
the Civil War in Spain stimulated dormant sentiments among Latin Americans
for the spiritual mother country. Many expressed these feelings through direct
military involvement in the International Brigades, while others lent moral
support through their writings. In all, national consciousness, as well as international bonds, were reinforced.

Similar sentiments had already been voiced by prominent *pensadores* of each   *27*
nation. Writers and essayists, such as José Martí, Eugenio María de Hostos, and
Lola Rodríguez de Tió, had applauded unity and solidarity among Latins
regardless of where they resided. Others, particularly the essayists who honed
the genre as a vehicle of protest, noted and articulated the irreconcilable
differences between North and South America. José Enrique Rodó, Uruguayan-
born and one of the most outspoken critics of U.S. policies, underscored its
crude materialism by comparing it with the idealism and superior cultural values
of Spanish-America in *Ariel*. Rubén Darío warned against U.S. penetration,
while José Martí, among the first to denounce imperialism, observed and rejected capitalism firsthand, during his years in New York. Like Martí, many of
the *pensadores* visited the New York *colonias*. Their words and those of their Latin
compatriots were known and internalized within the migrant community.

The 1920s, characterized in Puerto Rico by a period of search and indeci-   *28*
sion, gave way to the dissemination of a new consciousness throughout Latin
America. In the wake of the Mexican Revolution, the philosopher José Vasconcelos postulated his theory of the "new man" in his *Cosmic Race*. An affirmation
of *mestizaje* formed the crux of his lectures at the University of Puerto Rico,

24. Among the community leaders who articulated such attitudes were Jesús Colón, Bernardo Vega,
and Carlos Tapia.

where he was a visiting lecturer.[25] The desire to stimulate national awareness and the continual search for a Latin American identity, as well as an openness toward the rest of the Spanish-speaking world, structured the literary focus of Juan Carlos Mariátegui, a Peruvian; Juan Marinello, a Cuban; Manuel Ugarte, an Argentinian; Pedro Henríquez Ureña, a Dominican; and Gabriela Mistral, a Chilean. In Puerto Rico the publication of Antonio S. Pedreira's *Insularismo* and the *Prontuario Histórico de Puerto Rico* of Tomás Blanco set the stage for explaining the Puerto Rican experience on the island and within a hemispheric perspective. At the same time, the rise of the Nationalist Party under Pedro Albizu Campos, in direct response to North American colonialism, expressed the movement on the political front.

29   The 1930s witnessed a further strengthening of the cultural bonds between Puerto Rico and Latin America when such writers as Mariano Picón Salas, Germán Arciniegas, and Fernando Ortiz lived, lectured, taught, and traveled on the island. Along with native writers, they collaborated on the journals *Asomante*, *La Torre*, and *Sin Nombre*, which were read on both sides of the ocean. These conveyed the message of common roots, brotherhood, nationhood, and unity. As one scholar stated:

> I do not share the thesis of the cultural isolation of Puerto Rico. Sporadic separations, yes, but never a total disjuncture. Alienation might exist on an international level, on official planes. . . . But here there have always been people preoccupied with stretching the bonds with the Spanish American and Antillean countries. And you cannot attempt to study [Puerto Rican] letters, thought, theater, music, and art, history or even the ideas that shake up the modern university without taking into account the multiple contacts established.[26]

Conclusions

30   Undoubtedly the ties between Puerto Rico and the rest of the Spanish-speaking world were repeated to some extent in the New York *colonias*. In their attempts to cope with the difficult U.S. racial, class, and economic reality, Puerto Ricans created communities that reflected those they knew on the island. Our brief overview of the early Puerto Rican community in New York indicates that it encompassed formal and informal institutions that, more often than not, included Hispanics of other countries. Solidarity, particularly on political or cultural issues, was openly demonstrated by the advocacy and organizational positions taken by community groups.

31   By the 1950s, when the largest migration of Puerto Ricans left the island for continental shores, the U.S. presence in Puerto Rico was well entrenched.

25. Arturo Morales Carrión, "Puerto Rico en el Caribe," in *El Nuevo Día*, July 8, 1984, pp. 12–15.
26. Ibid.

For those born, educated, and drafted under the American flag, affiliations with other Latinos were somewhat obscured and less understood. This turn of events was further qualified by the social significance placed on race and class in the United States, which motivated some Puerto Ricans to align along racial rather than cultural classifications. The consequence, in part, was reflected among New York Hispanics by a limited historical memory, a decline in organizational interaction, and a lack of appreciation for the benefits of solidarity.

More recently, university-based programs have begun to emphasize com- 32
monalities in the U.S. experience of Spanish-speaking people. Their history has formed the focus of numerous studies. Support for bilingual education programs and an awareness of Hispanics as a potentially dynamic force in U.S. politics have motivated collaborative efforts. Productive political coalitions have already surfaced in major urban centers. Clearly, the collective ethnic image of U.S. Latinos has not totally disappeared: it has merely entered another historical phase. �֍

RESPONDING

1. In a journal entry, discuss the role your use of language plays in helping you relate to and feel close to others. You might consider the language you use with your family or with specific friends.

2. Working individually or in a group, summarize Sánchez Korrol's support for her statement that "current research on the Puerto Rican experience, before and immediately after World War II, confirms the presence of a collective ethnic image and suggests its roots were far more extensive than previously imagined" (paragraph 2).

3. Choose one of the features of daily life mentioned by Sánchez Korrol, such as the newspaper or the music store, and in an essay explain its role in creating a sense of community for Puerto Ricans living away from the island.

4. Sánchez Korrol argues that "in their attempts to cope with the difficult U.S. racial, class, and economic reality, Puerto Ricans created communities that reflected those they knew on the island" (paragraph 30). Using examples from the readings and your own experience, explain the economic, social, and psychological circumstances that motivated Puerto Ricans to create a replica of island life in the United States.

⁜

CONNECTING

Critical Thinking and Writing

1.   For many Puerto Ricans in New York, Puerto Rico continues to occupy an important place in their thoughts and dreams. Compare the different attitudes toward Puerto Rico held by the characters in the selections by Thomas, Mohr, and Cofer.

2.   Families such as Thomas's and the family Mohr describes support each other emotionally as well as economically. Using examples from the readings, write an essay discussing the importance of this emotional support for family members.

3.   Many of the readings describe situations involving insider/outsider relationships. Write an essay discussing those relationships using specific examples from the readings, especially those of Colón and Espada.

4.   Most Puerto Ricans immigrants settled in New York City. Speculate about the attraction of that particular large urban area as compared to a smaller town or a rural area. Compare conditions and opportunities in the city with those encountered by groups such as the Mexican immigrants, who often settled in farming communities.

5.   Design your own essay topic based on a issue emerging from these readings that engaged your interest.

6.   People moving to a new country often have a difficult time adjusting because they speak a different language or dialect or have different customs or a different culture. Compare the experiences of European immigrants, such as Constantine Panunzio in Chapter 1, with the experiences of Puerto Ricans, such as Colón.

7.   Many of the readings in this text describe situations in which workers are exploited or their opportunities limited. Write an essay arguing for or against the idea that much of that exploitation was based on racism.

8.   Write an essay defining what it means to be educated and illustrating your definition with examples from the readings and from your own observations. In your definition, does being educated include being "street smart" as well as "book smart"? Consider basic skills learned in school and those learned through

experience. For example, Piri Thomas's mother, although not formally educated, is well informed about her own culture.

9.   Compare the working conditions of the *tabaqueros* with conditions for other immigrant groups such as the Chinese railroad workers in Chapter 2. How do you account for the differences?

10. Using examples from this reading as well as other readings in this book and your own experience, write an essay discussing the role of language and culture in forging bonds between immigrant groups.

11. Compare the living conditions described by Espada with those of early European immigrants.

For Further Research

1.   Research the current political situation in Puerto Rico. Consider the likelihood of statehood as well as what other options are available for the territory.

2.   Investigate the current demographics of Puerto Ricans in the United States. How many people come to the continental United States each year? Where do they settle? What reasons do they have for leaving the island? Compare those reasons to those of other current immigrant groups, for example, those from Latin America.

REFERENCES AND ADDITIONAL SOURCES

Acosta-Belén, Edna, and Barbara R. Sjòstrom,, eds. *The Hispanic Experience in the United States: Contemporary Issues and Perspectives.* New York: Praeger, 1988.

Algarin, Miguel, and Miguel Pinero, eds. *Nuyorican Poetry: An Anthology of Puerto Rican Words and Feelings.* New York: William Morrow, 1975.

Centro de Estudios Puertorriqueños, Oral History Task Force. *Labor Migration under Capitalism: The Puerto Rican Experience.* New York: Monthly Review Press, 1979.

Cordasco, Francesco, and Eugene Bucchioni, eds. *The Puerto Rican Experience: A Sociological Sourcebook.* Totowa, N.J.: Rowman and Littlefield, 1973.

——. *The Puerto Ricans, 1493–1973: A Chronology and Fact Book.* Dobbs Ferry, N.Y.: Oceana, 1973.

Dietz, James. *Economic History of Puerto Rico: Institutional Change and Capitalist Development.* Princeton, N.J.: Princeton University Press, 1986.

Fitzpatrick, Joseph P. *Puerto Rican Americans: The Meaning of Migration to the Mainland.* Englewood Cliffs, N.J.: Prentice-Hall, 1971, 2nd. edition 1987.

Garcia-Passalacqua, Juan Manuel. *Puerto Rico: Equality and Freedom at Issue.* New York: Praeger, 1984.

Hauberg, Clifford A. *Puerto Rico and the Puerto Ricans.* New York: Twayne, 1974. New York: Hippocrene Books, 1984.

Hernández, Alvarez, José. *Return Migration to Puerto Rico.* Berkeley: Institute of International Studies, University of California, 1967. Westport, Conn.: Greenwood Press, 1976.

Jennings, James, and Monte Rivera. *Puerto Rican Politics in Urban America.* Westport, Conn.: Greenwood Press, 1984.

Kanellos, Nicholas, ed. *Biographical Dictionary of Hispanic Literature in the United States: The Literature of Puerto Ricans, Cuban Americans, and Other Hispanic Writers.* Westport, Conn.: Greenwood Press, 1989.

Lopez, Adalberto, ed. *The Puerto Ricans: Their History, Culture and Society.* Cambridge, Mass.: Schenkman, 1980.

Mohr, Eugene V. *The Nuyorican Experience: Literature of the Puerto Rican Minority.* Westport, Conn.: Greenwood Press, 1982.

Morales Carrión, Arturo. *Puerto Rico: A Political and Cultural History.* New York: Norton, 1983. Nashville, T.N.: American Association for State and Local History, 1983.

Padilla, Elena. *Up from Puerto Rico.* New York: Columbia University Press, 1958.

Rodriquez, Clara E., et al., eds. *The Puerto Rican Struggle: Essays on Survival in the U.S.* Maplewood, N.J.: Waterfront, 1984.

Rodriguez de Laguna, Asela. *Images and Identities: The Puerto Rican in Two World Contexts.* New York: Puerto Rican Migration Research Consortium, 1980. New Brunswick, N.J.: Transaction Books, 1987.

Sánchez Korrol, Virginia E. *From Colonia to Community: The History of Puerto Ricans in New York City, 1917–1948.* Westport, Conn.: Greenwood Press, 1983.

Steven-Arroyo, Anthony M., and Ana María Díaz Ramírez. "Puerto Ricans in the States," in *The Minority Report*, 2nd ed., edited by A. G. Dworkin and R. J. Dworkin. New York: Holt, Rinehart and Winston, pp. 196–232.

United States Commission on Civil Rights. *Puerto Ricans in the Continental United States: An Uncertain Future.* Washington, D.C.: Government Printing Office, The U.S. Commission on Civil Rights, 1976.

Weisskoff, Richard. *Factories and Food Stamps: The Puerto Rican Model of Development.* Baltimore: Johns Hopkins University Press, 1985.

Young Lords Party. *Palante: Young Lords Party.* New York: McGraw-Hill, 1971.

5

JAPANESE AMERICANS

In Camp, In Community

⊹

Above: Posting of Civilian Exclusion Order #5.
Opposite: Heart Mountain, Wyoming. Japanese American internment
camp, with tarpaper-covered barracks housing 10,000 citizens.
(National Archives)

SETTING THE HISTORICAL AND CULTURAL CONTEXT

IN HER BOOK *Nisei Daughter*, Monica Sone quotes her brother's question: "Doesn't my citizenship mean a single blessed thing to anyone?" This question, rhetorical as it was, helps to dramatize the sense of exasperation and outrage felt by Japanese Americans when they learned that they would have to leave their homes and businesses and move to remote camps, ostensibly to protect national security. This forced resettlement, known as the Internment, followed the United States's declaration of war against Japan. The Internment affected both Japanese nationals and those persons of Japanese ancestry who were also American citizens. Many people, both within and outside the Japanese community, look back on this action, like the attack on Pearl Harbor itself, as an event that, in the words of President Franklin Delano Roosevelt, "would live in infamy."

The Internment was not, of course, the first time that persons of Japanese origin had suffered because of their race and country of origin. Japanese nationals were prohibited by their government from emmigrating until 1885. When the first group did arrive, they encountered a country reluctant to accept more foreigners. Exclusionists, including such influential people as the writer Jack London and Senator Henry Cabot Lodge, campaigned to have quotas set on immigrants of non-European origin. They sought to extend to the Japanese the Chinese Exclusion Acts of 1882 and 1890, which had been directed at Chinese immigration.

The situation worsened in 1905, when Japan defeated Russia in the Russo-Japanese War; the United States now perceived Japan as a Pacific threat. Exclusionists pressured the federal government to negotiate restrictive quotas with the emperor of Japan. These negotiations resulted in the Gentlemen's Agreement, which was announced in 1908. The agreement stipulated how many Japanese would be allowed to immigrate to the United States each year; it also prohibited unskilled workers (a large percentage of those who would typically emigrate) from coming to America.

Once in the United States, Japanese immigrants faced discrimination in employment and education. Not only did unions exclude them, but they were often barred from holding professional positions as well. School districts, such as those of San Francisco, attempted to segregate Japanese students from white students. This segregation order was ordered stopped in 1906 by President Theodore Roosevelt, who was concerned about its effect on the American government's relations with Japan. Similar policies remained in effect in other communities as late as 1936, however, when they were declared unconstitutional by the U.S. Supreme Court. Between 1910 and 1920, "protective" leagues, special-interest groups motivated by economic fears and racial prejudice, pressured the legislature further to restrict the economic power of Japanese immigrants. As a result of such pressure, the Alien Land Act, passed in 1913, prohibited these immigrants from owning land, deeding it to their relatives, or leasing land for more than three years. Stricter legislation passed in 1920 prevented the Japanese from leasing any farmland.

Unlike European immigrants, Japanese immigrants were prevented by law from becoming naturalized American citizens. Citing a 1790 law that restricted citizenship to whites, the courts and the Justice Department denied citizenship to both the Chinese (in 1882) and the Japanese (in 1906 and 1913); this restriction was upheld by the Supreme Court as late as 1922, when the Court ruled that Takao Ozawa was ineligible for citizenship because of his race. In 1924 Congress passed the Immigration Act of 1924, which allowed only those immigrants racially eligible for citizenship to enter the country. This act cut off immigration from Japan almost completely.

These legal and social restrictions helped determine the composition of the Japanese American community before World War II. The first wave of immigration, which took place between 1885 (when the emperor lifted his ban on emigration) and 1907 (when the Gentleman's Agreement was signed), brought primarily unmarried, unskilled workers who planned to return to Japan after achieving economic success. Those who were married often planned to settle in the United States and send to Japan for their wives. After 1907, immigrants from Japan were primarily skilled workers who established themselves in business or in agriculture.

The Immigration Act of 1924 changed the shape of the Japanese American community. Because no new Japanese immigrants were allowed to enter the country, a gap in age and culture developed between the dwindling Issei (first generation immigrants, born in Japan) and the increasing Nisei (second-generation, born in the United States). At the same time, the discrimination experienced in the larger society led the Japanese community to hold itself separate. For this reason the community retained much of its cultural heritage and identity longer than most other immigrant groups. Children were taught Japanese language and culture in schools established and supported by their parents; many children were also sent to Japan to complete their education.

Despite restrictive laws and discriminatory practices, members of the Japanese community did find employment. Many worked in agriculture, commercial fishing, and canning. Japanese immigrants helped the fishing and canning industries to thrive in Southern California and throughout the Pacific Northwest; moreover, Japanese farmers were responsible for a large percentage of the berries and vegetables grown in California. At the same time, other Japanese immigrants helped to establish an urban service economy. They worked in and later established their own small restaurants, hotels, and shops, which primarily served the immigrant population, and in gardening and laundry services for those outside their own community. While some immigrants, such as George Shima and Masajiro Furiya, became wealthy as a result of wise financial investments, many other newcomers prospered in less dramatic ways. They saved money and purchased property, putting the deeds in the names of their American-born children. Many retained their belief that hard work and academic achievement would lead to success.

This belief was tested when the United States entered World War II on December 8, 1941. Anti-Japanese sentiment among whites, less often expressed since the passage of the Immigration Act of 1924, reemerged. This sentiment affected the treatment of individuals of Japanese descent not only by the general public but by the United States government as well. Some special interest groups, as well as some members of Congress and of the American military, held the Japanese American community responsible for the Japanese government's surprise attack on Pearl Harbor, the American naval headquarters in Hawaii. Rumors circulated that Japanese immigrants, both in Hawaii and on the mainland, had been in communication with the Japanese military forces and that they had been involved in directing planes and in transmitting information to the Japanese forces. Furthermore, early victories by the emperor's army in the Pacific made some Americans fearful that the West Coast might be vulnerable to attack.

These fears, along with the prevalent racial stereotypes of the time, caused the United States government to treat Japanese Americans differently from German Americans and Italian Americans, even though the United States was also at war with Germany and Italy. Because some officers feared that Japanese Americans living on the West Coast could sabotage military installations, the military was able to pressure the executive branch of government to deny Japanese Americans many of their constitutional rights. Despite the strong protests of the United States attorney general, the government authorized extensive searches of private residences and businesses for anything that might be considered contraband. The homes of both Japanese immigrants and Japanese American citizens were searched, often in the middle of the night. As Monica Sone describes, few personal possessions were considered above suspicion; the presence of cameras or radios, Japanese newspapers, books, or magazines—or the absence of such objects—made ordinary families subject to further government surveillance. Those who did not answer questions to the satisfaction of the authorities could be detained for further questioning. As a result, many Japanese and Japanese American heads of households, some of whom spoke little English, were rounded up and detained by the Federal Bureau of Investigation.

This search and seizure was only a prelude to the more extensive violation of rights that members of the Japanese community experienced as the war continued. Some were subjected to verbal and physical abuse; others had their homes and businesses vandalized and even destroyed. When the military, wary of Japanese living along the Pacific coast, asked them to move to areas farther inland, those who relocated were abused and threatened by the residents of the inland areas. Understandably, only a small number of Japanese Americans volunteered for the relocation program.

The military then asked President Franklin Roosevelt to begin a forced evacuation. General John DeWitt, an army officer with no combat experience but evidently a very strong anti-Asian bias, called for internment. On February 19, 1942, Roosevelt signed Executive Order 9066, which authorized the removal of anyone considered to be a risk to national security from military areas. DeWitt, who was given the authority to oversee the evacuation of the West Coast, stated that all persons of Japanese ancestry would be removed "in the interest of military necessity." On March 18, Roosevelt established the War Relocation Authority (WRA) to handle this evacuation.

Those subject to the internment order—both Japanese immigrants and American citizens of Japanese descent, or, in the contemporary vernacular, "aliens" and "nonaliens"—were given only a few days to leave their homes and move to designated camps. Because they were allowed to take only their bedding and a few suitcases, the Japanese had to sell their homes, businesses, and other property at great loss or entrust them to fate or neighbors. After reporting to a local pickup area, they were taken first by bus and then by train to one of ten internment camps located in remote sections of California and Arizona and, later, in Colorado, Utah, Idaho, and Arkansas.

Life in the camps was dismal. Dwellings consisted of hastily constructed barracks or other makeshift structures, such as recently cleared livestock exhibition halls. Barbed wire and watchtowers marked the perimeter of the camps. The barracks offered little comfort and lacked adequate heat and privacy; internees often had to use some of their blankets to shield the windows from searchlights. They stood in line for meals, eating in communal kitchens where the food allotment was less than fifty cents per person per day. Bathroom facilities were often latrines without running water. In addition to lacking personal comforts, internees were subject to curfews, monitoring, and arbitrary searches. There were usually meager "work opportunities" for adults and minimal education for children. This environment and the deprivation of basic rights it represented contributed to the disillusionment and restless despair described by those sent to the camps. "The Legend of Miss Sasagawara" examines the effects of this regimentation and lack of privacy on the internees, illustrating how such a routine can affect an individual's dignity and sense of order.

In 1943—one year after the internment order—the United States Army invited male internees eighteen years old or older to serve in special units of the armed forces. When the army distributed loyalty questionnaires to all candidates and to the rest of the interned population, it found more than 17,000 men eligible for service. Many of these recruits went on to fight in the war, some earning medals for their courage. Other young men refused military service, feeling that they could not fight for a country that had refused to recognize their own rights as citizens. These people, called "No-no Boys," were segregated from the rest of the internees. The section from John Okada's *No-no Boy* contrasts those who retained their loyalty with those who were so offended by having their loyalty questioned that they renounced their American citizenship.

In 1945, in the case of *Endo* v. *the United States,* the Supreme Court unanimously ruled that the prolonged internment of Japanese nationals who posed no threat to the national security had been unconstitutional. This ruling brought the Internment to an end. But it was difficult for the Japanese American community to feel much sense of vindication. When the internees returned from the camps, they found much of their property gone, often sold to pay back taxes. Their businesses and farms had often been dissolved or were in other hands. And in the larger society, prejudice against people of Japanese ancestry remained.

In recent years the American government has begun to acknowledge that the Internment was unjust. The Civil Liberties Act of 1988 awarded the 60,000 former internees alive on the day of signing $1.25 billion in reparations. In October 1990 Attorney General Dick Thornberg offered an apology and the first set of reparation checks to members of the Japanese American community who had been interned during World War II. Speaking for the entire nation, President George Bush asserted, "We can never fully right the wrongs of the past . . . but we can take a clear stand for justice and recognize that serious injustices were done to Japanese Americans during World War II."

For many Japanese Americans, however, the pain of the Internment did not end with the closing of the camps. Lawson Fusao Inada's poem "Concentration Constellation" shows the hold that the past still has on the Japanese American community, to such a degree that the western landscape can be viewed as a constellation, each point of which marks the site of an internment camp. In their essays, Garrett Hongo and Ronald Takaki treat the burden of internment for those who experienced it and the generations that follow. If Takaki stresses the importance of "overcoming the silence" that has marked the community's response to the Internment, Hongo's essay "Kubota" examines the reciprocal nature of the debts each generation owes the other, lest the Internment be forgotten. In his or her own way, each of these writers reveals the difficulty that many still face in attempting to come to terms with the Internment.

BEGINNING: Pre-reading/Writing

Imagine yourself in the following situation. A government agency has informed you that you must leave your home in seven days and go to an internment camp. You can bring only two small suitcases and a bag of bedding with you. How do you react to what is happening? What will you do? What will you take with you and why? Share your choices with the class.

Executive Order 9066, which was signed by President Franklin D. Roosevelt on February 19, 1942, gave the secretary of war the power to evacuate from specific military areas any residents who were considered to be risks to national security. Although the act did not mention any ethnic group, it was applied almost exclusively to Japanese Americans. Almost immediately after the order was signed, the military officer in charge ordered the evacuation of people of Japanese ancestry.

On March 18, Roosevelt established the War Relocation Authority (WRA) to take charge of this evacuation. The injustice of the Internment was not acknowledged by Congress until the 1980s, when it was ordered that reparations be paid.

⁜

JAPANESE RELOCATION ORDER

February 19, 1942
(Federal Register, Vol. VII, No. 38)

ALARMED BY THE SUPPOSED DANGER of Japanese invasion of the Pacific coast after Pearl Harbor and under the apprehension that all persons of Japanese ancestry were a potential threat to the United States, the War Department persuaded the President to authorize the evacuation of some 112,000 West Coast Japanese, two-thirds of them American citizens to "relocation" centers. A Congressional Resolution of March 21, 1942, made it a misdemeanor "to knowingly enter, remain in, or leave prescribed military areas" contrary to the orders of the commanding officer of the area. This Act which, in perspective seems to have been wholly unnecessary, has been called by E. S. Corwin "the most drastic invasion of the rights of citizens of the U.S. by their own government that has thus far occurred in the history of our nation." See Doc. No. 547 and M. Grodzins, *Americans Betrayed.* 1

Executive Order
Authorizing the Secretary of War to Prescribe Military Areas

Whereas the successful prosecution of the war requires every possible protection against espionage and against sabotage to national-defense materials, national-defense premises, and national-defense utilities. . . . 2

Now, therefore, by virtue of the authority vested in me as President of the United States, and Commander in Chief of the Army and Navy, I hereby authorize and direct the Secretary of War, and the Military Commanders whom he may from time to time designate, whenever he or any designated Com- 3 mander deems such action necessary or desirable, to prescribe military areas in such places and of such extent as he or the appropriate Military Commander may determine, from which any or all persons may be excluded, and with respect to which, the right of any person to enter, remain in, or leave shall be subject to whatever restrictions the Secretary of War or the appropriate Military Commander may impose in his discretion. The Secretary of War is hereby authorized to provide for residents of any such area who are excluded therefrom, such transportation, food, shelter, and other accommodations as may be necessary, in the judgment of the Secretary of War or the said Military Commander, and until other arrangements are made, to accomplish the purpose of this order. The designation of military areas in any region or locality shall supersede designations of prohibited and restricted areas by the Attorney General under the Proclamations of December 7 and 8, 1941, and shall supersede the responsibility and authority of the Attorney General under the said Proclamations in respect of such prohibited and restricted areas.

4   I hereby further authorize and direct the Secretary of War and the said Military Commanders to take such other steps as he or the appropriate Military Commander may deem advisable to enforce compliance with the restrictions applicable to each Military area hereinabove authorized to be designated, including the use of Federal troops and other Federal Agencies, with authority to accept assistance of state and local agencies.

5   I hereby further authorize and direct all Executive Departments, independent establishments and other Federal Agencies, to assist the Secretary of War or the said Military Commanders in carrying out this Executive Order, including the furnishing of medical aid, hospitalization, food, clothing, transportation, use of land, shelter, and other supplies, equipment, utilities, facilities, and services. . . . ✛

FRANKLIN D. ROOSEVELT

RESPONDING

1. Imagine that you are a native-born American of Japanese descent. The year is 1942 and you live in California. In a journal entry, write your reaction to the Japanese Relocation Order.

2. Working individually or in a group, list the powers that the order gives to the "appropriate Military Commander" (paragraph 3) Then explain the government's reasons for issuing the order. How does the act directly or indirectly indicate that the Japanese will be forced to live in relocation centers?

3. This act has been called "the most drastic invasion of the rights of citizens of the U.S. by their own government that has thus far occurred in the history of our nation" by the legal historian E. S. Corwin. Explain this statement and argue for or against its conclusion. Support your argument with examples from the introduction to the chapter and your own knowledge of history and current events. ✣

MONICA SONE

Monica Sone, born Kazuko Itoi in 1919, grew up in Seattle, Washington, where her family was in the hotel business until they were forced to evacuate. After the war she attended Hanover College and did graduate work in psychology at Case Western Reserve University.

In the following selection from her book Nisei Daughter *(1953), Sone recounts the changes in the country and in the Japanese American community after the attack on Pearl Harbor. The chapter also raises some uncomfortable questions about the relationship between national security and personal liberty during times of war.*

❖

PEARL HARBOR ECHOES IN SEATTLE

1   ON A PEACEFUL SUNDAY MORNING, December 7, 1941, Henry, Sumi and I were at choir rehearsal singing ourselves hoarse in preparation for the annual Christmas recital of Handel's "Messiah." Suddenly Chuck Mizuno, a young University of Washington student, burst into the chapel, gasping as if he had sprinted all the way up the stairs.

2   "Listen, everybody!" he shouted. "Japan just bombed Pearl Harbor . . . in Hawaii! It's war!"

3   The terrible words hit like a blockbuster, paralyzing us. Then we smiled feebly at each other, hoping this was one of Chuck's practical jokes. Miss Hara, our music director, rapped her baton impatiently on the music stand and chided him, "Now Chuck, fun's fun, but we have work to do. Please take your place. You're already half an hour late."

4   But Chuck strode vehemently back to the door. "I mean it, folks, honest! I just heard the news over my car radio. Reporters are talking a blue streak. Come on down and hear it for yourselves."

5   With that, Chuck swept out of the room, a swirl of young men following in his wake. Henry was one of them. The rest of us stayed, rooted to our places like a row of marionettes. I felt as if a fist had smashed my pleasant little existence, breaking it into jigsaw puzzle pieces. An old wound opened up again, and I found myself shrinking inwardly from my Japanese blood, the blood of an enemy. I knew instinctively that the fact that I was an American by birthright was not going to help me escape the consequences of this unhappy war.

6   One girl mumbled over and over again, "It can't be, God, it can't be!" Someone else was saying, "What a spot to be in! Do you think we'll be considered Japanese or Americans?"

A boy replied quietly, "We'll be Japs, same as always. But our parents are   7
enemy aliens now, you know."

A shocked silence followed. Henry came for Sumi and me. "Come on, let's   8
go home," he said.

We ran trembling to our car. Usually Henry was a careful driver, but that   9
morning he bore down savagely on the accelerator. Boiling angry, he shot us
up Twelfth Avenue, rammed through the busy Jackson Street intersection, and
rocketed up the Beacon Hill bridge. We swung violently around to the left of
the Marine Hospital and swooped to the top of the hill. Then Henry slammed
on the brakes and we rushed helter-skelter up to the house to get to the radio.
Asthma skidded away from under our trampling feet.

Mother was sitting limp in the huge armchair as if she had collapsed there,   10
listening dazedly to the turbulent radio. Her face was frozen still, and the only
words she could utter were, "*Komatta neh, komatta neh*. How dreadful, how
dreadful."

Henry put his arms around her. She told him she first heard about the attack   11
on Pearl Harbor when one of her friends phoned her and told her to turn on
the radio.

We pressed close against the radio, listening stiffly to the staccato outbursts   12
of an excited reporter: "The early morning sky of Honolulu was filled with the
furious buzzing of Jap Zero planes for nearly three hours, raining death and
destruction on the airfields below. . . . A warship anchored beyond the Harbor
was sunk. . . ."

We were switched to the White House. The fierce clack of teletype ma-   13
chines and the babble of voices surging in and out from the background almost
drowned out the speaker's terse announcements.

With every fiber of my being I resented this war. I felt as if I were on fire.   14
"Mama, they should never have done it," I cried. "Why did they do it? Why?
Why?"

Mother's face turned paper white. "What do you know about it? Right or   15
wrong, the Japanese have been chafing with resentment for years. It was bound
to happen, one time or another. You're young, Ka-chan, you know very little
about the ways of nations. It's not as simple as you think, but this is hardly the
time to be quarreling about it, is it?"

"No, it's too late, too late!" and I let the tears pour down my face.   16

Father rushed home from the hotel. He was deceptively calm as he joined   17
us in the living room. Father was a born skeptic, and he believed nothing unless
he could see, feel and smell it. He regarded all newspapers and radio news with
deep suspicion. He shook his head doubtfully. "It must be propaganda. With
the way things are going now between America and Japan, we should expect
the most fantastic rumors, and this is one of the wildest I've heard yet." But we
noticed that he was firmly glued to the radio. It seemed as if the regular Sunday
programs, sounding off relentlessly hour after hour on schedule, were trying to
blunt the catastrophe of the morning.

18   The telephone pealed nervously all day as people searched for comfort from each other. Chris called, and I told her how miserable and confused I felt about the war. Understanding as always, Chris said, "You know how I feel about you and your family, Kaz. Don't, for heaven's sake, feel the war is going to make any difference in our relationship. It's not your fault, nor mine! I wish to God it could have been prevented." Minnie called off her Sunday date with Henry. Her family was upset and they thought she should stay close to home instead of wandering downtown.

19   Late that night Father got a shortwave broadcast from Japan. Static sputtered, then we caught a faint voice, speaking rapidly in Japanese. Father sat unmoving as a rock, his head cocked. The man was talking about the war between Japan and America. Father bit his lips and Mother whispered to him anxiously, "It's true, then, isn't it, Papa? It's true?"

20   Father was muttering to himself, "So they really did it!" Now having heard the news in their native tongue, the war had become a reality to Father and Mother.

21   "I suppose from now on, we'll hear about nothing but the humiliating defeats of Japan in the papers here," Mother said, resignedly.

22   Henry and I glared indignantly at Mother, then Henry shrugged his shoulders and decided to say nothing. Discussion of politics, especially Japan versus America, had become taboo in our family for it sent tempers skyrocketing. Henry and I used to criticize Japan's aggressions in China and Manchuria while Father and Mother condemned Great Britain and America's superior attitude toward Asiatics and their interference with Japan's economic growth. During these arguments, we had eyed each other like strangers, parents against children. They left us with a hollow feeling at the pit of the stomach.

23   Just then the shrill peel of the telephone cut off the possibility of a family argument. When I answered, a young girl's voice fluttered through breathily, "Hello, this is Taeko Tanabe. Is my mother there?"

24   "No, she isn't, Taeko."

25   "Thank you," and Taeko hung up before I could say another word. Her voice sounded strange. Mrs. Tanabe was one of Mother's poet friends. Taeko called three more times, and each time before I could ask her if anything was wrong, she quickly hung up. The next day we learned that Taeko was trying desperately to locate her mother because FBI agents had swept into their home and arrested Mr. Tanabe, a newspaper editor. The FBI had permitted Taeko to try to locate her mother before they took Mr. Tanabe away while they searched the house for contraband and subversive material, but she was not to let anyone else know what was happening.

26   Next morning the newspapers fairly exploded in our faces with stories about the Japanese raids on the chain of Pacific islands. We were shocked to read Attorney General Biddle's announcement that 736 Japanese had been picked up in the United States and Hawaii. Then Mrs. Tanabe called Mother about her husband's arrest, and she said at least a hundred others had been taken from

our community. Messrs. Okayama, Higashi, Sughiri, Mori, Okada—we knew them all.

"But why were they arrested, Papa? They weren't spies, were they?" 27

Father replied almost curtly, "Of course not! They were probably taken for 28 questioning."

The pressure of war moved in on our little community. The Chinese consul 29 announced that all the Chinese would carry identification cards and wear "China" badges to distinguish them from the Japanese. Then I really felt left standing out in the cold. The government ordered the bank funds of all Japanese nationals frozen. Father could no longer handle financial transactions through his bank accounts, but Henry, fortunately, was of legal age so that business could be negotiated in his name.

In the afternoon President Roosevelt's formal declaration of war against 30 Japan was broadcast throughout the nation. In grave, measured words, he described the attack on Pearl Harbor as shameful, infamous. I writhed involuntarily. I could no more have escaped the stab of self-consciousness than I could have changed my Oriental features.

Monday night a complete blackout was ordered against a possible Japanese 31 air raid on the Puget Sound area. Mother assembled black cloths to cover the windows and set up candles in every room. All radio stations were silenced from seven in the evening till morning, but we gathered around the dead radio anyway, out of sheer habit. We whiled away the evening reading instructions in the newspapers on how to put out incendiary bombs and learning about the best hiding places during bombardments. When the city pulled its switches at blackout hour and plunged us into an ominous dark silence, we went to bed shivering and wondering what tomorrow would bring. All of a sudden there was a wild screech of brakes, followed by the resounding crash of metal slamming into metal. We rushed out on the balcony. In the street below we saw dim shapes of cars piled grotesquely on top of each other, their soft blue headlights staring helplessly up into the sky. Angry men's voices floated up to the house. The men were wearing uniforms and their metal buttons gleamed in the blue lights. Apparently two police cars had collided in the blackout.

Clutching at our bathrobes we lingered there. The damp winter night hung 32 heavy and inert like a wet black veil, and at the bottom of Beacon Hill, we could barely make out the undulating length of Rainier Valley, lying quietly in the somber, brooding silence like a hunted python. A few pinpoints of light pricked the darkness here and there like winking bits of diamonds, betraying the uneasy vigil of a tense city.

It made me positively hivey the way the FBI agents continued their raids 33 into Japanese homes and business places and marched the Issei men away into the old red brick immigration building, systematically and efficiently, as if they were stocking a cellarfull of choice bottles of wine. At first we noted that the men arrested were those who had been prominent in community affairs, like Mr. Kato, many times president of the Seattle Japanese Chamber of Commerce, and Mr. Ohashi, the principal of our Japanese language school, or individuals whose business was directly connected with firms in Japan; but as time went on, it became less and less apparent why the others were included in these raids.

34   We wondered when Father's time would come. We expected momentarily to hear strange footsteps on the porch and the sudden demanding ring of the front doorbell. Our ears became attuned like the sensitive antennas of moths, translating every soft swish of passing cars into the arrival of the FBI squad.

35   Once when our doorbell rang after curfew hour, I completely lost my Oriental stoicism which I had believed would serve me well under the most trying circumstances. No friend of ours paid visits at night anymore, and I was sure that Father's hour had come. As if hypnotized, I walked woodenly to the door. A mass of black figures stood before me, filling the doorway. I let out a magnificent shriek. Then pandemonium broke loose. The solid rank fell apart into a dozen separate figures which stumbled and leaped pell-mell away from the porch. Watching the mad scramble, I thought I had routed the FBI agents with my cry of distress. Father, Mother, Henry and Sumi rushed out to support my wilting body. When Henry snapped on the porch light, one lone figure crept out from behind the front hedge. It was a newsboy who, standing at a safe distance, called in a quavering voice, "I . . . I came to collect for . . . for the *Times*."

36   Shaking with laughter, Henry paid him and gave him an extra large tip for the terrible fright he and his bodyguards had suffered at the hands of the Japanese. As he hurried down the walk, boys of all shapes and sizes crawled out from behind trees and bushes and scurried after him.

37   We heard all kinds of stories about the FBI, most of them from Mr. Yorita, the grocer, who now took twice as long to make his deliveries. The war seemed to have brought out his personality. At least he talked more, and he glowed, in a sinister way. Before the war Mr. Yorita had been uncommunicative. He used to stagger silently through the back door with a huge sack of rice over his shoulders, dump it on the kitchen floor and silently flow out of the door as if he were bored and disgusted with food and the people who ate it. But now Mr. Yorita swaggered in, sent a gallon jug of soy sauce spinning into a corner, and launched into a comprehensive report of the latest rumors he had picked up on his route, all in chronological order. Mr. Yorita looked like an Oriental Dracula, with his triangular eyes and yellow-fanged teeth. He had a mournfully long sallow face and in his excitement his gold-rimmed glasses constantly slipped to the tip of his long nose. He would describe in detail how some man had been awakened in the dead of night, swiftly handcuffed, and dragged from out of his bed by a squad of brutal, tight-lipped men. Mr. Yorita bared his teeth menacingly in his most dramatic moments and we shrank from him instinctively. As he backed out of the kitchen door, he would shake his bony finger at us with a warning of dire things to come. When Mother said, "Yorita-san, you must worry about getting a call from the FBI, too," Mr. Yorita laughed modestly, pushing

his glasses back up into place. "They wouldn't be interested in anyone as insignificant as myself!" he assured her.

But he was wrong. the following week a new delivery boy appeared at the 38 back door with an airy explanation, "Yep, they got the old man, too, and don't ask me why! The way I see it, it's subversive to sell soy sauce now."

The Matsuis were visited, too, Shortly after Dick had gone to Japan, Mr. 39 Matsui had died and Mrs. Matsui had sold her house. Now she and her daughter and youngest son lived in the back of their little dry goods store on Jackson Street. One day when Mrs. Matsui was busy with the family laundry, three men entered the shop, nearly ripping off the tiny bell hanging over the door. She hurried out, wiping sudsy, reddened hands on her apron. At best Mrs. Matsui's English was rudimentary, and when she became excited, it deteriorated into Japanese. She hovered on her toes, delighted to see new customers in her humble shop. "Yes, yes, something you want?"

"Where's Mr. Matsui?" a steely-eyed man snapped at her. 40

Startled, Mrs. Matsui jerked her thumb toward the rear of the store and 41 said, "He not home."

"What? Oh, in there, eh? Come on!" The men tore the faded print curtain 42 aside and rushed into the back room. "Don't see him. Must be hiding."

They jerked open bedroom doors, leaped into the tiny bathroom, flung 43 windows open and peered down into the alley. Tiny birdlike Mrs. Matsui rushed around after them. "No, no! Whatsamalla, whatsamalla!"

"Where's your husband! Where is he?" one man demanded angrily, flinging 44 clothes out of the closet.

"Why you mix 'em all up? He not home, not home." She clawed at the 45 back of the burly men like an angry little sparrow, trying to stop the holocaust in her little home. One man brought his face down close to hers, shouting slowly and clearly, "WHERE IS YOUR HUSBAND? YOU SAID HE WAS IN HERE A MINUTE AGO!"

"Yes, yes, not here. *Mah, wakara nai hito da neh.* Such stupid men." 46

Mrs. Matsui dove under a table, dragged out a huge album and pointed at 47 a large photograph. She jabbed her gnarled finger up toward the ceiling, saying, "Heben! Heben!"

The men gathered around and looked at a picture of Mr. Matsui's funeral. 48 Mrs. Matsui and her two children were standing by a coffin, their eyes cast down, surrounded by all their friends, all of whom were looking down. The three men's lips formed an "Oh." One of them said, "We're sorry to have disturbed you. Thank you, Mrs. Matsui, and good-by." They departed quickly and quietly.

Having passed through this baptism, Mrs. Matsui became an expert on the 49 FBI, and she stood by us, rallying and coaching us on how to deal with them. She said to Mother, "You must destroy everything and anything Japanese which may incriminate your husband. It doesn't matter what it is, if it's printed or made in Japan, destroy it because the FBI always carries off those items for evidence."

50   In fact all the women whose husbands had been spirited away said the same thing. Gradually we became uncomfortable with our Japanese books, magazines, wall scrolls and knickknacks. When Father's hotel friends, Messrs. Sakaguchi, Horiuchi, Nishibue and a few others vanished, and their wives called Mother weeping and warning her again about having too many Japanese objects around the house, we finally decided to get rid of some of ours. We knew it was impossible to destroy everything. The FBI would certainly think it strange if they found us sitting in a bare house, totally purged of things Japanese. But it was as if we could no longer stand the tension of waiting, and we just had to do something against the black day. We worked all night, feverishly combing through bookshelves, closets, drawers, and furtively creeping down to the basement furnace for the burning. I gathered together my well-worn Japanese language schoolbooks which I had been saving over a period of ten years with the thought that they might come in handy when I wanted to teach Japanese to my own children. I threw them into the fire and watched them flame and shrivel into black ashes. But when I came face to face with my Japanese doll which Grandmother Nagashima had sent me from Japan, I rebelled. It was a gorgeously costumed Miyazukai figure, typical of the lady in waiting who lived in the royal palace during the feudal era. The doll was gowned in an elegant purple silk kimono with the long, sweeping hemline of its period and sashed with rich-embroidered gold and silver brocade. With its black, shining coiffed head bent a little to one side, its delicate pink-tipped ivory hand holding a red lacquer message box, the doll had an appealing, almost human charm. I decided to ask Chris if she would keep it for me. Chris loved and appreciated beauty in every form and shape, and I knew that in her hands, the doll would be safe and enjoyed.

51   Henry pulled down from his bedroom wall the toy samurai sword he had brought from Japan and tossed it into the flames. Sumi's contributions to the furnace were books of fairy tales and magazines sent to her by her young cousins in Japan. We sorted out Japanese classic and popular music from a stack of records, shattered them over our knees and fed the pieces to the furnace. Father piled up his translated Japanese volumes of philosophy and religion and carted them reluctantly to the basement. Mother had the most to eliminate, with her scrapbooks of poems cut out from newspapers and magazines, and her private collection of old Japanese classic literature.

52   It was past midnight when we finally climbed upstairs to bed. Wearily we closed our eyes, filled with an indescribable sense of guilt for having destroyed the things we loved. This night of ravage was to haunt us for years. As I lay struggling to fall asleep, I realized that we hadn't freed ourselves at all from fear. We still lay stiff in our beds, waiting.

53   Mrs. Matsui kept assuring us that the FBI would get around to us yet. It was just a matter of time and the least Mother could do for Father was to pack

a suitcase for him. She said that the men captured who hadn't been prepared had grown long beards, lived and slept in the same clothes for days before they were permitted visits from their families. So Mother dutifully packed a suitcase for Father with toilet articles, warm flannel pajamas, and extra clothes, and placed it in the front hall by the door. It was a personal affront, the way it stood there so frank and unabashedly. Henry and I said that it was practically a confession that Papa was a spy. "So please help yourself to him, Mr. FBI, and God speed you."

Mother was equally loud and firm, "No, don't anyone move it! No one thought that Mr. Kato or the others would be taken, but they're gone now. Why should we think Papa's going to be an exception?" 54

Henry threw his hands up in the air and muttered about the odd ways of the Japanese. 55

Every day Mrs. Matsui called Mother to check Father in; then we caught the habit and started calling him at the hotel every hour on the hour until he finally exploded. "Stop this nonsense! I don't know which is more nerve-wracking, being watched by the FBI or by my family!" 56

When Father returned home from work, a solicitous family eased him into his favorite armchair, arranged pillows behind his back, and brought the evening paper and slippers to him. Mother cooked Father's favorite dishes frenziedly, night after night. It all made Father very uneasy. 57

We had a family conference to discuss the possibility of Father and Mother's internment. Henry was in graduate school and I was beginning my second year at the university. We agreed to drop out should they be taken and we would manage the hotel during our parents' absence. Every week end Henry and I accompanied Father to the hotel and learned how to keep the hotel books, how to open the office safe, and what kind of linen, paper towels, and soap to order. 58

Then a new menace appeared on the scene. Cries began to sound up and down the coast that everyone of Japanese ancestry should be taken into custody. For years the professional guardians of the Golden West had wanted to rid their land of the Yellow Peril, and the war provided an opportunity for them to push their program through. As the chain of Pacific islands fell to the Japanese, patriots shrieked for protection from us. A Californian sounded the alarm: "The Japanese are dangerous and they must leave. Remember the destruction and the sabotage perpetrated at Pearl Harbor. Notice how they have infiltrated into the harbor towns and taken our best land." 59

He and his kind refused to be comforted by Edgar Hoover's special report to the War Department stating that there had not been a single case of sabotage committed by a Japanese living in Hawaii or on the Mainland during the Pearl Harbor attack or after. I began to feel acutely uncomfortable for living on Beacon Hill. The Marine Hospital rose tall and handsome on our hill, and if I stood on the west shoulder of the Hill, I could not help but get an easily photographed view of the Puget Sound Harbor with its ships snuggled against the docks. And Boeing airfield, a few miles south of us, which had never 60 bothered me before, suddenly seemed to have moved right up into my back yard, daring me to take just one spying glance at it.

61   In February, Executive Order No. 9066 came out, authorizing the War Department to remove the Japanese from such military areas as it saw fit, aliens and citizens alike. Even if a person had a fraction of Japanese blood in him, he must leave on demand.

62   A pall of gloom settled upon our home. We couldn't believe that the government meant that the Japanese-Americans must go, too. We had heard the clamoring of superpatriots who insisted loudly, "Throw the whole kaboodle out. A Jap's a Jap, no matter how you slice him. You can't make an American out of little Jap Junior just by handing him an American birth certificate." But we had dismissed these remarks as just hot blasts of air from an overheated patriot. We were quite sure that our rights as American citizens would not be violated, and we would not be marched out of our homes on the same basis as enemy aliens.

63   In anger, Henry and I read and reread the Executive Order. Henry crumpled the newspaper in his hand and threw it against the wall. "Doesn't my citizenship mean a single blessed thing to anyone? Why doesn't somebody make up my mind for me? First they want me in the army. Now they're going to slap an alien 4-C on me because of my ancestry. What the hell!"

64   Once more I felt like a despised, pathetic two-headed freak, a Japanese and an American, neither of which seemed to be doing me any good. The Nisei leaders in the community rose above their personal feelings and stated that they would co-operate and comply with the decision of the government as their sacrifice in keeping with the country's war effort, thus proving themselves loyal American citizens. I was too jealous of my recently acquired voting privilege to be gracious about giving in, and felt most unco-operative. I noticed wryly that the feelings about the Japanese on the Hawaiian Islands were quite different from those on the West Coast. In Hawaii, a strategic military outpost, the Japanese were regarded as essential to the economy of the island and powerful economic forces fought against their removal. General Delos Emmons, in command of Hawaii at the time, lent his authoritative voice to calm the fears of the people on the island and to prevent chaos and upheaval. General Emmons established martial law, but he did not consider evacuation essential for the security of the island.

65   On the West Coast, General, J. L. DeWitt of the Western Defense Command did not think martial law necessary, but he favored mass evacuation of the Japanese and Nisei. We suspected that pressures from economic and political interests who would profit from such a wholesale evacuation influenced this decision.

66   Events moved rapidly. General DeWitt marked off Western Washington, Oregon, and all of California, and the southern half of Arizona as Military Area No. 1, hallowed ground from which we must remove ourselves as rapidly as possible. Unfortunately we could not simply vanish into thin air, and we had

no place to go. We had no relatives in the east we could move in on. All our relatives were sitting with us in the forbidden area, themselves wondering where to go. The neighboring states in the line of exit for the Japanese protested violently at the prospect of any mass invasion. They said, very sensibly, that if the Coast didn't want the Japanese hanging around, they didn't either.

A few hardy families in the community liquidated their property, tied suitcases all around their cars, and sallied eastward. They were greeted by signs in front of store windows, "Open season for Japs!" and "We kill rats and Japs here." On state lines, highway troopers swarmed around the objectionable migrants and turned them back under governor's orders.   67

General DeWitt must have finally realized that if he insisted on voluntary mass evacuation, hundreds and thousands of us would have wandered back and forth, clogging the highways and pitching tents along the roadside, eating and sleeping in colossal disorder. He suddenly called a halt to voluntary movement, although most of the Japanese were not budging an inch. He issued a new order, stating that no Japanese could leave the city, under penalty of arrest. The command had hatched another plan, a better one. The army would move us out as only the army could do it, and march us in neat, orderly fashion into assembly centers. We would stay in these centers only until permanent camps were set up inland to isolate us.   68

The orders were simple: 69

Dispose of your homes and property. Wind up your businesses. Register the family. One seabag of bedding, two suitcases of clothing allowed per person. People in District #1 must report at 8th and Lane Street, 8 p.m. on April 28.

I wanted no part of this new order. I had read in the papers that the Japanese from the state of Washington would be taken to a camp in Puyallup, on the state fairgrounds. The article apologetically assured the public that the camp would be temporary and that the Japanese would be removed from the fairgrounds and parking lots in time for the opening of the annual State Fair. It neglected to say where we might be at the time when those fine breeds of Holstein cattle and Yorkshire hogs would be proudly wearing their blue satin ribbons.   70

We were advised to pack warm, durable clothes. In my mind, I saw our permanent camp sprawled out somewhere deep in a snow-bound forest, an American Siberia. I saw myself plunging chest deep in the snow, hunting for small game to keep us alive. I decided that one of my suitcases was going to hold nothing but vitamins from A to Z. I thought of sewing fur-lined hoods and parkas for the family. I was certain this was going to be a case of sheer animal survival.   71

One evening Father told us that he would lose the management of the hotel unless he could find someone to operate it for the duration, someone intelligent   72 and efficient enough to impress Bentley Agent and Company. Father said, "Sam, Joe, Peter, they all promised to stay on their jobs, but none of them can read or write well enough to manage the business. I've got to find a responsible party with experience in hotel management, but where?"

73 Sumi asked, "What happens if we can't find anyone?"

74 "I lose my business and my livelihood. I'll be saying good-by to a lifetime of labor and all the hopes and plans I had for the family."

75 We sagged. Father looked at us thoughtfully, "I've never talked much about the hotel business to you children, mainly because so much of it has been an uphill climb of work and waiting for better times. Only recently I was able to clear up the loans I took out years ago to expand the business. I was sure that in the next five or ten years I would be getting returns on my long-range investments, and I would have been able to do a lot of things eventually. . . . Send you through medical school," Father nodded to Henry, "and let Kazu and Sumi study anything they liked." Father laughed a bit self-consciously as he looked at Mother. "And when all the children had gone off on their own, I had planned to take Mama on her first real vacation, to Europe as well as Japan."

76 We listened to Father wide-eyed and wistful. It had been a wonderful, wonderful dream.

77 Mother suddenly hit upon a brilliant idea. She said maybe the Olsens, our old friends who had once managed the Camden Apartments, might be willing to run a hotel. The Olsens had sold the apartment and moved to Aberdeen. Mother thought that perhaps Marta's oldest brother, the bachelor of the family, might be available. If he refused, perhaps Marta and her husband might consider the offer. We rushed excitedly to the telephone to make a long-distance call to the Olsens. After four wrong Olsens, we finally reached Marta.

78 "Marta? Is this Marta?"

79 "Yes, this is Marta."

80 I nearly dove into the mouthpiece, I was so glad to hear her voice. Marta remembered us well and we exchanged news about our families. Marta and her husband had bought a small chicken farm and were doing well. Marta said, "I come from the farm ven I vas young and I like it fine. I feel more like home here. How's everybody over there?"

81 I told her that we and all the rest of the Japanese were leaving Seattle soon under government order on account of the war. Marta gasped, "Everybody? You mean the Saitos, the Fujinos, Watanabes, and all the rest who were living at the Camden Apartments, too?"

82 "Yes, they and everyone else on the West Coast."

83 Bewildered, Marta asked where we were going, what we were going to do, would we ever return to Seattle, and what about Father's hotel. I told her about our business situation and that Father needed a hotel manager for the duration. Would she or any of her brothers be willing to accept such a job? There was a silence at the other end of the line and I said hastily, "This is a very sudden

call, Marta. I'm sorry I had to surprise you like this, but we felt this was an emergency and . . ."

84   Marta was full of regrets. "Oh, I vish we could do someting to help you folks, but my husband and I can't leave the farm at all. We don't have anyone here to help. We do all the work ourselves. Magnus went to Alaska last year. He has a goot job up there, some kind of war work. My other two brothers have business in town and they have children so they can't help you much."

85   My heart sank like a broken elevator. When I said, "Oh . . ." I felt the family sitting behind me sink into a gloomy silence. Our last hope was gone. We finally said good-by, Marta distressed at not being able to help, and I apologized for trying to hoist our problem on them.

86   The next week end Marta and Karl paid us a surprise visit. We had not seen them for nearly two years. Marta explained shyly, "It was such a nice day and we don't go novair for a long time, so I tole Karl, 'Let's take a bus into Seattle and visit the Itois.'"

87   We spent a delightful Sunday afternoon taking about old times. Mother served our guests her best green tea and, as we relaxed, the irritating presence of war vanished. When it was time for them to return home, Marta's sparkling blue eyes suddenly filled. "Karl and I, we feel so bad about the whole ting, the war and everyting, we joost had to come out to see you and say 'good by.' God bless you. Maybe we vill see you again back home here. Anyvay, we pray for it."

88   Marta and Karl's warmth and sincerity restored a sense of peace into our home, an atmosphere which had disappeared ever since Pearl Harbor. They served to remind us that in spite of the bitterness war had brought into our lives, we were still bound to our home town. Bit by bit, I remembered our happy past, the fun we had growing up along the colorful brash waterfront, swimming through the white-laced waves of Puget Sound, and lolling luxuriously on the tender green carpet of grass around Lake Washington from where we could see the slick, blue-frosted shoulders of Mount Rainier. There was too much beauty surrounding us. Above all, we must keep friends like Marta and Karl, Christine, Sam, Peter and Joe, all sterling products of many years of associations. We could never turn our faces away and remain aloof forever from Seattle. ✣

RESPONDING

1. Have you ever felt that you had your rights taken away unfairly by a social institution, family, or a friend? Write a letter of protest to the individual or institution who you felt treated you unjustly.

2. Working individually or in a group, outline the changes that took place in

the lives of the Sone family from the bombing of Pearl Harbor to the evacuation of the Japanese Americans.

3. In an essay, compare the attitudes and reactions of different members of the Sone family to the United States and Japan before and after Pearl Harbor or before and after the evacuation order. Does the older generation have a markedly different attitude from that of the younger generation?

4. Sone states that the internment of her family violated their rights as American citizens. Using examples from her autobiography and other readings such as the Bill of Rights, write an essay agreeing or disagreeing with her statement.

JOHN OKADA

Born in Seattle, Washington, in 1923, John Okada served in the army during World War II. After earning a bachelor's degree from the University of Washington and a master's degree from Columbia University, he worked as a reference librarian and a technical writer. He died of a heart attack in 1971. Although Okada did not enjoy great fame during his lifetime, he is now considered by many to be one of the most important Japanese American writers.

The following excerpt from No-no Boy, *first published in 1957, describes some of the conflicts within the Japanese community at the time of the war. In the passage, the main character begins to see how one's sense of loyalty is very often a function of one's position in society. He also discovers how people use both ideology and emotion to justify their decisions.*

✠

From NO-NO BOY

"ICHIRO." 1

He propped himself up on an elbow and looked at her. She had hardly 2 changed. Surely, there must have been a time when she could smile and, yet, he could not remember.

"Yeah?" 3

"Lunch is on the table." 4

As he pushed himself off the bed and walked past her to the kitchen, she 5 took broom and dustpan and swept up the mess he had made.

There were eggs, fried with soy sauce, sliced cold meat, boiled cabbage, 6 and tea and rice. They all ate in silence, not even disturbed once by the tinkling of the bell. The father cleared the table after they had finished and dutifully retired to watch the store. Ichiro had smoked three cigarettes before his mother ended the silence.

"You must go back to school." 7

He had almost forgotten that there had been a time before the war when 8 he had actually gone to college for two years and studiously applied himself to courses in the engineering school. The statement staggered him. Was that all there was to it? Did she mean to sit there and imply that the four intervening years were to be casually forgotten and life resumed as if there had been no four years and no war and no Eto who had spit on him because of the thing he had done?

"I don't feel much like going to school." 9

"What will you do?" 10

11 "I don't know."

12 "With an education, your opportunities in Japan will be unlimited. You must go and complete your studies."

13 "Ma," he said slowly, "Ma, I'm not going to Japan. Nobody's going to Japan. The war is over. Japan lost. Do you hear? Japan lost."

14 "You believe that?" It was said in the tone of an adult asking a child who is no longer a child if he really believed that Santa Claus was real.

15 "Yes, I believe it. I know it. America is still here. Do you see the great Japanese army walking down the streets? No. There is no Japanese army any more."

16 "The boat is coming and we must be ready."

17 "The boat?"

18 "Yes." She reached into her pocket and drew out a worn envelope.

19 The letter had been mailed from São Paulo, Brazil, and was addressed to a name that he did not recognize. Inside the envelope was a single sheet of flimsy, rice paper covered with intricate flourishes of Japanese characters.

20 "What does it say?"

21 She did not bother to pick up the letter. "To you who are a loyal and honorable Japanese, it is with humble and heartfelt joy that I relay this momentous message. Word has been brought to us that the victorious Japanese government is presently making preparations to send ships which will return to Japan those residents in foreign countries who have steadfastly maintained their faith and loyalty to our Emperor. The Japanese government regrets that the responsibilities arising from the victory compel them to delay in the sending of the vessels. To be among the few who remain to receive this honor is a gratifying tribute. Heed not the propaganda of the radio and newspapers which endeavor to convince the people with lies about the allied victory. Especially, heed not the lies of your traitorous countrymen who have turned their backs on the country of their birth and who will suffer for their treasonous acts. The day of glory is close at hand. The rewards will be beyond our greatest expectations. What we have done, we have done only as Japanese, but the government is grateful. Hold your heads high and make ready for the journey, for the ships are coming."

22 "Who wrote that?" he asked incredulously. It was like a weird nightmare. It was like finding out that an incurable strain of insanity pervaded the family, an intangible horror that swayed and taunted beyond the grasp of reaching fingers.

23 "A friend in South America. We are not alone."

24 "We *are* alone," he said vehemently. "This whole thing is crazy. You're crazy. I'm crazy. All right, so we made a mistake. Let's admit it."

25 "There has been no mistake. The letter confirms."

26 "Sure it does. It proves there's crazy people in the world besides us. If Japan won the war, what the hell are we doing here? What are you doing running a grocery store? It doesn't figure. It doesn't figure because we're all wrong. The

minute we admit that, everything is fine. I've had a lot of time to think about all this. I've thought about it, and every time the answer comes out the same. You can't tell me different any more."

She sighed ever so slightly. "We will talk later when you are feeling better." 27 Carefully folding the letter and placing it back in the envelope, she returned it to her pocket. "It is not I who tell you that the ship is coming. It is in the letter. If you have come to doubt your mother—and I'm sure you do not mean it even if you speak in weakness—it is to be regretted. Rest a few days. Think more deeply and your doubts will disappear. You are my son, Ichiro."

No, he said to himself as he watched her part the curtains and start into 28 the store. There was a time when I was your son. there was a time that I no longer remember when you used to smile a mother's smile and tell me stories about gallant and fierce warriors who protected their lords with blades of shining steel and about the old woman who found a peach in the stream and took it home and when her husband split it in half, a husky little boy tumbled out to fill their hearts with boundless joy. I was that boy in the peach and you were the old woman and we were Japanese with Japanese feelings and Japanese pride and Japanese thoughts because it was all right then to be Japanese and feel and think all the things that Japanese do even if we lived in America. Then there came a time when I was only half Japanese because one is not born in America and raised in America and taught in America and one does not speak and swear and drink and smoke and play and fight and see and hear in America among Americans in American streets and houses without becoming American and loving it. But I did not love enough, for you were still half my mother and I was thereby still half Japanese and when the war came and they told me to fight for America, I was not strong enough to fight you and I was not strong enough to fight the bitterness which made the half of me which was you bigger than the half of me which was America and really the whole of me that I could not see or feel. Now that I know the truth when it is too late and the half of me which was you is no longer there, I am only half of me and the half that remains is American by law because the government was wise and strong enough to know why it was that I could not fight for America and did not strip me of my birthright. But it is not enough to be American only in the eyes of the law and it is not enough to be only half an American and know that it is an empty half. I am not your son and I am not Japanese and I am not American. I can go someplace and tell people that I've got an inverted stomach and that I am an American, true and blue and Hail Columbia, but the army wouldn't have me because of the stomach. That's easy and I would do it, only I've got to convince myself first and that I cannot do. I wish with all my heart that I were Japanese or that I were American. I am neither and I blame you and I blame myself and I blame the world which is made up of many countries which fight with each other and kill and hate and destroy but not enough, so that they must kill and hate and destroy again and again and again. It is so easy and simple that I cannot understand it at all. And the reason I do not understand it is because I do not understand you who were the half of me that is no more and because I do not understand what it was about that half that made me destroy the half of me which was American and the half which might have become the whole of me if I had said yes I will go and fight in your army because that is what I believe and want and cherish and love . . .

29   Defeatedly, he crushed the stub of a cigarette into an ash tray filled with many other stubs and reached for the package to get another. It was empty and he did not want to go into the store for more because he did not feel much like seeing either his father or mother. He went into the bedroom and tossed and groaned and half slept.

30   Hours later, someone shook him awake. It was not his mother and it was not his father. The face that looked down at him in the gloomy darkness was his brother's.

31   "Taro," he said softly, for he had hardly thought of him.

32   "Yeah, it's me," said his brother with unmistakable embarrassment. "I see you got out."

33   "How've you been?" He studies his brother, who was as tall as he but skinnier.

34   "Okay. It's time to eat." He started to leave.

35   "Taro, wait."

36   His brother stood framed in the light of the doorway and faced him.

37   "How've you been?" he repeated. Then he added quickly for fear of losing him: "No, I said that before and I don't mean it the way it sounds. We've got things to talk about. Long time since we saw each other."

38   "Yeah, it's been a long time."

39   "How's school?"

40   "Okay."

41   "About through with high school?"

42   "Next June."

43   "What then? College?"

44   "No, army."

45   He wished he could see his face, the face of the brother who spoke to him as though they were strangers—because that's what they were.

46   "You could get in a year or two before the draft," he heard himself saying in an effort to destroy the wall that separated them. "I read where you can take an exam now and get a deferment if your showing is good enough. A fellow's got to have all the education he can get, Taro."

47   "I don't want a deferment. I want in."

48   "Ma know?"

49   "Who cares?"

50   "She won't like it."

51   "Doesn't matter."

"Why so strong about the army? Can't you wait? They'll come and get you soon enough." 52

"That isn't soon enough for me." 53

"What's your reason?" 54

He waited for an answer, knowing what it was and not wanting to hear it. 55

"Is it because of me? What I did?" 56

"I'm hungry," his brother said and turned into the kitchen. 57

His mother had already eaten and was watching the store. He sat opposite his brother, who wolfed down the food without looking back at him. It wasn't more than a few minutes before he rose, grabbed his jacket off a nail on the wall, and left the table. The bell tinkled and he was gone. 58

"Don't mind him," said the father apologetically. "Taro is young and restless. He's never home except to eat and sleep." 59

"When does he study?" 60

"He does not." 61

"Why don't you do something about it?" 62

"I tell him. Mama tells him. Makes no difference. It is the war that has made them that way. All the people say the same thing. The war and the camp life. Made them wild like cats and dogs. It is hard to understand." 63

"Sure," he said, but he told himself that he understood, that the reason why Taro was not a son and not a brother was because he was young and American and alien to his parents, who had lived in America for thirty-five years without becoming less Japanese and could speak only a few broken words of English and write it not at all, and because Taro hated that thing in his elder brother which had prevented him from thinking for himself. And in his hate for that thing, he hated his brother and also his parents because they had created the thing with their eyes and hands and minds which had seen and felt and thought as Japanese for thirty-five years in an America which they rejected as thoroughly as if they had never been a day away from Japan. That was the reason and it was difficult to believe, but it was true because he was the emptiness between the one and the other and could see flashes of the truth that was true for his parents and the truth that was true for his brother. 64

"Pa," he said. 65

"Ya, Ichiro." He was swirling a dishcloth in a pan of hot water and working up suds for the dishes. 66

"What made you and Ma come to America?" 67

"Everyone was coming to America." 68

"Did you have to come?" 69

"No. We came to make money." 70

"Is that all?" 71

"Ya, I think that was why we came." 72

"Why to make money?" 73

"There was a man in my village who went to America and made a lot of 74 money and he came back and bought a big piece of land and he was very comfortable. We came so we could make money and go back and buy a piece of land and be comfortable too."

75   "Did you ever think about staying here and not going back?"

76   "No."

77   He looked at his father, who was old and bald and washing dishes in a kitchen that was behind a hole in the wall that was a grocery store. "How do you feel about it now?"

78   "About what?"

79   "Going back."

80   "We are going."

81   "When?"

82   "Oh, pretty soon."

83   "How soon?"

84   "Pretty soon."

85   There didn't seem to be much point in pursuing the questioning. He went out to the store and got a fresh pack of cigarettes. His mother was washing down the vegetable stand, which stood alongside the entrance. Her thin arms swabbed the green-painted wood with sweeping, vigorous strokes. There was a power in the wiry, brown arms, a hard, blind, unreckoning force which coursed through veins of tough bamboo. When she had done her work, she carried the pail of water to the curb outside and poured it on the street. Then she came back through the store and into the living quarters and emerged once more dressed in her coat and hat.

86   "Come, Ichiro," she said, "we must go and see Kumasaka-san and Ashida-san. They will wish to know that you are back."

87   The import of the suggested visits made him waver helplessly. He was too stunned to voice his protest. The Kumasakas and the Ashidas were people from the same village in Japan. The three families had been very close for as long as he could recall. Further, it was customary among the Japanese to pay ceremonious visits upon various occasions to families of close association. This was particularly true when a member of one of the families either departed on an extended absence or returned from an unusually long separation. Yes, he had been gone a long time, but it was such a different thing. It wasn't as if he had gone to war and returned safe and sound or had been matriculating at some school in another city and come home with a sheepskin *summa cum laude*. He scrabbled at the confusion in his mind for the logic of the crazy business and found no satisfaction.

88   "Papa," his mother shouted without actually shouting.

89   His father hastened out from the kitchen and Ichiro stumbled in blind fury after the woman who was only a rock of hate and fanatic stubbornness and was, therefore, neither woman nor mother.

90   They walked through the night and the city, a mother and son thrown together for a while longer because the family group is a stubborn one and does

not easily disintegrate. The woman walked ahead and the son followed and no word passed between them. They walked six blocks, then six more, and still another six before they turned in to a three-story frame building.

The Ashidas, parents and three daughters, occupied four rooms on the second floor. 91

"Mama," screamed the ten-year-old who answered the knock, "Mrs. Yamada." 92

A fat, cheerful-looking woman rushed toward them, then stopped, flushed and surprised. "Ichiro-san. You have come back." 93

He nodded his head and heard his mother say, with unmistakable exultation: "Today, Ashida-san. Just today he came home." 94

Urged by their hostess, they took seats in the sparsely furnished living room. Mrs. Ashida sat opposite them on a straight-backed kitchen chair and beamed. 95

"You have grown so much. It is good to be home, is it not, Ichiro-san?" She turned to the ten-year-old who gawked at him from behind her mother: "Tell Reiko to get tea and cookies." 96

"She's studying, Mama." 97

"You mustn't bother," said his mother. 98

"Go now, I know she is only listening to the radio." The little girl fled out of the room. 99

"It is good to see you again, Ichiro-san. You will find many of your young friends already here. All the people who said they would never come back to Seattle are coming back. It is almost like it was before the war. Akira-san—you went to school with him I think—he is just back from Italy, and Watanabe-san's boy came back from Japan last month. It is so good that the war is over and everything is getting to be like it was before." 100

"You saw the pictures?" his mother asked. 101

"What pictures?" 102

"You have not been to the Watanabes'?" 103

"Oh, yes, the pictures of Japan." She snickered. "He is such a serious boy. He showed me all the pictures he had taken in Japan. He had many of Hiroshima and Nagasaki and I told him that he must be mistaken because Japan did not lose the war as he seems to believe and that he could not have been in Japan to take pictures because, if he were in Japan, he would not have been permitted to remain alive. He protested and yelled so that his mother had to tell him to be careful and then he tried to argue some more, but I asked him if he was ever in Japan before and could he prove that he was actually there and he said again to look at the pictures and I told him that what must really have happened was that the army only told him he was in Japan when he was someplace else, and that it was too bad he believed the propaganda. Then he got so mad his face went white and he said: 'How do you know you're you? Tell me how you know you're you!' If his mother had not made him leave the room, he might even have struck me. It is not enough that they must willingly take up arms against their uncles and cousins and even brothers and sisters, but they no longer have 104 respect for the old ones. If I had a son and he had gone in the American army to fight Japan, I would have killed myself with shame."

105 "They know not what they do and it is not their fault. It is the fault of the parents. I've always said that Mr. Watanabe was a stupid man. Gambling and drinking the way he does. I am almost ashamed to call them friends." Ichiro's mother looked at him with a look which said I am a Japanese and you are my son and have conducted yourself as a Japanese and I know no shame such as other parents do because their sons were not really their sons or they would not have fought against their own people.

106 He wanted to get up and dash out into the night. The madness of his mother was in mutual company and he felt nothing but loathing for the gentle, kindly-looking Mrs. Ashida, who sat on a fifty-cent chair from Goodwill Industries while her husband worked the night shift at a hotel, grinning and bowing for dimes and quarters from rich Americans whom he detested, and couldn't afford to take his family on a bus ride to Tacoma but was waiting and praying and hoping for the ships from Japan.

107 Reiko brought in a tray holding little teacups and a bowl of thin, round cookies. She was around seventeen with little bumps on her chest which the sweater didn't improve and her lips heavily lipsticked a deep red. She said "Hi" to him and did not have to say look at me, I was a kid when you saw me last but now I'm a woman with a woman's desires and a woman's eye for men like you. She set the tray on the table and gave him a smile before she left.

108 His mother took the envelope from São Paulo out of her dress pocket and handed it to Mrs. Ashida.

109 "From South America."

110 The other woman snatched at the envelope and proceeded to read the contents instantly. Her face glowed with pride. She read it eagerly, her lips moving all the time and frequently murmuring audibly. "Such wonderful news," she sighed breathlessly as if the reading of the letter had been a deep emotional experience. "Mrs. Okamoto will be eager to see this. Her husband, who goes out of the house whenever I am there, is threatening to leave her unless she gives up her nonsense about Japan. Nonsense, he calls it. He is no better than a Chinaman. This will show him. I feel so sorry for her."

111 "It is hard when so many no longer believe," replied his mother, "but they are not Japanese like us. They only call themselves such. It is the same with the Teradas. I no longer go to see them. The last time I was there Mr. Terada screamed at me and told me to get out. They just don't understand that Japan did not lose the war because Japan could not possibly lose. I try not to hate them but I have no course but to point them out to the authorities when the ships come."

112 "It's getting late, Ma." He stood up, sick in the stomach and wanting desperately to smash his way out of the dishonest, warped, and uncompromising

world in which defeated people like his mother and the Ashidas walked their perilous tightropes and could not and would not look about them for having to keep their eyes fastened to the taut, thin support.

"Yes," his mother replied quickly, "forgive us for rushing, for you know that I enjoy nothing better than a visit with you, but we must drop in for a while on the Kumasakas." 113

"Of course. I wish you could stay longer, but I know that there will be plenty of opportunities again. You will come again, please, Ichiro-san?" 114

Mumbling thanks for the tea, he nodded evasively and hurried down the stairs. Outside, he lit a cigarette and paced restlessly until his mother came out. 115

"A fine woman," she said without stopping. 116

He followed, talking to the back of her head: "Ma, I don't want to see the Kumasakas tonight. I don't want to see anybody tonight. We'll go some other time." 117

"We won't stay long." 118

They walked a few blocks to a freshly painted frame house that was situated behind a neatly kept lawn. 119

"Nice house," he said. 120

"They bought it last month." 121

"Bought it?" 122

"Yes." 123

The Kumasakas had run a dry-cleaning shop before the war. Business was good and people spoke of their having money, but they lived in cramped quarters above the shop because, like most of the other Japanese, they planned someday to return to Japan and still felt transients even after thirty or forty years in America and the quarters above the shop seemed adequate and sensible since the arrangement was merely temporary. That, he thought to himself, was the reason why the Japanese were still Japanese. They rushed to America with the single purpose of making a fortune which would enable them to return to their own country and live adequately. It did not matter when they discovered that fortunes were not for the mere seeking or that their sojourns were spanning decades instead of years and it did not matter that growing families and growing bills and misfortunes and illness and low wages and just plain hard luck were constant obstacles to the realization of their dreams. They continued to maintain their dreams by refusing to learn how to speak or write the language of America and by living only among their own kind and by zealously avoiding long-term commitments such as the purchase of a house. But now, the Kumasakas, it seemed, had bought this house, and he was impressed. It could only mean that the Kumasakas had exchanged hope for reality and, late as it was, were finally sinking roots into the land from which they had previously sought not nourishment but only gold. 124

Mrs. Kumasaka came to the door, a short, heavy woman who stood solidly on feet planted wide apart, like a man. She greeted them warmly but with a 125 sadness that she would carry to the grave. When Ichiro had last seen her, her hair had been pitch black. Now it was completely white.

126   In the living room Mr. Kumasaka, a small man with a pleasant smile, was sunk deep in an upholstered chair, reading a Japanese newspaper. It was a comfortable room with rugs and soft furniture and lamps and end tables and pictures on recently papered walls.

127   "Ah, Ichiro, it is nice to see you looking well," Mr. Kumasaka struggled out of the chair and extended a friendly hand. "Please, sit down."

128   "You've got a nice place," he said, meaning it.

129   "Thank you," the little man said. "Mama and I, we finally decided that America is not so bad. We like it here."

130   Ichiro sat down on the sofa next to his mother and felt strange in this home which he envied because it was like millions of other homes in America and could never be his own.

131   Mrs. Kumasaka sat next to her husband on a large, round hassock and looked at Ichiro with lonely eyes, which made him uncomfortable.

132   "Ichiro came home this morning." It was his mother, and the sound of her voice, deliberately loud and almost arrogant, puzzled him. "He has suffered, but I make no apologies for him or for myself. If he had given his life for Japan, I could not be prouder."

133   "Ma," he said, wanting to object but not knowing why except that her comments seemed out of place.

134   Ignoring him, she continued, not looking at the man but at his wife, who now sat with head bowed, her eyes emptily regarding the floral pattern of the carpet. "A mother's lot is not an easy one. To sleep with a man and bear a son is nothing. To raise the child into a man one can be proud of is not play. Some of us succeed. Some, of course, must fail. It is too bad, but that is the way of life."

135   "Yes, yes, Yamada-san," said the man impatiently. Then, smiling, he turned to Ichiro: "I suppose you'll be going back to the university?"

136   "I'll have to think about it," he replied, wishing that his father was like this man who made him want to pour out the turbulence in his soul.

137   "He will go when the new term begins. I have impressed upon him the importance of a good education. With a college education, one can go far in Japan." His mother smiled knowingly.

138   "Ah," said the man as if he had not heard her speak. "Bobbie wanted to go to the university and study medicine. He would have made a fine doctor. Always studying and reading, is that not so, Ichiro?"

139   He nodded, remembering the quiet son of the Kumasakas, who never played football with the rest of the kids on the street or appeared at dances, but could talk for hours on end about chemistry and zoology and physics and other courses which he hungered after in high school.

140   "Sure, Bob always was pretty studious." He knew, somehow, that it was not the right thing to say, but he added: "Where is Bob?"

His mother did not move. Mrs. Kumasaka uttered a despairing cry and bit 141
her trembling lips.

The little man, his face a drawn mask of pity and sorrow, stammered: 142
"Ichiro, you—no one has told you?"

"No. What? No one's told me anything." 143

"Your mother did not write you?" 144

"No. Write about what?" He knew what the answer was. It was in the 145
whiteness of the hair of the sad woman who was the mother of the boy named
Bob and it was in the engaging pleasantness of the father which was not really
pleasantness but a deep understanding which had emerged from resignation to
a loss which only a parent knows and suffers. And then he saw the picture on
the mantel, a snapshot, enlarged many times over, of a grinning youth in
uniform who had not thought to remember his parents with a formal portrait
because he was not going to die and there would be worlds of time for pictures
and books and other obligations of the living later on.

Mr. Kumasaka startled him by shouting toward the rear of the house: "Jun! 146
Please come."

There was the sound of a door opening and presently there appeared a 147
youth in khaki shirt and wool trousers, who was a stranger to Ichiro.

"I hope I haven't disturbed anything, Jun," said Mr. Kumasaka. 148

"No, it's all right. Just writing a letter." 149

"This is Mrs. Yamada and her son Ichiro. They are old family friends." 150

Jun nodded to his mother and reached over to shake Ichiro's hand. 151

The little man waited until Jun had seated himself on the end of the sofa. 152
"Jun is from Los Angeles. He's on his way home from the army and was good
enough to stop by and visit us for a few days. He and Bobbie were together.
Buddies—is that what you say?"

"That's right," said Jun. 153

"Now, Jun." 154

"Yes?" 155

The little man looked at Ichiro and then at his mother, who stared stonily 156
at no one in particular.

"Jun, as a favor to me, although I know it is not easy for you to speak of 157
it, I want you to tell us about Bobbie."

Jun stood up quickly. "Gosh, I don't know." He looked with tender concern 158
at Mrs. Kumasaka.

"It is all right, Jun. Please, just this once more." 159

"Well, okay." He sat down again, rubbing his hands thoughtfully over his 160
knees. "The way it happened, Bobbie and I, we had just gotten back to the rest
area. Everybody was feeling good because there was a lot of talk about the
Germans' surrendering. All the fellows were cleaning their equipment. We'd
been up in the lines for a long time and everything was pretty well messed up.
When you're up there getting shot at, you don't worry much about how crummy
your things get, but the minute you pull back, they got to have inspection. So,

we were cleaning things up. Most of us were cleaning our rifles because that's something you learn to want to do no matter how anything else looks. Bobbie was sitting beside me and he was talking about how he was going to medical school and become a doctor—"

161   A sob wrenched itself free from the breast of the mother whose son was once again dying, and the snow-white head bobbed wretchedly.

162   "Go on, Jun," said the father.

163   Jun looked away from the mother and at the picture on the mantel. "Bobbie was like that. Me and the other guys, all we talked about was drinking and girls and stuff like that because it's important to talk about those things when you make it back from the front on your own power, but Bobbie, all he thought about was going to school. I was nodding my head and saying yeah, yeah, and then there was this noise, kind of a pinging noise right close by. It scared me for a minute and I started to cuss and said, 'Gee, that was damn close,' and looked around at Bobbie. He was slumped over with his head between his knees. I reached out to hit him, thinking he was fooling around. Then, when I tapped him on the arm, he fell over and I saw the dark spot on the side of his head where the bullet had gone through. That was all. Ping, and he's dead. It doesn't figure, but it happened just the way I've said."

164   The mother was crying now, without shame and alone in her grief that knew no end. And in her bottomless grief that made no distinction as to what was wrong and what was right and who was Japanese and who was not, there was no awareness of the other mother with a living son who had come to say to her you are with shame and grief because you were not Japanese and thereby killed your son but mine is big and strong and full of life because I did not weaken and would not let my son destroy himself uselessly and treacherously.

165   Ichiro's mother rose and, without a word, for no words would ever pass between them again, went out of the house which was a part of America.

166   Mr. Kumasaka placed a hand on the rounded back of his wife, who was forever beyond consoling, and spoke gently to Ichiro: "You don't have to say anything. You are truly sorry and I am sorry for you."

167   "I didn't know," he said pleadingly.

168   "I want you to feel free to come and visit us whenever you wish. We can talk even if your mother's convictions are different."

169   "She's crazy. Mean and crazy. Goddamned Jap!" He felt the tears hot and stinging.

170   "Try to understand her."

171   Impulsively, he took the little man's hand in his own and held it briefly. Then he hurried out of the house which could never be his own.

172   His mother was not waiting for him. He saw her tiny figure strutting into the shadows away from the illumination of the street lights and did not attempt to catch her. ❖

RESPONDING

1. Have you ever found yourself in serious conflict over a matter of conscience with a person whose opinion you valued such as a parent, teacher, religious leader, or special friend? Did the conflict produce inner turmoil? What was the outcome?

2. The story presents two contrasting attitudes toward Japan and America. Working individually or in a group, analyze the reasons for each point of view and present them to the class.

3. What is Ichiro's attitude toward his mother? Does it change in the course of the story? Write the dialogue that might have taken place between Ichiro and his mother on the way home from the Kumasakas'.

4. Ichiro's statement "I wish with all my heart that I were Japanese or that I were American" (paragraph 28) expresses his inner conflict. In an essay, explain the divided loyalties that pull him in different directions.

HISAYE YAMAMOTO

Hisaye Yamamoto, who was born in Redondo Beach, California, in 1921, spent the war years interned with her family in Arizona. After the war she attended college and wrote for the Los Angeles Tribune. *Since that time, Yamamoto has published short stories in such journals as* The Kenyon Review, Amerasia Journal, The Partisan Review, Arizona Quarterly, *and* Counterpoint. *Much of her writing was collected in the volume* Seventeen Syllables and Other Stories, *published in 1989.*

"The Legend of Miss Sasagawara," from Seventeen Syllables, *uses the concrete details of fiction to examine the effects of the camp's regimented life on one of its inmates; in a more general sense the story might be said to comment on the consequences of the Internment for many Japanese American young people who came of age during this period.*

⁜

THE LEGEND OF MISS SASAGAWARA

1 EVEN IN THAT UNLIKELY PLACE OF WIND, sand, and heat, it was easy to imagine Miss Sasagawara a decorative ingredient of some ballet. Her daily costume, brief and fitting closely to her trifling waist, generously billowing below, and bringing together arrestingly rich colors like mustard yellow and forest green, appeared to have been cut from a coarse-textured homespun; her shining hair was so long it wound twice about her head to form a coronet; her face was delicate and pale, with a fine nose, pouting bright mouth, and glittering eyes; and her measured walk said, "Look, I'm *walking*!" as though walking were not a common but a rather special thing to be doing. I first saw her so one evening after mess, as she was coming out of the women's latrine going toward her barracks, and after I thought I was out of hearing, I imitated the young men of the Block (No. 33), and gasped, "Wow! How much does *she* weigh?"

2 "Oh, haven't you heard?" said my friend Elsie Kubo, knowing very well I had not. "That's Miss Sasagawara."

3 It turned out Elsie knew all about Miss Sasagawara, who with her father was new to Block 33. Where had she accumulated all her items? Probably a morsel here and a morsel there, and, anyway, I forgot to ask her sources, because the picture she painted was so distracting: Miss Sasagawara's father was a Buddhist minister, and the two had gotten permission to come to this Japanese evacuation camp in Arizona from one further north, after the death there of Mrs. Sasagawara. They had come here to join the Rev. Sasagawara's brother's family, who lived in a neighboring Block, but there had been some trouble

between them, and just this week the immigrant pair had gotten leave to move over to Block 33. They were occupying one end of the Block's lone empty barracks, which had not been chopped up yet into the customary four apartments. The other end had been taken over by a young couple, also newcomers to the Block, who had moved in the same day.

"And do you know what, Kiku?" Elsie continued. "Oooh, that gal is really   4
temperamental. I guess it's because she was a ballet dancer before she got stuck in camp, I hear people like that are temperamental. Anyway, the Sasakis, the new couple at the other end of the barracks, think she's crazy. The day they all moved in, the barracks was really dirty, all covered with dust from the dust storms and everything, so Mr. Sasaki was going to wash the whole barracks down with a hose, and he thought he'd be nice and do the Sasagawaras' side first. You know, do them a favor. But do you know what? Mr. Sasaki got the hose attached to the faucet outside and started to go in the door, and he said all the Sasagawaras' suitcases and things were on top of the Army cots and Miss Sasagawara was trying to clean the place out with a pail of water and a broom. He said, 'Here let me flush the place out with a hose for you; it'll be faster.' And she turned right around and screamed at him, 'What are you trying to do? Spy on me? Get out of here or I'll throw this water on you!' He said he was so surprised he couldn't move for a minute, and before he knew it, Miss Sasagawara just up and threw that water at him, pail and all. Oh, he said he got out of that place fast, but fast. Madwoman, he called her."

But Elsie had already met Miss Sasagawara, too, over at the apartment of   5
the Murakamis, where Miss Sasagawara was borrowing Mrs. Murakami's Singer, and had found her quite amiable. "She said she was thirty-nine years old—imagine, thirty-nine, she looks so young, more like twenty-five; but she said she wasn't sorry she never got married, because she's had her fun. She said she got to go all over the country a couple of times, dancing in the ballet."

And after we emerged from the latrine, Elsie and I, slapping mosquitoes in   6
the warm, gathering dusk, sat on the stoop of her apartment and talked awhile, jealously of the scintillating life Miss Sasagawara had led until now and nostalgically of the few ballets we had seen in the world outside. (How faraway Los Angeles seemed!) But we ended up as we always did, agreeing that our mission in life, pushing twenty as we were, was first to finish college somewhere when and if the war ever ended and we were free again, and then to find good jobs and two nice, clean young men, preferably handsome, preferably rich, who would cherish us forever and a day.

My introduction, less spectacular, to the Rev. Sasagawara came later, as I   7
noticed him, a slight and fragile-looking old man, in the Block mess hall (where I worked as a waitress, and Elsie, too) or in the laundry room or going to and from the latrine. Sometimes he would be farther out, perhaps going to the post office or canteen or to visit friends in another Block or on some business to the Administration buildings, but wherever he was headed, however doubtless his destination, he always seemed to be wandering lostly. This may have been

because he walked so slowly, with such negligible steps, or because he wore perpetually an air of bemusement, never talking directly to a person, as though, being what he was, he could not stop for an instant his meditation on the higher life.

8   I noticed, too, that Miss Sasagawara never came to the mess hall herself. Her father ate at the tables reserved for the occupants, mostly elderly, of the end barracks known as the bachelors' dormitory. After each meal, he came up to the counter and carried away a plate of food, protected with one of the pinkish apple wrappers we waitresses made as wrinkleless as possible and put out for napkins, and a mug of tea or coffee. Sometimes Miss Sasagawara could be seen rinsing out her empties at the one double-tub in the laundry that was reserved for private dishwashing.

9   If any one in the Block or in the entire camp of 15,000 or so people had talked at any length with Miss Sasagawara (everyone happening to speak of her called her that, although her first name, Mari, was simple enough and rather pretty) after her first and only visit to use Mrs. Murakami's sewing machine, I never heard of it. Nor did she ever willingly use the shower room, just off the latrine, when anyone else was there. Once, when I was up past midnight writing letters and went for my shower, I came upon her under the full needling force of a steamy spray, but she turned her back to me and did not answer my surprised hello. I hoped my body would be as smooth and spare and well-turned when I was thirty-nine. Another time Elsie and I passed in front of the Sasagawara apartment, which was really only a cubicle because the once-empty barracks had soon been partitioned off into six units for families of two, and we saw her there on the wooden steps, sitting with her wide, wide skirt spread splendidly about her. She was intent on peeling a grapefruit, which her father had probably brought to her from the mess hall that morning, and Elsie called out, "Hello there!" Miss Sasagawara looked up and stared, without recognition. We were almost out of earshot when I heard her call, "Do I know you?" and I could have almost sworn that she sounded hopeful, if not downright wistful, but Elsie, already miffed at having expended friendliness so unprofitably, seemed not to have heard, and that was that.

10   Well, if Miss Sasagawara was not one to speak to, she was certainly one to speak of, and she came up quite often as topic for the endless conversations which helped along the monotonous days. My mother said she had met the late Mrs. Sasagawara once, many years before the war, and to hear her tell it, a sweeter, kindlier woman there never was. "I suppose," said my mother, "that I'll never meet anyone like her again; she was a lady in every sense of the word." Then she reminded me that I had seen the Rev. Sasagawara before. Didn't I remember him as one of the three bhikshus who had read the sutras at Grandfather's funeral?

11   I could not say that I did. I barely remembered Grandfather, my mother's father. The only thing that came back with clarity was my nausea at the wake and the funeral, the first and only ones I had ever had occasion to attend, because it had been reproduced several times since—each time, in fact, that I had crossed

again the actual scent or suspicion of burning incense. Dimly I recalled the inside of the Buddhist temple in Los Angeles, an immense, murky auditorium whose high and huge platform had held, centered in the background, a great golden shrine touched with black and white. Below this platform, Grandfather, veiled by gauze, had slept in a long grey box which just fitted him. There had been flowers, oh, such flowers, everywhere. And right in front of Grandfather's box had been the incense stand, upon which squatted two small bowls, one with a cluster of straw-thin sticks sending up white tendrils of smoke, the other containing a heap of coarse, grey powder. Each mourner in turn had gone up to the stand, bowing once, his palms touching in prayer before he reached it; had bent in prayer over the stand; had taken then a pinch of incense from the bowl of crumbs and, bowing over it reverently, cast it into the other, the active bowl; had bowed, the hands praying again; had retreated a few steps and bowed one last time, the hands still joined, before returning to his seat. (I knew the ceremony well from having been severely coached in it on the evening of the wake.) There had been tears and tears and here and there a sudden sob.

And all this while, three men in black robes had been on the platform, one standing in front of the shining altar, the others sitting on either side, and the entire trio incessantly chanting a strange, melifluous language in unison. From time to time there had reverberated through the enormous room, above the singsong, above the weeping, above the fragrance, the sharp, startling whang of the gong. $\qquad$ 12

So, one of those men had been Miss Sasagawara's father. . . . This information brought him closer to me, and I listened with interest later when it was told that he kept here in his apartment a small shrine, much more intricately constructed than that kept by the usual Buddhist household, before which, at regular hours of the day, he offered incense and chanted, tinkling (in lieu of the gong) a small bell. What did Miss Sasagawara do at these prayer periods, I wondered; did she participate, did she let it go in one ear and out the other, or did she abruptly go out on the steps, perhaps to eat a grapefruit? $\qquad$ 13

Elsie and I tired one day of working in the mess hall. And this desire for greener fields came almost together with the Administration announcement that henceforth the wages of residents doing truly vital labor, such as in the hospital or on the garbage trucks that went from mess hall to mess hall, would be upped to nineteen dollars a month instead of the common sixteen. $\qquad$ 14

"Oh, I've always wanted to be a nurse!" Elsie confided, as the Block manager sat down to his breakfast after reading out the day's bulletin in English and Japanese. $\qquad$ 15

"What's stopped you?" I asked. $\qquad$ 16

"Mom," Elsie said. "She thinks it's dirty work. And she's afraid I'll catch something. But I'll remind her of the extra three dollars." $\qquad$ 17

"It's never appealed to me much, either," I confessed. "Why don't we go over to garbage? It's the same pay." $\qquad$ 18

Elsie would not even consider it. "Very funny. Well, you don't have to be $\qquad$ 19 a nurse's aide, Kiku. The hospital's short all kinds of help. Dental assistants, receptionists. . . . Let's go apply after we finish this here."

20   So, willy-nilly, while Elsie plunged gleefully into the pleasure of wearing a trim blue-and-white striped seersucker, into the duties of taking temperatures and carrying bedpans, and into the fringe of medical jargon (she spoke very casually now of catheters, enemas, primiparas, multiparas), I became a relief receptionist at the hospital's front desk, taking my hours as they were assigned. And it was on one of my midnight-to-morning shifts that I spoke to Miss Sasagawara for the first time.

21   The cooler in the corridor window was still whirring away (for that desert heat in summer had a way of lingering intact through the night to merge with the warmth of the morning sun), but she entered bundled in an extraordinarily long black coat, her face made petulant, not unprettily, by lines of pain.

22   "I think I've got appendicitis," she said breathlessly, without preliminary.

23   "May I have your name and address?" I asked, unscrewing my pen.

24   Annoyance seemed to outbalance agony for a moment, but she answered soon enough, in a cold rush, "Mari Sasagawara, Thirty-three-seven C."

25   It was necessary also to learn her symptoms, and I wrote down that she had chills and a dull aching at the back of her head, as well as these excruciating flashes in her lower right abdomen.

26   "I'll have to go wake up the doctor. Here's a blanket, why don't you lie down over there on the bench until he comes?" I suggested.

27   She did not answer, so I tossed the Army blanket on the bench, and when I returned from the doctors' dormitory, after having tapped and tapped on the door of young Dr. Moritomo, who was on night duty, she was still standing where I had left her, immobile and holding onto the wooden railing shielding the desk.

28   "Dr. Moritomo's coming right away," I said. "Why don't you sit down at least?"

29   Miss Sasagawara said, "Yes," but did not move.

30   "Did you walk all the way?" I asked incredulously, for Block 33 was a good mile off, across the canal.

31   She nodded, as if that were not important, also as if to thank me kindly to mind my own business.

32   Dr. Moritomo (technically, the title was premature; evacuation had caught him with a few months to go on his degree), wearing a maroon bathrobe, shuffled in sleepily and asked her to come into the emergency room for an examination. A short while later, he guided her past my desk into the laboratory, saying he was going to take her blood count.

33   When they came out, she went over to the electric fountain for a drink of water, and Dr. Moritomo said reflectively, "Her count's all right. Not appendicitis. We should keep her for observation, but the general ward is pretty full, isn't it? Hm, well, I'll give her something to take. Will you tell one of the boys to take her home?

This I did, but when I came back from arousing George, one of the 34
ambulance boys, Miss Sasagawara was gone, and Dr. Moritomo was coming out
of the laboratory where he had gone to push out the lights. "Here's George,
but that girl must have walked home," I reported helplessly.

"She's in no condition to do that. George, better catch up with her and 35
take her home," Dr. Moritomo ordered.

Shrugging, George strode down the hall; the doctor shuffled back to bed; 36
and soon there was the shattering sound of one of the old Army ambulances
backing out of the hospital drive.

George returned in no time at all to say that Miss Sasagawara had refused 37
to get on the ambulance.

"She wouldn't even listen to me. She just kept walking and I drove alongside 38
and told her it was Dr. Moritomo's orders, but she wouldn't even listen to me."

"She wouldn't?"
39

"I hope Doc didn't expect me to drag her into the ambulance." 40

"Oh, well," I said. "I guess she'll get home all right. She walked all the way 41
up here."

"Cripes, what a dame!" George complained, shaking his head as he started 42
back to the ambulance room. "I never heard of such a thing. She wouldn't even
listen to me."

Miss Sasagawara came back to the hospital about a month later. Elsie was 43
the one who rushed up to the desk where I was on day duty to whisper, "Miss
Sasagawara just tried to escape from the hospital!"

"Escape? What do you mean, escape?" I said. 44

"Well, she came in last night, and they didn't know what was wrong with 45
her, so they kept her for observation. And this morning, just now, she ran out
of the ward in just a hospital nightgown and the orderlies chased after her and
caught her and brought her back. Oh, she was just fighting them. But once
they got her back to bed, she calmed down right away, and Miss Morris asked
her what was the big idea, you know, and do you know what she said? She
said she didn't want any more of those doctors pawing her. *Pawing* her,
imagine!"

After an instant's struggle with self-mockery, my curiosity led me down the 46
entrance corridor after Elsie into the longer, wider corridor admitting to the
general ward. The whole hospital staff appeared to have gathered in the room
to get a look at Miss Sasagawara, and the other patients, or those of them that
could, were sitting up attentively in their high, white, and narrow beds. Miss
Sasagawara had the corner bed to the left as we entered and, covered only by
a brief hospital apron, she was sitting on the edge with her legs dangling over
the side. With her head slightly bent, she was staring at a certain place on the
floor, and I knew she must be aware of that concentrated gaze, of trembling old
Dr. Kawamoto (he had retired several years before the war, but he had been
drafted here), of Miss Morris, the head nurse, of Miss Bowman, the nurse in

charge of the general ward during the day, of the other patients, of the nurse's aides, of the orderlies, and of everyone else who tripped in and out abashedly on some pretext or other in order to pass by her bed. I knew this by her smile, for as she continued to look at that same piece of the floor, she continued, unexpectedly, to seem wryly amused with the entire proceedings. I peered at her wonderingly through the triangular peephole created by someone's hand on hip, while Dr. Kawamoto, Miss Morris, and Miss Bowman tried to persuade her to lie down and relax. She was as smilingly immune to tactful suggestions as she was to tactless gawking.

47   There was no future to watching such a war of nerves as this; and besides, I was supposed to be at the front desk, so I hurried back in time to greet a frantic young mother and father, the latter carrying their small son who had had a hemorrhage this morning after a tonsillectomy yesterday in the outpatient clinic.

48   A couple of weeks later on the late shift I found George, the ambulance driver, in high spirits. This time he had been the one selected to drive a patient to Phoenix, where special cases were occasionally sent under escort, and he was looking forward to the moment when, for a few hours, the escort would permit him to go shopping around the city and perhaps take in a new movie. He showed me the list of things his friends had asked him to bring back for them, and we laughed together over the request of one plumpish nurse's aide for the biggest, richest chocolate cake he could find.

49   "You ought to have seen Mabel's eyes while she was describing the kind of cake she wanted," he said. "Man, she looked like she was eating it already!"

50   Just then one of the other drivers, Bobo Kunitomi, came up and nudged George, and they withdrew a few steps from my desk.

51   "Oh, I ain't particularly interested in that," I heard George saying.

52   There was some murmuring from Bobo, of which I caught the words, "Well, hell, you might as well, just as long as you're getting to go out there."

53   George shrugged, then nodded, and Bobo came over to the desk and asked for pencil and paper. "This is a good place. . . ." he said, handing George what he had written.

54   Was it my imagination, or did George emerge from his chat with Bobo a little ruddier than usual? "Well, I guess I better go get ready," he said, taking leave. "Oh, anything you want, Kiku? Just say the word."

55   "Thanks, not this time," I said. "Well, enjoy yourself."

56   "Don't worry," he said. "I will!"

57   He had started down the hall when I remembered to ask, "Who are you taking, anyway?"

58   George turned around. "Miss Sa-sa-ga-wa-ra," he said, accenting every syllable. "Remember that dame? The one who wouldn't let me take her home?"

59   "Yes," I said. "What's the matter with her?"

60   George, saying not a word, pointed at his head and made several circles in the air with his first finger.

"Really?" I asked.   61

Still mum, George nodded in emphasis and pity before he turned to go.   62

How long was she away? It must have been several months, and when,   63
towards late autumn, she returned at last from the sanitarium in Phoenix,
everyone in Block 33 was amazed at the change. She said hello and how are
you as often and easily as the next person, although many of those she greeted
were surprised and suspicious, remembering the earlier rebuffs. There were
some who never did get used to Miss Sasagawara as a friendly being.

One evening when I was going toward the latrine for my shower, my   64
youngest sister, ten-year-old Michi, almost collided with me and said excitedly,
"You going for your shower now, Kiku?"

"You want to fight about it?" I said, making fists.   65

"Don't go now, don't go now! Miss Sasagawara's in there," she whispered   66
wickedly.

"Well," I demanded. "What's wrong with that, honey?"   67

"She's scary. Us kids were in there and she came in and we finished, so we   68
got out, and she said, 'Don't be afraid of me. I won't hurt you.' Gee, we weren't
even afraid of her, but when she said that, gee!"

"Oh, go home and go to bed," I said.   69

Miss Sasagawara was indeed in the shower and she welcomed me with a   70
smile. "Aren't you the girl who plays the violin?"

I giggled and explained. Elsie and I, after hearing Menuhin on the radio,   71
had in a fit of madness sent to Sears and Roebuck for beginners' violins that
cost five dollars each. We had received free instruction booklets, too, but unable
to make heads or tails from them, we contented ourselves with occasionally
taking the violins out of their paper bags and sawing every which way away.

Miss Sasagawara laughed aloud—a lovely sound. "Well, you're just about   72
as good as I am. I sent for a Spanish guitar. I studied it about a year once, but
that was so long ago I don't remember the first thing and I'm having to start
all over again. We'd make a fine orchestra."

That was the only time we really exchanged words and some weeks later I   73
understood she had organized a dancing class from among the younger girls in
the Block. My sister Michi, becoming one of her pupils, got very attached to
her and spoke of her frequently at home. So I knew that Miss Sasagawara and
her father had decorated their apartment to look oh, so pretty, that Miss
Sasagawara had a whole big suitcase full of dancing costumes, and that Miss
Sasagawara had just lots and lots of books to read.

The fruits of Miss Sasagawara's patient labor were put on show at the Block   74
Christmas party, the second such observance in camp. Again, it was a gay, if
odd, celebration. The mess hall was hung with red and green crepe paper
streamers and the greyish mistletoe that grew abundantly on the ancient mesquite surrounding the camp. There were even electric decorations on the token
Christmas tree. The oldest occupant of the bachelors' dormitory gave a tremu-

lous monologue in an exaggerated Hiroshima dialect; one of the young boys wore a bow-tie and whispered a popular song while the girls shrieked and pretended to be growing faint; my mother sang an old Japanese song; four of the girls wore similar blue dresses and harmonized on a sweet tune; a little girl in a grass skirt and a superfluous brassiere did a hula; and the chief cook came out with an ample saucepan and, assisted by the waitresses, performed the familiar *dojo-sukui*, the comic dance about a man who is merely trying to scoop up a few loaches from an uncooperative lake. Then Miss Sasagawara shooed her eight little girls, including Michi, in front, and while they formed a stiff pattern and waited, self-conscious in the rustly crepe paper dresses they had made themselves, she set up a portable phonograph on the floor and vigorously turned the crank.

75   Something was past its prime, either the machine or the record or the needle, for what came out was a feeble rasp but distantly related to the Mozart minuet it was supposed to be. After a bit I recognized the melody; I had learned it as a child to the words,

> When dames wore hoops and powdered hair,
> And very strict was e-ti-quette,
> When men were brave and ladies fair,
> They danced the min-u-et. . . .

And the little girls, who might have curtsied and stepped gracefully about under Miss Sasagawara's eyes alone, were all elbows and knees as they felt the Block's one-hundred-fifty or more pairs of eyes on them. Although there was sustained applause after their number, what we were benevolently approving was the great effort, for the achievement had been undeniably small. Then Santa came with a pillow for a stomach, his hands each dragging a bulging burlap bag. Church people outside had kindly sent these gifts, Santa announced, and every recipient must write and thank the person whose name he would find on an enclosed slip. So saying, he called by name each Block child under twelve and ceremoniously presented each eleemosynary package, and a couple of the youngest children screamed in fright at this new experience of a red and white man with a booming voice.

76   At the last, Santa called, "Miss Mari Sasagawara!" and when she came forward in surprise, he explained to the gathering that she was being rewarded for her help with the Block's younger generation. Everyone clapped and Miss Sasagawara, smiling graciously, opened her package then and there. She held up her gift, a peach-colored bath towel, so that it could be fully seen, and everyone clapped again.

77   Suddenly I put this desert scene behind me. The notice I had long awaited, of permission to relocate to Philadelphia to attend college, finally came, and there was a prodigious amount of packing to do, leave papers to sign, and goodbyes to say. And once the wearying, sooty train trip was over, I found myself

in an intoxicating new world of daily classes, afternoon teas, and evening concerts, from which I dutifully emerged now and then to answer the letters from home. When the beautiful semester was over, I returned to Arizona, to that glowing heat, to the camp, to the family; for although the war was still on, it had been decided to close down the camps, and I had been asked to go back and spread the good word about higher education among the young people who might be dispersed in this way.

Elsie was still working in the hospital, although she had applied for entrance into the cadet nurse corps and was expecting acceptance any day, and the long conversations we held were mostly about the good old days, the good old days when we had worked in the mess hall together, the good old days when we had worked in the hospital together.

78

"What ever became of Miss Sasagawara?" I asked one day, seeing the Rev. Sasagawara go abstractedly by. "Did she relocate somewhere?"

79

"I didn't write you about her, did I?" Elsie said meaningfully. "Yes, she's relocated all right. Haven't seen her around, have you?"

80

"Where did she go?"

81

Elsie answered offhandedly. "California."

82

"California?" I exclaimed. "We can't go back to California. What's she doing in California?"

83

So Elsie told me: Miss Sasagawara had been sent back there to a state institution, oh, not so very long after I had left for school. She had begun slipping back into her aloof ways almost immediately after Christmas, giving up the dancing class and not speaking to people. Then Elsie had heard a couple of very strange, yes, very strange things about her. One thing had been told by young Mrs. Sasaki, that next-door neighbor of the Sasagawaras.

84

Mrs. Sasaki said she had once come upon Miss Sasagawara sitting, as was her habit, on the porch. Mrs. Sasaki had been shocked to the core to see that the face of this thirty-nine-year-old woman (or was she forty now?) wore a beatific expression as she watched the activity going on in the doorway of her neighbors across the way, the Yoshinagas. This activity had been the joking and loud laughter of Joe and Frank, the young Yoshinaga boys, and three or four of their friends. Mrs. Sasaki would have let the matter go, were it not for the fact that Miss Sasagawara was so absorbed a spectator of this horseplay that her head was bent to one side and she actually had one finger in her mouth as she gazed, in the manner of a shy child confronted with a marvel. "What's the matter with you, watching the boys like that?" Mrs. Sasaki had cried. "You're old enough to be their mother!" Startled, Miss Sasagawara had jumped up and dashed back into her apartment. And when Mrs. Sasaki had gone into hers, adjoining the Sasagawaras', she had been terrified to hear Miss Sasagawara begin to bang on the wooden walls with something heavy like a hammer. The banging, which sounded as though Miss Sasagawara were using all her strength on each blow, had continued wildly for at least five minutes. Then all had been still.

85

The other thing had been told by Joe Yoshinaga who lived across the way from Miss Sasagawara. Joe and his brother slept on two Army cots pushed

86

together on one side of the room, while their parents had a similar arrangement on the other side. Joe had standing by his bed an apple crate for a shelf, and he was in the habit of reading his sports and western magazines in bed and throwing them on top of the crate before he went to sleep. But one morning he had noticed his magazines all neatly stacked inside the crate, when he was sure he had carelessly thrown some on top the night before, as usual. This happened several times, and he finally asked his family whether one of them had been putting his magazines away after he fell asleep. They had said no and laughed, telling him he must be getting absent-minded. But the mystery had been solved late one night, when Joe gradually awoke in his cot with the feeling that he was being watched. Warily he had opened one eye slightly and had been thoroughly awakened and chilled in the bargain by what he saw. For what he saw was Miss Sasagawara sitting there on his apple crate, her long hair all undone and flowing about her. She was dressed in a white nightgown and her hands were clasped on her lap. And all she was doing was sitting there watching him, Joe Yoshinaga. He could not help it, he had sat up and screamed. His mother, a light sleeper, came running to see what had happened, just as Miss Sasagawara was running out the door, the door they had always left unlatched or even wide open in summer. In the morning Mrs. Yoshinaga had gone straight to the Rev. Sasagawara and asked him to do something about his daughter. The Rev. Sasagawara, sympathizing with her indignation in his benign but vague manner, had said he would have a talk with Mari.

87   And, concluded Elsie, Miss Sasagawara had gone away not long after. I was impressed, although Elsie's sources were not what I would ordinarily pay much attention to, Mrs. Sasaki, that plump and giggling young woman who always felt called upon to explain that she was childless by choice, and Joe Yoshinaga, who had a knack of blowing up, in his drawling voice, any incident in which he personally played even a small part (I could imagine the field day he had had with this one). Elsie puzzled aloud over the cause of Miss Sasagawara's derangement and I, who had so newly had some contact with the recorded explorations into the virgin territory of the human mind, sagely explained that Miss Sasagawara had no doubt looked upon Joe Yoshinaga as the image of either the lost lover or the lost son. But my words made me uneasy by their glibness, and I began to wonder seriously about Miss Sasagawara for the first time.

88   Then there was this last word from Miss Sasagawara herself, making her strange legend as complete as I, at any rate, would probably ever know it. This came some time after I had gone back to Philadelphia and the family had joined me there, when I was neck deep in research for my final paper. I happened one day to be looking through the last issue of a small poetry magazine that had suspended publication midway through the war. I felt a thrill of recognition at the name, Mari Sasagawara, signed to a long poem, introduced as ". . . the first published poem of a Japanese-American woman who is, at present, an evacuee from the West Coast making her home in a War Relocation center in Arizona."

89   It was a *tour de force*, erratically brilliant and, through the first readings, tantalizingly obscure. It appeared to be about a man whose lifelong aim had

been to achieve Nirvana, that saintly state of moral purity and universal wisdom. This man had in his way certain handicaps, all stemming from his having acquired, when young and unaware, a family for which he must provide. The day came at last, however, when his wife died and other circumstances made it unnecessary for him to earn a competitive living. These circumstances were considered by those about him as sheer imprisonment, but he had felt free for the first time in his long life. It became possible for him to extinguish within himself all unworthy desire and consequently all evil, to concentrate on that serene, eight-fold path of highest understanding, highest mindedness, highest speech, highest action, highest livelihood, highest recollectedness, highest endeavor, and highest meditation.

This man was certainly noble, the poet wrote, this man was beyond censure. 90 The world was doubtless enriched by his presence. But say that someone else, someone sensitive, someone admiring, someone who had not achieved this sublime condition and who did not wish to, were somehow called to companion such a man. Was it not likely that the saint, blissfully bent on cleansing from his already radiant soul the last imperceptible blemishes (for, being perfect, would he not humbly suspect his own flawlessness?) would be deaf and blind to the human passions rising, subsiding, and again rising, perhaps in anguished silence, within the selfsame room? The poet could not speak for others, of course; she could only speak for herself. But she would describe this man's devotion as a sort of madness, the monstrous sort which, pure of itself, might possibly bring troublous, scented scenes to recur in the other's sleep. ✤

RESPONDING

1. In a journal entry, discuss the conditions of internment that you would have found most difficult. Would the rationale behind the internment affect your response to the physical surroundings?

2. Choose one of the characters in the story and write an informal essay explaining his or her reaction to the internment. Working individually or in a group, share and classify the responses of the inmates.

3. In an essay, argue that Miss Sasagawara's problems did or did not stem from the internment. Use examples from the reading to support your argument.

4. Write an essay analyzing Miss Sasagawara's poem as it is described in the story's next-to-last paragraph. What or who do you think the characters in the poem represent? Could they represent or symbolize more than one thing? You might research the eightfold path and its implications about reactions to imprisonment. Consider the title of the story. Why does the author call it a legend?

LAWSON FUSAO INADA

The poet and essayist Lawson Fusao Inada was born in 1938 in Fresno, California. He studied at the University of California in Berkeley, Fresno State College, and the University of Oregon, from which he earned his M.F.A. in 1966. He has held teaching positions at several universities, including Southern Oregon State College in Ashland and the University of Hawaii. His writing has appeared in such journals as Amerasia Journal, Bridge, *and* The Iowa Review. *His poems, which are widely anthologized, have been collected in two volumes,* Before the War: Poems as They Happened *(1971) and* Legends from Camp: Poems *(1992). He also coedited the anthologies,* Aiiieeeee: An Anthology of Asian-American Writers *(1974, 1982) and* The Big Aiiieeeee: An Anthology of Chinese American and Japanese American Literature *(1992).*

In the poem that follows, the western landscape is presented as a constellation, each point of which marks the site of an internment camp. The poem is just one illustration of the way in which the camp image continues to be found in Japanese American literature, long after the closing of the camps.

⁜

CONCENTRATION CONSTELLATION

In this earthly configuration,
we have, not points of light,
but prominent barbs of dark.

It's all right there on the map.
It's all right there in the mind.
Find it. If you care to look.

Begin between the Golden State's
highest and lowest elevations
and name that location

Manzanar. Rattlesnake a line
southward to the zone
of Arizona, to the home
of natives on the reservation,
and call those *Gila, Poston.*

Then just take you time
winding your way across
the Southwest expanse, the Lone
Star State of Texas, gathering
up a mess of blues as you
meander around the banks
of the humid Mississippi; yes,
just make yourself at home
in the swamps of Arkansas,
for this is *Rohwer* and *Jerome*.

By now, you weary of the way.
It's a big country, you say.
It's a big history, hardly
halfway through—with *Amache*
looming in the Colorado desert,
Heart Mountain high in wide
Wyoming, *Minidoka* on the moon
of Idaho, then down to Utah's
jewel of *Topaz* before finding
yourself at northern California's
frozen shore of *Tule Lake* . . .

Now regard what sort of shape
this constellation takes.
It sits there like a jagged scar,
massive, on the massive landscape.
It lies there like the rusted wire
of a twisted and remembered fence. ✛

RESPONDING

1. In a journal entry, tell about a place that has positive and negative associations for you.

2. Working individually or in a group, plot the camps on a map of the United States. What do the locations of the camps suggest? Explain why you think those locations were chosen. Use information from the introduction to the chapter and the readings to support your explanation.

3. In an essay, compare the image of a constellation of stars and the image of the constellation of camps. Why do you think the author choose to call the camps "concentration constellation"?

GARRETT HONGO

Garrett Hongo was born in 1951 in Volcano, Hawaii. After graduating from Pomona College in 1973, he pursued graduate study at the University of Michigan and the University of California, Irvine, from which he earned an M.F.A. in 1980. He has taught at several universities, including the University of Oregon, Eugene; the University of California, Irvine; the University of Southern California; and the University of Missouri. In addition to contributing essays to numerous journals, Hongo has published two collections of poetry, Yellow Light *(1982) and* The River of Heaven *(1988). His work has been awarded prizes from the National Endowment for the Arts and the Academy of American Poets, among others.*

Hongo's essay "Kubota" recounts some of his grandfather's experiences during and after World War II and explores the ways in which his grandfather's story—and other such narratives—are both a burden for and a gift to the generations that follow.

KUBOTA

1 ON DECEMBER 8, 1941, the day after the Japanese attack on Pearl Harbor in Hawaii, my grandfather barricaded himself with his family—my grandmother, my teenage mother, her two sisters and two brothers—inside of his home in La'ie, a sugar plantation village on Oahu's North Shore. This was my maternal grandfather, a man most villagers called by his last name, Kubota. It could mean either "Wayside Field" or else "Broken Dreams," depending on which ideograms he used. Kubota ran La'ie's general store, and the previous night, after a long day of bad news on the radio, some locals had come by, pounded on the front door, and made threats. One was said to have brandished a machete. They were angry and shocked, as the whole nation was in the aftermath of the surprise attack. Kubota was one of the few Japanese Americans in the village and president of the local Japanese language school. He had become a target for their rage and suspicion. A wise man, he locked all his doors and windows and did not open his store the next day, but stayed closed and waited for news from some official.

2 He was a *kibei*, a Japanese American born in Hawaii (a U.S. territory then, so he was thus a citizen) but who was subsequently sent back by his father for formal education in Hiroshima, Japan, their home province. *Kibei* is written with two ideograms in Japanese: one is the word for "return" and the other is the word for "rice." Poetically, it means one who returns from America, known as

the Land of Rice in Japanese (by contrast, Chinese immigrants called their new home Mountain of Gold).

Kubota was graduated from a Japanese high school and then came back to Hawaii as a teenager. He spoke English—and a Hawaiian creole version of it at that—with a Japanese accent. But he was well liked and good at numbers, scrupulous and hard working like so many immigrants and children of immigrants. Castle & Cook, a grower's company that ran the sugarcane business along the North Shore, hired him on first as a stock boy and then appointed him to run one of its company stores. He did well, had the trust of management and labor—not an easy accomplishment in any day—married, had children, and had begun to exert himself in community affairs and excel in his own recreations. He put together a Japanese community organization that backed a Japanese language school for children and sponsored teachers from Japan. Kubota boarded many of them, in succession, in his own home. This made dinners a silent affair for his talkative, Hawaiian-bred children, as their stern *sensei*, or teacher, was nearly always at table and their own abilities in the Japanese language were as delinquent as their attendance. While Kubota and the *sensei* rattled on about things Japanese, speaking Japanese, his children hurried through their suppers and tried to run off early to listen to the radio shows.

After dinner, while the *sensei* graded exams seated in a wicker chair in the spare room and his wife and children gathered around the radio in the front parlor, Kubota sat on the screened porch outside, reading the local Japanese newspapers. He finished reading about the same time as he finished the tea he drank for his digestion—a habit he'd learned in Japan—and then he'd get out his fishing gear and spread it out on the plank floors. The wraps on his rods needed to be redone, gears in his reels needed oil, and, once through with those tasks, he'd painstakingly wind on hundreds of yards of new line. Fishing was his hobby and his passion. He spent weekends camping along the North Shore beaches with his children, setting up umbrella tents, packing a rice pot and hibachi along for meals. And he caught fish. *Ulu'a* mostly, the huge surf-feeding fish known on the mainland as the jack crevalle, but he'd go after almost anything in its season. In Kawela, a plantation-owned bay nearby, he fished for mullat Hawaiian-style with a throw net, stalking the bottom-hugging, gray-backed schools as they gathered at the stream mouths and in the freshwater springs. In an outrigger out beyond the reef, he'd try for *aku*—the skipjack tuna prized for steaks and, sliced raw and mixed with fresh seaweed and cut onions, for *sashimi* salad. In Kahaluu and Ka'awa and on an offshore rock locals called Goat Island, he loved to go torching, stringing lanterns on bamboo poles stuck in the sand to attract *kumu'u*, the red goatfish, as they schooled at night just inside the reef. But in Lai'e on Laniloa Point near Kahuku, the northernmost tip of Oahu, he cast twelve- and fourteen-foot surf rods for the huge, varicolored, and fast-running *ulu'a* as they ran for schools of squid and baitfish just beyond the biggest breakers and past the low sand flats wadable from the shore to nearly a half mile out. At sunset, against the western light, he looked as if he walked on water as he came back, fish and rods slung over his shoulders, stepping along the rock and coral path just inches under the surface of a running tide.

5 　　When it was torching season, in December or January, he'd drive out the afternoon before and stay with old friends, the Tanakas or Yoshikawas, shop-keepers like him who ran stores near the fishing grounds. They'd have been preparing for weeks, selecting and cutting their bamboo poles, cleaning the hurricane lanterns, tearing up burlap sacks for the cloths they'd soak with kerosene and tie onto sticks they'd poke into the soft sand of the shallows. Once lit, touched off with a Zippo lighter, these would be the torches they'd use as beacons to attract the schooling fish. In another time, they might have made up a dozen paper lanterns of the kind mostly used for decorating the summer folk dances outdoors on the grounds of the Buddhist church during O-Bon, the Festival for the Dead. But now, wealthy and modern and efficient killers of fish, Tanaka and Kubota used rag torches and Colemans and cast rods with tips made of Tonkin bamboo and butts of American-spun fiberglass. After just one good night, they might bring back a prize bounty of a dozen burlap bags filled with scores of bloody, rigid fish delicious to eat and even better to give away as gifts to friends, family, and special customers.

6 　　It was a Monday night, the day after Pearl Harbor, and there was a rattling knock at the front door. Two FBI agents presented themselves, showed iden-tification, and took my grandfather in for questioning in Honolulu. He didn't return home for days. No one knew what had happened or what was wrong. But there was a roundup going on of all those in the Japanese-American community suspected of sympathizing with the enemy and worse. My grandfa-ther was suspected of espionage, of communicating with offshore Japanese submarines launched from the attack fleet days before war began. Torpedo planes and escort fighters, decorated with the insignia of the Rising Sun, had taken an approach route from northwest of Oahu directly across Kahuku Point and on toward Pearl. They had strafed an auxiliary air station near the fishing grounds my grandfather loved and destroyed a small gun battery there, killing three men. Kubota was known to have sponsored and harbored Japanese na-tionals in his own home. He had a radio. He had wholesale access to firearms. Circumstances and an undertone of racial resentment had combined with war-time hysteria in the aftermath of the tragic naval battle to cast suspicion on the loyalties of my grandfather and all other Japanese Americans. The FBI reached out and pulled hundreds of them in for questioning in dragnets cast throughout the West Coast and Hawaii.

7 　　My grandfather was lucky; he'd somehow been let go after only a few days. Others were not as fortunate. Hundreds, from small communities in Washing-ton, California, Oregon, and Hawaii, were rounded up and, after what appeared to be routine questioning, shipped off under Justice Department orders to holding centers in Leuppe on the Navaho reservation in Arizona, in Fort Missoula in Montana, and on Sand Island in Honolulu Harbor. There were

other special camps on Maui in Ha'iku and on Hawaii—the Big Island—in my own home village of Volcano.

Many of these men—it was exclusively the Japanese-American men sus- 8 pected of ties to Japan who were initially rounded up—did not see their families again for more than four years. Under a suspension of due process that was only after the fact ruled as warranted by military necessity, they were, if only temporarily, "disappeared" in Justice Department prison camps scattered in particularly desolate areas of the United States designated as militarily "safe." These were grim forerunners of the assembly centers and concentration camps for the 120,000 Japanese-American evacuees that were to come later.

I am Kubota's eldest grandchild, and I remember him as a lonely, habitually 9 silent old man who lived with us in our home near Los Angeles for most of my childhood and adolescence. It was the fifties, and my parents had emigrated from Hawaii to the mainland in the hope of a better life away from the old sugar plantation. After some success, they had sent back for my grandparents and taken them in. And it was my grandparents who did the work of the household while my mother and father worked their salaried city jobs. My grandmother cooked and sewed, washed our clothes, and knitted in the front room under the light of a huge lamp with a bright three-way bulb. Kubota raised a flower garden, read up on soils and grasses in gardening books, and planted a zoysia lawn in front and a dichondra one in back. He planted a small patch near the rear block wall with green onions, eggplant, white Japanese radishes, and cucumber. While he hoed and spaded the loamless, clayey earth of Los Angeles, he sang particularly plangent songs in Japanese about plum blossoms and bamboo groves.

Once, in the mid-sixties, after a dinner during which, as always, he had been 10 silent while he worked away at a meal of fish and rice spiced with dabs of Chinese mustard and catsup thinned with soy sauce, Kubota took his own dishes to the kitchen sink and washed them up. He took a clean jelly jar out of the cupboard—the glass was thick and its shape squatty like an old-fashioned. He reached around to the hutch below where he kept his bourbon. He made himself a drink and retired to the living room where I was expected to join him for "talk story," the Hawaiian idiom for chewing the fat.

I was a teenager and, though I was bored listening to stories I'd heard often 11 enough before at holiday dinners, I was dutiful. I took my spot on the couch next to Kubota and heard him out. Usually, he'd tell me about his schooling in Japan where he learned judo along with mathematics and literature. He'd learned the *soroban* there—the abacus, which was the original pocket calculator of the Far East—and that, along with his strong, judo-trained back, got him his first job in Hawaii. This was the moral. "Study *ha-ahd,*" he'd say with pidgin emphasis. "Learn read good. Learn speak da kine *good* English." The message is the familiar one taught to any children of immigrants: succeed through education. And imitation. But this time, Kubota reached down into his past and told me a different story. I was thirteen by then, and I suppose he thought me ready for it. He told me about Pearl Harbor, how the planes flew in wing after wing of formations over his old house in La'ie in Hawaii, and how, the next day, after Roosevelt had made his famous "Day of Infamy" speech about the treachery of the Japanese, the FBI agents had come to his door and taken him in, hauled him off to Honolulu for questioning, and held him without charge for several days. I thought he was lying. I thought he was making up a kind of horror story to shock me and give his moral that much more starch. But it was true. I asked around. I brought it up during history class in junior high school, and my teacher, after silencing me and stepping me off to the back of the room, told me that it was indeed so. I asked my mother and she said it was true. I asked my schoolmates, who laughed and ridiculed me for being so ignorant. We lived in a Japanese-American community, and the parents of most of my classmates were the *nisei* who had been interned as teenagers all through the war. But there was a strange silence around all of this. There was a hush, as if one were invoking the ill powers of the dead when one brought it up. No one cared to speak about the evacuation and relocation for very long. It wasn't in our history books, though we were studying World War II at the time. It wasn't in the family albums of the people I knew and whom I'd visit staying over weekends with friends. And it wasn't anything that the family talked about or allowed me to keep bringing up either. I was given the facts, told sternly and pointedly that "it was war" and that "nothing could be done." "*Shikatta ga nai*" is the phrase in Japanese, a kind of resolute and determinist pronouncement on how to deal with inexplicable tragedy. I was to know it but not to dwell on it. Japanese Americans were busy trying to forget it ever happened and were having a hard enough time building their new lives after "camp." It was as if we had no history for four years and the relocation was something unspeakable.

12   But Kubota would not let it go. In session after session, for months it seemed, he pounded away at his story. He wanted to tell me the names of the FBI agents. He went over their questions and his responses again and again. He'd tell me how one would try to act friendly toward him, offering him cigarettes while the other, who hounded him with accusations and threats, left the interrogation room. Good cop, bad cop, I thought to myself, already superficially streetwise from stories black classmates told of the Watts riots and from my having watched too many episodes of *Dragnet* and *The Mod Squad*. But Kubota was not interested in my experiences. I was not made yet, and he was determined that his stories be part of my making. He spoke quietly at first, mildly, but once into his narrative and after his drink was down, his voice would rise and quaver with resentment and he'd make his accusations. He gave his testimony to me and I held it at first cautiously in my conscience like it was an heirloom too delicate to expose to strangers and anyone outside of the world Kubota made with his words. "I give you story now," he once said, "and you learn speak good, eh?" It was my job, as the disciple of his preaching I had then become, Ananda to his Buddha, to reassure him with a promise. "You learn

speak good like the Dillingham," he'd say another time, referring to the wealthy scion of the grower family who had once run, unsuccessfully, for one of Hawaii's first senatorial seats. Or he'd then invoke a magical name, the name of one of his heroes, a man he thought particularly exemplary and righteous. "Learn speak dah good Ing-rish like *Mistah Inouye*," Kubota shouted. "He *lick* dah Dillingham even in debate. I saw on *terre-bision* myself." He was remembering the debates before the first senatorial election just before Hawaii was admitted to the Union as its fiftieth state. "You *tell* story," Kubota would end. And I had my injunction.

The town we settled in after the move from Hawaii is called Gardena, the independently incorporated city south of Los Angeles and north of San Pedro harbor. At its northern limit, it borders on Watts and Compton, black towns. To the southwest are Torrance and Redondo Beach, white towns. To the rest of L.A., Gardena is primarily famous for having legalized five-card draw poker after the war. On Vermont Boulevard, its eastern border, there is a dingy little Vegas-like strip of card clubs with huge parking lots and flickering neon signs that spell out "The Rainbow" and "The Horseshoe" in timed sequences of varicolored lights. The town is only secondarily famous as the largest community of Japanese Americans in the United States outside of Honolulu, Hawaii. When I was in high school there, it seemed to me that every *sansei* kid I knew wanted to be a doctor, an engineer, or a pharmacist. Our fathers were gardeners or electricians or nurserymen or ran small businesses catering to other Japanese Americans. Our mothers worked in civil service for the city or as cashiers for Thrifty Drug. What the kids wanted was a good job, good pay, a fine home, and no troubles. No one wanted to mess with the law—from either side—and no one wanted to mess with language or art. They all talked about getting into the right clubs so that they could go to the right schools. There was a certain kind of sameness, an intensely enforced system of conformity. Style was all. Boys wore moccasin-sewn shoes from Flagg Brothers, black A-1 slacks, and Kensington shirts with high collars. Girls wore their hair up in stiff bouffants solidified in hair-spray and knew all the latest dances from the slauson to the funky chicken. We did well in chemistry and in math, no one who was Japanese but me spoke in English class or in history unless called upon, and no one talked about World War II. The day after Robert Kennedy was assassinated, after winning the California Democratic primary, we worked on calculus and elected class coordinators for the prom, featuring the 5th Dimension. We avoided grief. We avoided government. We avoided strong feelings and dangers of any kind. Once punished, we tried to maintain a concerted emotional and social discipline and would not willingly seek to fall out of the narrow margin of protective favor again.

But when I was thirteen, in junior high, I'd not understood why it was so difficult for my classmates, those who were themselves Japanese American, to talk about the relocation. They had cringed, too, when I tried to bring it up during our discussions of World War II. I was Hawaiian-born. They were mainland-born. Their parents had been in camp, had been the ones to suffer the complicated experience of having to distance themselves from their own history and all things Japanese in order to make their way back and into the American social and economic mainstream. It was out of this sense of shame and a fear of stigma I was only beginning to understand that the *nisei* had silenced themselves. And, for their children, among whom I grew up, they wanted no heritage, no culture, no contact with a defiled history. I recall the silence very well. The Japanese-American children around me were burdened in a way I was not. Their injunction was silence. Mine was to speak.

15   Away at college, in another protected world in its own way as magical to me as the Hawaii of my childhood, I dreamed about my grandfather. Tired from studying languages, practicing German conjugations or scripting an army's worth of Chinese ideograms on a single sheet of paper, Kubota would come to me as I drifted off into sleep. Or I would walk across the newly mown ball field in back of my dormitory, cutting through a street-side phalanx of ancient eucalyptus trees on my way to visit friends off campus, and I would think of him, his anger, and his sadness.

16   I don't know myself what makes someone feel that kind of need to have a story they've lived through be deposited somewhere, but I can guess. I think about *The Illiad, The Odyssey, The Peloponnesian Wars* of Thucydides, and a myriad of the works of literature I've studied. A character, almost a *topoi* he occurs so often, is frequently the witness who gives personal testimony about an event the rest of his community cannot even imagine. The sibyl is such a character. And Procne, the maid whose tongue is cut out so that she will not tell that she has been raped by her own brother-in-law, the king of Thebes. There are the dime novels, the epic blockbusters Hollywood makes into mini-series, and then there are the plain, relentless stories of witnesses who have suffered through horrors major and minor that have marked and changed their lives. I myself haven't talked to Holocaust victims. But I've read their survival stories and their stories of witness and been revolted and moved by them. My father-in-law, Al Thiessen, tells me his war stories again and again and I listen. A Mennonite who set aside the strictures of his own church in order to serve, he was a Marine codeman in the Pacific during World War II, in the Signal Corps on Guadalcanal, Morotai, and Bougainville. He was part of the island-hopping maneuver MacArthur had devised to win the war in the Pacific. He saw friends die from bombs which exploded not ten yards away. When he was with the 298th Signal Corps attached to the Thirteenth Air Force, he saw plane after plane come in and crash, just short of the runway, killing their crews, setting the jungle ablaze with oil and gas fires. Emergency wagons would scramble, bounding over newly bulldozed land men used just the afternoon before for a football game. Every time we go fishing together, whether it's in a McKenzie boat drifting for salmon in Tillamook Bay or taking a lunch break from wading the riffles of a stream in the Cascades, he tells me about what happened to him and the young men in his unit. One was a Jewish boy from

Brooklyn. One was a foul-mouthed kid from Kansas. They died. And he *has* to tell me. And I *have* to listen. It's a ritual payment the young owe their elders who have survived. The evacuation and relocation is something like that.

Kubota, my grandfather, had been ill with Alzheimer's disease for some time before he died. At the house he'd built on Kamehameha Highway in Hau'ula, a seacoast village just down the road from La'ie where he had his store, he'd wander out from the garage or greenhouse where he'd set up a workbench, and trudge down to the beach or up toward the line of pines he'd planted while employed by the Work Projects Administration during the thirties. Kubota thought he was going fishing. Or he thought he was back at work for Roosevelt, planting pines as a windbreak or soilbreak on the windward flank of the Ko'olau Mountains, emerald monoliths rising out of sea and cane fields from Waialua to Kaneohe. When I visited, my grandmother would send me down to the beach to fetch him. Or I'd run down Kam Highway a quarter mile or so and find him hiding in the cane field by the roadside, counting stalks, measuring circumferences in the claw of his thumb and forefinger. The look on his face was confused or concentrated, I didn't know which. But I guessed he was going fishing again. I'd grab him and walk him back to his house on the highway. My grandmother would shut him in a room.

Within a few years, Kubota had a stroke and survived it, then he had another one and was completely debilitated. The family decided to put him in a nursing home in Kahuku, just set back from the highway, within a mile or so of Kahuku Point and the Tanaka Store where he had his first job as a stock boy. He lived there three years, and I visited him once with my aunt. He was like a potato that had been worn down by cooking. Everything on him—his eyes, his teeth, his legs and torso—seemed like it had been sloughed away. What he had been was mostly gone now and I was looking at the nub of a man. In a wheelchair, he grasped my hands and tugged on them—violently. His hands were still thick and, I believed, strong enough to lift me out of my own seat into his lap. He murmured something in Japanese—he'd long ago ceased to speak any English. My aunt and I cried a little, and we left him.

I remember walking out on the black asphalt of the parking lot of the nursing home. It was heat-cracked and eroded already, and grass had veined itself into the interstices. There were coconut trees around, a cane field I could see across the street, and the ocean I knew was pitching a surf just beyond it. The green Ko'olaus came up behind us. Somewhere nearby, alongside the beach, there was an abandoned airfield in the middle of the canes. As a child, I'd come upon it playing one day, and my friends and I kept returning to it, day after day, playing war or sprinting games or coming to fly kites. I recognize it even now when I see it on TV—it's used as a site for action scenes in the detective shows Hollywood always sets in the islands: a helicopter chasing the hero racing away in a Ferrari, or gun dealers making a clandestine rendezvous on the abandoned runway. It was the old airfield strafed by Japanese planes the day the major flight attacked Pearl Harbor. It was the airfield the FBI thought my grandfather had targeted in his night fishing and signaling with the long surf poles he'd stuck in the sandy bays near Kahuku Point.

20   Kubota died a short while after I visited him, but not, I thought, without giving me a final message. I was on the mainland, in California studying for Ph.D. exams, when my grandmother called me with the news. It was a relief. He'd suffered from his debilitation a long time and I was grateful he'd gone. I went home for the funeral and gave the eulogy. My grandmother and I took his ashes home in a small, heavy metal box wrapped in a black *furoshiki*, a large silk scarf. She showed me the name the priest had given to him on his death, scripted with a calligraphy brush on a long, narrow talent of plain wood. Buddhist commoners, at death, are given priestly names, received symbolically into the clergy. The idea is that, in their next life, one of scholarship and leisure, they might meditate and attain the enlightenment the religion is aimed at. "*Shaku Shūchi*," the ideograms read. It was Kubota's Buddhist name, incorporating characters from his family and given names. It meant "Shining Wisdom of the Law." He died on Pearl Harbor Day, December 7, 1983.

21   After years, after I'd finally come back to live in Hawaii again, only once did I dream of Kubota, my grandfather. It was the same night I'd heard HR 442, the redress bill for Japanese Americans, had been signed into law. In my dream that night Kubota was "torching," and he sang a Japanese song, a querulous and wavery folk ballad, as he hung paper lanterns on bamboo poles stuck into the sand in the shallow water of the lagoon behind the reef near Kahuku Point. Then he was at a work table, smoking a hand-rolled cigarette, letting it dangle from his lips Bogart-style as he drew, daintily and skillfully, with a narrow trim brush, ideogram after ideogram on a score of paper lanterns he had hung in a dark shed to dry. He had painted a talismanic mantra onto each lantern, the ideogram for the word "red" in Japanese, a bit of art blended with some superstition, a piece of sympathetic magic appealing to the magenta coloring on the rough skins of the schooling, night-feeding fish he wanted to attract to his baited hooks. He strung them from pole to pole in the dream then, hiking up his khaki worker's pants so his white ankles showed and wading through the shimmering black waters of the sand flats and then the reef. "The moon is leaving, leaving," he sang in Japanese. "Take me deeper in the savage sea." He turned and crouched like an ice racer then, leaning forward so that his unshaven face almost touched the light film of water. I could see the light stubble of beard like a fine, gray ash covering the lower half of his face. I could see his gold-rimmed spectacles. He held a small wooden boat in his cupped hands and placed it lightly on the sea and pushed it away. One of his lanterns was on it and, written in small neat rows like a sutra scroll, it had been decorated with the silvery names of all our dead. ✢

RESPONDING

1. Imagine that you were Kubota. Write a journal entry about your reaction to being taken in for questioning by FBI agents the day after Pearl Harbor.

2. Working individually or in a group, retell historical events that were especially important to you or your family members. Were these events adequately covered in your history classes in elementary school, high school, college?

3. Hongo ends his essay by recounting a dream. Write your own essay explaining the significance of the dream and its message to the reader.

4. According to Hongo, what cultural factors resulted in the Japanese American silence about the Internment? In an essay, explore that silence and its effect on the young. What difference, if any, has breaking the silence made? Refer to the introduction to the chapter and outside knowledge if necessary.

RONALD TAKAKI

Ronald Takaki, who was born in 1939, is the grandson of Japanese immigrants who settled in Hawaii. He earned his bachelor's degree from the College of Wooster and his doctorate from the University of California at Berkeley, where he is currently a professor of ethnic studies. Takaki has written and edited several books on ethnic issues, including A Pro-Slavery Crusade: The Agitation to Open the African Slave Trade *(1971),* Violence in the Black Imagination *(1972),* Iron Cages: Plantation Life and Labor in Hawaii, From Different Shores: Perspectives on Race and Ethnicity in America, *and* A Different Mirror: A History of Multicultural America.

The excerpt that follows is from Strangers from a Different Shore: A History of Asian Americans *(1989). In the passage, the author reflects on the Internment and its effects on the Japanese American community. Takaki calls on the people victimized by the Internment to "break the silence" in which they have lived for too long.*

⌗

ROOTS

1   To confront the current problems of racism, Asian Americans know they must remember the past and break the silence. This need was felt deeply by Japanese Americans during the hearings before the commission reviewing the issue of redress and reparations for Japanese Americans interned during World War II. Memories of the internment nightmare have haunted the older generation like ghosts. But the former prisoners have been unable to exorcise them by speaking out and ventilating their anger.

> When we were children,
> you spoke Japanese
> in lowered voices
> between yourselves.
>
> Once you uttered secrets
> which we should not know,
> were not to be heard by us.
> When you spoke
> of some dark secret,
> you would admonish us,
> "Don't tell it to anyone else."

It was a suffocated vow of silence.
What we have come to know
yet cannot tell
lingers like voiceless ghosts
wandering in our memory
as though memory is
desert bleached by
years of cruel exile.

It is the language
the silence within myself
I cannot fill with words,
the sound of mournful music
distantly heard.[1]

"Stigmatized," the ex-internees have been carrying the "burdens of shame" [2] for over forty painful years. "They felt like a rape victim," explained Congressman Norman Mineta, a former internee of the Heart Mountain internment camp. "They were accused of being disloyal. They were the victims but they were on trial and they did not want to talk about it." But Sansei, or third-generation Japanese Americans, want their elders to tell their story. Warren Furutani, for example, told the commissioners that young people like himself had been asking their parents to tell them about the concentration camps and to join them in pilgrimages to the internment camp at Manzanar. "Why? Why!" their parents would reply defensively. "Why would you want to know about it? It's not important, we don't need to talk about it." But, Furutani continued, they need to tell the world what happened during those years of infamy.[2]

Suddenly, during the commission hearings, scores of Issei and Nisei came [3] forward and told their stories. "For over thirty-five years I have been the stereotype Japanese American," Alice Tanabe Nehira told the commission. "I've kept quiet, hoping in due time we will be justly compensated and recognized for our years of patient effort. By my passive attitude, I can reflect on my past years to conclude that it doesn't pay to remain silent." The act of speaking out has enabled the Japanese-American community to unburden itself of years of anger and anguish. Sometimes their testimonies before the commission were long and the chair urged them to conclude. But they insisted the time was theirs. "Mr. Commissioner," protested poet Janice Mirikitani,

1. Richard Oyama, poem published in *Transfer 38* (San Francisco, 1979), p. 43, reprinted in Elaine Kim, *Asian American Literature: An Introduction to the Writings and Their Social Context* (Philadelphia, 1982), pp. 308–309.
2. Congressman Robert Matsui, speech in the House of Representatives on bill 442 for redress and reparations, September 17, 1987, *Congressional Record* (Washington, 1987), p. 7584; Congressman Norman Mineta, interview with author, March 26, 1988; Warren Furutani, testimony, reprinted in *Amerasia*, vol. 8, no. 2 (1981), p. 104.

> So when you tell me my time is
> up I tell you this.
> Pride has kept my lips
> pinned by nails,
> my rage confined.
> But I exhume my past
> to claim this time.[3]

4   The former internees finally had spoken, and their voices compelled the nation to redress the injustice of internment. In August 1988, Congress passed a bill giving an apology and a payment of $20,000 to each of the survivors of the internment camps. When President Ronald Reagan signed the bill into law, he admitted that the United States had committed "a grave wrong," for during World War II, Japanese Americans had remained "utterly loyal" to this country. "Indeed, scores of Japanese Americans volunteered for our Armed Forces— many stepping forward in the internment camps themselves. The 442nd Regimental Combat Team, made up entirely of Japanese Americans, served with immense distinction to defend this nation, their nation. Yet, back at home, the soldiers' families were being denied the very freedom for which so many of the soldiers themselves were laying down their lives." Then the president recalled an incident that happened forty-three years ago. At a ceremony to award the Distinguished Service Cross to Kazuo Masuda, who had been killed in action and whose family had been interned, a young actor paid tribute to the slain Nisei soldier. "The name of that young actor," remarked the president, who had been having trouble saying the Japanese names, "—I hope I pronounce this right—was Ronald Reagan." The time had come, the present acknowledged, to end "a sad chapter in American history."[4]

5   Asian Americans have begun to claim their time not only before the commission on redress and reparations but elsewhere as well—in the novels of Maxine Hong Kingston and Milton Murayama, the plays of Frank Chin and Philip Gotanda, the scholarly writings of Sucheng Chan and Elaine Kim, the films of Steve Okazaki and Wayne Wang, and the music of Hiroshima and Fred Houn. Others, too, have been breaking silences. Seventy-five-year-old Tomo Shoji, for example, had led a private life, but in 1981 she enrolled in an acting course because she wanted to try something frivolous and to take her mind off her husband's illness. In the beginning, Tomo was hesitant, awkward on the stage. "Be yourself," her teacher urged. Then suddenly she felt something surge through her, springing from deep within, and she began to tell funny and also sad stories about her life. Now Tomo tours the West Coast, a wonderful

---

3. Alice Tanabe Nehira, testimony, reprinted in *Amerasia*, vol. 8, no. 2 (1981), p. 93; Janice Mirikitani, "Breaking Silences," reprinted ibid., p. 109.
4. "Text of Reagan's Remarks," reprinted in *Pacific Citizen*, August 19–26, 1988, p. 5; *San Francisco Chronicle*, August 5 and 11, 1988.

wordsmith giving one-woman shows to packed audiences of young Asian Americans. "Have we really told our children all we have gone through?" she asks. Telling one of her stories, Tomo recounts: "My parents came from Japan and I was born in a lumber camp. One day, at school, my class was going on a day trip to a show, and I was pulled aside and told I would have to stay behind. All the white kids went." Tomo shares stories about her husband: "When I first met him, I thought, 'wow.' Oh, he was so macho! And he wanted his wife to be a good submissive wife. But then he married me." Theirs had been at times a stormy marriage. "Culturally we were different because he was Issei and I was American, and we used to argue a lot. Well, one day in 1942 right after World War II started he came home and told me we had to go to an internment camp. 'I'm not going to camp because I'm an American citizen,' I said to him. 'You have to go to camp, but not me.' Well you know what, that was one time my husband was right!" Tomo remembers the camp: "We were housed in barracks, and we had no privacy. My husband and I had to share a room with another couple. So we hanged a blanket in the middle of the room as a partition. But you could hear everything from the other side. Well, one night, while we were in bed, my husband and I got into an argument, and I dumped him out of the bed. The other couple thought we were making violent love." As she stands on the stages and talks stories excitedly, Tomo cannot be contained: "We got such good, fantastic stories to tell. All our stories are different."[5]

Today, young Asian Americans want to listen to these stories—to shatter images of themselves and their ancestors as "strangers" and to understand who they are as Asian Americans. "What don't you know?" their elders ask. Their question seems to have a peculiar frame: it points to the blank areas of collective memory. And the young people reply that they want "to figure out how the invisible world the emigrants built around [their] childhoods fit in solid America." They wanted to know more about their "no name" Asian ancestors. They want to decipher the signs of the Asian presence here and there across the landscape of America—railroad tracks over high mountains, fields of cane virtually carpeting entire islands, and verdant agricultural lands.

> Deserts to farmlands
> Japanese-American
> Page in history.[6]

They want to know what is their history and "what is the movies." They want to trace the origins of terms applied to them. "Why are we called 'Oriental'?" they question, resenting the appellation that has identified Asians

5. Tomo Shoji, "Born Too Soon . . . It's Never Too Late: Growing Up Nisei in Early Washington," presentations at the University of California, Berkeley, September 19, 1987, and the Ohana Cultural Center, Oakland, California, March 4, 1988.
6. Kingston, *The Woman Warrior*, p. 6; poem in Kazuo Ito, *Issei: A History of Japanese Immigrants in North America* (Seattle, 1973), p. 493.

as exotic, mysterious, strange, and foreign. "The word 'orient' simply means 'east.' So why are Europeans 'West' and why are Asians 'East'? Why did empire-minded Englishmen in the sixteenth century determine that Asia was 'east' of London? Who decided what names would be given to the different regions and peoples of the world? Why does 'American' usually mean 'white'?" Weary of Eurocentric history, young Asian Americans want their Asian ancestral lives in America chronicled, "given the name of a place." They have earned the right to belong to specific places like Washington, California, Hawaii, Punnene, Promontory Point, North Adams, Manzanar, Doyers Street. "And today, after 125 years of our life here," one of them insists, "I do not want just a home that time allowed me to have." Seeking to lay claim to America, they realize they can no longer be indifferent to what happened in history, no longer embarrassed by the hardships and humiliations experienced by their grandparents and parents.

> My heart, once bent and cracked, once
> ashamed of your China ways.
> Ma, hear me now, tell me your story
> again and again.[7] ✛

RESPONDING

1. Takaki writes that young Asians ask Americans, "Why are we called Oriental?" (paragraph 7). Who gave them this name and what are its implications? Think about the connotations of names of groups. In a journal entry, explain the role of names in forming group images and individual identities. Consider the effect of derogatory names on children.

2. Working individually or in a group, discuss the role of being a witness to a historical event. Is it important to "testify"? Support your opinion with examples from the readings or your own knowledge.

3. Explain why Congressman Norman Mineta said that ex-internees have been "'stigmatized' . . . carrying the 'burdens of shame' for over forty painful years" (paragraph 2). What did the Japanese Americans feel ashamed about? Using information from the readings and your own knowledge of human nature, write an essay discussing the fact that though they were the victims

7. Kingston, *The Woman Warrior*, p. 6; Robert Kwan, "Asian v. Oriental: A Difference that Counts," *Pacific Citizen*, April 25, 1980; Sir James Augustus Henry Murry (ed.), *The Oxford English Dictionary* (Oxford, 1933); vol. 7, p. 200; Aminur Rahim, "Is Oriental an Occident?" in *The Asiandian*, vol. 5, no. 1, April 1983, p. 20; Shawn Wong, *Homebase* (New York, 1979), p. 111; Nellie Wong, "From a Heart of Rice Straw," in Nellie Wong, *Dreams in Harrison Railroad Park* (Berkeley, 1977), p. 41.

of an injustice they felt shame rather than anger. Does Japanese culture help explain this reaction or are feelings of shame and guilt typical reactions of victims?

4. In an essay, explain what caused Japanese Americans finally to break their silence about the internment years. Discuss the role of their stories in helping the younger generation understand themselves and their heritage.

⊹

CONNECTING

Critical Thinking and Writing

1.   Reread the Internment Order. Why did the United States government think that the Japanese in America, including American citizens of Japanese descent, were a security risk? Did these reasons justify the government's actions? Many Japanese Americans as well as others have charged that the public's fears were based on racial prejudice. Write an essay supporting or refuting these charges.

2.   Every individual represented in this chapter was influenced by the internment experience. Compare the varying responses to the Internment on two or more characters in these selections. Or write an essay classifying the range of responses to the Internment as exemplified in these readings.

3.   For many of these authors, loyalty is an important issue. Reflect on the question of whom you owe loyalty to, your government, your parents, your friends? When loyalties conflict, which has first priority?

4.   Language is often an important part of a person's identity. Compare the role of language in shaping and preserving the identity of at least two individuals in the readings in this and other chapters. For example, you might compare the significance in her life of Sone's native Japanese to the significance in her life of Mora's native Chicano Spanish (see Chapter 7).

5.   Many of these readings deal with the issue of trying to adapt to a new culture while retaining your own. Write an essay comparing the responses to this challenge of at least two individuals in the readings in this and other chapters.

6.   Many of the readings in this text deal with the relationships between parents and children, old ways and new. Analyze the difficulties of communication that can develop between parents who were raised in one culture and children raised in another.

7.   Write an essay agreeing or disagreeing with the statement that it is difficult to be a part of two cultures. Use the readings in this book and your own and your friends' experiences to support your argument.

8.   Being pulled between two cultures is a theme that recurs throughout this

text. Write an essay discussing what it means to be bicultural. You can use examples from the text as well as your own experience.

9. Do your possessions define you? Describe the possessions that are most important to you and reveal most about your personality and history. Do their possessions define the Sone family? What about the family being evicted in the excerpt from Ellison's *Invisible Man* in Chapter 6?

10. Use the readings in this and other sections to illustrate how personal ambitions can come into conflict with cultural expectations.

11. Compare Kubota's or Miss Sasagawara's reaction to the tragedy of the Internment with *The Shawl*'s Rosa to the Holocaust in Chapter 9.

12. Write an essay discussing the role of the witness to history. Do different cultures have different interpretations of that role? Have those interpretations changed over time? What effect does the act of testifying to historical events have on the younger generation? Consider the reaction of Japanese Americans to the Internment, African Americans to slavery, Latin Americans to massacres in their native countries, or survivors to the Holocaust.

13. Using your school library, research the history of the struggle of Japanese Americans to obtain justice for the wrongs done to them during the internment period. Read the 1988 newspaper articles reporting the quest for an apology and reparations. What was the reaction of the Japanese American community when reparations were finally made? Were the reparations considered satisfactory?

For Further Research

1. Research current laws protecting citizen's rights. Are there laws that would now prevent the internment of U.S. citizens? What organizations work to protect individuals and groups? Are there enough safeguards in our current system? What is your evaluation and what suggestions for changes would you make?

2. Though their families and friends were in internment camps, many Japanese Americans enlisted in the army and fought for the United States in Europe. Some units were cited for exceptional bravery. Examine the war record of one of those units.

3. The treatment of German Americans during World War II was quite different from the treatment of Japanese Americans. After studying the opinions of historians, sociologists, politicians, and victims about the reasons for the vastly different treatment of each group, write an essay trying to account for these differences.

REFERENCES AND ADDITIONAL SOURCES

Broom, Leonard. *The Managed Casualty: The Japanese-American Family in World War II.* Berkeley: University of California Press, 1973.

Christgau, John. *Enemies: World War II Alien Internment.* Ames: Iowa State University Press, 1985.

Collins, Donald E. *Native American Aliens: Disloyalty and the Renunciation of Citizenship by Japanese Americans During World War II.* Westport, Conn.: Greenwood Press, 1985.

Daniels, Roger. *Concentration Camps: North America: Japanese in the United States & Canada During World War II.* Malabar, Fla.: R. E. Kreiger, 1981, 1989.

Herman, Masako. *The Japanese in America, 1843–1973: A Chronology and Fact Book.* Dobbs Ferry, N.Y.: Oceana, 1974.

Inada, Lawson. *Before the War: Poems as They Happened.* New York: Morrow, 1971.

Peter Irons, ed. *Justice Delayed: The Record of the Japanese American Internment Cases.* Middleton, Conn.: Wesleyan University Press, 1989.

Kim, Elaine. "Japanese American Portraits," in *Asian American Literature: An Introduction to the Writings and Their Social Context.* Philadelphia: Temple University Press, 1982, 1984.

Montero, Darrel. *Japanese Americans: Changing Patterns of Ethnic Affiliation over Three Generations.* Boulder, Colo.: Westview Press, 1980.

Myer, Dillon S. *Uprooted Americans: The Japanese Americans and the War Relocation Authority During World War II.* Tucson: University of Arizona Press, 1971, 1972.

Nagata, Donna K. *Legacy of Injustice: Exploring the Cross-Generational Impact of the Japanese American Internment.* New York: Plenum Press, 1993.

Takaki, Ronald. *Strangers from a Different Shore: A History of Asian Americans.* Boston: Little, Brown, 1989; New York: Penguin, 1993.

Taylor, Sandra C. *Jewel of the Desert: Japanese American Internment at Topaz.* Berkeley: University of California Press, 1993.

Uchida, Yoshiko. *Desert Exile: The Uprooting of a Japanese-American Family.* Seattle: University of Washington Press, 1982, 1991.

Weglyn, Michi. *Years of Infamy: The Untold Story of America's Concentration Camps.* New York: Morrow, 1976.

Wilson, Robert A., and Bill Hosokawa. *East to America: A History of the Japanese in the United States.* New York: Morrow, 1980.

6

AFRICAN AMERICANS

The Struggle for Civil Rights

Above: Freedom Riders' bus burned in Alabama in May, 1961.
(Courtesy, The Birmingham News)
Opposite: March from Selma to Montgomery, in summer of 1965.
(© James H. Karales)

SETTING THE HISTORICAL AND CULTURAL CONTEXT

In Gwendolyn Brooks's poem "The Chicago Defender Sends a Man to Little Rock," the speaker begins by describing what might be considered a typical community of the late 1950s:

> In Little Rock the people bear
> Babes, and comb and part their hair
> And watch the want ads, put repair
> To roof and latch. While wheat toast burns
> A woman waters multiferns. . . .
>
> In Little Rock the people sing
> Sunday hymns like anything,
> Through Sunday pomp and polishing.

It becomes all the more inexplicable that this community, which seemed so "like people everywhere," engaged in a kind of unspeakable cruelty toward a group of African American students who, supported by the Supreme Court ruling against segregated schools, had sought admission to the local high school. As the speaker of the poem, a reporter who was himself injured while covering the event, recounts:

> And true, they are hurling spittle, rock,
> Garbage and fruit in Little Rock.
> And I saw coiling storm a-writhe
> On bright madonnas. And a scythe
> Of men harassing brownish girls.
> (The bows and barrettes in the curls
> And braids declined away from joy.)
>
> I saw a bleeding brownish boy . . .

In the poem, people who observe conventions of duty and civility with members of their own race seem to think little of committing acts of brutality in their dealings with people from another race.

In a literal sense, Brooks's poem has its grounding in the incidents of 1957, when a group of African American students was beaten by an angry mob after they attempted to gain admission to Little Rock's formerly segregated Central High School. In another sense, the poem reflects the widespread injustice that prompted many African Americans, both adults and children, to work for civil rights. This struggle involved the courts, the Congress, and the White House; it took place in offices, in churches, and in the streets, and it brought together people from different backgrounds who were willing to risk their social position and their very lives for their ideals.

For many African Americans, the promise of America has been, in the words of Martin Luther King, Jr., a "promissory note" on which the nation has "defaulted." Brought to the United States in chains, they remained—even a century after the Emancipation Proclamation—"crippled by the manacles of segregation and the chains of discrimination."

After the Civil War, three important amendments were added to the Constitution. The Thirteenth Amendment (1865) outlawed slavery throughout the nation, not just in the areas specified in the Emancipation Proclamation. The Fourteenth Amendment (1868) guaranteed all Americans due process of law, and the Fifteenth Amendment (1870) extended to African Americans the right to vote. Moreover, the Civil Rights Act of 1875 guaranteed all Americans equal access to public accommodations. As early as the late 1870s, however, these acts were weakened because of inadequate enforcement by the federal government and the very narrow interpretation given them by the Supreme Court. Not only was the Civil Rights Act of 1875 rendered invalid because of lack of federal support, but the Supreme Court's rulings, which allowed private organizations and individuals to continue to discriminate on the basis of race, substantially weakened the constitutional amendments.

Throughout the period after Reconstruction, southern legislatures drafted laws to circumvent and even nullify the rights guaranteed to African Americans under the Constitution. These "Jim Crow" laws were intended to keep public facilities segregated on the basis of color. African Americans were forced to ride in the back of buses, to drink from segregated fountains, and even to step off sidewalks in order to make room for Caucasians. More important, they were forced to attend segregated schools whose facilities and programs were later shown to be inferior to those of the "Caucasian" schools. African Americans had no way to nullify these laws despite the Fifteenth Amendment guarantees. Poll taxes and grandfather clauses, which made the right to vote dependent on whether one's ancestors had voted, systematically excluded African Americans from voting in many southern states. In addition, "literacy tests," which required applicants to read and interpret orally sections from their state constitution, allowed examiners to fail whomever they wished.

The situation in the North was only somewhat better. Although many states had outlawed segregation, they retained restrictive covenants and other barriers to full integration. Few schools in the North, for example, were actually integrated. As late as the 1940s restaurants in Chicago and other northern cities would serve African Americans only after being targeted by demonstrators. African Americans experienced discrimination in many regions of the country as the United States prepared to enter World War II. The nation's armed forces remained segregated. Moreover, defense industries exercised restrictive hiring policies, offering African Americans only janitorial and other low-status positions.

The "Letter from Birmingham Jail" notes that "privileged groups seldom give up their privileges voluntarily." For over a century, African Americans attempted to gain the rights guaranteed them by federal law. In many places throughout the South there were sporadic demonstrations against discriminatory legislation and attempts to mobilize through boycott. The migration north of large numbers of African Americans created in urban areas concentrated populations with a strengthened sense of political purpose. Organizations such as the NAACP and the National Urban League were established, and their publications announced a new political and cultural awakening. Yet the period preceding World War II was marked by an especially strong demand by African Americans for equal rights.

Much of the political action of the 1940s can be credited to the work of A. Philip Randolph, who, as editor of *The Messenger* and president of the Brotherhood of Sleeping Car Porters, had been politically active since the Harlem Renaissance. In 1941 Randolph organized 100,000 people to march on Washington to protest segregation in the government and discriminatory hiring practices in the defense industries. This group called off its march only after it had received a commitment from President Franklin D. Roosevelt to the cause of civil rights. Executive Order 8802 outlawed discrimination in defense industries and in government hiring. Later that year the federal government established the Fair Employment Practices Commission. Full integration of the armed forces, however, was not accomplished until the Korean War, which began in 1950.

During the 1950s, organizations such as the NAACP Legal Defense Fund began to challenge the continued existence of segregated schools. The prevailing doctrine, derived from the Supreme Court decision in *Plessy* v. *Ferguson* in 1896, had allowed so-called "separate but equal schools." Civil rights groups were encouraged, however, by the court's 1950 ruling in *Sweatt* v. *Painter*. Although this decision did not overturn the Plessy ruling, Sweatt forced school districts to prove that separate facilities were indeed equal. It was in the 1954 case of *Brown* v. *The Board of Education of Topeka*, that the doctrine of separate but equal was successfully challenged for the first time. Led by Thurgood Marshall (who would later become a justice of the Supreme Court), the plaintiffs argued against the doctrine in *Plessy* on educational, psychological, and economic grounds. In a unanimous ruling, the Supreme Court reversed the *Plessy* decision, declaring that separate educational facilities were inherently unequal and therefore unconstitutional.

The *Brown* decision, important as it was, did not end racial segregation in schools. Many southerners protested against the ruling; others sought ways to evade or defer it. More than a hundred southern congressmen signed a letter denouncing the decision, and several southern governors attempted to block its implementation. In 1957 Governor Orval Faubus ordered the Arkansas National Guard to prevent the court-ordered integration of Little Rock's Central High School; after President Eisenhower forced him to rescind the order, an angry mob formed to take the guardsmen's place and several African American students were severely beaten. Eisenhower then sent in federal troops and the National Guard to force integration; it was the first time since Reconstruction that federal troops had played such a role. In 1962, as James Meredith, aided by Medgar Evers and others from the NAACP, attempted to register at the University of Mississippi, a mob encouraged by the defiant speeches of Governor Ross Barnett rioted; federal troops had to be called in to quell the unrest. In 1963 Alabama's governor, George Wallace, stood in a doorway, barring two students from registering at the University of Alabama; it took the intervention of the Justice Department before the students were admitted. In other areas, school districts encouraged parents to send their children to private schools, which remained segregated. In Virginia, the public schools were closed and much of their property was given to private schools; as a result, many African American children were kept out of school for up to two years.

African Americans also had to demand their rights to public transportation. Although the Supreme Court had outlawed segregation in interstate transportation, most public transportation within individual southern states was segregated. African Americans, who paid the same fare as Caucasians, had to sit in the back of the bus; furthermore, when there was a shortage of seats for Caucasians, the African Americans riders were expected to give up theirs. On December 5, 1955, Mrs. Rosa Parks protested this form of discrimination by refusing to give her seat to a Caucasian. Her nonviolent civil disobedience led to her arrest and imprisonment; it also marked the beginning of a thirteen-month boycott of the bus system organized largely by Dr. Martin Luther King, Jr., president of the Southern Christian Leadership Conference (SCLC). There had been earlier protests against this form of discrimination, including a boycott of a Louisiana bus system, but the Montgomery boycott of 1955 was the first such demonstration to succeed. During the early 1960s, Freedom Riders—African Americans and Caucasians organized by CORE (Congress of Racial Equality)—rode southern buses to protest the continued illegal segregation in interstate transportation. Freedom Riders also participated in education and voter registration drives.

During the 1950s and early 1960s, African Americans continued to be refused service at the lunch counters of many department stores. In 1960, members of the Student Nonviolent Coordinating Committee (SNCC) sat in at a local lunch counter in Greensboro, North Carolina. They manned the counters around the clock in shifts until they were finally served. The sit-in, begun by four college freshmen, was repeated with success at lunch counters, libraries, swimming pools, theaters, and other public facilities throughout the

South. In these protests and others, African Americans demonstrated the power of nonviolent direct action.

The protests against desegregation culminated in the great March on Washington in August 1963. Organized to promote congressional passage of the Civil Rights Act, the march featured addresses by activists John Lewis and Bayard Rustin, among others, and Martin Luther King, Jr.'s now famous "I Have a Dream" speech. The major television and radio networks provided extensive coverage of the event. When the Civil Rights Act was passed in 1964, it was considered the furthest-reaching legislation in the nation's history. The Voting Rights Act the following year established federal offices to monitor the registration of African American voters, as well as to regulate and to prevent abuses by registrars.

Each victory was achieved because of the courage of the activists involved. Those sitting in at lunch counters were subjected to beatings and arrest; activists had food, ammonia, and other substances poured on them, and lighted cigarettes were ground into their backs. Leaders found their homes, churches, and families threatened and at times attacked. Freedom Riders traveling the South by bus were stoned and beaten; their buses were burned by angry mobs. In Birmingham during the administration of Public Safety Commissioner Eugene "Bull" Connor, police fought protesters—both adults and children—with fire hoses, attack dogs, and savage beatings. In 1965 demonstrators marching through Selma, Alabama, were driven back by tear gas and attacked by sheriff's officers. Such scenes, which were often televised, exposed the brutality with which civil rights activists were treated in the South.

Many civil rights activists died for their belief. In 1963, Medgar Evers, who had helped James Meredith gain admission to the University of Mississippi, was gunned down in front of his home. A year later, also in Mississippi, three Freedom Riders—Andrew Goodman, Michael Schwerner, and James Chaney, two Caucasians and an African American—disappeared. They had been investigating a church fire when they were apprehended by local authorities; after being turned over to a mob, they were murdered. In 1968, while leading a strike of sanitation workers in Memphis, Martin Luther King, Jr., was assassinated. James Farmer's selection explains what happened to Chaney, Goodman, and Schwerner. Gwendolyn Brooks celebrates people of vision and courage who suffered in the name of civil rights.

The numerous and mounting pressures on the civil rights movement, the slow progress to equality, and the high price paid for small gains caused divisions in the movement. The nonviolent action advocated by SCLC and CORE was rejected by Stokely Carmichael, SNCC, and other African American leaders. Malcolm X, one of the most influential of these leaders, questioned the achievements of the civil rights movement. In the selection in this chapter, Malcolm X returns to the question of justice and dignity. In his words, "A desegregated cup of coffee, a theater, public toilets—the whole range of hypocritical 'integration'" could be seen as inadequate "atonement" for the nation's treatment of African Americans.

In his essay "What's in a Name? Some Meanings of Blackness," Henry Louis Gates, Jr., asserts, "To declare that race is a trope, however, is not to deny its palpable force in the life of every African-American who tries to function every day in a still very racist America." Despite many accomplishments, the goals of the civil rights movement have yet to be achieved. As activists point out, the rates of poverty, unemployment, infant mortality, and crime remain higher in African American communities than in the majority culture. African Americans now have greater opportunities to serve in public office and to participate in the political process, yet neither the government nor the private sector has been able to stop the deterioration of many African American urban areas or counteract the extreme poverty of many rural areas; some of the effects of this continued poverty and inequality is dramatized in Toni Cade Bambara's short story "The Lesson." Despite the victories of the 1960s, African Americans in the 1990s still have to demand the right to join exclusive business and social clubs. And cities from Brooklyn to Los Angeles have been touched by racial violence. As pundits and politicians repeat the question of Rodney King—"can we all get along?"—it becomes more apparent that the struggle against prejudice and injustice is far from being won.

BEGINNING: Pre-reading/Writing

Before reading the selections in this chapter, try to determine how much you actually know about the civil rights movement of the 1960s and its leaders by listing events leading up to and taking place during the struggle for civil rights. Working with the class, construct a time line of significant events. As you read the selections in this chapter and learn more about the civil rights movement, revise your time line as necessary.

In 1954 the Supreme Court ruled that the school board of Topeka, Kansas, had violated the law when it had ordered children to attend racially segregated schools. In their unanimous decision, the justices said that segregation by race violated the constitutional guarantee of equal protection under the law. The court reversed the earlier decision of Plessy v. Ferguson *(1896), which had permitted "separate but equal" schools.*

⁜

From BROWN v. THE BOARD OF EDUCATION OF TOPEKA

1   THESE CASES COME TO US from the States of Kansas, South Carolina, Virginia, and Delaware. They are premised on different facts and different local conditions, but a common legal question justifies their consideration together in this consolidated opinion.

2   In approaching this problem, we cannot turn the clock back to 1868 when the Amendment was adopted, or even to 1896 when *Plessy* v. *Ferguson* was written. We must consider public education in the light of its full development and its present place in American life throughout the Nation. Only in this way can it be determined if segregation in public schools deprives these plaintiffs of the equal protection of the laws.

3   Today, education is perhaps the most important function of state and local governments. Compulsory school attendance laws and the great expenditures for education both demonstrate our recognition of the importance of education to our democratic society. It is required in the performance of our most basic public responsibilities, even service in the armed forces. It is the very foundation of good citizenship. Today it is a principal instrument in awakening the child to cultural values, in preparing him for later professional training, and in helping him to adjust normally to his environment. In these days, it is doubtful that any child may reasonably be expected to succeed in life if he is denied the opportunity of an education. Such an opportunity, where the state has undertaken to provide it, is a right which must be made available to all on equal terms.

4   We come then to the question presented: Does segregation of children in public schools solely on the basis of race, even though the physical facilities and other "tangible" factors may be equal, deprive the children of the minority group of equal educational opportunities? We believe that it does.

5   In *Sweatt* v. *Painter,* . . . in finding that a segregated law school for Negroes could not provide them equal educational opportunities, this Court relied in large part on "those qualities which are incapable of objective measurement but which make for greatness in a law school." In *McLaurin* v. *Oklahoma State Regents,* . . . the Court, in requiring that a Negro admitted to a white graduate

school be treated like all other students, again resorted to intangible considerations: ". . . his ability to study, to engage in discussions and exchange views with other students, and, in general, to learn his profession." Such considerations apply with added force to children in grade and high schools. To separate them from others of similar age and qualifications solely because of their race generates a feeling of inferiority as to their status in the community that may affect their hearts and minds in a way unlikely ever to be undone. The effect of this separation on their educational opportunities was well stated by a finding in the Kansas case by a court which nevertheless felt compelled to rule against the Negro plaintiffs:

> Segregation of white and colored children in public schools has a detrimental effect upon the colored children. The impact is greater when it has the sanction of the law; for the policy of separating the races is usually interpreted as denoting the inferiority of the Negro group. A sense of inferiority affects the motivation of a child to learn. Segregation with the sanction of the law, therefore, has a tendency to retard the educational and mental development of Negro children and to deprive them of some of the benefits they would receive in a racially integrated school system.

Whatever may have been the extent of psychological knowledge at the time of *Plessy* v. *Ferguson*, this finding is amply supported by modern authority. Any language in *Plessy* v. *Ferguson* contrary to this finding is rejected.

We conclude that in the field of public education the doctrine of "separate but equal" has no place. Separate educational facilities are inherently unequal. Therefore, we hold that the plaintiffs and others similarly situated for whom the actions have been brought are, by reason of the segregation complained of, deprived of the equal protection of the laws guaranteed by the Fourteenth Amendment. . . . ✠

6

RESPONDING

1. In a journal entry, explain the significance of the Fourteenth Amendment to the Constitution in your own words.

2. Working individually or in a group, define "segregation," "*de facto* segregation," and "separate but equal." Discuss the ways in which these policies were implemented in many school systems.

3. List the reasons that the justices give to support their statement that "today, education is perhaps the most important function of state and local govern-

ments" (paragraph 3). Which of these reasons do you think is most persuasive and important? Write an essay supporting your choice.

4. Using arguments from the decision as well as your own knowledge and experience, write an essay in which you agree or disagree that "in the field of public education the doctrine of 'separate but equal' has no place" (paragraph 6). Consider, as well, whether the same arguments apply to private education.

RALPH ELLISON

Ralph Ellison, who was born in Oklahoma City, Oklahoma, in 1914, studied at the Tuskegee Institute in Alabama and served in the merchant marines during World War II. After the war he taught at several major universities, including the University of Chicago, UCLA, Yale, New York University, and Bard College. His publications included the novel Invisible Man *(1952), the essay collections* Shadow and Art *(1964) and* Going to the Territory *(1986), as well as essays, articles, and short stories in many periodicals. Ralph Ellison died in 1994.*

In the following excerpt from Invisible Man, *the narrator describes his feelings as he joins a group of people witnessing the eviction of an elderly couple. In its depiction of the couple's attempt to retain their dignity at this moment of crisis, the passage raises troubling questions about the nature of justice and leadership.*

⸙

From INVISIBLE MAN

THE WIND DROVE ME INTO A SIDE STREET where a group of boys had set a packing box afire. The gray smoke hung low and seemed to thicken as I walked with my head down and eyes closed, trying to avoid the fumes. My lungs began to pain; then emerging, wiping my eyes and coughing, I almost stumbled over it: It was piled in a jumble along the walk and over the curb into the street, like a lot of junk waiting to be hauled away. Then I saw the sullen-faced crowd, looking at a building where two white men were toting out a chair in which an old woman sat; who, as I watched, struck at them feebly with her fists. A motherly-looking old woman with her head tied in a handkerchief, wearing a man's shoes and a man's heavy blue sweater. It was startling: The crowd watched silently, the two white men lugging the chair and trying to dodge the blows and the old woman's face streaming with angry tears as she thrashed at them with her fists. I couldn't believe it. Something, a sense of foreboding, filled me, a quick sense of uncleanliness.

"Leave us alone," she cried, "leave us alone!" as the men pulled their heads out of range and sat her down abruptly at the curb, hurrying back into the building.

What on earth, I thought, looking about me. What on earth? The old woman sobbed, pointing to the stuff piled along the curb. "Just look what they doing to us. Just look," looking straight at me. And I realized that what I'd taken for junk was actually worn household furnishings.

4   "Just look at what they doing," she said, her teary eyes upon my face.

5   I looked away embarrassed, staring into the rapidly growing crowd. Faces were peering sullenly from the windows above. And now as the two men reappeared at the top of the steps carrying a battered chest of drawers, I saw a third man come out and stand behind them, pulling at his ear as he looked out over the crowd.

6   "Shake it up, you fellows," he said, "shake it up. We don't have all day."

7   Then the men came down with the chest and I saw the crowd give way sullenly, the men trudging through, grunting and putting the chest at the curb, then returning into the building without a glance to left or right.

8   "Look at that," a slender man near me said. "We ought to beat the hell out of those paddies!"

9   I looked silently into his face, taut and ashy in the cold, his eyes trained upon the men going up the steps.

10   "Sho, we ought to stop 'em," another man said, "but ain't that much nerve in the whole bunch."

11   "There's plenty nerve," the slender man said. "All they need is someone to set it off. All they need is a leader. You mean *you* don't have the nerve."

12   "Who me?" the man said. "Who me?"

13   "Yes, you."

14   "Just look," the old woman said, "just look," her face still turned toward mine. I turned away, edging closer to the two men.

15   "Who are those men?" I said, edging closer.

16   "Marshals or something. I don't give a damn who they is."

17   "Marshals, hell," another man said. "Those guys doing all the toting ain't nothing but trusties. Soon as they get through they'll lock 'em up again."

18   "I don't care who they are, they got no business putting these old folks out on the sidewalk."

19   "You mean they're putting them out of their apartment?" I said. "They can do that up *here*?"

20   "Man, where *you* from?" he said, swinging toward me. "What does it look like they puttin' them out of, a Pullman car? They being evicted!"

21   I was embarrassed; others were turning to stare. I had never seen an eviction. Someone snickered.

22   "Where did *he* come from?"

23   A flash of heat went over me and I turned. "Look, friend," I said, hearing a hot edge coming into my voice. "I asked a civil question. If you don't care to answer, don't, but don't try to make me look ridiculous."

24   "Ridiculous? Hell, all scobos is ridiculous. Who the hell is you?"

25   "Never mind, I am who I am. Just don't beat up your gums at me," I said, throwing him a newly acquired phrase.

26   Just then one of the men came down the steps with an armful of articles, and I saw the old woman reach up, yelling, "Take your hands off my Bible!" And the crowd surged forward.

The white man's hot eyes swept the crowd. "Where, lady?" he said. "I don't   27
see any Bible."

And I saw her snatch the Book from his arms, clutching it fiercely and   28
sending forth a shriek. "They can come in your home and do what they want
to you," she said. "Just come stomping in and jerk your life up by the roots!
But this here's the last straw. They ain't going to bother with my Bible!"

The white man eyed the crowd. "Look, lady," he said, more to the rest of   29
us than to her, "I don't want to do this, I *have* to do it. They sent me up here
to do it. If it was left to me, you could stay here till hell freezes over . . ."

"These white folks, Lord. These white folks," she moaned, her eyes turned   30
toward the sky, as an old man pushed past me and went to her.

"Hon, Hon," he said, placing his hand on her shoulder. "It's the agent, not   31
these gentlemen. He's the one. He says it's the bank, but you know he's the
one. We've done business with him for over twenty years."

"Don't tell me," she said. "It's all the white folks, not just one. They all   32
against us. Every stinking low-down one of them."

"She's right!" a hoarse voice said. "She's right! They *all* is!"   33

Something had been working fiercely inside me, and for a moment I had   34
forgotten the rest of the crowd. Now I recognized a self-consciousness about
them, as though they, we, were ashamed to witness the eviction, as though we
were all unwilling intruders upon some shameful event; and thus we were careful
not to touch or stare too hard at the effects that lined the curb; for we were
witnesses of what we did not wish to see, though curious, fascinated, despite
our shame, and through it all the old female, mind-plunging crying.

I looked at the old people, feeling my eyes burn, my throat tighten. The   35
old woman's sobbing was having a strange effect upon me—as when a child,
seeing the tears of its parents, is moved by both fear and sympathy to cry. I
turned away, feeling myself being drawn to the old couple by a warm, dark,
rising whirlpool of emotion which I feared. I was wary of what the sight of them
crying there on the sidewalk was making me begin to feel. I wanted to leave,
but was too ashamed to leave, was rapidly becoming too much a part of it to
leave.

I turned aside and looked at the clutter of household objects which the two   36
men continued to pile on the walk. And as the crowd pushed me I looked down
to see looking out of an oval frame a portrait of the old couple when young,
seeing the sad, stiff dignity of the faces there; feeling strange memories awakening that began an echoing in my head like that of a hysterical voice stuttering
in a dark street. Seeing them look back at me as though even then in that
nineteenth-century day they had expected little, and this with a grim, unillu-
sioned pride that suddenly seemed to me both a reproach and a warning. My
eyes fell upon a pair of crudely carved and polished bones, "knocking bones,"
used to accompany music at country dances, used in black-face minstrels; the
flat ribs of a cow, a steer or sheep, flat bones that gave off a sound, when struck,
like heavy castanets (had he been a minstrel?) or the wooden block of a set of

drums. Pots and pots of green plants were lined in the dirty snow, certain to die of the cold; ivy, canna, a tomato plant. And in a basket I saw a straightening comb, switches of false hair, a curling iron, a card with silvery letters against a background of dark red velvet, reading "God Bless Our Home"; and scattered across the top of a chiffonnier were nuggets of High John the Conqueror, the lucky stone; and as I watched the white men put down a basket in which I saw a whiskey bottle filled with rock candy and camphor, a small Ethiopian flag, a faded tintype of Abraham Lincoln, and the smiling image of a Hollywood star torn from a magazine. And on a pillow several badly cracked pieces of delicate china, a commemorative plate celebrating the St. Louis World Fair . . . I stood in a kind of daze, looking at an old folded lace fan studded with jet and mother-of-pearl.

37   The crowd surged as the white men came back, knocking over a drawer that spilled its contents in the snow at my feet. I stooped and started replacing the articles: a bent Masonic emblem, a set of tarnished cuff links, three brass rings, a dime pierced with a nail hole so as to be worn about the ankle on a string for luck, an ornate greeting card with the message "Grandma, I love you" in childish scrawl; another card with a picture of what looked like a white man in black-face seated in the door of a cabin strumming a banjo beneath a bar of music and the lyric "Going back to my old cabin home"; a useless inhalant, a string of bright glass beads with a tarnished clasp, a rabbit foot, a celluloid baseball scoring card shaped like a catcher's mitt, registering a game won or lost years ago; an old breast pump with rubber bulb yellowed with age, a worn baby shoe and a dusty lock of infant hair tied with a faded and crumpled blue ribbon. I felt nauseated. In my hand I held three lapsed life insurance policies with perforated seals stamped "Void"; a yellowing newspaper portrait of a huge black man with the caption: MARCUS GARVEY[1] DEPORTED.

38   I turned away, bending and searching the dirty snow for anything missed by my eyes, and my fingers closed upon something resting in a frozen footstep: a fragile paper, coming apart with age, written in black ink grown yellow. I read: FREE PAPERS. *Be it known to all men that my negro, Primus Provo, has been freed by me this sixth day of August, 1859. Signed: John Samuels. Macon* . . . I folded it quickly, blotting out the single drop of melted snow which glistened on the yellowed page, and dropped it back into the drawer. My hands were trembling, my breath rasping as if I had run a long distance or come upon a coiled snake in a busy street. *It has been longer than that, further removed in time*, I told myself, and yet I knew that it hadn't been. I replaced the drawer in the chest and pushed drunkenly to the curb.

39   But it wouldn't come up, only a bitter spurt of gall filled my mouth and splattered the old folk's possessions. I turned and stared again at the jumble, no

1. Marcus Garvey (1887–1940), Jamaican-born Black Nationalist leader deported to Jamaica for mail fraud.

longer looking at what was before my eyes, but inwardly-outwardly, around a corner in the dark, far-away-and-long-ago, not so much of my own memory as of remembered words, of linked verbal echoes, images, heard even when not listening at home. And it was as though I myself was being dispossessed of some painful yet precious thing which I could not bear to lose; something confounding, like a rotted tooth that one would rather suffer indefinitely than endure the short, violent eruption of pain that would mark its removal. And with this sense of dispossession came a pang of vague recognition: this junk, these shabby chairs, these heavy, old-fashioned pressing irons, zinc wash tubs with dented bottoms— all throbbed within me with more meaning than there should have been: *And why did I, standing in the crowd, see like a vision my mother hanging wash on a cold windy day, so cold that the warm clothes froze even before the vapor thinned and hung stiff on the line, and her hands white and raw in the skirt-swirling wind and her gray head bare to the darkened sky—why were they causing me discomfort so far beyond their intrinsic meaning as objects? And why did I see them now as behind a veil that threatened to lift, stirred by the cold wind in the narrow street?*

A scream, "I'm going in!" spun me around. The old couple were on the 40 steps now, the old man holding her arm, the white men leaning forward above, and the crowd pressing me closer to the steps.

"You can't go in, lady," the man said. 41

"I want to pray!" she said. 42

"I can't help it, lady. You'll have to do your praying out here." 43

"I'm go'n in!" 44

"Not in here!" 45

"All we want to do is go in and pray," she said, clutching her Bible. "It ain't 46 right to pray in the street like this."

"I'm sorry," he said. 47

"Aw, let the woman go in to pray," a voice called from the crowd. "You got 48 all their stuff out here on the walk—what more do you want, blood?"

"Sure, let them old folks pray." 49

"That's what's wrong with us now, all this damn praying," another voice 50 called.

"You don't go back, see," the white man said. "You were legally evicted." 51

"But all we want to do is go in an' kneel on the floor," the old man said. 52 "We been living right here for over twenty years. I don't see why you can't let us go just for a few minutes . . ."

"Look, I've told you," the man said. "I've got my orders. You're wasting 53 my time."

"We go'n in!" the woman said. 54

It happened so suddenly that I could barely keep up with it: I saw the old 55 woman clutching her Bible and rushing up the steps, her husband behind her and the white man stepping in front of them and stretching out his arm. "I'll jug you," he yelled, "by God, I'll jug you!"

56   "Take your hands off that woman!" someone called from the crowd.

57   Then at the top of the stairs they were pushing against the man and I saw the old woman fall backwards, and the crowd exploded.

58   "Get that paddie sonofabitch!"

59   "He struck her!" a West Indian woman screamed into my ear. "The filthy brute, he struck her!"

60   "Stand back or I'll shoot," the man called, his eyes wild as he drew a gun and backed into the doorway where the two trusties stood bewildered, their arms full of articles. "I swear I'll shoot. You don't know what you're doing, but I'll shoot!"

61   They hesitated. "Ain't but six bullets in that thing," a little fellow called. "Then what you going to do?"

62   "Yeah, you damn sho caint hide."

63   "I advise you to stay out of this," the marshal called.

64   "Think you can come up here and hit one of our women, you a fool."

65   "To hell with all this talk, let's rush that bastard!"

66   "You better think twice," the white man called.

67   I saw them start up the steps and felt suddenly as though my head would split. I knew that they were about to attack the man and I was both afraid and angry, repelled and fascinated. I both wanted it and feared the consequences, was outraged and angered at what I saw and yet surged with fear; not for the man or of the consequences of an attack, but of what the sight of violence might release in me. And beneath it all there boiled up all the shock-absorbing phrases that I had learned all my life. I seemed to totter on the edge of a great dark hole.

68   "No, no," I heard myself yelling. "Black men! Brothers! Black Brothers! That's not the way. We're law-abiding. We're a law-abiding people and a slow-to-anger people."

69   Forcing my way quickly through the crowd, I stood on the steps facing those in front, talking rapidly without thought but out of my clashing emotions. "We're a law-abiding people and a slow-to-anger people . . ." They stopped, listening. Even the white man was startled.

70   "Yeah, but we mad now," a voice called out.

71   "Yes, you're right," I called back. "We're angry, but let us be wise. Let us, I mean let us not . . . Let us learn from that great leader whose wise action was reported in the newspaper the other day . . ."

72   "What, mahn? Who?" a West Indian voice shouted.

73   "Come on! To hell with this guy, let's get that paddie before they send him some help . . ."

74   "No, wait," I yelled. "Let's follow a leader, let's organize. *Organize.* We need someone like that wise leader, you read about him, down in Alabama. He was strong enough to choose to do the wise thing in spite of what he felt him-self . . ."

"Who, mahn? Who?"

This was it, I thought, they're listening, eager to listen. Nobody laughed. If they laugh, I'll die! I tensed my diaphragm.

"That wise man," I said, "you read about him, who when that fugitive escaped from the mob and ran to his school for protection, that wise man who was strong enough to do the legal thing, the law-abiding thing, to turn him over to the forces of law and order . . ."

"Yeah," a voice rang out, "yeah, so they could lynch his ass."

Oh, God, this wasn't it at all. Poor technique and not at all what I intended.

"He was a wise leader," I yelled. "He was within the law. Now wasn't that the wise thing to do?"

"Yeah, he was wise all right," the man laughed angrily. "Now get out of the way so we can jump this paddie."

The crowd yelled and I laughed in response as though hypnotized.

"But wasn't that the human thing to do? After all, he had to protect himself because—"

"He was a handkerchief-headed rat!" a woman screamed, her voice boiling with contempt.

"Yes, you're right. He was wise and cowardly, but what about us? What are we to do?" I yelled, suddenly thrilled by the response. "Look at him," I cried.

"Yes, just look at him!" an old fellow in a derby called out as though answering a preacher in church.

"And look at that old couple . . ."

"Yeah, what about Sister and Brother Provo?" he said. "It's an ungodly shame!"

"And look at their possessions all strewn there on the sidewalk. Just look at their possessions in the snow. How old are you, sir?" I yelled.

"I'm eighty-seven," the old man said, his voice low and bewildered.

"How's that? Yell so our slow-to-anger brethren can hear you."

"I'm *eighty-seven years old!*"

"Did you hear him? He's eighty-seven. Eighty-seven and look at all he's accumulated in eighty-seven years, strewn in the snow like chicken guts, and we're a law-abiding, slow-to-anger bunch of folks turning the other cheek every day in the week. What are we going to do? What would you, what would I, what would he have done? *What is to be done?* I propose we do the wise thing, the law-abiding thing. Just look at this junk! Should two old folks live in such junk, cooped up in a filthy room? It's a great danger, a fire hazard! Old cracked dishes and broken-down chairs. Yes, yes, yes! Look at that old woman, somebody's mother, somebody's grandmother, maybe. We call them 'Big Mama' and they spoil us and—*you* know, *you* remember . . . Look at her quilts and broken-down shoes. I know she's somebody's mother because I saw an old breast pump fall into the snow, and she's somebody's grandmother, because I saw a card that read 'Dear Grandma' . . . But we're law-abiding . . . I looked into a basket and

I saw some bones, not neckbones, but rib bones, knocking bones . . . This old couple used to dance . . . I saw—What kind of work do you do, Father?" I called.

94   "I'm a day laborer . . ."

95   ". . . A day laborer, you heard him, but look at his stuff strewn like chitterlings in the snow . . .Where has all his labor gone? Is he lying?"

96   "Hell, no, he ain't lying."

97   "Naw, suh!"

98   "Then where did his labor go? Look at his old blues records and her pots of plants, they're down-home folks, and everything tossed out like junk whirled eighty-seven years in a cyclone. Eighty-seven years, and *poof*! like a snort in a wind storm. Look at them, they look like my mama and my papa and my grandma and grandpa, and I look like you and you look like me. Look at them but remember that we're a wise, law-abiding group of people. And remember it when you look up there in the doorway at that law standing there with his forty-five. Look at him, standing with his blue steel pistol and his blue serge suit. Look at him! You don't see just one man dressed in one blue serge suit, or one forty-five, you see ten for every one of us, ten guns and ten warm suits and ten fat bellies and ten million laws. *Laws*, that's what we call them down South! Laws! And we're wise, and law-abiding. And look at this old woman with her dog-eared Bible. What's she trying to bring off here? She's let her religion go to her head, but we all know that religion is for the heart, not for the head. 'Blessed are the pure in heart,' it says. Nothing about the poor in head. What's she trying to do? What about the clear of head? And the clear of eye, the ice-water-visioned who see too clear to miss a lie? Look out there at her cabinet with its gaping drawers. Eighty-seven years to fill them, and full of brick and brack, a bricabrac, and she wants to break the law . . . What's happened to them? They're our people, your people and mine, your parents and mine. What's happened to 'em?"

99   "I'll tell you!" a heavyweight yelled, pushing out of the crowd, his face angry. "Hell, they been dispossessed, you crazy sonofabitch, get out the way!"

100   "Dispossessed?" I cried, holding up my hand and allowing the word to whistle from my throat. "That's a good word, 'Dispossessed'! 'Dispossessed,' eighty-seven years and dispossessed of what? They ain't *got* nothing, they caint *get* nothing, they never *had* nothing. So who was dispossessed?" I growled. "We're law-abiding. So who's being dispossessed? Can it be us? These old ones are out in the snow, but we're here with them. Look at their stuff, not a pit to hiss in, not a window to shout the news and us right with them. Look at them, not a shack to pray in or an alley to sing the blues! They're facing a gun and we're facing it with them. They don't want the world, but only Jesus. They only want Jesus, just fifteen minutes of Jesus on the rug-bare floor . . . How about it, Mr. Law? Do we get our fifteen minutes worth of Jesus? You got the world, can we have our Jesus?"

101   "I got my orders, Mac," the man called, waving the pistol with a sneer.

"You're doing all right, tell 'em to keep out of this. This is legal and I'll shoot if I have to . . ."

"But what about the prayer?" 102

"They don't go back!" 103

"Are you positive?" 104

"You could bet your life," he said. 105

"Look at him," I called to the angry crowd. "With his blue steel pistol and 106 his blue serge suit. You heard him, he's the law. He says he'll shoot us down because we're a law-abiding people. So we've been dispossessed, and what's more, he thinks he's God. Look up there backed against the post with a criminal on either side of him. Can't you feel the cold wind, can't you hear it asking, 'What did you do with your heavy labor? What did you do?' When you look at all you haven't got in eighty seven years you feel ashamed—"

"Tell 'em about it, brother," an old man interrupted. "It makes you feel 107 you ain't a man."

"Yes, these old folks had a dream book, but the pages went blank and it 108 failed to given them the number. It was called the Seeing Eye, The Great Constitutional Dream Book, The Secrets of Africa, The Wisdom of Egypt—but the eye was blind, it lost its luster. It's all cataracted like a cross-eyed carpenter and it doesn't saw straight. All we have is the Bible and this Law here rules that out. So where do we go? Where do we go from here, without a pot—"

"We going after that paddie," the heavyweight called, rushing up the steps. 109

Someone pushed me. "No, wait," I called. 110

"Get out the way now." 111

There was a rush against me and I fell, hearing a single explosion, backward 112 into a whirl of milling legs, overshoes, the trampled snow cold on my hands. Another shot sounded above like a bursting bag. Managing to stand, I saw atop the steps the fist with the gun being forced into the air above the crowd's bobbing heads and the next instant they were dragging him down into the snow; punching him left and right, uttering a low tense swelling sound of desperate effort; a grunt that exploded into a thousand softly spat, hate-sizzling curses. I saw a woman striking with the pointed heel of her shoe, her face a blank mask with hollow black eyes as she aimed and struck, aimed and struck, bringing spurts of blood, running along beside the man who was dragged to his feet now as they punched him gauntlet-wise between them. Suddenly I saw a pair of handcuffs arc gleaming into the air and sail across the street. A boy broke out of the crowd, the marshal's snappy hat on his head. The marshal was spun this way and that, then a swift tattoo of blows started him down the street. I was beside myself with excitement. The crowd surged after him, milling like a huge man trying to turn in a cubbyhole—some of them laughing, some cursing, some intently silent.

"The brute struck that gentle woman, poor thing!" the West Indian woman 113 chanted. "Black men, did you ever see such a brute? Is he a gentleman, I ask you? The brute! Give it back to him, black men. Repay the brute a thousandfold!

Give it back to him unto the third and fourth generations. Strike him, our fine black men. Protect your black women! Repay the arrogant creature to the third and fourth generations!"

114 "We're dispossessed," I sang at the top of my voice, "dispossessed and we want to pray. Let's go in and pray. Let's have a big prayer meeting. But we'll need some chairs to sit in . . . rest upon as we kneel. We'll need some chairs!"

115 "Here's some chairs down here," a woman called from the walk. "How 'bout taking in some chairs?"

116 "Sure," I called, "take everything. Take it all, hide that junk! Put it back where it came from. It's blocking the street and the sidewalk, and that's against the law. We're law-abiding, so clear the street of the debris. Put it out of sight! Hide it, hide their shame! Hide *our* shame!

117 "Come on, men," I yelled, dashing down the steps and seizing a chair and starting back, no longer struggling against or thinking about the nature of my action. The others followed, picking up pieces of furniture and lugging it back into the building.

118 "We ought to done this long ago," a man said.

119 "We damn sho should."

120 "I feel so good," a woman said, "I feel so *good*!"

121 "Black men, I'm proud of you," the West Indian woman shrilled. "Proud!"

122 We rushed into the dark little apartment that smelled of stale cabbage and put the pieces down and returned for more. Men, women and children seized articles and dashed inside shouting, laughing. I looked for the two trusties, but they seemed to have disappeared. Then, coming down into the street, I thought I saw one. He was carrying a chair back inside.

123 "So you're law-abiding too," I called, only to become aware that it was someone else. A white man but someone else altogether.

124 The man laughed at me and continued inside. And when I reached the street there were several of them, men and women, standing about, cheering whenever another piece of furniture was returned. It was like a holiday. I didn't want it to stop.

125 "Who are those people?" I called from the steps.

126 "What people?" someone called back.

127 "*Those*," I said, pointing.

128 "You mean those ofays?"

129 "Yes, what do they want?"

130 "We're friends of the people," one of the white men called.

131 "Friends of what people?" I called, prepared to jump down upon him if he answered, "*You* people."

132 "We're friends of *all* the common people," he shouted. "We came up to help."

133 "We believe in brotherhood," another called.

134 "Well, pick up that sofa and come on," I called. I was uneasy about their presence and disappointed when they all joined the crowd and starting lugging the evicted articles back inside. Where had I heard of them?

"Why don't we stage a march?" one of the white men called, going past.   135

"Why don't we march!" I yelled out to the sidewalk before I had time to   136
think.

They took it up immediately.   137

"Let's march . . ."   138

"It's a good idea."   139

"Let's have a demonstration . . ."   140

"Let's parade!"   141

I heard the siren and saw the scout cars swing into the block in the same   142
instant. It was the police! I looked into the crowd, trying to focus upon their
faces, hearing someone yell, "Here come the cops," and others answering, "Let
'em come!"

Where is all this leading? I thought, seeing a white man run inside the   143
building as the policemen dashed from their cars and came running up.

"What's going on here?" a gold-shield officer called up the steps.   144

It had become silent. No one answered.   145

"I said, what's going on here," he repeated. "You," he called, pointing   146
straight at me.

"We've . . . we've been clearing the sidewalk of a lot of junk," I called, tense   147
inside.

"What's that?" he said.   148

"It's a clean-up campaign," I called, wanting to laugh. "These old folks had   149
all their stuff cluttering up the sidewalk and we cleared the street . . ."

"You mean you're interfering with an eviction," he called, starting through   150
the crowd.

"He ain't doing nothing," a woman called from behind me.   151

I looked around, the steps behind were filled with those who had been   152
inside.

"We're all together," someone called, as the crowd closed in.   153

"Clear the streets," the officer ordered.   154

"That's what we were doing," someone called from back in the crowd.   155

"Mahoney!" he bellowed to another policeman, "send in a riot call!"   156

"What riot?" one of the white men called to him. "There's no riot."   157

"If I say there's a riot, there's a riot," the officer said. "And what are you   158
white people doing up here in Harlem?"

"We're citizens. We go anywhere we like."   159

"Listen! Here come some more cops!" someone called.   160

"Let them come!"   161

"Let the Commissioner come!"   162

It became too much for me. The whole thing had gotten out of hand. What   163
had I said to bring on all this? I edged to the back of the crowd on the steps
and backed into the hallway. Where would I go? I hurried up to the old couple's
apartment. But I can't hide here, I thought, heading back for the stairs.

"No. You can't go that way," a voice said.   164

I whirled. It was a white girl standing in the door.   165

166   "What are you doing in here?" I shouted, my fear turning to feverish anger.

167   "I didn't mean to startle you," she said. "Brother, that was quite a speech you made. I heard just the end of it, but you certainly moved them to action . . ."

168   "Action," I said, "action—"

169   "Don't be modest, brother," she said, "I heard you."

170   "Look, Miss, we'd better get out of here," I said, finally controlling the throbbing in my throat. "There are a lot of policemen downstairs and more coming."

171   "Oh, yes. You'd better go over the roof," she said. "Otherwise, someone is sure to point you out."

172   "Over the roof?"

173   "It's easy. Just go up to the roof of the building and keep crossing until you reach the house at the end of the block. Then open the door and walk down as though you've been visiting. You'd better hurry. The longer you remain unknown to the police, the longer you'll be effective."

174   Effective? I thought. What did she mean? And what was this "brother" business?

175   "Thanks," I said, and hurried for the stairs.

176   "Good-bye," her voice rose fluidly behind me. I turned, glimpsing her white face in the dim light of the darkened doorway.

177   I took the flight in a bound and cautiously opened the door, and suddenly the sun flared bright on the roof and it was windy cold. Before me the low, snow-caked walls dividing the buildings stretched hurdle-like the long length of the block to the corner, and before me empty clotheslines trembled in the wind. I made my way through the wind-carved snow to the next roof and then to the next, going with swift caution. Planes were rising over an airfield far to the southeast, and I was running now and seeing all the church steeples rising and falling and stacks with smoke leaning sharp against the sky, and below in the street the sound of sirens and shouting. I hurried. Then, climbing over a wall I looked back, seeing a man hurrying after me, slipping, sliding, going over the low dividing walls of the roofs with puffing, bustling effort. I turned and ray, trying to put the rows of chimneys between us, wondering why he didn't yell "Halt!" or shout, or shoot. I ran, dodging behind an elevator housing, then dashing to the next roof, going down, the snow cold to my hands, knees striking, toes gripping, and up and running and looking back, seeing the short figure in black still running after. The corner seemed a mile away. I tried to count the number of roofs that bounced before me yet to be crossed. Getting to seven, I ran, hearing shouts, more sirens, and looking back and him still behind me, running in a short-legged scramble, still behind me as I tried to open the door of a building to go down and finding it stuck and running once more, trying to zig-zag in the snow and feeling the crunch of gravel underneath, and behind me still, as I swung over a partition and went brushing past a huge cote and arousing a flight of frantic white birds, suddenly as large as buzzards as they beat furiously against my eyes, dazzling the sun as they fluttered up and away

and around in a furious glide and me running again and looking back and for a split second thinking him gone and once more seeing him bobbing after. Why doesn't he shoot? Why? If only it were like at home where I knew someone in *all* the houses, knew them by sight and by name, by blood and by background, by shame and pride, and by religion.

It was a carpeted hall and I moved down with pounding heart as a dog set up a terrific din within the top apartment. Then I moved quickly, my body like glass inside as I skipped downward off the edges of the stairs. Looking down the stairwell I saw pale light filtering through the door glass, far below. But what had happened to the girl, had she put the man on my trail? What was she doing there? I bounded down, no one challenging me, and I stopped in the vestibule, breathing deeply and listening for his hand upon the door above and brushing my clothing into order. Then I stepped into the street with a nonchalance copied from characters I had seen in the movies. No sound from above, not even the malicious note of the barking dog. ✚

RESPONDING

1. Describe how the narrator's feelings about his identity change during the course of this incident in a journal entry.

2. Working as an individual or in a group, examine events in this narrative as they occur chronologically and explain how each subsequent event escalates hostilities. Identify the interchanges that particularly move the onlookers to anger.

3. The narrator in this selection says, "it was as though I myself was being dispossessed of some painful yet precious thing which I could not bear to lose" (paragraph 39). In an essay, explain why the narrator identifies with the couple being evicted and feels himself to be dispossessed.

4. Compare the narrator's speech to the crowd to Marc Antony's speech to the crowd in Shakespeare's *Julius Caesar*. What techniques do they both use to move the crowd to action?

Friends, Romans, countrymen, lend me your ears!
I come to bury Caesar, not to praise him.
The evil that men do lives after them,
The good is oft interred with their bones;
So are they all, all honorable men,
Come I to speak of Caesar's funeral.
He was my friend, faithful and just to me;

But Brutus says he was ambitious,
And Brutus is an honorable man.
He hath brought many captives home to Rome,
Whose ransoms did the general coffers fill;
Did this in Caesar seem ambitious?
When that the poor have cried, Caesar hath wept;
Ambition should be made of sterner stuff:
Yet Brutus says he was ambitious,
And Brutus is an honorable man.
You all did see that on the Lupercal
I thrice presented him a kingly crown,
Which he did thrice refuse. Was this ambition?
Yet Brutus says he was ambitious,
And sure he is an honorable man.
I speak not to disprove what Brutus spoke,
But here I am to speak what I do know.
You all did love him once, not without cause;
What cause withholds you then to mourn for him?
O judgment! thou [art] fled to brutish beasts,
And men have lost their reason. Bear with me,
My heart is in the coffin there with Caesar,
And I must pause till it come back to me.

—WILLIAM SHAKESPEARE

JAMES FARMER

James Farmer was born in Marshall, Texas, in 1920. He studied at Wiley College in Texas before pursuing graduate studies in religion at Howard University, where he earned a degree in divinity in 1941.

Even while attending school, Farmer was active in religious and civil rights groups, including the Christian Youth Movement, the National Council of Methodist Youth, and the Christian Youth Council of America. His involvement in civil rights led to his co-founding of the Congress of Racial Equality (CORE) in 1942, the first African American protest organization to adopt the methods of nonviolent resistance advocated by Gandhi. A year later, in a Chicago restaurant, Farmer organized the first successful sit-in demonstration. In 1961 CORE introduced the Freedom Ride to Alabama and Mississippi. After this period, Farmer worked as an adviser in the Johnson and Nixon administrations. He currently teaches and lectures on the civil rights movement. His publications include Freedom When? *(1965),* Lay Bare the Heart: The Autobiography of the Civil Rights Movement *(1986), and many magazine articles.*

The following chapter from Lay Bare the Heart *describes the way in which peaceful demonstrators sometimes met with violence. The passage serves as a reminder that some civil rights workers made the ultimate sacrifice for their beliefs.*

✤

"TOMORROW IS FOR OUR MARTYRS"

IT HAD BEEN A CALM DAY in the office, if any days could be considered calm in 1
the frenetic atmosphere in which we functioned. There had been no major crises; no mass arrests or calls for immediate bail money; no libel suits had been filed against any of our chapters; no scandals were threatening to erupt in the press; the sky had not fallen that day. Such tranquility was rare, particularly in the freedom summer of 1964 when CORE and SNCC had drawn hundreds of young volunteers into Mississippi, blanketing the state with voter registration workers.

I went home the evening of June 21, 1964, with a sense of well-being, 2
cherishing the night of easy sleep that lay ahead.

Gretchen, now an old dog, labored to get on the bed and snuggle in her 3
favorite spot on the pillows between Lula's head and mine. ("I always knew some bitch would come between us," Lula had once said.) At 3:00 A.M.,

the bedside phone rang. Cursing the intrusion, I growled hello into the receiver.

4   CORE's Mississippi field secretary, George Raymond, spoke into the phone: "Jim, three of our guys, Schwerner, Goodman, and Chaney, are missing. They left Meridian yesterday afternoon to go over to the town of Philadelphia in Neshoba County to look at the ruins of the church where they had been teaching voter registration courses. You know that church was burned down a week ago. They were supposed to return by sundown, but they're not back yet. Can you come down right away?"

5   "Don't jump to conclusions, George," I said. "It's only been a few hours. Maybe they stopped to visit some friends for dinner and decided to take a nap before driving home."

6   "Face facts, Jim," Raymond shouted into the phone. "Our guys and gals don't just stop over and visit friends or take a nap without calling in. Those three are responsible guys; they wouldn't be nine hours late without calling us. That is, if they could call."

7   "Okay, I'll be on the next plane to Meridian," I said. "I'll call you back in a few minutes to let you know the time of arrival."

8   I wanted company going to Neshoba County, so I called Dick Gregory at his home in Chicago, waking him up. Before he answered the phone, I glanced at Lula and saw that she was wide awake, watching with no sign of emotion.

9   "Hey, big daddy," said Gregory. "What's happening?"

10 "Three of my guys are missing in Mississippi," I said.

11 After a brief silence, Gregory said, "Okay, I know you're going down there. I'll meet you there. What airport do I fly to?"

12 Meridian, though close to Neshoba County, was an island of relative sanity in Mississippi. At the airport when we arrived were a few dozen city policemen with rifles. They were there to ensure my safety. I was given a police escort to the small, unpretentious black hotel. Immediately, I was closeted with George Raymond; Mickey Schwerner's wife, Rita; and several other CORE people in Meridian.

13 It was early evening on the day after the disappearance, and still there was no word. We were certain our colleagues were dead. Rita, no more than five feet tall and less than a hundred pounds, was dry-eyed and rational. When Mickey had accepted the assignment, both of them were well aware of the risks. Mickey was a social worker from New York who had joined the CORE staff several months earlier. Rita intended to study law.

14 The local and state officials were showing no interest in locating the men or their bodies. We had alerted the FBI, but there was not yet any evidence of their involvement in the search. A nearby U.S. military unit had just been called in to search some of the swamps for bodies, but the results thus far were negative. The CORE car in which the men had been riding when last seen—a white Ford station wagon—had not been found.

15 As we discussed things that might be done to aid the search, Rita suggested

that going through the ashes at the city dump where trash was burned might possibly yield some fragments of metal that could be identified as having belonged to one of the three men. Nothing more helpful than that came immediately to mind.

I told them that on the following morning, I intended to go into Philadel- 16 phia in Neshoba County to talk with Sheriff Lawrence Rainey and Deputy Sheriff Cecil Price about the disappearance of the men. Considering the racist reputation of the sheriff and his deputy, all agreed that one or both of them knew something about the disappearance of our friends.

George Raymond told us that Dick Gregory had called to say that he would 17 be joining me in Meridian early the next morning.

"Good," I said. "Let's time my trip to Philadelphia so that Dick can go 18 along with me."

Early the next morning, after Gregory's arrival, he and I sat in the small 19 hotel office on the ground floor with Raymond and one or two other CORE staffers. There was also a lieutenant of the Meridian City Police. Outside the building were several uniformed policemen and two squad cars, with others ready if needed.

The police official asked me what our plans were and I told him of my 20 intention to talk with Rainey and Price in their office. He let out a low whistle. "Farmer," he said, "you can't go over there. That's Neshoba County. That's real red-neck territory. We cain't protect you outside of Meridian."

"Lieutenant, we do appreciate the protection the city is giving us and we 21 want to thank you for it. However, we're not asking for protection, and certainly not from the Meridian police, when we go into Neshoba County. Mr. Gregory and I will go to Neshoba County this morning to try to see the sheriff and his deputy. That is our right and our duty, and we intend to exercise it."

The lieutenant shook his head and then made a phone call to a Mr. 22 Snodgrass, head of the Mississippi State Police. I knew Snodgrass and had always respected him. He was a conscientious law enforcement officer and, I felt, a humane one. At the various marches and demonstrations CORE had held in Mississippi, when Snodgrass personally was present, I had felt a little more at ease.

This time, I could hear Snodgrass shouting over the phone from ten feet 23 away: "He can't go over there. They'll kill him in that place. We can't protect him."

The lieutenant handed me the phone. "Mr. Snodgrass wants to talk to you." 24

Still shouting, Snodgrass said, "Farmer, don't go over there. That's one of 25 the worst red-neck areas in this state. They would just as soon kill you as look at you. We cannot protect you over there."

"Mr. Snodgrass, we have not asked for your protection. This is something 26 we have to do, protection or not."

"Okay, okay," Snodgrass replied. "What time are you going?" 27

"We're leaving here in about an hour and a half," I said and hung up. 28

29   We left Meridian in a caravan of five cars, with an escort of city police cars. Dick Gregory and I were in the lead car. Our escort left us at the Meridian city limits.

30   At the Neshoba County line, there was a roadblock with two sheriff's cars and one unmarked vehicle. A hefty middle-aged man, stereotypical of the "Negro-hating" southern sheriff of that day—chewing either a wad of tobacco or the end of a cigar, I forget which—swaggered up to our lead car. He was closely followed by an equally large but younger deputy sheriff.

31   The middle-aged man spoke to me: "Whut's yo' name?"

32   "James Farmer, and this gentleman is Mr. Dick Gregory, the entertainer and social critic."

33   "Where yo' think you goin'?"

34   "Mr. Gregory and I are going to Philadelphia."

35   "Whut yo' gon' do there?"

36   "We are going to talk to Sheriff Rainey and Deputy Price."

37   "Whut yo' wanna talk ta them 'bout?"

38   "We are going to talk with them about the disappearance of three of the staff members of the organization I head: Michael Schwerner, Andrew Goodman, and James Chaney."

39   "Well, Ah'm Sheriff Rainey and this heah's mah deputy, Deputy Price. Y'all wanna talk ta us heah?"

40   "No. We want to talk to you in your office."

41   "Awright, folla me."

42   "Just a moment," I said, "let me pass the word back down the line that we're all going to Philadelphia."

43   "Naw. Jus' you and this heah man can come," he said, pointing to Gregory. "The rest of them boys'll have to wait heah."

44   I glanced at the unmarked car and saw that leaning against it was Mr. Snodgrass, watching the scene closely.

45   Gregory and I followed Rainey and Price into town. Outside the courthouse were several hundred shirt-sleeved white men, standing with assorted weapons in hand. Surrounding the courthouse, though, were state police with rifles pointed at the crowd. State police also flanked the sidewalk leading to the steps of the building.

46   Gregory and I followed Rainey and Price up those steps and into the courthouse. We followed them to an elevator, and as the doors closed behind us, we thought of the same thing simultaneously. We never should have gotten into that box with those two men. They could have killed us and said that we had jumped them and that they had to shoot us in self-defense. And there would have been no witnesses. But it was too late now. We shrugged our shoulders.

47   To our relief, the door opened on the second floor without event, and we followed the two men down the hallway to an office at its end. Rainey introduced the three men seated in that office as the city attorney of Philadelphia, the county attorney of Neshoba, and Mr. Snodgrass of the state police. Snodgrass

merely nodded at the introduction, and looked sharply at the faces of the other men in the room.

Rainey cleared his throat and rasped, "Ah've got laryngitis or somethin'. This heah man will tall fer me." He was pointing at the county attorney. I nodded, but thought it strange that I had not noticed the impaired throat during our conversation at the roadblock. [48]

The county attorney squinted his eyes, and said to me, "Well, we're all heah. What was it you wanted to talk to the sheriff and his deputy about?" [49]

I told him that, as national director of CORE, I was charged with responsibility for the supervision of all members of the CORE staff. Three members of that staff had been missing for thirty-six hours. Mr. Gregory and I were there, I said, to try to find out what had happened to them and whether they were alive or dead. Specifically, I indicated I wanted to ask Deputy Price a question. [50]

Price then sat upright in this seat. Deputy Price had given conflicting stories to the press, I pointed out. First, he had said he never saw the men, then he said he had arrested them and released them in the evening. I wanted to know the true story. [51]

The attorney looked at Price and the deputy spoke: "Ah'll tell ya the God's truth. Ah did see them boys. I arrested them for speedin' and took them ta jail—" [52]

"What time did you arrest them?" I said. [53]

"It was about three or three-thirty. Yeah, closer to three-thirty when Ah arrested them. Ah kept them in jail till 'bout six-thirty or seven in the evenin'—" [54]

"Why would you keep men in jail for three and a half hours for speeding?" [55]

"Ah had to find out how much the justice of the peace was gonna fine them. The justice of the peace was not at home, so Ah had to wait till he got home. He fined them fifteen dollars. That colored boy, Chaney, who wuz drivin' the car, didn't have no fifteen dollars, but one of them Jew boys, Schwerner, had fifteen an' he paid the fine. Then, I took them boys out to the edge of town and put them in their car and they headed for Meridian. Ah sat in mah car and watched their taillights as long as Ah could see them. An' they were goin' toward Meridian. Then Ah turned around and came back into town, and that was the last Ah seen of them boys. Now, that's the God's truth." [56]

"At this moment," I said, "I have about fifteen young men waiting at the county line. They are friends and coworkers of Mickey Schwerner, Jim Chaney, and Andy Goodman. They want to join in the search for their missing colleagues." [57]

"What would they do? Where would they look?" the county attorney asked, rather anxiously, I felt. Could it have been he thought we might have gotten some clue as to where the bodies could be found? [58]

"They would look anywhere and everywhere that bodies could be hidden or disposed of—in the woods, the swamps, the rivers, whatever." [59]

"No!" he said. "We can't let them go out there by themselves without any supervision." [60]

61   "Oh, they'll be supervised," I replied. "I'll go with them."

62   "And I'll be with them, too," Gregory added.

63   "No, no! I can't let you do that. This is private property all around heah and the owners could shoot you for trespassing. We don't want anything to happen to you down here," he said.

64   "Something already *has* happened to three of our brothers. I'll take my chances," I said.

65   "No, these swamps around here are very dangerous," the attorney said. "They've got water moccasins, rattlesnakes, copperheads, and everything else in them. Like I said, we don't want anything to happen to you. We won't allow you to do it."

66   "Then," I said, "I have another question. We heard over the car radio coming here that the car in which the men were riding, that white Ford station wagon, has been found burned out on the other side of town, the opposite side from Meridian. That automobile belonged to the organization I serve as national director, and I want to look at what is left of it."

67   "No," said the county lawyer emphatically. "We can't let you do that either. You might destroy fingerprints or some other evidence that will be useful to Sheriff Rainey or Deputy Price in solving this crime—if there has been a crime. You know, those boys may have decided to go up north or someplace and have a short vacation. They'll probably be coming back shortly."

68   Dick Gregory, who had shown masterful restraint thus far, rose to his feet. He began speaking to the assembled men, pointing his finger at them, looking at each one with sharp eyes, and speaking with an even sharper tongue. He made it clear that he thought someone there knew much more about the disappearance of the three men than was being told. He said that we were not going to let this matter rest but were going to get to the bottom of it, and the guilty persons were going to pay for their crimes.

69   I felt this was neither the time nor the place to have a showdown with Rainey and Price. Yet, I was struggling with my own feelings. I was not Christ. I was not Gandhi. I was not King. I wanted to kill those men—not with bullets, but with my fingers around their throats, squeezing tighter as I watched life ebb from their eyes.

70   Back in Meridian, I called a meeting of the CORE staff and summer volunteers. Our embattled southern staff evidenced little of the black/white tension so prevalent in the North. At the meeting, I announced that I wanted two volunteers for an extraordinarily important and dangerous mission. The qualifications for the volunteers were that they had to be black, male, and young. I wanted them to slip into Philadelphia in Neshoba County in the dead of night, not going by the main highway but by side routes. They would very quietly disappear into the black community of Philadelphia, see a minister, and ask if he could find a family for them to stay with.

71   They would have to do all they could to keep the officials from knowing

that they were there or of their mission. I believed that the black community would take them in, for that is an old tradition among blacks—the extended family. They would have to try not to be conspicuous, but to disappear into the woodwork, so to speak, until they were trusted by the blacks in Philadelphia.

In all probability, George Raymond and I believed, some person or persons 72
in the black community knew what had happened to the three men. Someone in that community always does, but no one would tell the FBI or any city or state officials, for fear of retribution.

When accepted and trusted, our men were to begin asking discreet ques- 73
tions. When any information was secured, they were to communicate that to me. If they did so by phone, it was to be from a phone booth and not the same one each time. If by letter, the message should be mailed from another town, and without a return address on the envelope. If they had any reason to believe that Rainey or Price knew of their presence or mission, they were to contact me immediately by phone.

Practically all hands went up. Everyone wanted to go. When George 74
Raymond and I selected two, most others felt let down and angry.

The two volunteers left the meeting, packed small suitcases, and surrepti- 75
tiously moved into Philadelphia. It was about two weeks before I began getting reports. Those reports from eyewitnesses of various parts of the tragedy indicated a clear scenario, the stage for which had been set by an earlier report from another source.

A black maid in Meridian had told us of overhearing a phone call from a 76
black Meridian man who was speaking in an open telephone booth. The man allegedly fingered the three young CORE men. The maid, of course, did not know to whom the call was made, but we suspected it was either to Sheriff Rainey or Deputy Price. The caller said that the three guys, two Jews and one colored, were in a white '62 Ford station wagon. He also gave the license number of the car. He said the three had just left Meridian, heading for Philadelphia.

The scenario as told to the CORE volunteers by various eyewitnesses was 77
as follows: when Schwerner, Goodman, and Chaney entered Philadelphia, they were trailed by Deputy Price, who kept his distance. When they stopped at the charred ruins of the small black church on the other side of town, Price parked at a distance and watched them. As they got back into the car to drive on, Deputy Price, according to the witnesses, closed in on them.

James Chaney, who was driving the car, saw Price in his rearview mirror 78
and, knowing Price's reputation as a "nigger killer," sped up.

Price then shot a tire on the Ford wagon and it came to a halt. The men 79
were arrested and taken to jail, as Price had said. Also, as the deputy had told us, he took them out of jail about sundown, but there the similarity between the deputy's story and fact seemed to end.

He took them to the other side of town, not the Meridian side, and turned 80
them over to a waiting mob in a vacant field. The three men were pulled into

the field and pushed beneath a large tree. There, members of the mob held Schwerner and Goodman while the other mobsters beat Chaney without mercy. He was knocked down, stomped, kicked, and clubbed. Schwerner broke away from his captives and tried to help Chaney. He was then clubbed once on the head and knocked unconscious. Seconds later, he revived and was again held by members of the mob while the beating of Chaney continued.

81   By this time Chaney appeared dead, and the beating stopped. Members of the mob huddled, and then Deputy Price, who was also in the group, went back to his car and drove away. The mob remained there, holding Schwerner and Goodman and looking at the prone form of Chaney on the ground.

82   A little while later, Price returned and said something to the members of the mob. They then dragged Schwerner and Goodman and Chaney's body to a car and threw them into it. The car drove off.

83   The latter scene was allegedly witnessed by two blacks crossing different corners of the field at about the same time, on the way to church for a prayer meeting.

84   We turned this information over to the FBI.

85   It was weeks later—August fifth—when I received a call from Deke DeLoach, then assistant to the director at FBI headquarters in Washington, D.C.

86   DeLoach said, "Mr. Farmer, since Schwerner, Goodman, and Chaney were members of your staff, I wanted you to be the first to know. We have found the bodies. An informant told us to look under a fake dam. We drove in a bulldozer and with the first scoop of earth uncovered the three bodies. Though they were badly decomposed, there was every evidence that Chaney had received the most brutal beating imaginable. It seemed that every bone in his body was broken. He was beaten to death. Each of the other two was shot once in the heart."

87   Months later, on October 3, 1964, the FBI arrested a group of men and charged them with conspiracy to violate the civil rights of the dead trio—the only charge available to the federal government, since murder is a state charge. Mississippi never charged them with murder.

88   Among those arrested and convicted of conspiracy, in addition to Deputy Price, was a minister of the gospel. When he prayed to his God, did he feel remorse? Or had he silenced the still, small voice within his soul?

89   Evil societies always kill their consciences.

90   We, who are the living, possess the past. Tomorrow is for our martyrs. ✠

RESPONDING

1.   Imagine that you were James Farmer. What fears might you have had about going to Mississippi? Write a letter to your family explaining why you must go.

2. Members of the African American community possessed information about the killings of Chaney, Schwerner, and Goodman but didn't come forward immediately. Working individually or in a group, discuss the reasons why having such information would be dangerous. What difficulties would African Americans have in getting the information to someone they could trust? Farmer implies that the three civil rights workers were "fingered" by someone who was African American. What might explain such a betrayal? Why might some members of the African American community cooperate with a white sheriff?

3. Describe the circumstances when Farmer says, "I was not Christ. I was not Gandhi. I was not King" (paragraph 69). Why was it especially hard for him to practice nonviolence at that moment? Using your own knowledge and any relevant readings, write an essay speculating about the arguments that figures such as Christ, Ghandi, or King would present for "turning the other cheek."

4. African American and Caucasian members of CORE and other groups that went into the South to register voters willingly risked their lives. Does such idealism exist in America today? In an essay, support your position using examples from the readings, current events, and personal feelings and experiences.

MARTIN LUTHER KING, JR.

Martin Luther King, Jr., the son, grandson, and greatgrandson of Baptist ministers, was born in Atlanta, Georgia, in 1929. After graduating from Morehouse College in 1951, he earned a doctorate from Boston University in 1955. In that year he also led the Montgomery bus boycott; two years later he founded the Southern Christian Leadership Conference (SCLC). During this time and throughout the 1960s, King worked vigorously to organize and promote boycotts and voter registration drives in the South. Because of the leadership and self-sacrifice he displayed on behalf of the civil rights movement, he received the 1964 Nobel Prize for Peace, the youngest person ever to receive this honor. King was assassinated in 1968.

The "Letter from Birmingham Jail," which uses the techniques of deductive argument to outline his position, is one of Dr. King's most important works.

⁜

LETTER FROM BIRMINGHAM JAIL*

April 16, 1963

MY DEAR FELLOW CLERGYMEN:

1 WHILE CONFINED HERE IN THE BIRMINGHAM CITY JAIL, I came across your recent statement calling my present activities "unwise and untimely." Seldom do I pause to answer criticism of my work and ideas. If I sought to answer all the criticisms that cross my desk, my secretaries would have little time for anything other than such correspondence in the course of the day, and I would have no time for constructive work. But since I feel that you are men of genuine good will and that your criticisms are sincerely set forth, I want to try to answer your statement in what I hope will be patient and reasonable terms.

2 I think I should indicate why I am here in Birmingham, since you have been influenced by the view which argues against "outsiders coming in." I have the honor of serving as president of the Southern Christian Leadership Conference, an organization operating in every southern state, with headquarters in Atlanta,

---

*Author's Note: This response to a published statement by eight fellow clergymen from Alabama (Bishop C. C. J. Carpenter, Bishop Joseph A. Durick, Rabbi Hilton L. Grafman, Bishop Paul Hardin, Bishop Holan B. Harmon, the Reverend George M. Murray, the Reverend Edward V. Ramage and the Reverend Earl Stallings) was composed under somewhat constricting circumstances. Begun on the margins of the newspaper in which the statement appeared while I was in jail, the letter was continued on scraps of writing paper supplied by a friendly Negro trusty, and concluded on a pad my attorneys were eventually permitted to leave me. Although the text remains in substance unaltered, I have indulged in the author's prerogative of polishing it for publication.

Georgia. We have some eighty-five affiliated organizations across the South, and one of them is the Alabama Christian Movement for Human Rights. Frequently we share staff, educational and financial resources with our affiliates. Several months ago the affiliate here in Birmingham asked us to be on call to engage in a nonviolent direct-action program if such were deemed necessary. We readily consented, and when the hour came we lived up to our promise. So I, along with several members of my staff, am here because I was invited here. I am here because I have organizational ties here.

But more basically, I am in Birmingham because injustice is here. Just as the prophets of the eighth century B.C. left their villages and carried their "thus said the Lord" far beyond the boundaries of their home towns, and just as the Apostle Paul left his village of Tarsus and carried the gospel of Jesus Christ to the far corners of the Greco-Roman world, so am I compelled to carry the gospel of freedom beyond my own home town. Like Paul, I must constantly respond to the Macedonian call for aid.

Moreover, I am cognizant of the interrelatedness of all communities and states. I cannot sit idly by in Atlanta and not be concerned about what happens in Birmingham. Injustice anywhere is a threat to justice everywhere. We are caught in an inescapable network of mutuality, tied in a single garment of destiny. Whatever affects one directly, affects all indirectly. Never again can we afford to live with the narrow, provincial "outside agitator" idea. Anyone who lives inside the United States can never be considered an outsider anywhere within its bounds.

You deplore the demonstrations taking place in Birmingham. But your statement, I am sorry to say, fails to express a similar concern for the conditions that brought about the demonstrations. I am sure that none of you would want to rest content with the superficial kind of social analysis that deals merely with effects and does not grapple with underlying causes. It is unfortunate that demonstrations are taking place in Birmingham, but it is even more unfortunate that the city's white power structure left the Negro community with no alternative.

In any nonviolent campaign there are four basic steps: collection of the facts to determine whether injustices exist; negotiation; self-purification; and direct action. We have gone through all these steps in Birmingham. There can be no gainsaying the fact that racial injustice engulfs this community. Birmingham is probably the most thoroughly segregated city in the United States. Its ugly record of brutality is widely known. Negroes have experienced grossly unjust treatment in the courts. There have been more unsolved bombings of Negro homes and churches in Birmingham than in any other city in the nation. These are the hard, brutal facts of the case. On the basis of these conditions, Negro leaders sought to negotiate with the city fathers. But the latter consistently refused to engage in good-faith negotiation.

Then, last September, came the opportunity to talk with leaders of Birmingham's economic community. In the course of the negotiations, certain promises were made by the merchants—for example, to remove the stores' humiliating racial signs. On the basis of these promises, the Reverend Fred Shuttlesworth and the leaders of the Alabama Christian Movement for Human Rights agreed to a moratorium on all demonstrations. As the weeks and months went by, we realized that we were the victims of a broken promise. A few signs, briefly removed, returned; the others remained.

8   As in so many past experiences, our hopes had been blasted, and the shadow of deep disappointment settled upon us. We had no alternative except to prepare for direct action, whereby we would present our very bodies as a means of laying our case before the conscience of the local and the national community. Mindful of the difficulties involved, we decided to undertake a process of self-purification. We began a series of workshops on nonviolence, and we repeatedly asked ourselves: "Are you able to accept blows without retaliating?" "Are you able to endure the ordeal of jail?" We decided to schedule our direct-action program for the Easter season, realizing that except for Christmas, this is the main shopping period of the year. Knowing that a strong economic-withdrawal program would be the by-product of direct action, we felt that this would be the best time to bring pressure to bear on the merchants for the needed change.

9   Then it occurred to us that Birmingham's mayoral election was coming up in March, and we speedily decided to postpone action until after election day. When we discovered that the Commissioner of Public Safety, Eugene "Bull" Connor, had piled up enough votes to be in the run-off, we decided again to postpone action until the day after the run-off so that the demonstrations could not be used to cloud the issues. Like many others, we waited to see Mr. Connor defeated, and to this end we endured postponement after postponement. Having aided in the community need, we felt that our direct-action program could be delayed no longer.

10   You may well ask: "Why direct action? Why sit-ins, marches and so forth? Isn't negotiation a better path?" You are quite right in calling for negotiation. Indeed, this is the very purpose of direct action. Nonviolent direct action seeks to create such a crisis and foster such a tension that a community which has constantly refused to negotiate is forced to confront the issue. It seeks so to dramatize the issue that it can no longer be ignored. My citing the creation of tension as part of the work of the nonviolent-resister may sound rather shocking. But I must confess that I am not afraid of the word "tension." I have earnestly opposed violent tension, but there is a type of constructive, nonviolent tension which is necessary for growth. Just as Socrates felt that it was necessary to create a tension in the mind so that individuals could rise from the bondage of myths and half-truths to the unfettered realm of creative analysis and objective appraisal, so must we see the need for nonviolent gadflies to create the kind of tension in society that will help men rise from the dark depths of prejudice and racism to the majestic heights of understanding and brotherhood.

11   The purpose of our direct-action program is to create a situation so crisis-packed that it will inevitably open the door to negotiation. I therefore concur

with you in your call for negotiation. Too long has our beloved Southland been bogged down in a tragic effort to live in monologue rather than dialogue.

One of the basic points in your statement is that the action that I and my associates have taken in Birmingham is untimely. Some have asked: "Why don't you give the new city administration time to act?" The only answer that I can give to this query is that the new Birmingham administration must be prodded about as much as the outgoing one, before it will act. We are sadly mistaken if we feel that the election of Albert Boutwell as mayor will bring the millennium to Birmingham. While Mr. Boutwell is a much more gentle person than Mr. Connor, they are both segregationists, dedicated to maintenance of the status quo. I have hope that Mr. Boutwell will be reasonable enough to see the futility of massive resistance to desegregation. But he will not see this without pressure from devotees of civil rights. My friends, I must say to you that we have not made a single gain in civil rights without determined legal and nonviolent pressure. Lamentably, it is an historical fact that privileged groups seldom give up their privileges voluntarily. Individuals may see the moral light and voluntarily give up their unjust posture; but, as Reinhold Niebuhr has reminded us, groups tend to be more immoral than individuals.

We know through painful experience that freedom is never voluntarily given by the oppressor; it must be demanded by the oppressed. Frankly, I have yet to engage in a direct-action campaign that was "well timed" in the view of those who have not suffered unduly from the disease of segregation. For years now I have heard the word "Wait!" It rings in the ear of every Negro with piercing familiarity. This "Wait" has almost always meant "Never." We must come to see, with one of our distinguished jurists, that "justice too long delayed is justice denied."

We have waited for more than 340 years for our constitutional and God-given rights. The nations of Asia and Africa are moving with jetlike speed toward gaining political independence, but we still creep at horse-and-buggy pace toward gaining a cup of coffee at a lunch counter. Perhaps it is easy for those who have never felt the stinging darts of segregation to say, "Wait." But when you have seen vicious mobs lynch your mothers and fathers at will and drown your sisters and brothers at whim; when you have seen hate-filled policemen curse, kick and even kill your black brothers and sisters; when you see the vast majority of your twenty million Negro brothers smothering in an airtight cage of poverty in the midst of an affluent society; when you suddenly find your tongue twisted and your speech stammering as you seek to explain to your six-year-old daughter why she can't go to the public amusement park that has just been advertised on television, and see tears welling up in her eyes when she is told that Funtown is closed to colored children, and see ominous clouds of inferiority beginning to form in her little mental sky, and see her beginning to distort her personality by developing an unconscious bitterness toward white people; when you have to concoct an answer for a five-year-old son who is asking: "Daddy, why do white people treat colored people so mean?"; when you take a cross-country drive and find it necessary to sleep night after night in the uncomfortable corners of your automobile because no motel will accept you; when you are humiliated day in and day out by nagging signs reading "white" and "colored"; when your first name becomes "nigger," your middle name becomes "boy" (however old you are) and your last name becomes "John," and your wife and mother are never given the respected title "Mrs."; when you are harried by day and haunted by night by the fact that you are a Negro, living constantly at tiptoe stance, never quite knowing what to expect next, and are plagued with inner fears and outer resentments; when you are forever fighting a degenerating sense of "nobodiness"—then you will understand why we find it difficult to wait. There comes a time when the cup of endurance runs over, and men are no longer willing to be plunged into the abyss of despair. I hope, sirs, you can understand our legitimate and unavoidable impatience.

15   You express a great deal of anxiety over our willingness to break laws. This is certainly a legitimate concern. Since we so diligently urge people to obey the Supreme Court's decision of 1954 outlawing segregation in the public schools, at first glance it may seem rather paradoxical for us consciously to break laws. One may well ask: "How can you advocate breaking some laws and obeying others?" The answer lies in the fact that there are two types of laws: just and unjust. I would be the first to advocate obeying just laws. One has not only a legal but a moral responsibility to obey just laws. Conversely, one has a moral responsibility to disobey unjust laws. I would agree with St. Augustine that "an unjust law is no law at all."

16   Now, what is the difference between the two? How does one determine whether a law is just or unjust? A just law is a man-made code that squares with the moral law or the law of God. An unjust law is a code that is out of harmony with the moral law. To put it in the terms of St. Thomas Aquinas: An unjust law is a human law that is not rooted in eternal law and natural law. Any law that uplifts human personality is just. Any law that degrades human personality is unjust. All segregation statutes are unjust because segregation distorts the soul and damages the personality. It gives the segregator a false sense of superiority and the segregated a false sense of inferiority. Segregation, to use the terminology of the Jewish philosopher Martin Buber, substitutes an "I—it" relationship for an "I–thou" relationship and ends up relegating persons to the status of things. Hence segregation is not only politically, economically and sociologically unsound, it is morally wrong and sinful. Paul Tillich has said that sin is separation. Is not segregation an existential expression of man's tragic separation, his awful estrangement, his terrible sinfulness? Thus it is that I can urge men to obey the 1954 decision of the Supreme Court, for it is morally right; and I can urge them to disobey segregation ordinances, for they are morally wrong.

17   Let us consider a more concrete example of just and unjust laws. An unjust law is a code that a numerical or power majority group compels a minority group to obey but does not make binding on itself. This is *difference* made legal.

By the same token, a just law is a code that a majority compels a minority to follow and that it is willing to follow itself. This is *sameness* made legal.

Let me give another explanation. A law is unjust if it is inflicted on a minority that, as a result of being denied the right to vote, had no part in enacting or devising the law. Who can say that the legislature of Alabama which set up that state's segregation laws was democratically elected? Throughout Alabama all sorts of devious methods are used to prevent Negroes from becoming registered voters, and there are some counties in which, even though Negroes constitute a majority of the population, not a single Negro is registered. Can any law enacted under such circumstances be considered democratically structured? 18

Sometimes a law is just on its face and unjust in its application. For instance, I have been arrested on a charge of parading without a permit. Now, there is nothing wrong in having an ordinance which requires a permit for a parade. But such an ordinance becomes unjust when it is used to maintain segregation and to deny citizens the First-Amendment privilege of peaceful assembly and protest. 19

I hope you are able to see the distinction I am trying to point out. In no sense do I advocate evading or defying the law, as would the rabid segregationist. That would lead to anarchy. One who breaks an unjust law must do so openly, lovingly, and with a willingness to accept the penalty. I submit that an individual who breaks a law that conscience tells him is unjust, and who willingly accepts the penalty of imprisonment in order to arouse the conscience of the community over its injustice, is in reality expressing the highest respect for law. 20

Of course, there is nothing new about this kind of civil disobedience. It was evidenced sublimely in the refusal of Shadrach, Meshach and Abednego to obey the laws of Nebuchadnezzar, on the ground that a higher moral law was at stake. It was practiced superbly by the early Christians, who were willing to face hungry lions and the excruciating pain of chopping blocks rather than submit to certain unjust laws of the Roman Empire. To a degree, academic freedom is a reality today because Socrates practiced civil disobedience. In our own nation, the Boston Tea Party represented a massive act of civil disobedience. 21

We should never forget that everything Adolf Hitler did in Germany was "legal" and everything the Hungarian freedom fighters did in Hungary was "illegal." It was "illegal" to aid and comfort a Jew in Hitler's Germany. Even so, I am sure that, had I lived in Germany at the time, I would have aided and comforted my Jewish brothers. If today I lived in a Communist country where certain principles dear to the Christian faith are suppressed, I would openly advocate disobeying that country's antireligious laws. 22

I must make two honest confessions to you, my Christian and Jewish brothers. First, I must confess that over the past few years I have been gravely disappointed with the white moderate. I have almost reached the regrettable conclusion that the Negro's great stumbling block in his stride toward freedom is not the White Citizen's Counciler or the Ku Klux Klanner, but the white 23 moderate, who is more devoted to "order" than to justice; who prefers a negative peace which is the absence of tension to a positive peace which is the presence of justice; who constantly says: "I agree with you in the goal you seek, but I cannot agree with your methods of direct action"; who paternalistically believes he can set the timetable for another man's freedom; who lives by a mythical concept of time and who constantly advises the Negro to wait for a "more convenient season." Shallow understanding from people of good will is more frustrating than absolute misunderstanding from people of ill will. Lukewarm acceptance is much more bewildering than outright rejection.

24   I had hoped that the white moderate would understand that law and order exist for the purpose of establishing justice and that when they fail in this purpose they become the dangerously structured dams that block the flow of social progress. I had hoped that the white moderate would understand that the present tension in the South is a necessary phase of the transition from an obnoxious negative peace, in which the Negro passively accepted his unjust plight, to a substantive and positive peace, in which all men will respect the dignity and worth of human personality. Actually, we who engage in nonviolent direct action are not the creators of tension. We merely bring to the surface the hidden tension that is already alive. We bring it out in the open, where it can be seen and dealt with. Like a boil that can never be cured so long as it is covered up but must be opened with all its ugliness to the natural medicines of air and light, injustice must be exposed, with all the tension its exposure creates, to the light of human conscience and the air of national opinion before it can be cured.

25   In your statement you assert that our actions, even though peaceful, must be condemned because they precipitate violence. But is this a logical assertion? Isn't this like condemning a robbed man because his possession of money precipitated the evil act of robbery? Isn't this like condemning Socrates because his unswerving commitment to truth and his philosophical inquiries precipitated the act by the misguided populace in which they made him drink hemlock? Isn't this like condemning Jesus because his unique God-consciousness and never-ceasing devotion to God's will precipitated the evil act of crucifixion? We must come to see that, as the federal courts have consistently affirmed, it is wrong to urge an individual to cease his efforts to gain his basic constitutional rights because the quest may precipitate violence. Society must protect the robbed and punish the robber.

26   I had also hoped that the white moderate would reject the myth concerning time in relation to the struggle for freedom. I have just received a letter from a white brother in Texas. He writes: "All Christians know that the colored people will receive equal rights eventually, but it is possible that you are in too great a religious hurry. It has taken Christianity almost two thousand years to accomplish what it has. The teachings of Christ take time to come to earth." Such an attitude stems from a tragic misconception of time, from the strangely irrational notion that there is something in the very flow of time that will

inevitably cure all ills. Actually, time itself is neutral; it can be used either destructively or constructively. More and more I feel that the people of ill will have used time much more effectively than have the people of good will. We will have to repent in this generation not merely for the hateful words and actions of the bad people but for the appalling silence of the good people. Human progress never rolls in on wheels of inevitability; it comes through the tireless efforts of men willing to be co-workers with God, and without this hard work, time itself becomes an ally of the forces of social stagnation. We must use time creatively, in the knowledge that the time is always ripe to do right. Now is the time to make real the promise of democracy and transform our pending national elegy into a creative psalm of brotherhood. Now is the time to lift our national policy from the quicksand of racial injustice to the solid rock of human dignity.

You speak of our activity in Birmingham as extreme. At first I was rather disappointed that fellow clergymen would see my nonviolent efforts as those of an extremist. I began thinking about the fact that I stand in the middle of two opposing forces in the Negro community. One is a force of complacency, made up in part of Negroes who, as a result of long years of oppression, are so drained of self-respect and a sense of "somebodiness" that they have adjusted to segregation; and in part of a few middle-class Negroes who, because of a degree of academic and economic security and because in some ways they profit by segregation, have become insensitive to the problems of the masses. The other force is one of bitterness and hatred, and it comes perilously close to advocating violence. It is expressed in the various black nationalist groups that are springing up across the nation, the largest and best-known being Elijah Muhammad's Muslim movement. Nourished by the Negro's frustration over the continued existence of racial discrimination, this movement is made up of people who have lost faith in America, who have absolutely repudiated Christianity, and who have concluded that the white man is an incorrigible "devil." [27]

I have tried to stand between these two forces, saying that we need emulate neither the "do-nothingism" of the complacent nor the hatred and despair of the black nationalist. For there is the more excellent way of love and nonviolent protest. I am grateful to God that, through the influence of the Negro church, the way of nonviolence became an integral part of our struggle. [28]

If this philosophy had not emerged, by now many streets of the South would, I am convinced, be flowing with blood. And I am further convinced that if our white brothers dismiss as "rabble-rousers" and "outside agitators" those of us who employ nonviolent direct action, and if they refuse to support our nonviolent efforts, millions of Negroes will, out of frustration and despair, seek solace and security in black-nationalist ideologies—a development that would inevitably lead to a frightening racial nightmare. [29]

Oppressed people cannot remain oppressed forever. The yearning for freedom eventually manifests itself, and that is what has happened to the American Negro. Something within has reminded him of his birthright of freedom, and [30] something without has reminded him that it can be gained. Consciously or unconsciously, he has been caught up by the *Zeitgeist*, and with his black brothers of Africa and his brown and yellow brothers of Asia, South America and the Caribbean, the United States Negro is moving with a sense of great urgency toward the promised land of racial justice. If one recognizes this vital urge that has engulfed the Negro community, one should readily understand why public demonstrations are taking place. The Negro has many pent-up resentments and latent frustrations, and he must release them. So let him march; let him make prayer pilgrimages to the city hall; let him go on freedom rides—and try to understand why he must do so. If his repressed emotions are not released in nonviolent ways, they will seek expression through violence; this is not a threat but a fact of history. So I have not said to my people: "Get rid of your discontent." Rather, I have tried to say that this normal and healthy discontent can be channeled into the creative outlet of nonviolent direct action. And now this approach is being termed extremist.

31 But though I was initially disappointed at being categorized as an extremist, as I continued to think about the matter I gradually gained a measure of satisfaction from the label. Was not Jesus an extremist for love: "Love your enemies, bless then that curse you, do good to them that hate you, and pray for them which despitefully use you, and persecute you." Was not Amos an extremist for justice: "Let justice roll down like waters and righteousness like an ever-flowing stream." Was not Paul an extremist for the Christian gospel: "I bear in my body the marks of the Lord Jesus." Was not Martin Luther an extremist: "Here I stand; I cannot do otherwise, so help me God." And John Bunyan: "I will stay in jail to the end of my days before I make a butchery of my conscience." And Abraham Lincoln: "This nation cannot survive half slave and half free." And Thomas Jefferson: "We hold these truths to be self-evident, that all men are created equal . . ." So the question is not whether we will be extremists, but what kind of extremists we will be. Will we be extremists for hate or for love? Will we be extremists for the preservation of injustice or for the extension of justice? In that dramatic scene on Calvary's hill three men were crucified. We must never forget that all three were crucified for the same crime—the crime of extremism. Two were extremists for immorality, and thus fell below their environment. Two were extremists for immorality, and thus fell below their environment. The other, Jesus Christ, was an extremist for love, truth and goodness, and thereby rose above his environment. Perhaps the South, the nation and the world are in dire need of creative extremists.

32 I had hoped that the white moderate would see this need. Perhaps I was too optimistic; perhaps I expected too much. I suppose I should have realized that few members of the oppressor race can understand the deep groans and passionate yearnings of the oppressed race, and still fewer have the vision to see that injustice must be rooted out by strong, persistent and determined action. I am thankful, however, that some of our white brothers in the South have grasped the meaning of this social revolution and committed themselves to it. They are still all too few in quantity, but they are big in quality. Some—such

as Ralph McGill, Lillian Smith, Harry Golden, James McBride Dabbs, Ann Braden and Sarah Patton Boyle—have written about our struggle in eloquent and prophetic terms. Others have marched with us down nameless streets of the South. They have languished in filthy, roach-infested jails, suffering the abuse and brutality of policemen who view them as "dirty nigger-lovers." Unlike so many of their moderate brothers and sisters, they have recognized the urgency of the moment and sensed the need for powerful "action" antidotes to combat the disease of segregation.

33 Let me take note of my other major disappointment. I have been so greatly disappointed with the white church and its leadership. Of course, there are some notable exceptions. I am not unmindful of the fact that each of you has taken some significant stands on this issue. I commend you, Reverend Stallings, for your Christian stand on this past Sunday, in welcoming Negroes to your worship service on a nonsegregated basis. I commend the Catholic leaders of this state for integrating Spring Hill College several years ago.

34 But despite these notable exceptions, I must honestly reiterate that I have been disappointed with the church. I do not say this as one of those negative critics who can always find something wrong with the church. I say this as a minister of the gospel, who loves the church; who was nurtured in its bosom; who has been sustained by its spiritual blessings and who will remain true to it as long as the cord of life shall lengthen.

35 When I was suddenly catapulted into the leadership of the bus protest in Montgomery, Alabama, a few years ago, I felt we would be supported by the white church. I felt that the white ministers, priests and rabbis of the South would be among our strongest allies. Instead, some have been outright opponents, refusing to understand the freedom movement and misrepresenting its leaders; all too many others have been more cautious than courageous and have remained silent behind the anesthetizing security of stained-glass windows.

36 In spite of my shattered dreams, I came to Birmingham with the hope that the white religious leadership of this community would see the justice of our cause and, with deep moral concern, would serve as the channel through which our just grievances could reach the power structure. I had hoped that each of you would understand. But again I have been disappointed.

37 I have heard numerous southern religious leaders admonish their worshippers to comply with a desegregation decision because it is the law, but I have longed to hear white ministers declare: "Follow this decree because integration is morally right and because the Negro is your brother." In the midst of blatant injustices inflicted upon the Negro, I have watched white churchmen stand on the sideline and mouth pious irrelevancies and sanctimonious trivialities. In the midst of a mighty struggle to rid our nation of racial and economic injustice, I have heard many ministers say: "Those are social issues, with which the gospel has no real concern." And I have watched many churches commit themselves to a completely otherworldly religion which makes a strange, un-Biblical distinction between body and soul, between the sacred and the secular.

38 I have traveled the length and breadth of Alabama, Mississippi and all the

other southern states. On sweltering summer days and crisp autumn mornings I have looked at the South's beautiful churches with their lofty spires pointing heavenward. I have beheld the impressive outlines of her massive religious-education buildings. Over and over I have found myself asking: "What kind of people worship here? Who is their God? Where were their voices when the lips of Governor Barnett dripped with words of interposition and nullification? Where were they when Governor Wallace gave a clarion call for defiance and hatred? Where were their voices of support when bruised and weary Negro men and women decided to rise from the dark dungeons of complacency to the bright hills of creative protest?"

39   Yes, these questions are still in my mind. In deep disappointment I have wept over the laxity of the church. But be assured that my tears have been tears of love. There can be no deep disappointment where there is not deep love. Yes, I love the church. How could I do otherwise? I am in the rather unique position of being the son, the grandson and the great-grandson of preachers. Yes, I see the church as the body of Christ. But, oh! How we have blemished and scarred the body through social neglect and through fear of being nonconformists.

40   There was a time when the church was very powerful—in the time when the early Christians rejoiced at being deemed worthy to suffer for what they believed. In those days the church was not merely a thermometer that recorded the ideas and principles of popular opinion; it was a thermostat that transformed the mores of society. Whenever the early Christians entered a town, the people in power became disturbed and immediately sought to convict the Christians for being "disturbers of the peace" and "outside agitators." But the Christians pressed on, in the conviction that they were "a colony of heaven," called to obey God rather than man. Small in number, they were big in commitment. They were too God-intoxicated to be "astronomically intimidated." By their effort and example they brought an end to such ancient evils as infanticide and gladiatorial contests.

41   Things are different now. So often the contemporary church is a weak, ineffectual voice with an uncertain sound. So often it is an archdefender of the status quo. Far from being disturbed by the presence of the church, the power structure of the average community is consoled by the church's silent—and often even vocal—sanction of things as they are.

42   But the judgment of God is upon the church as never before. If today's church does not recapture the sacrificial spirit of the early church, it will lose its authenticity, forfeit the loyalty of millions, and be dismissed as an irrelevant social club with no meaning for the twentieth century. Every day I meet young people whose disappointment with the church has turned into outright disgust.

43   Perhaps I have once again been too optimistic. Is organized religion too inextricably bound to the status quo to save our nation and the world? Perhaps I must turn my faith to the inner spiritual church, the church within the church, as the true *ekklesia* and the hope of the world. But again I am thankful to God

that some noble souls from the ranks of organized religion have broken loose
from the paralyzing chains of conformity and joined us as active partners in the
struggle for freedom. They have left their secure congregations and walked the
streets of Albany, Georgia, with us. They have gone down the highways of the
South on tortuous rides for freedom. Yes, they have gone to jail with us. Some
have been dismissed from their churches, have lost the support of their bishops
and fellow ministers. But they have acted in the faith that right defeated is
stronger than evil triumphant. Their witness has been the spiritual salt that has
preserved the true meaning of the gospel in these troubled times. They have
carved a tunnel of hope through the dark mountain of disappointment.

I hope the church as a whole will meet the challenge of this decisive hour.   44
But even if the church does not come to the aid of justice, I have no despair
about the future. I have no fear about the outcome of our struggle in Birmingham, even if our motives are at present misunderstood. We will reach the goal
of freedom in Birmingham and all over the nation, because the goal of America
is freedom. Abused and scorned though we may be, our destiny is tied up with
America's destiny. Before the pilgrims landed at Plymouth, we were here. Before
the pen of Jefferson etched the majestic words of the Declaration of Independence across the pages of history, we were here. For more than two centuries
our forebears labored in this country without wages; they made cotton king;
they built the homes of their masters while suffering gross injustice and shameful
humiliation—and yet out of a bottomless vitality they continued to thrive and
develop. If the inexpressible cruelties of slavery could not stop us, the opposition
we now face will surely fail. We will win our freedom because the sacred heritage
of our nation and the eternal will of God are embodied in our echoing demands.

Before closing I feel impelled to mention one other point in your statement   45
that has troubled me profoundly. You warmly commended the Birmingham
police force for keeping "order" and "preventing violence." I doubt that you
would have so warmly commended the police force if you had seen its dogs
sinking their teeth into unarmed, nonviolent Negroes. I doubt that you would
so quickly commend the policemen if you were to observe their ugly and
inhuman treatment of Negroes here in the city jail; if you were to watch them
push and curse old Negro women and young Negro girls; if you were to see
them slap and kick old Negro men and young boys; if you were to observe
them, as they did on two occasions, refuse to give us food because we wanted
to sing our grace together. I cannot join you in your praise of the Birmingham
police department.

It is true that the police have exercised a degree of discipline in handling   46
the demonstrators. In this sense they have conducted themselves rather "nonviolently" in public. But for what purpose? To preserve the evil system of
segregation. Over the past few years I have consistently preached that nonviolence demands that the means we use must be as pure as the ends we seek. I
have tried to make clear that it is wrong to use immoral means to attain moral
ends. But now I must affirm that it is just as wrong, or perhaps even more so,

to use moral means to preserve immoral ends. Perhaps Mr. Connor and his policemen have been rather nonviolent in public, as was Chief Pritchett in Albany, Georgia, but they have used the moral means of nonviolence to maintain the immoral end of racial injustice. As T. S. Eliot has said: "The last temptation is the greatest treason: To do the right deed for the wrong reason."

47   I wish you had commended the Negro sit-inners and demonstrators of Birmingham for their sublime courage, their willingness to suffer and their amazing discipline in the midst of great provocation. One day the South will recognize its real heroes. They will be the James Merediths, with the noble sense of purpose that enables them to face jeering and hostile mobs, and with the agonizing loneliness that characterizes the life of the pioneer. They will be old, oppressed, battered Negro women, symbolized in a seventy-two-year-old woman in Montgomery, Alabama, who rose up with a sense of dignity and with her people decided not to ride segregated buses, and who responded with ungrammatical profundity to one who inquired about her weariness: "My feets is tired, but my soul is at rest." They will be the young high school and college students, the young ministers of the gospel and a host of their elders, courageously and nonviolently sitting in at lunch counters and willingly going to jail for conscience' sake. One day the South will know that when these disinherited children of God sat down at lunch counters, they were in reality standing up for what is best in the American dream and for the most sacred values in our Judaeo-Christian heritage, thereby bringing our nation back to those great wells of democracy which were dug deep by the founding fathers in their formulation of the Constitution and the Declaration of Independence.

48   Never before have I written so long a letter. I'm afraid it is much too long to take your precious time. I can assure you that it would have been much shorter if I had been writing from a comfortable desk, but what else can one do when he is alone in a narrow jail cell, other than write long letters, think long thoughts and pray long prayers?

49   If I have said anything in this letter that overstates the truth and indicates an unreasonable impatience, I beg you to forgive me. If I have said anything that understates the truth and indicates my having a patience that allows me to settle for anything less than brotherhood, I beg God to forgive me.

50   I hope this letter finds you strong in the faith. I also hope that circumstances will soon make it possible for me to meet each of you, not as an integrationist or a civil-rights leader but as a fellow clergyman and a Christian brother. Let us all hope that the dark clouds of racial prejudice will soon pass away and the deep fog of misunderstanding will be lifted from our fear-drenched communities, and in some not too distant tomorrow the radiant stars of love and brotherhood will shine over our great nation with all their scintillating beauty.

51   Yours for the cause of Peace and Brotherhood,

MARTIN LUTHER KING, JR. ✠

RESPONDING

1. In your opinion, has the hope Dr. King expressed in the penultimate paragraph of the letter been realized? Write a journal entry supporting your position with examples from your reading or experience or from television news reports or special programs.

2. Working individually or in a group, discuss the reasons that Dr. King was in jail if he was fighting injustice.

3. Argue for or against the following proposition: "an individual who breaks a law that conscience tells him is unjust, and who willingly accepts the penalty of imprisonment in order to arouse the conscience of the community over its injustice, is in reality expressing the highest respect for law" (paragraph 20).

4. Write an essay agreeing or disagreeing with the following statement: "Injustice anywhere is a threat to justice everywhere. We are caught in an inescapable network of mutuality, tied in a single garment of destiny. Whatever affects one directly, affects all indirectly" (paragraph 4).

Malcolm X

Malcolm X was born Malcolm Little in Omaha, Nebraska, in 1925. When the author was only six years old, his father was murdered—apparently by members of the Ku Klux Klan. He left school in the eighth grade and became involved in crime; he was imprisoned for burglary and larceny in 1946. While in prison, Malcolm Little studied the teachings of Mohammed and became a Black Muslim minister; he also changed his name to Malcolm X in order to eliminate his slave name. After his release from prison in 1952, he worked first as an evangelist for the Nation of Islam, and later as the leader of the Muslim Mosque and the Organization of Afro-American Unity. He also became a major spokesman for the Black separatist movement. In 1965, he was assassinated.

Alex P. Haley, with whom Malcolm X collaborated on his Autobiography *(1965) was born in Ithaca, New York, in 1921. He served as a journalist in the Coast Guard for twenty years before beginning work as a free-lance writer in 1959. His most famous work,* Roots *(1976), won a Pulitzer Prize. Alex Haley died in 1992.*

This excerpt from Malcolm X's Autobiography *examines the injustices endured by African Americans and takes issue with those who rely on nonviolence as a means of obtaining equality.*

✜

From THE AUTOBIOGRAPHY OF MALCOLM X

1 I must be honest. Negroes—Afro-Americans—showed no inclination to rush to the United Nations and demand justice for themselves here in America. I really had known in advance that they wouldn't. The American white man has so thoroughly brainwashed the black man to see himself as only a domestic "civil rights" problem that it will probably take longer than I live before the Negro sees that the struggle of the American black man is international.

2 And I had known too, that Negroes would not rush to follow me into the orthodox Islam which had given me the insight and perspective to see that the black men and white men truly could be brothers. America's Negroes—especially older Negroes—are too indelibly soaked in Christianity's double standard of oppression.

3 So, in the "public invited" meetings which I began holding each Sunday afternoon or evening in Harlem's well-known Audubon Ballroom, as I addressed predominantly non-Muslim Negro audiences, I did not immediately attempt to press the Islamic religion, but instead to embrace all who sat before me:

"—not Muslim, nor Christian, Catholic, nor Protestant . . . Baptist nor   4
Methodist, Democrat nor Republican, Mason nor Elk! I mean the black people
of America—and the black people all over this earth! Because it is as this
collective mass of black people that we have been deprived not only of our civil
rights, but even of our human rights, the right to human dignity. . . ."

On the streets, after my speeches, in the faces and the voices of the people   5
I met—even those who would pump my hands and want my autograph—I would
feel the wait-and-see attitude. I would feel—and I understood—their uncertainty about where I stood. Since the Civil War's "freedom," the black man has
gone down so many fruitless paths. His leaders, very largely, had failed him.
The religion of Christianity had failed him. The black man was scarred, he was
cautious, he was apprehensive.

I understood it better now than I had before. In the Holy World, away   6
from America's race problem, was the first time I ever had been able to think
clearly about the basic divisions of white people in America, and how their
attitudes and their motives related to, and affected Negroes. In my thirty-nine
years on this earth, the Holy City of Mecca had been the first time I had ever
stood before the Creator of All and felt like a complete human being.

In that peace of the Holy World—in fact, the very night I have mentioned   7
when I lay awake surrounded by snoring brother pilgrims—my mind took me
back to personal memories I would have thought were gone forever . . . as far
back, even, as when I was just a little boy, eight or nine years old. Out behind
our house, out in the country from Lansing, Michigan, there was an old, grassy
"Hector's Hill," we called it—which may still be there. I remembered there in
the Holy World how I used to lie on top of Hector's Hill, and look up at the
sky, at the clouds moving over me, and daydream, all kinds of things. And then,
in a funny contrast of recollections, I remembered how years later, when I was
in prison, I used to lie on my cell bunk—this would be especially when I was
in solitary: what we convicts called "The Hole"—and I would picture myself
talking to large crowds. I don't have any idea why such previsions came to me.
But they did. To tell that to anyone then would have sounded crazy. Even I
didn't have, myself, the slightest inkling. . . .

In Mecca, too, I had played back for myself the twelve years I had spent   8
with Elijah Muhammad[1] as if it were a motion picture. I guess it would be
impossible for anyone ever to realize fully how complete was my belief in Elijah
Muhammad. I believed in him not only as a leader in the ordinary *human* sense,
but also I believed in him as a *divine* leader. I believed he had no human
weaknesses or fault, and that, therefore, he could make no mistakes and that he
could do no wrong. There on a Holy World hilltop, I realized how very
dangerous it is for people to hold any human being in such esteem, especially
to consider anyone some sort of "divinely guided" and "protected" person.

[1.] Elijah Mohammed (1896–1975), a leader of the Black Muslim faith in the U.S. Malcolm X began
corresponding with him soon after his conversion.

9   My thinking had been opened up wide in Mecca. In the long letters I wrote to friends, I tried to convey to them my new insights into the American black man's struggle and his problems, as well as the depths of my search for truth and justice.

10   "I've had enough of someone else's propaganda," I had written to these friends. "I'm for truth, no matter who tells it. I'm for justice, no matter who it is for or against. I'm a human being first and foremost, and as such I'm for whoever and whatever benefits humanity *as a whole.*"

11   Largely, the American white man's press refused to convey that I was now attempting to teach Negroes a new direction. With the 1964 "long, hot summer" steadily producing new incidents, I was constantly accused of "stirring up Negroes." Every time I had another radio or television microphone at my mouth, when I was asked about "stirring up Negroes" or "inciting violence," I'd get hot.

12   "It takes no one to stir up the sociological dynamite that stems from the unemployment, bad housing, and inferior education already in the ghettoes. This explosively criminal condition has existed for so long, it needs no fuse; it fuses itself; it spontaneously combusts from within itself. . . ."

13   They called me "the angriest Negro in America." I wouldn't deny that charge. I spoke exactly as I felt. "I *believe* in anger. The Bible says there is a *time* for anger." They called me a "teacher, a fomentor of violence." I would say point blank, "That is a lie. I'm not for wanton violence, I'm for justice. I feel that if white people were attacked by Negroes—if the forces of law prove unable, or inadequate, or reluctant to protect those whites from those Negroes—then those white people should protect and defend themselves from those Negroes, using arms if necessary. And I feel that when the law fails to protect Negroes from whites' attack, then those Negroes should use arms, if necessary, to defend themselves."

14   "Malcolm X Advocates Armed Negroes!"

15   What was wrong with that? I'll tell you what was wrong. I was a black man talking about physical defense against the white man. The white man can lynch and burn and bomb and beat Negroes—that's all right: "Have patience" . . . "The customs are entrenched" . . . "Things are getting better."

16   Well, I believe it's a crime for anyone who is being brutalized to continue to accept that brutality without doing something to defend himself. If that's how "Christian" philosophy is interpreted, if that's what Gandhian philosophy teaches, well, then, I will call them criminal philosophies.

17   I tried in every speech I made to clarify my new position regarding white people—"I don't speak against the sincere, well-meaning, good white people. I have learned that there *are* some. I have learned that not all white people are racists. I am speaking against and my fight is against the white *racists.* I firmly believe that Negroes have the right to fight against these racists, by any means that are necessary."

But the white reporters kept wanting me linked with that word "violence." I doubt if I had one interview without having to deal with that accusation. 18

"I *am* for violence if non-violence means we continue postponing a solution to the American black man's problem—just to *avoid* violence. I don't go for non-violence if it also means a delayed solution. To me a delayed solution is a non-solution. Or I'll say it another way. If it must take violence to get the black man his human rights in this country, I'm *for* violence exactly as you know the Irish, the Poles, or Jews would be if they were flagrantly discriminated against. I am just as they would be in that case, and they would be for violence—no matter what the consequences, no matter who was hurt by the violence." 19

White society *hates* to hear anybody, especially a black man, talk about the crime the white man has perpetrated on the black man. I have always understood that's why I have been so frequently called "a revolutionist." It sounds as if *I* have done some crime! Well, it may be the American black man does need to become involved in a *real* revolution. The word for "revolution" in German is *Umwälzung.* What it means is a complete overturn—a complete change. The overthrow of King Farouk in Egypt and the succession of President Nasser is an example of a true revolution. It means the destroying of an old system, and its replacement with a new system. Another example is the Algerian revolution, led by Ben Bella; they threw out the French who had been there over 100 years. So how does anybody sound talking about the Negro in America waging some "revolution"? Yes, he is condemning a system—but he's not trying to overturn the system, or to destroy it. The Negro's so-called "revolt" is merely an asking to be *accepted* into the existing system! A *true* Negro revolt might entail, for instance, fighting for separate black states within this country—which several groups and individuals have advocated, long before Elijah Muhammad came along. 20

When the white man came into this country, he certainly wasn't demonstrating any "non-violence." In fact, the very man whose name symbolizes non-violence here today has stated: 21

"Our nation was born in genocide when it embraced the doctrine that the original American, the Indian, was an inferior race. Even before there were large numbers of Negroes on our shores, the scar of racial hatred had already disfigured colonial society. From the sixteenth century forward, blood flowed in battles over racial supremacy. We are perhaps the only nation which tried as a matter of national policy to wipe out its indigenous population. Moreover, we elevated that tragic experience into a noble crusade. Indeed, even today we have not permitted ourselves to reject or to feel remorse for this shameful episode. Our literature, our films, our drama, our folklore all exalt it. Our children are still taught to respect the violence which reduced a red-skinned people of an earlier culture into a few fragmented groups herded into impoverished reservations." 22

"Peaceful coexistence!" That's another one the white man has always been 23 quick to cry. Fine! But what have been the deeds of the white man? During his entire advance through history, he has been waving the banner of Christianity . . . and carrying in his other hand the sword and the flintlock.

24   You can go right back to the very beginning of Christianity. Catholicism, the genesis of Christianity as we know it to be presently constituted, with its hierarchy, was conceived in Africa—by those whom the Christian church calls "The Desert Fathers." The Christian church became infected with racism when it entered white Europe. The Christian church returned to Africa under the banner of the Cross—conquering, killing, exploiting, pillaging, raping, bullying, beating—and teaching white supremacy. This is how the white man thrust himself into the position of leadership of the world—through the use of naked physical power. And he was totally inadequate spiritually. Mankind's history has proved from one era to another that the true criterion of leadership is spiritual. Men are attracted by spirit. By power, men are *forced*. Love is engendered by spirit. By power, anxieties are created.

25   I am in agreement one hundred per cent with those racists who say that no government laws ever can *force* brotherhood. The only true world solution today is governments guided by true religion—of the spirit. Here in race-torn America, I am convinced that the Islam religion is desperately needed, particularly by the American black man. The black man needs to reflect that he has been America's most fervent Christian—and where has it gotten him? In fact, in the white man's hands, in the white man's interpretation . . . where has Christianity brought this *world*?

26   It has brought the non-white two-thirds of the human population to rebellion. Two-thirds of the human population today is telling the one-third minority white man, "Get out!" And the white man is leaving. And as he leaves, we see the non-white peoples returning in a rush to their original religions, which had been labeled "pagan" by the conquering white man. Only one religion—Islam— had the power to stand and fight the white man's Christianity for a *thousand years!* Only Islam could keep white Christianity at bay.

27   The Africans are returning to Islam and other indigenous religions. The Asians are returning to being Hindus, Buddhists and Muslims.

28   As the Christian Crusade once went East, now the Islamic Crusade is going West. With the East—Asia—closed to Christianity, with Africa rapidly being converted to Islam, with Europe rapidly becoming un-Christian, generally today it is accepted that the "Christian" civilization of America—which is propping up the white race around the world—is Christianity's remaining strongest bastion.

29   Well, if *this* is so—if the so-called "Christianity" now being practiced in America displays the best that world Christianity has left to offer—no one in his right mind should need any much greater proof that very close at hand is the *end* of Christianity.

30   Are you aware that some Protestant theologians, in their writings, are using the phrase "post-Christian era"—and they mean *now*?

And what is the greatest single reason for this Christian church's failure? 31
It is its failure to combat racism. It is the old "You sow, you reap" story. The
Christian church sowed racism—blasphemously; now it reaps racism.

Sunday mornings in this year of grace 1965, imagine the "Christian con- 32
science" of congregations guarded by deacons barring the door to black would-
be worshipers, telling them, "You can't enter *this* House of God!"

Tell me, if you can, a sadder irony than that St. Augustine, Florida—a city 33
named for the black African saint who saved Catholicism from heresy—was
recently the scene of bloody race riots.

I believe that God now is giving the world's so-called "Christian" white 34
society its last opportunity to repent and atone for the crimes of exploiting and
enslaving the world's non-white peoples. It is exactly as when God gave Pharaoh
a chance to repent. But Pharaoh persisted in his refusal to give justice to those
whom he oppressed. And, we know, God finally destroyed Pharaoh.

Is white America really sorry for her crimes against the black people? Does 35
white America have the capacity to repent—and to atone? Does the capacity to
repent, to atone, exist in a majority, in one-half, in even one-third of American
white society?

Many black men, the victims—in fact most black men—would like to be 36
able to forgive, to forget, the crimes.

But most American white people seem not to have it in them to make any 37
serious atonement—to do justice to the black man.

Indeed, how *can* white society atone for enslaving, for raping, for unman- 38
ning, for otherwise brutalizing *millions* of human beings, for centuries? What
atonement would the God of Justice demand for the robbery of the black
people's labor, their lives, their true identities, their culture, their history—and
even their human dignity?

A desegregated cup of coffee, a theater, public toilets—the whole range of 39
hypocritical "integration"—these are not atonement.

After a while in America, I returned abroad—and this time, I spent eighteen 40
weeks in the Middle East and Africa.

The world leaders with whom I had private audiences this time included 41
President Gamal Abdel Nasser, of Egypt; President Julius K. Nyerere, of
Tanzania; President Nnamoi Azikiwe, of Nigeria; Osagyefo Dr. Kwame Nkrumah, of Ghana; President Sekou Touré, of Guinea; President Jomo Kenyatta,
of Kenya; and Prime Minister Dr. Milton Obote, of Uganda.

I also met with religious leaders—African, Arab, Asian, Muslim, and non- 42
Muslim. And in all of these countries, I talked with Afro-Americans and whites
of many professions and backgrounds.

An American white ambassador in one African country was Africa's most 43
respected American ambassador: I'm glad to say that this was told to me by one
ranking African leader. We talked for an entire afternoon. Based on what I had
heard of him, I had to believe him when he told me that as long as he was on
the African continent, he never thought in terms of race, that he dealt with

human beings, never noticing their color. He said he was more aware of language differences than of color differences. He said that only when he returned to America would he become aware of color differences.

44　　I told him, "What you are telling me is that it isn't the American white *man* who is a racist, but it's the American political, economic, and social *atmosphere* that automatically nourishes a racist psychology in the white man." He agreed.

45　　We both agreed that American society makes it next to impossible for humans to meet in America and not be conscious of their color differences. And we both agreed that if racism could be removed, America could offer a society where rich and poor could truly live like human beings.

46　　That discussion with the ambassador gave me a new insight—one which I like: that the white man is *not* inherently evil, but America's racist society influences him to act evilly. The society has produced and nourishes a psychology which brings out the lowest, most base part of human beings.

47　　I had a totally different kind of talk with another white man I met in Africa—who, to me, personified exactly what the ambassador and I had discussed. Throughout my trip, I was of course aware that I was under constant surveillance. The agent was a particularly obvious and obnoxious one; I am not sure for what agency, as he never identified it, or I would say it. Anyway, this one finally got under my skin when I found I couldn't seem to eat a meal in the hotel without seeing him somewhere around watching me. You would have thought I was John Dillinger or somebody.

48　　I just got up from my breakfast one morning and walked over to where he was and I told him I knew he was following me, and if he wanted to know anything, why didn't he ask me. He started to give me one of those too-lofty-to-descend-to-you attitudes. I told him then right to his face he was a fool, that he didn't know me, or what I stood for, so that made him one of those people who let somebody else do their thinking; and that no matter what job a man had, at least he ought to be able to think for himself. That stung him; he let me have it.

49　　I was, to hear him tell it, anti-American, un-American, seditious, subversive, and probably Communist. I told him that what he said only proved how little he understood about me. I told him that the only thing the F.B.I., the C.I.A., or anybody else could ever find me guilty of, was being open-minded. I said I was seeking for the truth, and I was trying to weigh—objectively—everything in its own merit. I said what I was against was strait-jacketed thinking, and strait-jacketed societies. I said I respected every man's right to believe whatever his intelligence tells him is intellectually sound, and I expect everyone else to respect my right to believe likewise. ✤

RESPONDING

1. Clarify Malcolm X's position on nonviolence and on the appropriate use of violence. Write a journal entry responding to his statement that "when the law fails to protect Negroes from whites' attack, then those Negroes should use arms, if necessary, to defend themselves" (paragraph 13).

2. Individually or in a group, list Malcolm X's criticisms of the Christian church. Discuss the validity of his charges.

3. In an essay, discuss Malcolm X's solution to the problems of the "black man" worldwide. Analyze the strengths and weaknesses of that solution.

4. Argue for or against the position that Malcolm X states in the following passage: "it's the American political, economic, and social *atmosphere* that automatically nourishes a racist psychology in the white man . . . American society makes it next to impossible for humans to meet in America and not be conscious of their color differences" (paragraphs 44–45).

GWENDOLYN BROOKS

The poet Gwendolyn Brooks was born in Topeka, Kansas, in 1917. After graduating from Wilson Junior College, she worked as a book reviewer for the New York Times *and the* New York Herald Tribune. *During the late 1930s she joined the NAACP; she has remained active in the civil rights movement since that time. Her publications include* A Street in Bronzeville *(1945),* Annie Allen *(1949),* The Bean Eaters *(1960),* Selected Poems *(1963),* In the Mecca *(1968),* Family Pictures *(1970),* To Disembark *(1981), and* The Near-Johannesburg Boy and Other Poems *(1986). Brooks's work has been awarded the prize of the American Academy of Arts and Letters (1946), Guggenheim Fellowships (1946 and 1947), and the Pulitzer Prize for Poetry (1950). In 1968 Brooks was named the poet laureate of Illinois. In that post, as writer in residence at several universities, and as distinguished professor of the arts at the City College of New York, she has worked to make young people more aware of their talents as writers.*

"The Chicago Defender Sends a Man to Little Rock" explores the effects of prejudice and injustice on the children who are its victims.

THE CHICAGO DEFENDER SENDS A MAN TO LITTLE ROCK

FALL, 1957

In Little Rock the people bear
Babes, and comb and part their hair
And watch the want ads, put repair
To roof and latch. While wheat toast burns
A woman waters multiferns.

Time upholds or overturns
The many, tight, and small concerns.

In Little Rock the people sing
Sunday hymns like anything,
Through Sunday pomp and polishing.

And after testament and tunes,
Some soften Sunday afternoons
With lemon tea and Lorna Doones.

I forecast
And I believe
Come Christmas Little Rock will cleave
To Christmas tree and trifle, weave,
From laugh and tinsel, texture fast.

In Little Rock is baseball; Barcarolle.
That hotness in July . . . the uniformed figures raw and
    implacable
And not intellectual,
Batting the hotness or clawing the suffering dust.
The Open Air Concert, on the special twilight green . . .
When Beethoven is brutal or whispers to lady-like air.
Blanket-sitters are solemn, as Johann troubles to lean
To tell them what to mean. . . .

There is love, too, in Little Rock. Soft women softly
Opening themselves in kindness,
Or, pitying one's blindness,
Awaiting one's pleasure
In azure
Glory with anguished rose at the root. . . .
To wash away old semi-discomfitures.
They re-teach purple and unsullen blue.
The wispy soils go. And uncertain
Half-havings have they clarified to sures.

In Little Rock they know
Not answering the telephone is a way of rejecting life,
That it is our business to be bothered, is our business
To cherish bores or boredom, be polite
To lies and love and many-faceted fuzziness.

I scratch my head, massage the hate-I-had.
I blink across my prim and pencilled pad.
The saga I was sent for is not down.
Because there is a puzzle in this town.
The biggest News I do not dare
Telegraph to the Editor's chair:
"They are like people everywhere."

The angry Editor would reply
In hundred harryings of Why.
And true, they are hurling spittle, rock,
Garbage and fruit in Little Rock.
And I saw coiling storm a-writhe
On bright madonnas. And a scythe
Of men harassing brownish girls.
(The bows and barrettes in the curls
And braids declined away from joy.)

I saw a bleeding brownish boy. . . .

The lariat lynch-wish I deplored.

The loveliest lynchee was our Lord. ✠

RESPONDING

1. In your journal, describe an incident of injustice about which you or someone you know became aware. What response did you or your friend have? Did you try to rectify what you felt was wrong? Were you successful or unsuccessful?

2. Working individually or in a group, describe the people to whom the poet refers. Do they include the entire population of Little Rock?

3. Write a profile of the speaker. Who is he? Whom does he work for? Is he Caucasian or African American? How does he feel about what is happening? Use evidence from the poem to support your claims.

4. Explain why the poem begins with the date "Fall, 1957." Is it necessary to know about the events in Little Rock in order to understand the poem? What else does the poet expect her audience to know? Review the introduction to the chapter and do outside research as needed. Then, write an essay discussing the ways in which the additional knowledge changed your response to the poem.

Toni Cade Bambara

The poet, novelist, and short-story writer Toni Cade Bambara was born in New York City in 1939. After receiving her bachelor's degree from Queens College in 1959, she studied in Florence and Paris before returning to New York to earn her master's degree from New York University in 1964. Her works include the short-story collections Gorilla, My Love *(1972) and* The Sea Birds Are Still Alive *(1977) and the novel* The Salt Eaters *(1980). She has also contributed to many anthologies and short-story collections.*

In "The Lesson," from Gorilla, My Love, *the characters are taken on a journey to a toy store, which prompts them to examine the value systems at work in the dominant culture and in their own lives.*

❖

THE LESSON

BACK IN THE DAYS when everyone was old and stupid or young and foolish and me and Sugar were the only ones just right, this lady moved on our block with nappy hair and proper speech and no makeup. And quite naturally we laughed at her, laughed the way we did at the junk man who went about his business like he was some big-time president and his sorry-ass horse his secretary. And we kinda hated her too, hated the way we did the winos who cluttered up our parks and pissed on our handball walls and stank up our hallways and stairs so you couldn't halfway play hide-and-seek without a goddamn gas mask. Miss Moore was her name. The only woman on the block with no first name. And she was black as hell, cept for her feet, which were fish-white and spooky. And she was always planning these boring-ass things for us to do, us being my cousin, mostly, who lived on the block cause we all moved North the same time and to the same apartment then spread out gradual to breathe. And our parents would yank our heads into some kinda shape and crisp up our clothes so we'd be presentable for travel with Miss Moore, who always looked like she was going to church, though she never did. Which is just one of things the grown-ups talked about when they talked behind her back like a dog. But when she came calling with some sachet she'd sewed up or some gingerbread she'd made or some book, why then they'd all be too embarrassed to turn her down and we'd get handed over all spruced up. She'd been to college and said it was only right that she should take responsibility for the young ones' education, and she not even related by marriage or blood. So they'd go for it. Specially Aunt Gretchen. She was the main gofer in the family. You got some old dumb shit foolishness you want somebody to go for, you send for Aunt Gretchen. She been screwed into the go-along for so long, it's a blood-deep natural thing with her. Which

1

is how she got saddled with me and Sugar and Junior in the first place while our mothers were in a la-de-da apartment up the block having a good ole time.

2   So this one day Miss Moore rounds us all up at the mailbox and it's puredee hot and she's knockin herself out about arithmetic. And school suppose to let up in summer I heard, but she don't never let up. And the starch in my pinafore scratching the shit outta me and I'm really hating this nappy-head bitch and her goddamn college degree. I'd much rather go to the pool or to the show where it's cool. So me and Sugar leaning on the mailbox being surly, which is a Miss Moore word. And Flyboy checking out what everybody brought for lunch. And Fat Butt already wasting his peanut-butter-and-jelly sandwich like the pig he is. And Junebug punchin on Q.T.'s arm for potato chips. And Rosie Giraffe shifting from one hip to the other waiting for somebody to step on her foot or ask her if she from Georgia so she can kick ass, preferably Mercedes'. And Miss Moore asking us do we know what money is, like we a bunch of retards. I mean real money, she say, like it's only poker chips or monopoly papers we lay on the grocer. So right away I'm tired of this and say so. And would much rather snatch Sugar and go to the Sunset and terrorize the West Indian kids and take their hair ribbons and their money too. And Miss Moore files that remark away for next week's lesson on brotherhood, I can tell. And finally I saw we oughta get to the subway cause it's cooler and besides we might meet some cute boys. Sugar done swiped her mama's lipstick, so we ready.

3   So we heading down the street and she's boring us silly about what things cost and what our parents make and how much goes for rent and how money ain't divided up right in this country. And then she gets to the part about we all poor and live in the slums, which I don't feature. And I'm ready to speak on that, but she steps out in the street and hails two cabs just like that. Then she hustles half the crew in with her and hands me a five-dollar bill and tells me to calculate 10 percent tip for the driver. And we're off. Me and Sugar and Junebug and Flyboy hangin out the window and hollering to everybody, putting lipstick on each other cause Flyboy a faggot anyway, and making farts with our sweaty armpits. But I'm mostly trying to figure how to spend this money. But they all fascinated with the meter ticking and Junebug starts laying bets as to how much it'll read when Flyboy can't hold his breath no more. Then Sugar lays bets as to how much it'll be when we get there. So I'm stuck. Don't nobody want to go for my plan, which is to jump out at the next light and run off to the first bar-b-que we can find. Then the driver tells us to get the hell out cause we there already. And the meter reads eighty-five cents. And I'm stalling to figure out the tip and Sugar say give him a dime. And I decide he don't need it bad as I do, so later for him. But then he tries to take off with Junebug foot still in the door so we talk about his mama something ferocious. Then we check out that we on Fifth Avenue and everybody dressed up in stockings. One lady in a fur coat, hot as it is. White folks crazy.

4   "This is the place," Miss Moore say, presenting it to us in the voice she uses at the museum. "Let's look in the windows before we go in."

"Can we steal?" Sugar asks very serious like she's getting the ground rules squared away before she plays. "I beg your pardon," say Miss Moore, and we fall out. So she leads us around the windows of the toy store and me and Sugar screamin, "This is mine, that's mine, I gotta have that, that was made for me, I was born for that," till Big Butt drowns us out. 5

"Hey, I'm goin to buy that there." 6

"That there? You don't even know what it is, stupid." 7

"I do so," he say punchin on Rosie Giraffe. "It's a microscope." 8

"Watcha gonna do with a microscope, fool?" 9

"Look at things." 10

"Like what, Ronald?" ask Miss Moore. And Big Butt ain't got the first notion. So here go Miss Moore gabbing about the thousands of bacteria in a drop of water and the somethinorother in a speck of blood and the million and one living things in the air around us is invisible to the naked eye. And what she say that for? Junebug go to town on that "naked" and we rolling. Then Miss Moore ask what it cost. So we all jam into the window smudgin it up and the price tag say $300. So then she ask how long'd take for Big Butt and Junebug to save up their allowances. "Too long," I say. "Yeh," adds Sugar, "outgrown it by that time." And Miss Moore say no, you never outgrow learning instruments. "Why, even medical students and interns and," blah, blah, blah. And we ready to choke Big Butt for bringing it up in the first damn place. 11

"This here costs four hundred eighty dollars," say Rosie Giraffe. So we pile up all over her to see what she pointin out. My eyes tell me it's a chunk of glass cracked with something heavy, and different-color inks dripped into the splits, then the whole thing put into a oven or something. But for $480 it don't make sense. 12

"That's a paperweight made of semi-precious stones fused together under tremendous pressure," she explains slowly, with her hands doing the mining and all the factory work. 13

"So what's a paperweight?" asks Rosie Giraffe. 14

"To weigh paper with, dumbbell," say Flyboy, the wise man from the East. 15

"Not exactly," say Miss Moore, which is what she say when you warm or way off too. "It's to weigh paper down so it won't scatter and make your desk untidy." So right away me and Sugar curtsy to each other and then to Mercedes who is more the tidy type. 16

"We don't keep paper on top of the desk in my class," say Junebug, figuring Miss Moore crazy or lyin one. 17

"At home, then," she say. "Don't you have a calendar and a pencil case and a blotter and a letter-opener on your desk at home where you do your home-work?" And she know damn well what our homes look like cause she nosys around in them every chance she gets. 18

"I don't even have a desk," say Junebug. "Do we?" 19

"No. And I don't get no homework neither," say Big Butt. 20

"And I don't even have a home," say Flyboy like he do at school to keep 21 the white folks off his back and sorry for him. Send this poor kid to camp posters, is his specialty.

22 "I do," says Mercedes. "I have a box of stationery on my desk and a picture of my cat. My godmother bought the stationery and the desk. There's a big rose on each sheet and the envelopes smell like roses."

23 "Who wants to know about your smelly-ass stationery," say Rosie Giraffe fore I can get my two cents in.

24 "It's important to have a work area all your own so that . . ."

25 "Will you look at this sailboat, please," say Flyboy, cuttin her off and pointin to the thing like it was his. So once again we tumble all over each other to gaze at this magnificent thing in the toy store which is just big enough to maybe sail two kittens across the pond if you strap them to the posts tight. We all start reciting the price tag like we in assembly. "Handcrafted sailboat of fiberglass at one thousand one hundred ninety-five dollars."

26 "Unbelievable," I hear myself say and am really stunned. I read it again for myself just in case the group recitation put me in a trance. Same thing. For some reason this pisses me off. We look at Miss Moore and she lookin at us, waiting for I dunno what.

27 "Who'd pay all that when you can buy a sailboat set for a quarter at Pop's, a tube of glue for a dime, and a ball of string for eight cents? "It must have a motor and a whole lot else besides," I say. "My sailboat cost me about fifty cents."

28 "But will it take water?" say Mercedes with her smart ass.

29 "Took mine to Alley Pond Park once," say Flyboy. "String broke, Lost it. Pity."

30 "Sailed mine in Central Park and it keeled over and sank. Had to ask my father for another dollar."

31 "And you got the strap," laugh Big Butt. "The jerk didn't even have a string on it. My old man wailed on his behind."

32 Little Q.T. was staring hard at the sailboat and you could see he wanted it bad. But he too little and somebody'd just take it from him. So what the hell. "This boat for kids, Miss Moore?"

33 "Parents silly to buy something like that just to get all broke up," say Rosie Giraffe.

34 "That much money it should last forever," I figure.

35 "My father'd buy it for me if I wanted it."

36 "Your father, my ass," say Rosie Giraffe getting a chance to finally push Mercedes.

37 "Must be rich people shop here," say Q.T.

38 "You are a very bright boy," say Flyboy. "What was your first clue?" And he rap him on the head with the back of his knuckles, since Q.T. the only one he could get away with. Though Q.T. liable to come up behind you years later and get his licks in when you half expect it.

39 "What I want to know is," I say to Miss Moore though I never talk to her,

I wouldn't give the bitch that satisfaction, "is how much a real boat costs? I figure a thousand'd get you a yacht any day."

"Why don't you check that out," she says, "and report back to the group?" 40 Which really pains my ass. If you gonna mess up a perfectly good swim day least you could do is have some answers. "Let's go in," she say like she got something up her sleeve. Only she don't lead the way. So me and Sugar turn the corner to where the entrance is, but when we get there I kinda hang back. Not that I'm scared, what's there to be afraid of, just a toy store. But I feel funny, shame. But what I got to be shamed about? Got as much right to go in as anybody. But somehow I can't seem to get hold of the door, so I step away for Sugar to lead. But she hangs back too. And I look at her and she looks at me and this is ridiculous. I mean, damn, I have never ever been shy about doing nothing or going nowhere. But then Mercedes steps up and then Rosie Giraffe and Big Butt crowd in behind and shove, and next thing we all stuffed into the doorway with only Mercedes squeezing past us, smoothing out her jumper and walking right down the aisle. Then the rest of us tumble in like a glued-together jigsaw done all wrong. And people lookin at us. And it's like the time me and Sugar crashed into the Catholic church on a dare. But once we got in there and everything so hushed and holy and the candles and the bowin and the handkerchiefs on all the drooping heads, I just couldn't go through with the plan. Which was for me to run up to the altar and do a tap dance while Sugar played the nose flute and messed around in the holy water. And Sugar kept givin me the elbow. Then later teased me so bad I tied her up in the shower and turned it on and locked her in. And she'd be there till this day if Aunt Gretchen hadn't finally figured I was lyin about the boarder takin a shower.

Same thing in the store. We all walkin on tiptoe and hardly touchin the 41 games and puzzles and things. And I watched Miss Moore who is steady watchin us like she waitin for a sign. Like Mama Drewery watches the sky and sniffs the air and takes note of just how much slant is in the bird formation. Then me and Sugar bump smack into each other, so busy gazing at the toys, 'specially the sailboat. But we don't laugh and go into our fat-lady bump-stomach routine. We just stare at that price tag. Then Sugar run a finger over the whole boat. And I'm jealous and want to hit her. Maybe not her, but I sure want to punch somebody in the mouth.

"Watcha bring us here for, Miss Moore?" 42

"You sound angry, Sylvia. Are you mad about something?" Givin me one 43 of them grins like she tellin a grown-up joke that never turns out to be funny. And she's lookin very closely at me like maybe she plannin to do my portrait from memory. I'm mad, but I won't give her that satisfaction. So I slouch around the store being very bored and say, "Let's go."

Me and Sugar at the back of the train watchin the tracks whizzin by large 44 then small then gettin gobbled up in the dark. I'm thinkin about this tricky toy I saw in the store. A clown that somersaults on a bar then does chin-ups just cause you yank lightly at his leg. Cost $35. I could see me askin my mother for a $35 birthday clown. "You wanna who that costs what?" she'd say, cocking her head to the side to get a better view of the hole in my head. Thirty-five dollars could buy new bunk beds for Junior and Gretchen's boy. Thirty-five dollars and the whole household could go visit Granddaddy Nelson in the country. Thirty-five dollars would pay for the rent and the piano bill too. Who are these people that spend that much for performing clowns and $1,000 for toy sailboats? What kinda work they do and how they live and how come we ain't in on it? Where we are is who we are, Miss Moore always pointin out. But it don't necessarily have to be that way, she always adds then waits for somebody to say that poor people have to wake up and demand their share of the pie and don't none of us know what kind of pie she talkin about in the first damn place. But she ain't so smart cause I still got her four dollars from the taxi and she sure ain't gettin it. Messin up my day with this shit. Sugar nudges me in my pocket and winks.

45   Miss Moore lines us up in front of the mailbox where we started from, seem like years ago, and I got a headache for thinkin so hard. And we lean all over each other so we can hold up under the draggy-ass lecture she always finishes us off with at the end before we thank her for borin us to tears. But she just looks at us like she readin tea leaves. Finally she say, "Well, what did you think of F.A.O. Schwarz?"

46   Rosie Giraffe mumbles, "White folks crazy."

47   "I'd like to go there again when I get my birthday money," says Mercedes, and we shove her out the pack so she has to lean on the mailbox by herself.

48   "I'd like a shower. Tiring day," say Flyboy.

49   Then Sugar surprises me by sayin, "You know, Miss Moore, I don't think all of us here put together eat in a year what that sailboat costs." And Miss Moore lights up like somebody goosed her. "And?" she say, urging Sugar on. Only I'm standin on her foot so she don't continue.

50   "Imagine for a minute what kind of society it is in which some people can spend on a toy what it would cost to feed a family of six or seven. What do you think?"

51   "I think," say Sugar pushing me off her feet like she never done before, cause I whip her ass in a minute, "that this is not much of a democracy if you ask me. Equal chance to pursue happiness means an equal crack at the dough, don't it?" Miss Moore is besides herself and I am disgusted with Sugar's treachery. So I stand on her foot one more time to see if she'll shove me. She shuts up, and Miss Moore looks at me, sorrowfully I'm thinkin. And somethin weird is goin on, I can feel it in my chest.

52   "Anybody else learn anything today?" lookin dead at me. I walk away and Sugar has to run to catch up and don't even seem to notice when I shrug her arm off my shoulder.

53   "Well, we got four dollars, anyway," she says.

54   "Uh hunh."

55   "We could go to Hascombs and get half a chocolate layer and then go to the Sunset and still have plenty money for potato chips and ice-cream sodas."

"Uh hunh." 56

"Race you to Hascombs," she say. 57

We start down the block and she gets ahead which is O.K. by me cause I'm 58
goin to the West End and then over to the Drive to think this day through.
She can run if she want to and even run faster. But ain't nobody gonna beat me
at nuthin. ✠

RESPONDING:

1. In a journal entry, speculate about the life of the narrator since the story
    took place. Do you think the experience had an effect on her future? Why
    or why not?

2. Working individually or in a group, retell the story from the point of view
    of another character. Share your versions with the class. Explain why you
    think the character you chose would have responded the way he or she did.

3. Write an essay explaining Sylvia's change of attitude. How does she feel
    when she first enters the toy store? How does she feel at the end of the
    story? What lesson does she learn?

4. Write an essay discussing the meaning of the story's last line. What does
    Sylvia have to think over? Who is the "nobody" in that line? Could it refer
    to anyone other than Sugar?

Henry Louis Gates, Jr.

The critic and literary theorist Henry Louis Gates, Jr., was born in 1950 in Keyser, West Virginia. He earned his bachelor's degree in history from Yale University in 1973 and his master's and doctoral degrees from Clare College, University of Cambridge in 1975 and 1979. He has held professorships at Yale University, Cornell University, Duke University, and Harvard University. Among his publications are Figures in Black: Words, Signs, and the Racial Self *(1987),* The Signifying Monkey: Toward a Theory of Afro-American Literary Criticism *(1987), and* Loose Canons: Notes on the Culture Wars *(1992). Gates has also edited several volumes, including* Black Literature and Literary Theory *(1984),* "Race," Writing and Difference *(1986), and* The Classic Slave Narratives *(1987). His research and writing have earned him awards from the Ford Foundation, the MacArthur Foundation, and the National Endowment for the Humanities, among others.*

In the following essay, from Loose Canons, *Gates explores some of the personal and theoretical assumptions connected with the process of naming. More specifically, he invites readers to consider the relationships between specific names or modes of classification and the value systems associated with them.*

✠

"WHAT'S IN A NAME?"
SOME MEANINGS OF BLACKNESS

The question of color takes up much space in these pages, but the question of color, especially in this country, operates to hide the graver questions of the self.

—JAMES BALDWIN, 1961

. . . blood, darky, Tar Baby, Kaffir, shine . . . moor, blackamoor, Jim Crow, spook . . . quadroon, meriney, red bone, high yellow . . . Mammy, porch monkey, home, homeboy, George . . . spear-chucker, schwarze, Leroy, Smokey . . . mouli, buck, Ethiopian, brother, sistah. . . .

—TREY ELLIS, 1989

I HAD FORGOTTEN THE INCIDENT COMPLETELY, until I read Trey Ellis's essay,   1
"Remember My Name," in a recent issue of the *Village Voice* (June 13, 1989).
But there, in the middle of an extended italicized list of the bynames of "the
race" ("the race" or "our people" being the terms my parents used in polite or
reverential discourse, "jigaboo" or "nigger" more commonly used in anger, jest,
or pure disgust) it was: "George." Now the events of that very brief exchange
return to mind so vividly that I wonder why I had forgotten it.

My father and I were walking home at dusk from his second job. He   2
"moonlighted" as a janitor in the evenings for the telephone company. Every
day but Saturday, he would come home at 3:30 from his regular job at the paper
mill, wash up, eat supper, then at 4:30 head downtown to his second job. He
used to make jokes frequently about a union official who moonlighted. I never
got the joke, but he and his friends thought it was hilarious. All I knew was that
my family always ate well, that my brother and I had new clothes to wear, and
that all of the white people in Piedmont, West Virginia, treated my parents with
an odd mixture of resentment and respect that even we understood at the time
had something directly to do with a small but certain measure of financial
security.

He had left a little early that evening because I was with him and I had to   3
be in bed early. I could not have been more than five or six, and we had stopped
off at the Cut-Rate Drug Store (where no black person in town but my father
could sit down to eat, and eat off real plates with real silverware) so that I could
buy some caramel ice cream, two scoops in a wafer cone, please, which I was
busy licking when Mr. Wilson walked by.

Mr. Wilson was a very quiet white man, whose stony, brooding, silent   4
manner seemed designed to scare off any overtures of friendship, even from
white people. He was Irish, as was one third of our village (another third being
Italian), the more affluent among whom sent their children to "Catholic School"
across the bridge in Maryland. He had white straight hair, like my Uncle Joe,
whom he uncannily resembled, and he carried a black worn metal lunch pail,
the kind that Riley carried on the television show. My father always spoke to
him, and for reasons that we never did understand, he always spoke to my father.

"Hello, Mr. Wilson," I heard my father say.   5

"Hello, George."   6

I stopped licking my ice cream cone and asked my Dad in a loud voice why   7
Mr. Wilson had called him "George."

"Doesn't he know your name, Daddy? Why don't you tell him your name?   8
Your name isn't George."

For a moment I tried to think of who Mr. Wilson was mixing Pop up with.   9
But we didn't have any Georges among the colored people in Piedmont; nor
were there colored Georges living in the neighboring towns and working at the
mill.

"Tell him your name, Daddy."   10

11   "He knows my name, boy," my father said after a long pause. "He calls all colored people George."

12   A long silence ensued. It was "one of those things," as my mom would put it. Even then, that early, I knew when I was in the presence of "one of those things," one of those things that provided a glimpse, through a rent curtain, at another world that we could not affect but that affected us. There would be a painful moment of silence, and you would wait for it to give way to a discussion of a black superstar such as Sugar Ray or Jackie Robinson.

13   "Nobody hits better in a clutch than Jackie Robinson."

14   "That's right. Nobody."

15   I never again looked Mr. Wilson in the eye.

16   But I loved the names that we gave ourselves when no white people were around. And I have to confess that I have never really cared too much about what we called ourselves publicly, except when my generation was fighting the elders for the legitimacy of the word black as our common, public name. "I'd rather they called me 'nigger,'" my Uncle Raymond would say again and again. "I can't *stand* the way they say the word *black*. And, by the way," he would conclude, his dark brown eyes flashing as he looked with utter disgust at my tentative Afro, "when are you going to get that nappy shit *cut*?"

17   There was enough in our public name to make a whole generation of Negroes rail against our efforts to legitimize, to naturalize, the word *black*. Once we were black, I thought, we would be free, inside at least, and maybe from inside we would project a freedom outside of ourselves. "Free your mind," the slogan went, "and your behind will follow." Still, I value those all-too-rare, precious moments when someone "slips" in the warmth and comfort of intimacy, and says the dreaded words: "Was he colored?"

18   I knew that there was power in our name, enough power so that the prospect frightened my maternal uncles. To open the "Personal Statement" for my Yale admission application in 1968, I had settled upon the following: "My grandfather was colored, my father is Negro, and I am black." (If that doesn't grab them, I thought, then nothing will.) I wonder if my daughters, nine years hence, will adapt the line, identifying themselves as "I am an African-American." Perhaps they'll be Africans by then, or even feisty rapper-dappers. Perhaps by that time, the most radical act of naming will be a return to "colored."

19   I began to learn about the meanings of blackness—or at least how to give voice to what I had experienced—when I went off to Yale. The class of 1973 was the first at Yale to include a "large" contingent of "Afro-Americans," the name we quickly and comfortably seized upon at New Haven. Like many of us in those years, I gravitated to courses in Afro-American studies, at least one per semester, despite the fact that I was pre-med, like almost all the other black kids at Yale—that is, until the ranks were devastated by organic chemistry. (Pre-law was the most common substitute.) The college campus, then, was a refuge from

explicit racism, freeing us to read and write about our "racial" selves, to organize for recruitment of minority students and faculty, and to demand the constitutional rights of the Black Panther Party for Self-Defense—an action that led, at New Haven at least, to a full-fledged strike in April of 1970, two weeks before Nixon and Kissinger invaded Cambodia. The campus was our sanctuary, where we could be as black as the ace of spades and nobody seemed to mind.

Today the white college campus is a rather different place. Black studies,   20 where it has survived—and it has survived only at those campuses where *someone* believed enough in its academic integrity to insist upon a sound academic foundation—is entering its third decade. More black faculty members are tenured than ever before, despite the fact that only eight hundred or so Afro-Americans took the doctorate in 1989, and fully half of these were in education. Yet for all the gains that have been made, racial tensions on college campuses appear to be on the rise. The dream of the university as a haven of racial equity, as an ultimate realm beyond the veil, has not been realized. Racism on our college campuses has become a palpable, ugly thing.

Even I—despite a highly visible presence as a faculty member at Cornell—   21 have found it necessary to cross the street, hum a tune, or smile when confronting a lone white woman in a campus building or on the Commons late at night. (Once a white coed even felt it necessary to spring from an elevator that I was about to enter, in the very building where my department is housed.) Nor can I help but feel some humiliation as I try to put a white person at ease in a dark place on campus at night, coming from nowhere, confronting that certain look of panic in his or her eyes, trying to think grand thoughts like Du Bois but —for the life of me—looking to him or her like Willie Horton. Grinning, singing, scratching my head, I have felt like Steppin Fetchit with a Ph.D. So much for Yale; so much for Cambridge.

The meanings of blackness are vastly more complex, I suspect, than they ever   22 have been before in our American past. But how to explain? I have often imagined encountering the ghost of the great Du Bois, riding on the shoulders of the Spirit of Blackness.

"Young man," he'd say, "what has happened in my absence? Have things   23 changed?"

"Well, sir," I'd respond, "your alma mater, Fair Harvard, has a black studies   24 department, a Du Bois Research Center, and even a Du Bois Professor of History. Your old friend Thurgood Marshall sits like a minotaur as an associate justice on the Supreme Court. Martin Luther King's birthday is a *federal* holiday, and a black man you did not know won several Democratic presidential primaries last year. Black women novelists adorn the *New York Times* best-seller lists, and the number one television show in the country is a situation comedy concerning the lives and times of a refined Afro-African obstetrician and his lovely wife, who is a senior partner in a Wall Street law firm. Sammy Davis, Jr.'s second autobiography has been widely—"

25 "Young man, I have come a long way. Do not trifle with the Weary Traveler."

26 "I would not think of it, sir. I revere you, sir, why, I even—"

27 "How many of them had to die? How many of our own? Did Nkrumah and Azikwe send troops? Did a nuclear holocaust bring them to their senses? When Shirley Graham and I set sail for Ghana, I pronounced all hope for our patient people doomed."

28 "No, sir," I would respond. "The gates of segregation fell rather quickly after 1965. A new middle class defined itself, a talented tenth, the cultured few, who, somehow, slipped through the cracks."

29 "Then the preservation of the material base proved to be more important then the primal xenophobia that we had posited?"

30 "That's about it, Doctor. But regular Negroes still catch hell. In fact, the ranks of the black underclass have never been larger."

31 I imagine the great man would heave a sigh, as the Spirit of Blackness galloped away.

32 From 1831, if not before, to 1965, an ideology of desegregation, of "civil rights," prevailed among our thinkers. Abolitionists, Reconstructors, neoabolitionists, all shared one common belief: If we could only use the legislature and the judiciary to create and interpret the laws of desegregation and access, all else would follow. As it turns out, it was vastly easier to dismantle the petty forms of apartheid in this country (housing, marriage, hotels, and restaurants) that anyone could have possibly believed it would be, *without* affecting the larger patterns of inequality. In fact, the economic structure has not changed one jot, in any fundamental sense, except that black adult and teenage unemployment are much higher now than they have been in my lifetime. Considering the out-of-wedlock birthrate, the high school dropout rate, and the unemployment figures, the "two nations" predicted by the Kerner Commission in 1968 may be upon us. And the conscious manipulation of our public image, by writers, filmmakers, and artists, which many of us *still* seem to think will bring freedom, has had very little impact in palliating our structural social problems. What's the most popular television program in South Africa? The "Cosby Show." Why not?

33 Ideology, paradoxically, was impoverished when we needed it most, during the civil rights movement of the early 1960s. Unable to theorize what Cornel West calls "the racial problematic," unwilling (with very few exceptions) to theorize class, and scarcely able even to contemplate the theorizing of the curious compound effect of class-cum-race, we have—since the day after the signing of the Civil Rights Act of 1965—utterly lacked any instrumentality of ideological analysis, beyond the attempts of the Black Power and Black Aesthetic movements, to *invert* the signification of "blackness" itself. Recognizing that what

had passed for "the human," or "the universal" was in fact white essentialism, we substituted one sort of essentialism (that of "blackness") for another. That, we learned quickly enough, was just not enough. But it led the way to a gestural politics captivated by fetishes and feel-bad rhetoric. The ultimate sign of our sheer powerlessness is all of the attention that we have given, in the past few months, to declaring the birth of the African-American and pronouncing the Black Self dead. Don't we have anything better to do?

Now, I myself happen to like African-American, especially because I am, 34 as a scholar, an Africanist as well as an African-Americanist. Certainly the cultural continuities among African, Caribbean, and black American cultures cannot be denied. (The irony is that we often thought of ourselves as "African" until late into the nineteenth century. The death of the African was declared by the Park school of sociology in the first quarter of this century, which thought that the hyphenated ethnicity of the Negro American would prove to be ultimately liberating.) But so tame and unthreatening is a politics centered on onomastics that even the *New York Times*, in a major editorial, declared its support of this movement:

> If Mr. Jackson is right and blacks now prefer to be called African-Americans, it is a sign not just of their maturity but of the nation's success. . . . Blacks may now feel comfortable enough in their standing as citizens to adopt the family surname: American. And their first name, African, conveys a pride in cultural heritage that all Americans cherish. The late James Baldwin once lamented, "Nobody knows my name." Now everyone does. (December 22, 1988)

To which one young black writer, Trey Ellis, responded recently: "When somebody tries to tell me what to call myself in all uses just because they come to some decision at a cocktail party to which I wasn't even invited, my mama raised me to tell them to kiss my ass" (*Village Voice*, June 13, 1989). As he says, sometimes African-American jut won't do.

Ellis's amused rejoinder speaks of a very different set of concerns and makes 35 me think of James Baldwin's prediction of the coming of a new generation that would give voice to blackness:

> While the tale of how we suffer, and how we are delighted, and how we may triumph is never new, it always must be heard. There isn't any other to tell, it's the only light we've got in all this darkness. . . . And this tale, according to that face, that body, those strong hands on those strings, has another aspect in every country, and a new depth in every generation. (*The Price of the Ticket*)

In this spirit, Ellis has declared the birth of a "New Black Aesthetic" movement, comprising artists and writers who are middle-class, self-confident, and secure with black culture, and not looking over their shoulders at white people, wondering whether or not the Mr. Wilsons of their world will call them George. Ellis sees creative artists such as Spike Lee, Wynton Marsalis, Anthony Davis, August Wilson, Warrington Hudlin, Joan Armatrading, and Lisa and Kelly Jones as representatives of a new generation who, commencing with the publication in 1978 of Toni Morrison's *Song of Solomon* (for Ellis, a founding gesture) "no longer need to deny or suppress any part of our complicated and sometimes contradictory cultural baggage to please either white people or black. The culturally mulatto *Cosby* girls are equally as black as a black teenage welfare mother" ("The New Black Aesthetic," *Before Columbus Review*, May 14, 1989). And Ellis is right: something quite new is afoot in African-American letters.

36   In a recent *New York Times Book Review* of Maxine Hong Kingston's new novel, Le Anne Schreiber remarks, "Wittman Ah Singh can't be Chinese even if he wants to be. . . . He is American, as American as Jack Kerouac or James Baldwin or Allen Ginsberg." I remember a time, not so very long ago, when almost no one would have thought of James Baldwin as typifying the "American." I think that even James Baldwin would have been surprised. Certainly since 1950, the meanings of blackness, as manifested in the literary tradition, have come full circle.

37   Consider the holy male trinity of the black tradition: Wright, Ellison, and Baldwin. For Richard Wright, "the color curtain"—as he titled a book on the Bandung Conference in 1955 when the "Third World" was born—was something to be rent asunder by something he vaguely called the "Enlightenment." (It never occurred to Wright, apparently, that the sublime gains in intellection in the Enlightenment took place simultaneously with the slave trade in African human beings, which generated an unprecedented degree of wealth and an unprecedentedly large leisure and intellectual class.) Wright was hardly sentimental about black Africa and the Third World: he actually told the first Conference of Negro-African Writers and Artists in Paris in 1956 that colonialism had been "liberating, since it smashed old traditions and destroyed old gods, freeing Africans from the 'rot' of their past," their "irrational past" (James Baldwin, *Nobody Knows My Name*). Despite the audacity of this claim, however, Wright saw himself as chosen "in some way to inject into the American consciousness" a cognizance of "other people's mores or national habits" ("I Choose Exile," unpublished essay). Wright claimed that he was "split": "I'm black. I'm a man of the West. . . . I see and understand the non- or anti-Western point of view." But, Wright confessed, "when I look out upon the vast stretches of this earth inhabited by brown, black and yellow men . . . my reactions and attitudes are those of the West" (*White Man, Listen!*). Wright never had clearer insight into himself, although his unrelentingly critical view of Third World cultures may make him a problematic figure among those of us bent upon decentering the canon.

38   James Baldwin, who in *Nobody Knows My Name*, parodied Wright's 1956

speech, concluded that "this was, perhaps, a tactless way of phrasing a debatable idea." Blackness, for Baldwin, was a sign, a sign that signified through the salvation of the "gospel impulse," as Craig Werner characterizes it, seen in his refusal "to create demons, to simplify the other in a way that would inevitably force him to simplify himself. . . . The gospel impulse—its refusal to accept oppositional thought; its complex sense of presence; its belief in salvation— sounds in Baldwin's voice no matter what his particular vocabulary at a particular moment" (Craig Werner, "James Baldwin: Politics and the Gospel Impulse," *New Politics* [Winter 1989]). Blackness, if it would be anything, stood as the saving grace of both white *and* black America.

Ralph Ellison, ever the trickster, felt it incumbent upon him to show that blackness was a metaphor of the human condition, and yet to do so through a faithful adherence to its particularity. Nowhere is this idea rendered more brilliantly than in his sermon "The Blackness of Blackness," the tradition's classic critique of blackness as an essence: 39

> "Brothers and sisters, my text this morning is the 'Blackness of Blackness.'"
> And a congregation of voices answered: "That blackness is most black, brother, most black . . ."
> "In the beginning . . ."
> "At the very start," they cried.
> ". . . there was blackness . . ."
> "Preach it . . ."
> "and the sun . . ."
> "The sun, Lawd . . ."
> ". . . was bloody red . . ."
> "Red . . ."
> "Now black is . . ." the preacher shouted.
> "Bloody . . ."
> "I said black is . . ."
> "Preach it, brother . . ."
> ". . . an' black ain't . . ."
> "Red, Lawd, red: He said it's red!"
> "Amen, brother . . ."
> "Black will git you . . ."
> "Yes, it will . . ."
> ". . . an' black won't . . ."
> "Naw, it won't!"
> "It do . . ."
> "It do, Lawd . . ."
> ". . . an' it don't."
> "Hallelujah . . ."

"It'll put you, glory, glory, Oh my Lawd, in the WHALE'S BELLY."

"Preach it, dear brother . . ."

". . . an' make you tempt . . ."

"Good God a-mighty!"

"Old aunt Nelly!"

"Black will make you . . ."

"Black . . ."

". . . or black will un-make you."

"Ain't it the truth, Lawd?"

(*Invisible Man*)

Ellison parodies the idea that blackness can underwrite a metaphysics or even a negative theology, that it can exist outside and independent of its representation.

40   And it is out of this discursive melee that so much contemporary African-American literature has developed.

41   The range of representation of the meanings of blackness among the post–*Song of Solomon* (1978) era of black writing can be characterized—for the sake of convenience—by the works of C. Eric Lincoln (*The Avenue, Clayton City*); Trey Ellis's manifesto, "The New Black Aesthetic"; and Toni Morrison's *Beloved*, in many ways the Ur-text of the African-American experience.

42   Each of these writers epitomizes the points of a post–Black Aesthetic triangle, made up of the realistic representation of black vernacular culture: the attempt to preserve it for a younger generation (Lincoln), the critique through parody of the essentialism of the Black Aesthetic (Ellis), and the transcendence of the ultimate horror of the black past—slavery—through myth and the supernatural (Morrison).

43   The first chapter of Eric Lincoln's first novel, *The Avenue, Clayton City* (1988), contains an extended recreation of the African-American ritual of signifying, which is also known as "talking that talk," "the dozens," "nasty talk," and so on. To render the dozens in such wonderful detail, of course, is a crucial manner of preserving it in the written cultural memory of African-Americans. This important impulse to preserve (by recording) the vernacular links Lincoln's work directly to that of Zora Neale Hurston. Following the depiction of the ritual exchange, the narrator of the novel analyzes its import in the following way:

But it was playing the dozens that perplexed and worried Dr. Tait the most of all when he first tuned in on what went on under the streetlight. Surely it required the grossest level of depravity to indulge in such willful vulgarity. He had thought at first that Guts Gallimore's appraisal of talking that talk as "nasty" was too generous to be useful. . . . But the truth of the matter was that in spite of his disgust, the twin insights of agony and intellection had eventually paid off, for suddenly not only the language but the logic of the whole streetlight ritual finally became clear to him. What he was observing from the safety and the anonymity of his cloistered front porch was nothing less than a teenage rite of passage. A very critical *black* rite of passage! How could he not have recognized it for so long? The public deprecation of black men and women was, of course, taken for granted in Clayton City, and everywhere else within the experience of the Flame Gang. But when those black men and women were one's fathers, mothers, and sisters, how could one approaching manhood accept that deprecation and live with it? To be a *man* implied responsibilities no colored man in Clayton City could meet, so the best way to deal with the contradiction was to deny it. Talkin' that talk—that is, disparaging one's loved ones within the in-group—was an obvious expression of self-hatred, but it also undercut the white man's style of black denigration by presupposing it, and to some degree narcotizing the black boys who were on the way to manhood from the pain of their impotence. After all, *they had said it first!* Playing the dozens, Tait reasoned, was an effort to prepare one to be able to "take it." Anyone who refused to play the dozens was unrealistic, for the dozens were a fact of life for every black man. They were implicit in the very structure of black-white relations, and if one didn't "play," he could "pat his foot" while the play went on, over and around him. No one could exempt himself from the cultural vulgarity of black debasement, no matter how offensive it might be.

Trey Ellis, whose first novel, *Platitudes*, is a satire on contemporary black cultural politics, is an heir of Ishmael Reed, the tradition's great satirist. Ellis describes the relation of what he calls "The New Black Aesthetic" (NBA) to the black nationalism of the sixties, engaged as it is in the necessary task of critique and revision:

Yet ironically, a telltale sign of the work of the NBA is our parodying of the black nationalist movement: Eddie Murphy, 26, and his old *Saturday Night Live* character, prison poet Tyrone Green, with his hilariously awful angry black poem, "Cill [*sic*] My Landlord," ("See his dog Do he bite?"); fellow Black Packer Keenan Wayans' upcoming blaxploitation parody *I'ma Get You Sucka!*; playwright George Wolfe, and his parodies of both "A Raisin in the Sun" and "For Colored girls . . ." in his hit play "The Colored Museum" ("Enter Walter-Lee-Beau-Willie-Jones. . . . His brow is heavy from 300 years of oppression."); filmmaker Reginald Hudlin, 25, and his sacrilegious *Reggie's World of Soul* with its fake commercial for a back scratcher, spatula and toilet bowl brush all with black clenched fists for their handle ends; and Lisa Jones' character Clean Mama King who is available for both sit-ins and film walk-ons. There is now such a strong and vast body of great black work that the corny or mediocre doesn't need to be coddled. NBA artists aren't afraid to publicly flout the official, positivist black party line.

This generation, Ellis continues, cares less about what white people think than any other in the history of Africans in this country: "The New Black Aesthetic says you just have to *be* natural, you don't necessarily have to *wear* one."

45   Ellis dates the beginning of this cultural movement to the publication of *Song of Solomon* in 1978. Morrison's blend of magical realism and African-American mythology proved compelling: this brilliantly rendered book was an overnight bestseller. Her greatest artistic achievement, however, and most controversial, is her most recent novel, *Beloved*, which won the 1988 Pulitzer Prize for Fiction.

46   In *Beloved*, Morrison has found a language that gives voice to the unspeakable horror and terror of the black past, our enslavement in the New World. Indeed, the novel is an allegorical representation of this very unspeakability. It is one of the few treatments of slavery that escapes the pitfalls of *kitsch*. Toni Morrison's genius is that she has found a language by which to thematize this very unspeakability of slavery:

> Everybody knew what she was called, but nobody knew her name. Disremembered and unaccounted for, she cannot be lost because no one is looking for her, and even if they were, how can they call her if they don't know her name? Although she has claim, she is not claimed. In the place where long grass opens, the girl who waited to be loved and cry shame erupts into her separate parts, to make it easy for the chewing laughter to swallow her all away.
>
> It was not a story to pass on.
>
> They forgot her like a bad dream. After they made up their tales, shaped and decorated them, those that saw her that day on the porch quickly and deliberately forgot her. It took longer for those who had spoken to her, lived with her, fallen in love with her, to forget, until they realized they couldn't remember or repeat a single thing she said, and began to believe that, other than what they themselves were thinking, she hadn't said anything at all. So, in the end, they forgot her too. Remembering seemed unwise. They never knew where or why she crouched, or whose was the underwater face she needed like that. Where the memory of the smile under her chin might have been and was not, a latch latched and lichen attached its apple-green bloom to the metal. What made her think her fingernails could open locks the rain rained on?
>
> It was not a story to pass on.

Only by stepping outside the limitations of realism and entering a realm of myth could Morrison, a century after its abolition, give a voice to the silence of enslavement.

For these writers, in their various ways, the challenge of the black creative intelligence is no longer to *posit* blackness, as it was in the Black Arts movement of the sixties, but to render it. Their goal seems to be to create a fiction *beyond* the color line, one that takes the blackness of the culture for granted, as a springboard to write about those human emotions that we share with everyone else, and that we have always shared with each other, when no white people are around. They seem intent, paradoxically on escaping the very banality of blackness that we encountered in so much Black Arts poetry, by *assuming* it as a legitimate grounds for the creation of art. 47

To declare that race is a trope, however, is not to deny its palpable force in the life of every African-American who tries to function every day in a still very racist America. In the fact of Anthony Appiah's and my own critique of what we might think of as "black essentialism," Houston Baker demands that we remember what we might characterize as the "taxi fallacy." 48

Houston, Anthony, and I emerge from the splendid isolation of the Schomburg Library and stand together on the corner of 135th Street and Malcolm X Boulevard attempting to hail a taxi to return to the Yale Club. With the taxis shooting by us as if we did not exist, Anthony and I cry out in perplexity, "But sir, it's only a trope." 49

If only that's *all* it was. 50

My father, who recently enjoyed his seventh-sixth birthday, and I attended a basketball game at Duke this past winter. It wasn't just any game; it was "the" game with North Carolina, the ultimate rivalry in American basketball competition. At a crucial juncture of the game, one of the overly avid Duke fans bellowing in our section of the auditorium called J. R. Reid, the Carolina center, "rubber lips." 51

"Did you hear what he said?" I asked my father, who wears *two* hearing aids. 52

"I heard it. Ignore it, boy." 53

"I can't, Pop," I replied. Then, loud-talking all the way, I informed the crowd, while ostensibly talking only to my father, that we'd come too far to put up with shit like this, that Martin Luther King didn't die in vain, and we won't tolerate this kind of racism again, etc., etc., etc. Then I stood up and told the guy not to say those words ever again. 54

You could have cut the silence in our section of that auditorium with a knife. After a long silence, my Dad leaned over and whispered to me, "Nigger, is you *crazy*? We am in de Souf." We both burst into laughter. 55

Even in the South, though, the intrusion of race into our lives usually takes more benign forms. One day my wife and my father came to lunch at the 56

National Humanities Center in Research Triangle Park, North Carolina. The following day, the only black member of the staff cornered me and said that the kitchen staff had a bet, and that I was the only person who could resolve it. Shoot, I said. "Okay," he said. "The bet is that your Daddy is Mediterranean—Greek or Eyetalian, and your wife is High Yellow." "No," I said, "it's the other way around: my dad is black; my wife is white."

57   "Oh, yeah," he said, after a long pause, looking at me through the eyes of the race when one of us is being "sadiddy," or telling some kind of racial lie. "You, know, *brother*," he said to me in a low but pointed whisper, "we black people got ways to *tell* these things, you know." Then he looked at me to see if I was ready to confess the truth. Indeterminacy had come home to greet me.

58   What, finally, is the meaning of blackness for my generation of African-American scholars? I think many of us are trying to work, rather self-consciously, within the tradition. It has taken white administrators far too long to realize that the recruitment of black faculty members is vastly easier at those institutions with the strongest black studies departments, or at least with the strongest representation of other black faculty. Why? I think the reason for this is that many of us wish to be a part of a community, of something "larger" than ourselves, escaping the splendid isolation of our studies. What can be lonelier than research, except perhaps the terror of the blank page (or computer screen)? Few of us—and I mean *very few*—wish to be the "only one" in town. I want my own children to grow up in the home of intellectuals, but with black middle-class values as common to them as the air they breathe. This I cannot achieve alone. I seek out, eagerly, the company of other African-American academics who have paid their dues; who understand the costs, and the pleasures, of achievement; who care about "the race"; and who are determined to leave a legacy of self-defense against racism in all of its pernicious forms.

59   Part of this effort to achieve a sense of community is understanding that our generation of scholars is just an extension of other generations, of "many thousands gone." We are no smarter than they; we are just a bit more fortunate, in some ways, the accident of birth enabling us to teach at "white" research institutions, when two generations before we would have been teaching at black schools, overworked and underfunded. Most of us define ourselves as extensions of the tradition of scholarship and academic excellence epitomized by figures such as J. Saunders Redding, John Hope Franklin, and St. Clair Drake, merely to list a few names. But how are we *different* from them?

60   A few months ago I heard Cornel West deliver a memorial lecture in honor of James Snead, a brilliant literary critic who died of cancer this past spring at the age of thirty-five. Snead graduated valedictorian of his class at Exeter, then summa cum laude at Yale. Fluent in German, he wrote his Scholar of the House "essay" on the uses of repetition in Thomas Mann and William Faulkner. (Actually, this "essay" amounted to some six hundred pages, and the appendices were written in German.) He was also a jazz pianist and composer and worked

as an investment banker in West Germany, after he took the Ph.D. in English literature at the University of Cambridge. Snead was a remarkable man.

West, near the end of his memorial lecture, told his audience that he had been discussing Snead's life and times with St. Clair Drake, as Drake lay in bed in a hospital recovering from a mild stroke that he had experienced on a flight from San Francisco to Princeton, where Drake was to lecture. When West met the plane at the airport, he rushed Drake to the hospital, and sat with him through much of the weekend. 61

West told Drake how Snead was, yes, a solid race man, how he loved the tradition and wrote about it, but that his real goal was to redefine *American Studies* from the vantage point of African-American concepts and principles. For Snead, taking the black mountaintop was not enough; he wanted the entire mountain range. "There is much about Dr. Snead that I can understand," Drake told West. "But then again," he concluded, "there is something about his enterprise that is quite unlike ours." Our next move within the academy, our next gesture, is to redefine the whole, simultaneously institutionalizing African-American studies. The idea that African-American culture is exclusively a thing apart, separate from the whole, having no influence on the shape and shaping of American culture, is a racialist fiction. There can be no doubt that the successful attempts to "decenter" the canon stem in part from the impact that black studies programs have had upon traditional notions of the "teachable," upon what, properly, constitutes the universe of knowledge that the well-educated should know. For us, and for the students that we train, the complex meaning of blackness is a vision of America, a refracted image in the American looking-glass. 62

Snead's project, and Ellis's—the project of a new generation of writers and scholars—is about transcending the I-got-mine parochialism of a desperate era. It looks beyond that overworked master plot of victims and victimizers so carefully scripted in the cultural dominant, beyond the paranoid dream of cultural autarky, and beyond the seductive ensolacements of nationalism. Their story—and it is a new story—is about elective affinities, unburdened by an ideology of descent; it speaks of blackness without blood. And this *is* a story to pass on. ✛ 63

RESPONDING

1. In a journal entry, tell about a time you or someone you know spoke out against injustice or insensitivity as Gates speaks out at the basketball game at Duke. Or speculate about how you would have reacted if someone insulted a group to which you belong.

2.   Working individually or in a group, list and try to define the following terms in the essay: black essentialism, canon, rite of passage, signifying onomastics. Compare your definitions with your classmates' and check them with outside sources.

3.   In an essay, explain what Gates means when he says that "certainly since 1950, the meanings of blackness, as manifested in the literary tradition, have come full circle" (paragraph 36).

4.   Gates states that "the dream of the university as a haven of racial equity, as an ultimate realm beyond the veil, has not been realized. Racism on our college campuses has become a palpable, ugly thing" (paragraph 20). Write an essay agreeing or disagreeing; use evidence from outside information and your own experience.

✥

CONNECTING

Critical Thinking and Writing

1.   Argue for or against the position that though morality cannot be controlled by legislation, the passage of laws can gradually change attitudes.

2.   Write an essay discussing the shift in focus that took place in the civil rights movement after 1965. What civil rights issues seem most important today?

3.   Write an essay comparing Farmer's reflection that "evil societies always kill their consciences" (paragraph 89) with King's statement that "groups tend to be more immoral than individuals" (paragraph 12). You may use examples from this text or from your own knowledge and experience.

4.   Watch the 1988 film *Mississippi Burning*, which tells the story of the murders of Schwerner, Chaney, and Goodman, and compare its account of events with Farmer's. Some social and film critics were very unhappy with the movie version. Read reviews by both African American and Caucasian critics and summarize their comments. Write your own review of the film considering the reviews you read and Farmer's essay.

5.   Apply King's argument defending the breaking of an unjust law to a current issue. Present the case both for and against such an action. Be sure to consider the restrictions King placed on the lawbreaker.

6. See Spike Lee's film *Do the Right Thing* and compare the circumstances surrounding the conflict in the film with the situation described by Ellison. Compare the origin of the conflict in these two cases. Should we view these disturbances as civil disobedience protests or criminal activities?

7. Compare the changes in living and working conditions, education, and political activity for an African American person living in Montgomery, Alabama, in 1965 and today. Research and describe the role of specific legislation in effecting changes in the living conditions for African Americans in the South.

8. Discuss the current status of African Americans in the United States. Argue that King's dream of an America where "all men are created equal" has or has not become a reality.

9. Compare the issues that were important to African Americans during the Harlem Renaissance with the issues that were important to African Americans in the 1960s. Consider what issues changed, if they changed, and how they changed. Did the participants in the debate change?

10. Discuss the parallels and differences between the Black Power movement and the Red Power movement discussed in chapter eight.

11. Using information from your reading in this text and elsewhere, argue that a nonviolent restructuring of society is or is not possible.

12. Write about a time when you or someone you know has been torn between a violent and a nonviolent reaction to a situation or solution to a problem. What choice did you or your friend make? Was it the most effective choice? Why or why not?

13. The theme of injustice is a theme that runs through many of the selections in this book. Choose an individual or an ethnic group and write an essay about the suffering he or it endured as a victim of injustice.

14. Many of the selections in this text describe responses to injustice. Discuss the ways in which one or more groups in this text have tried to gain acceptance and equality.

For Further Research

1. Many of the readings in this chapter focus on the contributions of men, specifically African American leaders, or the role and fate of the African American man. Research and describe the role of women in the civil rights movement.

Consider the contributions of Septima Clark, Rosa Parks, Fannie Lou Hamer, or Coretta King.

2. Research the history of civil disobedience both in America and around the world. Select a country such as India or South Africa and compare nonviolent protest in that country with the nonviolent movement in the United States.

3. Investigate the legacies of major civil rights figures such as Martin Luther King, Jr., James Farmer, or Malcolm X. Compare their methods and discuss their relative successes and failures.

REFERENCES AND ADDITIONAL SOURCES

Adera, Malaika. *Up South: Stories, Studies, and Letters of this Century's Black Migrations.* New York: The New Press, 1993.

Armah, Ayi Kwei. *The Beautyful Ones are Not Yet Born.* New York: Collier Books, 1968.

Bambara, Toni Cade. *Gorilla, My Love.* New York: Random House, 1981.

———. *The Sea Birds Are Still Alive.* New York: Random House, 1974.

Bates, Daisy. *The Long Shadow of Little Rock: A Memoir.* New York: David McKay, 1962. Fayetteville: University of Arkansas Press, 1987.

Branch, Taylor, *Parting the Waters: American in the King Years, 1954–63.* New York: Simon and Schuster, 1988, 1989 (1st Touchstone ed.).

Brooks, Thomas R. *Walls Come Tumbling Down: A History of the Civil Rights Movement: 1940–1970.* Englewood Cliffs, N.J.: Prentice-Hall, 1974.

Buchanan, A. Russell. *Black Americans in World War II.* Claremont, Calif.: Regina Books, 1977; Santa Barbara: Clio Books, 1977.

Clark, B. Kenneth. *The Negro Protest.* Boston: Beacon Press, 1963.

Clark, Septima. *Echo in My Soul.* New York: Dutton, 1962.

Coleman, Wanda. *A War of Eyes and Other Stories.* Santa Rosa, Calif.: Black Sparrow Press, 1988.

Farmer, James. *Lay Bare the Heart: The Autobiography of the Civil Rights Movement.* New York: New American Library, 1986.

Franklin, John Hope. *From Slavery to Freedom: A History of Negro Americans.* New York: Knopf, 1988.

Friedman, Lawrence M. *A History of American Law.* 2nd ed. New York: Simon and Schuster, Touchstone, 1973, 1986; New York: Oceana Publications, 1990.

Gates, Henry Louis, Jr. *Figures in Black: Words, Signs, and the "Racial" Self.* New York: Oxford University Press, 1987.

George, Lynell. *No Crystal Stair: African Americans in the City of Angels.* New York: Verso, 1992.

Holt, Thomas C. "Afro Americans," in *Harvard Encyclopedia of American Ethnic Groups.* Cambridge: Harvard University Press, 1980.

Jones, Jacqueline. *Labor of Love, Labor of Sorrow: Black Women, Work, & the Family from Slavery to the Present.* New York: Basic Books, 1985; New York: Random, 1986.

Killens, John Oliver, and Jerry W. Ward, Jr., eds. *Black Southern Voices: An Anthology of Fiction, Poetry, Drama, Nonfiction, and Critical Essays.* New York: Meridian, 1992.

King, Martin Luther, Jr. *A Testament of Hope: The Essential Writings of Martin Luther King, Jr.* Ed. James Melvin Washington. San Francisco: Harper & Row, 1986.

———. *The Trumpet of Conscience.* New York: Harper & Row, 1967.

Kluger, Richard. *Simple Justice: The History of Brown v. Board of Education and Black America's Struggle for Equality.* New York: Knopf, 1976; New York: Vintage,1977.

Malcolm X. *Malcolm X Speaks.* Ed. George Breitman. New York: Merit, 1965; New York: Grove Weidenfield, 1990.

Moody, Anne. *Coming of Age in Mississippi.* New York: Dell, 1976, 1980.

Morrison, Toni. *Jazz.* New York: Plume Books, 1992.

Oates, Stephen B. *Let the Trumpet Sound: The Life of Martin Luther King, Jr.* New York: Harper & Row, 1982; New York: New American Library, 1988.

Smythe, Mabel M. *The Black American Reference Book.* Englewood Cliffs, N.J.: Prentice-Hall, 1976.

Thurman, Wallace. *The Blacker the Berry.* New York: Arno Press and the New York Times, 1969.

Williams, Juan. *Eyes on the Prize: America's Civil Rights Years, 1954–65.* New York: Viking, 1987; New York: Penguin, 1988.

Woodward, C. Vann. *The Strange Career of Jim Crow.* New York: Oxford University Press, 1955, 3rd rev. ed. 1974.

7

CHICANOS

*Negotiating Political and
Cultural Boundaries*

✛

Above: César Chávez addressing United Farmworkers Union Members.
(© Victor Aleman/2 Mun-Dos Communications)
Opposite: Cinco de Mayo Market, East Los Angeles. *(Photograph:
Melba Levick)*

SETTING THE HISTORICAL AND CULTURAL CONTEXT

IN HIS POEM "I am Joaquín," Rodolfo Gonzalez writes of the need to establish an identity within a collective experience:

> My fathers
>   have lost the economic battle
> and won
>   the struggle of cultural survival . . .
> And now I must choose
>   between the paradox
>   of the victory of the spirit
> [and] the sterilization of the soul
> and a full stomach.

Gonzalez depicts the Chicanos as struggling with irreconcilable, opposing goals: to enjoy economic success in the majority culture is to gain "a full stomach" but to lose one's soul. For the speaker, the struggle to maintain cultural identity, to survive as a culture, requires a process of retreat and separation:

> I withdraw to the safety
> within the circle of life
> MY OWN PEOPLE

In this withdrawal, Joaquín, the speaker, finds his own reason for being.

When it was first published in 1967, "I am Joaquín" was considered a very influential poem. Its author, Rodolfo "Corky" Gonzalez, had led demonstrations for Chicano rights throughout the Southwest. In a larger sense, the poem helped to dramatize the struggle for dignity and cultural awareness in which many Chicanos were engaged during the late 1960s and early 1970s. They sought "the victory of the spirit" within the collective *raza*, the ideal of the homeland called Aztlán. To search for Aztlán, the mythic homeland of the Aztec peoples, is to seek one's identity in the civilizations of the Mexican Indians that had shaped the Southwest and Mesoamerica centuries before the arrival of the Spanish conquistadors. These native peoples included the Mayans, the Pueblos, and the Aztecs. The Mayans of Yucatan and Central America had established a network of cities, a system of mathematics, and a calendar that predated the Gregorian calendar used in Western Europe by 1,000 years. The Pueblos of the Southwest, who emerged as a culture around A.D. 500, were known for their pottery and weaving. The Aztec civilization of central Mexico, which had many urban centers, was known for its use of astronomy, its system of barter, and its military prowess. A polytheistic culture, the Aztecs relied on human sacrifice to appease the anger of their deities. Although the classic Mayan culture had disappeared by the time the conquistadors reached the continent in the 1500s, the Pueblo and Aztec civilizations were still flourishing.

Spanish explorers were attracted to this continent for several reasons. Explorers and adventurers such as Hernán Cortés and Francisco Vásquez de Coronado sought natural resources and the promise of the Seven Cities of Gold. When he arrived in continental Yucatán in search of laborers, Cortés was treated well by the Mayans, whose legends taught them to be wary of "bearded strangers." He was given Malinche, an Aztec noblewoman who had been sold into slavery, as a translator and mistress. Within two years, however, Cortés had conquered Montezuma's Aztec Empire and had claimed its territory and minerals for the Spanish. In Chicano culture, therefore, "la Malinche" has come to signify a betrayal. In many Chicano works, *la Malinche* represents one who sacrifices cultural affiliation for advancement within the larger society. Recently, Chicano and Chicana writers and artists have reconsidered these views of Malinche, challenging them as prejudices of a traditional patriarchal culture.

The period of Spanish conquest and settlement was recorded in the journals and histories of Bernal Díaz del Castillo and Bartolomé de las Casas. Explorers and missionaries had strategic, economic, and cultural motives for settling the area. Strategists sought a protective buttress for Mexican territory farther south. Those looking for wealth, either for themselves or for the Spanish crown, were drawn by the area's minerals and other natural resources. Missionaries who accompanied many expeditions wanted to convert the native population to Catholicism.

There has been much controversy about the role of the Spanish explorers and missionaries in the economic and cultural development of the Southwest. Some credit the missionaries with educating native peoples about methods of irrigation and planning and ascribe to the intermarriage of explorers and American Indians the formation of the *mestizo* (mixed) culture. Other historians view the Spanish expeditions as having primarily deleterious effects on the native population. They point to the large numbers of American Indians who perished after the arrival of the Spanish, both from diseases against which they had no immunity and from the *encomienda* system of forced labor sanctioned by the Catholic Church. Despite the protests of the missionary Bartolomé de las Casas, who chronicled the abuse of the native population in his letters of protest to the Spanish government, the conditions continued for some time afterward.

Spanish settlements extended throughout the area that now comprises Texas, New Mexico, Arizona, and California. Despite the success of the *hacienda* system in California, the rest of the viceroyalty of Nueva España remained sparsely populated by Novohispanos. The Spanish, and later the

Mexican government, which had declared independence from Spain in 1821, offered *norteamericanos* grants of property and livestock to establish settlements in certain parts of the territory. After the discovery of mineral reserves and good fur-trapping areas, the population increased dramatically. In Austin Colony (now in Texas), for example, the population of *norteamericanos* increased during the 1820s from 300 families to more than 25,000 people.

Political factors also affected the settlement of the territory. Many property owners in what is now Texas also owned slaves, a violation of Mexican law; they were therefore eager to secede from Mexico and have their territory admitted to the United States as a "slave state." Many other Americans also subscribed to the doctrine of Manifest Destiny—the belief that the United States had the right and duty to settle the entire North American continent. Other peoples, even those whose claims on the land had predated those of the Americans, were often viewed as obstacles to achieving this objective. This doctrine coupled with the discovery of gold in California helped to determine the fate of the southwest territory.

During the mid-nineteenth century, Euro American settlers in both Texas and California revolted against Mexico. Texas declared its independence from Mexico and established itself as a republic in 1836; it immediately sought annexation by the United States. In California, Euro American settlers led by John Charles Frémont and others moved against Mexican authorities and established the Bear Flag Republic. These hostilities led to the United States–Mexican War in 1846 and, two years later, the defeat of Mexican military forces. When it signed the Treaty of Guadalupe Hidalgo in 1848, Mexico surrendered all claims to Texas and ceded to the United States government much of the territory that now comprises Arizona, New Mexico, Utah, Nevada, and California. For this territory the United States paid $15 million. The treaty promised those living in the territory the choice of remaining there as American citizens or leaving for Mexico. All citizens living in the area were guaranteed property rights and the freedom to choose their own language, religion, and culture. For many Chicanos, the Treaty of Guadalupe Hidalgo represents a turning point in relations between Mexico and the United States. Because of the treaty, Mexico lost approximately half its territory to those to whom it had once granted generous settlement rights. For this reason, many Chicanos regard the border between Mexico and the United States as arbitrary and irrelevant.

Immigration laws notwithstanding, the migration of people across the border, which began long before the United States–Mexican War, continues to the present day. A great influx of immigrants, for example, occurred during the period between 1910 and 1920 as a result of the Mexican Revolution. Yet it could also be said that it is the demands of the American economy that actually determine the fate of these workers. During times of labor shortage, migrant workers are tolerated, even encouraged; indeed, many service industries in the Southwest depend for their survival on this cheap labor.

When the U.S. economy weakens, however, and the demand for jobs by the white population increases, restrictions against Mexican migrant workers are more rigorously enforced. During the early years of the Great Depression, for example, more than 500,000 Mexicans or people of Mexican descent—one third of the Chicano population—were deported or repatriated to Mexico. Many of the deportees were United States citizens.

Migrant workers in the Southwest have also suffered from substandard working conditions. This group of workers, responsible for much of the labor needed to build the railroads, work the mines, and cultivate the fields, has had few of the safeguards to which Euro American workers are accustomed. Migrants have worked long hours without breaks, earning wages far below the minimum wage given to other workers. Frequently they have had to house their families in shacks, without electricity or indoor plumbing, for months on end while they did their seasonal labor. The economic power of landowners, combined with the workers' frequent migrations and their marginal legal status, has discouraged unionizing and collective bargaining efforts.

Despite a long history of political and labor activism, therefore, conditions changed only slowly. During the 1960s and 1970s, César Chávez and his followers drew the country's attention to the farmworkers' struggle by leading *huelgas*, or strikes, against the growers. The group also organized a nationwide boycott of California grapes, the largest such boycott in American history. These combined actions led to the recognition of the United Farm Workers Union and contracts for its members. By fasting and using boycotts and strikes, the group continues to work for the rights of farmworkers despite declining membership. Recently the union has protested the exposure of field workers to potentially carcinogenic pesticides. The migrant workers in industry have fared worse; despite recent efforts at immigration reform, many people still work long hours in the modern equivalent of the nineteenth-century sweatshop.

Several of the selections in this chapter either directly address or gain their inspiration from the migrant worker. César Chávez's essay provides us with a firsthand account of the struggle to organize the farmworkers. The situation of the migrant worker is presented from a different perspective in the Tomás Rivera excerpt, "Christmas Eve." Rivera, who was raised in a family of migrant workers who traveled from South Texas to the Midwest as farm laborers, considers the psychological effects of this lifestyle on the wife of a migrant worker. The migrant worker and the Mexican immigrant also appear in the work of Ana Castillo and Pat Mora. Castillo's "Napa, California" pays tribute to the farmworkers and reflects on the cycle of their lives—with one day following the other while "the land . . . in turn waits for us." Mora's poems, "Illegal Alien" and "Legal Alien," consider the situation of the undocumented worker from a personal, rather than a legal or political perspective.

The recent history of the Southwest suggests that it is not only the migrant workers whose rights have been ignored. Despite the rights guaranteed by the Treaty of Guadalupe Hidalgo and the Constitution of the United States, Chicanos have suffered discrimination and sometimes violence at the hands of the dominant culture. The Texas Rangers, the state's principal law-enforcement officers, became notorious for their cruel and arbitrary treat-ment of people of Mexican descent; indeed, some historians claim that there were more lynchings of Mexicans in the Southwest than of African Ameri-cans in the South. Despite guarantees of freedom of language, Chicano chil-dren in California were routinely segregated from Anglo children during the nineteenth century; even twenty years ago they were still subject to punish-ment for speaking Spanish.

Beginning in the 1950s and intensifying during the 1960s and 1970s, Chicanos more forcefully asserted their rights as citizens. Organizations such as the Mexican American Political Association and MECHA (Movimiento Estudiantíl Chicano de Aztlán) were founded to represent the interests of Chicano constituents. Striking students in cities such as Los Angeles de-manded that Chicanos be given more say in their education; students and other activists organized the Chicano Moratorium to protest the war in Viet-nam. The Mexican American Legal Defense and Education Fund was estab-lished to provide legal assistance for people who felt their civil rights were being violated.

Along with this political activism there emerged a heightened cultural awareness. The term "Chicano," which became popular during this time, dramatized the sense of self-definition that was critical to the movement. The word embodied an attempt to move beyond the hyphenated appellation "Mexican-American" to a term that more strongly suggested ethnic identity and pride. The Chicano Renaissance, as this movement was often called, used literature, music, and art to signal a rebirth of cultural identity.

Much of the writing of that cultural movement has addressed the issue of the border. As Héctor Calderón explains in the essay that closes this chap-ter, "Whenever Chicanas or Chicanos write on behalf of their community, the border has always loomed in the background." Much Chicano literature explores the border as an image and with it accompanying issues of owner-ship, entitlement, loyalty, and identity. In the chapter from Arturo Islas's *Mi-grant Souls*, the act of border crossing prompts the characters to address is-sues related to identity and affiliation. The selection from Graciela Limón's novel *In Search of Bernabé* presents the border from another perspective; here the main character is a Chicana at ease on both sides of the border who uses her knowledge to act as a *coyota*, one who helps others—in this case refugees from the repression of El Salvador—enter the country secretly and without legal sanction. Sandra Cisneros's story, "Woman Hollering Creek," illustrates how the border image has been extended beyond legal and political con-structs to embrace cultural and personal values as well.

Héctor Calderón's essay, "Reinventing the Border," explores the image of the border and the act of border crossing in both personal and analytical terms. For Calderón, the importance of preserving heritage goes beyond writing the cultural history. In an essay that acts out a kind of disciplinary and stylistic border crossing, Calderón calls attention to "a centuries-old border culture with new social and economic realities . . . reasserting itself on the U.S. national scene" and invites his readers to consider the implications of that *mestizo* presence and its reassertion of self in economic, political, and cultural terms.

Today the Chicano community continues to confront economic, political, and other cultural borders. It has participated in the national debates over bilingualism, affirmative action, and the status of the undocumented worker. Yet in negotiating those borders, there is the ability to assert some control: In the words of Joaquín, "The odds are great/ but my spirit is strong . . . [and] I shall endure."

BEGINNING: Pre-reading/Writing

Imagine that the place where you are living suddenly becomes part of another country and culture. What aspects of your life might change? How hard do you think it will be to make those changes? Write a journal entry expressing your feelings about the situation and your plans for the future. Share your entries with the class.

The Treaty of Guadalupe Hidalgo, ratified in 1848, brought an end to the Mexican-American War. As a part of the treaty, Mexico ceded to the United States much of the territory now referred to as the American Southwest, with the understanding that Mexican nationals living in the territory would be guaranteed their rights to property, religion, and liberty. However, the specific provisions guarding these rights were never passed by the U.S. Congress. The excerpt below shows the treaty as passed by Congress, followed by the original version of Article IX and the excised Article X.

⁜

From THE TREATY OF GUADALUPE HIDALGO*

Articles 8–15

Article VIII

1   MEXICANS NOW ESTABLISHED IN TERRITORIES previously belonging to Mexico, and which remain for the future within the limits of the United States, as defined by the present treaty, shall be free to continue where they now reside, or to remove at any time to the Mexican Republic, retaining the property which they possess in the said territories, or disposing thereof, and removing the proceeds wherever they please, without their being subjected, on this account, to any contribution, tax or charge whatever.

2   Those who shall prefer to remain in the said territories, may either retain the title and rights of Mexican citizens, or acquire those of citizens of the United States. But they shall be under the obligation to make their election within one year from the date of the exchange of ratifications of this treaty: and those who shall remain in the said territories, after the expiration of that year, without having declared their intention to retain the character of Mexicans, shall be considered to have elected to become citizens of the United States.

3   In the said territories, property of every kind, now belonging to Mexicans, not established there, shall be inviolably respected. The present owners, the heirs of these and all Mexicans who may hereafter acquire said property by contract, shall enjoy with respect to it, guarantees equally ample as if the same belonged to citizens of the United States.

*Reprinted from Hunter Miller, ed., *Treaties and Other International Acts of the United States of America*, Vol. 5 (Washington, D.C.: Government Printing Office, 1937).

Article IX

The Mexicans who, in the territories aforesaid, shall not preserve the character   4
of citizens of the Mexican Republic, conformably with what is stipulated in the
preceding article, shall be incorporated into the Union of the United States and
be admitted, at the proper time (to be judged of by the Congress of the United
States) to the enjoyment of all the rights of citizens of the United States
according to the principles of the Constitution; and in the mean time shall be
maintained and protected in the free enjoyment of their liberty and property,
and secured in the free exercise of their religion without restriction.

   [*One of the amendments of the Senate struck out Article 10.*]   5

Article XI

Considering that a great part of the territories which, by the present Treaty,   6
are to be comprehended for the future within the limits of the United States,
is now occupied by savage tribes, who will hereafter be under the exclusive
control of the Government of the United States, and whose incursions within
the territory of Mexico would be prejudicial in the extreme; it is solemnly agreed
that all such incursions shall be forcibly restrained by the Government of the
United States, whensoever this may be necessary; and that when they cannot
be prevented, they shall be punished by the said Government, and satisfaction
for the same shall be exacted; all in the same way, and with equal diligence and
energy, as if the same incursions were meditated or committed within its own
territory against its own citizens.

   It shall not be lawful, under any pretext whatever, for any inhabitant of the   7
United States, to purchase or acquire any Mexican or any foreigner residing in
Mexico, who may have been captured by Indians inhabiting the territory of
either of the two Republics, nor to purchase or acquiring horses, mules, cattle
or property of any kind, stolen within Mexican territory by such Indians.

   And, in the event of any person or persons, captured within Mexican   8
Territory by Indians, being carried into the territory of the United States, the
Government of the latter engages and binds itself in the most solemn manner,
so soon as it shall know of such captives being within its territory, and shall be
able so to do, through the faithful exercise of its influence and power, to rescue
them and return them to their country, or deliver them to the agent or
representative of the Mexican Government. The Mexican Authorities will, as
far as practicable, give to the Government of the United States notice of such
captures; and its agent shall pay the expenses incurred in the maintenance and
transmission of the rescued captives; who, in the mean time, shall be treated
with the utmost hospitality by the American authorities at the place where they
may be. But if the Government of the United States, before receiving such
notice from Mexico, should obtain intelligence through any other channel, of

the existence of Mexican captives within its territory, it will proceed forthwith to effect their release and delivery to the Mexican agent, as above stipulated.

9 For the purpose of giving to these stipulations the fullest possible efficacy, thereby affording the security and redress demanded by their true spirit and intent, the Government of the United States will now and hereafter pass, without unnecessary delay, and always vigilantly enforce, such laws as the nature of the subject may require. And finally, the sacredness of this obligation shall never be lost sight of by the said Government, when providing for the removal of the Indians from any portion of the said territories, or for its being settled by citizens of the United States; but on the contrary special care shall then be taken not to place its Indian occupants under the necessity of seeking new homes, by committing those invasions which the United States have solemnly obliged themselves to restrain.

Article XII

10 In consideration of the extension acquired by the boundaries of the United States, as defined in the fifth Article of the present treaty, the Government of the United States engages to pay to that of the Mexican Republic the sum of fifteen Millions of Dollars.

11 Immediately after this treaty shall have been duly ratified by the Government of the Mexican Republic, the sum of three millions of dollars shall be paid to the said Government by that of the United States at the city of Mexico, in the gold or silver coin of Mexico. The remaining twelve millions of dollars shall be paid at the same place and in the same coin, in annual instalments of three millions of dollars each, together with interest on the same at the rate of six per centum per annum. This interest shall begin to run upon the whole sum of twelve millions, from the day of the ratification of the present treaty by the Mexican Government, and the first of the instalments shall be paid at the expiration of one year from the same day. Together with each annual instalment, as it falls due, the whole interest accruing on such instalment from the beginning shall also be paid.

Article XIII

12 The United States engage moreover, to assume and pay to the claimants all amounts now due them, and those hereafter to become due, by reason of the claims already liquidated and decided against the Mexican Republic, under the conventions between the two Republics severally concluded on the eleventh day of April eighteen hundred and thirty-nine, and on the thirtieth day of January eighteen hundred and forty-three: so that the Mexican Republic shall be absolutely exempt for the future, from all expense whatever on account of the said claims.

Article XIV

The United States do furthermore discharge the Mexican Republic from all   13
claims of citizens of the United States, not heretofore decided against the
Mexican Government, which may have arisen previously to the date of the
signature of this treaty: which discharge shall be final and perpetual, whether
the said claims be rejected or be allowed by the Board of Commissioners
provided for in the following Article, and whatever shall be the total amount
of those allowed.

Article XV

The United States, exonerating Mexico from all demands on account of the   14
claims of their citizens mentioned in the preceding Article, and considering
them entirely and forever cancelled, whatever their amount may be, undertake
to make satisfaction for the same, to an amount not exceeding three and one
quarter millions of Dollars. To ascertain the validity and amount of those claims,
a Board of Commissioners shall be established by the Government of the United
States, whose awards shall be final and conclusive: provided that in deciding
upon the validity of each claim, the board shall be guided and governed by the
principles and rules of decision prescribed by the first and fifth Articles of the
unratified convention, concluded at the City of Mexico on the twentieth day of
November, one thousand eight hundred and forty-three; and in no case shall
an award be made in favour of any claim not embraced by these principles and
rules.

If, in the opinion of the said Board of Commissioners, or of the claimants,   15
any books, records or documents in the possession or power of the Government
of the Mexican Republic, shall be deemed necessary to the just decision of any
claim, the Commissioners or the claimants, through them, shall, within such
period as Congress may designate, make an application in writing for the same,
addressed to the Mexican Minister for Foreign Affairs, to be transmitted by the
Secretary of State of the United States; and the Mexican Government engages,
at the earliest possible moment after the receipt of such demand, to cause any
of the books, records or documents, so specified, which shall be in their
possession or power (or authenticated Copies or extracts of the same) to be
transmitted to the said Secretary of State, who shall immediately deliver them
over to the said Board of Commissioners: provided that no such application
shall be made, by, or at the instance of, any claimant, until the facts which it is
expected to prove by such books, records or documents, shall have been stated
under oath or affirmation.

Articles 9 and 10 Before Senate Amendment

Article IX

16   The Mexicans who, in the territories aforesaid, shall not preserve the character of citizens of the Mexican Republic, conformably with what is stipulated in the preceding Article, shall be incorporated into the Union of the United States, and admitted as soon as possible, according to the principles of the Federal Constitution, to the enjoyment of all the rights of citizens of the United States. In the mean time, they shall be maintained and protected in the enjoyment of their liberty, their property, and the civil rights now vested in them according to the Mexican laws. With respect to political rights, their condition shall be on an equality with that of the inhabitants of the other territories of the United States; and at least equally good as that of the inhabitants of Louisiana and the Floridas, when these provinces, by transfer from the French Republic and the Crown of Spain, became territories of the United States.

17   The same most ample guaranty shall be enjoyed by all ecclesiastics and religious corporations or communities, as well in the discharge of the offices of their ministry, as in the enjoyment of their property of every kind, whether individual or corporate. This guaranty shall embrace all temples, houses and edifices dedicated to the Roman Catholic worship; as well as all property destined to its support, or to that of schools, hospitals and other foundations for charitable or beneficent purposes. No property of this nature shall be considered as having become the property of the American Government, or as subject to be, by it, disposed of or diverted to other uses.

18   Finally, the relations and communication between the Catholics living in the territories aforesaid, and their respective ecclesiastical authorities shall be open, free and exempt from all hindrance whatever, even although such authorities should reside within the limits of the Mexican Republic, as defined by this treaty; and this freedom shall continue, so long as a new demarcation of ecclesiastical districts shall not have been made, conformably with the laws of the Roman Catholic Church.

Article X

19   All grants of land made by the Mexican Government or by the competent authorities, in territories previously appertaining to Mexico, and remaining for the future within the limits of the United States, shall be respected as valid, to the same extent that the same grants would be valid, if the said territories had remained within the limits of Mexico. But the grantees of lands in Texas, put in possession thereof, who, by reason of the circumstances of the country since the beginning of the troubles between Texas and the Mexican Government, may have been prevented from fulfilling all the conditions of their grants, shall be under the obligation to fulfill the said conditions within the periods limited

in the same respectively; such periods to be now counted from the date of the exchange of ratifications of this treaty: in default of which the said grants shall not be obligatory upon the State of Texas, in virtue of the stipulations contained in this Article.

The foregoing stipulation in regard to grantees of land in Texas, is extended   20 to all grantees of land in the territories aforesaid, elsewhere than in Texas, put in possession under such grants; and, in default of the fulfillment of the conditions of any such grant, within the new period, which, as is above stipulated, begins with the day of the exchange of ratifications of this treaty, the same shall be null and void.

The Mexican Government declares that no grant whatever of lands in Texas   21 has been made since the second day of March one thousand eight hundred and thirty-six; and that no grant whatever of lands in any of the territories aforesaid has been made since the thirteenth day of May one thousand eight hundred and forty-six. ✛

RESPONDING

1. In a journal entry, explain one of the effects of the treaty on people living in the region.

2. Working individually or in a group, identify on a map the parts of the United States that were originally settled by Mexico. Speculate on the reasons those particular areas would have been settled.

3. Write an essay explaining how regions of the United States that were originally settled by Mexico became American territory.

4. In an essay, discuss the effects of the Treaty of Guadalupe Hidalgo on Mexicans living in the disputed area. What rights were they guaranteed? What did they have to give up? In your opinion, was the treaty fair to Mexican citizens? To Americans? Support your answer with examples from the treaty and your own knowledge.

Cesar Chavez

César Chávez (1927–1993) was best known as the founder of the United Farm Workers Union. Born in San Jose, California to a family of migrant workers, he experienced firsthand the deplorable working conditions of seasonal laborers. During the mid-1960s and early 1970s his union organized boycotts of California table grapes and nonunion lettuce. During the 1980s the union focused attention on the use of dangerous pesticides in the fields, documenting and publicizing the extraordinary number of miscarriages and cancerous tumors occurring among farmworkers exposed to these chemicals.

In the essay that follows, first published in Ramparts *magazine in 1966, Chávez talks about his early involvement in the farmworkers' cause. In describing the attempt to obtain support from various community groups, the essay suggests the special demands that leadership makes on an individual.*

✠

THE ORGANIZER'S TALE

1 IT REALLY STARTED FOR ME 16 years ago in San Jose, California, when I was working on an apricot farm. We figured he was just another social worker doing a study of farm conditions, and I kept refusing to meet with him. But he was persistent. Finally, I got together some of the rough element in San Jose. We were going to have a little reception for him to teach the *gringo* a little bit of how we felt. There were about 30 of us in the house, young guys mostly. I was supposed to give them a signal—change my cigarette from my right hand to my left, and then we were going to give him a lot of hell. But he started talking and the more he talked, the more wide-eyed I became and the less inclined I was to give the signal. A couple of guys who were pretty drunk at this time still wanted to give the *gringo* the business, but we got rid of them. This fellow was making a lot of sense, and I wanted to hear what he had to say.

2 His name was Fred Ross, and he was an organizer for the Community Service Organization (CSO) which was working with Mexican-Americans in the cities. I became immediately really involved. Before long I was heading a voter registration drive. All the time I was observing the things Fred did, secretly, because I wanted to learn how to organize, to see how it was done. I was impressed with his patience and understanding of people. I thought this was a tool, one of the greatest things he had.

3 It was pretty rough for me at first. I was changing and had to take a lot of ridicule from the kids my age, the rough characters I worked with in the fields. They would say, "Hey, big shot. Now that you're a *politico*, why are you working

here for 65 cents an hour?" I might add that our neighborhood had the highest percentage of San Quentin graduates. It was a game among the *pachucos* in the sense that we defended ourselves from outsiders, although inside the neighborhood there was not a lot of fighting.

After six months of working every night in San Jose, Fred assigned me to   4
take over the CSO chapter in Decoto. It was a tough spot to fill. I would suggest something, and people would say, "No, let's wait till Fred gets back," or "Fred wouldn't do it that way." This is pretty much a pattern with people, I discovered, whether I was put in Fred's position, or later, when someone else was put in my position. After the Decoto assignment I was sent to start a new chapter in Oakland. Before I left, Fred came to a place in San Jose called the Hole-in-the-Wall and we talked for half an hour over coffee. He was in a rush to leave, but I wanted to keep him talking; I was scared of my assignment.

There were hard times in Oakland. First of all, it was a big city and I'd get   5
lost every time I went anywhere. Then I arranged a series of house meetings. I would get to the meeting early and drive back and forth past the house, too nervous to go in and face the people. Finally I would force myself to go inside and sit in a corner. I was quite thin then, and young, and most of the people were middle-aged. Someone would say, "Where's the organizer?" And I would pipe up, "Here I am." Then they would say in Spanish—these were very poor people and we hardly spoke anything but Spanish—"Ha! This *kid?*" Most of them said they were interested, but the hardest part was to get them to start pushing themselves, on their own initiative.

The idea was to set up a meeting and then get each attending person to   6
call his own house meeting, inviting new people—a sort of chain letter effect. After a house meeting, I would lie awake going over the whole thing, playing the tape back, trying to see why people laughed at one point, or why they were for one thing and against another. I was also learning to read and write, those late evenings. I had left school in the 7th grade after attending 67 different schools, and my reading wasn't the best.

At our first organizing meeting we had 368 people: I'll never forget it   7
because it was very important to me. You eat your heart out; the meeting is called for 7 o'clock and you start to worry about 4. You wait. Will they show up? Then the first one arrives. By 7 there are only 20 people, you have everything in order, you have to look calm. But little by little they filter in and at a certain point you know it will be a success.

After four months in Oakland, I was transferred. The chapter was beginning   8
to move on its own, so Fred assigned me to organize the San Joaquin Valley. Over the months I developed what I used to call schemes or tricks—now I call them techniques—of making initial contacts. The main thing in convincing someone is to spend time with him. It doesn't matter if he can read, write or even speak well. What is important is that he is a man and second, that he has shown some initial interest. One good way to develop leadership is to take a man with you in your car. And it works a lot better if you're doing the driving;

that way you are in charge. You drive, he sits there, and you talk. These little things were very important to me; I was caught in a big game by then, figuring out what makes people work. I found that if you work hard enough you can usually shake people into working too, those who are concerned. You work harder and they work harder still, up to a point and then they pass you. Then, of course, they're on their own.

9   I also learned to keep away from the established groups and so-called leaders, and to guard against philosophizing. Working with low-income people is very different from working with the professionals, who like to sit around talking about how to play politics. When you're trying to recruit a farmworker, you have to paint a little picture, and then you have to color the picture in. We found out that the harder a guy is to convince, the better leader or member he becomes. When you exert yourself to convince him, you have his confidence and he has good motivation. A lot of people who say OK right away wind up hanging around the office, taking up the workers' time.

10   During the McCarthy era in one Valley town, I was subjected to a lot of redbaiting. We had been recruiting people for citizenship classes at the high school when we got into a quarrel with the naturalization examiner. He was rejecting people on the grounds that they were just parroting what they learned in citizenship class. One day we had a meeting about it in Fresno, and I took along some of the leaders of our local chapter. Some redbaiting official gave us a hard time, and the people got scared and took his side. They did it because it seemed easy at the moment, even though they knew that sticking with me was the right thing to do. It was disgusting. When we left the building they walked by themselves ahead of me as if I had some kind of communicable disease. I had been working with these people for three months and I was very sad to see that. It taught me a great lesson.

11   That night I learned that the chapter officers were holding a meeting to review my letters and printed materials to see if I really was a Communist. So I drove out there and walked right in on their meeting. I said, "I hear you've been discussing me, and I thought it would be nice if I was here to defend myself. Not that it matters that much to you or even to me, because as far as I'm concerned you are a bunch of cowards." At that they began to apologize. "Let's forget it," they said. "You're a nice guy." But I didn't want apologies. I wanted a full discussion. I told them I didn't give a damn, but that they had to learn to distinguish fact from what appeared to be a fact because of fear. I kept them there till two in the morning. Some of the women cried. I don't know if they investigated me any further, but I stayed on another few months and things worked out.

12   This was not an isolated case. Often when we'd leave people to themselves they would get frightened and draw back into their shells where they had been all the years. And I learned quickly that there is no real appreciation. Whatever you do, and no matter what reasons you may give to others, you do it because you want to see it done, or maybe because you want power: And there shouldn't

be any appreciation, understandably. I know good organizers who were destroyed, washed out, because they expected people to appreciate what they'd done. Anyone who comes in with the idea that farmworkers are free of sin and that the growers are all bastards, either has never dealt with the situation or is an idealist of the first order. Things don't work that way.

For more than 10 years I worked for the CSO. As the organization grew, we found ourselves meeting in fancier and fancier motels and holding expensive conventions. Doctors, lawyers and politicians began joining. They would get elected to some office in the organization and then, for all practical purposes, leave. Intent on using the CSO for their own prestige purposes, these "leaders," many of them, lacked the urgency we had to have. When I became general director I began to press for a program to organize farmworkers into a union, an idea most of the leadership opposed. So I started a revolt within the CSO. I refused to sit at the head table at meetings, refused to wear a suit and tie, and finally I even refused to shave and cut my hair. It used to embarrass some of the professionals. At every meeting I got up and gave my standard speech: we shouldn't meet in fancy motels, we were getting away from the people, farmworkers had to be organized. But nothing happened. In March of '62 I resigned and came to Delano to begin organizing the Valley on my own.

By hand I drew a map of all the towns between Arvin and Stockton—86 of them, including farming camps—and decided to hit them all to get a small nucleus of people working in each. For six months, I traveled around, planting an idea. We had a simple questionnaire, a little card with space for name, address and how much the worker thought he ought to be paid. My wife, Helen, mimeographed them, and we took our kids for two or three day jaunts to these towns, distributing the cards door-to-door and to camps and groceries.

Some 80,000 cards were sent back from eight Valley counties. I got a lot of contacts that way, but I was shocked at the wages the people were asking. The growers were paying $1 and $1.15, and maybe 95 per cent of the people thought they should be getting only $1.25. Sometimes people scribbled messages on the cards: "I hope to God we win" or "Do you think we can win?" or "I'd like to know more." So I separated the cards with the pencilled notes, got in my car and went to those people.

We didn't have any money at all in those days, none for gas and hardly any for food. So I went to people and started asking for food. It turned out to be about the best thing I could have done, although at first it's hard on your pride. Some of our best members came in that way. If people give you their food, they'll give you their hearts. Several months and many meetings later we had a working organization, and this time the leaders were the people.

None of the farmworkers had collective bargaining contracts, and I thought it would take ten years before we got that first contract. I wanted desperately to get some color into the movement, to give people something they could identify with, like a flag. I was reading some books about how various leaders discovered what colors contrasted and stood out the best. The Egyptians had found that a red field with a white circle and a black emblem in the center crashed into your eyes like nothing else. I wanted to use the Aztec eagle in the center, as on the Mexican flag. So I told my cousin Manuel, "Draw an Aztec eagle." Manuel had a little trouble with it, so we modified the eagle to make it easier for people to draw.

18   The first big meeting of what we decided to call the National Farm Workers Association was held in September 1962, at Fresno, with 287 people. We had our huge red flag on the wall, with paper tacked over it. When the time came, Manuel pulled a cord ripping the paper off the flag and all of a sudden it hit the people. Some of them wondered if it was a Communist flag, and I said it probably looked more like a neo-Nazi emblem than anything else. But they wanted an explanation. So Manuel got up and said, "When that damn eagle flies—that's when the farmworkers' problems are going to be solved."

19   One of the first things I decided was that outside money wasn't going to organize people, at least not in the beginning. I even turned down a grant from a private group—$50,000 to go directly to organize farmworkers—for just this reason. Even when there are no strings attached, you are still compromised because you feel you have to produce immediate results. This is bad, because it takes a long time to build a movement, and your organization suffers if you get too far ahead of the people it belongs to. We set the dues at $42 a year per family, really a meaningful dues, but of the 212 we got to pay, only 12 remained by June of '63. We were discouraged at that, but not enough to make us quit.

20   Money was always a problem. Once we were facing a $180 gas bill on a credit card I'd got a long time ago and was about to lose. And we *had* to keep that credit card. One day my wife and I were picking cotton, pulling bolls, to make a little money to live on. Helen said to me, "Do you put all this in the bag, or just the cotton?" I thought she was kidding and told her to throw the whole boll in so that she had nothing but a sack of bolls at the weighing. The man said, "Whose sack is this?" I said, well, my wife's, and he told us we were fired. "Look at all that crap you brought in," he said. Helen and I started laughing. We were going anyway. We took the $4 we had earned and spent it at a grocery store where they were giving away a $100 prize. Each time you shopped they'd give you one of the letters of M-O-N-E-Y or a flag: you had to have M-O-N-E-Y plus the flag to win. Helen had already collected the letters and just needed the flag. Anyway, they gave her the ticket. She screamed, "A flag? I don't believe it," ran in and got the $100. She said "Now we're going to eat steak." But I said no, we're going to pay the gas bill. I don't know if she cried, but I think she did.

21   It was rough in those early years. Helen was having babies and I was not there when she was at the hospital. But if you haven't got your wife behind you, you can't do many things. There's got to be peace at home. So I did, I think, a fairly good job of organizing her. When we were kids, she lived in Delano and I came to town as a migrant. Once on a date we had a bad experience about segregation at a movie theater, and I put up a fight. We were together then,

and still are. I think I'm more of a pacifist than she is. Her father, Fabela, was a colonel with Pancho Villa in the Mexican Revolution. Sometimes she gets angry and tells me, "These scabs—you should deal with them sternly," and I kid her, "It must be too much of that Fabela blood in you."

The movement really caught on in '64. By August we had a thousand members. We'd had a beautiful 90-day drive in Corcoran, where they had the Battle of the Corcoran Farm Camp 30 years ago, and by November we had assets of $25,000 in our credit union, which helped to stabilize the membership. I had gone without pay the whole of 1963. The next year the members voted me a $40 a week salary, after Helen had to quit working in the fields to manage the credit union.

Our first strike was in May of '65, a small one but it prepared us for the big one. A farmworker from McFarland named Epifanio Camacho came to see me. He said he was sick and tired of how people working the roses were being treated, and he was willing to "go the limit." I assigned Manuel and Gilbert Padilla to hold meetings at Camacho's house. The people wanted union recognition, but the real issue, as in most cases when you begin, was wages. They were promised $9 a thousand, but they were actually getting $6.50 and $7 for grafting roses. Most of them signed cards giving us the right to bargain for them. We chose the biggest company, with about 85 employees, not counting the irrigators and supervisors, and we held a series of meetings to prepare the strike and call the vote. There would be no picket line; everyone pledged on their honor not to break the strike.

Early on the first morning of the strike, we sent out 10 cars to check the people's homes. We found lights in five or six homes and knocked on the doors. The men were getting up and we'd say, "Where are you going?" They would dodge, "Oh, uh . . . I was just getting up, you know." We'd say, "Well, you're not going to work, are you?" And they'd say no. Dolores Huerta, who was driving the green panel truck, saw a light in one house where four rose-workers lived. They told her they were going to work, even after she reminded them of their pledge. So she moved the truck so it blocked their driveway, turned off the key, put it in her purse and sat there alone.

That morning the company foreman was madder than hell and refused to talk to us. None of the grafters had shown up for work. At 10:30 we started to go to the company office, but it occurred to us that maybe a woman would have a better chance. So Dolores knocked on the office door, saying, "I'm Dolores Huerta from the National Farm Workers Association." "Get out!" the man said, "you Communist. Get out!" I guess they were expecting us, because as Dolores stood arguing with him the cops came and told her to leave. She left.

For two days the fields were idle. On Wednesday they recruited a group of Filipinos from out of town who knew nothing of the strike, maybe 35 of them. They drove through escorted by three sheriff's patrol cars, one in front, one in the middle and one at the rear with a dog. We didn't have a picket line, but we parked across the street and just watched them go through, not saying a word.

All but seven stopped working after half an hour, and the rest had quit by mid-afternoon.

27 The company made an offer the evening of the fourth day, a package deal that amounted to a 120 per cent wage increase, but no contract. We wanted to hold out for a contract and more benefits, but a majority of the rose-workers wanted to accept the offer and go back. We are a democratic union so we had to support what they wanted to do. They had a meeting and voted to settle. Then we had a problem with a few militants who wanted to hold out. We had to convince them to go back to work, as a united front, because otherwise they would be canned. So we worked—Tony Orendain and I, Dolores and Gilbert, Jim Drake and all the organizers—knocking on doors till two in the morning, telling people, "You have to go back or you'll lose your job." And they did. They worked.

28 Our second strike, and our last before the big one at Delano, was in the grapes at Martin's Ranch last summer. The people were getting a raw deal there, being pushed around pretty badly. Gilbert went out to the field, climbed on top of a car and took a strike vote. They voted unanimously to go out. Right away they started bringing in strikebreakers, so we launched a tough attack on the labor contractors, distributed leaflets portraying them as really low characters. We attacked one—Luis Campos—so badly that he just gave up the job, and he took 27 of his men out with him. All he asked was that we distribute another leaflet reinstating him in the community. And we did. What was unusual was that the grower would talk to us. The grower kept saying, "I can't pay. I just haven't got the money." I guess he must have found the money somewhere, because we were asking $1.40 and we got it.

29 We had just finished the Martin strike when the Agricultural Workers Organizing Committee (AFL-CIO) started a strike against the grape growers, DiGiorgio, Schenley liquors and small growers, asking $1.40 an hour and 25 cents a box. There was a lot of pressure from our members for us to join the strike, but we had some misgivings. We didn't feel ready for a big strike like this one, one that was sure to last a long time. Having no money—just $87 in the strike fund—meant we'd have to depend on God knows who.

30 Eight days after the strike started—it takes time to get 1,200 people together from all over the Valley—we held a meeting in Delano and voted to go out. I asked the membership to release us from the pledge not to accept outside money, because we'd need it now, a lot of it. The help came. It started because of the close, and I would say even beautiful relationship that we've had with the Migrant Ministry for some years. They were the first to come to our rescue, financially and in every other way, and they spread the word to other bene-factors.

31 We had planned, before, to start a labor school in November. It never happened, but we have the best labor school we could ever have, in the strike. The strike is only a temporary condition, however. We have over 3,000 members spread out over a wide area, and we have to service them when they have

problems. We get letters from New Mexico, Colorado, Texas, California, from farmworkers saying, "We're getting together and we need an organizer." It kills you when you haven't got the personnel and resources. You feel badly about not sending an organizer because you look back and remember all the difficulty you had in getting two or three people together, and here *they're* together. Of course, we're training organizers, many of them younger than I was when I started in CSO. They can work 20 hours a day, sleep four, and be ready to hit it again; when you get to 39 it's a different story.

The people who took part in the strike and the march have something more than their material interest going for them. If it were only material, they wouldn't have stayed on the strike long enough to win. It is difficult to explain. But it flows out in the ordinary things they say. For instance, some of the younger guys are saying, "Where do you think's going to be the next strike?" I say, "Well, we have to win in Delano." They say, "We'll win, but where do we go next?" I say, "Maybe most of us will be working in the fields." They say, "No, I don't want to go and work in the fields. I want to organize. There are a lot of people that need our help." So I say, "you're going to be pretty poor then, because when you strike you don't have much money." They say they don't care about that. 32

And others are saying, "I have friends who are working in Texas. If we could only help them." It is bigger, certainly, than just a strike. And if this spirit grows within the farm labor movement, one day we can use the force that we have to help correct a lot of things that are wrong in this society. But that is for the future. Before you can run, you have to learn to walk. 33

There are vivid memories from my childhood—what we had to go through because of low wages and the conditions, basically because there was no union. I suppose if I wanted to be fair I could say that I'm trying to settle a personal score. I could dramatize it by saying that I want to bring social justice to farmworkers. But the truth is that I went through a lot of hell, and a lot of people did. If we can even the score a little for the workers then we are doing something. Besides, I don't know any other work I like to do better than this. I really don't, you know. ✢ 34

RESPONDING

1. Write a journal entry identifying the techniques Chavez learned that helped him become a labor organizer.

2. Working individually or in a group, pool information about the McCarthy era. Explain what Chavez means when he says he was "subjected to a lot of redbaiting" (paragraph 10).

3. Chávez says, "Whatever you do, and no matter what reasons you may give to others, you do it because you want to see it done, or maybe because you want power" (paragraph 12). In an essay, agree or disagree with this statement. Use examples from the essay to support your argument.

4. Review the philosophy, focus, and methods of the organization Chávez founded. Write an essay that discusses the advantages and disadvantages of his method of going directly to the people.

TOMAS RIVERA

Tomás Rivera was born in Crystal City, Texas, in 1935, the child of migrant workers who had emigrated from Mexico. He spent his childhood working on farms from Texas to the Midwest. Rivera earned a bachelor's degree from Southwest Texas State University in 1964, as well as a master's degree in educational administration and a doctorate in Romance languages and literature from the University of Oklahoma.

From 1957 until his death in 1984, Rivera held several university teaching and administrative positions in Texas and California. In 1980 he was named chancellor of the University of California at Riverside; he was the youngest person and the first member of a minority group to earn this position. Tomás Rivera died in 1984, at the age of forty-eight.

Rivera's most famous work, Y no se lo tragó la tierra (. . . And the Earth Did Not Part, *1969), examines the experience of a migrant family. While most of the book's chapters focus on the thoughts of a young boy, the excerpted chapter centers on the reactions of the family's mother. As it describes the townspeople's treatment of this woman, the passage asks us to consider the ways in which economic and political issues can affect both families and individual lives.*

⁜

LA NOCHE BUENA

1 La noche buena se aproximaba y la radio igualmente que la comioneta de la bocina que anunciaba las películas del Teatro Ideal parecían empujarla con canción, negocio y bendición. Faltaban tres días para la noche buena cuando doña María se decidió comprarles algo a sus niños. Esta sería la primera vez que les compraría juguetes. Cada añoy se proponía a hacerlo pero siempre terminaba diciéndose que no, que no podían. Su esposo de todas maneras les traía dulces y nueces a cado uno así que racionalizaba que en realidad no les faltaba nada. Sin embargo cada navidad preguntaban los niños por sus juguetes. Ella siempre los apaciguaba con lo de siempre. Les decía que se esperaran hasta el seis de enero, el día de los reyes magos y así para cuando se llegaba ese día ya hasta se les había olvidado todo a los niños. También había notado que sus hijos apreciaban menos y menos la venida de don Chon la noche de navidad cuando venía con el costal de naranjas y nueces.

—Pero, ¿por qué a nosotros no nos trae nada Santo Clos?
—¿Cómo que no? ¿Luego cuando viene y les trae naranjas y nueces?
—No, pero ése es don Chon.
—No, yo digo lo que siempre aparece debajo de la máquina de coser.
—Ah, eso lo trae papá, apoco cree que no sabemos. ¿Es que no somos buenos como los demás?
—Sí, sí son buenos, pero . . . pues espérense hasta el día de los reyes magos. Ese es el día en que de veras vienen los juguetes y los regalos. Allá en México no viene Santo Clos sino los reyes magos. Y no vienen hasta el seis de enero. Así que ése sí es el mero día.
—Pero, lo que pasa es que se les olvida. Porque a nosotros nunca nos han dado nada ni en la noche buena ni en el día de los reyes magos.
—Bueno, pero a lo mejor esta ves sí.
—Pos sí, ojalá.

2 Por eso se decidió comprarles algo. Pero no tenían dinero para gastar en juguetes. Su esposo trabajaba casi las diez y ocho horas lavando platos y haciendo de comer en un restaurante. No tenía tiempo de ir al centro para comprar juguetes. Además tenían que alzar cada semana para poder pagar para la ida al norte. Ya les cobraban por los niños aunque fueran parados todo el camino hasta Iowa. Así que les costaba bastante para hacer el viaje. De todas maneras le propuso a su esposa esa noche, cuando llegó bien cansado del trabajo, que les compraran algo.

CHRISTMAS EVE

CHRISTMAS EVE WAS APPROACHING. The radio as well as the loudspeaker on the   1
pickup truck that advertised the movies for the Teatro Ideal seemed to draw it
closer with songs, business, and prayers. It was three days before Christmas
when doña María decided to buy something for her children. This would be
the first time that she had bought toys for them. She planned to do it every
year, but she always wound up convincing herself that they could not afford it.
Her husband brought candies and nuts for each one of them, so she rationalized
that they weren't missing anything. Still, every Christmas day the children
would ask for their toys. She always placated them with the same story. She
would tell them to wait until the sixth of January, the day of the Reyes Magos.
By the time the day arrived the children had completely forgotten about toys.
She had also noticed that her children appreciated less and less each year the
visit by don Chon with his sack of oranges and nuts.

"But why doesn't Santa Clause bring us anything?"

"What do you mean? What about the oranges and nuts that he brings
you?"

"No, that's don Chon who brings them."

"No, I mean what is always left under the sewing machine."

"Oh, father brings that, don't think we don't know. Aren't we as good as
the other children?"

"Yes, of course you are, but why don't you wait until the day of the Reyes
Magos. That's really the day when toys and other gifts should be given. In
Mexico it isn't Santa Claus who brings toys, but the Reyes Magos. And they
don't come until the sixth of January. So, you see, that is the real day."

"But what happens is that you forget all about it. We've never received
anything either on Christmas Eve or on the day of the Reyes Magos."

"Well, maybe this time you will."

"Yes, I really hope so."

She decided to buy something for them. But she didn't have any money to   2
spend on toys. Her husband worked almost eighteen hours washing dishes and
cooking in a restaurant. He didn't have time to go downtown to buy toys.
Furthermore, every week they had to save some money to pay for the trip north.
They had to pay the children's fare even if they had to stand up all the way to
Iowa. It was very expensive for them to make the trip. In spite of all this, that
night when her husband arrived tired from work she suggested that they buy
something for them.

—Fíjate, viejo, que los niños quieren algo para crismes.

—¿Y luego las naranjas y las nueces que les traigo?

—Pos, sí, pero ellos quieren juguetes. Ya no se conforman con comida. Es que están más grandes y ven más.

—No necesitan nada.

—¿A poco tú no tenías juguetes cuando eras niño?

—Sabes que yo mismo los hacía de barro—caballitos, soldaditos. . . .

—Pos sí, pero aquí es distinto, como ven muchas cosas . . . ándale vamos a comprarles algo . . . yo misma voy al Kres.

—¿Tú?

—Sí, yo.

—¿No tienes miedo ir al centro? ¿Te acuerdas allá en Wilmar, Minesóra, cómo te perdiste en el centro? ¿'Tas segura que no tienes miedo?

—Sí, sí me acuerdo pero me doy ánimo. Yo voy. Ya me estuve dando ánimo todo el día y estoy segura que no me pierdo aquí. Mira, salgo a la calle. De aquí se ve la hielería. Son cuatro cuadras nomás, según me dijo doña Regina. Luego cuando llegue a la hielería volteo a la derecha y dos cuadras más y estoy en el centro. Allí está el Kres. Luego salgo del Kres, voy hacia la hielería y volteo para esta calle y aquí me tienes.

—De veras que no estaría difícil. Pos sí. Bueno, te voy a dejar dinero sobre la mesa cuando me vaya por la mañana. Pero tienes cuidado, vieja, en estos días hay mucha gente en el centro.

3   Era que doña María nunca salía de casa sola. La única vez que salía era cuando iba a visitar a su papá y a su hermana quienes vivían en la siguiente cuadra. Sólo iba a la iglesia cuando había difuntito y a veces cuando había boda. Pero iba siempre con su esposo así que nunca se fijaba por donde iba. También su esposo le traía siempre todo. El era el que compraba la comida y la ropa. En realidad no conocía el centro aun estando solamente a seis cuadras de su casa. El camposanto quedaba por el lado opuesto al centro, la iglesia también quedaba por ese rumbo. Pasaban por el centro sólo cuando iban de pasada para San Antonio o cuando iban o venían del norte. Casi siempre era de madrugada o de noche. Pero ese día traía ánimo y se preparó para ir al centro.

4   El siguiente día se levantó, como lo hacía siempre, muy temprano y ya cuando había despachado a su esposo y a los niños recogió el dinero de sobre la mesa y empezó a prepararse para ir al centro. No le llevó mucho tiempo.

—Yo no sé por qué soy tan miedosa yo, Dios mío. Si el centro está solamente a seis cuadras de aquí. Nomás me voy derechito y luego volteo a la derecha al pasar los traques. Luego, dos cuadras, y allí está el Kres. De allá para acá ando

"Look, viejo, the children would like something for Christmas."

"What about the oranges and nuts that I bring them?"

"Well, yes, but they want toys. They won't settle for food. They're older now, and they are aware of more things."

"They're not in need of anything."

"Don't tell me you didn't have any toys when you were a child."

"You know, I used to make them myself, out of clay. I'd make little horses, little soldiers. . . ."

"Well, yes, but it's different here since they see many things . . . come on, let's go buy something for them . . . I'll go to Kress myself."

"You?"

"Yes, me."

"Aren't you afraid to go downtown? Don't you remember what happened in Wilmar, Minnesota, when you got lost downtown? Are you sure you're not afraid?"

"Yes, yes, I remember, but I'll try to get up my courage. I'll go. I've been building up courage all day and I'm sure that I won't get lost. Look, all I have to do is go out to the street. I can see the ice plant from here. It's only four blocks away, according to doña Regina. When I get to the ice plant I'll turn right and two blocks more I'll be downtown. Kress is right there. Then I leave Kress, head toward the ice plant, turn into this street and here I am."

"It really won't be difficult at all. Alright, I'll leave you some money on the table when I leave in the morning. But be careful, vieja, there are a lot of people in town these days."

The fact was that doña María never went out of the house by herself. The only time she left the house was when she visited her father and her sister who lived a block away. She went to church only when someone passed away or sometimes when there was a wedding. But she always went with her husband, so she never noticed where she was going. Also, her husband always brought everything to her. He was the one who brought food and clothing. In reality she had never been downtown even though it was just six blocks away from her house. The cemetery was in the opposite direction from the downtown area, as was the church. They crossed the downtown area only when they were on their way to San Antonio or when they were on their way back from up north. Somehow it was always at dawn or during the night. But that day she had built up her courage and she got ready to go downtown. 3

The following day she got up very early, as she always did, and after she had sent off her husband and the children she picked up the money from the table and started to ready herself to go downtown. It didn't take her very long. 4

las dos cuadras, y luego volteo a la izquierda y luego hasta que llegue aquí otra vez. Dios quiera y no me vaya a salir algún perro. Al pasar los traques que no vaya a venir un tren y me pesque en medio . . . Ojalá y no me salga un perro . . . Ojalá y no venga un tren por los traques.

5   La distancia de su casa al ferrocarril la anduvo rapidamente. Se fue en medio de la calle todo el trecho. Tenía miedo andar por la banqueta. Se le hacía que la mordían los perros o que alguien la cogia. En realidad solamente había un perro en todo el trecho y la mayor parte de la gente ni se dio cuenta de que iba al centro. Ella, sin embargo, seguía andando por en medio de la calle y tuvo suerte de que no pasara un solo mueble si no no hubiera sabido que hacer. Al llegar al ferrocarril le entró el miedo. Oía el movimiento y el pitido de los trenes y esto la desconcertaba. No se animaba a cruzar los rieles. Parecía que cada vez que se animaba se oía el pitido de un tren y se volvía a su lugar. Por fin venció el miedo, cerró los ojos y pasó sobre los rieles. Al pasar se le fue quitando el miedo. Volteó a la derecha.

6   Las aceras estaban repletas de gente y se le empezaron a llenar los oídos de ruido, un ruido que después de entrar no quería salir. No reconocía a nadie en la banqueta. Le entraron ganas de regresarse pero alguien la empujó hacia el centro y los oídos se le llenaban más y más de ruido. Sentía miedo y más y más se le olvidaba la razón por la cual estaba allí entre el gentío. En medio de dos tiendas donde había una callejuela se detuvo para recuperar el ánimo un poco y se quedó viendo un rato a la gente que pasaba.

—Dios mío, ¿qué me pasa? Ya me empiezo a sentir como me sentí en Wilmar. Ojalá y no me vaya a sentir mal. A ver. Para allá queda la hielería. No, para allá. No, Dios mío, ¿qué me pasa? A ver. Venía andando de allá para acá. Así que queda para allá. Mejor me hubiera quedado en casa. Oiga, perdone usted, ¿dónde está el Kres, por favor? . . . Gracias.

7   Se fue andando hasta donde le habían indicado y entró. El ruido y la apretura de la gente era peor. Le entró más miedo y ya lo único que quería era salirse de la tienda pero ya no veía la puerta. Sólo veía cosas sobre cosas, gente sobre gente. Hasta oía hablar a las cosas. Se quedó parada un rato viendo vacíamente a lo que estaba enfrente de ella. Era que ya no sabía los nombres de las cosas. Unas personas se le quedaban viendo unos segundos otras solamente la empujaban para un lado. Permaneció así por un rato y luego empezó a andar de nuevo. Reconoció unos juguetes y los echó en su bolsa, luego vio una cartera y también la echó a la bolsa. De pronto ya no oía el ruido de la gente aunque sí veía todos los movimientos de sus piernas, de sus brazos, de la boca, de sus

"I don't know why I'm so timid, my God. Downtown is only six blocks away. I just go straight and I turn right when I cross the tracks. Then two blocks and there is Kress. On the way back I walk two blocks and then I turn left and then straight home. God willing I won't meet any dogs on the way. I'll be careful when I cross the tracks, or a train might come along and catch me in the middle of the tracks . . . I hope I don't meet any dogs . . . I hope there is no train."

Rapidly she walked the distance from her house to the railroad tracks. The entire distance she walked along the middle of the street. She was afraid to walk on the sidewalk. She was afraid of being bitten by dogs or of being accosted by someone. Actually there was only one dog along the entire route, and most of the people didn't even notice that she was going downtown. However, she kept on walking in the middle of the street, lucky that not a single car came along, otherwise she would not have known what to do. As she approached the railroad track she became afraid. She could hear movements and the whistles of the trains, and this unsettled her. She didn't dare cross the tracks. It seemed as though every time she built up enough courage to do so she heard a train whistle and she retreated. Finally she overcame her fear, closed her eyes and crossed the tracks. Her fear left her as she crossed the tracks. She turned to her right.

The streets were full of people and her ears became crowded with noise that once inside refused to leave. She didn't recognize anyone on the sidewalk. She felt the urge to go home, but someone pushed her toward downtown as more and more noises crowded into her ears. She was afraid. More and more she was forgetting the reason for being there among so many people. To regain her courage she stopped in an alley that separated two stores and for a while she looked at the people who passed by.

She felt the urge to go home, but someone pushed her toward downtown as more and more noises crowded into her ears. She was afraid. More and more she was forgetting the reason for being there among so many people. To regain her courage she stopped in an alley that separated two stores and for a while she looked at the people who passed by.

"My God, what's wrong with me? I'm beginning to feel the same way I felt in Wilmar. I hope I don't get sick. Let's see. The ice plant is in that direction. No, it's this other way. No, my God, what's happening to me? Let's see. I came from that direction toward here, so, it's in that direction. I should have stayed at home. Excuse me, can you tell me where Kress is, please? . . . Thank you."

She walked to the place that was pointed out to her and she went in. The noise was worse and the crowd was thicker. She became even more afraid and the only thing she wanted to do was to leave the store but she couldn't find the door. She only saw things piled on top of things, people piled on top of people.

ojos. Pero no oía nada. Por fin preguntó que dónde quedaba la puerta, la salida. Le indicaron y empezó a andar hacia aquel rumbo. Empujó y empujó gente hasta que llegó a empujar la puerta y salió.

8   Apenas había estado unos segundos en la acera tratando de reconocer dónde estaba, cuando sintió que alguien la cogió fuerte del brazo. Hasta la hicieron que diera un gemido.

—Here she is . . . these damn people, always stealing something, stealing. I've been watching you all along. Let's have that bag.

—¿Pero . . .?

9   Y ya no oyó nada por mucho tiempo. Sólo vio que el cemento de la acera se vino a sus ojos y que una piedrita se le metió en el ojo y le calaba mucho. Sentía que la estiraban de los brazos y aun cuando la voltearon boca arriba veía a todos muy retirados. Se veía a sí misma. Se sentía hablar pero ni ella sabía lo que decía pero sí se veía mover la boca. También veía puras caras desconocidas. Luego vio al empleado con la pistola en la cartuchera y le entró un miedo terrible. Fue cuando se volvió a acordar de sus hijos. Le empezaron a salir las lágrimas y lloró. Luego ya no supo nada. Sólo se sentía andar en un mar de gente. Los brazos la rozaban como si fueran olas.

—De a buena suerte que mi compadre andaba por allí. El fue el que me fue a avisar al restaurante. ¿Cómo te sientes?

—Yo creo que estoy loca, viejo.

—Por eso te pregunté que si no te irías a sentir mal como en Wilmar.

—¿Qué va a ser de mis hijos con una mamá loca? Con una loca que ni siquiera sabe hablar ni ir el centro.

—De todos modos, fui a traer al notario público. Y él fue el que fue conmigo a la cárcel. El le explicó todo al empleado. Que se te había volado la cabeza. Y que te daban ataques de nervios cuando andabas entre mucha gente.

—¿Y si me mandan a un manicomio? Yo no quiero dejar a mis hijos. Por favor, viejo, no vayas a dejar que me manden, que no me lleven. Mejor no hubiera ido al centro.

—Pos nomás quédate aquí dentro de la casa y no te salgas del solar. Que al cabo no hay necesidad. Yo te traigo todo lo que necesites. Mira, ya no llores, ya no llores. No, mejor llora, para que te desahogues. Les voy a decir a los muchachos que ya no te anden fregando con Santo Clos. Les voy a decir que no hay para que no te molesten con eso ya.

—No, viejo, no seas malo. Díles que si no les trae nada en noche buena que es porque les van a traer algo los reyes magos.

She could even hear the different things speak. She stood there for a while, emptily looking at what was in front of her. She could no longer remember the names of things. A few people stared at her for a second or so, others shoved her aside. She remained fixed in that position for a while and then started to walk again. She was able to make out some toys and she put them in her shopping bag; then she saw a wallet and put that in her shopping bag, too. Suddenly the noise of the crowd stopped, even though she could still see all the movements of their legs, their arms, their mouths and their eyes. But she couldn't hear anything. She finally asked where the door was, the way out. They pointed it out to her and she began to walk in that direction. She pushed and pushed people aside until finally she was pushing on the door and went out.

She had been outside only for a few seconds, on the sidewalk, trying to get   8
her bearings when she felt someone grab her strongly by the arm. The force with which she was seized forced a moan out of her.

"Here she is . . . these damn people, always stealing something, always stealing. I've been watching you all along. Let's have that bag."

"But . . .?"

And she didn't hear anything else for a long time. She only saw the sidewalk   9
cement rush to her eyes and a small pebble lodge in her eye and felt its irritation. She felt someone pull her arms, and when she was turned face up the people appeared elongated in shape. She looked at herself. She was aware that she was speaking but not even she understood what she was saying, even though she could see her lips move. Also, all the faces that she saw were unfamiliar to her. She then saw the store guard with a gun in his holster and she became terrified. It was then that she remembered her children. Tears rolled out and she cried. Then everything went blank. She was only aware of walking in a sea of people. Their arms touched her like ocean waves.

"It was a good thing my compadre was around. He was the one who rushed over to the restaurant with the news. How do you feel?"

"I think I'm insane, viejo."

"That's why I asked if you thought you might get sick as you did in Wilmar."

"What will become of my children with an insane mother like me? With an insane woman who can't even express herself nor go downtown?"

"I brought along the notary public just in case. He was the one who went with me to the jailhouse. He explained everything to the guard, that your thoughts became confused. And that you became very nervous when you were in a crowd."

"What if they send me to the insane asylum? I don't want to leave my

—Pero . . . Bueno, como tú quieras. Yo creo que siempre lo mejor es tener esperanzas.

10   Los niños que estaban escondidos detrás de la puerta oyeron todo pero no comprendieron muy bien. Y esperaron el día de los reyes magos como todos los años. Cuando llegó y pasó aquel día sin regalos no preguntaron nada. ✚

children alone. Please, viejo, don't let them send me; don't let them take me. I shouldn't have gone downtown."

"Well, just stay here in the house and don't leave the yard. There is no need for you to go out anyway. I'll bring everything you need. Look, don't cry, don't cry. Well, maybe you should cry, it will ease your pain. I'm going to tell the boys not to bother you anymore about Santa Claus. I'll tell them there is no Santa Claus so they won't bother you with that anymore."

"No, viejo, don't be mean. Tell them that if they didn't get anything for Christmas it's because the Reyes Magos will bring them something."

"But . . . well, whatever you say. I guess it's always best to have hope."

The children, who had been hiding behind the door, heard everything even though they didn't understand too well. And they waited the coming of the Reyes Magos just as they did every year. When that day arrived and there were no gifts they didn't question anything.

RESPONDING

1. Have you ever been afraid to do something or tried to do something that was very threatening and failed in the attempt? Write a journal entry abut this experience and compare it to doña María's experience. How did you feel about yourself? Did you try again? How does doña María feel about her attempt to go to the store? Do you think she will try again?

2. Working individually or in a group, describe the attitude of the person who stopped doña María outside the store. What do this person's comments reveal about attitudes toward the migrant community?

3. In an essay, discuss Rivera's attitude toward doña María. Is he sympathetic or unsympathetic? How does he try to get the reader to share his viewpoint? Use examples from the text to support your opinion.

4. Imagine that you are one of the following people in the crowd around doña María: a local banker, the store owner, the guard, a friend of doña María's, a migrant worker, one of doña María'a children, a local newsman, a newsman from a large metropolitan area, a civil rights worker. Write a letter to a friend or a letter to the editor of the local paper about the incident.

ANA CASTILLO

Born in Chicago in 1953, Ana Castillo earned a bachelor's degree from Northwestern University in 1975. In addition to serving as a reviewer for and associate editor of Third Woman Magazine *and as coeditor of* Humanizarte Magazine, *she has contributed poems and short stories to several anthologies and literary journals, among them* The Third Woman *and* Woman of Her Word. *Her publications include the poetry collections* Otro Canto *(1977),* The Invitation *(1979),* Women Are Not Roses *(1984), and* My Father was a Toltec: Poems *(1988), as well as the novels* The Mixquiahuala Letters *(1986),* Sapogonia *(1989), and* So Far from God *(1993). She has recently completed a nonfiction work,* Massacre of the Dreamers: Reflections on Mexican Indian Women in the United States *(1994). Castillo has been the recipient of several grants and awards, including a grant from the National Endowment for the Arts.*

In Castillo's poems, the struggle of the migrant workers provides a focal point for reflecting on the relationship between labor and dignity. "Napa, California," for example, considers the people's attitudes toward their leader and the reasons they follow him.

❖

NAPA, CALIFORNIA

Dedicado al Sr. Chávez, sept. '75

We pick
  the bittersweet grapes
  at harvest
  one
    by
      one
with leather worn hands
        as they pick
          at our dignity
          and wipe our pride
          away
          like the sweat we wipe
          from our sun-beaten brows
          at midday

In fields
  so vast
  that our youth seems
  to pass before us
  and we have grown
  very
    very
      old
        by dusk . . .
        (*bueno pues, ¿qué vamos a hacer, Ambrosio?*
        ¡bueno pues, seguirle, compadre, seguirle!
        ¡Ay, Mama!
        Sí pues, ¿qué vamos a hacer, compadre?
        ¡Seguirle, Ambrosio, seguirle!)[1]
We pick
  with a desire
  that only survival
  inspires
While the end
  of each day only brings
  a tired night
  that waits for the sun
  and the land
  that in turn waits
  for us . . . ✠

RESPONDING

1. Reread the translation of the Spanish text. Why do you think the author includes several lines in Spanish? In a journal entry, discuss your reaction when you first read these lines.

2. Understanding a poem often means understanding references the poem makes to events and people. Working individually or in a group, research the title and dedication of the poem. Why did the poet choose "Napa," "Sr. Chávez," "sept. '75?" Reflect on the role of titles and the information they

1 Well then, what are we going to do, Ambrosio?
Well then, follow him, my good friend, follow him!
Mama!
Yes, well, what are we going to do, friend?
Follow him, Ambrosio, follow him!

provide the reader. Think of alternate titles for this poem. What response might these titles produce in a reader?

3. Who is the "we" in the poem? Write a profile of these people based on information from the poem.

4. Recopy one stanza of the poem into conventional prose sentences. How is the effect different? In an essay, discuss the reasons the poet may have written the stanzas in the form she did.

PAT MORA

Although Pat Mora now lives in the Midwest, she incorporates much of the heritage of her native Southwest in her writing. Born in El Paso, Texas, she earned her master's degree from the University of Texas at El Paso in 1967. Since the late 1960s she has worked in the academic and cross-cultural fields, first by teaching English and later by working in university administration. In 1986 she was awarded a Kellogg National Fellowship to study cultural conservation issues; in 1994 she was awarded a fellowship from the National Endowment for the Arts. In addition to contributing poetry to numerous journals and anthologies, Mora has published two collections of poems, Chants *(1984) and* Borders *(1986), which have received several awards, and an essay collection* Nepantla: Essays from the Land in the Middle *(1993), among other works.*

The following poems, from Chants, *explore the effects of economic and cultural boundaries on both the speaker and the audience.*

✜

ILLEGAL ALIEN

Socorro, you free me
to sit in my yellow kitchen
waiting for a poem
while you scrub and iron.

Today you stand before me
holding cleanser and sponge
and say you can't sleep at night.
"My husband's fury is a fire.
His fist can burn.
We don't fight with words
on that side of the Rio Grande."

Your eyes fill. I want
to comfort you, but my arms
feel heavy, unaccustomed
to healing grown-up bodies.

I offer foolish questions
when I should hug you hard,
when I should dry your eyes, my
    sister,
sister because we are both women,
both married, both warmed
by Mexican blood.

It is not cool words you need
but soothing hands.
My plastic band-aid doesn't fit
your hurt.
I am the alien here. ✜

RESPONDING

1. In a journal entry, discuss the bond created between the speaker and Socorro. Does it make them responsible for each other? In what way?

2. We know what the speaker has to say but not what Socorro is thinking. Working with a partner, each taking one role, write a dialogue between Socorro and the speaker. Share your dialogue with your classmates.

3. In an essay, discuss the relationship between the two women. What does the relationship mean to the speaker? What images in the poem help the reader understand the poet's attitude toward the speaker and Socorro?

4. Imagine that Socorro has written to one of the following people for help in dealing with her physically abusive husband: her mother, a social worker, Dear Abby, a religious leader, an administrator of a shelter for battered women. Write a reply from the point of view of that person.

LEGAL ALIEN

Bi-lingual. Bi-cultural,
able to slip from "How's life?"
to *"Me'stan volviendo loca,"*
able to sit in a paneled office
drafting memos in smooth English,
able to order in fluent Spanish
at a Mexican restaurant,
American but hyphenated,
viewed by Anglos as perhaps exotic,
perhaps inferior, definitely different,
viewed by Mexicans as alien.
(their eyes say, "You may speak
Spanish but you're not like me")
an American to Mexicans
a Mexican to Americans
a handy token
sliding back and forth
between the fringes of both worlds
by smiling
by masking the discomfort
of being pre-judged
Bi-laterally. ✠

RESPONDING

1. In a journal entry, tell about a time when you or someone you know felt torn between two traditions, two sets of beliefs, or two cultures.

2. Working individually or in a group, list the advantages and disadvantages of being bicultural in the United States today. Compare notes with the class. Write an essay presenting your conclusions.

3. Is "legal alien" a contradiction in terms? In an essay, discuss what the speaker means when she calls herself a legal alien.

4. The speaker believes that being "bi-cultural" means that you aren't really accepted by either culture. Write an essay agreeing or disagreeing. Support your position by referring to the poem, other readings in the text, or your own experience.

ELENA

My Spanish isn't enough.
I remember how I'd smile
listening to my little ones,
understanding every word they'd say,
their jokes, their songs, their plots.
  Vamos a pedirle dulces a mamá. Vamos.
But that was in Mexico.
Now my children go to American high schools.
They speak English. At night they sit around
the kitchen table, laugh with one another.
I stand by the stove and feel dumb, alone.
I bought a book to learn English.
My husband frowned, drank more beer.
My oldest said, "*Mamá*, he doesn't want you
to be smarter than he is." I'm forty,
embarrassed at mispronouncing words,
embarrassed at the laughter of my children,
the grocer, the mailman. Sometimes I take
my English book and lock myself in the bathroom,
say the thick words softly,
for if I stop trying, I will be deaf
when my children need my help. ✢

RESPONDING

1. In a journal entry, tell about a time when you or someone you know felt inadequate or out of touch with a situation.

2. Working individually or in a group, identify Elena's problem and suggest solutions. Share these with the class.

3. The poem suggests a conflict that arises between Elena's husband and herself. Write a scene in which this conflict unfolds.

4. Write an essay discussing the difficulties of moving to a new country and learning a new language. You may use information from the poem, other readings, or your own experience.

Arturo Islas

Arturo Islas was born in El Paso, Texas, in 1938. He earned his bachelor's, master's, and doctoral degrees from Stanford University, where he served on the faculty as a professor of English. In addition to contributing several essays, short stories, poems, and reviews to literary journals, Islas published two novels, The Rain God *(1984) and* Migrant Souls *(1988). He was awarded the Woodrow Wilson Fellowship (1963–1964), the Carnegie Mellon Faculty Award (1974), and the Dinkelspiel Award for Outstanding Service to Undergraduate Education (1976), among others. Arturo Islas died in 1991.*

The following excerpt, from Migrant Souls, *uses the backdrop of the Thanksgiving holiday celebration to examine issues of heritage and cultural tradition.*

✠

From MIGRANT SOULS

AFTER THE WAR, their mother took to raising chickens and pigeons in order to   1
save money. Josie saw their neighbors enjoying life and thought that her mother had gone crazy. Eduviges had even bought a live duck from God knows where and kept it until the Garcias next door began complaining about all the racket it made at night. Josie and Serena had become attached to it, so much so that when it appeared piecemeal in a *mole poblano,* both of them refused to eat it.

"It's too greasy," Josie said, holding back her tears and criticizing her   2
mother's cooking instead.

"Then let your sisters have your portion. Eat the beans," Sancho said from   3
behind the hunting magazine that was his bible.

"I don't want it," Serena said, her tears falling unchecked. "Poor don Pato.   4
He didn't make that much noise. The Garcias are louder than he ever was."

Ofelia was dutifully, even happily, chewing away. "I think he's delicious,"   5
she said.

Josie glared at her and held her hands tightly under the table and away from   6
the knife next to her plate. In her mind, she was dumping its contents into Ofelia's lap.

Eduviges stared at her husband until the silence made him glance up from   7
his magazine. "Well," she said, "if your little darlings won't eat what I raise, slaughter, and cook with my own hands, let them live on beans. I know Josie likes chicken well enough. And pigeon stew. From now on, she can do the killing before she eats them. Let's see how she likes it."

And then speaking to Josie directly, she added, "This is not a restaurant,   8 young lady. You have to eat what I serve you. And that's that." She said nothing to Serena, who was blowing her nose loudly into a paper napkin and now glaring at her in an accusing way.

9   "Leave her alone," Sancho said, meaning Josie. "The child liked that dumb duck, that's all. She doesn't have to eat him if she doesn't want to." These words caused Josie to leave the table in tears, followed by Serena, now struck by another fit of weeping. Ofelia kept eating and asked that her sisters' portions be passed to her.

10   "Of course, darling," Eduviges said. Sancho returned to his magazine.

11   In their bedroom, Josie and Serena held each other until they stopped crying. "I'll never forgive her for killing him," Josie said.

12   "Oh, Josie, don't say that. I was crying because of the way you were looking at Ofelia and Mother. We can always get another duck."

13   After don Pato's transformation, their mother stuck to chickens and pigeons. Atoning for her harshness toward Josie, she cooked omelets and looked the other way whenever Serena slipped Josie a piece of chicken. But for Thanksgiving in 1947, Eduviges, in a fit of guilt, decided to bake a turkey with all the trimmings. She had memorized the recipes in the glossy American magazines while waiting her turn at the Safeway checkout counter.

14   Because the girls were in public school and learning about North American holidays and customs, Eduviges thought her plan would please them. It did and even Josie allowed her mother to embrace her in that quick, embarrassed way she had of touching them. As usual, Sancho had no idea why she was going to such lengths preparing for a ritual that meant nothing to him.

15   "I don't see why we can't have the enchiladas you always make," he said. "I don't even like turkey. Why don't you let me bring you a nice, fat pheasant from the Chihuahua mountains? At least it'll taste like something. Eating turkey is going to turn my girls into little *gringos*. Is that what you want?"

16   "Oh, Daddy, please! Everybody else is going to have turkey." The girls, wearing colored paper headdresses they had made in art class, were acting out the Pocahontas story and reciting from "Hiawatha" in a hodgepodge of Indian sentiment that forced Sancho to agree in order to keep them quiet.

17   "All right, all right," he said, "Just stop all the racket, please. And Serena, *querida*, don't wear that stuff outside the house or they'll pick you up and send you to a reservation. That would be okay with me, but your mother wouldn't like it."

18   Serena and Josie gave each other knowing glances. "They" were the *migra*, who drove around in their green vans, sneaked up on innocent dark-skinned people, and deported them. Their neighbor down the block—Benito Cruz, who was lighter-skinned than Serena and did not look at all like an Indian—had been picked up three times already, detained at the border for hours, and then released with the warning that he was to carry his identification papers at all times. That he was an American citizen did not seem to matter to the immigration officers.

The Angel children were brought up on as many deportation stories as fairy   19
tales and family legends. The latest border incident had been the discovery of
twenty-one young Mexican males who had been left to asphyxiate in an airtight
boxcar on their way to pick cotton in the lower Rio Grande Valley.

When they read the newspaper articles about how the men died, both Josie   20
and Serena thought of the fluttering noises made by the pigeons their mother
first strangled and then put under a heavy cardboard box for minutes that
seemed eternal to the girls. They covered their ears to protect their souls from
the thumping and scratching noises of the doomed birds.

Even their mother had shown sympathy for the Mexican youths, especially   21
when it was learned that they were not from the poorest class. "I feel very bad
for their families," she said, "Their mothers must be in agony."

What about their fathers? Josie felt like asking but did not. Because of the   22
horror she imagined they went through, Josie did not want to turn her own
feelings for the young men into yet another argument with her mother about
"wetbacks" or about who did and did not "deserve" to be in the United States.

In the first semester of seventh grade, Josie had begun to wonder why being   23
make-believe North American Indians seemed to be all right with their mother.
"Maybe it was because those Indians spoke English," Josie said to Serena.
Mexican Indians were too close to home and the truth, and the way Eduviges
looked at Serena in her art class getup convinced Josie she was on the right
track.

That year on the Saturday before Thanksgiving, their mother and father   24
took them across the river in search of the perfect turkey. Sancho borrowed his
friend Tacho Morales' pickup and they drove down the valley to the Zaragoza
crossing. It was closer to the ranch where Eduviges had been told the turkeys
were raised and sold for practically nothing. Josie and Serena sat in the front
seat of the pickup with their father. Eduviges and Ofelia followed them in the
Chevy in case anything went wrong.

Sancho was a slower, more patient driver than their mother, who turned   25
into a speed demon with a sharp tongue behind the wheel. More refined than
her younger sisters, Ofelia was scandalized by every phase that came out of
Eduviges' mouth when some sorry driver from Chihuahua or New Mexico got
in her way.

"Why don't they teach those imbecile cretins how to drive?" she said loudly   26
in Spanish, window down and honking. Or, "May all your teeth fall out but one
and may that ache until the day you die" to the man who pulled out in front
of her without a signal.

Grateful that her mother was being good for once and following slowly and   27
at a safe distance behind the pickup, Ofelia dozed, barely aware of the clear day
so warm for November. Only the bright yellow leaves of the cottonwood trees
reminded her that it was autumn. They clung to the branches and vibrated in
the breeze, which smelled of burning mesquite and Mexican alders. As they
followed her father away from the mountains and into the valley, Ofelia began

to dream they were inside one of Mama Chona's Mexican blue clay bowls, suspended in midair while the sky revolved around them.

28   To Josie and Serena, it seemed their father was taking forever to get to where they were going. "Are we there yet?" they asked him until he told them that if they asked again, he would leave them in the middle of nowhere and not let their mother rescue them. The threat only made them laugh more and they started asking him where the middle of nowhere was until he, too, laughed with them.

29   "The middle of nowhere, smart alecks, is at the bottom of the sea and so deep not even the fish go there," Sancho said, getting serious about it.

30   "No, no," Serena said, "It's in the space between two stars and no planets around."

31   "I already said the middle of nowhere is in Del Sapo, Texas," Josie said, not wanting to get serious.

32   "I know, I know. It's in the Sahara Desert where not even the tumbleweeds will grow," their father said.

33   "No, Daddy. It's at the top of Mount Everest." Serena was proud of the B she had gotten for her report on the highest mountain in the world. They fell silent and waited for Josie to take her turn.

34   "It's here," Josie said quietly and pointed to her heart.

35   "Oh, for heaven's sake, Josie, don't be so dramatic. You don't even know what you are saying," Serena said. Their father changed the subject.

36   When they arrived at the ranch, he told Eduviges and the girls that the worst that could happen on their return was that the turkey would be taken away from them. But the girls, especially, must do and say exactly as he instructed them.

37   Their mother was not satisfied with Sancho's simple directions and once again told them about the humiliating body search her friend from New Mexico, *la señora* Moulton, had been subjected to at the Santa Fe Street bridge. She had just treated her daughter Ethel and her granddaughters, Amy and Mary Ann, to lunch at the old Central Cafe in Juarez. When *la señora* had been asked her citizenship, she had replied in a jovial way, "Well, what do I look like, sir?"

38   They made her get out of the car, led her to a special examining cell, ordered her to undress, and made her suffer unspeakable mortifications while her relatives waited at least four hours in terror, wondering if they would ever see her again or be allowed to return to the country of their birth. Then, right on cue, Josie and Serena said along with Eduviges, "And they were Anglos and blond!"

39   While their parents were bargaining for the bird, the girls looked with awe upon the hundreds of adult turkeys kept inside four large corrals. As they walked by each enclosure, one of the birds gobbled and the rest echoed its call until the racket was unbearable. Serena was struck by an attack of giggles.

40   "They sure are stupid," Josie said in Spanish to their Mexican guide.

41   "They really are," he said with a smile. "When it rains, we have to cover the coops of the younger ones so they won't drown." He was a dark red color and very shy. Josie liked him instantly.

"How can they drown?" Serena asked him. "The river is nowhere near here.   42
Does it flood?"

"No," the young man said, looking away from them. "Not from the Rio   43
Bravo. From the rain itself. They stretch their necks, open their beaks wide and
let it pour in until they drown. They keel over all bloated. That's how stupid
they are." He bent his head back and showed them as they walked by an
enclosure. "Gobble, gobble," the guide called and the turkeys answered hysteri-
cally.

Josie and Serena laughed all the way back to the pickup. Ofelia had not   44
been allowed to join them because of the way their mother thought the guide
was looking at her. She was dreaming away in the backseat of the Chevy while
their father struggled to get the newly bought and nervous turkey into a slatted
crate. Eduviges was criticizing every move he made. At last, the creature was in
the box and eerily silent.

"Now remember, girls," Sancho said, wiping his face, "I'll do all the talking   45
at the bridge. You just say 'American' when the time comes. Not another word,
you hear? Think about Mrs. Moulton, Josie," He gave her a wink.

The turkey remained frozen inside the crate. Sancho lifted it onto the   46
pickup, covered it with a yellow plastic tablecloth they used on picnics, and told
Serena to sit on top of it with her back against the rear window.

"Serena," he said, "I'd hate to lose you because of this stupid bird, but if   47
you open your mouth except to say 'American,' I won't be responsible for what
happens. Okay?" He kissed her on the cheek as if in farewell forever, Josie
thought, looking at them from the front seat. She was beginning to wish they
had not begged so successfully for a traditional North American ceremony.
Nothing would happen to Ofelia, of course. She was protected in their mother's
car and nowhere near the turkey. Josie felt that Serena was in great peril and
made up her mind to do anything to keep her from harm.

On the way to the bridge, Josie made the mistake of asking her father if   48
they were aliens. Sancho put his foot on the brake so hard that Eduviges almost
rear-ended the truck. He looked at Josie very hard and said, "I do not ever want
to hear you use that word in my presence again. About anybody. We are not
aliens. We are American citizens of Mexican heritage. We are proud of both
countries and have never and will never be that word you just said to me."

"Well," Josie said. Sancho knew she was not afraid of him. He pulled the   49
truck away from the shoulder and signaled for his wife to continue following
them. "That's what they call Mexican people in all the newspapers. And Kathy
Jarvis at school told me real snotty at recess yesterday that we were nothing but
a bunch of resident aliens."

After making sure Eduviges was right behind them, Sancho said in a calmer,   50
serious tone, "Josie, I'm warning you. I do not want to hear those words again.
Do you understand me?"

"I'm only telling you what Kathy told me. What did she mean? Is she   51
right?"

"Kathy Jarvis is an ignorant little brat. The next time she tells you that, you   52 tell her that Mexican and Indian people were in this part of the country long before any *gringos*, Europeans (he said 'Yurrup-beans') or anyone else decided it was theirs. That should shut her up. If it doesn't, tell her those words are used by people who think Mexicans are not human beings. That goes for the newspapers, too. They don't think anyone is human." She watched him look straight ahead, then in the rearview mirror, then at her as he spoke.

53   "Don't you see, Josie? When people call Mexicans those words, it makes it easier for them to deport or kill them. Aliens come from outer space." He paused. "Sort of like your mother's family, the blessed Angels, who think they come from heaven. Don't tell her I said that."

54   Before he made that last comment, Josie was impressed by her father's tone. Sancho seldom became that passionate in their presence about any issue. He laughed at the serious and the pompous and especially at religious fanatics.

55   During their aunt Jesus Maria's visits, the girls and their cousins were sent out of the house in the summer or to the farthest room away from the kitchen in the winter so that they would not be able to hear her and Sancho arguing about God and the Church. Unnoticed, the children sneaked around the house and crouched in the honeysuckle under the kitchen window, wide open to the heat of July. In horror and amusement, they listened to Jesus Maria tell Sancho that he would burn in hell for all eternity because he did not believe in an afterlife and dared to criticize the infallibility of the Pope.

56   "It's because they're afraid of dying that people make up an afterlife to believe in," Sancho said.

57   "That's not true. God created Heaven, Hell, and Purgatory before He created man. And you are going to end up in Hell if you don't start believing what the Church teaches us." Jesus Maria was in her glory defending the teachings of Roman Catholicism purged by the fires of the Spanish Inquisition.

58   "Oh, Jessie—" he began.

59   "Don't call me that. My name is Jesus Maria and I am proud of it." She knew the children were listening.

60   "Excuse me, Jesus Maria," he said with a flourish. "I just want to point out to you that it's hotter here in Del Sapo right now than in hell." He saw her bristle but went on anyway. "Haven't you figured it out yet? This is hell and heaven and purgatory right here. How much worse, better, or boring can the afterlife be?" Sancho was laughing at his own insight.

61   "If you are going to start joking about life-and-death matters, I simply won't talk about anything serious with you again," their aunt said. They knew she meant it. "I, like the Pope, am fighting for your everlasting soul, Sancho. If I did not love you because you are my sister's husband, I would not be telling you these things."

62   "Thank you, Jessie. I appreciate your efforts and love. But the Pope is only a man. He is not Christ. Don't you read history? All most popes have cared about is money and keeping the poor in rags so that they can mince about in gold lamé dresses."

"Apostate!" their aunt cried. 63

"What's that?" Serena whispered to Josie. 64

"I don't know but it sounds terrible. We'll look it up in the dictionary as 65 soon as they stop." They knew the arguing was almost over when their aunt began calling their father names. Overwhelmed by the smell of the honeysuckle, the children ran off to play kick the can. Later, when Josie looked up the word "apostate," she kept its meaning to herself because she knew that Serena believed in an afterlife and would be afraid for her father.

That one word affected her father more than another was a mystery to 66 Josie. She loved words and believed them to be more real than whatever they described. In her mind, she, too, suspected that she was an apostate but, like her father, she did not want to be an alien.

"All right, Daddy, I promise I won't say that word again. And I won't tell 67 Mother what you said about the Angels."

They were now driving through the main streets of Juarez, and Sancho was 68 fighting to stay in his lane. "God, these Mexicans drive like your mother," he said with affection.

At every intersection, young Indian women with babies at their breast 69 stretched out their hands. Josie was filled with dread and pity. One of the women knocked on her window while they waited for the light to change. She held up her baby and said, "*Señorita, por favor. Dinero para el niño.*" Her hair was black and shiny and her eyes as dark as Josie's. The words came through the glass in a muted, dreamlike way. Silent and unblinking, the infant stared at Josie. She had a quarter in her pocket.

"Don't roll down the window or your mother will have a fit," Sancho said. 70 He turned the corner and headed toward the river. The woman and child disappeared. Behind them, Eduviges kept honking almost all the way to the bridge.

"I think it was blind," Josie said. Her father did not answer and looked 71 straight ahead.

The traffic leading to the declaration points was backed up several blocks, 72 and the stop-and-go movement as they inched their way to the American side was more than Josie could bear. She kept looking back at Serena, who sat like a *Virgen de Guadalupe* statue on her yellow plastic-covered throne.

Knowing her sister, Josie was certain that Serena was going to free the 73 turkey, jump out of the truck with it, gather up the beggarly women and children, and disappear forever into the sidestreets and alleys of Juarez. They drove past an old Indian woman, her long braids silver gray in the sun, begging in front of Curley's Club. And that is how Josie imagined Serena years from that day—an ancient and withered creature, bare feet crusted with clay, too old to recognize her little sister. The vision made her believe that the middle of nowhere was exactly where she felt it was. She covered her chest with her arms.

"What's the matter? Don't tell me you're going to be sick," her father said. 74

75   "No. I'm fine. Can't you hurry?"

76   Seeing the fear in her face, Sancho told her gently that he had not yet figured out how to drive through cars without banging them up. Josie smiled and kept her hands over her heart.

77   When they approached the border patrolman's station, the turkey began gobbling away. "Oh, no," Josie cried and shut her eyes in terror for her sister.

78   "Oh, shit," her father said. "I hate this god-damned bridge." At that moment, the officer stuck his head into the pickup and asked for their citizenship.

79   "American," said Sancho.

80   "American," said Josie.

81   "Anything to declare? Any liquor or food?" he asked in an accusing way. While Sancho was assuring him that there was nothing to declare, the turkey gobbled again in a long stream of high-pitched gurgles that sent shivers up and down Josie's spine. She vowed to go into the cell with Serena when the search was ordered.

82   "What's that noise?" the patrolman wanted to know. Sancho shrugged and gave Josie and then the officer a look filled with the ignorance of the world.

83   Behind them, Serena began gobbling along with the bird and it was hard for them to tell one gobble from the another. Their mother pressed down on the horn of the Chevy and made it stick. Eduviges was ready to jump out of the car and save her daughter from a fate worse than death. In the middle of the racket, the officer's frown was turning into anger and he started yelling at Serena.

84   "American!" she yelled back and gobbled.

85   "What have you got there?" The officer pointed to the plastic-covered crate.

86   "It's a turkey," Serena shouted. "It's American, too." She kept gobbling along with the noise of the horn. Other drivers had begun honking with impatience.

87   The patrolman looked at her and yelled, "Sure it is! Don't move," he shouted toward Sancho.

88   Eduviges had opened the hood and was pretending not to know what to do. Rushing toward the officer, she grabbed him by the sleeve and pulled him away from the pickup. Confused by the din, he made gestures that Sancho took as permission to drive away. "Relax, *señora*. Please let go of my arm."

89   In the truck, Sancho was laughing like a maniac and wiping the tears and his nose on his sleeve. "Look at that, Josie. The guy is twice as big as your mother."

90   She was too scared to laugh and did not want to look. Several blocks into South Del Sapo, she was still trembling. Serena kept on gobbling in case they were being followed by the *migra* in unmarked cars.

91   Fifteen minutes later, Eduviges and Ofelia caught up with them on Alameda Street. Sancho signaled his wife to follow him into the vacant lot next to Don

Luis Leal's Famous Tex-Mex Diner. They left the turkey unattended and silent once more.

"Dumb bird," Sancho said. With great ceremony, he treated them to *menudo* 92 and *gorditas* washed down with as much Coca-Cola as they could drink. ✛

RESPONDING

1. "The Angel children were brought up on as many deportation stories as fairy tales and family legends" (paragraph 19). In a journal entry, discuss the possible psychological effects of such stories on young children.

2. Working individually or in a group, list examples of the bicultural aspects of the Angel family's lifestyle. Discuss the advantages and disadvantages of being bicultural.

3. Taking the turkey over the border could be viewed as humorous, serious, or even frightening depending on your point of view. Imagine you are one of the characters in the story such as Sancho, Eduviges, Serena, the patrolman, or an onlooker and write a letter reporting the incident to a friend.

4. Explain Sancho's reaction to the term "aliens" (paragraph 53). How does he define the term, and why is it so offensive to him? Write an essay explaining why his reaction is or is not excessive.

SANDRA CISNEROS

Born in Chicago in 1954, the poet and short-story writer Sandra Cisneros earned her bachelor's degree from Loyola University of Chicago in 1976 and her master's degree from the University of Iowa Writers Workshop in 1978. While teaching at the Latino Youth Alternative High School and working as a counselor in the Educational Opportunities Program at Loyola University of Chicago during the early 1980s, she served as an artist in residence for the Illinois Arts Council. Cisneros has also held teaching and administrative positions in Texas, teaching creative writing at the Austin Women's Peace House, serving as an artist-in-the-schools, and directing the Guadalupe Cultural Arts Center in San Antonio. Since 1988 she has been a guest writer in residence at the University of California at Berkeley, the University of California at Irvine, and the University of Michigan.

Her published works include the poetry volumes Bad Boys *(1980) and* My Wicked, Wicked Ways *(1987), the young adult novel* The House on Mango Street *(1983), and the short-story collection* Woman Hollering Creek and Other Stories *(1992). Her writing has earned her numerous fellowships and awards, among them the Roberta Holloway lectureship at the University of California at Berkeley (1988), two National Endowment for the Arts Creative Writing Fellowships (1982 and 1988), and the Before Columbus Book Award (1985).*

"Woman Hollering Creek" explores the way in which one character looks for strength in other people and in herself when she needs to make changes in her life.

❖

WOMAN HOLLERING CREEK

1   THE DAY DON SERAFÍN gave Juan Pedro Martínez Sánchez permission to take Cleófilas Enriqueta DeLeón Hernández as his bride, across her father's threshold, over several miles of dirt road and several miles of paved, over one border and beyond to a town four hours from the Rio Grande in the E.E.U.U., did he divine already the morning his daughter would raise her hand over her eyes, look south, and dream of returning to the chores that never ended, six good-for-nothing brothers, and one old man's complaints.

2   He had said, after all, in the hubbubb of parting: I am your father, I will never abandon you. He *had* said that, hadn't he, when he hugged and then let her go. But at the moment Cleófilas was busy looking for Chela, her maid of

honor, to fulfill their bouquet conspiracy. She would not remember her father's parting words until three years had passed since holding that ragged face in her hands. I am your father, I will never abandon you.

Only now that she was a mother, now when she and Juan Pedrito sat by   3
the creek's edge, did she remember. When a man and a woman love each other, how sometimes that love sours. But a parent's love for a child, a child's for its parents, was another thing entirely.

This is what Cleófilas thought evenings when Juan Pedro did not come   4
home, and she lay on her side of the bed listening to the hollow roar of the interstate, a distant dog barking, the pecan trees rustling like ladies in stiff petticoats—shh-shh-shh, shh-shh-shh, soothing her to sleep.

In the town where she grew up, there isn't very much to do except accompany   5
the aunts and godmothers to the house of one or the other to play cards. Or walk to the cinema to see this week's film again speckled and with one hair quivering annoyingly on the screen. Or to the center of town to order a milkshake that will appear in a day and a half as a pimple on her backside. Or to the girlfriend's house to watch the latest telenovela episode and try to copy the way the women comb their hair, wear their make-up.

But what Cleófilas has been waiting for, has been whispering and sighing   6
and giggling for, has been anticipating since she was old enough to lean against the window displays of gauze and butterflies and lace, is passion. Not the kind on the cover of the ¡Alarma! magazines, mind you, where the lover is photographed with the bloody fork she used to salvage her good name. But passion in its purest crystalline essence. The kind the books and songs and telenovelas describe when one finds, finally, the great love of one's life, and does whatever one can, must do, at whatever the cost. Tú o Nadie. You or No One. The title of the current favorite telenovela. The beautiful Lucía Méndez having to put up with all kinds of hardships of the heart, separation and betrayal, and loving, always loving no matter what, because *that* is the most important thing, and did you see Lucía Méndez on the Bayer aspirin commercials, wasn't she lovely? Does she dye her hair do you think? Cleófilas is going to go to the farmacia and buy a hair rinse because her girlfriend Chela will apply it, it's not that difficult at all. Because you didn't watch last night's episode when Lucía confessed she loved him more than anyone in her life. In her life! And she sings the song "You or No One" in the beginning and end of the show. Tú o Nadie. Somehow one ought to live one's life like that, don't you think? You or no one. Because to suffer for love is good. The pain all sweet somehow, in the end.

Seguin. She had liked the sound of it. Far away and lovely. Not like   7
Monclova, Coahuila. Ugly.

Seguín, Tejas. A nice sterling ring to it. The tinkle of money. She would   8
get to wear outfits like the women on the tele, like Lucía Méndez. And have a lovely house, and wouldn't Chela be jealous.

9 And yes, they will drive all the way to Laredo to get her wedding dress. That's what they say. Because Juan Pedro wants to get married right away, without a long engagement since he can't take off too much time from work. He has a very important position in Seguin with, with . . . a beer company I think. Or was it tires? Yes, he has to be back. So they will get married in the spring when he can take off work, and then they will drive off in his new pickup—did you see it?—to their new home in Seguin. Well, not exactly new, but they're going to repaint the house. You know newlyweds. New paint and new furniture. Why not? He can afford it. And later on add maybe a room or two for the children. May they be blessed with many. Well, you'll see. Cleófilas has always been so good with her sewing machine. A little whirr, whirr, whirr of the machine and ¡zas! Miracles. She's always been so clever that girl. Poor thing. And without even a mama to advise her on things like her wedding night. Well, may God help her. What with a father with a head like a burro, and those six clumsy brothers. Well, what do you think. Yes, I'm going to the wedding. Of course! The dress I want to wear just needs to be altered a teensy bit to bring it up to date. See, I saw a new style last night that I thought would suit me. Did you watch last night's episode of "And the Rich Also Cry"? Well, did you notice the dress the mother was wearing.

10 La mujer gritando. Such a funny name for such a lovely arroyo. Though no one could say whether the woman had hollered from anger or pain. The natives only knew the arroyo one crossed on the way to San Antonio, and then once again on the way back, was called Woman Hollering, a name no one from these parts questioned, little less understood. Pues, allá de los Indios, quien sabe—who knows, the townspeople shrugged, because it was of no concern to their lives how this trickle of water received its curious name.

11 What do you want to know for? Trini the laundromat attendant asked in the same gruff Spanish she always used whenever she gave Cleófilas change or yelled at her for something. First for putting too much soap in the machines. Later, for sitting on a washer. And still later, after Juan Pedrito was born, for not understanding that in this country you cannot let your baby walk around with no diaper and his pee-pee hanging out, it wasn't nice, entiendes? Pues.

12 How could Cleófilas explain to a woman like this why the name Woman Hollering fascinated her. Well, there was no sense talking to Trini.

13 On the other hand there were the neighbor ladies, one on either side of the house they rented near the arroyo. The woman Soledad on the left, the woman Dolores on the right.

14 The neighbor lady Soledad liked to call herself a widow though how she came to be one was a mystery. Her husband had either died, or run away with an ice house floozie, or simply had gone out for cigarettes one afternoon and never come back. It was hard to say which since Soledad, as a rule, didn't mention him.

15 In the other house lives la señora Dolores, kind and very sweet, but her

house smelled too much of incense and candles from the altars that burned continuously in memory of two sons who had died in the last war and one husband who had died shortly after from grief. The neighbor lady Dolores divided her time between the memory of these men and her garden, famous for its sunflowers—so tall they had to be supported with broom handles and old boards; red red cockscombs, fringed and bleeding a thick menstrual color; and, especially, roses whose sad scent reminded Cleófilas of the dead. Each Sunday la señora Dolores clipped the most beautiful of these flowers and arranged them on three modest headstones at the Seguin cemetery.

The neighbor ladies, Soledad, Dolores, they might've known once the name   16 of the arroyo before it turned English but they did not know now. They were too busy remembering the men who had left either through choice or circumstance and would never come back.

Pain or rage, Cleófilas wondered when she drove over the bridge the first   17 time as a newlywed and Juan Pedro had pointed it out. La mujer gritando, he had said, and she had laughed. Such a funny name for a creek so pretty and full of happily ever after.

The first time she had been so surprised she didn't cry out nor try to defend   18 herself. She had always said she would strike back if a man, any man, were to touch her.

But when the moment came, and he slapped her once, and then again, and   19 again, until the lip split and bled an orchid of blood, she didn't fight back, she didn't break into tears, she didn't run away as she imagined she might when she saw such things in the telenovelas.

In her own home her parents had never raised a hand to each other nor to   20 their children. Although she admitted she may have been brought up a little leniently as an only daughter—la consentida, the princess—there were some things she would never tolerate. Ever.

Instead, when it happened the first time, when they were barely man and   21 wife, she had been so stunned, it left her speechless, motionless, numb. She had done nothing but reach up to the heat on her mouth and stare at the blood on her hand as if even then she didn't understand

She could think of nothing to say, said nothing. Just stroked the dark curls   22 of the man who wept and would weep like a child, his tears of repentance and shame, this time and each.

The men at the ice house. From what she can tell, from the times during her   23 first year when still a newlywed she is invited and accompanies her husband, sits mute beside their conversation, waits and sips a beer until it grows warm, twists a paper napkin into a knot, then another into a fan, one into a rose, nods her head, smiles, yawns, politely grins, laughs at the appropriate moments, leans against her husband's sleeve, tugs at his elbow, and finally becomes good at predicting where the talk will lead.

From this Cleófilas concludes each is nightly trying to find the truth lying   24 at the bottom of the glass like a gold doubloon on the sea bottom. They want to tell each other what they want to tell themselves. But what is bumping like a helium balloon at the ceiling of the brain never finds its way out. It bubbles and rises, it gurgles in the throat, it rolls across the surface of the tongue, and erupts from the lips—a belch.

25   If they are lucky, there are tears at the end of the long night. At any given moment, the fists try to speak. They are dogs chasing their own tail before lying down to sleep, trying to find a way, a route, an out, and—finally—get some peace.

26   In the morning sometimes before he opens his eyes. Or after they have finished loving. Or at times when he is simply across from her at the table putting pieces of food into his mouth and chewing. Cleófilas thinks, this is the man I have waited my whole life for.

27   Not that he isn't a good man. She has to remind herself why she loves him when she changes the baby's Pampers, or when she mops the bathroom floor, or tries to make the curtains for the doorways without doors, or whiten the linen. Or wonder a little when he kicks the refrigerator and says he hates this shitty house and is going out where he won't be bothered with the baby's howling and her suspicious questions, and her requests to fix this and this and this because if she had any brains in her head she'd realize he's been up before the rooster earning his living to pay for the food in her belly and the roof over her head and would have to wake up again early the next day so why can't you just leave me in peace, woman.

28   He is not very tall, no, and he doesn't look like the men on the telenovelas. His face still scarred from acne. And he has a bit of a belly from all the beer he drinks. Well, he's always been husky.

29   This man who farts and belches and snores as well as laughs and kisses and holds her. Somehow this husband whose whiskers she finds each morning in the sink, whose shoes she must air each evening on the porch, this husband who cuts his fingernails in public, laughs loudly, curses like a man, and demands each course of dinner be served on a separate plate like at his mother's, as soon as he gets home, on time or late, and who doesn't care at all for music or telenovelas or romance or roses or the moon floating pearly over the arroyo, or through the bedroom window for that matter, shut the blinds and go back to sleep, this man, this father, this rival, this keeper, this lord, this master, this husband till kingdom come.

30   Slender like a hair. A washed cup set back on the shelf wrong side up. Her lipstick, and body talc, and hair brush all arranged in the bathroom a different way.

31   No. Her imagination. The house the same as always. Nothing.

32   Coming home from the hospital with her new son, her husband. Something comforting in discovering her house slippers beneath the bed, the faded housecoat where she left it on the bathroom hook. Her pillow. Their bed.

Sweet sweet homecoming. Sweet as the scent of face powder in the air,   33
jasmine, sticky liquor.

Smudged fingerprint on the door. Crushed cigarette in a glass. Wrinkle in   34
the brain crumpling to a crease.

Sometimes she thinks of her father's house. But how could she go back there?   35
What a disgrace. What would the neighbors say? Coming home like that with
one baby on her hip and one in the oven. Where's your husband?

The town of gossips. The town of dust and despair. Which she has traded   36
for this town of gossips. This town of dust, despair. Houses further apart
perhaps, though no more privacy because of it. No leafy zocalo in the center
of the town, though the murmur of talk is clear enough all the same. No huddled
whispering on the church steps each Sunday. Because here the whispering begins
at sunset at the ice house instead.

This town with its silly pride for a bronze pecan the size of a baby carriage   37
in front of the city hall. T.V. repair shop, drug store, hardware, dry cleaners,
chiropractor's, liquor store, bail bonds, empty storefront and nothing, nothing,
nothing of interest. Nowhere one could walk to any rate. Because the towns
here are built so that you have to depend on husbands. Or you stay home. Or
you drive. If you're rich enough to own, allowed to drive, your own car.

There is no place to go. Unless one counts the neighbor ladies. Soledad on   38
one side, Dolores on the other. Or the creek.

Don't go out there after dark, mi'jita. Stay near the house. No es bueno   39
para la salud. Mala suerte. Bad luck. Mal aire. You'll get sick and the baby too.
You'll catch a fright wandering about in the dark, and then you'll see how right
we were.

The stream sometimes only a muddy puddle in the summer, though now   40
in the springtime, because of the rains, a good-size alive thing, a thing with a
voice all its own, all day and all night calling in its high, silver voice. Is it La
Llorona, the weeping woman? La Llorona who drowned her own children.
Perhaps La Llorona is the one they named the creek after, she thinks, remembering all the stories she learned as a child.

La Llorona calling to her. She is sure of it. Cleófilas sets the baby's Donald   41
Duck blanket on the grass. Listens. The day sky turning to night. The baby
pulling up fistfuls of grass and laughing. La Llorona. Wonders if something as
quiet as this drives a woman to the darkness under the trees.

What she needs is . . . and made a gesture as if to yank a woman's buttocks to   42
his groin. Maximiliano the foul-smelling fool from across the road said this and
set the men laughing, but Cleófilas just muttered *grosero* and went on washing
dishes.

She knew he said it not because it was true, but more because it was he   43
who needed to sleep with a woman, instead of drinking each night at the ice
house and stumbling home alone.

44   Maximiliano who was said to have killed his wife in an ice house brawl when she came at him with a mop. I had to shoot, he had said, she was armed.

45   Their laughter outside the kitchen window. Her husband's, his friends'. Manolo, Beto, Efrain, el Perico. Maximiliano.

46   Was Cleófilas just exaggerating as her husband always said? It seemed the newspapers were full of such stories. This woman found on the side of the interstate. This one pushed from a moving car. This one's cadaver, this one unconscious, this one beaten blue. Her ex-husband, her husband, her lover, her father, her brother, her uncle, her friend, her co-worker. Always. The same grisly news in the pages of the daily, She dunked a glass under the soapy water for a moment—shivered.

47   He had thrown a book. Hers. From across the room. A hot welt across the cheek. She could forgive that. But what stung more was the fact it was *her* book, a love story by Corin Tellado, what she loved most now that she lived in the U.S., without a television set, without the telenovelas.

48   Except now and again when her husband was away and she could manage it, the few episodes glimpsed at the neighbor lady Soledad's house because Dolores didn't care for that sort of thing, though Soledad was often kind enough to retell what had happened on what episode of "Maria de Nadie," the poor Argentine county girl who had the ill fortune of falling in love with the beautiful son of the Arrocha family, the very family she worked for, whose roof she slept under and whose floors she vacuumed, while in that same house, with the dustbrooms and floor cleaners as witnesses, the square-jawed Juan Carlos Arrocha had uttered words of love, I love you, Maria, listen to me, mi querida, but it was she who had to say no, no, we are not of the same class, and remind him it was not in his place nor hers to fall in love, while all the while her heart was breaking, can you imagine.

49   Cleófilas thought her life would have to be like that, like a telenovela, only now the episodes got sadder and sadder. And there were no commercials in between for comic relief. And no happy ending in sight. She thought this when she sat with the baby out by the creek behind the house. Cleófilas de . . .? But somehow she would have to change her name to Topazio, or Yesenia, Cristal, Adriana, Stefania, Andrea, something more poetic than Cleófilas. Everything happened to women with names like jewels. But what happened to Cleófilas? Nothing. But a crack in the face.

50   Because the doctor has said so. She has to go. To make sure the new baby is alright, so there won't be any problems when he's born, and the appointment card says next Tuesday. Could he please take her. And that's all.

51   No, she won't mention it. She promises. If the doctor asks she can say she fell down the front steps or slipped when she was out in the back yard, slipped out back, she could tell him that. She has to go back next Tuesday, Juan Pedro, please, for the new baby. For their child.

She could write to her father and ask maybe for money, just a loan, for the   52
new baby's medical expenses. Well then if he'd rather she didn't. All right, she
won't. Please don't anymore. Please don't. She knows it's difficult saving money
with all the bills they have, but how else are they going to get out of debt with
the truck payments. And after the rent and the food and the electricity and the
gas and the water and the who-knows-what, well, there's hardly anything left.
But please, at least for the doctor visit. She won't ask for anything else. She has
to. Why is she so anxious? Because.

Because she is going to make sure the baby is not turned around backwards   53
this time to split her down the center. Yes. Next Tuesday at 5:30. I'll have Juan
Pedrito dressed and ready. But those are the only shoes he has. I'll polish them,
and we'll be ready. As soon as you come from work. We won't make you
ashamed.

Felice? It's me, Graciela.   54

No, I can't talk louder. I'm at work.   55

Look, I need kind of a favor. There's a patient, a lady here who's got a   56
problem.

Well, wait a minute. Are you listening to me or what?   57

I can't talk real loud 'cause her husband's in the next room.   58

Well, would you just listen.   59

I was going to do this sonogram on her—she's pregnant, right?—and she   60
just starts crying on me. Hijole, Felice! This poor lady's got black-and-blue
marks all over. I'm not kidding.

From her husband. Who else? Another one of those brides from across the   61
border. And her family's all in Mexico.

Shit. You think they're going to help her? Give me a break. This lady   62
doesn't even speak English. She hasn't been allowed to call home or write or
nothing. That's why I'm calling you.

She needs a ride.   63

Not to Mexico, you goof. Just to the Greyhound. In San Anto.   64

No, just a ride. She's got her own money. All you'd have to do is drop her   65
off in San Antonio on your way home. Come on, Felice. Please? If we don't
help her, who will? I'd drive her myself, but she needs to be on that bus before
her husband gets home from work. What do you say?

I don't know. Wait.   66

Right away she says. Tomorrow even.   67

Well, if tomorrow's no good for you . . .   68

It's a date, Felice. Thursday. At the Cash N Carry off I-80. Noon. She'll   69
be ready.

Oh, and her name's Cleófilas.   70

I don't know. One of those Mexican saints I guess. A martyr or something.   71

Cleófilas. C-L-E-O-F-I-L-A-S. Cle. O. Fi. Las. Write it down.   72

Thanks, Felice, When her kid's born she'll name her after us, right?   73

74   Yeah, you got it. A regular soap opera sometimes. Que vida, comadre. Bueno bye.

75   All morning that flutter of half fear, half doubt. At any moment Juan Pedro might appear in the doorway. On the street. At the Cash N Carry. Like in the dreams she dreamed.

76   There was that to think about, yes, until the woman in the pickup drove up. Then there wasn't time to think about anything but the pickup pointed towards San Antonio. Put your bags in the back and get in.

77   But when they drove across the arroyo, the driver opened her mouth and let out a yell as loud as any mariachi. Which startled not only Cleófilas, but Juan Pedrito as well.

78   Pues, look how cute. I scared you two, right? Sorry. Should've warned you. Every time I cross that bridge I do that. Because of the name, you know. Woman Hollering. Pues, I holler. She said this in a Spanish pocked with English and laughed. Did you ever notice, Felice continued, how nothing around here is named after a woman. Really. Unless she's the Virgin. I guess you're only famous if you're a virgin. She was laughing again.

79   That's why I like the name of that arroyo. Makes you want to holler like Tarzan, right?

80   Everything about this woman, this Felice, amazed Cleófilas. The fact that she drove a pickup. A pickup mind you, but when Cleófilas asked if it was her husband's, she said she didn't have a husband. The pickup was hers. She herself had chosen it. She herself was paying for it.

81   I used to have a Pontiac Sunbird. But those cars are for viejas. Pussy cars. Now this here is a *real* car.

82   What kind of talk was that coming from a woman, Cleófilas thought. But then again, Felice was like no woman she'd ever met. Can you imagine. When we crossed the arroyo she just started yelling like a crazy, she would say later to her father and brothers. Just like that. Who would've thought.

83   Who would've? Pain or rage perhaps but not a hoot like the one Felice had just let go. Makes you want to holler like Tarzan, Felice had said.

84   Then Felice began laughing again, but it wasn't Felice laughing. It was gurgling out of her own throat, a long ribbon of laughter, like water. ✥

RESPONDING

1. Cleófilas acts to remove herself and her child from a dangerous situation. Write about a time when you or someone you know or have read about took a risk to make a bad situation better.

2. Working individually or in a group, discuss the pros and cons of the options

available to Cleófilas. Which option would you have chosen if you were in her situation?

3.   Why does Cleófilas think that "Felice was like no woman she'd ever met" (paragraph 82)? Is that observation a compliment or a criticism? Explain Cleófilas's attitude toward Felice in an essay.

4.   Analyze the appeal of the telenovelas for Cleófilas. If her story appeared on a soap opera, how might the ending differ? Write an alternate ending for the story. Discuss the new possible endings with the class. In an essay, explain which ending you like best and why.

Graciela Limon

The critic and novelist Graciela Limón, who was born in East Los Angeles in 1938, earned her bachelor's degree from Marymount College, her master's from the University of the Américas, Mexico City, and her doctorate from UCLA in 1975. Since 1975 she has taught at Loyola Marymount University (Los Angeles), where she is currently chair of the Department of Modern Languages. She has published several fictional works, including Maria de Belen: The Autobiography of an Indian Woman *(1990),* In Search of Bernabé *(1993) which was awarded an American Bach Award in 1994, and* The Memories of Ana Calderón *(1994). Her work has been praised for its stark realism.*

The following selection is from In Search of Bernabé, *a novel inspired by the author's own journey to San Salvador as a part of the delegation in honor of the memory of four priests and their housekeepers who were murdered in 1989. This section explores the meaning of the border for newer immigrants.*

⊞

From IN SEARCH OF BERNABE

III

1   Most of the passengers planned to continue north but others, forced to stay in Mexico City because they had run short of money, began their farewells as soon as they got off the bus. Luz stood on the fringe of the bustling group staring vacantly around her. The cardboard box that held her things was on the pavement next to her feet. She had reached the end of the line, and she felt lost. At that moment Arturo approached her attempting an awkward goodbye.

2   "Bueno, Doña Luz, hasta la próxima . . ."

3   "Wait a minute!"

4   She gazed into his eyes with an intensity that made him shuffle nervously. Different thoughts were flashing through Luz's mind: Arturo wanted to reach Los Angeles, but didn't have the money. She had money, but not enough for the both of them. He had to stay in Mexico City, and her ticket took her only to Mexico City. He was alone, and she didn't want to be alone.

5   Luz walked to a nearby bench taking her box with one hand and Arturo's arm with the other one. She sat down and motioned him to join her. She paused to look around as she absorbed the disappointment stamped on the faces of so

many people. From the way a man on her right was embracing his children, Luz sensed they were soon to be parted. In front of her was a woman whose stooped head betrayed her loneliness.

Luz was quiet for a long time before she spoke. "Arturo, look around us! Everywhere there's sadness because people are separating from each other. You lost your money because I fought with the official. At least, I think that's why he took your money." 6

"No. That's not the reason. He would have taken it anyway." 7

"Well, maybe. Anyway, let me speak. I haven't told you that when I began my trip I really didn't know where I was going. All I knew was that I was looking for my son. Why did I head for Mexico City? I wasn't sure of that either. Perhaps it was because in my heart I hoped he would be doing what you are doing: heading north." 8

Luz sighed deeply. She was aware that Arturo was listening intently. "Now that I've reached this city, things have become a little bit clearer for me." Suddenly shifting her body to face Arturo she said, "Hijo, I want to go to Los Angeles. I think that maybe I'll find Bernabé there. Let me go with you." 9

Arturo jerked his head showing surprise. He was about to speak when Luz put her hand to his mouth. "I don't think I have enough money to go to Los Angeles right away. But even if I did, I don't want to go alone. So, let's stay here together, Arturo. I'll help you save money, and then we'll make our way up there. What do you say?" 10

He was smiling but his eyes contradicted his lips. Luz thought she understood and said, "Don't worry, Arturo. I can take care of myself. I won't be a burden." 11

He fastened his gaze on his feet. "I know you can take care of yourself. That's not it." Then looking at her he said, "Doña Luz, I hear Los Angeles is a big city." 12

"¿Y qué? So is Mexico City." 13

"Chances are that it will be impossible for you to find. . . ." 14

"I know! I know!" Luz was irked by the reality of his words. "But I must do it, Arturo, or else I'll stop breathing." 15

Arturo looked at her for a while. Then he smiled broadly as he shook his head in affirmation. Encouraged by this sudden turn, Luz rose to her feet, straightening her rumpled dress. She looked around as if searching for someone in particular. After a few minutes her eyes rested on a man, and motioning to Arturo to follow her, she approached the stranger. The man wore simple trousers, a white shirt, huaraches, and a straw sombrero which he carried in rough brown hands. 16

"Buenas tardes, Señor. May I speak to you for a moment?" 17

The man wrinkled his forehead in surprise but, with a smile, he responded, "Como no, Señora." 18

"Señor, this is my friend, Arturo Escutia." 19

Both men shook hands. 20

21   "Señor, as you probably can tell, we've come a long way . . . and we, well . . . we were wondering if you know . . ."

22   "You're from the south, aren't you?"

23   "Yes."

24   "And you need to find work so you can buy a ticket to finish your trip."

25   "Are there many like us?"

26   "Yes. Many."

27   The man gave them instructions on how to go to a laundry owned by a Spaniard. They would find the business in Colonia Cuauhtémoc, a district not far from the station. There, the man told Luz and Arturo, they would find temporary work.

28   "Muchas gracias, Señor, y hasta luego."

29   "¡Para servirles, Señora!"

30   Turning to Arturo, Luz said, "¡*Vámonos!*" as she tugged at his sleeve.

31   "But Doña Luz, why should we believe this man? How do we know he is telling the truth?"

32   "I know in my heart it's the truth. Now, let's go, Arturo. Every minute is important."

33   Luz picked up her belongings and Arturo followed her as she headed for the exit. When they walked through the wide doors of the station into a milling crowd, Luz instructed Arturo to ask someone how to find Colonia Cuauhtémoc; she would do the same.

34   No one paid attention to Luz or Arturo; they were pushed aside or ignored. A few passersbys shook their head negatively, others muttered unintelligible words. Finally a man, after taking a long pause to look in several directions, pointed towards the city's eastern district. Neither Luz nor Arturo questioned the instructions, and picking up their bundles, they walked for nearly an hour until Luz, fatigued and breathing heavily, stopped suddenly.

35   "Arturo, I have a strange feeling. Something tells me that this isn't the way to the laundry. Look. It's almost dark. Even if we did find the place I'm sure no one would be there now. We'd better think of something else to do."

36   "Let's go back to the station and spend the night there."

37   Luz and Arturo returned to the terminal in search of a bench or vacant corner in which to sleep but the station was jammed with transients and weary travelers who eyed one another suspiciously. The scramble for space was made more difficult by the station guards who shooed away anyone who looked like an overnighter. To evade the watchmen, those people searching for a place pretended to be waiting for a bus while they snatched short spurts of sleep.

38   "Hijo, we'll have to sleep standing up. There's nothing else to do. Tomorrow will come soon, and things will be better."

39   Next day, as daylight filtered through the city's thick layer of smoke and fog, Luz and Arturo began their search. This time Luz was intent on not burning her energy following ill-given instructions. By noon, she and Arturo had found their way to the laundry.

The owner of Lavandería La Regenta provided work for Luz and Arturo   40
without questions, and even though it turned out that the wages were low, the
work hours were regular. In the beginning Luz, who had only washed clothes
by hand, felt intimidated by the oversized machine she was instructed to operate.
But she forced herself to overcome her fears by following the instructions given
by the owner, even though the machine's grinding noises rattled her nerves.

Arturo, who was assigned to be a helper on the laundry's delivery truck,   41
had to deal with the weakness he still felt in his arms and legs. But like Luz, he
too forced himself to forget everything and do his work. He liked the job
because it took him deep into the city, where he felt sheltered by anonymity.

Luz and Arturo found a room in Colonia Cuauhtémoc the same day they   42
landed their jobs. The accommodations were meager. The room provided only
two cots along with a nightstand and a kitchenette, but they were grateful
because they had a place to stay when they were not working. Together they
began to save the few *pesos* that remained after they paid rent and bought food.

In the beginning, saving money was especially hard because they and other   43
Central Americans were routinely hunted out by Mexican immigration agents.
The harassment posed by the agents of *la Migra*, who sniffed out the foreigners'
telltale timidity, was constant and efficient. The pattern was always the same.

"Nombre y documentos, por favor."   44

Money seemed to be the only thing that mattered to the immigration   45
agents, and like the other workers, Luz and Arturo frequently found themselves
cornered by them and forced to produce whatever *pesos* they had. Once, Arturo
had to hide an entire day in a post office while a patrol car cruised the district.
As a result, he was docked a full day's wages.

Luz was frustrated by the intimidation, for she felt that the prospect of   46
reaching Los Angeles was slipping away. She could think of nothing else to do,
however; so, she resorted to tricks such as crying out loud, then shouting that
she was a poor, solitary, penniless woman who wanted to be friends with the
mexicanos while she spent a short time in their land. Even though it worked a
few times, Luz decided to abandon this tactic because she realized it only
embarrassed the officials into leaving her alone, and she feared they would pick
on her even more out of spite.

She decided to try another way. Luz began by offering gifts of food or drink   47
as a substitute for the money demanded by the agents. She also approached
them as if they had been her friends for years, using words and tones she had
picked up from fellow Mexican workers.

"¿Qué tal, mi sargento? Beautiful day, isn't it? All of you here are so lucky.   48
No wonder everyone in the world loves you. Here, try this little nothing that
I made for you today. How's the family? I hear you have a beautiful wife and
intelligent kids."

These words were always followed by Luz's loud, contagious laughter. The   49
ploy not only worked once or twice; its effects lasted. Soon those men looked
for Luz among the piles of soiled sheets and pillowcases, not for her money,

but for her food and flattery, and her loud laughter. Her success with offering food to *la Migra* made Luz think about peddling food to her fellow workers. She started a small business and soon she and Arturo were able to begin saving for their trek north.

50   They lived in Mexico City for more than a year, working every day except Sundays. When they finally had enough *pesos* to buy their tickets to Tijuana and to pay for the coyote who would guide them across the border into the United States, they felt they were ready to leave Mexico City. On the day their bus left the terminal at dawn, Luz and Arturo were so filled with anxiety that neither dared to share this with the other.

IV

51   Luz and Arturo arrived at the Tijuana bus terminal forty hours later, exhausted and bloated from sitting in their cramped seat. As soon as they stepped out of the bus, they were approached by a woman who asked them if they wanted to cross the border that night. Without waiting for an answer, she told them she could be their guide. The price was five hundred American dollars apiece.

52   Luz stared at the woman for a few moments, caught off guard by the suddenness of what was happening. More than her words, it was the woman's appearance that held Luz's attention. She was about thirty-five. Old enough, Luz figured, to have experience in her business. The woman was tall and slender, yet her body conveyed a muscular strength that gave Luz the impression that she would be able to lead them across the border.

53   The coyota returned Luz's gaze, evidently allowing time for the older woman to make up her mind. She took a step closer to Luz, who squinted as she concentrated on the woman's face. Luz regarded her dark skin and high forehead, and the deeply set eyes that steadily returned her questioning stare. With a glance, she took in the coyota's faded levis and plaid shirt under a shabby sweatshirt, and her eyes widened when she saw the woman's scratched, muddy cowboy boots. She had seen only men wear such shoes.

54   Luz again looked into the woman's eyes. She was tough, and Luz knew that she had to drive a hard bargain. She began to cry. "¡Señora, por favor! Have a heart! How can you charge so much? We're poor people who have come a long way. Where do you think we can find so many dólares? All we have is one hundred dollars to cover the two of us. Please! For the love of your mamacita!"

55   The woman crossed her arms over her chest and laughed out loud as she looked into Luz's eyes. She spoke firmly. "Señora, I'm not in the habit of eating fairy tales for dinner. You've been in Mexico City for a long time. I have eyes, don't I? I can tell that you're not starving. Both of you have eaten a lot of enchiladas and tacos. Just look at those nalgas!"

56   She gave Luz a quick, hard smack on her behind. Then, ignoring the older woman's look of outrage, the coyota continued to speak rapidly. "Look, Señora.

Just to show you that I have feelings, I'll consider guiding the both of you at the reduced rate of seven hundred dollars. Half now; the rest when I get you to Los Angeles. Take it or leave it!"

Luz knew that she was facing her match. She answered with one word. 57 "Bueno."

The coyota led them to a man who was standing nearby. He was wearing 58 a long overcoat, inappropriate for the sultry weather in Tijuana. The coat had a purpose though, for it concealed deep inner pockets which were filled with money. The coyota pulled Luz nearer to the man, then whispered into her ear. "This man will change your *pesos* into American dollars. A good rate, I guarantee."

When Arturo began to move closer, the coyota turned on him. "You stay 59 over there!"

Arturo obeyed. 60

Even though she felt distrust, Luz decided that she and Arturo had no 61 alternative. However, she needed to speak with him, so she pulled him to the side. "Hijo, we're taking a big chance. We can be robbed, even killed. Remember the stories we've been hearing since we left home. But what can we do? We need someone to help us get across, so what does it matter if it's this one, or someone else? What do you say?"

Arturo agreed with her. "Let's try to make it to the other side. The sooner 62 the better. I think you made a good bargain. We have the money, don't we?"

"With a little left over for when we get to Los Angeles." 63

Before they returned to where the others were waiting, she turned to a wall. 64 She didn't want anyone to see what she was doing. Luz withdrew the amount of *pesos* she estimated she could exchange for a little more than seven hundred American dollars. She walked over to the money vendor, and no sooner had the man placed the green bills on her palm, then she heard the coyota's sharp voice. "Three hundred and fifty dollars, por favor!"

She signaled Luz and Arturo to follow her to a waiting car. They went as 65 far as Mesa Otay, the last stretch of land between Mexico and California. There, the coyota instructed them to wait until it got dark. Finally, when Luz could barely see her hand in front of her, the woman gave the signal. "¡Vámonos!"

They walked together under the cover of darkness. As Luz and Arturo 66 trekked behind the woman, they sensed that they were not alone, that other people were also following. Suddenly someone issued a warning, "¡La Migra! ¡Cuidado!" The coyota turned with unexpected speed, and murmured one word, "¡Abajo!"

All three fell to the ground, clinging to it, melting into it, hoping that it 67 would split open so that they could crawl into its safety. Unexpectedly a light flashed on. Like a giant eye, it seemed to be coming from somewhere in the sky, slowly scanning the terrain. No one moved. All that could be heard were the crickets and the dry grass rasping in the mild breeze. The light had not detected the bodies crouched behind bushes and rocks. It flashed out as suddenly as it had gone on.

68 "¡Vámonos!" The coyota was again on her feet and moving. They continued in the dark for hours over rough, rocky terrain. The coyota was sure footed but Luz and Arturo bumped into rocks and tripped over gopher holes. Luz had not rested or eaten since she had gotten off the bus. She was fatigued but she pushed herself fearing she would be left behind if she stopped. Arturo was exhausted too, but he knew that he still had reserves of energy, enough for himself and for Luz.

69 Dawn was breaking as they ascended a hill. Upon reaching the summit, they were struck with awe at the sight that spread beneath their feet. Their heavy breathing stopped abruptly as their eyes glowed in disbelief. Below, even though diffused by dawn's advancing light, was an illuminated sea of streets and buildings. A blur of neon formed a mass of light and color, edged by a highway that was a ribbon of liquid silver. Luz and Arturo wondered if fatigue had caused their eyes to trick them because as far as they could see there was brilliance, limited only in the distance by a vast ocean. To their left, they saw the lights of San Diego unfolding beneath them, and their hearts stopped when they realized that farther north, where their eyes could not see, was their destination.

70 Without thinking, Luz and Arturo threw their arms around one another and wept.

V

71 The lights of San Diego receded behind them. The coyota had guided Luz and Arturo over an inland trail, taking them past the U.S. Immigration station at San Onofre, and then down to connect with the highway. A man in a car was waiting for them a few yards beyond Las Pulgas Road on California Interstate 5.

72 The driver got out of the car as they approached, extending a rough hand first to Luz, and then to Arturo. "Me llamo Ordaz."

73 Ordaz turned to the coyota and spoke in English. His words were casual, as if he had seen her only hours before. "You're late. I was beginning to worry."

74 "The old bag slowed me down."

75 The coyota spoke to the man in English, knowing that her clients were unable to understand her. Then, she switched to Spanish to introduce herself to Luz and Arturo. "Me llamo Petra Traslaviña. I was born back in San Ysidro on a dairy farm. I speak English and Spanish."

76 There was little talk among them beyond this first encounter. The four piled into a battered Pontiac station wagon, and with Ordaz at the wheel, they headed north. The woman pulled out a pack of Mexican cigarettes, smoking one after the other, until Ordaz started to cough. He opened the window complaining, "Por favor, Petra, you wanna choke us to death?"

"Shut up!" she retorted rapidly, slurring the English *sh*. 77

The phrase engraved itself in Luz's memory. She liked the sound of it. She 78 liked its effect even more, since she noticed that Ordaz was silenced by the magical phrase. Inwardly, Luz practiced her first English words, repeating them over and again under her breath.

Luz and Arturo were quiet during the trip mainly because they were 79 frightened by the speed at which Ordaz was driving. As she looked out over the coyota's shoulder, Luz knew that she didn't like what she was feeling and hearing. She even disliked the smell of the air, and she felt especially threatened by the early morning fog. When the headlights of oncoming cars broke the grayness, her eyes squinted with pain.

The hours seemed endless, and they were relieved when Ordaz finally 80 steered the Pontiac off the freeway and onto the streets of Los Angeles. Like children, Luz and Arturo looked around, craning their necks, curiously peering through the windows and seeing that people waited for their turn to step onto the street. Luz thought it was silly the way those people moved in groups. No one ran out onto the street, leaping, jumping, dodging cars as happened in Mexico City and back home. Right away, she missed the vendors peddling wares, and the stands with food and drink.

Suddenly, Luz was struck by the thought that she didn't know where the 81 coyota was taking them. As if reading Luz's mind, the woman asked, "Do you have a place you want me to take you to?"

Rattled by the question, Luz responded timidly. "No. We didn't have time 82 to think."

"I thought so. It's the same with all of you." 83

The coyota was quiet for a while before she whispered to Ordaz, who shook 84 his head in response. They engaged in a heated exchange of words in English, the driver obviously disagreeing with what the coyota was proposing. Finally, seeming to have nothing more to say, Ordaz shrugged his shoulders, apparently accepting defeat. The coyota turned to her passengers.

"Vieja, I know of a place where you two can find a roof and a meal until 85 you find work. But . . ." She was hesitating. "¡Mierda! . . . just don't tell them I brought you. They don't like me because I charge you people money."

What she said next was muttered and garbled. Luz and Arturo did not 86 understand her so they kept quiet, feeling slightly uneasy and confused. By this time Ordaz was on Cahuenga Boulevard in Hollywood. He turned up a short street, and pulled into the parking lot of Saint Turibius Church, where the battered wagon spurted, then came to a stand-still.

"Hasta aquí. You've arrived." 87

The coyota was looking directly at Luz, who thought she detected a warning 88 sign in the woman's eyes. "It was easy this time, Señora. Remember, don't get caught by *la Migra*, because it might not be so good the next time around. But if that happens, you know that you can find me at the station in Tijuana."

89   Again, the coyota seemed to be fumbling for words. Then she said, "Just don't get any funny ideas hanging around these people. I mean, they love to call themselves voluntarios, and they'll do anything for nothing. Yo no soy así. I'll charge you money all over again, believe me!"

90   The coyota seemed embarrassed. Stiffly, she shifted in her seat, pointing at a two-story, Spanish-style house next to the church.

91   "See that house?"

92   Luz nodded.

93   "Bueno. Just walk up to the front door, knock, and tell them who you are, and where you're from. They'll be good to you. But, as I already told you, don't mention me."

94   She turned to Arturo. "Take care of yourself, Muchacho. I've known a few like you who have gotten themselves killed out there."

95   With her chin, she pointed toward the street. When Arturo opened his mouth to speak, the coyota cut him off curtly. "My three hundred and fifty dollars, por favor."

96   She stretched out her hand in Luz's direction without realizing that her words about other young men who resembled Arturo had had an impact on Luz. "Petra, have you by any chance met my son? His name is Bernabé and he looks like this young man."

97   The coyota looked into Luz's eyes. When she spoke her voice was almost soft. "They all look like Arturo, Madre. They all have the same fever in their eyes. How could I possibly know your son from all the rest?"

98   Luz's heart shuddered when the coyota called her madre. Something told her that the woman did know Bernabé. This thought filled her with new hope, and she gladly reached into her purse. She put the money into the coyota's hand, saying, "Hasta pronto. I hope, Petra, that our paths will cross again sooner or later."

99   Luz and Arturo were handed the small bundles they had brought with them from Mexico City. As they stepped out of the car, the engine cranked on, backfiring loudly. When it disappeared into the flow of traffic, both realized that even though only three days had passed since they had left Mexico, they had crossed over into a world unknown to them. They were aware that they were facing days and months, perhaps even years, filled with dangers neither of them could imagine.

100   Feeling apprehensive they were silent as they approached the large house that their guide had pointed out. They didn't know that the building had been a convent and that it was now a refuge run by priests and other volunteers. Neither realized that they were entering a sanctuary for the displaced and for those without documents or jobs. When they were shown in, Luz and Arturo were surprised at how warmly they were received. No one asked any questions. Afterwards, they were given food to eat and a place to sleep. ✠

RESPONDING

1. In a journal entry, explain how Petra does or does not fit your expectations of a person who leads people across the border into the United States illegally.

2. Working individually or in a group, list the arguments for or against open borders. Share your ideas with the class.

3. In an essay, compare Petra and Luz. How would you describe the two women? Do they share more similarities or differences? How do you account for the differences?

4. Write Petra's biography. How and why do you think she become a coyota? Or write a story about what you think will happen to Luz or Arturo in Los Angeles.

HECTOR CALDERON

Héctor Calderón was born in the California border town of Calexico in 1945. He earned undergraduate degrees from UCLA (1968) and California State University of Los Angeles (1972), a master's degree from the University of California at Irvine (1975), and a doctorate in Latin American literature and comparative literature from Yale University (1981). He has taught at Stanford, Yale, and Scripps College, and is currently professor of Spanish American and Chicano Literature at UCLA. Calderón has published numerous articles in his field and is the author of Conciencia y lenguaje en el "Quijote" y "El obsceno pájaro de la noche" *(1987), and he is coeditor of* Criticism in the Borderlands: Studies in Chicano Literature, Culture, and Ideology *(1991). Currently he is at work on* Contemporary Chicano Narrative: A Tradition and Its Forms.*

The following essay was written specifically for this book in 1990. Here Calderón uses his childhood experiences of growing up in a California border town as a backdrop for exploring Chicano heritage.

⁜

REINVENTING THE BORDER

I

The creators of borders . . . are . . . great pretenders. They post their projects in the world with the sturdiest available signs and hope that conventions (or, in the instance of California, a language law) will keep them in place. But even as the first stakes are driven, the earth itself, in all its intractable shiftiness, moves toward displacement.[1]

1 For the first eighteen years of my life the border, the line or *la línea*, was a daily presence. From the north end of the Imperial Valley in Brawley, Highway 86 winds down past agricultural fields and several cities—Imperial, El Centro, and Heber—to arrive eventually (as Highway 111) at the very limits of the American Southwest at the border, at Calexico, California. I, who grew up on Highway 111, also Imperial Avenue, four blocks from *la línea*, would rather think of the border not as a limit but as both a cultural and historical crossroads; for Calexico, like no other border town I know, has a mirror held up to it in Mexicali, Baja

---

1. Houston A. Baker, Jr., "LimIts of the Border." (unpublished)

California. Both cities have been historical and cultural reflections of each other; both the same, yet quite different.

Calexico began in the 1890s as an encampment for laborers in a water diversion project that was to transform an area of the Sonora desert into one of the most productive agricultural regions of both the United States and Mexico. Mexicali, which had been an early extension of Calexico, rapidly outgrew its sister city. By the 1950s, and throughout my childhood, Calexico remained a dusty border town of eleven thousand, while Mexicali, the capital of Baja California del Norte, was a thriving (as only Mexican cities can thrive), tumultuous city of one hundred thousand. Nowadays, Calexico boasts a population of twenty-two thousand; I would wager that the population of Mexicali and its surrounding valleys is close to one million, with both its economy and its population boosted by assembly plants, *maquiladoras*, built since 1968 by U.S. companies on the Mexican side under the Border Industrial Program.

Both cities, ingeniously named around 1900 by a Mr. L. M. Holt, are, in fact, a single economic entity separated by a fence constructed in this century. Commercial traffic has flowed more or less freely across the border. Many Mexican families from Calexico, including mine, would "cross the line" into Mexicali three or four days of the week, whether to visit relatives, to shop or dine, or to seek any number of professional or medical services. The Mexicali upper crust would frequent our Calexico stores, while the lower class would compete with us for jobs as clerks, domestics, and, most important of all, agricultural workers. At 4:00 A.M. the sleeping border town would awaken, and the Calexico downtown, the four blocks on Second Street, would be busier than at any other time of the day with both foot and auto traffic on the way to "The Hole," *el hoyo*. At El Hoyo, labor contractors and their hawkers awaited men, women, and children, in summer taking them as far north as Indio to harvest Thompson seedless grapes and in winter as near as the outskirts of Holtville or El Centro to pick carrots or lettuce. The Imperial Valley, you see, has a year-around growing season; it is where the "sun spends the winter"; it is also where migrant worker families would return from northern California, from as far as Napa and California's central valley, to work on winter crops.

During the 1940s and '50s in this poor, working-class town, we were reminded of both what we were and what we were not. To the Euro-American minority of ranchers, shopkeepers, clerks, teachers, and government officials, we were not real Americans: we were foreigners, Mexicans. To our brothers and sisters on the other side of the line, we were *pochos*: inauthentic, Americanized Mexicans, identifiable by our mutilated pachuco Spanish and our dress, "con lisas y tramados y calcos siempre bien shiniados."[2] I grew up *mestizo* and *rascuachi*, impure and lower class, in Calecia (Calexico) and Chikis (Mexicali), listening with my family to Spanish-language radio on XECL, enjoying the

2

3

4

2. With *lisas* and *tramados* and always well-shined shoes. *Lisas* are a special type of loose fitting, long sleeve shirt worn buttoned to the neck. *Tramados* are baggy khaki pants.

African rhythms of the mambo and the chachachá; the great big bands of Luis Alcaraz and Pérez Prado; the German-influenced Banda de Sinaloa; the border *corridos* and *norteña* polkas sung by the Alegres de Terán; the national idols of mariachi music, Jorge Negrete, Pedro Infante, Lola Beltrán, José Alfredo Jiménez, Amalia Mendoza; the romantic ballads composed by Augustín Lara interpreted by the Trío Los Panchos, Pedro Vargas, or Toña la Negra. Fridays were reserved for the Aztec Theatre, where we both laughed and cried to Mexican films by the exiled Spanish director Luis Buñuel or starring the Mexican national hero Cantinflas.

5   Many of our daily and seasonal activities were still dictated by Mexican oral and cultural traditions handed down to our family by our grandmother. Before we acquired a television set, our grandmother would narrate tales every night. However, our world was rapidly changing. The alternative to the Mexican radio station, XECL, was the appropriately named KROP of Brawley, on which we listened to R&B and rockabilly as they become rock 'n roll. We danced to James Brown, Little Richard, Chuck Berry, Laverne Baker, Buddy Holly and Ritchie Valens, the Platters, doo-wop, and Elvis and the Everlys—even Hank Williams and Patsy Cline on the "West Side of Your Hit Parade." We really hit the big time when the Ike and Tina Turner Revue came to the El Centro National Guard Armory and Little Richard played at the Mexicali Gimnasio. And yes, the Cisco Kid was a friend of mine.

6   This multicultural lens through which we viewed our world certainly made us "Mexicans" different from Euro-American Calexicans. However, in school we were told, assured, that we were white, Spanish, descendants of the conquistadors. Many years later, as I read my birth certificate, I think about how much our world has changed, for my race in 1945 was identified as white. But despite this, and even though we were legal citizens and should have been treated equally, we attended school in segregated classrooms. We were still, after all, foreigners, the children of Mexicans who had arrived in large numbers in the first decades of this century to play a significant role as agricultural laborers in a region that was undergoing a major economic transformation. My parents arrived shortly after the Mexican Revolution.[3] My mother belonged to a migrant worker family that traveled up and down California's central valley; my father, like all the males in his family, worked for the Southern Pacific Railroad.

7   These ethnic and class contradictions come back to me as I recall our most important annual festive occasion: the parade and pageant known as the Calexico Desert Cavalcade. Begun in the Depression years to boost the morale of the border community, the pageant was the invention of a Mrs. Keller, who had the support of the editor of the Calexico *Chronicle*, the local newspaper, and of the president of the Chamber of Commerce and representatives of the city's service clubs. This reenactment of California's past began, in the words of the organ-

3. Mexican Revolution of 1910.

izing committee, "with the stout-hearted pioneers who brought God and civilization to the Southwest." My fourth-grade experience is especially memorable: dressed like all my classmates as a Plains Indian in feathers and buckskin, I fell in behind the gallant Juan Bautista de Anza and kindly, black-robed padres as we paraded past our two important side-by-side architectural landmarks, the neo-Spanish Hotel de Anza and the mission-like Our Lady of Guadalupe Catholic Church, on our way to Monterrey in Alta California. That de Anza did not establish a Mexican settlement in the area in 1775 was not important to some Calexicans. Actually, de Anza had the more important task of establishing an overland route from what is now southern Arizona to Alta California, a task made easier by existing Native American trails. It also did not matter to the Cavalcade organizers that their activities made no sense given the cultural, historical, and economic realities of this overwhelmingly Mexican town. The Cavalcade probably made no sense either to Mrs. Yokum, Pete Emmett, or Lucille, our African American neighbors, or to Mar Chan, our corner grocer.

We in the Southwest were never so different from our friends and relatives   8
across the border in Mexico as when we asserted this, our Spanish heritage. Though biologically and culturally we were indistinct from one another—we were all Mexican *mestizos*—we had different national cultural heritages and ideologies imposed from above by educators, civic leaders, and government officials. Just a short distance across the border, buildings and monuments bore the names of Mexican revolutionary leaders like Obregón and Cárdenas. Not Spanish, but Native American culture had been purified into their norm of the classic after the Mexican Revolution of 1910. From José Vasconcelos's *La raza cósmica (The Cosmic Race)* of 1926 to Octavio Paz's *El laberinto de la soledad (The Labyrinth of Solitude)* of 1949, Native American culture was not only Mexico's historical base, but also its possibility for the future. In the idealized Mexican historical drama, Cuauhtémoc, Fallen Eagle, the last Aztec emperor, became the nation's hero, and Cortés, Spanish conqueror, became the archvillain. These different popular and intellectual traditions reveal why, until the Chicano movement of the 1960s, one side of the border was "Spanish" and the other "Mexican," although we shared the same Mexican-*mestizo* culture.

II

Perhaps the single most influential agent of Euro-American cultural domination   9
was Charles F. Lummis, whose lifelong activities and writings changed the image of a region, Mexican America, that had been acquired through military conquest some thirty-six years prior to his arrival in Santa Fe, New Mexico, in 1884. In 1925, three years before his death, Lummis boasted in *Mesa, Cañon and Pueblo*, that he had been the first to apply the generic name "Southwest," or more specifically, "Spanish Southwest," to the million square miles that include New Mexico, Arizona, southern California, and parts of Colorado, Utah, and Texas.

In a span of nine years, from 1891 to 1899, Lummis published eleven books, changing what was a physical and cultural desert into a land internationally known for its seductive natural and cultural attractions. Though in truth an amateur inclined toward self-promotion and melodramatic and hyperbolic writing, Lummis became the founder of the "Southwest genre," recognized by both professionals and the popular media as the undisputed authority on the history, anthropology, and folklore of the Southwest.

10 In the West, Lummis discovered for his readers a culture much like that of the fictional characters and settings of romantic literature. Unlike the East, the West had an authentic folk culture of simple and picturesque, yet dignified, souls still existing in a pastoral or agricultural mode of production undisturbed by the modern world. So taken was Lummis by the alien culture he encountered that he adopted it as his own; he learned Spanish, took on the name of Don Carlos, and was fond of posing for photographs in Spanish, Western, Apache, and Navajo attire. He was a promoter of "Spanish" architecture and established the Landmarks Club to revive the California missions. He founded the Southwest Museum in Los Angeles to house his collections of Native American artifacts.

11 Like other foreigners who make native culture their own, however, Lummis also had a conservative and patronizing side. He was intent on writing only about the most folkloric and romantic elements of Native American and *mestizo* culture. Thus in his first books, *A New Mexico David* (1891) and *The Land of Poco Tiempo* (1893), Lummis reveals his attraction to courtly dons, beautiful, dark-eyed Spanish señoritas, innocent Indian children, kind Mexican peons, witches, liturgical feast days, medieval-style penitents, haciendas, burros, carretas, and sunshine. Charmed by his "child-hearted" Spanish, Lummis became an apologist for the Spanish conquest of the Americas. His early book, *The Spanish Pioneers* (1893), is a history of the heroic padres and gallant Spaniards who brought God and civilization to the Americas.

12 Of course, the past was not just a romance, and the present was more than Mexicans resting against adobe. This strategy of glorifying the past ignored the historical fact that the land upon which Lummis set foot in 1884 was conquered Mexican territory. For Lummis, it was as if Spain had become the United States without centuries of racial and cultural mixture. Yet Lummis's view of the conquest and colonization of Arizona, California, New Mexico, and Texas as the golden age of Hispanic culture in the Southwest became a standard interpretation of Euro-American and Hispanic academic scholarship early in the twentieth century, and it continues to flourish in the popular imagination in literature, mass media images and Hollywood films and in the celebrations of Spanish fiesta days throughout the Southwest.

III

13 But what about the cultural changes during the viceroyalty of New Spain and the young Mexican nation? These changes created new American cultural

traditions throughout the years from the conquest of Mexico in 1521 to the establishment of Santa Fe in 1610 and down to the growth of Arizona, California, New Mexico, and Texas in the twentieth century. On these issues virtually nothing was written in the United States until the reinvention of the border from a Chicano perspective. I am referring to Américo Paredes's ground-breaking study in 1958, *"With His Pistol in His Hand": A Border Ballad and Its Hero.* As the title indicates, the book is a study of folk balladry along the Texas lower Rio Grande border, from the two Laredos in the north to Brownsville and Matamoros on the Gulf of Mexico. As a work of scholarship—it was Paredes's doctoral dissertation, presented in 1956 to the English department at the University of Texas at Austin—it did not differ from traditional studies. The author established a theory of genesis for border balladry, tracing its development from its origins in the Spanish *romance* to the Texas-Mexican *corrido*. But the book was more than this; it was a highly conscious, imaginative act of resistance that established for Chicanos a definition for the border, which is to say, not as a line but as Greater Mexico, a historically determined geopolitical zone of military, cultural, and linguistic conflict. For me, when I came upon Paredes's book by accident as a student at UCLA in 1965, it was the answer to the silencing of our voices, the stereotyping of our culture, and the reification of our history that resulted from the Southwest genre.

It is difficult to describe the complexity of Paredes's study. It is a hybrid   14
form, blurring the boundaries between genres and disciplines; it is part history, anthropology, folklore, and fiction. It is a reconstruction of the history of the lower Río Grande Valley from Spanish colonization in 1749 to the displacement of a Mexican ranching culture by large-scale farming in the 1930s and '40s to the migrant worker culture of the post–World War II era. A graduate student at Austin faced up to the myth of the Texas Rangers and the white supremacist attitudes of Texas scholar Walter Prescott Webb, who had written in *The Texas Rangers* (1936) that Mexican blood "was no better than ditch water." Paredes dared to utter the unspeakable: that the development of a Texas-Mexican pastoral mode of production, a ranching culture, that had emerged from the mixture of Spanish and Native American elements and was beginning to extend up from the Rio Grande to the Nueces River, was cut short in 1836 and 1848 by a "restless and acquisitive people, exercising the rights of conquest."

"With His Pistol in His Hand" is also a theory of culture by a native   15
anthropologist who understood that culture is not necessarily consensual but conflictual. Given the current temper of anthropological studies, in which the question of the objective gaze of the observer is being displaced by the acknowledgement of the institutional and political situation of the discipline, Paredes was ahead of his time. He turned his scholarly attention to the voices of his people, to the *corridos*, the ballads, that he had heard as a child, and chose to study the "Corrido de Gregorio Cortez," the ballad of a Texas-Mexican vaquero who in 1901 had been wrongly accused of killing an Anglo sheriff. Unlike earlier scholars, Paredes studied the oral tradition in its context, to understand how it

had developed. According to Paredes, after 1836 the Spanish *romance* developed into the *corrido* as a result of the border conflicts that became its dominant theme: the protagonist of the *corrido* defends his rights with his pistol in his hand. Other border heroes preceded and followed Cortez: Juan Nepomuceno Cortina, from Brownsville, who led a rebellion in 1859; Catarino Garza, of Brownsville-Matamoros, who was probably the first to rise up against the Mexican dictator Porfirio Diaz in 1890; and Aniceto Pizaña, who led a 1915 rebellion against the state of Texas.

16   While most critics of Chicano literature have focused their attention on Gregorio Cortez as the complete and legitimate Texas-Mexican persona whose life of struggle was worthy of being told, I would rather think of Paredes as the writer who made the Chicano genre possible. After poking fun at the biased scholarship of his "objective" colleagues at the University of Texas in Chapter I, "The Country," the Texas-Mexican trickster Paredes disappears in Chapter II, "The Legend of Gregorio Cortez," giving way to a third-person plural narrative, told in the anonymous voices of the elders of the tribe who gather at night to tell the legend. Paredes transcribes and translates a group storytelling performance, so that, through his individual talents and inventive energy as a writer, the interests of the community are represented. As the elders relive the exploits of Gregorio Cortez, in a retelling spiced with humor and linguistic jokes, the hero becomes the embodiment of the cultural values that developed during a history of conflict and resistance. In Chapter IV, "The Hero's Progress," Paredes returns to this storytelling situation, explaining that the legend as it appears in Chapter II is his own creation; he put together those parts that seemed to him furthest removed from fact and the most revealing of folk attitudes. This narrative stance, with its folkloric, anthropological, and historical elements, seems to me the inner form of much of Chicano literature, from Tomás Rivera's *y no se lo tragó la tierra/And the Earth Did Not Part* (1971) and Rolando Hinojosa's *Klail City Death Trip Series* (1973–1989) to Sandra Cisneros's *The House on Mango Street* and Gloria Anzaldúa's *Borderlands/La Frontera: The New Mestiza* (1987).

IV

17   Whenever Chicanas or Chicanos write on behalf of their community, the border has always loomed in the background. This is true whether it is a real historical or cultural crossing back and forth between the United States and Mexico or a crossing of more symbolic barriers, as in confronting issues of racism and language, gender, sexual, and class differences. These issues found their way to paper in the early work of Jovita González (1930), Américo Paredes (1958), and Ernesto Galarza (1964), and also appear in the work of the writers of the Chicano movement selected for this volume.

18   Given these scholarly and creative traditions and the national and international preoccupation with the question of the border, it is not surprising that

the Chicana lesbian activist Gloria Anzaldúa in her *Borderlands/La Frontera: The New Mestiza* (1987) should combine an autobiographical account with a reconceptualization of the border. Hers is a new historical and metaphorical version. For her, borders are established to protect what is "ours" from danger, from the "alien," because they are also places inhabited by what is forbidden. For those in power, border zones are inhabited by Chicanos, African Americans, Native Americans, Asian Americans, mulattos, *mestizos*, gays, lesbians, "wetbacks," illegals—in short, all those who are judged to be illegitimate. To sum up in another way, borders are those spaces, both geographical and conceptual, where the contradictions of power and repression, resistance and rebellion, are painfully visible.

To really know border zones, one has to overcome barriers, to be *atravesada*, 19 a border crosser. Anzaldúa is a border writer who lives her contradictions at various levels. She is no longer a quiet woman. She speaks out and confronts her own Texas-Mexican patriarchal and heterosexist culture. She writes in both English and Spanish to find her own voice and rejects any linguistic inferiority imposed by nationalists from both sides of the border. As she explains, Chicano language was invented to communicate realities and values belonging to a border zone.

Like Paredes before her, Anzaldúa retells the history of Anglo-Texan 20 domination of the Río Grande border; however, she bears witness to land fraud and usurpation suffered by both of her grandmothers. As she matured through the decade of the fifties, she saw her borderlands parcelled out for the benefit of U.S. companies. Like other Texas-Mexican families displaced from their ancestral homeland, the Anzaldúas became sharecroppers. The transformation of the Río Grande Valley did not stop at *la línea*. Nowadays, observes Anzaldúa, U.S. companies (RCA, Fairchild, Litton, Zenith, Motorola, among others) control the border economy through their assembly plants, the *maquiladoras*, whose workforces are mostly women. These new industrial forces have displaced older rural social and cultural structures.

V

Anzaldúa's account should be inserted within a new historical problematic along 21 the border: The dividing lines between north and south, First and Third World, are being effaced even as I write. We are witnessing dramatic demographic changes in the West and Southwest, and in northern Mexico, that will play a decisive role in the development of Chicano-Latino culture. Since the 1950s the population of major Mexican border towns, from Tijuana, on the Pacific Ocean, to Matamoros, on the Gulf of Mexico, has more than quadrupled, because women, men, and children from Mexico, Central America, and the Caribbean are flocking to these cities as points of entry into the United States, to work in U.S. assembly plants on the Mexican side, or to take advantage of a growing international business and tourist trade. As if in a García Márquez tale, one of the largest flea markets in the Southwest has sprung up in an empty field on the outskirts of Calexico. The promise of inexpensive U.S. products offered by Asian entrepreneurs from Los Angeles draws Mexican nationals from isolated areas, who must travel days to reach Calexico. I heard from a touring Japanese family that some street vendors in Tijuana now speak Japanese. I imagine similar border crossings occur in Texas, New Mexico, and Arizona.

22   This multicultural world will have its effect on Mexico. Because of U.S. cultural and economic influence (U.S. assembly plants are now being constructed in the interior of Mexico), we hear from a frank Mexican historian that every Mexican national is a potential Chicano. Similar phenomena are occurring on the northern side of the border. California, we are told, is fast becoming a Third World state; soon after the year 2000, the Euro-American population will reach minority status. In the late 1970s, I taught as a substitute teacher in a Hollywood elementary school whose administrators had to deal with fifteen different languages. I have even heard that there exists in Los Angeles a community of Mexicans who speak their native *quiché* Maya. A recent concert of Filipino popular music in a white suburb of Los Angeles drew 10,000. It is therefore not surprising to read reports that if current population trends and birthrates continue, California will experience a complete reversal from its 1945 ratio of whites to nonwhites. Thus, a centuries-old border culture with new social and economic realities, extending from San Francisco in the West and Chicago in the Midwest to Mexico, Central America, and the Caribbean, is reasserting itself on the U.S. national scene.

23   However, we should not be totally celebratory of a multicultural United States. To understand the economic realities of the expanding border zone, we should also be aware that the gap between privileged and underprivileged along the border and in this country—including Chicanos and millions of Mexicans and other Latino and Third World groups—has never been greater. There exists the real possibility that some regions of this country, especially California, like the Third World countries in Latin America and, indeed, South Africa, will be composed of a ruling minority and an underprivileged majority. Although these political and economic problems will not be solved in the very near future, it is true at this moment that we can no longer ignore the centuries old Mexican-*mestizo* presence in the Southwest. ✛

RESPONDING

1. Calderón reports that many of his daily and seasonal activities as a child were "dictated by Mexican oral and written traditions handed down to our family by our grandmother" (paragraph 5). Write a journal essay about the influence of cultural or family traditions on your childhood.

2. Working individually or in a group, define "border." Compare your definition with Calderón's. Are there many different kinds of borders?

3. Write an essay explaining what Calderón means when he says "we were reminded of both what we were and what we were not" (paragraph 4). Support your explanation with evidence from the essay.

4. In an essay, discuss the way in which Lummis romanticized the Southwest. Compare his version of history with the presentations in the other readings in this chapter.

⁜

CONNECTING

Critical Thinking and Writing

1.   Analyze the role economic realities play in the lives of the characters in this section. How do the financial situations limit or restrict their choices?

2.   A variety of women characters appear in this chapter. Choose two and compare their ways of coping with life's challenges. Or classify the women according to the way they respond to difficult situations. What elements might account for these different responses? Consider the women's personalities, characters, social circumstances, education, and economic situations.

3.   Compare the images of the traditional roles of men and women that emerge from the readings in this chapter. Which characters conform and which rebel against these roles?

4.   Eduviges in *Migrant Souls* has very different attitudes toward American Indians and Mexican Indians. Compare these attitudes and explain why someone might find her statements ironic. Do you think her views are widespread in American society?

5.   Write an essay speculating about how Sancho in *Migrant Souls* might react to Mora's poems "Legal Alien" and "Illegal Alien."

6.   Compare Cleófilas's situation in "Woman Hollering Creek" and Graciela's response to it with Socorro's situation and the speaker's response in Mora's poem "Illegal Alien."

7.   Working in a group, generate a list of essay questions based on issues raised in this chapter. Share your list with the class. Choose one question and answer it in an essay.

8.   Many of the older generation portrayed in these stories are bewildered by the changes taking place around them, though some accept change more easily than others. Compare the different ways the older people in the readings in this text deal with adjusting to life in America.

9.   Examine the role economic realities play in the lives of the early immigrants, American Indians, or any other group and compare their circumstances with those of Chicanos in the 1940s and '50s.

10. Compare the conflicts experienced by the speaker of "Legal Alien" and Ichiro in the excerpt from *No-no Boy* in chapter five because they are bicultural.

11. Using information from the readings, identify gender roles in two particular cultures during a specific period such as the Chicanos in the forties and fifties, Jews in the late 1800s, or Japanese in the thirties and forties and compare them to each other. Or identify gender roles for one group during a specific period and compare them to gender roles for that group in the present.

12. Compare barriers that Chicanos faced in the 1950s with the problems faced by other groups such as early immigrants, Japanese Americans during World War II, or blacks before desegregation. What barriers still exist today that might prevent people from getting an education in spite of their desire to do so? Write an essay presenting the problems and suggesting solutions.

13. Adjusting to a new country means adjusting to a new culture and often a new language. For older people such an adjustment is often difficult, while younger people frequently adapt more quickly. This can cause conflict between the new values the children hold and the traditional values parents retain. Write an essay illustrating the difficulties that arise within families when children begin to move away from the beliefs of their parents. Use examples from this chapter and others in the text.

For Further Research

1. Research the current situation of migrant workers. Who are they? What are their working conditions? What organizations support them? What is their legal status?

2. Research the Chicano Moratorium Movement.

3. Explore the concept of *la raza* and its implication for various Chicano communities.

REFERENCES AND ADDITIONAL SOURCES

Arce, Carlos H. "A Reconsideration of Chicano Culture and Identity." *Daedalus*, Spring 1981: 177–92.

Aztlán: Essay on the Chicano Homeland. Ed. Rudolfo A. Anaya and Franscisco Lomeli. Albuquerque: University of New Mexico Press, 1989.

Bruce-Novoa, Juan D. *Chicano Authors: Inquiry by Interview.* Austin: University of Texas Press, 1980.

———. *Chicano Poetry: A Response to Chaos*. Austin: University of Texas Press, 1982.

———. *RetroSpace: Collected Essays on Chicano Literature, Theory, and History*. Houston: Arte Publico Press, 1990.

Calderón, Héctor. "At the Crossroads of History, on the Borders of Change: Chicano Literary Studies Past, Present and Future." *Left Politics and the Literary Profession*. Edited by M. Bella Mirabella and Lennard J. Davis. New York: Columbia University Press, 1990.

Candelaria, Nash. *Not By the Sword*. Ypsilanti, Mich.: Bilingual Press, 1982.

Castro, Tony. *Chicano Power: The Emergence of Mexican America*. New York: Saturday Review, 1974.

Durán, Livie Isauro, and J. Russell Bernard. *Introduction to Chicano Studies: A Reader*. New York: Macmillan, 1973.

Estrada, Leobardo F., et al. "Chicanos in the United States: A History of Exploitation and Resistance." *Daedalus*, Spring 1981: 103–32.

Garlaza, Ernesto. *Merchants of Labor: The Mexican Bracero Story: An Account of the Managed Migration of the Mexican Farm Workers in California, 1942–1960*. Charlotte and Santa Barbara: McNally and Loftin, 1964; McNally and Loftin, West, 1978.

Hernández, Guillermo. *Chicano Satire: A Study in Literary Culture*. Austin: University of Texas Press, 1991.

Herrera-Sobek, Maria. *Northward Bound: The Mexican Immigrant Experience in Ballad and Song*. Bloomington, Ind.: Indiana University Press, 1993.

———, and Helena Maria Viramontes, eds., *Chicana Creativity and Criticism: Charting New Frontiers in American Literature*. Houston: Arte Publico Press, 1988.

Limón, Graciela. *In Search of Bernabé*. Houston: Arte Publico Press, 1993.

López, Tiffany Ana, ed. and with an intro. *Growing up Chicano: An Anthology*. New York: Morrow, 1993.

McWilliams, Carey. *North from Mexico: The Spanish Speaking People of the United States*. Philadelphia: JB Lippincott Co., 1949; Westport, Conn.: Greenwood Press, 1968, 1990.

Meier, Matt S., and Feliciano Rivera. *The Chicanos: A History of Mexican Americans*. New York: Hill and Wang, 1972.

Moquin, Wayne, and Charles Van Doren, eds. *A Documentary History of the Mexican Americans*. New York: Praeger, 1971, New York: Bantam, 1972.

Paredes, Raymúnd. "The Evolution of Chicano Literature." *Three American Literatures: Essays in Chicano, Native American, and Asian-American Literature for Teachers of American Literature*. Edited by Houston A. Baker, Jr. New York: Modern Language Association of America, 1982.

Rendon, Armando. *Chicano Manifesto*. New York: Macmillan, 1971; New York: Collier, 1972.

Saldívar, Ramon. *Chicano Narrative: The Dialectics of Difference*. Madison, Wis.: University of Wisconsin Press, 1990.

Samora, Julian, and Patricia Simon. *A History of the Mexican-American People*. Notre Dame, Ind.: University of Notre Dame Press, 1977. Rev. ed. 1993

Servin, Manuel P. *An Awkward Minority: The Mexican Americans*. New York: Macmillan, 1974. (2nd ed); Beverly Hills, CA: Glencoe Press, 1974 (2nd ed.).

Soto, Gary, ed. *Pieces of the Heart: New Chicano Fiction*. San Francisco: Chronicle Books, 1993.

Tatum, Charles M. *Chicano Literature*. Boston: Twayne, 1982.

8

AMERICAN INDIANS

Reclaiming Cultural Heritage

Above: Anasazi ruins, Arizona. *(© 1982 Jonathan A. Meyers)*
Opposite: Traditional Apache ceremony marking a young woman's
coming of age. *(Bill Gillette/Stock Boston)*

SETTING THE HISTORICAL AND CULTURAL CONTEXT

In James Welch's poem "Plea to Those Who Matter," the speaker dramatizes the pressure to assimilate:

> Don't ignore me. I'll build my face a different way,
> a way to make you know that I am no longer
> proud, my name not strong enough to stand alone.
> If I lie and say you took me for a friend,
> patched together in my thin bones,
> will you help me be cunning and noisy as the wind?

Welch's poem uses irony to identify ways in which American Indians have been asked to substitute dominant culture stereotypes for traditional systems and beliefs. To obtain property and mineral rights belonging to American Indians, Euro Americans have often coerced tribes into signing treaties against their best interests and have then refused to honor the terms of these agreements. In the interest of acculturation, the majority culture has penalized those natives who have attempted to retain their cultural identity. In recent years, however, American Indians have been somewhat more successful in their struggle to obtain their rights.

American Indian cultures had established highly structured systems long before the coming of the Europeans. Indians often lived communally and participated in trade with other tribes. This communal attitude toward the land contrasted with the notion of individual property rights accepted by most Euro Americans.

The history of the relationships between American Indian peoples and European settlers is a very complex subject. Even the designation of each group as a "tribe" or as a separate "nation" is an issue that was subject to much legal interpretation and debate. (In the 1830s, for example, Supreme Court justice John Marshall referred to Indians in one opinion as being "dependent domestic nations," while he stressed their capacity for self-government in another opinion.) Moreover, many native communities signed treaties with and received recognition from both state and federal governments. Although we cannot recount the histories of each of these relationships here, we will describe some crucial events from the period of the United States's rapid western expansion in the nineteenth century to the emergence of an American Indian rights movement in the twentieth century.

In her book *American Indian Literatures*, A. LaVonne Brown Ruoff comments on the history of relations between American Indians and Euro Americans: "Whites' settlement in Indian territory was inevitably followed by attempts to expand their land holdings and Indians' determined efforts to retain their ancestral land." The desire for land often caused the Euro Americans to ignore the terms of earlier treaties. Some of the earliest groups of European settlers negotiated with many of the Indian groups as separate nations, giving them some payment or remuneration for lands ceded; this practice became less common, however, by the end of the eighteenth century. After the United States had defeated the British in the War of 1812, agrarian and commercial interests sought to force the Indians from rich farmland in the south and east and from western territories not yet settled or extensively explored. Although Indian nations had earlier been able to exercise some influence over the Euro Americans because of their past alliances with the British, they found themselves in a strategically weaker position after the British defeat. Andrew Jackson made expansion a central point in his campaign for president; in addition, other government officials pressured on both the state and federal levels to have Indians removed from lands the whites viewed as desirable.

The Indian Removal Act of 1830 is but one example of the federal government's denying Euro American Indians what they had been promised in earlier treaties. The Removal Act gave the federal government power to force those native peoples living east of the Mississippi River to move to a designated Indian territory in the West. Although the language of the act provides for an "exchange" of lands, the process is described more often as a forced removal, by which most of the Indians were made to move westward against their wills.

The "Trail of Tears"—the forced migration of the so-called Five Civilized Tribes—dramatizes the dehumanizing nature of the process. The Five Civilized Tribes was a confederation of the Cherokees, Chickasaws, Choctaws, Creeks, and Seminoles living in the southeast that had been given the name by Euro Americans themselves. When the rich land they occupied became particularly desirable for the cultivation of cotton and other crops, these Indians found themselves regarded as obstacles to the expansion of agriculture in the southeast. Through coercion and bribery, and often despite the protests of their leaders, Indian communities were forced from the lands of their ancestors and made to travel long distances to the newly designated Indian Territory in the west. Although a few groups, such as the Eastern Band of the Cherokees, were able to hide in North Carolina and later sneak back to their own lands, many other tribes were forced out permanently. As they made their ways west, often in the winter months, they were exposed to cold weather, contaminated provisions, and disease. Many starved to death or perished from infectious diseases to which their systems had no immunity. In the Cherokee nation, for example, 4,000 Indians died; huge numbers of Choctaws, Creeks, and other tribes also died along the way. Midwest Indian nations and tribes were also forced from their lands to territories farther west: The Potawatomis had to resettle in Kansas, and the Kickapoos were moved to Missouri. Once they were settled in Indian Territory, tribes attempted to reestablish themselves culturally by forming schools, governmental systems, and the like. After a few decades, however, many tribes found that the assurances contained in the Indian Removal Act could easily be disregarded. For despite its promise that it "[would] forever secure and guaranty [the land] to them and their heirs," the federal government often continued to encroach on Indian territories and ways of life.

The next fifty years witnessed further assaults by Euro Americans on Indian territorial rights and cultural identity. The westward migration of settlers during the 1840s and 1850s increased the competition for land and for resources. Not only was land for grazing destroyed, but the buffalo herds upon which the Indians had become even more dependent for their food came to be depleted. Railroad companies, eager to encourage western expansion, crossed Indian territories with their lines. Furthermore, through such legislation as the Dawes Act of 1887 (also known as the General Allotment Act) and the Curtis Act of 1898, the government attempted to alter tribal customs and values. Under the Dawes Act, for example, Indians were allotted single plots of land—160 acres—in exchange for giving up Indian ways. The act changed the way Indians had to view land, forcing them to reject a communal attitude toward land for a more individualistic one. Indians were forced to abandon their traditional nomadic way of life and to adopt an agrarian culture on the much smaller parcels of land allotted them. Whereas Indians saw themselves attached to the land of their ancestors, the act weakened those ties. Provisions in the law also caused Indians to be exploited by unscrupulous agents, who could cheat them or their heirs of their property. At first some tribes were exempted from the Allotment Act because of previous treaties with the government; the Curtis Act of 1898, however, eliminated those exemptions. The act also dissolved the governments of any tribes who did not cooperate with the Dawes Act, thereby stripping them of power.

Government Americanization programs prevented many Indians from exercising tribal customs and religion. Children were often taken from their parents and sent to foster parents and boarding schools in distant states, where they were required to speak English and adopt the ways of Euro Americans. Leslie Marmon Silko's short story uses the language of fiction to convey the suffering that such a separation can cause.

Indians were not granted citizenship until 1924. Until the 1930s, American Indians had to ask permission if they wanted to leave their reservations. Those living in Arizona and New Mexico remained disfranchised—they were not allowed to vote—until the late 1940s.

The period between 1930 and 1945 saw some improvement in the status of American Indians. The Bureau of Indian Affairs instituted reforms that would provide them greater autonomy. The Indian Reorganization Act (IRA) of 1934, for example, gave tribes greater control over their property and funds and the administration of social programs. There was a general movement away from coerced assimilation toward what IRA director John Mills called "cultural pluralism."

Many of these reforms of the Indian Reorganization Act were undermined, however, by the termination policy that began in 1953, during the Eisenhower administration. This policy was designed to get the government "out of the Indian business": to dissolve the reservations, relocate their residents, and allocate private property—all largely without the consent of the people affected. Administered by Dillon S. Myer, who had run the Japanese American internment camps during World War II, the termination policy caused an erosion of tribal authority and further loss of American Indians' control of land, since much of their former reservation territory was signed over to Caucasians.

The termination policy was renounced by the Kennedy administration, which took office in 1960. Relations between the federal government and American Indian groups changed to reflect the growing appreciation among the citizens of the United States of the values of pluralism. The government promised to help American Indians preserve their cultural heritage; it also pledged to negotiate any changes in treaties or contracts directly with the native peoples involved. There was also growing awareness that governmental policies toward American Indians could not be imposed from without—as had been typically done in the past—but had to be based on the initiative and cooperation of the people affected.

In 1961, the American Indian Chicago Conference, a meeting of more than 450 delegates from ninety tribes, issued a formal Declaration of Indian Purpose, which reaffirmed the resolve of American Indians for self-determination. The conference also advocated the abandonment of the termination policy, the establishment of broad educational programs, and the reorganization of the federal government's Bureau of Indian Affairs to ensure more local control. At the same time, the Task Force on Indian Affairs, established by the Kennedy administration, recommended improvements in educational, employment, and industrial programs; the Task Force also advocated greater protection for the rights of off-reservation American Indians. A key objective was to attempt to address the extreme poverty found on many tribal reservations. The Economic Opportunity Act of 1964, part of the war on poverty initiated by the Kennedy administration and continued by the administration of President Lyndon B. Johnson, helped to address this need. This act stressed local initiative by encouraging the poor to help plan and administer the programs. Tribal governments were quick to set up community action programs.

The Civil Rights Act of 1968 was extended to protect the rights of American Indians. Although this law limited the powers to tribal governments, it did guarantee that the freedom from discrimination accorded by the Constitution would be fully applied to American Indians. In 1968, President Johnson created the National Council on Indian Opportunity. Chaired by Vice President Hubert Humphrey, the council emphasized American Indian leadership and initiative in solving their own problems. Many American Indians considered these reforms inadequate. Many who feared termination policies distrusted the federal government. President Johnson appointed Robert L. Bennett the first American Indian commissioner of Indian Affairs in a hundred years. But these acts alone could not counteract centuries of broken promises. The government could not earn the complete confidence of the tribes. While some American Indians waited for the government to enforce the Civil Rights Act, others took more direct action. In 1969 Red Power, a militant political group named after the Black Power movement, occupied Alcatraz Island in San Francisco Bay and attempted to convert it into an American Indian cultural and educational center. For many, the occupation came to symbolize the struggle for American Indian unity. Other protests followed, among them the 1972 march called the Trail of Broken Treaties, which culminated in an occupation of the Bureau of Indian Affairs building in Washington, D.C. In 1973 the American Indian Movement (AIM) seized the village of Wounded Knee on the Pine Ridge Reservation in South Dakota to call attention to the continuing problems faced by American Indians. (In 1890 Pine Ridge had been the site of the final large-scale massacre of American Indians by United States military forces.) Although AIM's action was condemned by many American Indians, the occupation lasted for more than seventy days.

During the 1970s and 1980s the government continued to endorse a policy of American Indian self-determination without termination. Under President Richard Nixon, procedural changes were made to improve the tribes' relationships with the government. Nixon's team on Indian affairs renounced the termination policy and restored sacred lands. The Alaska Native Claims Settlement Act passed in 1971 granted Alaskan Indians legal title to 40 million acres of land; the act also restored to legal status the previously terminated Menominee tribe. During this period the American Indian community assumed control of some federal programs and began to manage their own public schools. Relations continued to improve during the Carter administration, with the elevation of the Commissioner of Indian Affairs to an assistant secretary position. Additional legislation was passed, further guaranteeing the rights of American Indians and other peoples.

Despite these improvements, the situations on the reservations themselves were still cause for concern. Many American Indians felt that government schools inadequately addressed the varying educational and cultural needs of the tribes. There also arose a demand for an educational system to validate tribal culture and to keep native traditions alive. Many on the reservation called attention to the high rate of non–American Indian adoption of American Indian children. They pointed out that approximately one quarter of all American Indian children had been taken from their families and placed in foster or adoptive homes on the advice of the Bureau of Indian Affairs or state social workers. In 1978, Congress passed the Indian Child Welfare Act to protect the interest of these children and their families.

Since World War II, steady numbers of American Indians have migrated to the cities, where they have generally attained higher standards of living than those remaining on reservations. In so doing, however, they have too often lost the support of the tribe. Moreover, conflicts between the traditional and urban ways of life have contributed to the rise of alcoholism, crime, and mental illness among urban American Indians. But these conflicts have also led to the establishment of American Indian centers in many cities.

Some of the selections in this chapter examine the ways in which one can come to terms with history. James Welch's "Plea to Those Who Matter" addresses the assault on Indian culture. In their essay, Vine Deloria, Jr., and Clifford M. Lytle explore the background of treaty negotiations between Indians and the federal government, observing that there is "little mention of the complex of ideas that constitutes nationhood." The authors go on to explore the distinction between the physical ownership of land and the spiritual possession of it—a difference that helps to explain some of the differences between Indian and Euro American attitudes toward treaty negotiation. Other writings in the chapter reflect upon events and traditions of the past to suggest ways in which American Indian culture and traditions can blend with modern life. In her essay "Where I Come from Is Like This," Paula Gunn Allen expresses the desire of American Indian women to redefine themselves and "reconcile traditional tribal definitions of women with industrial and postindustrial non-Indian definitions" (paragraph 1). Rather than rejecting the past and tribal identity as limiting, she considers ways to integrate them into her present life. The essay by Greg Sarris considers the relationship between ethnic identity and other kinds of affiliation. The excerpt from Louise Erdrich's novel *Love Medicine* takes a wry approach to the effort to integrate the American Indian tradition with the perspective of mainstream culture. And the excerpt from N. Scott Momaday's *House Made of Dawn* contrasts an American Indian perception of language with that of the majority culture. Simon J. Ortiz explores some of the connections between the oral tradition and the "urge to write."

After many years of eroding autonomy, tribes are working toward becoming economically self-sufficient while maintaining sovereignty over their reservations and dealing effectively with the United States government. They also want to find ways to make decision-making processes more inclusive. American Indians are working to retain the traditions that have defined them for centuries.

BEGINNING: Pre-reading/Writing

Critics charge that American Indians have often been stereotyped in films and television as vicious savages or as romanticized innocents. Working individually or in a group, list the general characteristics attributed to Americans Indians in early Westerns, specific television series, and commercials. Has the portrayal changed over time? If so, in what ways? As you read the chapter, compare these depictions with those by American Indian authors.

The Indian Removal Act of 1830, passed during Andrew Jackson's administration, gave the president authority to transfer to the western territories any Indian tribes living in the East. The law dissolved tribal governments, but guaranteed that American Indians would hold the new territories "in perpetuity"—a promise soon forgotten. The passage of this bill led to the forced relocation of 1838. Because of the suffering it caused, the journey from the east to the so-called Indian Territories of the West is often called the "Trail of Tears."

⁜

From THE INDIAN REMOVAL ACT

CHAP. CXLVIII.—*An Act to provide for an exchange of lands with the Indians residing in any of the states or territories, and for their removal west of the river Mississippi.*

Be it enacted by the Senate and House of Representatives of the United States of America, in Congress assembled, That it shall and may be lawful for the President of the United States to cause so much of any territory belonging to the United States, west of the river Mississippi, not included in any state or organized territory, and to which the Indian title has been extinguished, as he may judge necessary, to be divided into a suitable number of districts, for the reception of such tribes or nations of Indians as may choose to exchange the lands where they now reside, and remove there; and to cause each of said districts to be so described by natural or artificial marks, as to be easily distinguished from every other.

SEC. 2. *And be it further enacted,* That it shall and may be lawful for the President to exchange any or all of such districts, so to be laid off and described, with any tribe or nation of Indians now residing within the limits of any of the states or territories, and with which the United States have existing treaties, for the whole or any part or portion of the territory claimed and occupied by such tribe or nation, within the bounds of any one or more of the states or territories, where the land claimed and occupied by the Indians, is owned by the United States, or the United States are bound to the state within which it lies to extinguish the Indian claim thereto.

SEC. 3. *And be it further enacted,* That in the making of any such exchange or exchanges, it shall and may be lawful for the President solemnly to assure the tribe or nation with which the exchange is made, that the United States will forever secure and guaranty to them, and their heirs or successors, the country so exchanged with them; and if they prefer it, that the United States will cause a patent or grant to be made and executed to them for the same: *Provided always,* That such lands shall revert to the United States, if the Indians become extinct, or abandon the same.

5   SEC. 4. *And be it further enacted*, That if, upon any of the lands now occupied by the Indians, and to be exchanged for, there should be such improvements as add value to the land claimed by any individual or individuals of such tribes or nations, it shall and may be lawful for the President to cause such value to be ascertained by appraisement or otherwise, and to cause such ascertained value to be paid to the person or persons rightfully claiming such improvements. And upon the payment of such valuation, the improvements so valued and paid for, shall pass to the United States, and possession shall not afterwards be permitted to any of the same tribe.

6   SEC. 5. *And be it further enacted*, That upon the making of any such exchange as is contemplated by this act, it shall and may be lawful for the President to cause such aid and assistance to be furnished to the emigrants as may be necessary and proper to enable them to remove to, and settle in, the country for which they may have exchanged; and also, to give them such aid and assistance as may be necessary for their support and subsistence for the first year after their removal.

7   SEC. 6. *And be it further enacted*, That it shall and may be lawful for the President to cause such tribe or nation to be protected, at their new residence, against all interruption or disturbance from any other tribe or nation of Indians, or from any other person or persons whatever.

8   SEC. 7. *And be it further enacted*, That it shall and may be lawful for the President to have the same superintendence and care over any tribe or nation in the country to which they may remove, as contemplated by this act, that he is now authorized to have over them at their present places of residence: *Provided*, That nothing in this act contained shall be construed as authorizing or directing the violation of any existing treaty between the United States and any of the Indian tribes.

9   SEC. 8. *And be it further enacted*, That for the purpose of giving effect to the provisions of this act, the sum of five hundred thousand dollars is hereby appropriated, to be paid out of any money in the treasury, not otherwise appropriated.

10 APPROVED, May 28, 1830. ✠

RESPONDING

1. In a journal entry, imagine that you are an American Indian reading this act today. How would you respond? What would your feeling be toward the United States?

2. Write an essay discussing the assumptions of the government implicit in the document about the future of American Indians. Support your opinions with evidence from the act.

3. Research the myth of the "vanishing American." Using evidence from the act, argue in an essay that the framers of the act did or did not give credence to this myth.

N. Scott Momaday

*N. Scott Momaday was born in Lawton, Oklahoma, in 1934, of Kiowa and
Cherokee parentage. As a child he lived on New Mexican reservations where
his parents taught school. He received his bachelor's degree from the University
of New Mexico in 1958 and later earned a master's degree and a doctorate
from Stanford University, where he studied with Yvor Winters. After teaching
literature at the University of California at Santa Barbara, New Mexico
State University, the University of California at Berkeley, and Stanford
University, he joined the faculty of the University of Arizona, where he is
currently professor of English.*

In addition to editing American Indian Authors, *Momaday has published
several volumes of poetry, fiction, and an autobiography that focuses on Native
American Culture. These works include* Journey of Tai-Me *(1968),* The
Way to Rainy Mountain *(1969),* House Made of Dawn *(1969),* Angle
of Geese and Other Poems *(1974),* The Names: A Memoir *(1976), and*
The Ancient Child *(1989). Momaday's writing has won him awards and
fellowships from the National Academy of American poets, the Whitney
Foundation, the Guggenheim Foundation, the Fulbright Foundation, and the
National Institute of Arts and Letters among others. His first novel,* House
Made of Dawn, *was awarded the Pulitzer Prize for Fiction in 1969.*

The following chapter from House Made of Dawn *considers different
attitudes toward language and religion in the Euro American and Native
American traditions.*

⁜

JANUARY 26

1 "My grandmother was a storyteller; she knew her way around words. She
never learned to read and write, but somehow she knew the good of reading
and writing; she had learned how to listen and delight. She had learned that in
words and in language, and there only, she could have whole and consummate
being. She told me stories, and she taught me how to listen. I was a child and
I listened. She could neither read nor write, you see, but she taught me how to
live among her words, how to listen and delight. 'Storytelling; to utter and to
hear . . .' And the simple act of listening is crucial to the concept of language,
more crucial even than reading and writing, and language in turn is crucial to
human society. There is proof of that, I think, in all the histories and prehistories
of human experience. When that old Kiowa woman told me stories, I listened

with only one ear. I was a child, and I took the words for granted. I did not know what all of them meant, but somehow I held on to them; I remembered them, and I remember them now. The stories were old and dear; they meant a great deal to my grandmother. It was not until she died that I knew how *much* they meant to her. I began to think about it, and then I knew. When she told me those old stories, something strange and good and powerful was going on. I was a child, and that old woman was asking me to come directly into the presence of her mind and spirit; she was taking hold of my imagination, giving me to share in the great fortune of her wonder and delight. She was asking me to go with her to the confrontation of something that was sacred and eternal. It was a timeless, *timeless* thing; nothing of her old age or of my childhood came between us.

"Children have a greater sense of the power and beauty of words than have 2 the rest of us in general. And if that is so, it is because there occurs—or reoccurs—in the mind of every child something like a reflection of all human experience. I have heard that the human fetus corresponds in its development, stage by stage, to the scale of evolution. Surely it is no less reasonable to suppose that the waking mind of a child corresponds in the same way to the whole evolution of human thought and perception.

"In the white man's world, language, too—and the way in which the white 3 man thinks of it—has undergone a process of change. The white man takes such things as words and literatures for granted, as indeed he must, for nothing in his world is so commonplace. On every side of him there are words by the millions, an unending succession of pamphlets and papers, letters and books, bills and bulletins, commentaries and conversations. He has diluted and multiplied the Word, and words have begun to close in upon him. He is sated and insensitive; his regard for language—for the Word itself—as an instrument of creation has diminished nearly to the point of no return. It may be that he will perish by the Word.

"But it was not always so with him, and it is not so with you. Consider for 4 a moment that old Kiowa woman, my grandmother, whose use of language was confined to speech. And be assured that her regard for words was always keen in proportion as she depended upon them. You see, for her words were medicine; they were magic and invisible. They came from nothing into sound and meaning. They were beyond price; they could neither be bought nor sold. And she never threw words away.

"My grandmother used to tell me the story of Tai-me, of how Tai-me came 5 to the Kiowas. The Kiowas were a sun dance culture, and Tai-me was their sun dance doll, their most sacred fetish; no medicine was ever more powerful. There is a story about the coming of Tai-me. This is what my grandmother told me:

Long ago there were bad times. The Kiowas were hungry and there was no 6 food. There was a man who heard his children cry from hunger, and he began to search for food. He walked four days and became very weak. On the fourth day he came to a great canyon. Suddenly there was thunder and lightning. A Voice spoke to him and said, "Why are you following me? What do you want?" The man was afraid. The thing standing before him had the feet of a deer, and its body was covered with feathers. The man answered that the Kiowas were hungry. "Take me with you," the Voice said, "and I will give you whatever you want." From that day Tai-me has belonged to the Kiowas.

7   "Do you see? There, far off in the darkness, something happened. Do you see? Far, far away in the nothingness something happened. There was a voice, a sound, a word—and everything began. The story of the coming of Tai-me has existed for hundreds of years by word of mouth. It represents the oldest and best idea that man has of himself. It represents a very rich literature, which, because it was never written down, was always but one generation from extinction. But for the same reason it was cherished and revered. I could see that reverence in my grandmother's eyes, and I could hear it in her voice." ✤

RESPONDING

1. Are stories an important way of transmitting knowledge in your family or among friends? In a journal entry, tell a story that teaches a cultural lesson.

2. Working individually or in a group, explain the ways in which the narrator believes the white man's use of "the word" differs from the Kiowas'. Use examples from the reading and your own knowledge to illustrate the differences. Write an essay agreeing or disagreeing with his conclusions.

3. The narrator argues that orality has more value than literacy. Using examples from the readings and outside knowledge, write an essay exploring the differences between oral and written use of language. Consider what happens when a story is written down. Is something gained? Lost?

LESLIE MARMON SILKO

The poet, novelist, and short-story writer Leslie Marmon Silko was born in New Mexico in 1948 of Laguna, Plains Indian, Mexican, and white ancestry. After earning her bachelor's degree from the University of New Mexico and attending law school, she devoted herself to writing, focusing primarily on American Indian themes. Silko's publications include Laguna Woman: Poems *(1974), the novels* Ceremony *(1977) and* Almanac of the Dead *(1991), and a poetry and short-story collection,* Storyteller *(1981). She was honored with grants from the National Endowment for the Arts in 1974 and the MacArthur Foundation in 1983, among others.*

   "Lullaby," from Storyteller, *describes an American Indian woman as she confronts government authorities whose language she cannot understand. At the same time, the story asks us to consider the ways in which language and power can be interconnected.*

⁛

LULLABY

THE SUN HAD GONE DOWN but the snow in the wind gave off its own light. It came in thick tufts like new wool—washed before the weaver spins it. Ayah reached out for it like her own babies had, and she smiled when she remembered how she had laughed at them. She was an old woman now, and her life had become memories. She sat down with her back against the wide cottonwood tree, feeling the rough bark on her back bones; she faced east and listened to the wind and snow sing a high-pitched Yeibechei song. Out of the wind she felt warmer, and she could watch the wide fluffy snow fill in her tracks, steadily, until the direction she had come from was gone. By the light of the snow she could see the dark outline of the big arroyo a few feet away. She was sitting on the edge of Cebellota Creek, where in the springtime the thin cows would graze on grass already chewed flat to the ground. In the wide deep creek bed where only a trickle of water flowed in the summer, the skinny cows would wander, looking for new grass along winding paths splashed with manure. 1

   Ayah pulled the old Army blanket over her head like a shawl. Jimmie's blanket—the one he had sent to her. That was a long time ago and the green wool was faded, and it was unraveling on the edges. She did not want to think about Jimmie. So she thought about the weaving and the way her mother had done it. On the tall wooden loom set into the sand under a tamarack tree for shade. She could see it clearly. She had been only a little girl when her grandma gave her the wooden combs to pull the twigs and burrs from the raw, freshly 2 washed wool. And while she combed the wool, her grandma sat beside her, spinning a silvery strand of yarn around the smooth cedar spindle. Her mother worked at the loom with yarns dyed bright yellow and red and gold. She watched them dye the yarn in boiling black pots full of beeweed petals, juniper berries, and sage. The blankets her mother made were soft and woven so tight that rain rolled off them like birds' feathers. Ayah remembered sleeping warm on cold windy nights, wrapped in her mother's blankets on the hogan's sandy floor.

3   The snow drifted now, with the northwest wind hurling it in gusts. It drifted up around her black overshoes—old ones with little metal buckles. She smiled at the snow which was trying to cover her little by little. She could remember when they had no black rubber overshoes; only the high buckskin leggings that they wrapped over their elkhide moccasins. If the snow was dry or frozen, a person could walk all day and not get wet; and in the evenings the beams of the ceiling would hang with lengths of pale buckskin leggings, drying out slowly.

4   She felt peaceful remembering. She didn't feel cold any more. Jimmie's blanket seemed warmer than it had ever been. And she could remember the morning he was born. She could remember whispering to her mother, who was sleeping on the other side of the hogan, to tell her it was time now. She did not want to wake the others. The second time she called to her, her mother stood up and pulled on her shoes; she knew. They walked to the old stone hogan together, Ayah walking a step behind her mother. She waited alone, learning the rhythms of the pains while her mother went to call the old woman to help them. The morning was already warm even before dawn and Ayah smelled the bee flowers blooming and the young willow growing at the springs. She could remember that so clearly, but his birth merged into the births of the other children and to her it became all the same birth. They named him for the summer morning and in English they called him Jimmie.

5   It wasn't like Jimmie died. He just never came back, and one day a dark blue sedan with white writing on its doors pulled up in front of the boxcar shack where the rancher let the Indians live. A man in a khaki uniform trimmed in gold gave them a yellow piece of paper and told them that Jimmie was dead. He said the Army would try to get the body back and then it would be shipped to them; but it wasn't likely because the helicopter had burned after it crashed. All of this was told to Chato because he could understand English. She stood inside the doorway holding the baby while Chato listened. Chato spoke English like a white man and he spoke Spanish too. He was taller than the white man and he stood straighter too. Chato didn't explain why; he just told the military man they could keep the body if they found it. The white man looked bewildered; he nodded his head and he left. Then Chato looked at her and shook his head, and then he told her, "Jimmie isn't coming home anymore," and when he spoke, he used the words to speak of the dead. She didn't cry then, but she hurt inside with anger. And she mourned him as the years passed, when a horse fell with Chato and broke his leg, and the white rancher told them he wouldn't

pay Chato until he could work again. She mourned Jimmie because he would have worked for his father then; he would have saddled the big bay horse and ridden the fence lines each day, with wire cutters and heavy gloves, fixing the breaks in the barbed wire and putting the stray cattle back inside again.

She mourned him after the white doctors came to take Danny and Ella 6 away. She was at the shack alone that day they came. It was back in the days before they hired Navajo women to go with them as interpreters. She recognized one of the doctors. She had seen him at the children's clinic at Cañoncito about a month ago. They were wearing khaki uniforms and they waved papers at her and a black ball-point pen, trying to make her understand their English words. She was frightened by the way they looked at the children, like the lizard watches the fly. Danny was swinging on the tire swing on the elm tree behind the rancher's house, and Ella was toddling around the front door, dragging the broomstick horse Chato made for her. Ayah could see they wanted her to sign the papers, and Chato had taught her to sign her name. It was something she was proud of. She only wanted them to go, and to take their eyes away from her children.

She took the pen from the man without looking at his face and she signed 7 the papers in three different places he pointed to. She stared at the ground by their feet and waited for them to leave. But they stood there and began to point and gesture at the children. Danny stopped swinging. Ayah could see his fear. She moved suddenly and grabbed Ella into her arms; the child squirmed, trying to get back to her toys. Ayah ran with the baby toward Danny; she screamed for him to run and then she grabbed him around his chest and carried him too. She ran south into the foothills of juniper trees and black lava rock. Behind her she heard the doctors running, but they had been taken by surprise, and as the hills became steeper and the cholla cactus were thicker, they stopped. When she reached the top of the hill, she stopped to listen in case they were circling around her. But in a few minutes she heard a car engine start and they drove away. The children had been too surprised to cry while she ran with them. Danny was shaking and Ella's little fingers were gripping Ayah's blouse.

She stayed up in the hills for the rest of the day, sitting on a black lava 8 boulder in the sunshine where she could see for miles all around her. The sky was light blue and cloudless, and it was warm for late April. The sun warmth relaxed her and took the fear and anger away. She lay back on the rock and watched the sky. It seemed to her that she could walk into the sky, stepping through clouds endlessly. Danny played with little pebbles and stones, pretending they were birds' eggs and then little rabbits. Ella sat at her feet and dropped fistfuls of dirt into the breeze, watching the dust and particles of sand intently. Ayah watched a hawk soar high above them, dark wings gliding; hunting or only watching, she did not know. The hawk was patient and he circled all afternoon before he disappeared around the high volcanic peak the Mexicans called Guadalupe.

9   Late in the afternoon, Ayah looked down at the gray boxcar shack with the paint all peeled from the wood; the stove pipe on the roof was rusted and crooked. The fire she had built that morning in the oil drum stove had burned out. Ella was asleep in her lap now and Danny sat close to her, complaining that he was hungry; he asked when they would go to the house. "We will stay up here until your father comes," she told him, "because those white men were chasing us." The boy remembered then and he nodded at her silently.

10   If Jimmie had been there he could have read those papers and explained to her what they said. Ayah would have known then, never to sign them. The doctors came back the next day and they brought a BIA policeman with them. They told Chato they had her signature and that was all they needed. Except for the kids. She listened to Chato sullenly; she hated him when he told her it was the old woman who died in the winter, spitting blood; it was her old grandma who had given the children this disease. "They don't spit blood" she said coldly. "The whites lie." She held Ella and Danny close to her, ready to run to the hills again. "I want a medicine man first," she said to Chato, not looking at him. He shook his head. "It's too late now. The policeman is with them. You signed the paper." His voice was gentle.

11   It was worse than if they had died: to lose the children and to know that somewhere, in a place called Colorado, in a place full of sick and dying strangers, her children were without her. There had been babies that died soon after they were born, and one that died before he could walk. She had carried them herself, up to the boulders and great pieces of the cliff that long ago crashed down from Long Mesa; she laid them in the crevices of sandstone and buried them in fine brown sand with round quartz pebbles that washed down the hills in the rain. She had endured it because they had been with her. But she could not bear this pain. She did not sleep for a long time after they took her children. She stayed on the hill where they had fled the first time, and she slept rolled up in the blanket Jimmie had sent her. She carried the pain in her belly and it was fed by everything she saw: the blue sky of their last day together and the dust and pebbles they played with; the swing in the elm tree and the broomstick horse choked life from her. The pain filled her stomach and there was no room for food or for her lungs to fill with air. The air and the food would have been theirs.

12   She hated Chato, not because he let the policeman and doctors put the screaming children in the government car, but because he had taught her to sign her name. Because it was like the old ones always told her about learning their language or any of their ways: it endangered you. She slept alone on the hill until the middle of November when the first snows came. Then she made a bed for herself where the children had slept. She did not lie down beside Chato again until many years later, when he was sick and shivering and only her body could keep him warm. The illness came after the white rancher told Chato he was too old to work for him anymore, and Chato and his old woman should be out of the shack by the next afternoon because the rancher had hired

new people to work there. That had satisfied her. To see how the white man repaid Chato's years of loyalty and work. All of Chato's fine-sounding English talk didn't change things.

It snowed steadily and the luminous light from the snow gradually diminished into the darkness. Somewhere in Cebolleta a dog barked and other village dogs joined with it. Ayah looked in the direction she had come, from the bar where Chato was buying the wine. Sometimes he told her to go on ahead and wait; and then he never came. And when she finally went back looking for him, she would find him passed out at the bottom of the wooden steps to Azzie's Bar. All the wine would be gone and most of the money too, from the pale blue check that came to them once a month in a government envelope. It was then that she would look at his face and his hands, scarred by ropes and the barbed wire of all those years, and she would think, this man is a stranger; for forty years she had smiled at him and cooked his food, but he remained a stranger. She stood up again, with the snow almost to her knees, and she walked back to find Chato.

It was hard to walk in the deep snow and she felt the air burn in her lungs. She stopped a short distance from the bar to rest and readjust the blanket. But this time he wasn't waiting for her on the bottom step with his old Stetson hat pulled down and his shoulders hunched up in his long wool overcoat.

She was careful not to slip on the wooden steps. When she pushed the door open, warm air and cigarette smoke hit her face. She looked around slowly and deliberately, in every corner, in every dark place that the old man might find to sleep. The bar owner didn't like Indians in there, especially Navajos, but he let Chato come in because he could talk Spanish like he was one of them. The men at the bar stared at her, and the bartender saw that she left the door open wide. Snowflakes were flying inside like moths and melting into a puddle on the oiled wood floor. He motioned to her to close the door, but she did not see him. She held herself straight and walked across the room slowly, searching the room with every step. The snow in her hair melted and she could feel it on her forehead. At the far corner of the room, she saw red flames at the mica window of the old stove door; she looked behind the stove just to make sure. The bar got quiet except for the Spanish polka music playing on the jukebox. She stood by the stove and shook the snow from her blanket and held it near the stove to dry. The wet wool smell reminded her of new-born goats in early March, brought inside to warm near the fire. She felt calm.

In past years they would have told her to get out. But her hair was white now and her face was wrinkled. They looked at her like she was a spider crawling slowly across the room. They were afraid; she could feel the fear. She looked at their faces steadily. They reminded her of the first time the white people brought her children back to her that winter. Danny had been shy and hid behind the thin white woman who brought them. And the baby had not known her until Ayah took her into her arms, and then Ella had nuzzled close to her as she had when she was nursing. The blonde woman was nervous and kept looking at a dainty gold watch on her wrist. She sat on the bench near the small window and watched the dark snow clouds gather around the mountains; she was worrying about the unpaved road. She was frightened by what she saw inside too: the strips of venison drying on a rope across the ceiling and the children jabbering excitedly in a language she did not know. So they stayed for only a few hours. Ayah watched the government car disappear down the road and she knew they were already being weaned from these lava hills and from this sky. The last time they came was in early June, and Ella stared at her the way the men in the bar were now staring. Ayah did not try to pick her up; she smiled at her instead and spoke cheerfully to Danny. When he tried to answer her, he could not seem to remember and he spoke English words with the Navajo. But he gave her a scrap of paper that he had found somewhere and carried in his pocket; it was folded in half, and he shyly looked up at her and said it was a bird. She asked Chato if they were home for good this time. He spoke to the white woman and she shook her head. "How much longer?" he asked, and she said she didn't know; but Chato saw how she stared at the boxcar shack. Ayah turned away then. She did not say good-bye.

17   She felt satisfied that the men in the bar feared her. Maybe it was her face and the way she held her mouth with teeth clenched tight, like there was nothing anyone could do to her now. She walked north down the road, searching for the old man. She did this because she had the blanket, and there would be no place for him except with her and the blanket in the old adobe barn near the arroyo. They always slept there when they came to Cebolleta. If the money and the wine were gone, she would be relieved because then they could go home again; back to the old hogan with a dirt roof and rock walls where she herself had been born. And the next day the old man could go back to the few sheep they still had, to follow along behind them, guiding them, into dry sandy arroyos where sparse grass grew. She knew he did not like walking behind old ewes when for so many years he rode big quarter-horses and worked with cattle. But she wasn't sorry for him; he should have known all along what would happen.

18   There had not been enough rain for their garden in five years; and that was when Chato finally hitched a ride into the town and brought back brown boxes of rice and sugar and big tin cans of welfare peaches. After that, at the first of the month they went to Cebolleta to ask the postmaster for the check; and then Chato would go to the bar and cash it. They did this as they planted the garden every May, not because anything would survive the summer dust, but because it was time to do this. The journey passed the days that smelled silent and dry like the caves above the canyon with yellow painted buffaloes on their walls.

19   He was walking along the pavement when she found him. He did not stop or turn around when he heard her behind him. She walked beside him and she

noticed how slowly he moved now. He smelled strong of woodsmoke and urine. Lately he had been forgetting. Sometimes he called her by his sister's name and she had been gone for a long time. Once she had found him wandering on the road to the white man's ranch, and she asked him why he was going that way; he laughed at her and said, "You know they can't run that ranch without me," and he walked on determined, limping on the leg that had been crushed many years before. Now he looked at her curiously, as if for the first time, but he kept shuffling along, moving slowly along the side of the highway. His gray hair had grown long and spread out on the shoulders of the long overcoat. He wore the old felt hat pulled down over his ears. His boots were worn out at the toes and he had stuffed pieces of an old red shirt in the holes. The rags made his feet look like little animals up to their ears in snow. She laughed at his feet; the snow muffled the sound of her laugh. He stopped and looked at her again. The wind had quit blowing and the snow was falling straight down; the southeast sky was beginning to clear and Ayah could see a star.

"Let's rest awhile," she said to him. They walked away from the road and up the slope to the giant boulders that had tumbled down from the red sandrock mesa throughout the centuries of rainstorms and earth tremors. In a place where the boulders shut out the wind, they sat down with their backs against the rock. She offered half of the blanket to him and they sat wrapped together.   20

The storm passed swiftly. The clouds moved east. They were massive and full, crowding together across the sky. She watched them with the feeling of horses—steely blue-gray horses startled across the sky. The powerful haunches pushed into the distances and the tail hairs streamed white mist behind them. The sky cleared. Ayah saw that there was nothing between her and the stars. The light was crystalline. There was no shimmer, no distortion through earth haze. She breathed the clarity of the night sky; she smelled the purity of the half moon and the stars. He was lying on his side with his knees pulled up near his belly for warmth. His eyes were closed now, and in the light from the stars and the moon, he looked young again.   21

She could see it descend out of the night sky: an icy stillness from the edge of the thin moon. She recognized the freezing. It came gradually, sinking snowflake by snowflake until the crust was heavy and deep. It had the strength of the stars in Orion, and its journey was endless. Ayah knew that with the wine he would sleep. He would not feel it. She tucked the blanket around him, remembering how it was when Ella had been with her; and she felt the rush so big inside her heart for the babies. And she sang the only song she knew to sing for babies. She could not remember if she had ever sung it to her children, but she knew that her grandmother had sung it and her mother had sung it: 22

> The earth is your mother,
> she holds you.
> The sky is your father,
> he protects you.
> Sleep,
> sleep.
> Rainbow is your sister,
>   she loves you.
> The winds are your brothers,
>   they sing to you.
> Sleep,
> sleep.
> We are together always
> We are together always
> There never was a time
> when this
> was not so. ❖

RESPONDING

1. The story takes place "back in the days before they hired Navajo women to go with them as interpreters." Ayah loses her children because she doesn't speak English and can't read the paper she is given to sign. In a journal entry, describe your reactions to the story's events. Or tell about a time when you or someone you know was in a situation where lack of understanding of language or customs created great difficulties.

2. Working with a partner, write a dialogue between Ayah and the doctors who come to take away her children. If they spoke her language, what argument might they give her to convince her to consent to having the children taken away for treatment? How might she respond?

3. Chato ends his life in rags, spending his government checks on alcohol. Discuss the causes of his difficulties in an essay. In your opinion, who is responsible for his problems?

4. Write an essay explaining Ayah's attitude toward life and death, illustrating your explanation with examples from the text.

James Welch

A poet of Blackfeet and Gros Ventre heritage, James Welch was born in Browning, Montana, in 1940. After growing up on Montana's Blackfeet and Fort Belknap reservations and in Minneapolis, he earned a bachelor's degree from the University of Montana. Welch's writing includes the fictional works Winter in the Blood *(1974),* The Death of Jim Loney *(1979),* Fools Crow *(1986), and* The Indian Lawyer *(1990) and the poetry collection* Riding the Earthboy 40 *(1971). He has received several awards, including a grant from the National Endowment for the Arts; in 1970 he was named to the NEA's literature panel.*

The poem that follows, from Riding the Earthboy 40, *examines the issues of tradition and identity, and the social pressures that threaten them.*

❖

PLEA TO THOSE WHO MATTER

You don't know I pretend my dumb.
My songs often wise, my bells could chase
the snow across these whistle-black plains.
Celebrate. The days are grim. Call your winds
to blast these bundled streets and patronize
my past of poverty and 4-day feasts.

Don't ignore me. I'll build my face a different way,
a way to make you know that I am no longer
proud, my name not strong enough to stand alone.
If I lie and say you took me for a friend,
patched together in my thin bones,
will you help me be cunning and noisy as the wind?

I have plans to burn my drum, move out
and civilize this hair. See my nose? I smash it
straight for you. These teeth? I scrub my teeth
away with stones. I know you help me now I matter.
And I—I come to you, head down, bleeding from my smile,
happy for the snow clean hands of you, my friends. ❖

RESPONDING

1. Have you or someone you know ever felt you had to change your appearance or behavior to please someone in authority? Write a journal entry about that experience or about your reaction to that solution to being different.

2. Individually or with a partner, write a dialogue between the speaker and an Indian rights activist.

3. In an essay, identify and describe the speaker in the poem. According to the poem, who are the ones who matter and how is the speaker willing to change to please them?

4. Write an essay explaining the attitude of the poet toward the speaker. Does he approve or disapprove of the speaker's behavior? Support your opinion by citing examples from the poem.

LOUISE ERDRICH

Louise Erdrich, who is of Turtle Mountain Chippewa and German ancestry, inherits a mixture of Ojibwa, Cree, French, and Plains traditions. She was born in Little Falls, Minnesota, in 1954 and grew up in Wahpeton, North Dakota. Erdrich received a bachelor's degree from Dartmouth College in 1976, and a master's degree from Johns Hopkins University in 1977. In addition to contributing to Atlantic Monthly, Chicago, The Kenyon Review, *and* North American Review, *Erdrich has published the poetry collection* Jacklight *(1984) as well as the novels* Love Medicine *(1984),* The Beet Queen *(1986), and* Tracks *(1988). Most recently she published the novel* Bingo Palace *(1994). Her work has earned her the National Book Critics' Circle Award (1984) and the O. Henry Award (1985).*

In the following selection from Love Medicine, *the young narrator, Lipsha Morrissey, describes his attitudes toward his extended family and the healing touch that he believes he has been given. The narrative provides a commentary not only on the Chippewa culture but on the culture beyond the Chippewa community.*

✛

From **LOVE MEDICINE**

LIPSHA MORRISSEY

I NEVER REALLY DONE MUCH with my life, I suppose. I never had a television. Grandma Kashpaw had one inside her apartment at the Senior Citizens, so I used to go there and watch my favorite shows. For a while she used to call me the biggest waste on the reservation and hark back to how she saved me from my own mother, who wanted to tie me in a potato sack and throw me in a slough. Sure, I was grateful to Grandma Kashpaw for saving me like that, for raising me, but gratitude gets old. After a while, stale. I had to stop thanking her. One day I told her I had paid her back in full by staying at her beck and call. I'd do anything for Grandma. She knew that. Besides, I took care of Grandpa like nobody else could, on account of what a handful he'd gotten to be.

But that was nothing, I know the tricks of mind and body inside out without ever having trained for it, because I got the touch. It's a thing you got to be born with. I got secrets in my hands that nobody ever knew to ask. Take Grandma Kashpaw with her tired veins all knotted up in her legs like clumps of blue snails. I take my fingers and I snap them on the knots. The medicine flows out of me. The touch. I run my fingers up the maps of those rivers of veins or I knock very gentle above their hearts or I make a circling motion on their stomachs, and it helps them. They feel much better. Some women pay me five dollars.

3   I couldn't do the touch for Grandpa, though. He was a hard nut. You know, some people fall right through the hole in their lives. It's invisible, but they come to it after time, never knowing where. There is this woman here, Lulu Lamartine, who always had a thing for Grandpa. She loved him since she was a girl and always said he was a genius. Now she says that his mind got so full it exploded.

4   How can I doubt that? I know the feeling when your mental power builds up too far. I always used to say that's why the Indians got drunk. Even statistically we're the smartest people on the earth. Anyhow with Grandpa I couldn't hardly believe it, because all my youth he stood out as a hero to me. When he started getting toward second childhood he went through different moods. He would stand in the woods and cry at the top of his shirt. It scared me, scared everyone, Grandma worst of all.

5   Yet he was so smart—do you believe it?—that he *knew* he was getting foolish.

6   He said so. He told me that December I failed school and come back on the train to Hoopdance. I didn't have nowhere else to go. He picked me up there and he said it straight out: "I'm getting into my second childhood." And then he said something else I still remember: "I been chosen for it. I couldn't say no." So I figure that a man so smart all his life—tribal chairman and the star of movies and even pictured in the statehouse and on cans of snuff—would know what he's doing by saying yes. I think he was called to second childhood like anybody else gets a call for the priesthood or the army or whatever. So I really did not listen too hard when the doctor said this was some kind of disease old people got eating too much sugar. You just can't tell me that a man who went to Washington and gave them bureaucrats what for could lose his mind from eating too much Milky Way. No, he put second childhood on himself.

7   Behind those songs he sings out in the middle of Mass, and back of those stories that everybody knows by heart, Grandpa is thinking hard about life. I know the feeling. Sometimes I'll throw up a smokescreen to think behind. I'll hitch up to Winnipeg and play the Space Invaders for six hours, but all the time there and back I will be thinking some fairly deep thoughts that surprise even me, and I'm used to it. As for him, if it was just the thoughts there wouldn't be no problem. Smokescreen is what irritates the social structure, see, and Grandpa has done things that just distract people to the point they want to throw him in the cookie jar where they keep the mentally insane. He's far from that, I know for sure, but even Grandma had trouble keeping her patience once he started sneaking off to Lamartine's place. He's not supposed to have his candy, and Lulu feeds it to him. That's *one* of the reasons why he goes.

8   Grandma tried to get me to put the touch on Grandpa soon after he began

stepping out. I didn't want to, but before Grandma started telling me again what a bad state my bare behind was in when she first took me home, I thought I should at least pretend.

I put my hands on either side of Grandpa's head. You wouldn't look at him ⁹ and say he was crazy. He's a fine figure of a man, as Lamartine would say, with all his hair and half his teeth, a beak like a hawk, and cheeks like the blades of a hatchet. They put his picture on all the tourist guides to North Dakota and even copied his face for artistic paintings. I guess you could call him a monument all of himself. He started grinning when I put my hands on his templates, and I knew right then he knew how come I touched him. I knew the smokescreen was going to fall.

And I was right: just for a moment it fell. ¹⁰

"Let's pitch whoopee," he said across my shoulder to Grandma. ¹¹

They don't use that expression much around here anymore, but for damn ¹² sure it must have meant something. It got her goat right quick.

She threw my hands off his head herself and stood in front of him, over- ¹³ matching him pound for pound, and taller too, for she had a growth spurt in middle age while he had shrunk, so now the length and breadth of her surpassed him. She glared and spoke her piece into his face about how he was off at all hours tomcatting and chasing Lamartine again and making a damn old fool of himself.

"And you got no more whoopee to pitch anymore anyhow!" she yelled at ¹⁴ last, surprising me so my jaw just dropped, for us kids all had pretended for so long that those rustling sounds we heard from their side of the room at night never happened. She sure had pretended it, up till now, anyway. I saw that tears were in her eyes. And that's when I saw how much grief and love she felt for him. And it gave me a real shock to the system. You see I thought love got easier over the years so it didn't hurt so bad when it hurt, or feel so good when it felt good. I thought it smoothed out and old people hardly noticed it. I thought it curled up and died, I guess. Now I saw it rear up like a whip and lash.

She loved him. She was jealous. She mourned him like the dead. ¹⁵

And he just smiled into the air, trapped in the seams of his mind. ¹⁶

So I didn't know what to do. I was in a laundry then. They was like parents ¹⁷ to me, the way they had took me home and reared me. I could see her point for wanting to get him back the way he was so at least she could argue with him, sleep with him, not be shamed out by Lamartine. She'd always love him. That hit me like a ton of bricks. For one whole day I felt this odd feeling that cramped my hands. When you have the touch, that's where longing gets you. I never loved like that. It made me feel all inspired to see them fight, and I wanted to go out and find a woman who I would love until one of us died or went crazy. But I'm not like that really. From time to time I heal a person all up good inside, however when it comes to the long shot I doubt that I got staying power.

18   And you need that, staying power, going out to love somebody. I know this
quality was not going to jump on me with no effort. So I turned my thoughts
back to Grandma and Grandpa. I felt her side of it with my hands and my
tangled guts, and I felt his side of it within the stretch of my mentality. He had
gone out to lunch one day and never came back. He was fishing in the middle
of Matchimanito. And there was big thoughts on his line, and he kept throwing
them back for even bigger ones that would explain to him, say, the meaning of
how we got here and why we have to leave so soon. All in all, I could not see
myself treating Grandpa with the touch, bringing him back, when the real part
of him had chose to be off thinking somewhere. It was only the rest of him that
stayed around causing trouble, after all, and we could handle most of it without
any problem.

19   Besides, it was hard to argue with his reasons for doing some things. Take
Holy Mass. I used to go there just every so often, when I got frustrated mostly,
because even though I know the Higher Power dwells everyplace, there's
something very calming about the cool greenish inside of our mission. Or so I
thought, anyway. Grandpa was the one who stripped off my delusions in this
matter, for it was he who busted right through what Father calls the sacred
serenity of the place.

20   We filed in that time. Me and Grandpa. We sat down on our pews. Then
the rosary got started up pre-Mass and that's when Grandpa filled up his chest
and opened his mouth and belted out them words.

21   HAIL MARIE FULL OF GRACE.

22   He had a powerful set of lungs.

23   And he kept on like that. He did not let up. He hollered and he yelled them
prayers, and I guess people was used to him by now, because they only muttered
theirs and did not quit and gawk like I did. I was getting red-faced, I admit. I
give him the elbow once or twice, but that wasn't nothing to him. He kept on.
He shrieked to heaven and he pleaded like a movie actor and he pounded his
chest like Tarzan in the Lord I Am Not Worthies. I thought he might hurt
himself. Then after a while I guess I got used to it, and that's when I wondered:
how come?

24   So afterwards I out and asked him, "How come? How come you yelled?"

25   "God don't hear me otherwise," said Grandpa Kashpaw.

26   I sweat. I broke right into a little cold sweat at my hairline because I knew
this was perfectly right and for years not one damn other person had noticed
it. God's been going deaf. Since the Old Testament, God's been deafening up
on us. I read, see. Besides the dictionary, which I'm constantly in use of, I had
this Bible once. I read it. I found there was discrepancies between then and now.
It struck me. Here Got used to raineth bread from clouds, smite the Phillipines,
sling fire down on red-light districts where people got stabbed. He even appeared in person every once in a while. God used to pay attention, is what I'm
saying.

27   Now there's your God in the Old Testament and there is Chippewa Gods

as well. Indian Gods, good and bad, like tricky Nanabozho or the water monster, Missepeshu, who lives over in Matchimanito. That water monster was the last God I ever heard to appear. It had a weakness for young girls and grabbed one of the Pillagers off her rowboat. She got to shore all right, but only after this monster had its way with her. She's an old lady now. Old Lady Pillager. She still doesn't like to see her family fish that lake.

Our Gods aren't perfect, is what I'm saying, but at least they come around. They'll do a favor if you ask them right. You don't have to yell. But you do have to know, like I said, how to ask in the right way. That makes problems, because to ask proper was an art that was lost to the Chippewas once the Catholics gained ground. Even now, I have to wonder if Higher Power turned it back, if we got to yell, or if we just don't speak its language. 28

I looked around me. How else could I explain what all I had seen in my short life—King smashing his fist in things, Gordie drinking himself down to the Bismarck hospitals, or Aunt June left by a white man to wander off in the snow. How else to explain the times my touch don't work, and farther back, to the old-time Indians who was swept away in the outright germ warfare and dirty-dog killing of the whites. In those times, us Indians was so much kindlier than now. 29

We took them in. 30

Oh yes, I'm bitter as an old cutworm just thinking of how they done to us and doing still. 31

So Grandpa Kashpaw just opened my eyes a little there. Was there any sense relying on a God whose ears was stopped? Just like the government? I says then, right off, maybe we got nothing but ourselves. And that's not much, just personally speaking. I know I don't got the cold hard potatoes it takes to understand everything. Still, there's things I'd like to do. For instance, I'd like to help some people like my Grandpa and Grandma Kashpaw get back some happiness within the tail ends of their lives. 32

I told you once before I couldn't see my way clear to putting the direct touch on Grandpa's mind, and I kept my moral there, but something soon happened to make me think a little bit of mental adjustment wouldn't do him and the rest of us no harm. 33

It was after we saw him one afternoon in the sunshine courtyard of the Senior Citizens with Lulu Lamartine. Grandpa used to like to dig there. He had his little dandelion fork out, and he was prying up them dandelions right and left while Lamartine watched him. 34

"He's scratching up the dirt, all right," said Grandma, watching Lamartine watch Grandpa out the window. 35

Now Lamartine was about half the considerable size of Grandma, but you would never think of sizes anyway. They were different in an even more noticeable way. It was the difference between a house fixed up with paint and picky fence, and a house left to weather away into the soft earth, is what I'm saying. Lamartine was jacked up, latticed, shuttered, and vinyl sided, while 36

Grandma sagged and bulged on her slipped foundations and let her hair go the silver gray of rain-dried lumber. Right now, she eyed the Lamartine's pert flowery dress with such a look it despaired me. I knew what this could lead to with Grandma. Alterating tongue storms and rock-hard silences was hard on a man, even one who didn't notice, like Grandpa. So I went fetching him.

37   But he was gone when I popped through the little screen door that led out on the courtyard. There was nobody out there either, to point which way they went. Just the dandelion fork quibbling upright in the ground. That gave me an idea. I snookered over to the Lamartine's door and I listened in first, then knocked. But nobody. So I went walking through the lounges and around the card tables. Still nobody. Finally it was my touch that led me to the laundry room. I cracked the door. I went in. There they were. And he was really loving her up good, boy, and she was going hell for leather. Sheets was flapping on the lines above, and washcloths, pillowcases, shirts was also flying through the air, for they was trying to clear out a place for themselves in a high-heaped but shallow laundry cart. The washers and dryers was all on, chock-full of quarters, shaking and moaning. I couldn't hear what Grandpa and the Lamartine was billing and cooing, and they couldn't hear me.

38   I didn't know what to do, so I went inside and shut the door.

39   The Lamartine wore a big curly light-brown wig. Looked like one of them squeaky little white-people dogs. Poodles they call them. Anyway, that wig is what saved us from the worse. For I could hardly shout and tell them I was in there, no more could I try and grab him. I was trapped where I was. There was nothing I could really do but hold the door shut. I was scared of somebody else upsetting in and really getting an eyeful. Turned out though, in the heat of the clinch, as I was trying to avert my eyes you see, the Lamartine's curly wig jumped off her head. And if you ever been in the midst of something and had a big change like that occur in the someone, you can't help know how it devastates your basic urges. Not only that, but her wig was almost with a life of its own. Grandpa's eyes were bugging at the change already, and swear to God if the thing didn't rear up and pop him in the face like it was going to start something. He scrambled up, Grandpa did, and the Lamartine jumped up after him all addled looking. They just stared at each other, huffing and puffing, with quizzical expression. The surprise seemed to drive all sense completely out of Grandpa's mind.

40   "The letter was what started the fire," he said. "I never would have done it."

41   "What letter?" said the Lamartine. She was stiff-necked now, and elegant, even bald, like some alien queen. I gave her back the wig. The Lamartine replaced it on her head, and whenever I saw her after that, I couldn't help thinking of her bald, with special powers, as if from another planet.

42   "That was a close call," I said to Grandpa after she had left.

43   But I think he had already forgot the incident. He just stood there all quiet and thoughtful. You really wouldn't think he was crazy. He looked like he was

just about to say something important, explaining himself. He said something, all right, but it didn't have nothing to do with anything that made sense.

He wondered where the heck he put his dandelion fork. That's when I decided about the mental adjustment. 44

Now what was mostly our problem was not so much that he was not all there, but that what was there of him often hankered after Lamartine. If we could put a stop to that, I thought, we might be getting someplace. But here, see, my touch was of no use. For what could I snap my fingers at to make him faithful to Grandma? Like the quality of staying power, this faithfulness was invisible. I know it's something that you got to acquire, but I never known where from. Maybe there's no rhyme or reason to it, like my getting the touch, and then again maybe it's a kind of magic. 45

It was Grandma Kashpaw who thought of it in the end. She knows things. Although she will not admit she has a scrap of Indian blood in her, there's no doubt in my mind she's got some Chippewa. How else would you explain the way she'll be sitting there, in front of her TV story, rocking in her armchair and suddenly she turns on me, her brown eyes hard as lake-bed flint. 46

"Lipsha Morrissey," she'll say, "you went out last night and got drunk." 47

How did she know that? I'll hardly remember it myself. Then she'll say she just had a feeling or ache in the scar of her hand or a creak in her shoulder. She is constantly being told things by little aggravations in her joints or by her household appliances. One time she told Gordie never to ride with a crazy Lamartine boy. She had seen something in the polished-up tin of her bread toaster. So he didn't. Sure enough, the time came we heard how Lyman and Henry went out of control in their car, ending up in the river. Lyman swam to the top, but Henry never made it. 48

Thanks to Grandma's toaster, Gordie was probably spared. 49

Someplace in the blood Grandma Kashpaw knows things. She also remembers things, I found. She keeps things filed away. She's got a memory like them video games that don't forget your score. One reason she remembers so many details about the trouble I gave her in early life is so she can flash back her total when she needs to. 50

Like now. Take the love medicine. I don't know where she remembered that from. It came tumbling from her mind like an asteroid off the corner of the screen. 51

Of course she starts out by mentioning the time I had this accident in church and did she leave me there with wet overhalls? No she didn't. And ain't I glad? Yes I am. Now what you want now, Grandma? 52

But when she mentions them love medicines, I feel my back prickle at the danger. These love medicines is something of an old Chippewa specialty. No other tribe has got them down so well. But love medicines is not for the layman to handle. You don't just go out and get one without paying for it. Before you get one, even, you should go through one hell of a lot of mental condensation. 53

You got to think it over. Choose the right one. You could really mess up your life grinding up the wrong little thing.

54   So anyhow, I said to Grandma I'd give this love medicine some thought. I knew the best thing was to go ask a specialist like Old Lady Pillager, who lives up in a tangle of bush and never shows herself. But the truth is I was afraid of her, like everyone else. She was known for putting the twisted mouth on people, seizing up their hearts. Old Lady Pillager was serious business, and I have always thought it best to steer clear of that whenever I could. That's why I took the powers in my own hands. That's why I did what I could.

55   I put my whole mentality to it, nothing held back. After a while I started to remember things I'd heard gossiped over.

56   I heard of this person once who carried a charm of seeds that looked like baby pearls. They was attracted to a metal knife, which made them powerful. But I didn't know where them seeds grew. Another love charm I heard about I couldn't go along with, because how was I suppose to catch frogs in the act, which it required. Them little creatures is slippery and fast. And then the powerfullest of all, the most extreme, involved nail clips and such. I wasn't anywhere near asking Grandma to provide me all the little body bits that this last love recipe called for. I went walking around for days just trying to think up something that would work.

57   Well I got it. If it hadn't been the early fall of the year, I never would have got it. But I was sitting underneath a tree one day down near the school just watching people's feet go by when something tells me, look up! Look up! So I look up, and I see two honkers, Canada geese, the kind with little masks on their faces, a bird what mates for life. I see them flying right over my head naturally preparing to land in some slough on the reservation, which they certainly won't get off of alive.

58   It hits me, anyway. Them geese, they mate for life. And I think to myself, just what if I went out and got a pair? And just what if I fed some part—say the goose heart—of the female to Grandma and Grandpa ate the other heart? Wouldn't that work? Maybe it's all invisible, and then maybe again it's magic. Love is a stony road. We know that for sure. If it's true that the higher feelings of devotion get lodged in the heart like people say, then we'd be home free. If not, eating goose heart couldn't harm nobody anyway. I thought it was worth my effort, and Grandma Kashpaw thought so, too. She had always known a good idea when she heard one. She borrowed me Grandpa's gun.

59   So I went out to this particular slough, maybe the exact same slough I never got thrown in by my mother, thanks to Grandma Kashpaw, and I hunched down in a good comfortable pile of rushes. I got my gun loaded up. I ate a few of these soft baloney sandwiches Grandma made me for lunch. And then I waited. The cattails blown back and forth above my head. Them stringy blue herons was spearing up their prey. The thing I know how to do best in this world, the thing I been training for all my life, is to wait. Sitting there and sitting there was no hardship on me. I got to thinking about some funny things that hap-

pened. There was this one time that Lulu Lamartine's little blue tweety bird, a paraclete, I guess you'd call it, flown up inside her dress and got lost within there. I recalled her running out into the hallway trying to yell something, shaking. She was doing a right good jig there, cutting the rug for sure, and the thing is it *never* flown out. To this day people speculate where it went. They fear she might perhaps of crushed it in her corsets. It sure hasn't ever yet been seen alive. I thought of funny things for a while, but then I used them up, and strange things that happened started weaseling their way into my mind.

I got to thinking quite naturally of the Lamartine's cousin named Wrist- 60
watch. I never knew what his real name was. They called him Wristwatch because he got his father's broken wristwatch as a young boy when his father passed on. Never in his whole life did Wristwatch take his father's watch off. He didn't care if it worked, although after a while he got sensitive when people asked what time it was, teasing him. He often put it to his ear like he was listening to the tick. But it was broken for good and forever, people said so, at least that's what they thought.

Well I saw Wristwatch smoking in his pickup one afternoon and by nine 61
that evening he was dead.

He died sitting at the Lamartine's table, too. As she told it, Wristwatch had 62
just eaten himself a good-size dinner and she said would he take seconds on the hot dish when he fell over to the floor. They turnt him over. He was gone. But here's the strange thing: when the Senior Citizens' orderly took the pulse he noticed that the wristwatch Wristwatch wore was now working. The moment he died the wristwatch started keeping perfect time. They buried him with the watch still ticking on his arm.

I got to thinking. What if some gravediggers dug up Wristwatch's casket 63
in two hundred years and that watch was still going? I thought what question they would ask and it was this: Whose hand wound it?

I started shaking like a piece of grass at just the thought. 64

Not to get off the subject or nothing. I was still hunkered in the slough. It 65
was passing late into the afternoon and still no honkers had touched down. Now I don't need to tell you that the waiting did not get to me, it was the chill. The rushes was very soft, but damp. I was getting cold and debating to leave, when they landed. Two geese swimming here and there as big as life, looking deep into each other's little pinhole eyes. Just the ones I was looking for. So I lifted Grandpa's gun to my shoulder and I aimed perfectly, and *blam! Blam!* I delivered two accurate shots. But the thing is, them shots missed. I couldn't hardly believe it. Whether it was that the stock had warped or the barrel got bent someways, I don't quite know, but anyway them geese flown off into the dim sky, and Lipsha Morrissey was left there in the rushes with evening fallen and his two cold hands empty. He had before him just the prospect of another day of bone-cracking chill in them rushes, and the thought of it got him depressed.

Now it isn't my style, in no way, to get depressed. 66

So I said to myself, Lipsha Morrissey, you're a happy S.O.B. who could be 67 covered up with weeds by now down at the bottom of this slough, but instead you're alive to tell the tale. You might have problems in life, but you still got the touch. You got the power, Lipsha Morrissey. Can't argue that. So put your mind to it and figure out how not to be depressed.

68   I took my advice. I put my mind to it. But I never saw at the time how my thoughts led me astray toward a tragic outcome none could have known. I ignored all the danger, all the limits, for I was tired of sitting in the slough and my feet were numb. My face was aching. I was chilled, so I played with fire. I told myself love medicine was simple. I told myself the old superstitions was just that—strange beliefs. I told myself to take the ten dollars Mary MacDonald had paid me for putting the touch on her arthritis joint, and the other five I hadn't spent yet from winning bingo last Thursday. I told myself to go down to the Red Owl store.

69   And here is what I did that made the medicine backfire. I took an evil shortcut. I looked at birds that was dead and froze.

70   All right. So now I guess you will say, "Slap a malpractice suit on Lipsha Morrissey."

71   I heard of those suits. I used to think it was a color clothing quack doctors had to wear so you could tell them from the good ones. Now I know better that it's law.

72   As I walked back from the Red Owl with the rock-hard, heavy turkeys, I argued to myself about malpractice. I thought of faith. I thought to myself that faith could be called belief against the odds and whether or not there's any proof. How does that sound? I thought how we might have to yell to be heard by Higher Power, but that's not saying it's not *there*. And that is faith for you. It's belief even when the goods don't deliver. Higher Power makes promises we all know they can't back up, but anybody ever go and slap an old malpractice suit on God? Or the U.S. government? No they don't. Faith might be stupid, but it gets us through. So what I'm heading at is this. I finally convinced myself that the real actual power to the love medicine was not the goose heart itself but the faith in the cure.

73   I didn't believe it, I knew it was wrong, but by then I had waded so far into my lie I was stuck there. And then I went one step further.

74   The next day, I cleaned the hearts away from the paper packages of gizzards inside the turkeys. Then I wrapped them hearts with a clean hankie and brung them both to get blessed up at the mission. I wanted to get official blessings from the priest, but when Father answered the door to the rectory, wiping his hands on a little towel, I could tell he was a busy man.

75   "Booshoo, Father," I said. "I got a slight request to make of you this afternoon."

76   "What is it?" he said.

77   "Would you bless this package?" I held out the hankie with the hearts tied inside it.

He looked at the package, questioning it. 78

"It's turkey hearts," I honestly had to reply. 79

A look of annoyance crossed his face. 80

"Why don't you bring this matter over to Sister Martin," he said. "I have 81
duties."

And so, although the blessing wouldn't be as powerful, I went over to the 82
Sisters with the package.

I rung the bell, and they brought Sister Martin to the door. I had her as a 83
music teacher, but I was always so shy then. I never talked out loud. Now, I
had grown taller than Sister Martin. Looking down, I saw that she was not
feeling up to snuff. Brown circles hung under her eyes.

"What's the matter?" she said, not noticing who I was. 84

"Remember me, Sister?" 85

She squinted up at me. 86

"Oh yes," she said after a moment. "I'm sorry, you're the youngest of the 87
Kashpaws. Gordie's brother."

Her faced warmed up. 88

"Lipsha," I said, "that's my name." 89

"Well, Lipsha," she said, smiling broadly at me now, "what can I do for 90
you?"

They always said she was the kindest-hearted of the Sisters up the hill, and 91
she was. She brought me back into their own kitchen and made me take a big
yellow wedge of cake and a glass of milk.

"Now tell me," she said, nodding at my package. "What have you got 92
wrapped up so carefully in those handkerchiefs?"

Like before, I answered honestly. 93

"Ah," said Sister Martin. "Turkey hearts." She waited. 94

"I hoped you could bless them." 95

She waited some more, smiling with her eyes. Kindhearted though she was, 96
I began to sweat. A person could not pull the wool down over Sister Martin. I
stumbled through my mind for an explanation, quick, that wouldn't scare her
off.

"They're a present," I said, "for Saint Kateri's statue." 97

"She's not a saint yet." 98

"I know," I stuttered on. "In the hopes they will crown her." 99

"Lipsha," she said, "I never heard of such a thing." 100

So I told her. "Well the truth is," I said, "it's a kind of medicine." 101

"For what?" 102

"Love." 103

"Oh Lipsha," she said after a moment, "you don't need any medicine. I'm 104
sure any girl would like you exactly the way you are."

I just sat there. I felt miserable, caught in my pack of lies. 105

"Tell you what," she said, seeing how bad I felt, "my blessing won't make 106
any difference anyway. But there is something you can do."

107   I looked up at her, hopeless.

108   "Just be yourself."

109   I looked down at my plate. I knew I wasn't much to brag about right then, and I shortly became even less. For as I walked out the door I stuck my fingers in the cup of holy water that was sacred from their touches. I put my fingers in and blessed the hearts, quick, with my own hand.

110   I went back to Grandma and sat down in her little kitchen at the Senior Citizens. I unwrapped them hearts on the table, and her hard agate eyes went soft. She said she wasn't even going to cook those hearts up but eat them raw so their power would go down strong as possible.

111   I couldn't hardly watch when she munched hers. Now that's true love. I was worried about how she would get Grandpa to eat his, but she told me she'd think of something and don't worry. So I did not. I was supposed to hide off in her bedroom while she put dinner on a plate for Grandpa and fixed up the heart so he'd eat it. I caught a glint of the plate she was making for him. She put that heart smack on a piece of lettuce like in a restaurant and then attached to it a little heap of boiled peas.

112   He sat down. I was listening in the next room.

113   She said, "Why don't you have some mash potato?" So he had some mash potato. Then she gave him a little piece of boiled meat. He ate that. Then she said, "Why you didn't never touch your salad yet. See that heart? I'm feeding you it because the doctor said your blood needs building up."

114   I couldn't help it, at that point I peeked through a crack in the door.

115   I saw Grandpa picking at that heart on his plate with a certain look. He didn't look appetized at all, is what I'm saying. I doubted our plan was going to work. Grandma was getting worried, too. She told him one more time, loudly, that he had to eat that heart.

116   "Swallow it down," she said. "You'll hardly notice it."

117   He just looked at her straight on. The way he looked at her made me think I was going to see the smokescreen drop a second time, and sure enough it happened.

118   "What you want me to eat this for so bad?" he asked her uncannily.

119   Now Grandma knew the jig was up. She knew that he knew she was working medicine. He put his fork down. He rolled the heart around his saucer plate.

120   "I don't want to eat this," he said to Grandma. "It don't look good."

121   "Why it's fresh grade-A," she told him. "One hundred percent."

122   He didn't ask percent what, but his eyes took on an even more warier look.

123   "Just go on and try it," she said, taking the salt shaker up in her hand. She was getting annoyed. "Not tasty enough? You want me to salt it for you?" She waved the shaker over his plate.

124   "All right, skinny white girl!" She had got Grandpa mad. Oopsy-daisy, he popped the heart into his mouth. I was about to yawn loudly and come out of the bedroom. I was about ready for this crash of wills to be over, when I saw

he was still up to his old tricks. First he rolled it into one side of his cheek. "Mmmmm," he said. Then he rolled it into the other side of his cheek. "Mmmmmmm," again. Then he stuck his tongue out with the heart on it and put it back, and there was no time to react. He had pulled Grandma's leg once too far. Her goat was got. She was so mad she hopped up quick as a wink and slugged him between the shoulderblades to make him swallow.

Only thing is, he choked. 125

He choked real bad. A person can choke to death. You ever sit down at a 126 restaurant table and up above you there is a list of instructions what to do if something slides down the wrong pipe? It sure makes you chew slow, that's for damn sure. When Grandpa fell off his chair better believe me that little graphic illustrated poster fled into my mind. I jumped out the bedroom. I done everything within my power that I could do to unlodge what was choking him. I squeezed underneath his rib cage. I socked him in the back. I was desperate. But here's the factor of decision: he wasn't choking on the heart alone. There was more to it than that. It was other things that choked him as well. It didn't seem like he wanted to struggle or fight. Death came and tapped his chest, so he went just like that. I'm sorry all through my body at what I done to him with that heart, and there's those who will say Lipsha Morrissey is just excusing himself off the hook by giving song and dance about how Grandpa gave up.

Maybe I can't admit what I did. My touch had gone worthless, that is true. 127 But here is what I seen while he lay in my arms.

You hear a person's life will flash before their eyes when they're in danger. 128 It was him in danger, not me, but it was *his* life come over me. I saw him dying, and it was like someone pulled the shade down in a room. He eyes clouded over and squeezed shut, but just before that I looked in. He was still fishing in the middle of Matchimanito. Big thoughts was on his line and he had half a case of beer in the boat. He waved at me, grinned, and then the bobber went under.

Grandma had gone out of the room crying for help. I bunched my force 129 up in my hands and I held him. I was so wound up I couldn't even breathe. All the moments he had spent with me, all the times he had hoisted me on his shoulders or pointed into the leaves was concentrated in that moment. Time was flashing back and forth like a pinball machine. Lights blinked and balls hopped and rubber bands chirped, until suddenly I realized the last ball had gone down the drain and there was nothing. I felt his force leaving him, flowing out of Grandpa never to return. I felt his mind weakening. The bobber going under in the lake. And I felt the touch retreat back into the darkness inside my body, from where it came.

One time, long ago, both of us were fishing together. We caught a big old 130 snapper what started towing us around like it was a motor. "This here fishline is pretty damn good," Grandpa said. "Let's keep this turtle on and see where he takes us." So we rode along behind that turtle, watching as from time to time it surfaced. The thing was just about the size of a washtub. It took us all around the lake twice, and as it was traveling, Grandpa said something as a joke.

"Lipsha," he said, "we are glad your mother didn't want you because we was always looking for a boy like you who would tow us around the lake."

131   "I ain't no snapper. Snappers is so stupid they stay alive when their head's chopped off," I said.

132   "That ain't stupidity," said Grandpa. "Their brain's just in their heart, like yours is."

133   When I looked up, I knew the fuse had blown between my heart and my mind and that a terrible understanding was to be given.

134   Grandma got back into the room and I saw her stumble. And then she went down too. It was like a house you can't hardly believe has stood so long, through years of record weather, suddenly goes down in the worst yet. It makes sense, is what I'm saying, but you still can't hardly believe it. You think a person you know has got through death and illness and being broke and living on commodity rice will get through anything. Then they fold and you see how fragile were the stones that underpinned them. You see how instantly the ground can shift you thought was solid. You see the stop signs and the yellow dividing markers of roads you traveled and all the instructions you had played according to vanish. You see how all the everyday things you counted on was just a dream you had been having by which you run your whole life. She had been over me, like a sheer overhang of rock dividing Lipsha Morrissey from outer space. And now she went underneath. It was as though the banks gave way on the shores of Matchimanito, and where Grandpa's passing was just the bobber swallowed under by his biggest thought, her fall was the house and the rock under it sliding after, sending half the lake splashing up to the clouds.

135   Where there was nothing.

136   You play them games never knowing what you see. When I fell into the dream alongside of both of them I saw that the dominions I had defended myself from anciently was but delusions of the screen. Blips of light. And I was scot-free now, whistling through space.

137   I don't know how I come back. I don't know from where. They was slapping my face when I arrived back at Senior Citizens and they was oxygenating her. I saw her chest move, almost unwilling. She sighed the way she would when somebody bothered her in the middle of a row of beads she was counting. I think it irritated her to no end that they brought her back. I knew from the way she looked after they took the mask off, she was not going to forgive them disturbing her restful peace. Nor was she forgiving Lipsha Morrissey. She had been stepping out onto the road of death, she told the children later at the funeral. I asked was there any stop signs or dividing markers on that road, but she clamped her lips in a vise the way she always done when she was mad.

138   Which didn't bother me. I knew when things had cleared out she wouldn't have no choice. I was not going to speculate where the blame was put for Grandpa's death. We was in it together. She had slugged him between the shoulders. My touch had failed him, never to return.

All the blood children and the took-ins, like me, came home from Minnea-   139
polis and Chicago, where they had relocated years ago. They stayed with friends
on the reservation or with Aurelia or slept on Grandma's floor. They were struck
down with grief and bereavement to be sure, every one of them. At the funeral
I sat down in the back of the church with Albertine. She had gotten all skinny
and ragged haired from cramming all her years of study into two or three. She
had decided that to be a nurse was not enough for her so she was going to be
a doctor. But the way she was straining her mind didn't look too hopeful. Her
eyes were bloodshot from driving and crying. She took my hand. From the back
we watched all the children and the mourners as they hunched over their
prayers, their hands stuffed full of Kleenex. It was someplace in that long sad
service that my vision shifted. I began to see things different, more clear. The
family kneeling down turned to rocks in a field. It struck me how strong and
reliable grief was, and death. Until the end of time, death would be our rock.

So I had perspective on it all, for death gives you that. All the Kashpaw   140
children had done various things to me in their lives—shared their folks with
me, loaned me cash, beat me up in secret—and I decided, because of death,
then and there I'd call it quits. If I ever saw King again, I'd shake his hand.
Forgiving somebody else made the whole thing easier to bear.

Everybody saw Grandpa off into the next world. And then the Kashpaws   141
had to get back to their jobs, which was numerous and impressive. I had a few
beers with them and I went back to Grandma, who had sort of got lost in the
shuffle of everybody being sad about Grandpa and glad to see one another.

Zelda had sat beside her the whole time and was sitting with her now. I   142
wanted to talk to Grandma, say how sorry I was, that it wasn't her fault, but
only mine. I would have, but Zelda gave me one of her looks of strict warning
as if to say, "I'll take care of Grandma. Don't horn in on the women."

If only Zelda knew, I thought, the sad realities would change her. But of   143
course I couldn't tell the dark truth.

It was evening, late. Grandma's light was on underneath a crack in the door.   144
About a week had passed since we buried Grandpa. I knocked first but there
wasn't no answer, so I went right in. The door was unlocked. She was there but
she didn't notice me at first. Her hands were tied up in her rosary, and her gaze
was fully absorbed in the easy chair opposite her, the one that had always been
Grandpa's favorite. I stood there, staring with her, at the little green nubs in
the cloth and plastic armrest covers and the sad little hair-tonic stain he had
made on the white doily where he laid his head. For the life of me I couldn't
figure what she was staring at. Thin space. Then she turned.

"He ain't gone yet," she said.   145

Remember that chill I luckily didn't get from waiting in the slough? I got   146
it now. I felt it start from the very center of me, where fear hides, waiting to
attack. It spiraled outward so that in minutes my fingers and teeth were shaking
and clattering. I knew she told the truth. She seen Grandpa. Whether or not

he had been there is not the point. She had *seen* him, and that meant anybody else could see him, too. Not only that but, as is usually the case with these ghosts, he had a certain uneasy reason to come back. And of course Grandma Kashpaw had scanned it out.

147   I sat down. We sat together on the couch watching his chair out of the corner of our eyes. She had found him sitting in his chair when she walked in the door.

148   "It's the love medicine, my Lipsha," she said. "It was stronger than we thought. He came back even after death to claim me to his side."

149   I was afraid. "We shouldn't have tampered with it," I said. She agreed. For a while we sat still. I don't know what she thought, but my head felt screwed on backward. I couldn't accurately consider the situation, so I told Grandma to go to bed. I would sleep on the couch keeping my eye on Grandpa's chair. Maybe he would come back and maybe he wouldn't. I guess I feared the one as much as the other, but I got to thinking, see, as I lay there in darkness, that perhaps even through my terrible mistakes some good might come. If Grandpa did come back, I thought he'd return in his right mind. I could talk with him. I could tell him it was all my fault for playing with power I did not understand. Maybe he'd forgive me and rest in peace. I hoped this. I calmed myself and waited for him all night.

150   He fooled me though. He knew what I was waiting for, and it wasn't what he was looking to hear. Come dawn I heard a blood-splitting cry from the bedroom and I rushed in there. Grandma turnt the lights on. She was sitting on the edge of the bed and her face looked harsh, pinched-up, gray.

151   "He was here," she said. "He came and laid down next to me in bed. And he touched me."

152   Her heart broke down. She cried. His touch was so cold. She laid back in bed after a while, as it was morning, and I went to the couch. As I lay there, falling asleep, I suddenly felt Grandpa's presence and the barrier between us like a swollen river. I felt how I had wronged him. How awful was the place where I had sent him. Behind the wall of death, he'd watched the living eat and cry and get drunk. He was lonesome, but I understood he meant no harm.

153   "Go back," I said to the dark, afraid and yet full of pity. "You got to be with your own kind now," I said. I felt him retreating, like a sigh, growing less. I felt his spirit as it shrunk back through the walls, the blinds, the brick courtyard of Senior Citizens. "Look up Aunt June," I whispered as he left.

154   I slept late the next morning, a good hard sleep allowing the sun to rise and warm the earth. It was past noon when I awoke. There is nothing, to my mind, like a long sleep to make those hard decisions that you neglect under stress of wakefulness. Soon as I woke up that morning, I saw exactly what I'd say to Grandma. I had gotten humble in the past week, not just losing the touch but getting jolted into the understanding that would prey on me from here on out. Your life feels different on you, once you greet death and understand your heart's position. You wear your life like a garment from the mission bundle sale

ever after—lightly because you realize you never paid nothing for it, cherishing because you know you won't ever come by such a bargain again. Also you have the feeling someone wore it before you and someone will after. I can't explain that, not yet, but I'm putting my mind to it.

"Grandma," I said, "I got to be honest about the love medicine." 155

She listened. I knew from then on she would be listening to me the way I 156 had listened to her before. I told her about the turkey hearts and how I had them blessed. I told her what I used as love medicine was purely a fake, and then I said to her what my understanding brought me.

"Love medicine ain't what brings him back to you, Grandma. No, it's 157 something else. He loved you over time and distance, but he went off so quick he never got the chance to tell you how he loves you, how he doesn't blame you, how he understands. It's true feeling, not no magic. No supermarket heart could have brung him back."

She looked at me. She was seeing the years and days I had no way of 158 knowing, and she didn't believe me. I could tell this. Yet a look came on her face. It was like the look of mothers drinking sweetness from their children's eyes. It was tenderness.

"Lipsha," she said, "you was always my favorite." 159

She took the beads off the bedpost, where she kept them to say at night, 160 and she told me to put out my hand. When I did this, she shut the beads inside of my fist and held them there a long minute, tight, so my hand hurt. I almost cried when she did this. I don't really know why. Tears shot up behind my eyelids, and yet it was nothing. I didn't understand, except her hand was so strong, squeezing mine.

The earth was full of life and there were dandelions growing out the window, 161 thick as thieves, already seeded, fat as big yellow plungers. She let my hand go. I got up. "I'll go out and dig a few dandelions," I told her.

Outside, the sun was hot and heavy as a hand on my back. I felt it flow 162 down my arms, out my fingers, arrowing through the ends of the fork into the earth. With every root I prized up there was return, as if I was kin to its secret lesson. The touch got stronger as I worked through the grassy afternoon. Uncurling from me like a seed out of the blackness where I was lost, the touch spread. The spiked leaves full of bitter mother's milk. A buried root. A nuisance people dig up and throw in the sun to wither. A globe of frail seeds that's indestructible. ❖

RESPONDING

1. In a journal entry discuss Lipsha's understanding of "the Higher Power." Is he referring to God in the Old Testament? Chippewa Gods? Something else?

2. Lipsha Morrissey describes human behavior by comparing it to things he sees in the world around him. Working individually or in a group, find some of his descriptions and discuss what they tell you about his daily life. Replace some of his descriptions with ones of your own that reflect your understanding of human behavior. How does your understanding differ from his?

3. The Catholic Church and the Chippewas' traditional beliefs comprise a great deal of Lipsha's worldview. In an essay, examine how the two belief systems influence his thinking and behavior and how he combines the two. Use examples from the story to support your assertions.

4. Grandpa Kashpaw's death gives Lipsha a new understanding of life, death, and love. Using examples from the reading, write an essay discussing the changes that take place in his understanding of life's milestones.

PAULA GUNN ALLEN

The novelist, essayist, and poet Paula Gunn Allen was born in 1939 in Cubero, New Mexico, of Laguna-Sioux and Lebanese-Jewish ancestry. She holds a doctorate from the University of New Mexico. In addition to serving as editor for Studies in American Indian Literature: Critical Essays and Course Designs *(1983), as well as editing* Spider Woman's Granddaughters: Traditional Tales and Contemporary Writing by Native American Women *(1989), she has published a novel,* The Woman Who Owned the Shadows *(1983), a book-length study,* The Sacred Hoop: Recovering the Feminine in American Indian Traditions *(1986),* Wyrds *(1987),* Grandmothers of the Light: A Medicine Woman's Sourcebook *(1991), and several volumes of poetry. In addition, she has been awarded a grant for creative writing from the National Endowment for the Arts and a fellowship for Native American Studies from the University of California at Los Angeles.*

"Where I Come from Is Like This," from The Sacred Hoop, *explores connections between ethnic identity and feminist ideology by tracing some of the stories that comprised the American Indian oral tradition Allen was exposed to as a child.*

✠

WHERE I COME FROM IS LIKE THIS

I

MODERN AMERICAN INDIAN WOMEN, like their non-Indian sisters, are deeply engaged in the struggle to redefine themselves. In their struggle they must reconcile traditional tribal definitions of women with industrial and postindustrial non-Indian definitions. Yet while these definitions seem to be more or less mutually exclusive, Indian women must somehow harmonize and integrate both in their own lives. 1

An American Indian woman is primarily defined by her tribal identity. In her eyes, her destiny is necessarily that of her people, and her sense of herself as a woman is first and foremost prescribed by her tribe. The definitions of woman's roles are as diverse as tribal cultures in the Americas. In some she is devalued, in others she wields considerable power. In some she is a familial/clan adjunct, in some she is as close to autonomous as her economic circumstances and psychological traits permit. But in no tribal definitions is she perceived in the same way as are women in western industrial and postindustrial cultures. 2

In the west, few images of women form part of the cultural mythos, and 3 these are largely sexually charged. Among Christians, the madonna is the female prototype, and she is portrayed as essentially passive: her contribution is simply that of birthing. Little else is attributed to her and she certainly possesses few of the characteristics that are attributed to mythic figures among Indian tribes. This image is countered (rather than balanced) by the witch-goddess/whore characteristics designed to reinforce cultural beliefs about women, as well as western adversarial and dualistic perceptions of reality.

4   The tribes see women variously, but they do not question the power of femininity. Sometimes they see women as fearful, sometimes peaceful, sometimes omnipotent and omniscient, but they never portray women as mindless, helpless, simple, or oppressed. And while the women in a given tribe, clan, or band may be all these things, the individual woman is provided with a variety of images of women from the interconnected supernatural, natural, and social worlds she lives in.

5   As a half-breed American Indian woman, I cast about in my mind for negative images of Indian women, and I find none that are directed to Indian women alone. The negative images I do have are of Indians in general and in fact are more often of males than of females. All these images come to me from non-Indian sources, and they are always balanced by a positive image. My ideas of womanhood, passed on largely by my mother and grandmothers, Laguna Pueblo women, are about practicality, strength, reasonableness, intelligence, wit, and competence. I also remember vividly the women who came to my father's store, the women who held me and sang to me, the women at Feast Day, at Grab Days, the women in the kitchen of my Cubero home, the women I grew up with; none of them appeared weak or helpless, none of them presented herself tentatively. I remember a certain reserve on those lovely brown faces; I remember the direct gaze of eyes framed by bright-colored shawls draped over their heads and cascading down their backs. I remember the clean cotton dresses and carefully pressed hand-embroidered aprons they always wore; I remember laughter and good food, especially the sweet bread and the oven bread they gave us. Nowhere in my mind is there a foolish woman, a dumb woman, a vain woman, or a plastic woman, though the Indian women I have known have shown a wide range of personal style and demeanor.

6   My memory includes the Navajo woman who was badly beaten by her Sioux husband; but I also remember that my grandmother abandoned her Sioux husband long ago. I recall the stories about the Laguna woman beaten regularly by her husband in the presence of her children so that the children would not believe in the strength and power of femininity. And I remember the women who drank, who got into fights with other women and with the men, and who often won those battles. I have memories of tired women, partying women, stubborn women, sullen women, amicable women, selfish women, shy women, and aggressive women. Most of all I remember the women who laugh and scold and sit uncomplaining in the long sun on feast days and who cook wonderful food on wood stoves, in beehive mud ovens, and over open fires outdoors.

Among the images of women that come to me from various tribes as well   7
as my own are White Buffalo Woman, who came to the Lakota long ago and
brought them the religion of the Sacred Pipe which they still practice; Tinotzin
the goddess who came to Juan Diego to remind him that she still walked the
hills of her people and sent him with her message, her demand and her proof
to the Catholic bishop in the city nearby. And from Laguna I take the images
of Yellow Woman, Coyote Woman, Grandmother Spider (Spider Old Woman),
who brought the light, who gave us weaving and medicine, who gave us life.
Among the Keres she is known as Thought Woman who created us all and who
keeps us in creation even now. I remember Iyatiku, Earth Woman, Corn
Woman, who guides and counsels the people to peace and who welcomes us
home when we cast off this coil of flesh as huskers cast off the leaves that wrap
the corn. I remember Iyatiku's sister, Sun Woman, who held metals and cattle,
pigs and sheep, highways and engines and so many things in her bundle, who
went away to the east saying that one day she would return.

II

Since the coming of the Anglo-Europeans beginning in the fifteenth century,   8
the fragile web of identity that long held tribal people secure has gradually been
weakened and torn. But the oral tradition has prevented the complete destruction of the web, the ultimate disruption of tribal ways. The oral tradition is
vital; it heals itself and the tribal web by adapting to the flow of the present
while never relinquishing its connection to the past. Its adaptability has always
been required, as many generations have experienced. Certainly the modern
American Indian woman bears slight resemblance to her forebears—at least on
superficial examination—but she is still a tribal woman in her deepest being.
Her tribal sense of relationship to all that is continues to flourish. And though
she is at times beset by her knowledge of the enormous gap between the life
she lives and the life she was raised to live, and while she adapts her mind and
being to the circumstances of her present life, she does so in tribal ways,
mending the tears in the web of being from which she takes her existence as
she goes.

My mother told me stories all the time, though I often did not recognize   9
them as that. My mother told me stories about cooking and childbearing; she
told me stories about menstruation and pregnancy; she told me stories about
gods and heroes, about fairies and elves, about goddesses and spirits; she told
me stories about the land and the sky, about cats and dogs, about snakes and
spiders; she told me stories about climbing trees and exploring the mesas; she
told me stories about going to dances and getting married; she told me stories
about dressing and undressing, about sleeping and waking; she told me stories
about herself, about her mother, about her grandmother. She told me stories
about grieving and laughing, about thinking and doing; she told me stories about
school and about people; about darning and mending; she told me stories about

turquoise and about gold; she told me European stories and Laguna stories; she told me Catholic stories and Presbyterian stories; she told me city stories and country stories; she told me political stories and religious stories. She told me stories about living and stories about dying. And in all of those stories she told me who I was, who I was supposed to be, who I came from, and who would follow me. In this way she taught me the meaning of the words she said, that all life is a circle and everything has a place within it. That's what she said and what she showed me in the things she did and the way she lives.

10   Of course, through my formal, white, Christian education, I discovered that other people had stories of their own—about women, about Indians, about fact, about reality—and I was amazed by a number of startling suppositions that others made about tribal customs and beliefs. According to the un-Indian, non-Indian view, for instance, Indians barred menstruating women from cere- monies and indeed segregated them from the rest of the people, consigning them to some space specially designed for them. This showed that Indians considered menstruating women unclean and not fit to enjoy the company of decent (nonmenstruating) people, that is, men. I was surprised and confused to hear this because my mother had taught me that white people had strange attitudes toward menstruation: they thought something was bad about it, that it meant you were sick, cursed, sinful, and weak and that you had to be very careful during that time. She taught me that menstruation was a normal occur- rence, that I could go swimming or hiking or whatever else I wanted to do during my period. She actively scorned women who took to their beds, who were incapacitated by cramps, who "got the blues."

11   As I struggled to reconcile these very contradictory interpretations of American Indians' traditional beliefs concerning menstruation. I realized that the menstrual taboos were about power, not about sin or filth. My conclusion was later borne out by some tribes' own explanations, which, as you may well imagine, came as quite a relief to me.

12   The truth of the matter as many Indians see it is that women who are at the peak of their fecundity are believed to possess power that throws male power totally out of kilter. They emit such force that, in their presence, any male- owned or -dominated ritual or sacred object cannot do its usual task. For instance, the Lakota say that a menstruating woman anywhere near a yuwipi man, who is a special sort of psychic, spirit-empowered healer, for a day or so before he is to do his ceremony will effectively disempower him. Conversely, among many if not most tribes, important ceremonies cannot be held without the presence of women. Sometimes the ritual woman who empowers the cere- mony must be unmarried and virginal so that the power she channels is unal- loyed, unweakened by sexual arousal and penetration by a male. Other ceremo- nies require tumescent women, others the presence of mature women who have borne children, and still others depend for empowerment on postmenopausal women. Women may be segregated from the company of the whole band or village on certain occasions, but on certain occasions men are also segregated.

In short, each ritual depends on a certain balance of power, and the positions of women within the phases of womanhood are used by tribal people to empower certain rites. This does not derive from a male-dominant view; it is not a ritual observance imposed on women by men. It derives from a tribal view of reality that distinguishes tribal people from feudal and industrial people.

Among the tribes, the occult power of women, inextricably bound to our 13 hormonal life, is thought to be very great; many hold that we possess innately the blood-given power to kill—with a glance, with a step, or with a judicious mixing of menstrual blood into somebody's soup. Medicine women among the Pomo of California cannot practice until they are sufficiently mature; when they are immature, their power is diffuse and is likely to interfere with their practice until time and experience have it under control. So women of the tribes are not especially inclined to see themselves as poor helpless victims of male domination. Even in those tribes where something akin to male domination was present, women are perceived as powerful, socially, physically, and metaphysically. In times past, as in times present, women carried enormous burdens with aplomb. We were far indeed from the "weaker sex," the designation that white aristocratic sisters unhappily earned for us all.

I remember my mother moving furniture all over the house when she 14 wanted it changed. She didn't wait for my father to come home and help—she just went ahead and moved the piano, a huge upright from the old days, the couch, the refrigerator. Nobody had told her she was too weak to do such things. In imitation of her, I would delight in loading trucks at my father's store with cases of pop or fifty-pound sacks of flour. Even when I was quite small I could do it, and it gave me a belief in my own physical strength that advancing middle age can't quite erase. My mother used to tell me about the Acoma Pueblo women she had seen as a child carrying huge ollas (water pots) on their heads as they wound their way up the tortuous stairwell carved into the face of the "Sky City" mesa, a feat I tried to imitate with books and tin buckets. ("Sky City" is the term used by the Chamber of Commerce for the mother village of Acoma, which is situated atop a high sandstone table mountain.) I was never very successful, but even the attempt reminded me that I was supposed to be strong and balanced to be a proper girl.

Of course, my mother's Laguna people are Keres Indian, reputed to be the 15 last extreme mother-right people on earth. So it is no wonder that I got notably nonwhite notions about the natural strength and prowess of women. Indeed, it is only when I am trying to get non-Indian approval, recognition, or acknowledgment that my "weak sister" emotional and intellectual ploys get the better of my tribal woman's good sense. At such times I forget that I just moved the piano or just wrote a competent paper or just completed a financial transaction satisfactorily or have supported myself and my children for most of my adult life.

Nor is my contradictory behavior atypical. Most Indian women I know are 16 in the same bicultural bind: we vacillate between being dependent and strong, self-reliant and powerless, strongly motivated and hopelessly insecure. We resolve the dilemma in various ways: some of us party all the time; some of us drink to excess; some of us travel and move around a lot; some of us land good jobs and then quit them; some of us engage in violent exchanges; some of us blow our brains out. We act in these destructive ways because we suffer from the societal conflicts caused by having to identify with two hopelessly opposed cultural definitions of women. Through this destructive dissonance we are unhappy prey to the self-disparagement common to, indeed demanded of, Indians living in the United States today. Our situation is caused by the exigencies of a history of invasion, conquest, and colonization whose searing marks are probably ineradicable. A popular bumper sticker on many Indian cars proclaims: "If You're Indian You're In," to which I always find myself adding under my breath, "Trouble."

III

17   No Indian can grow to any age without being informed that her people were "savages" who interfered with the march of progress pursued by respectable, loving, civilized white people. We are the villains of the scenario when we are mentioned at all. We are absent from much of white history except when we are calmly, rationally, succinctly, and systematically dehumanized. On the few occasions we are noticed in any way other than as howling, bloodthirsty beings, we are acclaimed for our noble quaintness. In this definition, we are exotic curios. Our ancient arts and customs are used to draw tourist money to state coffers, into the pocketbooks and bank accounts of scholars, and into support of the American-in-Disneyland promoters' dream.

18   As a Roman Catholic child I was treated to bloody tales of how the savage Indians martyred the hapless priests and missionaries who went among them in an attempt to lead them to the one true path. By the time I was through high school I had the idea that Indians were people who had benefited mightily from the advanced knowledge and superior morality of the Anglo-Europeans. At least I had, perforce, that idea to lay beside the other one that derived from my daily experience of Indian life, an idea less dehumanizing and more accurate because it came from my mother and the other Indian people who raised me. That idea was that Indians are a people who don't tell lies, who care for their children and their old people. You never see an Indian orphan, they said. You always know when you're old that someone will take care of you—one of your children will. Then they'd list the old folks who were being taken care of by this child or that. No child is ever considered illegitimate among the Indians, they said. If a girl gets pregnant, the baby is still part of the family, and the mother is too. That's what they said, and they showed me real people who lived according to those principles.

19   Of course the ravages of colonization have taken their toll; there are orphans in Indian country now, and abandoned, brutalized old folks; there are even

illegitimate children, though the very concept still strikes me as absurd. There are battered children and neglected children, and there are battered wives and women who have been raped by Indian men. Proximity to the "civilizing" effects of white Christians has not improved the moral quality of life in Indian country, though each group, Indian and white, explains the situation differently. Nor is there much yet in the oral tradition that can enable us to adapt to these inhuman changes. But a force is growing in that direction, and it is helping Indian women reclaim their lives. Their power, their sense of direction and of self will soon be visible. It is the force of the women who speak and work and write, and it is formidable.

Through all the centuries of war and death and cultural and psychic destruction have endured the women who raise the children and tend the fires, who pass along the tales and the traditions, who weep and bury the dead, who are the dead, and who never forget. There are always the women, who make pots and weave baskets, who fashion clothes and cheer their children on at powwow, who make fry bread and piki bread, and corn soup and chili stew, who dance and sing and remember and hold within their hearts the dream of their ancient peoples—that one day the woman who thinks will speak to us again, and everywhere there will be peace. Meanwhile we tell the stories and write the books and trade tales of anger and woe and stories of fun and scandal and laugh over all manner of things that happen every day. We watch and we wait.   20

My great-grandmother told my mother: Never forget you are Indian. And my mother told me the same thing. This, then, is how I have gone about remembering, so that my children will remember too. ✢   21

RESPONDING

1. Allen talks about the power of the oral tradition, the family stories passed down to her from her mother. Using examples from the reading, discuss the role of tradition in preserving a culture. Consider the stories, or traditions, that have been passed down in your family. Do your stories tell you, as Allen's told her, "who I was, who I was supposed to be, who I came from, and who would follow me" (paragraph 9)? Write or tell one of your own important family stories.

2. Allen asserts that "in the west, few images of women form part of the cultural mythos" (paragraph 3). Working individually or in a group, compare the way an American Indian woman is defined by her tribe with the way a woman is defined by western civilization. Summarize the most important differences and share these with the class. Do you agree or disagree with Allen's depiction of western women's roles in their culture?

3. How are women's and men's roles defined in your culture? Write an essay comparing current roles for men and women with those in your mother's and your grandmother's time.

4. According to Allen, "No Indian can grow to any age without being informed that her people were 'savages' who interfered with the march of progress pursued by respectable, loving, civilized white people" (paragraph 17). Consider the source or impetus behind such messages. In an essay, discuss the effects that such a portrayal might have on an American Indian's sense of identity and self-esteem.

GREG SARRIS

Greg Sarris, born in Santa Rosa, California, received his bachelor's degree from the University of California, Los Angeles (UCLA) in 1978 and his master's and doctoral degrees from Stanford University. He has taught at several institutions, including Stanford, the University of California, Santa Cruz, and UCLA, where he is currently associate professor of English and associate director of the American Indian Studies Center. He has won grants from the Institute for American Cultures and the Irvine Foundation, among others. His publications include Keeping the Slug Woman Alive: A Holistic Approach to American Indian Literature *(1994), as well as essays in many academic journals.*

The essay that follows, first published in Sequoia, *examines the issues of legitimacy, authority, and oppression as they relate to personal and collective identities.*

❖

BATTLING ILLEGITIMACY: SOME WORDS AGAINST THE DARKNESS

I HAVE HEARD THAT SOMEONE SAID to American Indian writer Louise Erdrich, "You don't look Indian." It was at a reading she gave, or perhaps when she received an award of some kind for her writing. Undoubtedly, whoever said this noted Erdrich's very white skin, her green eyes and her red hair. She retorted, "Gee, you don't look rude."

You don't look Indian.

How often I too have heard that. But unlike Erdrich, I never returned the insult, or challenged my interlocutors. Not with words anyway. I arranged the facts of my life to fit others' conceptions of what it is to be Indian. I used others' words, others' definitions. That way, if I didn't look Indian, I might still be Indian.

Well, I don't know if I am Indian, I said, or if I am, how much. I was adopted. I know my mother was white—Jewish, German, Irish. I was illegitimate. Father unknown. It was back in the fifties when having a baby without being married was shameful. My mother uttered something on the delivery table about the father being Spanish. Mexican maybe. Anyway, I was given up and adopted, which is how I got a name. For awhile things went well. Then they didn't. I found myself with other families, mostly on small ranches where I milked cows and worked with horses. I met a lot of Indians—Pomo Indians— and was taken in by one of the families. I learned bits and pieces of two Pomo languages. So if you ask, I call myself Pomo. But I don't know . . . My mother isn't around to ask. After she had me, she needed blood. The hospital gave her the wrong type and it killed her.

5 The story always went something like that. It is true, all of it, but arranged so that people might see how I fit. The last lines—about my mother—awe people and cause them to forget, or to be momentarily distracted, from their original concern about my not looking Indian. And I am illegitimate. That explains any crossing of borders, anything beyond the confines of definition. That is how I fit.

6 Last year I found my father. Well, I found out his name—Emilio. My mother's younger brother, my uncle, who I met recently, remembered taking notes from his sister to a "big Hawaiian type" on the football field. "I would go after school while the team was practicing," my uncle said. "The dude was big, dark. They called him Meatloaf. I think his name though was Emilio. Try Emilio."

7 To have a name, even a nickname, seemed unfathomable. To be thirty-six years old and for the first time to have a lead about a father somehow frightened me. You imagine all your life; you find ways to account for that which is missing, you tell stories, and now all that is leveled by a name.

8 In Laguna Beach I contacted the high school librarian and made arrangements to look through old yearbooks. It was just after a conference there in Southern California, where I had finished delivering a paper on American Indian education. I found my mother immediately, and while I was staring for the first time at an adult picture of my mother, a friend who was with me scanned other yearbooks for an Emilio. Already we knew by looking at the rows and rows of white faces, there wouldn't be too many Emilios. I was still gazing at the picture of my mother when my friend jumped. "Look," she said. She was tilting the book, pointing to a name. But already, even as I looked, a dark face caught my attention, and it was a face I saw myself in. Without a doubt. Darker, yes. But me nonetheless.

9 I interviewed several of my mother's and father's classmates. It was my mother's friends who verified what I suspected. Emilio Hilario was my father. They also told me that he had died, that I had missed him by about five years.

10 I had to find out from others what he couldn't tell me. I wanted to know about his life. Did he have a family? What was his ethnicity? Luckily I obtained the names of several relatives, including a half-brother and a grandmother. People were quick about that, much more so than about the ethnicity question. They often circumvented the question by telling stories about my father's athletic prowess and about how popular he was. A few, however, were more candid. His father, my grandfather, is Filipino. "A short Filipino man," they said. "Your father got his height from his mother. She was fairer." Some people said my grandmother was Spanish, others said she was Mexican or Indian. Even within the family, there is discrepancy about her ethnicity. Her mother was

definitely Indian, however. Coast Miwok from Tomales Bay just north of San Francisco, and just South of Santa Rosa, where I grew up. Her name was Rienette.

During the time my grandmother was growing up, probably when her mother—Rienette—was growing up too, even until quite recently, when it became popular to be Indian, Indians in California sometimes claimed they were Spanish. And for good reason. The prejudice against Indians was intolerable, and often only remnants of tribes, or even families, remained to face the hatred and discrimination. My grandmother spoke Spanish. Her sister, Juanita, married a Mexican and her children's children are proud *Chicanos* living in East Los Angeles. Rienette's first husband, my grandmother and her sister's father, was probably part Mexican or Portuguese—I'm not sure.

The story is far from complete. But how much Indian I am by blood is not the question whose answer concerns me now. Oh, I qualify for certain grants, and that is important. But knowing about my blood heritage will not change my complexion any more than it will my experience.

In school I was called the white beaner. This was not because some of my friends happened to be Mexican, but because the white population had little sense of the local Indians. Anyone with dark hair and skin was thought to be Mexican. A counselor once called me in and asked if my family knew I went around with Mexicans. "Yes," I said. "They're used to it." At the time, I was staying with an Indian family—the McKays—and Mrs. McKay was a mother to me. But I said nothing more then. I never informed the counselor that most of my friends, the people she was referring to, were Indian—Pomo Indian. Kashaya Pomo Indian. Sulfur Bank Pomo Indian. Coyote Valley Pomo Indian. Yokaya Pomo Indian. Point Arena Pomo Indian. Bodega Bay Miwok Indian. Tomales Bay Miwok Indian. And never mind that names such as Smith and Pinola are not Spanish (or Mexican) names.

As I think back, I said nothing more to the counselor not because I didn't want to cause trouble (I did plenty of that), but because, like most other kids, I never really knew a way to tamper with how the authorities—counselors, teachers, social workers, police—categorized us. We talked about our ethnicity amongst ourselves, often speculating who was more or less this or that. So many of us are mixed with other groups—white, Mexican, Spanish, Portuguese, Filipino. I know of an Indian family who is half Mexican and they identify themselves as Mexicans. In another family of the same admixture just the opposite is true. Yet for most of the larger white community, we were Mexican, or something.

And here I am with blue eyes and fair skin. If I was a white beaner, I was, more generally, a kid from the wrong side of the tracks. Hood. Greaser. Low Brow. Santa Rosa was a much smaller town then, the lines more clearly drawn between the haves and the have-nots, the non-colored and the colored. Suburban sprawl was just beginning; there was still the old downtown with its stone library and old Roman-columned courthouse. On the fringes of town lived the poorer folk. The civil rights movement had not yet engendered the ethnic pride typical of the late sixties and early seventies.

16   I remember the two guys who taught me to box, Manual and Robert. They said they were Portuguese, Robert part Indian. People whispered that they were black. I didn't care. They picked me out, taught me to box. That was when I was fourteen. By the time I was sixteen, I beat heads everywhere and every time I could. I looked for fights and felt free somehow in the fight. I say I looked for fights, but really, as I think about it, fights seemed to fine me. People said things, they didn't like me, they invaded my space. I had reason. So I fought. And afterwards I was somebody. Manny said I had a chip on my shoulder, which is an asset for a good fighter. "Hate in your eyes, brother," he told me. "You got hate in your eyes."

17   I heard a lot of "Indian" stories too. We used to call them old-time stories, those about Coyote and the creation. Then there were the spook stories about spook men and women and evil doings. I knew of a spook man, an old guy who would be sitting on his family's front porch one minute and then five minutes later, just as you were driving uptown, there he'd be sitting on the old court-house steps. The woman whose son I spent so much time with was an Indian doctor. She healed the sick with songs and prayer; she sucked pains from people's bodies. These are the things my professors and colleagues wanted to hear about.

18   I was different here too. I read books, which had something to do with my getting into college. But when I started reading seriously—about the middle of my junior year in high school—I used what I read to explain the world; I never engaged my experience to inform what I was reading. Again, I was editing my experience, and, not so ironically, I found meaning that way. And, not so ironically, the more I read the more I became separated from the world of my friends and what I had lived. So in college when I found people interested in my Indian experience as it related to issues of ecology, personal empowerment, and other world-views, I complied and told them what I "knew" of these things. In essence I shaped what I knew to fit the books and read the books to shape what I knew. The woman who was a mother to me came off as Castaneda's Don Juan. Think of the "separate reality" of her dream world, never mind what I remember about her—the long hours in the apple cannery, her tired face, her clothes smelling of rotten apples.

19   Now, as I sort through things, I am beginning to understand why I hated myself and those people at the university; how by sculpting my experience and their interests, I denied so much of my life, including the anger and self-hatred that seeps up from such denial. I wanted to strike back, beat the hell out of them; I imagined them angering me in some way I could recognize—maybe an insult, a push or shove—so that I could hurt them. Other times I just wanted them to be somewhere, perhaps outside the classroom, on a street, in a bar, where they came suddenly upon me and saw me fighting, pummelling some-

body. Anger is like a cork in water. Push it down, push it down, and still it keeps coming to the surface.

Describing her life experience in a short autobiographical piece entitled 20 "The Autobiography of a Confluence," Paula Gunn Allen says, "Fences would have been hard to place without leaving something out . . . Essentially, my life, like my work, is a journey-in-between, a road." Poet Wendy Rose writes about how she went to the Highland Games in Fresno to search for her Scottish roots: "It may have looked funny to all those Scots to see an Indian [Rose] looking for a booth with her clan's name on it." She adds: "The colonizer and the colonized meet in my blood. It is so much more complex than just white and Indian. I will pray about this, too." These American Indian writers, just as so many other ethnic minority American writers, are attempting to mediate the cultural variables that constitute their experience as Americans. They are attempting to redefine their experience based on the experience itself and not in terms of others' notions of that experience.

During the late sixties and early seventies, an odd reversal of affairs took 21 place. Where some Indian people once denied, or at least kept quiet their Indian heritage, they suddenly began denying that part which is white, Spanish, or whatever. The point here is that in the name of ethnic pride we begin to make illegitimate so much of what we are, and have been, about. We deny aspects of our history and experience that could enrich any understanding of what it means to be an American Indian in time, in history, and not just as some relic from a prelapserian past, as the dominant culture so often likes to see us. We in fact become oppressor-like; we internalize the oppression we have felt, and, ironically, using others' definitions, or even those created by ourselves, decide who is Indian and who is not. We perpetuate illegitimacy in our ranks.

But the danger isn't just for ourselves here. Ultimately, by accepting or 22 creating certain definitions by which we judge our own experiences, we allow others a definition by which we can be judged by them. Criteria that render certain kinds of experience illegitimate enable people to escape the broader, human issues in life as it is lived. They allow the phonies a way to dress up, showing how they are Indian, and they cheat the rest of us of a true and fully human and historical cultural identity. What we need are words—stories, poems, histories, biographies—that qualify and challenge given definitions, that allow all of us as students and teachers, Indians and non-Indians, the opportunity to examine our own framing devices in order that we might be able to see and consider the possibility of seeing beyond those frames. We need to make visible the heretofore illegitimate so that we might consider human experience in the broadest sense possible.

My father was a local hero, they say. He excelled in all sports, was voted 23 junior class president, and served as president of the local Hi-Y. He was charming, outgoing, women loved him. But there was the other side, the black-out drinking and violence. Like a Jekyll and Hyde, people told me. He would turn on a dime, get nasty and mean. He'd rip into people. Kick ass. You could see it coming in his eyes.

24   When my grandfather brought his family from East Los Angeles to Laguna Beach, there was only one other minority family in town—a black family. Grandpa worked as a cook at Victor Hugo's, a glamorous waterfront restaurant. He settled his family in a small house in "the canyon," where the black family and season migrant families lived at the time, and where Grandpa still lives today. While my father was exalted locally as an athlete, he was constantly reminded of his color and class. Behind his back, people referred to him as a "nigger." To his face, the fathers of girls he dated told him: "Go away. We aren't hiring any gardeners."

25   I don't need to probe far here to get the picture. Illegitimacy in any form cuts a wide swath. Those of us affected by it react in a number of ways. Our histories, if they are presented and examined honestly, tell the stories. For my father and me it was, among other things, violence. Unable to tell his story, unable to fill in those chasms between his acceptance and rejection by the world around him, my father fought, each blow a strike against the vast and imposing darkness. He became a professional boxer; in the Navy he was undefeated, and after he sparred with Floyd Patterson. He died at 52, three weeks before his fifty-third birthday, just five years before his first son would find his picture in a yearbook. He died of a massive heart attack, precipitated by years of chronic alcoholism.

26   Now sometimes I wonder at my being Filipino, for I am as much Filipino by one definition, that is by blood, as I am anything by that same definition. Grandpa came from a small village on the island of Panay in the South Central Philippines. He tells me I have second cousins who have never worn shoes and speak only the Bisian dialect of that island. Yet, if I am Filipino, I am a Filipino separated from my culture and to backtrack, or go back, to that culture, I must carry my life with me, as it has been lived—in Santa Rosa with Pomo Indians and all others, and in the various cities and universities where I have lived and worked.

27   "You have quite a legacy in that man," a friend of my father's said to me. "He was one hell of a guy."

28   Yes, I thought to myself, a legacy. Fitting in by not fitting in. Repression. Violence. Walls of oppressive darkness. The urge now, the struggle, the very need to talk about the spaces, to word the darkness. ✠

RESPONDING

1. Sarris uses storytelling to define who he is. In a journal entry, tell a story that defines who you are.

2. Working individually or in a group, trace Sarris's family tree. Discuss what defines our ethnicity—is it blood?—or culture—or upbringing?

3. In an essay, explain how Sarris felt he was shaping and changing his experience to fit others' expectations. According to Sarris, what are some of the problems with that strategy?

4. Sarris says, "We in fact become oppressor-like; we internalize the oppression we have felt, and, ironically, using others' definitions, or even those created by ourselves, decide who is Indian and who is not" (paragraph 21). Explain his position and write an essay agreeing or disagreeing with his conclusions.

SIMON J. ORTIZ

A poet and short-story writer of Acoma Pueblo heritage, Simon J. Ortiz was born in 1941 at the Pueblo of Acoma, near Albuquerque, New Mexico, where he was raised. He received a bachelor's degree from the University of New Mexico (1968), and a master's degree in fine arts from the University of Iowa (1969). Ortiz has served in the United States Army and has been on the faculty at institutions such as the University of New Mexico and Sinte Gleska College in South Dakota, teaching creative writing. Ortiz's publications include the collections of short fiction Howbah Indians *(1978) and* Fightin': New and Collected Stories *(1983) as well as the poetry collections* Going for the Rain *(1976),* A Good Journey *(1977), and* From Sand Creek *(1981). He has also edited a collection of short fiction entitled* Earth Power Coming *(1983).*

In the essay that follows, Ortiz explores how heritage is defined through language; moreover, his essay reveals the ability of language to express natural beauty and artistic vision.

⊞

THE LANGUAGE WE KNOW

1   I DON'T REMEMBER a world without language. From the time of my earliest childhood, there was language. Always language, and imagination, speculation, utters of sound. Words, beginnings of words. What would I be without language? My existence has been determined by language, not only the spoken but the unspoken, the language of speech and the language of motion. I can't remember a world without memory. Memory, immediate and far away in the past, something in a sinew, blood, ageless cell. Although I don't recall the exact moment I spoke or tried to speak, I know the feeling of something tugging at the core of the mind, something unutterable uttered into existence. It is language that brings us into existence. It is language that brings us into being in order to know life.

2   My childhood was the oral tradition of the Acoma Pueblo people— Aaquumeh hano—which included my immediate family of three older sisters, two younger sisters, two younger brothers, and my mother and father. My world was our world of the Aaquumeh in McCartys, one of the two villages descended from the ageless mother pueblo of Acoma. My world was our Eagle clan-people among other clans. I grew up in Deetziyamah, which is the Aaquumeh name for McCartys, which is posted at the exit off the present interstate highway in

western New Mexico. I grew up within a people who farmed small garden plots and fields, who were mostly poor and not well schooled in the American system's education. The language I spoke was that of a struggling people who held ferociously to a heritage, culture, language, and land despite the odds posed them by the forces surrounding them since A.D. 1540, the advent of Euro-American colonization. When I began school in 1948 at the BIA (Bureau of Indian Affairs) day school in our village, I was armed with the basic ABC's and the phrases "Good morning, Miss Oleman" and "May I please be excused to go to the bathroom," but it was an older language that was my fundamental strength.

In my childhood, the language we all spoke was Acoma, and it was a struggle   3
to maintain it against the outright threats of corporal punishment, ostracism, and the invocation that it would impede our progress towards Americanization. Children in school were punished and looked upon with disdain if they did not speak and learn English quickly and smoothly, and so I learned it. It has occurred to me that I learned English simply because I was forced to, as so many other Indian children were. But I know, also, there was another reason, and this was that I loved language, the sound, meaning, and magic of language. Language opened up vistas of the world around me, and it allowed me to discover knowledge that would not be possible for me to know without the use of language. Later, when I began to experiment with and explore language in poetry and fiction, I allowed that a portion of that impetus was because I had come to know English through forceful acculturation. Nevertheless, the under-lying force was the beauty and poetic power of language in its many forms that instilled in me the desire to become a user of language as a writer, singer, and storyteller. Significantly, it was the Acoma language, which I don't use enough of today, that inspired me to become a writer. The concepts, values, and philosophy contained in my original language and the struggle it has faced have determined my life and vision as a writer.

In Deetziyamah, I discovered the world of the Acoma land and people   4
firsthand through my parents, sisters, and brothers, and my own perceptions, voiced through all that encompasses the oral tradition, which is ageless for any culture. It is a small village, even smaller years ago, and like other Indian communities it is wealthy with its knowledge of daily event, history, and social system, all that make up a people who have a many-dimensioned heritage. Our family lived in a two-room home (built by my grandfather some years after he and my grandmother moved with their daughters from Old Acoma), which my father added rooms to later. I remember my father's work at enlarging our home for our growing family. He was a skilled stoneworker, like many other men of an older Pueblo generation who worked with sandstone and mud mortar to build their homes and pueblos. It takes time, persistence, patience, and the belief that the walls that come to stand will do so for a long, long time, perhaps even forever. I like to think that by helping to mix mud and carry stone for my father

and other elders I managed to bring that influence into my consciousness as a writer.

5   Both my mother and my father were good storytellers and singers (as my mother is to this day—my father died in 1978), and for their generation, which was born soon after the turn of the century, they were relatively educated in the American system. Catholic missionaries had taken both of them as children to a parochial boarding school far from Acoma, and they imparted their discipline for study and quest for education to us children when we started school. But it was their indigenous sense of gaining knowledge that was most meaningful to me. Acquiring knowledge about life was above all the most important item; it was a value that one had to have in order to be fulfilled personally and on behalf of his community. And this they insisted upon imparting through the oral tradition as they told their children about our native history and our community and culture and our "stories." These stories were common knowledge of act, event, and behavior in a close-knit pueblo. It was knowledge about how one was to make a living through work that benefited his family and everyone else.

6   Because we were a subsistence farming people, or at least tried to be, I learned to plant, hoe weeds, irrigate and cultivate corn, chili, pumpkins, beans. Through counsel and advice I came to know that the rain which provided water was a blessing, gift, and symbol and that it was the land which provided for our lives. It was the stories and songs which provided the knowledge that I was woven into the intricate web that was my Acoma life. In our garden and our cornfields I learned about the seasons, growth cycles of cultivated plants, what one had to think and feel about the land; and at home I became aware of how we must care for each other: All of this was encompassed in an intricate relationship which had to be maintained in order that life continue. After supper on many occasions my father would bring out his drum and sing as we, the children, danced to themes about the rain, hunting, land, and people. It was all that is contained within the language of oral tradition that made me explicitly aware of a yet unarticulated urge to write, to tell what I had learned and was learning and what it all meant to me.

7   My grandfather was old already when I came to know him. I was only one of his many grandchildren, but I would go with him to get wood for our households, to the garden to chop weeds, and to his sheep camp to help care for his sheep. I don't remember his exact words, but I know they were about how we must sacredly concern ourselves with the people and the holy earth. I know his words were about how we must regard ourselves and others with compassion and love; I know that his knowledge was vast, as a medicine man and an elder of his kiva, and I listened as a boy should. My grandfather represented for me a link to the past that is important for me to hold in my memory because it is not only memory but knowledge that substantiates my present existence. He and the grandmothers and grandfathers before him thought about us as they lived, confirmed in their belief of a continuing life,

and they brought our present beings into existence by the beliefs they held. The consciousness of that belief is what informs my present concerns with language, poetry, and fiction.

My first poem was for Mother's Day when I was in the fifth grade, and it 8
was the first poem that was ever published, too, in the Skull Valley School newsletter. Of course I don't remember how the juvenile poem went, but it must have been certain in its expression of love and reverence for the woman who was the most important person in my young life. The poem didn't signal any prophecy of my future as a poet, but it must have come from the forming idea that there were things one could do with language and writing. My mother, years later, remembers how I was a child who always told stories—that is, tall tales—who always had explanations for things probably better left unspoken, and she says that I also liked to perform in school plays. In remembering, I do know that I was coming to that age when the emotions and thoughts in me began to moil to the surface. There was much to experience and express in that age when youth has a precociousness that is broken easily or made to flourish. We were a poor family, always on the verge of financial disaster, though our parents always managed to feed us and keep us in clothing. We had the problems, unfortunately ordinary, of many Indian families who face poverty on a daily basis, never enough of anything, the feeling of a denigrating self-consciousness, alcoholism in the family and community, the feeling that something was falling apart though we tried desperately to hold it all together.

My father worked for the railroad for many years as a laborer and later as 9
a welder. We moved to Skull Valley, Arizona, for one year in the early 1950s, and it was then that I first came in touch with a non-Indian, non-Acoma world. Skull Valley was a farming and ranching community, and my younger brothers and sisters and I went to a one-room school. I had never really had much contact with white people except from a careful and suspicious distance, but now here I was, totally surrounded by them, and there was nothing to do but bear the experience and learn from it. Although I perceived there was not much difference between *them* and *us* in certain respects, there was a distinct feeling that we were not the same either. This thought had been inculcated in me, especially by an Acoma expression—*Gaimuu Mericano*—that spoke of the "fortune" of being an American. In later years as a social activist and committed writer, I would try to offer a strong positive view of our collective Indianness through my writing. Nevertheless, my father was an inadequately paid laborer, and we were far from our home land for economic-social reasons, and my feelings and thoughts about that experience during that time would become a part of how I became a writer.

Soon after, I went away from my home and family to go to boarding school, 10
first in Santa Fe and then in Albuquerque. This was in the 1950s, and this had been the case for the past half-century for Indians: We had to leave home in order to become truly American by joining the mainstream, which was deemed

to be the proper course of our lives. On top of this was termination, a U.S. government policy which dictated that Indians sever their relationship to the federal government and remove themselves from their lands and go to American cities for jobs and education. It was an era which bespoke the intent of U.S. public policy that Indians were no longer to be Indians. Naturally, I did not perceive this in any analytical or purposeful sense; rather, I felt an unspoken anxiety and resentment against unseen forces that determined our destiny to be un-Indian, embarrassed and uncomfortable with our grandparents' customs and strictly held values. We were to set our goals as American working men and women, singlemindedly industrious, patriotic, and unquestioning, building for a future which ensured that the United States was the greatest nation in the world. I felt fearfully uneasy with this, for by then I felt the loneliness, alienation, and isolation imposed upon me by the separation from my family, home, and community.

11   Something was happening; I could see that in my years at Catholic school and the U.S. Indian school. I remembered my grandparents' and parents' words: Educate yourself in order to help your people. In that era and the generation who had the same experience I had, there was an unspoken vow: We were caught in a system inexorably, and we had to learn that system well in order to fight back. Without the motive of a fight-back we would not be able to survive as the people our heritage had lovingly bequeathed us. My diaries and notebooks began then, and though none have survived to the present, I know they contained the varied moods of a youth filled with loneliness, anger, and discomfort that seemed to have unknown causes. Yet at the same time, I realize now, I was coming to know myself clearly in a way that I would later articulate in writing. My love of language, which allowed me to deal with the world, to delve into it, to experiment and discover, held for me a vision of awe and wonder, and by then grammar teachers had noticed I was a good speller, used verbs and tenses correctly, and wrote complete sentences. Although I imagine that they might have surmised this as unusual for an Indian student whose original language was not English, I am grateful for their perception and attention.

12   During the latter part of that era in the 1950s of Indian termination and the Cold War, a portion of which still exists today, there were the beginnings of a bolder and more vocalized resistance against the current U.S. public policies of repression, racism, and cultural ethnocide. It seemed to be inspired by the civil rights movement led by black people in the United States and by decolonization and liberation struggles worldwide. Indian people were being relocated from their rural homelands at an astonishingly devastating rate, yet at the same time they resisted the U.S. effort by maintaining determined ties with their heritage, returning often to their native communities, and establishing Indian centers in the cities they were removed to. Indian rural communities, such as Acoma Pueblo, insisted on their land claims and began to initiate legal battles in the areas of natural and social, political and economic human rights. By the

retention and the inspiration of our native heritage, values, philosophies, and language, we would know ourselves as a strong and enduring people. Having a modest and latent consciousness of this as a teenager, I began to write about the experience of being Indian in America. Although I had only a romanticized image of what a writer was, which came from the pulp rendered by American popular literature, and I really didn't know anything about writing, I sincerely felt a need to say things, to speak, to release the energy of the impulse to help my people.

My writing in my late teens and early adulthood was fashioned after the American short stories and poetry taught in the high schools of the 1940s and 1950s, but by the 1960s, after I had gone to college and dropped out and served in the military, I began to develop topics and themes from my Indian background. The experience in my village of Deetziyamah and Acoma Pueblo was readily accessible. I had grown up within the oral tradition of speech, social and religious ritual, elders' counsel and advice, countless and endless stories, everyday event, and the visual art that was symbolically representative of life all around. My mother was a potter of the well-known Acoma clayware, a traditional art form that had been passed to her from her mother and the generations of mothers before. My father carved figures from wood and did beadwork. This was not unusual, as Indian people know; there was always some kind of artistic endeavor that people set themselves to, although they did not necessarily articulate it as "Art" in the sense of Western civilization. One lived and expressed an artful life, whether it was in ceremonial singing and dancing, architecture, painting, speaking, or in the way one's social-cultural life was structured. When I turned my attention to my own heritage, I did so because this was my identity, the substance of who I was, and I wanted to write about what that meant. My desire was to write about the integrity and dignity of an Indian identity, and at the same time I wanted to look at what this was within the context of an America that had too often denied its Indian heritage.

To a great extent my writing was a natural political-cultural bent simply because I was nurtured intellectually and emotionally within an atmosphere of Indian resistance. Aacquu did not die in 1598 when it was burned and razed by European conquerors, nor did the people become hopeless when their children were taken away to U.S. schools far from home and new ways were imposed upon them. The *Aaquumeh hano*, despite losing much of their land and surrounded by a foreign civilization, have not lost sight of their native heritage. This is the factual case with most other Indian peoples, and the clear explanation for this has been the fight-back we have found it necessary to wage. At times, in the past, it was outright armed struggle, like that of present-day Indians in Central and South America with whom we must identify; currently, it is often in the legal arena, and it is in the field of literature. In 1981, when I was invited to the White House for an event celebrating American poets and poetry, I did not immediately accept the invitation. I questioned myself about the possibility that I was merely being exploited as an Indian, and I hedged against accepting.

But then I recalled the elders going among our people in the poor days of the 1950s, asking for donations—a dollar here and there, a sheep, perhaps a piece of pottery—in order to finance a trip to the nation's capital. They were to make another countless appeal on behalf of our people, to demand justice, to reclaim lost land even though there was only spare hope they would be successful. I went to the White House realizing that I was to do no less than they and those who had fought in the Pueblo Revolt of 1680, and I read my poems and sang songs that were later described as "guttural" by a Washington, D.C., newspaper. I suppose it is more or less understandable why such a view of Indian literature is held by many, and it is also clear why there should be a political stand taken in my writing and those of my sister and brother Indian writers.

15   The 1960s and afterward have been an invigorating and liberating period for Indian people. It has been only a little more than twenty years since Indian writers began to write and publish extensively, but we are writing and publishing more and more; we can only go forward. We come from an ageless, continuing oral tradition that informs us of our values, concepts, and notions as native people, and it is amazing how much of this tradition is ingrained so deeply in our contemporary writing, considering the brutal efforts of cultural repression that was not long ago outright U.S. policy. We were not to speak our languages, practice our spiritual beliefs, or accept the values of our past generations; and we were discouraged from pressing for our natural rights as Indian human beings. In spite of the fact that there is to some extent the same repression today, we persist and insist in living, believing, hoping, loving, speaking, and writing as Indians. This is embodied in the language we know and share in our writing. We have always had this language, and it is the language, spoken and unspoken, that determines our existence, that brought our grandmothers and grandfathers and ourselves into being in order that there be a continuing life. ✤

RESPONDING

1. When do you have the urge or the need to express yourself in writing? Do you write only when forced to do so by necessity or a class assignment? Do you write to communicate or for your own pleasure? Given a choice, would you prefer all your communication to be oral? In a journal entry, speculate about when and why you write.

2. Working individually or in a group, think about a recent event in your school, city, or country. Tell your version of the event to your group. Then write a version of the event. Compare the written and the spoken versions. How are they similar? In what ways are they different? What are the advantages and disadvantages of the written version?

3. Ortiz says that the "oral tradition . . . made me explicitly aware of a yet unarticulated urge to write" (paragraph 6). In an essay, explain and illustrate the influence of that tradition on his writing. Do you find it unusual that the spoken word was the stimulus for writing? What could he gain by writing that he couldn't achieve through telling a story aloud?

4. Ortiz believes Indians need a mainstream education in order to effect social change. In an essay, clarify Ortiz's views and give specific examples of the way in which he visualizes Indians using their education to fight injustice and preserve their cultural heritage. Then argue for or against his position.

VINE DELORIA, JR., AND CLIFFORD M. LYTLE

A member of the Sioux tribe, Vine Deloria, Jr., was born in Martin, South Dakota, in 1933. He earned his bachelor's degree from Iowa State University (1958), his master's from the Lutheran School of Theology (1963), and his law degree from the University of Colorado (1970). Since serving as director of the National Congress of American Indians, he has held teaching and research positions at several colleges and universities, including Colorado College, the University of Arizona, and the University of Colorado. His publications include Custer Died for Your Sins: An Indian Manifesto *(1969),* We Talk, You Listen: New Tribes, New Turf *(1970),* God is Red *(1973), and* Behind the Trail of Broken Treaties: An Indian Declaration of Independence *(1974). With Clifford Lytle, he has coauthored* American Indians, American Justice *(1983) and* The Nations Within: The Past and Future of American Indian Sovereignty *(1984), among others.*

Clifford M. Lytle, who was born in 1932, has written extensively on issues related to constitutional law and the history of the American justice system. He holds a bachelor's degree from Denison University, a legal degree from Case Western University, and a doctorate from the University of Pittsburgh. In addition to the books he has coauthored with Vine Deloria, Lytle has also written The Warren Court and Its Critics *(1968) and coauthored, with Richard Cortner,* Modern Constitutional Law *(1971) and* Constitutional Politics in Arizona *(1969), among other works.*

The selection that follows, from The Nations Within, *explores some of the negotiations that have taken place between the federal government and the tribes. As it examines the difference between nationhood and self-government, the selection assesses the implications of that distinction for American Indians and members of the dominant culture as well.*

✜

A STATUS HIGHER THAN STATES

1   IT MUST BE A BIT DISCONCERTING when the average American on vacation out west suddenly encounters a sign that boldly proclaims that the highway is entering an Indian "nation." We like to think of nations on a much larger scale—preferably an ocean away, with all the hustle and bustle of modern, industrial, institutional life. Nations have different languages, religions, customs, and holidays from our own; they represent a mass of people who have struggled for centuries to create institutions that presently serve them. Indian tribes have

some of the attributes we find familiar in other nations; language, religion, and social customs certainly set them apart from other Americans. But we miss the massive crowd of people, the well-developed lands, the military and economic power that we see in larger nations. And so, when the idea of Indian tribes as nations is voiced, many Americans laugh at the pretension, convinced that Indians have some primitive delusion of grandeur that has certainly been erased by history.

Indian affairs constitute but a minute part of the domestic American scene— so small a share, in fact, that federal Indian legislation no longer even rates a permanent subcommittee in either house of Congress. It is not difficult to see that although Indians are poor and generally live in isolated places in rural America, they are not in most respects radically different from other Americans living in the same circumstances. In fact, one might observe, most Indians are not distinguishable from other Americans except on those occasions when they shed working clothes and perform dances in fancy costumes for tourists—for a small entrance fee, of course. If this occasional ceremonial, the meaning of which has been lost in the past century and replaced by the commercial pow-wow, is all that distinguishes Indians from other Americans, why do Indians believe they are different? And why does the United States government treat them differently?

Modern social reality and historical political reality are rarely consonant with each other. Contemporary Indian communities, both reservation and urban, represent the continuing existence of a particular group of people who have traditionally had a moral and legal claim against the United States. The fact that many Indian tribes continue to exist unassimilated is not due to the practice of traditional ceremonies as much as it testifies to the complex of legal and political ideas that have surrounded Indians for two centuries and made them understand the world in much different terms from any other group of American citizens.

American Indians are unique in the world in that they represent the only aboriginal peoples still practicing a form of self-government in the midst of a wholly new and modern civilization that has been transported to their lands. Early in the period of discovery of the New World, the papacy articulated the Doctrine of Discovery, which announced that Christian princes discovering new lands had a recognized title to them, subject only to the willingness of the original inhabitants to sell their lands to the discoverer. Because of such principles—and in spite of the history of exploitation and conquest represented by American settlement of North America—American Indians have actually been treated considerably better than any other aboriginal group on any other continent.

The United States, after successfully revolting against the king of England, claimed to inherit Great Britain's right to buy the lands of the Indians, and this doctrine, modified to fit the internal, domestic law of the United States, has been the primary conceptual focus for all subsequent federal Indian law. Every legal doctrine that today separates and distinguishes American Indians from other Americans traces its conceptual roots back to the Doctrine of Discovery and the subsequent moral and legal rights and responsibilities of the United States with respect to Indians.

6   Under the Constitutions, Congress is given exclusive power to regulate commerce with foreign nations, among the several states, and with the Indian tribes.[1] Among other powers and privileges ceded to the national government with the adoption of the Constitution was the surrender by the states of the subject of Indians. New York State and several other former colonies—specifically, Virginia and Massachusetts—preserved the right to continue to deal with Indian tribes for whom they had already assumed some responsibility. But these relationships were themselves based upon the old Doctrine of Discovery and represented a long series of treaty agreements in which the colonies—now states, with the adoption of the Constitution—agreed to protect the tribes from the depredations of their own citizens. There is no inherent power in any of the fifty states to deal with Indians at all.

7   One good way to view the subsequent history of the United States is through the eyes of the federal government in dealing with Indians and Indian rights. Much of the federal-state conflict has revolved around the role of the federal government in protecting its primacy with respect to Indian affairs. Pressures on the frontier for free lands, the extension of slavery into land unsuitable for cotton production, the aggressive gold rushes, the need for a suitable water law on western lands, and the authorization and construction of railroads—all these activities were hampered by and influenced by the role of the federal government toward Indians. Settlement was chaotic, but in a sense systematically so, in that many activities were delayed while the government dealt with the tribes who occupied and defended various parts of the continent.

8   The Constitution mentions Indians as an identifiable group twice: once in the provision for determining representation in the Congress and the second time when this phrase is repeated in the Fourteenth Amendment. Indians in these instances are viewed as individuals: "Indians not taxed," a phrase that testifies to the idea that Indians, as individuals, could be assimiliated into the body politic, providing they assumed the ordinary citizenship responsibilities. In the world of Anglo-Saxon property owners this meant paying taxes. Indians not paying taxes are not to be enumerated when determining the population of each state, and the presumption is that those Indians immune from state and federal taxes are in some kind of political allegiance to their own tribes, submitting to whatever strictures that tribe or society is able to impose on its members. Therefore these Indians are outside the reach of American sovereignty and its taxing power.

9   This interpretation is further supported by the language of the Indian

---

1. U.S., *Constitution*, Art. 1, sec. 8, clause 3.

Citizenship Act of 1924,[2] which gives all Indians born within the territorial limits of the United States full citizenship but adds that such status does not infringe upon the rights to tribal and other property that Indians enjoy as members of their tribes. A dual citizenship exists here, which is not to be hindered in either respect: Indians are not to lose civil rights because of their status as members of a tribe, and members of a tribe are not to be denied their tribal rights because of their American citizenship. Unfortunately, this distinction has not often been preserved, and in the 1920s, and again in the 1950s, Congress attempted to sever unilaterally the political relationship between Indian tribes and the United States, using the citizenship of individual Indians as its excuse.

For a long time after the United States assumed primary control over its portion of North America, Indian tribes maintained their own civil and criminal jurisdiction. Tribal traditions and customs prevailed in instances of civil and social disorder. Some treaties—most notably those signed in 1867 and 1868 with the large tribes of the West (the Sioux, Cheyenne, Navajo, Ute, Crow, and Arapaho)—made provision for the Indians to continue to govern themselves according to ancient ways. The first article of these treaties generally recites a formula to the effect that the tribes can punish their own wrongdoers and they can pay indemnities to the United States instead of surrendering tribal members who have performed bad or injurious acts against citizens of the United States or members of other tribes.

In 1882 the Brule Sioux medicine man Crow Dog killed Spotted Tail, leader of the band and a chief who had counseled accommodation with the United States. Under traditional Sioux customs the relatives of the two men arranged for compensation for the death of Spotted Tail. Presents were exchanged, and the families believed they had solved the problems created by the killing. The federal attorney for Dakota Territory was aghast at the seemingly casual manner in which the Sioux dealt with this killing, and he soon charged Crow Dog with murder. The case reached the Supreme Court in 1883, and the conviction of Crow Dog by the territorial court was reversed on the grounds that the 1868 treaty had preserved for the Sioux the right to punish tribal members who had committed serious crimes. A great public outcry followed the decision, and in 1885 Congress passed the Seven Major Crimes Act,[3] which took away major criminal jurisdiction from Indian tribes.

Although the Seven Major Crimes Act was phrased to apply to all Indian tribes in their capacity as governments, it was not so applied. The Five Civilized Tribes—the Cherokee, Choctaw, Creek, Chickasaw, and Seminole—did not legally come under its provisions because of special laws which applied only to them. Neither, as a matter of practical fact, was it applied to the small groups of Indians in the Great Basin who had not yet moved to a reservation. Never-

10

11

12

2. U.S., *Statutes at Large*, 43:253.
3. Ibid., 23:362.

theless, for the majority of Indians living on the reservations, the passage of this act, coupled with a new aggressive attitude on the part of Indian agents assigned to them, quickly eroded the social cement that tribal custom had provided to tribal societies. Some tribes were able to maintain a form of religious continuity in ceremonies, but the major strength of tribal political unity was broken by the assumption of jurisdiction by federal and territorial courts over offenses committed by one Indian against another on the reservation.

13   In 1887 the General Allotment Act was passed, and shortly thereafter most of the reservations were subdivided into 160-acre tracts, which were distributed to tribal members. The remaining tribal lands were purchased by the United States at a minimum price and opened to settlement by whites, the purchase price sometimes deposited in the United States Treasury but more often distributed on a per-capita basis among tribal members. Allotment redirected the thrust of the federal-Indian relationship to that of property management, and with the need for supervision over the use of property came the expansion of the administrative structure of the Bureau of Indian Affairs. Tribal status became less important, and natural resources became the major concern of both Indians and federal bureaucrats.

14   In 1934, as a part of the New Deal efforts to grapple with the economic depression that had brought the country to a standstill, John Collier, commissioner of Indian Affairs, presented to Congress a major piece of reform legislation popularly called the Indian Reorganization Act (IRA). Under the provisions of this act any tribe or the people of any reservation could organize themselves as a business corporation, adopt a constitution and bylaws, and exercise certain forms of self-government. Although the IRA was designed to permit tribal governments to engage in some kinds of economic development and business enterprise, the failure of Congress to appropriate sufficient funds made the economic recovery of the tribes difficult and blunted their progress.

15   The postwar retrenchment of domestic social programs made it exceedingly difficult for tribes to continue the progress they had made under the IRA before the Second World War. In 1954, under the urging of Senator Arthur Watkins, Congress adopted a program of termination of federal supervision of Indians. In reality this policy meant termination of federal services to Indians; most of the tribes who lost their federal status did not escape from the burdens of wardship. They were usually placed under the supervision of one of the larger banks in the state in which they were located, and their property was managed for them by it.

16   With the advent of the New Frontier and Great Society programs, Indian tribes were declared eligible as local sponsoring agencies for the multitude of social welfare programs authored by Congress. The sixties' War on Poverty required that the poor be organized into Community Action Program (CAP) areas and that a CAP agency administer programs designed to eliminate poverty. The poverty programs were a welcome respite from decades of neglect. Educational services were expanded, some modern forms of economic development

were made available to the reservations, and housing was built for the first time since the Great Depression. By the early 1970s, tribes felt so confident in their own talents in management and political organization that they began to pressure the federal government to give them more flexibility in controlling the activities on their reservations. The 1972 Indian Education Act[4] and the Indian Self-determination and Education Act of 1975[5] were legislative expressions of the Indian desire for more freedom in the activities of government.

The major thrust of recent contemporary reform in Indian affairs was represented by the American Policy Review Commission resolution,[6] which established the American Indian Policy Review Commission (AIPRC), charged with surveying the conditions of Indians in the United States and making recommendations on how to improve federal Indian policy. The commission, popularly nicknamed the Abourezk Commission after the senator from South Dakota who had sponsored the measure in the Senate and had become co-chairman of the body, was subdivided into eleven task forces that investigated various topical subjects of importance to Indians—treaties, tribal government, economic development, education, and so forth.

The AIPRC devoted two years to this study and produced a massive report, running close to two thousand pages. The final report contained over two-hundred separate recommendations, the majority of which were simple housekeeping corrections that reflected the orientation of Bureau of Indian Affairs employees who had been borrowed to write the final draft of the commission's findings. The tone of the Abourezk Commission was very aggressive, and consequently the final report was divided into a majority and minority opinion, the conflict revolving around the degree to which the commission should endorse the idea of tribal sovereignty. Many of the Indians who had worked for the commission wanted a strong posture that conceived of tribes as dependent domestic nations. The minority, led by Congressman Lloyd Meeds of Washington, recognizing that the political climate was shifting away from militancy, sought to blunt the impact of the report. Shortly after the Abourezk Commission report was issued, the Indian subcommittees in the Senate and House Interior committees were abolished, making it difficult, if not impossible, to carry out the recommendations of the commission.

With the advent of the Carter and later Reagan administrations, Indian tribes shifted their attention to more practical programmatic considerations. Declining federal budgets for domestic social programs meant a drastic cutback in funds available to operate reservation programs, and unemployment rose swiftly on most reservations, which had depended on an expanding number of federal programs for meeting the employment needs of the tribe. Neither Carter nor Reagan disturbed the status of tribal governments with new policy consid-

4. Ibid., 86:334.
5. Ibid., 88:2203.
6. Ibid., 1910.

erations. They were content to admonish the tribes to enter the world of private enterprise and reduce their dependence on federal largess.

20   Recent federal policy has featured the slogan of a "government-to-government relationship," which is intended to represent the older idea that tribes have a special political status with respect to the United States. Few Indians or bureaucrats know exactly what this recent phrase is supposed to represent. Since tribes are very much dependent upon the federal government for their operating funds and for permission to exploit the natural resources present on their reservations, the idea of two governments meeting in some kind of contemporary contractual arrangement on anything approaching an equal bargaining position itself seems ludicrous. Nevertheless, the Indian leadership has insisted that this description of the federal-tribal relationship is accurate and describes precisely the framework they believe exists. It is no mistake, in view of the accommodations the tribes and the United States have worked out, that many tribes have erected signs proclaiming their nationhood, that traditional Indians believe themselves to be sovereign entities endowed with almost mystical political powers, and that groups of Indians have recently appeared on the world scene demanding some form of representation in the United Nations.

21   When we look back at the treaty negotiations between the United States and the respective Indian tribes, there is little mention of the complex of ideas that constitutes nationhood. Indeed, we find very little awareness in either the Indians or the American treaty commissioners that an important status was being changed by the agreement that people were then making. During the 1868 treaty negotiations with the Sioux and Arapaho, at times the American commissioners speak of the Sioux as a small nation that can be totally destroyed by the kind of warfare the United States was willing to wage were peace not forthcoming from the talks. Strangely, the Indians were not cowed by the threats of the treaty commissioners; they knew so little about the white man that they believed they could prevail if the whites wished to make war on them. So finally the United States signed the treaty and agreed to one of the most humiliating provisions it ever accepted. The forts on the Bozeman Trail were abandoned at the demand of Red Cloud that the Sioux hunting lands be kept inviolate, and as the soldiers departed, the Indians rushed into the stockades and burned them to the ground.

22   In almost every treaty, however, the concern of the Indians was the preservation of the people, and it is in this concept of the people that we find both the psychological and the political keys that unlock the puzzling dilemma of the present and enable us to understand why American Indians view the world as they do today. When we understand the idea of the people, we can also learn how the idea of the treaty became so sacred to Indians that even today, more than a century after most of the treaties were made, Indians still refer to the provisions as if the agreement were made last week. The treaty, for most tribes, was a sacred pledge made by one people to another and required no more than

the integrity of each party for enforcement. That the United States quickly insisted that the treaties should be interpreted rigidly as strictly legal documents has galled succeeding generations of Indians and made permanent peace between Indians and the federal government impossible.

The idea of the people is primarily a religious conception, and with most American Indians tribes it begins somewhere in the primordial mists. In that time the people were gathered together but did not yet see themselves as a distinct people. A holy man had a dream or a vision; quasi-mythological figures of cosmic importance revealed themselves, or in some other manner the people were instructed. They were given ceremonies and rituals that enabled them to find their place on the continent. Quite often they were given prophecies that informed them of the historical journey ahead. In some instances the people were told to migrate until a special place was revealed; in the interim, as with the Hebrews wandering in the deserts of Sinai, the older generation, which had lost faith, and the cynics and skeptics in the group would be eliminated until the people were strong enough to receive the message. 23

Tribal names generally reflect the basic idea that these particular people have been chosen from among the various peoples of the universe—including mammals, birds, and reptiles, as well as other humans,—to hold a special relationship with the higher powers. Thus, most tribal names can be interpreted simply to mean "the people." There are, of course, some variations that have arisen in the course of the Indian historical journey. The people who pierced their noses have now become the Nez Perce; the prosperous people have become the Gros Ventres; the allies, or friends, have become the Sioux; and some tribes have called themselves after the holy location where they finally came to rest—they are now the people who live at the lake, on the river, and so forth. 24

Because the tribes understood their place in the universe as one given specifically to them, they had no need to evolve special political institutions to shape and order their society. A council at which everyone could speak, a council to remind the people of their sacred obligations to the cosmos and to themselves, was sufficient for most purposes. The tribes needed no other form of government except the gentle reminder by elders of the tribe when the people were assembled to maintain their institutions. Indians had a good idea of nationhood, but they had no knowledge of the other attributes of political existence that other people saw as important. Most of all, Indians had no awareness of the complexity that plagued the lives of other peoples, in particular the Europeans. 25

First contact with Europeans shocked both the Indians and the explorers. The Indians watched without understanding as the residents in the European settlements, bowed before arbitrary authority with a meekness that the Indians loathed. They believed that the whites had surrendered all moral substance in exchange for security in the anonymity of institutional life. Many Indian nicknames spoke derisively of the whites as "people who take orders," or "people who march in a straight line." And most Indians had little respect for white 26 military leaders who commanded their soldiers to go to war while remaining safely in the rear. They might fear a white general, but they respected very few of them.

27   To the Europeans, Indians appeared as the lowest form of man. No formal institutions were apparent. Leaders seemed to come and go almost whimsically. One might be negotiating with one chief on one occasion and be faced with a different person for no apparent reason except that the Indian council had designated the new man to speak for them. In tracing the source of political authority, whites were really baffled. No one seemed to be in charge of anything. A promise need not even be written down, and there seemed to be no appeal to any formal authority when things went wrong. In frustration, an early painter designed the Iroquois chiefs "kings," because there seemed no way to describe their status within the tribe except through the medium of familiar English feudal terminology.

28   It was difficult for whites not to conclude that chiefs had some mystical but absolute power over other members of the tribe. Most important social/political positions of leadership in tribes depended upon the personal prestige and charisma of the individual. Even where a position as chief was a lifetime office, qualifications for filling the post were primarily those of personal integrity and honesty, so that respect rather than popularity was the criterion by which Indians selected who would lead them. When whites faced an Indian war party, they would note that the Indians fought with great vigor until their leader was killed. More often than not, the Indian spirit for the fight declined swiftly upon the death of the war chief, and the whites would win the day. This kind of behavior suggested an influence far beyond that of the hereditary European monarchs over their subjects.

29   The truth, not surprisingly, was somewhat less mysterious. Indian war parties most often were composed of individuals who had volunteered upon hearing the announcement, made by the village crier, that a certain warrior was thinking about leading a war party. No one had to go; there was never a draft in Indian society. But if the warrior had a good reputation and the adventure promised others a chance to distinguish themselves, and if they had confidence in the warrior, then a lot of men, particularly younger warriors, would clamor to be a part of the expedition. It is not difficult to imagine the trauma of seeing the leader of the war party, a man in whom the rest of the party had placed implicit trust, killed in a skirmish. Having lost their leader, the chances were that the Indians would quickly leave the field of combat, disheartened at the turn of events. Whites interpreted this kind of Indian behavior as a political/military defeat rather than the personal loss to the members of the war party that it really represented.

30   This kind of leadership and these kinds of informal governing institutions existed long ago, when Indian tribes were free to live as they wished. The substance of those days remained in Indian memories, but the political institutions and social customs changed quite rapidly as more contact with whites

occurred, so that we can speak of these things now as the spiritual but not the practical heritage of Indians. The important thing is that there was no doubt in the minds of most Indians that, whatever the Europeans might say or do, they were still a free people, that they controlled certain lands and territories, and that they had the capability of punishing their enemies for any transgressions they might suffer. With respect to the lands they lived on, many Indians felt a strong religious duty to protect their territory. Future generations would need the lands to live on, many previous generations had migrated long distances to arrive finally at the place where the people were intended to live. One could sell neither the future nor the past, and land cessions represented the loss of both future and past to most Indians.

The expanding white population did not see it the same way, however, and when faced with the unpleasant choice of ceding their lands or drowning in the tidal wave of settlers who stood poised on their borders, the Indians wisely surrendered their lands and reluctantly moved west, hoping to escape white civilization by staying away from it. The course of American history demonstrated that even this faint hope was illusory, and the result of constant moves and land cessions is our scattered bits and pieces of reservation land that dot the maps of western states today.   31

Although Indians surrendered the physical occupation and ownership of their ancestral lands, they did not abandon the spiritual possession that had been a part of them. Even today most Indians regard their homeland as the area where their tribe originally lived. The Cherokees recently filed suit to prevent the flooding of a part of the Little Tennessee River where the old Cherokee town of Tellico once stood. To most Americans, and certainly to the federal courts who heard the case, the claim of the Indians was remote, if it existed at all, geographical proximity being more tangible and comprehensible than spiritual beliefs. To the Cherokees who opposed the flooding of the area, however, there was no responsible course except to fight as best they were able to prevent the destruction of their town site.   32

Today a terrible divisiveness exists in many Indian tribes. After almost a century of regarding their reservations as a place to live, Indians are discovering that they are being prodded into leasing large portions of their lands so that others can exploit the mineral wealth that lies underneath the ground. Sometimes it is coal deposits, often oil or natural gas, and occasionally uranium and molybdenum. All of these resources bring immense wealth, and their removal always leaves some desolation that cannot easily be corrected. Sacredness and utility confront each other within the tribal psyche, and it is not at all certain how Indians will decide the issue. Most Indians are so desperately poor that any kind of income seems a godsend. On the other hand, ancient teachings inform Indians that the true mark of a civilization is its ability to live in a location with a minimum disruption of its features.   33

Strangely, in the old prophecies in many tribes the conditions of today are accurately forecast. "A time will come," these prophecies begin, and they speak   34 of the total desolation of the land and the abandonment of ceremonials and rituals. Religious gifts of power seem not to be eternal but only to be used within this particular segment of cosmic time. As this cycle of planetary history ends, the culture and traditions that enabled the people to live are changed, distorted, and worn out. When all resources are exhausted, there will be tremendous cosmic upheaval and a new heaven and earth will be created. The survivors of the catastrophe will then receive new prophecies and ceremonies that will enable the people to prosper in the radically changed world that has come to pass. While traditional Indians mourn each step of dissolution, they are also comforted with the thought that a completely new world is in the process of being created. The fact remains, however, that the experience of this generation is one of transformation, heartbreak, and confusion.

35   The idea of peoplehood, of nationality, has gradually been transformed over the past two centuries into a new idea, one derived primarily from the European heritage, and with a singular focus distinct from the old Indian culture and traditions. It is also important to understand the primacy of land in the Indian psychological makeup, because, as land is alienated, all other forms of social cohesion also begin to erode, land having been the context in which the other forms have been created. In such ideas lie the conceptual keys to understanding how the Indian experiences the world today.

36   With such understanding, we can see that the occupation of Wounded Knee in 1973 was far more traumatic for Indians than it was for whites, who might have felt a little disturbed at the idea of Indian militants taking up arms against the United States. Wounded Knee is symbolic of the conflict that is raging in Indian hearts everywhere. It arose basically over the question of how the Sioux, and by extension other Indians, should deal with the untenable situation created by the federal government in their communities. The tribes faced seemingly insoluble problems involving the form of tribal government; the claims filed against the United States that were not moving toward resolution; the use of land, tribal and individual, on the reservation; and the nature of education that Indians were receiving. Above all was the perennial dilemma of how Indians could pursue their own religious traditions in a world that refused to recognize the essential spiritual nature of life.

37   Politically the Wounded Knee occupation pitted traditional Indians and militants against the established tribal government, which had adopted a constitution and bylaws during the New Deal under somewhat less than promising circumstances. The traditional Sioux had always been suspicious of the new tribal government and frequently voiced their opposition to it. But since the tribal government was the only form of political participation that the United States government would recognize and deal with, the traditionals had little choice except to boycott the tribal government and then hope that some crumbs would fall from the table of government largess, which had become available

because of the existence of the tribal government—an uncomfortable dilemma, to be sure.

From the perspective of the protestors, the point at issue in Wounded Knee was the *form of government* that the Sioux would use to direct their own destiny. From the perspective of the established tribal government—and, by extension, the federal government—the point at issue was *the direction that the existing tribal government would take*. For the traditionals the issue was philosophical and, by extension, theological and sociological; for the tribal government the issue was pragmatic, programmatic, and operational. They believed that the larger questions were considered settled by the passage of time and by the changes that had already been wrought in many of the tribal members.

Supporters of the tribal government argued that only through the Indian Reorganization Act did the Indians have self-government and that attacking the existing tribal government was in essence advocating anarchy, a condition that the United States could not allow under any circumstances. The response of those people who supported the traditionals and militants was that self-government was a delusion, because the existing tribal government had been created by the United States simply to serve its own purposes, supplanting the traditional government and customs with an alien institution and its rules and regulations. Where, one Sunday during the seventy-one-day occupation, the Indian protestors announced that they constituted the "independent Oglala Nation" and declared that a state of war existed between that nation and the United States, few Americans realized that it represented deep and persistent conviction among the Oglalas.

Wounded Knee, in the end, represented the philosophical divisions within all Indian tribes, the collision between the political dilemma of nationhood and the adoption of self-government within the existing federal structure. The traditionals certainly focused on the morality of the case, but the incumbent tribal government, for all its faults, spoke with a bitter contemporary pragmatism that could not be ignored. Wounded Knee could have happened on any Indian reservation, and while the occupation was dragging out to its final spasms, even many a conservative Indian suggested that maybe such activities were necessary to awaken the bureau and the president to their responsibilities.

When we distinguish between nationhood and self-government, we speak of two entirely different positions in the world. *Nationhood* implies a process of decision making that is free and uninhibited within the community, a community in fact that is almost completely insulated from external factors as it considers its possible options. *Self-government*, on the other hand, implies a recognition by the superior political power that some measure of local decision making is necessary but that this process must be monitored very carefully so that its products are compatible with the goals and policies of the larger political power. *Self-government* implies that the people were previously incapable of making any decisions for themselves and are now ready to assume some, but not all, of the responsibilities of a municipality. Under self-government, however, the larger moral issues that affect a *people's* relationship with other people are presumed to be included within the responsibilities of the larger nation.

42 The postwar generation of Indians had been enthusiastic about self-government because it has represented a step forward from the absolute prostration the tribes suffered when the federal bureaucracy preempted all social and political functions on the reservations after the passage of the General Allotment Act. Thus, having a tribal government that did have minimum respect accorded it by the federal agencies that were charged with providing services to the tribe did help Indians regain a measure of self-respect that had been lacking for several generations.

43 It is a long step from a small group of people living in a rather primitive fashion on an undisturbed and undiscovered continent to the present immensely complicated network of reservations that constitutes the homelands of American Indians. Nevertheless, Indian tribal governments, as presently constituted, have many of the powers of nations and, more important, have the expectation that they will continue to enhance the political status they enjoy. With some exceptions, such as jurisdiction over major crimes, now fourteen in number, a standing army, coinage and postage, and other attributes of the truly independent nations, Indian tribes exercise in some respects more governing powers than local non-Indian municipalities and in other respects more important powers than the states themselves.

44 But such privileges do not assuage the needs of a spiritual tradition that remains very strong within most tribes and that needs to express itself in ways familiar to the people. Thus, Wounded Knee was the inevitable product of the experiment in self-government because it represented the first effort to establish the dignity of the tribe in a manner consonant with the people's memories of their older way of life.

45 To suggest now that the movement for self-government was wrong may shatter modern Indian beliefs and cause great consternation. Self-government was not wrong; it was simply inadequate. It was limited in a fundamental way because it circumscribed the area in which the people's aspirations could express themselves. Hence we *do not* say that the movement for self government was wrong or misguided; it certainly led to the present situation, which has both positive and negative dimensions. The task that Indians face today is tracing the roots of the idea of self-government to discover how and where it relates to the present aspirations of Indians and Indian tribes.

46 Self-government is not an Indian idea. It originates in the minds of non-Indians who have reduced the traditional ways to dust, or believe they have, and now wish to give, as a gift, a limited measure of local control and responsibility. Self-government is an exceedingly useful concept for Indians to use when dealing with the larger government because it provides a context within which negotiations can take place. Since it will never supplant the intangible, spiritual,

and emotional aspirations of American Indians, it cannot be regarded as the final solution to Indian problems. Because self-government is such a complex idea, because it has been a product of the historical process, and because it has received much of its substance from Indians in the course of its development, it is important that we trace the genesis and development of this idea and discover how it manifests itself in our lives today. ✜

RESPONDING

1. In a journal entry, rewrite in your own words the provisions of the agreements between the U.S. government and the Indian tribes presented in this reading.

2. Working individually or in a group, construct a time line that outlines the historical relationship between the American government and the Indian tribes. Place all the treaties and agreements on the time line.

3. The reading explains the differing points of view between traditional and militant Indians. Imagine that you are the spokesperson for either group and write a letter to uncommitted Indians trying to persuade them to adopt your point of view.

4. In an essay, agree or disagree that self-rule is an important component of Indian life. Be sure to support your argument with specific examples from the readings or outside knowledge.

✜

CONNECTING

Critical Thinking and Writing

1. Critics have called the period during which the readings in this chapter were written the American Indian Renaissance. Define *renaissance*. How do the readings in this chapter exemplify a renaissance?

2. For many groups tradition shapes understanding of the present. Using the readings in this chapter and your own experience, describe occasions in which traditional beliefs have helped individuals solve current problems or have created problems.

3. The earth itself is an important force in American Indian culture. Write an essay describing the role of the earth in the life of one or more of the characters in these readings.

4. Compare Lipsha Morrissey's understanding and acceptance of events at the end of the story "Love Medicine" with Ayah's understanding at the end of "Lullaby." What aspects of their responses are based on the teachings of their cultures? What might be considered universal? What aspects might be attributable to differences in personality or experience?

5. The character in Momaday's novel praises the oral ability of his grandmother. Orality, for him, is a positive. Is this always the case? Write an essay comparing the value of orality with the difficulties encountered by Ayah in "Lullaby" because of her reliance on orality alone.

6. Allen describes American Indian women as caught in a "bicultural bind" and as acting in "destructive ways because we suffer from the societal conflicts caused by having to identify with two hopelessly opposed cultural definitions of women" (paragraph 16). Explain those conflicting definitions and the ways in which the women in these selections deal successfully or unsuccessfully with the dilemmas.

7. Write an essay discussing the contributions American Indians made to new immigrants to America.

8. Refer to the pre-reading assignment and review the characteristics the media currently attributes to American Indians. Now that you have read the selections in this chapter, discuss the accuracy of these portrayals.

9. Storytelling and the oral tradition are an important part of many cultures. Momaday says that "'storytelling: to utter and to hear . . .' And the simple act of listening is crucial to the concept of language, more crucial even than reading and writing, and language in turn is crucial to human society" (paragraph 1). Discuss the importance of storytelling within a particular culture and support your points with examples from some of the readings in this text. Or compare the role of storytelling in American Indian culture with that of another culture such as the Chinese.

10. Ayah in the story "Lullaby" expresses the point of view that having contact with mainstream culture is dangerous when she says "learning their language or any of their ways: it endangered you" (paragraph 12). Explain her fears. What compromise do you think might exist between a position that advocates total isolation from mainstream culture and a position that accepts total loss of native culture? How could such a compromise be implemented?

11. Welch's poem reflects the pressure on American Indians to assimilate into mainstream society and culture. Describe ways in which the pressure American Indians feel differs from and is similar to those experienced by early-twentieth-century European immigrants or other groups.

12. Design your own essay question, relating a theme that emerges from the concerns of American Indians to a theme that is important to another group. You can use examples from the readings in this text or from outside knowledge and research.

For Further Research

1. Research the life of an American Indian leader such as Black Elk, Chief Joseph, or Geronimo. Look at novels and films treating events in that person's life. Compare the portrayals that emerge from the two forms of inquiry.

2. Many American Indians still live on reservations. Research the political, social, and economic structure of the reservation.

3. More than half of American Indians now live in cities. Research their social and economic situation. What factors cause people to leave the reservation? How successful are they in integrating into mainstream culture within urban areas? Are they able to live in cities and maintain their culture?

REFERENCES AND ADDITIONAL SOURCES

Apes, William (Pequot). *A Son of the Forest: The Experience of William Apes, a Native of the Forest, Comprising a Notice of the Pequot Tribe of Indians.* New York: published by author, 1829. Republished as *A Son of the Forest: The Experience of William Apes, a Native of the Forest*, 2nd ed. rev. and corr. New York: published by author, 1831.

Axtell, James. *The European & the Indian: Essays in the Ethnohistory of Colonial North America.* New York: Oxford University Press, 1981.

Champagne, Duane, ed. *The Native North American Almanac: A Reference Work on Native North Americans in the United States and Canada.* Detroit, Mich.: Gale Research, 1994.

Debo, Angie. *A History of the Indian in the United States,* vol. 106. The Civilizations of the American Indian Series. Norman, Okla.: University of Oklahoma Press, 1970.

Deloria, Vine, Jr. *Custer Died for Your Sins: An Indian Manifesto.* New York: Macmillan, 1969.

——, and Clifford M. Lytle. *American Indians, American Justice.* Austin: University of Texas Press, 1983.

Eagle, Adam Fortunate. *Alcatraz! Alcatraz!: The Indian Occupation of 1969–1971.* Berkeley: Heyday Books, 1992.

Fixico, Donald L. *Termination and Relocation: Federal Indian Policy, 1945–1960.* Albuquerque: University of New Mexico Press, 1986.

Green, Rayna, ed. *That's What She Said: Contemporary Poetry and Fiction by Native American Women.* Bloomington, Ind.: Indiana University Press, 1984.

Hagan, William T., *The Indian in American History* New York: Macmillan, 1963. Series: Service Center for Teachers of History. Vol. 50.

Hobson, Geary, ed. *The Remembered Earth. An Anthology of Contemporary Native American Literature.* Albuquerque: University of New Mexico Press, 1981.

Kehoe, Alice Beck. *North American Indians: A Comprehensive Account.* Englewood Cliffs, N.J.: Prentice Hall, 1992.

Larson, Charles. *American Indian Fiction.* Albuquerque: University of New Mexico Press, 1978.

Lerner, Andrea, ed. *Dancing on the Rim of the World: An Anthology of Contemporary Northwest Native American Writing.* Tucson: Sun Tracks: University of Arizona Press, 1990.

McNickle, D'Arcy. *Native American Tribalism: Indian Survivals and Renewals.* New York: Institute of Race Relations for Oxford University Press, 1973.

Mitchell, Lee C. *Witnesses to a Vanishing America: The Nineteenth-Century Response.* Princeton, N.J.: Princeton University Press, 1981.

Neihardt, John G. *Black Elk Speaks: Being the Life Story of a Holy Man of the Ogala Sioux.* Lincoln: University of Nebraska Press, 1961.

Niatum, Duane, ed. *Carriers of the Dream Wheel: Contemporary Native American Poetry.* New York: Harper & Row, 1975, 1981.

Oswalt, Wendell H. *This Land Was Theirs: A Study of the North American Indian.* New York: Wiley, 1966.

Prucha, Francis P. *The Great Father: The United States Government and the American Indians.* Lincoln: University of Nebraska Press, 1984.

Rosen, Charles. *The Man to Send the Rain Clouds.* New York: Vintage, 1975.

Ruoff, A. Lavonne Brown. *American Indian Literatures: An Introduction, Bibliographic Review, and Selected Bibliography.* New York: Modern Language Association, 1990.

Sarris, Greg. *Keeping the Slug Woman Alive.* Berkeley: University of California Press, 1993.

Starr, G. A. *Defoe and Spiritual Autobiography.* Princeton, N.J.: Princeton University Press, 1965.

Sturtevant, William C., and Wilcomb E. Washburn, eds. *History of Indian-White Relations*, Vol. 4, Handbook of North American Indians series. Washington, D.C.: Smithsonian, 1988.

Sturtevant, William C., and Wilcomb E. Washburn, eds. *History of Indian-White Relations*, Vol. 4, Handbook of North American Indians series. Washington, D.C.: Smithsonian, 1989.

Swann, Brian. *Song of the Sky: Versions of Native American Songs and Poems*, Ashuelot, N.H.: Four Zoahs Night House, 1985, rev. ed. Amherst: University of Massachusetts Press, 1993.

Thernstrom, Stephen, et al., eds. "American Indians," in *Harvard Encyclopedia of American Ethnic Groups*. Cambridge, Mass.: Harvard University Press, 1980.

Tyler, S. Lyman. *A History of Indian Policy*. Washington, D.C.: Government Printing Office, 1973.

Vogel, Virgil J. *This Country Was Ours: A Documentary History of the American Indian*. New York: Harper & Row, 1972.

Welch, James. *Fools Crow*. New York: Viking, 1986.

9

NEW IMMIGRANTS

Reviving, Reinventing, and Challenging the American Dream

✥

Above: Gert Jacobson, *Anywhere Europe*, a memorial to Holocaust victims. *(Yad Vashem History and Holocaust Art Museum, Jerusalem, no. 2626-3. Permission provided by sons Burt and Stuart Jacobson.)* *Opposite:* Vietnamese boat people on the way to Hong Kong, 1979. *(© 1979 Magnus Bartlett/Woodfin Camp and Associates)*

SETTING THE HISTORICAL AND CULTURAL CONTEXT

THE NOTION OF THE AMERICAN DREAM was been rediscovered, revived, and refashioned in the works of newer immigrants. In the excerpt from his novel *Our House in the Lost World*, Oscar Hijuelos describes a recent immigrant's reaction to the abundance of material goods that he finds in his relative's Americanized kitchen:

> There was so much of everything! Milk and wine and beer, steaks and rice and chicken and sausages and ham and plantains and ice cream and black bean soup and Pepsi Cola and Hershey chocolate bars and almond nougat, and popcorn, and Wise potato chips and Jiffy peanut butter, and rum and whiskey, marshmallows, spaghetti, flan and pasteles and chocolate cake and pie, more than enough to make them delirious. And even though the walls were cracked and it was dark, there was a television set and a radio and light-bulbs and toilet paper and pictures of the family and crucifixes and tooth-paste and soap and more.

The exhaustive list is both a celebration and a mocking of the limitless consumer opportunities the immigrant discovers. The profusion of material goods, the seemingly unlimited choices sharply contrast with the shortages and rationing of the old country.

But the new economic opportunity often brings with a new kind of confusion, as Hijuelos goes on to suggest: "It was 'Thank God for freedom and bless my family!' from Luisa's mouth, but her daughters were more cautious. . . . In the food-filled kitchen Alejo told them how happy he was to have them in his house, and they were happy because the old misery was over, but they were still without a home and in a strange world. Uncertainty showed in their faces." Hijuelos's characters and many others in this chapter are experiencing what Czeslaw Milosz has referred to as "a lost point of view." The readings in this chapter explore both the promise that America still holds for many recent immigrants and the difficulties they continue to face as they attempt to shape a new life for themselves and their families.

Since World War II persons of many nationalities have sought political, religious, or economic refuge in the United States. Among these were persons displaced by the war, including many survivors of the Holocaust. Refugees from oppressive regimes in China, the Soviet Union, Eastern Europe, and Greece sought political asylum in the late 1940s and early 1950s. During the 1960s Cubans took *vuelos de libertad* (freedom flights) to escape the regime of Fidel Castro; the Mariel boat lift of the late 1970s allowed other Cubans to leave their homeland. The fall of Saigon in 1975 led many Vietnamese to emigrate as well. During the late 1970s and 1980s Central Americans sought to escape dictatorial regimes and death squads. Since the massacre at Tiananmen Square in 1989, many Chinese nationals, already in the United States on student visas, have sought to extend their stays on the grounds of political asylum. The collapse of the Berlin Wall, the disintegration of the Soviet Union, and the ethnic wars that have been taking place throughout Eastern Europe have led other persons to seek entry.

During the last fifty years, the United States government has responded in a variety of ways to the demands of immigrants and refugees—the nation has seemed more welcoming at some times than at others. The federal government has passed legislation to increase quotas for some groups and to provide asylum for others. During the 1940s, for example, President Roosevelt ordered immigration quotas to be increased for persons fleeing political persecution. After World War II, the Truman administration granted new immigration privileges to so-called displaced persons; later, the Refugee Relief Act of 1953 allowed for the admission of other refugees. This process continued in the 1970s, with the admission of the Vietnamese "boat people" and the Mariel refugees from Cuba. After the Tiananmen Square massacre, President George Bush signed an executive order allowing some of the student refugees from China to remain in the United States after the time designated on their visas.

This country has long attempted to provide amnesty for persons seeking refuge from political persecution. Those who have entered the country illegally, but who feel that they are victims of political persecution, have sometimes been given refuge as well. The Immigration and Nationality Act of 1980, for example, outlines a procedure whereby those persons who fear for their lives can seek amnesty from deportation. Nonetheless, because of legislation dating back to the Cold War era, immigrants are still subject to deportation even after they have become American citizens. Many immigration policy experts contend that the enforcement and administration of immigration laws—with their continued focus on foreign policy toward the country of origin rather than the applicant's own situation—are often arbitrary and unfair.

Earlier chapters of this book have shown how the promise that America held out to immigrants was often threatened by periods of exclusionary legislation and antiimmigrant sentiment. During periods of austerity, for example, unions have regarded an influx of immigrant labor as threatening their job security. Politicians and other persons who have associated refugees and immigrants with the potential for subversive activity have lobbied to keep out of the country anyone who would question the government or participate in "un-American activities." Exclusionists have traditionally used isolated events as proof of a threat from "foreigners." Some of the more famous of these include the Haymarket Square riot of 1886, in which Irish and German immigrants involved in a Chicago labor protest were blamed for instigating a violent uprising that claimed several lives; the Sacco and Vanzetti case of

1920–1921, in which two Italian immigrants were executed for a murder they might not have committed; and the World Trade Center explosion of 1992, which incited anti-Arab sentiment and has been cited by many who would endorse stricter enforcement of immigration laws. During the late 1980s and early 1990s, there has been an increase in exclusionary legislation. During the 1992 presidential campaign, Patrick Buchanan sought the Republican nomination with an antiimmigrant platform. In 1993, California governor Pete Wilson introduced legislation that would bar the American-born children of undocumented immigrants from being considered American citizens. In that same year, Congress considered several bills that would extend the sponsorship period required for new immigrants. It is amidst this conflict between the country's promise as a land of inclusion and the pressure to exclude that many of the readings in this chapter find their place.

Several of the works in this chapter address the United States's traditional position as a refuge for those who have suffered religious or political persecution elsewhere. The excerpt from Cynthia Ozick's novella *The Shawl* presents the voice of Rosa, a survivor of the Holocaust, as she attempts to cope with what she has endured. For Rosa, the key is to refuse to accept other people's versions of her experience, to learn instead to write her own history, to assert control over how her history will be recorded. The issue of asserting control is central to Van Luu's essay on Vietnamese refugees who are confronting both the separation from their family and their own kind of "survival guilt."

Other readings explore the motivations of immigrants to seek refuge in the United States. While Oscar Hijuelos's text depicts the disillusionment with communism, the poetry of José Alejandro Romero describes in very graphic terms the massacre of innocents by the right-wing totalitarian regime that ruled El Salvador during the late 1970s and 1980s.

The consequences of immigration, on both economic and psychological levels, are addressed in other readings. Whereas Van Luu's essay discusses the difficulties that refugees from Vietnam sometimes have adjusting to the economic and familial realities of life in the new country, Czeslaw Milosz's essay explores in a more general way the situation of the immigrant or "exile," who is, by definition, "catapulted out of history" and made to experience a "loss of internal foundation." Bharati Mukherjee explores some of the consequences of this change in orientation and alteration in the pace of life, suggesting as well the ways in which one's habits, protocols, and rules of conduct become modified in the new surroundings. Indeed the tension in her story derives from a misinterpretation of those protocols.

In several of the readings, the issue is not so much a choice between one option and another but a negotiation among alternatives. Many of the works in this chapter, including those by Cathy Song and Naomi Shihab Nye, stress a kind of communal experience, a ritual act that helps to provide a sense of memory and affiliation. For some, the act of writing, of storytelling, can provide both continuity and escape. Language can also allow one to come to terms with what Nye has called "the burden and the gift" that is one's culture.

The act of writing is itself an act of exchange and transformation. The immigrant writer and the reader from the dominant culture exchange positions of marginality and centrality. At the same time there is another kind of transformation, a new kind of fusing. As Mukherjee says in the preface to one of her story collections, "I see my immigrant story replicated in a dozen American cities, and instead of seeing my Indianness as a fragile entity to be preserved . . . I see it now as a set of fluid identities to be celebrated. I see myself as in the tradition of other immigrant writers [telling] stories of broken identities and discarded languages, and the will to bond oneself to a new community, against the ever present fear of failure and betrayal." In this way the new immigrant participates in the continual transformation and enrichment of the multiethnic culture of the United States.

BEGINNING: Pre-reading/Writing

Throughout its history, the United States has often been a haven for citizens of other countries who are looking for improved political and economic conditions. Working individually or in a group, speculate about recent political and economic situations in specific countries that might make their citizens choose to emigrate. Discuss why they might choose to come to the United States, the possible problems of immigrating here, and the difficulties they would face once they arrive.

Some people immigrate to this country for political and religious reasons. In fleeing their repressive governments, they fear for their lives if they are denied entry to our country and are forced to return to their homelands. This section of the Immigration and Nationality Act outlines the procedures whereby individuals can apply for political asylum. If asylum is denied, the applicant may appeal the decision, first to the Immigration Court and then to the Board of Immigration Appeals. In rare cases, the appeal process has been taken as far as the Supreme Court.

⚜

From IMMIGRATION AND NATIONALITY ACT OF 1980

Asylum Procedure

1   Sec. 208. [8 U.S.C. 1158] (a) The Attorney General shall establish a procedure for an alien physically present in the United States or at a land border or port of entry, irrespective of such alien's status, to apply for asylum, and the alien may be granted asylum in the discretion of the Attorney General if the Attorney General determines that such alien is a refugee within the meaning of section 101(a)(42)(A).

2   (b) Asylum granted under subsection (a) may be terminated if the Attorney General, pursuant to such regulations as the Attorney General may prescribe, determines that the alien is no longer a refugee within the meaning of section 101(a)(42)(A) owing to a change in circumstances in the alien's country of nationality or, in the case of an alien having no nationality, in the country in which the alien last habitually resided.

3   (c) A spouse or child (as defined in section 101(b)(1)(A), (B), (C), (D), or (E)) of an alien who is granted asylum under subsection (a) may, if not otherwise eligible for asylum under such subsections, be granted the same status as the alien if accompanying, or following to join, such alien.

Adjustment of Status of Refugees

4   Sec. 209. [8 U.S.C. 1159] (a)(1) Any alien who has been admitted to the United States under section 207—

5   (A) whose admission has not been terminated by the Attorney General pursuant to such regulations as the Attorney General may prescribe,

6   (B) who has been physically present in the United States for at least one year, and

7   (C) who has not acquired permanent resident status, shall, at the end of such year period, return or be returned to the custody of the Service for

inspection and examination for admission to the United States as an immigrant in accordance with the provisions of sections 235, 236, and 237.

(2) Any alien who is found upon inspection and examination by an immigration officer pursuant to paragraph (1) or after a hearing before a special inquiry officer to be admissible (except as otherwise provided under subsection (c)) as an immigrant under this Act at the time of the alien's inspection and examination shall, notwithstanding any numerical limitation specified in this Act, be regarded as lawfully admitted to the United States for permanent residence as of the date of such alien's arrival into the United States. ✥

RESPONDING

1. In a journal entry, explain the provisions of the asylum regulations in your own words. If you were writing the law, how would you define "refugee"?

2. Working individually or in a group, discuss the reasons why your family members came to the United States. Was it hard for them to enter the country? What were immigration policies during that period? If you don't know the answers to these questions, consider *why* you don't know. Were your relatives unwilling to talk about their experiences? Why might that be?

3. Write about the experience of someone you know or have read, studied, or heard about who has had to seek asylum in the United States. What circumstances caused this person to leave his or her country? How do you think the circumstances of immigration affected his or her adjustment?

4. What do you think the United States policy should be regarding immigration? Who should be granted asylum? Choose a recent historical event such as the Tiananmen Square massacre and discuss whether we should give asylum to participants in that event.

CYNTHIA OZICK

Born in New York in 1928, Cynthia Ozick received her bachelor's degree from New York University in 1949 and her master's degree from Ohio State University in 1950. After teaching writing at New York University for a year, she devoted herself to writing full time. Since 1966 she has published both fiction and essays, including the novel Trust *(1966),* The Pagan Rabbi and Other Stories *(1971),* Bloodshed and Three Novellas *(1976),* Leviathan: Five Fictions *(1981),* Art and Ardor *(1983),* Metaphor and Memory *(1989), and* The Shawl: A Story and Novella *(1989).*

The following excerpt from the novella "Rosa," published in The Shawl, *represents the personal history of a Holocaust survivor. At issue is not only the speaker's need to reinterpret but also to come to terms with her past.*

⌗

From THE SHAWL

Department of Clinical Social Pathology
University of Kansas-Iowa

April 17, 1977

1 Dear Ms. Lublin:

Though I am not myself a physician, I have lately begun to amass survivor data as rather a considerable specialty. To be concrete: I am presently working on a study, funded by the Minew Foundation of the Kansas-Iowa Institute for Humanitarian Context, designed to research the theory developed by Dr. Arthur R. Hidgeson and known generally as Repressed Animation. Without at this stage going into detail, it may be of some preliminary use to you to know that investigations so far reveal an astonishing generalized minimalization during any extended period of stress resulting from incarceration, exposure, and malnutrition. We have turned up a wide range of neurological residues (including, in some cases, acute cerebral damage, derangement, disorientation, premature senility, etc.), as well as hormonal changes, parasites, anemia, thready pulse, hyperventilation, etc.; in children especially, temperatures as high as 108°, ascitic fluid, retardation, bleeding sores on the skin and in the mouth, etc. What is remarkable is that these are all *current conditions* in survivors and their families.

2 DISEASE, DISEASE! Humanitarian Context, what did it mean? An excitement over other people's suffering. They let their mouths water up. Stories about children running blood in America from sores, what muck. Consider also the special

word they used: *survivor*. Something new. As long as they didn't have to say *human being*. It used to be *refugee*, but by now there was no such creature, no more refugees, only survivors. A name like a number—counted apart from the ordinary swarm. Blue digits on the arm, what difference? They don't call you a woman anyhow. *Survivor*. Even when your bones get melted into the grains of the earth, still they'll forget *human being*. Survivor and survivor and survivor; always and always. Who made up these words, parasites on the throat of suffering!

For some months teams of medical paraphrasers have been conducting inter-   3
views with survivors, to contrast current medical paraphrase with conditions found more than three decades ago, at the opening of the camps. This, I confess, is neither my field nor my interest. My own concern, both as a scholar of social pathology and as a human being . . .

Ha! For himself it was good enough, for himself he didn't forget this word   4
human being!

. . . is not with medical nor even with psychological aspects of survivor data.   5

Data. Drop in a hole!   6

What particularly engages me for purposes of my own participation in the   7
study (which, by the way, is intended to be definitive, to close the books, so to speak, on this lamentable subject) is what I can only term the "metaphysical" side of the Repressed Animation (R.A.). It begins to be evident that prisoners gradually came to Buddhist positions. They gave up craving and began to function in terms of non-functioning, i.e., non-attachment. The Four Noble Truths in Buddhist thought, if I may remind you, yield a penetrating summary of the fruit of craving: pain. "Pain" in this view is defined as ugliness, age, sorrow, sickness, despair, and, finally, birth. Non-attachment is attained through the Eightfold Path, the highest stage of which is the cessation of all human craving, the loftiest rapture, one might say, of consummated indifference.

It is my hope that these speculations are not displeasing to you. Indeed, I   8
further hope that they may even attract you, and that you would not object to joining our study by means of an in-depth interview to be conducted by me at, if it is not inconvenient, your home. I should like to observe survivor syndrom-ing within the natural setting.

Home. Where, where?   9

As you may not realize, the national convention of the American Associa-   10
tion of Clinical Social Pathology has this year, for reasons of fairness to our

East Coast members, been moved from Las Vegas to Miami Beach. The convention will take place at a hotel in your vicinity about the middle of next May, and I would be deeply grateful if you could receive me during that period. I have noted via a New York City newspaper (we are not so provincial out here as some may think!) your recent removal to Florida; consequently you are ideally circumstanced to make a contribution to our R.A. study. I look forward to your consent at your earliest opportunity.

Very sincerely yours,
James W. Tree, Ph.D.

11 Drop in a hole! Disease! It comes from Stella, everything! Stella saw what this letter was, she could see from the envelope—Dr. Stella! Kansas–Iowa Clinical Social Pathology, a fancy hotel, this is the cure for the taking of a life! Angel of Death!

12 With these university letters Rosa had a routine: she carried the scissors over to the toilet bowl and snipped little bits of paper and flushed. In the bowl going down, the paper squares whirled like wedding rice.

13 But this one: drop in a hole with your Four Truths and your Eight Paths together! Non-attachment! She threw the letter into the sink; also its crowded envelope ("Please forward," Stella's handwriting instructed, pretending to be American, leaving out the little stroke that goes across the 7); she lit a match and enjoyed the thick fire. Burn, Dr. Tree, burn up with your Repressed Animation! The world is full of Trees! The world is full of fire! Everything, everything is on fire! Florida is burning!

14 Big flakes of cinder lay in the sink: black foliage, Stella's black will. Rosa turned on the faucet and the cinders spiraled down and away. Then she went to the round oak table and wrote the first letter of the day to her daughter, her healthy daughter, her daughter who suffered neither from thready pulse nor from anemia, her daughter who was a professor of Greek philosophy at Columbia University in New York City, a stone's throw—the philosophers' stone that prolongs life and transmutes iron to gold—from Stella in Queens!

Magda, my Soul's Blessing [Rosa wrote]:

15 Forgive me, my yellow lioness. Too long a time since the last writing. Strangers scratch at my life; they pursue, they break down the bloodstream's sentries. Always there is Stella. And so half a day passes without my taking up my pen to speak to you. A pleasure, the deepest pleasure, home bliss, to speak in our own language. Only to you. I am always having to write to Stella now, like a dog paying respects to its mistress. It's my obligation. She sends me money. She, whom I plucked out of the claws of all those Societies that came to us with bread and chocolate after the liberation! Despite everything, they were selling sectarian ideas; collecting troops for their armies. If not for me they

would have shipped Stella with a boatload of orphans to Palestine, to become God knows what, to live God knows how. A field worker jabbering Hebrew. It would serve her right. Americanized airs. My father was never a Zionist. He used to call himself a "Pole by right." The Jews, he said, didn't put a thousand years of brains and blood into Polish soil in order to have to prove themselves to anyone. He was the wrong sort of idealist, maybe, but he had the instincts of a natural nobleman. I could laugh at that now—the whole business—but I don't, because I feel too vividly what he was, how substantial, how not given over to any light-mindedness whatever. He had Zionist friends in his youth. Some left Poland early and lived. One is a bookseller in Tel Aviv. He specializes in foreign texts and periodicals. My poor little father. It's only history—an ad hoc instance of it, you might say—that made the Zionist answer. My father's ideas were more logical. He was a Polish patriot on a temporary basis, he said, until the time when the nation should lie down beside nation like the lily and the lotus. He was at bottom a prophetic creature. My mother, you know, published poetry. To you all these accounts must have the ring of pure legend.

Even Stella, who *can* remember, refuses. She calls me a parable-maker. She 16 was always jealous of you. She has a strain of dementia, and resists you and all other reality. Every vestige of former existence is an insult to her. Because she fears the past she distrusts the future—it, too, will turn into the past. As a result she has nothing. She sits and watches the present roll itself up into the past more quickly than she can bear. That's why she never found the one thing she wanted more than anything, an American husband. I'm immune to these pains and panics. Motherhood—I've always known this—is a profound distraction from philosophy, and all philosophy is rooted in suffering over the passage of time. I mean the *fact* of motherhood, the physiological fact. To have the power to create another human being, to be the instrument of such a mystery. To pass on a whole genetic system. I don't believe in God, but I believe, like the Catholics, in mystery. My mother wanted so much to convert; my father laughed at her. But she was attracted. She let the maid keep a statue of the Virgin and Child in the corner of the kitchen. Sometimes she used to go in and look at it. I can even remember the words of a poem she wrote about the heat coming up from the stove, from the Sunday pancakes—

> Mother of God, how you shiver
> in these heat-Ribbons!
> Our cakes rise to you
> and in the trance of His birthing
> you hide.

Something like that. Better than that, more remarkable. Her Polish was very dense. You had to open it out like a fan to get at all the meanings. She was exceptionally modest, but she was not afraid to call herself a symbolist.

17   I know you won't blame me for going astray with such tales. After all, you're always prodding me for these old memories. If not for you, I would have buried them all, to satisfy Stella. Stella Columbus! She thinks there's such a thing as the New World. Finally—at last, at last—she surrenders this precious vestige of your sacred babyhood. Here it is in a box right next to me as I write. She didn't take the trouble to send it by registered mail! Even though I told her and told her. I've thrown out the wrapping paper, and the lid is plastered down with lots of Scotch tape. I'm not hurrying to open it. At first my hunger was unrestrained and I couldn't wait, but nothing is nice now. I'm saving you; I want to be serene. In a state of agitation one doesn't split open a diamond. Stella says I make a relic of you. She has no heart. It would shock you if I told you even one of the horrible games I'm made to play with her. To soothe her dementia, to keep her quiet, I pretend you died! Yes! It's true! There's nothing, however crazy, I wouldn't say to her to tie up her tongue. She slanders. Everywhere there are slanders, and sometimes—my bright lips, my darling!—the slanders touch even you. My purity, my snowqueen!

18   I'm ashamed to give an example. Pornography. What Stella, that pornographer, has made of your father. She thieves all the truth, she robs it, she steals it, the robbery goes unpunished. She lies, and it's the lying that's rewarded. The New World! That's why I smashed up my store! Because here they make up lying theories. University people do the same: they take human beings for specimens. In Poland there used to be justice; here they have social theories. Their system inherits almost nothing from the Romans, that's why. Is it a wonder that the lawyers are no better than scavengers who feed on the droppings of thieves and liars? Thank God you followed your grandfather's bent and studied philosophy and not law.

19   Take my word for it, Magda, your father and I had the most ordinary lives—by "ordinary" I mean respectable, gentle, cultivated. Reliable people of refined reputation. His name was Andrzej. Our families had status. Your father was the son of my mother's closest friend. She was a converted Jew married to a Gentile: you can be a Jew if you like, or a Gentile, it's up to you. You have a legacy of choice, and they say choice is the only true freedom. We were engaged to be married. We would have been married. Stella's accusations are all Stella's own excretion. Your father was not a German. I was forced by a German, it's true, and more than once, but I was too sick to conceive. Stella has a naturally pornographic mind, she can't resist dreaming up a dirty sire for you, an S.S. man! Stella was with me the whole time, she knows just what I know. They never put me in their brothel either. Never believe this, my lioness,

my snowqueen! No lies come out of me to you. You are pure. A mother is the source of consciousness, of conscience, the ground of being, as philosophers say. I have no falsehoods for you. Otherwise I don't deny some few tricks: the necessary handful. To those who don't deserve the truth, don't give it. I tell Stella what it pleases her to hear. My child, perished. Perished. She always wanted it. She was always jealous of you. She has no heart. Even now she believes in my loss of you: and you a stone's throw from her door in New York! Let her think whatever she thinks; her mind is awry, poor thing; in me the strength of your being consumes my joy. Yellow blossom! Cup of the sun!

What a curiosity it was to hold a pen—nothing but a small pointed stick, after all, oozing its hieroglyphic puddles: a pen that speaks, miraculously, Polish. A lock removed from the tongue. Otherwise the tongue is chained to the teeth and the palate. An immersion into the living language: all at once this cleanliness, this capacity, this power to make a history, to tell, to explain. To retrieve, to reprieve!

To lie. ✠

20

21

RESPONDING

1. Rosa calls writing "this capacity, this power to make a history, to tell, to explain. To retrieve, to reprieve!" Write a journal entry explaining how her letter to Magda does all of these things. Discuss why and to whom Rosa is lying.

2. Dr. Tree asks Rosa to participate in his study of survivors. Working individually or in a group, discuss why Rosa is so angry at his letter and write the response she might send him. How do you think you would feel in her situation?

3. Write an essay that discusses the ethical issues involved in studies of victims of tragedies. What benefits might result from such studies? What harmful effects might they produce? How would you balance the knowledge that can be gained with the victim's right to privacy.?

4. Agree or disagree that events can be rewritten by individuals or by groups to distort history. Support your argument with incidents from the story, your own experience, or your knowledge of current events.

CATHY SONG

The Korean American poet Cathy Song was born in Honolulu, Hawaii, in 1955. She attended the University of Hawaii, graduated from Wellesley College in 1977, and received an M.A. in creative writing from Boston University in 1981. Her poems have appeared in many journals, among them Amerasia Journal, The American Poetry Review, Poetry, *and* The Seneca Review. *Moreover, she has published two collections of poetry,* Picture Bride *(1982) and* Frameless Windows, Squares of Light *(1988). She was selected as the winner of the Yale Series of Younger Poets Competition in 1982, which praised her poems for "remind[ing] a loud, indifferent, hard world of what truly matters to the human spirit."*

Song's poem "Easter: Wahiawa, 1959," which appears in Picture Bride, *explores the special significance of simple objects as parts of both a family ritual and a personal exchange between a young person and her grandfather.*

✤

EASTER: WAHIAWA, 1959

1

The rain stopped for one afternoon.
Father brought out
his movie camera and for a few hours
we were all together
under a thin film
that separated the rain showers
from that part of the earth
like a hammock
held loosely by clothespins.

Grandmother took the opportunity
to hang the laundry
and Mother and my aunts
filed out of the house
in pedal pushers and poodle cuts,
carrying the blue washed eggs.

Grandfather kept the children
penned in on the porch,
clucking at us in his broken English
whenever we tried to peek
around him. There were bread crumbs
stuck to his blue gray whiskers.

I looked from him to the sky,
a membrane of egg whites
straining under the weight
of the storm that threatened
to break.

We burst loose from Grandfather
when the mothers returned
from planting the eggs
around the soggy yard.
He followed us,
walking with stiff but sturdy legs.
We dashed and disappeared
into bushes,
searching for the treasures;
the hard-boiled eggs
which Grandmother had been simmering
in vinegar and blue color all morning.

2

When Grandfather was a young boy
in Korea,
it was a long walk
to the riverbank,
where, if he were lucky,
a quail egg or two
would gleam from the mud
like gigantic pearls.
He could never eat enough
of them.

It was another long walk
through the sugarcane fields
of Hawaii,
where he worked for eighteen years,
cutting the sweet stalks
with a machete. His right arm
grew disproportionately large
to the rest of his body.
He could hold three
grandchildren in that arm.

I want to think
that each stalk that fell
brought him closer
to a clearing,
to that palpable field
where from the porch
to the gardenia hedge
that day he was enclosed
by his grandchildren,
scrambling around him,
for whom he could at last buy
cratefuls of oranges,
basketfuls of sky blue eggs.

I found three that afternoon.
By evening, it was raining hard.
Grandfather and I skipped supper.
Instead, we sat on the porch
and I ate what he peeled
and cleaned for me.
The scattering of the delicate
marine-colored shells across his lap
was something like what the ocean gives
the beach after a rain. ✛

RESPONDING

1. Write a poem or a short story about a favorite relative.

2. Working in groups, read the poem aloud. Pay special attention to the way things look, sound, feel, and smell, and try to relay these perceptions using as much specific detail as you can. Listen to the language of the poem,

observing rhythms and recurring sounds. Where do these occur and what is their effect?

3. Discuss the time, the setting, and the activities presented in the poem in an essay. Why do you think Song chose to write about an Easter egg hunt?

4. The author gives the reader hints about the history of the family in the poem. Write a prose version that fills in the family history. Use clues in the poem to tell you who they are, where they originally came from, and what their lives are like. The poet speaks in the first person, but are these her family members and is this a real memory?

Oscar Hijuelos

Oscar Hijuelos was born in New York in 1951 of Cuban parentage. After earning his bachelor's and master's degrees from the City College of the City University of New York in 1975 and 1976, he worked in advertising, finally devoting himself to writing full time in 1984. His writing, which includes the novels Our House in the Lost World *(1983),* The Mambo Kings Play Songs of Love *(1989), and* The Fourteen Sisters of Emilio Montez O'Brien *(1993), as well as several short stories, has earned him several awards, among them a National Endowment for the Arts Creative Writing Fellowship (1985), an American Academy in Rome Fellowship in Literature (1985), and the Pulitzer Prize for Fiction (1990).*

"Visitors, 1965," from Our House in the Lost World, *reflects the experiences of some Cuban émigrés living in the United States. In this chapter the narrator explains the community's reactions to news of Fidel Castro's victory. The text's references to the overthrow of Batista, the Bay of Pigs invasion, and the rationing system help to provide the novel with a sense of historical context. At the same time, the narrative explores the ways in which such events are connected to each person's sense of personal and collective identity.*

⊞

VISITORS, 1965

1

1   DOWN IN THE COOL BASEMENT of the hotel restaurant, Alejo Santinio looked over a yellowed newspaper clipping dating back to 1961. He had not looked at it recently, although in the past had always been proud to show it to visitors. And why? Because it was a brief moment of glory. In the newspaper picture Alejo and his friend Diego were in their best dress whites standing before a glittering cart of desserts. Beside them was a fat, cheery beaming face, the Soviet premier Nikita Khrushchev, who was attending a luncheon in his honor at the hotel.

2   Alejo always told the story: The governor and mayor were there with the premier, who had "great big ears and a bright red nose." The premier had dined on a five-course meal. The waiters and cooks, all nervous wrecks, had fumbled around in the kitchen getting things into order. But outside they managed an orderly composed appearance. After the meal had been served, the cooks drew lots to see who would wheel out the dessert tray. Diego and Alejo won.

Alejo put on his best white uniform and apron and waited in the foyer,   3
chainsmoking nervously, while, outside, news reporters fired off their cameras
and bodyguards stood against the walls, watching. Alejo and Diego did not say
anything. Alejo was bewildered by the situation: Only in America could a worker
get so close to a fat little guy with enormous power. These were the days of the
new technology: mushroom-cloud bombs and satellites and missiles. And there
he was, a hick from a small town in Cuba, slicked up by America, thinking, "If
only my old compañeros could see me now! and my sisters and Mercedes."

When the time came, they went to the freezer, filled up shiny bowls with   4
ice cream, brought out the sauces and hot fudge, and loaded them all onto
a dessert cart. Alejo was in charge of cherries. They went out behind the
maître d' and stood before the premier's table. They humbly waited as the
smiling premier looked over the different cakes, tarts, pies, fruits, sauces, and
ice creams. Through a translator the premier asked for a bowl of chocolate and
apricot ice cream topped with hot fudge, cocoanut, and a high swirl of fresh
whipped cream. This being served, Alejo picked out the plumpest cherry from
a bowl and nimbly placed it atop the dessert.

Delighted, the premier whispered to the translator, who said, "The premier   5
wishes to thank you for this masterpiece."

As Diego and Alejo bowed, lightbulbs and cameras flashed all around them.   6
They were ready to wheel the cart back when the premier rose from the table
to shake Diego's and Alejo's hands. Then through the translator he asked a few
questions. To Alejo: "And where do you come from?"

"Cuba," Alejo answered in a soft voice.   7

"Oh yes, Cuba," the premier said in halting English. "I would like to go   8
there one day, Cuba." And he smiled and patted Alejo's back and then rejoined
the table. A pianist, a violinist, and a cellist played a Viennese waltz.

Afterward reporters came back into the kitchen to interview the two cooks,   9
and the next morning the *Daily News* carried a picture of Alejo, Diego, and
Khrushchev with a caption that read: DESSERT CHEFS CALL RUSKY PREMIER HEAP
BIG EATER! It made them into celebrities for a few weeks. People recognized
Alejo on the street and stopped to talk with him. He even went on a radio show
in the Bronx. The hotel gave him a five-dollar weekly raise, and for a while
Alejo felt important, and then it played itself out and became the yellowed
clipping, stained by grease on the basement kitchen wall.

In Alejo's locker Khrushchev turned up again, on the cover of a *Life*   10
magazine. He was posed, cheek against cheek, with the bearded Cuban premier
Fidel Castro. "What was going to happen in Cuba?" Alejo wondered. He shook
his head. "How could Cuba have gone 'red'?" It had been more than six years
since the fall of Batista on New Year's Eve, 1958, the year of getting rid of the
evil in Cuba, and now Alejo and Mercedes were going to sponsor the arrival of
Aunt Luisa, her daughters, and a son-in-law, Pedro. They were coming to the
United States via *un vuelo de la libertad*, or freedom flight, as the U.S. military
airplane trips from Havana to Miami were called. Khrushchev was going to eat

up Cuba like an ice cream sundae. Things had gotten out of hand, bad enough for Luisa, who had loved her life in Holguín, to leave. Gone were the days of the happy-go-lucky Cubans who went on jaunts to Miami and New York to have a high time ballroom hopping; gone were the days when Cubans came to the States to make money and see more of the world. Now Cubans were leaving because of Khrushchev's new pal, Fidel Castro, the Shit, as some Cubans called him.

2

11 Alejo had supported Castro during the days of the revolution. He had raised money for the pro-Castro Cubans in Miami by hawking copies of the *Sierra Maestra* magazine to pals on the street. This magazine was printed in Miami by pro-Castro Cubans and was filled with pictures of tortured heroes left on the streets or lying in the lightless mortuary rooms with their throats cut and their heads blood-splattered. They were victims of the crooked Batista regime, and now it was time for Batista and his henchmen to go! Alejo was not a political creature, but he supported the cause, of course, to end the injustices of Batista's rule. When someone brought him a box of Cuban magazines to sell, Alejo went down on Amsterdam Avenue and sold them to friends. Alejo always carried one of those magazines in his pocket, and he was persuasive, selling them. In his soft calm voice he would say, "Come on, it's only a dollar and for the cause of your countrymen's freedom!" And soon he would find himself inviting all the buyers back to his apartment, where they sat in the kitchen drinking and talking about what would save the world: "An honest man with a good heart, out of greed's reach," was the usual consensus. Political talk about Cuba always led to nostalgic talk, and soon Alejo's friends would soften up and bend like orchid vines, glorying in the lost joys of childhood. Their loves and regrets thickened in the room in waves, until they began singing along with their drinking and falling down. With their arms around each other and glasses raised, they toasted Fidel as "the hope for the future."

12 Alejo and Mercedes had been happy with the success of the revolution. The day Castro entered Havana they threw a party with so much food and drink that the next morning people had to cross into the street to get around the stacks of garbage bags piled on the sidewalk in front of the building. Inside, people were sprawled around everywhere. There were sleepers in the kitchen and in the hall, sleepers in the closet. There was a *dudduhduh* of a skipping needle over a phonograph record. A cat that had come in through the window from the alley was going around eating leftover scraps of food.

13 Soon the papers printed that famous picture of Castro entering Havana with his cowboy-looking friend, Camilio Cienfuegos, on a tank. They were like Jesus and John the Baptist in a Roman epic movie. The *Sierra Maestra* magazine would later feature a centerfold of Castro as Jesus Christ with his hair long and golden brown, almost fiery in a halo of light. And for the longest time Cubans,

Alejo and Mercedes among them, referred to Castro with great reverence and love, as if he were a saint.

In a few years, however, kids in the street started to write slogans like *Castro eats big bananas!* The New York press ran stories about the Castro visit to New York. Alejo and Hector stood on the corner one afternoon, watching his motorcade speed uptown to a Harlem hotel. There, the press said, Castro's men killed their own chickens and ate them raw. Castro even came to give a talk at the university. Alejo and Hector were among a crowd of admirers that clustered around him to get a look. Castro was very tall for a Cuban, six-feet-two. He was wearing a long raincoat and took sips from a bottle of Pepsi-Cola. He listened to questions intently, liked to smile, and kept reaching out to shake hands. He also signed an occasional autograph. He was, the newspapers said, unyielding in his support of the principles of freedom.   14

In time Castro announced the revolutionary program. Alejo read the *El Diario* accounts intently while Mercedes wandered around the apartment asking, "What's going to happen to my sisters?" By 1962, after the Bay of Pigs invasion and the beginning of the Cuban ration-card programs, an answer to her question came in the form of letters. Standing by the window Mercedes would read the same letter over and over again, sighing and saying out loud, "Oh my Lord! They are so unhappy!"   15

"Ma, what's going on?" Hector would ask her.   16

"Things are very bad. The Communists are very bad people. Your aunts have nothing to eat, no clothes to wear, no medicine. The Communists go around taking things away from people! And if you say anything they put you in jail!"   17

Mercedes's stories about the new life in Cuba made Hector think of a house of horrors. In his sleep he pictured faceless, cowled abductors roaming the streets of Holguín in search of victims to send to brainwashing camps. He pictured the ransacking of old mansions, the burning of churches, deaths by firing squads. He remembered back many years and saw the door of Aunt Luisa's house on Arachoa Street, and then he imagined guards smashing that door open to search Luisa's home.   18

All the news that came into the house in those letters fed such visions: "Ai, Hector, do you remember your cousin Paco? He has been sent to prison for a year, and all he did was get caught with a pound of sugar under his shirt!" A year later: "Oh your poor cousin Paco! He just came out of prison and now my sister can hardly recognize him. Listen to what Luisa says: 'He has lost most of his hair and is as thin as a skeleton with yellowed, jaundiced skin. He has aged twenty years in one.'" Another letter: "Dear sister, the headaches continue. Everything is upside down. You can't even go to church these days without someone asking, 'Where are you going?' Everyone in the barrio watches where you go. No one has any privacy. If you are not in the Party then you're no good. Many of them are Negroes, and now that they have the power, they are very bad to us. I don't know how long we can endure these humiliations. We   19 hope for Castro's fall." Another letter: "Dear sister, last week your niece Maria was kicked out of dental school, and do you know what for? Because she wouldn't recite 'Hail Lenin!' in the mornings with the other students. I went to argue with the headmaster of the school, but there was nothing I could do. On top of that, poor Rina's roof was high by lightning but she can't get the materials to fix it. When it rains the floors are flooded—all because she is not in the Party. . . . As usual I ask for your prayers and to send us whatever you can by way of clothing, food and medicine. Aspirins and penicillin are almost impossible to find these days, as are most other things. I know I'm complaining to you, but if you were here, you would understand. With much love, Luisa."

20   To help her sisters, Mercedes went from apartment to apartment asking neighbors for any clothing they might not need. These clothes were packed into boxes and sent down to Cuba at a cost of fifty dollars each. Mercedes paid for this out of her own pocket. She had been working at night cleaning in a nursery school since the days of Alejo's illness. Alejo too contributed. He came home with boxes of canned goods and soap and toothpaste from the hotel and he bought such items as rubbing alcohol, aspirins, mercurochrome, iodine, Tampax, Q-Tips, cotton, and toilet paper to send to Cuba.

21   "The world is going to the devil," Mercedes would say to Alejo as she packed one of the boxes. "Imagine having to use old newspapers for toilet paper! The Russians are the new masters, they have everything, but what do Luisa and Rina have? Nothing!"

22   Of the family, Mercedes was the most outspoken about the revolution. Alejo was very quiet in his views. He didn't like Castro, or, for that matter, Khrushchev. But he would never argue with a friend about politics. He was always more concerned about keeping his friendships cordial. To please two different sets of neighbors he subscribed to both the *Daily Worker* and the *Republican Eagle*. He read neither of them, but still would nod emphatically whenever he came upon these neighbors in the hallway and they bombarded him with their philosophies. "Certainly," Alejo would say to them, "why don't you come inside and have a drink with me?" When there was a gathering of visitors with different points of view, Alejo used liquor to keep the wagging tongues in line. Get them drunk and make them happy, was his motto.

23   But Mercedes didn't want to hear about Fidel Castro from anyone, not even from Señor Lopez, a union organizer and good friend of the family who lived in the building. He would come to the apartment to recount the declines in illiteracy, prostitution, and malnutrition in Cuba. "No more of this!" he would declare, showing Mercedes and Alejo and Hector a picture from *La Bohemia* of a decrepit old Negro man dying in bed, with bloated stomach, festering sores on his limbs, and a long gray worm literally oozing out of his navel. "You won't see this anymore now that Castro is in power!"

24   "And what about the decent people who supported Castro in the first place, and who now have nothing but troubles?" she would ask.

"Mercita, the revolution is the will of the majority of the Cuban people!" 25

"You mean the people who were the good-for-nothings?" 26

"No, the people who had nothing because they were allowed nothing." 27

"Oh yes? And what about my family?" 28

"Mercita, use your brains. I don't like to put it this way, but as the saying 29
goes, 'To make an omelet you have to break a few eggs.'"

"My family are not eggs! If you like eggs so much, why don't you go down 30
to Cuba and live there? Chickens have more to eat than what you would get.
Go there and see what freedom is like!"

By 1965 it was becoming clear that Castro was not going to fall from power. 31
Cubans who had been hoping for a counterrevolution were now growing
desperate to leave. Luisa and her family were among them. One evening an
errand boy from the corner drugstore knocked at the door. There was a call
from Cuba. Mercedes and Hector hurried down the hill. The caller was Aunt
Luisa. Her sad voice was so far away, interrupted by sonic hums and clicking
static echoes. It sounded like the voices of hens reciting numbers in Spanish.
With the jukebox going, it was a wonder that Luisa's voice could be heard over
mountains and rivers and across the ocean.

"How is it over there now?" Mercedes asked. 32

"It's getting worse here. There are too many headaches. We want to leave. 33
Pedro, Virginia's husband, lost his mechanic's shop. There is no point in our
staying."

"Who wants to come?" 34

"Me, Pedro, Virginia, and Maria." 35

"And what about Rina?" 36

"She is going to stay for the time being with Delores and her husband." 37
Delores was Rina's daughter. She had a doctorate in pedagogy that made her a
valuable commodity in those days of literacy programs. "Delores has been
appointed to a government post and she is too afraid to refuse the Party, for
fear they will do something to Rina or to her husband. But we will come. I have
the address of the place where you must write for the sponsorship papers. We've
already put our name on the government waiting list. When our name reaches
the top of the list we'll be able to go."

The only other way was to fly either to Mexico or Spain, but at a cost of 38
two thousand dollars per person to Mexico, three thousand dollars per person
to Spain. The family did not have that kind of money.

Mercedes then gave Hector the telephone. He listened to his aunt's soft 39
voice, saying, "We will be with you soon, and you will know your family again.
Pray for us so that we will be safe," Her voice sounded weak. There was clicking,
like a plug being pulled. Perhaps someone was listening in the courthouse, where
the call was being made.

Luisa spoke with Mercedes for another minute, and then their time was up 40
and Mercedes and Hector returned home.

41   Alejo took care of the paperwork. He wrote to immigration authorities in Miami for their visas and for the special forms that would be mailed out by him, approved by the U.S. Immigration Department, and sent to Cuba.

42   In February 1966 Luisa and her daughters and son-in-law left Cuba. First they waited in front of the house on Arachoa Street in Holguín, where they had all been living, for the army bus that would take them on the ten-hour journey west to Havana. When they arrived at the José Martí Airport, they waited in a wire-fenced compound. A Cuban official went over their papers and had them stand in line for hours before they boarded the military transport jet to America.

43   On the day that Alejo looked at the clipping of Khrushchev again, they received word that Luisa and her daughters and a son-in-law were coming, and a sort of shock wave of apprehension and hope passed through them.

3

44   For Hector the prospect of Aunt Luisa's arrival stirred up memories. He began to make a conscious effort to be "Cuban," and yet the very idea of *Cubanness* inspired fear in him as if he would grow ill from it, as if micróbios would be transmitted by the very mention of the word *Cuba*. He was a little perplexed because he also loved the notion of Cuba to an extreme. In Cuba there were so many pleasant fragrances, like the small of Luisa's hair and the damp clay ground of the early morning. Cuba was where Mercedes had once lived a life of style and dignity and happiness. And it was the land of happy courtship with Alejo and the land where men did not fall down. Hector was tired of seeing Mercedes cry and yell. He was tired of her moroseness and wanted the sadness to go away. He wanted the apartment to be filled with beams of sunlight, like in the dream house of Cuba.

45   He was sick at heart for being so Americanized, which he equated with being fearful and lonely. His Spanish was unpracticed, practically nonexistent. He had a stutter, and saying a Spanish word made him think of drunkenness. A Spanish sentence wrapped around his face, threatened to peel off his skin and send him falling to the floor like Alejo. He avoided Spanish even though that was all he heard at home. He read it, understood it, but he grew paralyzed by the prospect of the slightest conversation.

46   "Hablame en espanol!" Alejo's drunken friends would challenge him. But Hector always refused and got lost in his bedroom, read *Flash* comic books. And when he was around the street Ricans, they didn't want to talk Spanish with Whitey anyway, especially since he was not getting high with them, just getting drunk now and then, and did not look like a hood but more like a goody-goody, round-faced mama's boy: a dark dude, as they used to say in those days.

47   Even Horacio had contempt for Hector. Knowing that Hector was nervous in the company of visitors, he would instigate long conversations in Spanish. When visiting men would sit in the kitchen speaking about politics, family, and Cuba, Horacio would play the patrón and join them, relegating Hector to the

side, with the women. He had disdain for his brother and for the ignorance Hector represented. He was now interested in "culture." He had returned from England a complete European who listened to Mozart instead of diddy-bop music. His hair was styled as carefully as Beau Brummell's. His wardrobe consisted of English tweed jackets and fine Spanish shoes; his jewelry, his watches, his cologne, everything was very European and very far from the gutter and the insecurity he had left behind. As he put it, "I'm never going to be fuckin' poor again."

He went around criticizing the way Mercedes kept house and cooked, the way Alejo managed his money (buying everything with cash and never on credit) and the amounts of booze Alejo drank. But mostly he criticized Hector. The day he arrived home from the Air Force and saw Hector for the first time in years, his face turned red. He could not believe his eyes. Hector was so fat that his clothes were bursting at the seams, and when Hector embraced him, Horacio shook his head and said, "Man, I can't believe this is my brother." 48

And now the real Cubans, Luisa and her daughters and son-in-law, were coming to find out what a false life Hector led. Hector could not sleep at night, thinking of it. He tried to remember his Spanish, but instead of sentences, pictures of Cuba entered into his mind. But he did not fight this. He fantasized about Cuba. He wanted the pictures to enter him, as if memory and imagination would make him more of a man, a Cuban man. 49

The day before Luisa arrived he suddenly remembered his trip to Cuba with Mercedes and Horacio in 1954. He remembered looking out the window of the plane and seeing fire spewing from the engines on the wing. To Cuba. To Cuba. Mercedes was telling him a story when the plane abruptly plunged down through some clouds and came out into the night air again. Looking out the window he saw pearls in the ocean and the reflection of the moon in the water. For a moment he saw a line of three ships, caravels with big white sails like Columbus's ships, and he tugged at Mercedes's arm. She looked but did not see them. And when he looked again, they were gone. 50

Hector tried again for a genuine memory. Now he saw Luisa's house on Arachoa Street, the sun a haze bursting through the trees. 51

"Do you remember a cat with one eye in Cuba?" he asked Horacio, who was across the room reading *Playboy* magazine. 52

"What?" he said with annoyance. 53

"In Cuba, wasn't there a little cat who used to go in and out of the shadows and bump into things? You know, into the steps and into the walls, because it only had one eye. And then Luisa would come out and feed it bits of meat?" 54

"You can't remember anything. Don't fool yourself," he replied. 55

But Hector could not stop himself. He remembered bulldozers tearing up the street and that sunlight again, filtering through the flower heads, and flamingos of light on the walls of the house. He remembered the dog with the pathetic red dick running across the yard. Then he remembered holding an enormous, trembling white sunhat. His grandmother, Doña Maria, was sitting 56 nearby in a blue-and-white dotted dress, and he took the sunhat to show her. But it wasn't a sunhat. It was an immense white butterfly. "¡Ai, que linda!" Doña Maria said. "It's so pretty, but maybe we should let the poor thing go." And so Hector released the butterfly and watched it rise over the house and float silently away.

57   Then he saw Doña Maria, now dead, framed by a wreath of orchids in the yard, kissing him—so many kisses, squirming kisses—and giving advice. She never got over leaving Spain for Cuba and would always remain a proud Spaniard. "Remember," she had told Hector. "You're Spanish first and then Cuban."

58   He remembered sitting on the cool steps to Luisa's kitchen and watching the road where the bulldozers worked. A turtle was crawling across the yard, and iguanas were licking up the sticky juice on the kitchen steps. Then he heard Luisa's voice: "Come along, child," she called. "I have something for you." And he could see her face again through the screen door, long and wistful.

59   Inside, she had patted Hector's head and poured him a glass of milk. Cuban milk alone was sour on the tongues of children, but with the Cuban magic potion, which she added, it was the most delicious drink Hector ever tasted. With deep chocolate and nut flavors and traces of orange and mango, the bitter with the sweet, the liquid went down his throat, so delicious. "No child, drink that milk," Luisa said. "Don't forget your *tia*. She loves you."

60   Then a bam! bam! came from the television and Hector could hear voices of neighbors out in the hallway. No, he wasn't used to hearing Luisa's niceties anymore, and he couldn't remember what was in the milk, except that it was Cuban, and then he wondered what he would say to his aunt and cousins, whether he would smile and nod his head or hide as much as possible, like a turtle on a hot day.

4

61   It was late night when a van pulled up to the building and its four exhausted passengers stepped onto the sidewalk. Seeing the arrival from the window, Mercedes was in a trance for a moment and then removed her apron and ran out, almost falling down the front steps, waving her arms and calling, "Aaaaiiii, aaaaiiii, aaaaiiii! Oh my God! My God! My God," and giving many kisses. Alejo followed and hugged Pedro. The female cousins waited humbly, and then they began kissing Mercedes and Alejo and Hector and Horacio, their hats coming off and teeth chattering and hair getting all snarled like ivy on an old church . . . kisses, kisses, kisses . . . into the warm lobby with its deep, endless mirrors and the mailbox marked *Delgado/Santinio*. The female cousins, like china dolls, were incredibly beautiful, but struck dumb by the snow and the new world, silent because there was something dreary about the surroundings. They were thinking Alejo had been in this country for twenty years, and yet what did he

have? But no one said this. They just put hands on hands and gave many kisses and said, "I can't believe I'm seeing you here." They were all so skinny and exhausted-looking, Luisa, Virginia, Maria, and Pedro. They came holding cloth bags with all their worldly possessions: a few crucifixes, a change of clothing, aspirins given to them at the airport, an album of old photographs, prayer medals, a Bible, a few Cuban coins from the old days, and a throat-lozenge tin filled with some soil from Holguín, Oriente province, Cuba.

After kissing and hugging them Alejo took them into the kitchen where they almost died: There was so much of everything! Milk and wine and beer, steaks and rice and chicken and sausages and ham and plantains and ice cream and black bean soup and Pepsi Cola and Hershey chocolate bars and almond nougat, and popcorn and Wise potato chips and Jiffy peanut butter, and rum and whiskey, marshmallows, spaghetti, flan and pasteles and chocolate cake and pie, more than enough to make them delirious. And even though the walls were cracked and it was dark, there was a television set and a radio and lightbulbs and toilet paper and pictures of the family and crucifixes and toothpaste and soap and more.

It was "Thank God for freedom and bless my family" from Luisa's mouth, but her daughters were more cautious. Distrusting the world, they approached everything timidly. In the food-filled kitchen Alejo told them how happy he was to have them in his house, and they were happy because the old misery was over, but they were still without a home and in a strange world. Uncertainty showed in their faces.

Pedro, Virginia's husband, managed to be the most cheerful. He smoked and talked up a storm about the conditions in Cuba and the few choices the Castro government had left to them. Smoking thick, black cigars, Horacio and Alejo nodded and agreed, and the conversation went back and forth and always ended with "What are you going to do?"

"Work until I have something," was Pedro's simple answer.

It was such a strong thing to say that Hector, watching from the doorway, wanted to be like Pedro. And from time to time, Pedro would look over and wink and flash his Victor Mature teeth.

Pedro was about thirty years old and had been through very bad times, including the struggle in 1957 and 1958 to get Castro into power. But wanting to impress Hector with his cheeriness, Pedro kept saying things in English to Hector like, "I remember Elvis Presley records. Do you know *You're My Angel Baby*?" And Hector would not even answer that. But Pedro would speak on, about the brave Cubans who got out of Cuba in the strangest ways. His buddy back in Holguín stole a small airplane with a few friends and flew west to Mexico, where they crash-landed their plane on a dirt road in the Yucatán. He ended up in Mexico City, where he found work in the construction business. He was due in America soon and would one day marry Maria, who wanted a brave man. These stories only made Hector more and more silent.

68   As for his female cousins, all they said to him was: "Do you want to eat?" or "Why are you so quiet?" And sometimes Horacio answered for him, saying: "He's just dumb when it comes to being Cuban."

69   Aunt Luisa, with her good heart, really didn't care what Hector said or didn't say. Each time she encountered him in the morning or the afternoons, she would take his face between her hands and say, "Give me a kiss and say 'Tia, I love you.'" And not in the way Alejo used to, falling off a chair and with his eyes desperate, but sweetly. Hector liked to be near Luisa with her sweet angelic face.

70   He felt comfortable enough around Aunt Luisa to begin speaking to her. He wasn't afraid because she overflowed with warmth. One day while Aunt Luisa was washing dishes, Hector started to think of her kitchen in Cuba. He remembered the magic Cuban drink.

71   "Auntie," he asked her. "Do you remember a drink that you used to make for me in the afternoons in Cuba? What was it? It was the most delicious chocolate but with Cuban spices."

72   She thought about it. "Chocolate drink in the afternoon? Let me see . . ." She wiped a plate clean in the sink. She seemed perplexed and asked, "And it was chocolate?"

73   "It was Cuban chocolate. What was it?"

74   She thought on it again and her eyes grew big and she laughed, slapping her knee. "Ai, bobo. It was Hershey syrup and milk!"

75   After that he didn't ask her any more questions. He just sat in the living room listening to her tell Mercedes about her impressions of the United States. For example, after she had sat out on the stoop or gazed out the window for a time, she would make a blunt declaration: "There are a lot of airplanes in the sky." But usually when Mercedes and Luisa got to talking, they drifted toward the subject of spirits and ghosts. When they were little girls spiritualism was very popular in Cuba. All the little girls were half mediums, in those days. And remembering this with great laughter, Luisa would say, "If only we could have seen what would happen to Papa! Or that Castro would turn out to be so bad!"

76   "Yes, Papa, that would have been something," Mercedes answered with wide hopeful eyes. "But Castro is something else. What could a few people do about him?"

77   "Imagine if you're dead in Cuba," said Luisa, "and you wake up to that mess. What would you do?"

78   "I would go to Miami, or somewhere like that."

79   "Yes, and you would go on angel wings."

80   It was Luisa's ambition to ignore America and the reality of her situation completely. So she kept taking Mercedes back to the old days: "You were such a prankster, so mischievous! You couldn't sit down for a moment without being up to something. Poor Papa! What he had to do with you!" And then, turning to Hector, she would add, "Look at your Mama. This innocent over here was the fright of us all. She was always imagining things. Iguanas, even little baby

iguanas, were dragons. A rustle in the bushes was ghosts of fierce Indians looking for their bones!" She laughed. "There are ghosts, but not as many as she saw. She was always in trouble with Papa. He was very good to her but also strict. But his punishments never stopped your mother. My, but she was a fresh girl!"

When she wasn't talking to Mercedes, Luisa watched the Spanish channel   81
on the television, or ate, or prayed. Pedro went out with Alejo and Horacio, looking for work. Maria and Virginia helped with the housecleaning and the cooking, and then they studied their books. They were very quiet, like felines, moving from one spot to another without a sound. Sometimes everyone went out to the movies; Alejo paid for it. Or they all went downtown to the department stores to buy clothing and other things they needed. Again, Alejo paid for everything, angering Mercedes, for whom he bought nothing.

"I know you're trying to be nice to my family, but remember we don't have   82
money."

Still, he was generous with them, as if desperate to keep Luisa and her   83
daughters in the apartment. Their company made him as calm and happy as a mouse. Nothing pleased Alejo more than sitting at the head of the dinner table, relishing the obvious affection that Luisa and her daughters and son-in-law felt for him. At meals Alejo would make toast after toast to their good health and long life, drink down his glass of rum or whiskey quickly, and then fill another and drink that and more. Mercedes always sat quietly wondering, "What does my sister really think of me for marrying him?" while Hector waited for Alejo suddenly to fall off his chair, finally showing his aunt and cousins just who the Santinios really were.

One night Alejo fell against the table and knocked down a big stack of   84
plates. The plates smashed all around Alejo, who was on the floor. Hector scrambled to correct everything before Virginia and Maria and Pedro came to look. He scrambled to get Alejo up before they saw him. He pulled with all his strength, the way he and Horacio used to, but Alejo weighed nearly three hundred pounds. As the cousins watched in silence, Hector wished he could walk through the walls and fly away. He thought that now they would know one of his secrets, that the son is like the father. He tried again to pull Alejo up and had nearly succeeded when Pedro appeared and, with amazing strength, wrapped his arms around Alejo's torso and heaved him onto a chair with one pull.

Hector hadn't wanted them to see this, because then they might want to   85
leave and the apartment would be empty of Pedro and Luisa and her daughters. those fabulous beings. He didn't want them to see the dingy furniture and the cracking walls and the cheap decorative art, plaster statues, and mass-produced paintings. He didn't want them to see that he was an element in this world, only as good as the things around him. He wanted to be somewhere else, be someone else, a Cuban . . . And he didn't want the family perceived as the poor relations with the drunk father. So he tried to laugh about Alejo and eventually went to bed, leaving Luisa and Pedro and his cousins still standing in the hall.

Eventually, they did move away. Virginia and Maria found work in a factory in Jersey City, and Pedro came home one evening with the news that he had landed a freight dispatcher's job in an airport. Just like that. He had brought home a big box of pastries, sweet cakes with super-sweet cream, chocolate eclairs, honey-drenched cookies with maraschino cherries in their centers.

86   As Alejo devoured some of these, he said to Pedro, "Well, that's good. You're lucky to have such good friends here. Does it pay you well?"

87   Pedro nodded slightly and said, "I don't know, it starts out at seven thousand dollars a year, but it will get better."

88   Alejo also nodded, but he was sick because after twenty years in the same job he did not make that much, and this brought down his head and made him yawn. He got up and went to his bedroom where he fell asleep.

89   A few months later, they were ready to rent a house in a nice neighborhood in Jersey. The government had helped them out with some emergency funds. ("We never asked the government for even a penny," Mercedes kept saying to Alejo.) Everyone but Luisa was bringing home money. They used that money to buy furniture and to send Virginia to night computer school taught by Spanish instructors. Instead of being cramped up in someone else's apartment with rattling pipes and damp plaster walls that seemed ready to fall in, they had a three-story house with a little yard and lived near many Cubans who kept the sidewalks clean and worked hard, so their sick hearts would have an easier time of it.

90   Hector was bereft at their leaving, but more than that he was astounded by how easily they established themselves. One day Pedro said, "I just bought a car." On another, "I just got a color TV." In time they would be able to buy an even larger house. The house would be filled with possessions: a dishwasher, a washing machine, radios, a big stereo console, plastic-covered velour couches and chairs, electric clocks, fans, air conditioners, hair dryers, statues, crucifixes, lamps and electric-candle chandeliers, and more. One day they would have enough money to move again, to sell the house at a huge profit and travel down to Miami to buy another house there. They would work like dogs, raise children, prosper. They did not allow the old world, the past, to hinder them. They did not cry but walked straight ahead. They drank but did not fall down. Pedro even started a candy and cigarette business to keep him busy in the evenings, earning enough money to buy himself a truck.

91   "Qué bueno," Alejo would say.

92   "This country's wonderful to new Cubans," Mercedes kept repeating. But then she added, "They're going to have everything, and we . . . what will we have?" And she would go about sweeping the floor or preparing chicken for dinner. She would say to Alejo, "Doesn't it hurt you inside?"

93   Alejo shrugged. "No, because they have suffered in Cuba."

94   He never backed off from that position and always remained generous to them, even after their visits became less frequent, even when they came only once a year. And when Pedro tried to repay the loans, Alejo always waved the

money away. By this time Virginia was pregnant, so Alejo said, "Keep it for the baby."

"You don't want the money?" 95

"Only when you don't need it. It's important for you to have certain things now." 96

But Mercedes stalked around the apartment, screaming, "What about the pennies I saved? What about us?" ✣ 97

RESPONDING

1. In a journal entry, explain Horacio's definition of "culture" (paragraph 47). Compare his definition with other definitions of "culture."

2. Compare Alejo and Mercedes's attitudes toward the Cuban revolution before and after Castro came to power. Working in pairs, write a dialogue between Alejo or Mercedes and a supporter of the revolution, their neighbor, Señor Lopez.

3. Hector is "sick at heart for being so Americanized, which he equated with being fearful and lonely" (paragraph 45). Using examples from the reading, write an essay explaining the ways in which Hector is Americanized. Compare his feelings about America with his feelings about Cuba. What does Cuba seem to represent to him?

4. Why is Mercedes angry at the end of the story? Compare the situation for the new immigrants arriving in 1965 with that of immigrants arriving twenty years earlier. Why do you think Pedro and his family become prosperous while Alejo and his family remain poor? Using information from the reading, your own knowledge, and any relevant news coverage you have seen or reading you have done, speculate about each family's reception in the new country.

VAN B. LUU

Van B. Luu left Vietnam at the age of twelve. She holds a bachelor's degree from the University of California, Berkeley. Her work has appeared in Making Waves: An Anthology of Writings by and About Asian American Women.

In the essay that follows, Van Luu makes use of traditional academic resources—books, journal articles, doctoral dissertations, and government documents. She also includes information obtained through interviews she conducted in Vietnamese with some of the refugees themselves. In this way, her essay provides a unique perspective on the issues faced by one group of immigrant women.

⊞

THE HARDSHIPS OF ESCAPE FOR VIETNAMESE WOMEN

1   AT PRESENT ONLY A LIMITED AMOUNT of research is being done on Vietnamese refugee women. In writing this essay, which is based on personal interviews and research, I hope to contribute some knowledge and understanding to the study of these women's lives and experiences in America. In addition to their stressful escape, they are also facing new challenges during their resettlement. What makes these experiences significant is that they have a great impact on the women's mental health. In this essay, I will focus on the external causes of mental health problems rather than their psychological manifestations. Understanding the evacuation and resettlement of Vietnamese women is a necessary prerequisite to understanding their needs and problems. Thus, I will examine the problem from the period of the women's escape to their present situation. And since the majority of problems are experienced by the women who have come to America in recent years, I will concentrate on them in this discussion.

2   Ever since the Communists took over South Vietnam in 1975, thousands of Vietnamese refugees have left their country in search of freedom. Despite the increasing risks and dangers such as piracy, a majority of people, 575,000 in total, have fled by sea.[1] After arriving at an asylum camp in Hong Kong, Malaysia, the Philippines, or Thailand, they hope they will be able to resettle in new countries—Japan, France, Canada, and especially the United States, the nation most willing to accept refugees. By the end of 1981, over 450,000

---

1. U.S. Committee for Refugees, *Vietnamese Boat People: Pirates' Vulnerable Prey* (Washington, D.C., February 1984), I. [Author's note]

refugees had resettled in the United States; approximately 45 percent of these people are women.[2] Only recently have the women been recognized as a vulnerable group that needs special programs and attention. In addition to their poor mental health resulting from the traumatic experiences during their escapes, many Vietnamese women also suffer emotional problems during their adjustment in the United States.

Leaving Their Homes

Vietnamese women—both those who work in the home and those outside the home—experience a great deal of grief and loss.[3] The separation from family, in many ways, causes depression among the Vietnamese women. Because of the high cost of leaving the country—approximately two thousand dollars per person is charged by boat owners—usually only wealthy families can afford to raise enough money to transport the entire family. Other families must decide which member has the most potential in their future endeavors and transport him or her out of the country, leaving the less promising relatives at home. This has created a dilemma because Vietnamese families are traditionally close-knit: name, status, and personal as well as financial support all come from the family.[4] As in other Asian cultures, children are expected to take care of their aged parents to "compensate the gift of birth and upbringing."[5] It is very common to find several generations living together under one roof.

After settling in America, the Vietnamese women, as well as the men, often feel guilty about leaving their relatives behind. According to Dr. Le Tai Rieu, director of Indo-Chinese Mental Health Projects in San Francisco, the Vietnamese refugees are plagued by "survivor's guilt"—they feel that they have run away while their relatives are still suffering.[6] Some women save money from work and often send gifts through the black market such as medicine and, if possible, currency, so their relatives can pay for the passage of the remaining family members. However, many times their dreams of reuniting with their relatives are very difficult to fulfill because the passage to the asylum camp is unsafe. Consequently, the Vietnamese women feel helpless and continue to bear depression and guilt as the years go by in the new land.

The ability to finance an escape to foreign countries does not guarantee admission into asylum camps. Hong Kong, Malaysia, the Philippines, and Thailand were chosen by the refugees as sites for the camps because of their

2. Lani Davidson, "Women Refugees: Special Needs and Programs," *Journal of Refugee Resettlement* I (1981): 17. [Author's note]
3. Kasumi Hirayama, "Effects of the Employment of Vietnamese Refugee Wives on Their Family Roles and Mental Health" (Ph.D. diss., University of Pennsylvania, 1980), 156.
4. Lynelle Burmark-Parasurman, *Interfacing Two Cultures: Vietnamese and Americans* (California: Alameda County, 1982), 58.
5. Burmark-Parasurman, *Interfacing Two Cultures*, 58.
6. Bill Soiffer, "Viet Mental Health Project in a Bind," *San Francisco Chronicle*, 14 January 1980, 7.

proximity to the escape points, which are located mostly along the southern coast of Vietnam. (Some refugees have also found ways of leaving the country by land route, walking through Laos and Cambodia with paid guides who speak several languages and lead them to safety in Thailand.) In recent years many countries that experienced an early influx of refugees have begun to deny admissions. In 1979 Malaysia refused entry to 55,000 refugees, and Indonesia deployed a twenty-four vessel force to prevent refugees from reaching its soil.[7] Apparently these governments are afraid of the economic problems in feeding and housing the refugees, as well as the interethnic conflict resulting from longstanding tension among these countries' peoples. However, their efforts to stem the migration have not been successful due to the refugees' desperation to find shelter after their long struggle for survival during their exodus.

Robbery and Violence at Sea

6   The interval between deciding to leave their homes and arriving in a safe camp can be long and very harrowing. The boats in which the refugees escape are small and in poor condition; they can easily be sunk en route to the asylum camps. Sometimes sinking boats have been saved in time by passing vessels; sometimes not. This tragedy resulted in 150,000 refugee deaths in the ocean from May 1975 to mid-1979.[8] The fortunate refugees who survive the exodus still must face the possibility of witnessing the deaths of their family members or other passengers. In one case, Tran Hue Hue, a sixteen-year-old girl, was the only survivor out of fifty people during the escape in 1980. She suffered the traumatic experiences of watching both her brother and aunt pass away and being stranded on a tiny atoll before her rescue. Despite the long years spent resettling in her new country, Tran Hue Hue still suffers from the grief of her lost relatives.

7   Since 1978 one of the main hindrances to safe passage has been piracy. Many people believe that refugees carry fortunes in gold, jewelry, and U.S. dollars, and that "collectively the wealth could be substantial, especially when in 1978 the boats became larger and started carrying not a few score but as many as 600 to 700 people."[9] With the lure of their potential wealth, these refugees on the rickety boats are brutally attacked by the pirates in the waters joining Vietnam's Mekong Delta, the coasts of southern Thailand, and northeast Malaysia. Some pirates rob but provide food and water in return. However, in recent years the incidence of violent attacks has increased dramatically, with the pirates using a variety of weapons—including guns, daggers, knives, and even

---

7. Scott Stone and John McGowan, *Wrapped in the Wind Shawl: Refugees of Southeast Asia and the Western World* (San Rafael: Presidio Press, 1980), 39.
8. Bruce Grant, *The Boat People: An Age Investigation of Bruce Grant* (New York: Penguin Books, 1979), 80.
9. Ibid., 63–64.

hammers—to attack the defenseless refugees. U.S. refugee officials interviewing the victims often write the initials "RPM" in their case histories. "RPM" stands for "rape, pillage, and murder," a summary of the dreadful experiences of these newcomers.[10]

Female Vietnamese refugees are in a particularly vulnerable situation, one that began back in their old country where they were oppressed in the traditional caste system. There these women held an inferior status and had fewer privileges than men. Usually the males were encouraged to get a good education while the females were expected to take care of the household and later become good wives and mothers. In addition, the importance of *noi doi tong duaon*, that is, carrying the family name from one generation to the next through the male heir, led to the increasing practice of bigamy until just recently. Pressure from the society as well as from the family often made women share their husbands with others; it was not surprising to see men with three or four wives living under one roof. Many women had a hard time getting out of this unwanted situation because when a woman married, she became part of the husband's family. To leave their husbands, even in instances of bad marriages, was a great risk because they feared slander, which was very difficult to withstand in the caste society of Vietnam. At present the women are found to be less oppressed than in the past, but problems still exist.

Even after leaving their country, the ordeal of Vietnamese women may continue because they are subjected to risks of sexual abuse. They suffer not only from the terrible journey to the asylum camps, but also from rape and violence at the hands of Thai fishermen, otherwise known as "sea pirates." Nhat Tien, a famous Vietnamese writer and an expert on the Vietnamese refugee issue, says that "these women deserve very special consideration and assistance, much different from that prescribed for ordinary boat people, special materials as well as psychological and emotional support necessary to enable them to stand secure and build a fine new life in the U.S."[11]

In a personal interview[12] Mrs. L., a thirty-three-year-old nurse, described her painful experiences during her escape in 1983:

> Staying on the boat was very uncomfortable, because sixty-six people had been crammed together in a small boat. There was neither food, drinks, nor shelter. We had to wait until the rain came to get fresh water. One day, the boat suddenly stopped moving and a storm arrived. The men teamed up to work on the engine and at the same time they tried to scoop the water out of the boat. No other women helped out, except me. As I was scooping out the water, I had a sudden impulse to smear my face with black oil from the engine. I looked filthy and

10. Ibid., 65.
11. Nhat Tien, Thuy Vu, and Duong Phuc, "Report on the Kro-Kra Trial" (Unpublished report compiled by the Boat People S.O.S. Committee, San Diego, 1980).
12. This and subsequent interviews were conducted in Vietnamese by the author in 1985.

disgusting. Up until now, I do not know why I did that, but it surely saved me from the pirates who later attacked our boat.

11   About twenty pirates from two boats set upon the refugees' vessel. Armed with guns, hammers, and large metal bars, they demanded gold, money, and other valuables. They carefully searched both the boats and the people to make sure Mrs. L. and her fellow escapees had not hidden anything from them. Then the pirates, satisfied with their booty, turned their attention to the women on board.

> Everyone felt so helpless since we were unarmed. After searching, the pirates started the rape and abuse of the women. They took all of them, except me, to the back of the boat and raped them. I was so lucky because I looked so ugly and filthy. I fainted and couldn't see anything. . . . I closed my eyes really tight to stop myself from witnessing the horrible scene, but I could not help hearing the moans and groans, and especially the beggings for mercy by those poor women. There were thirteen or fourteen women altogether, whose ages ranged from fifteen to early forties. I really felt sorry for a young girl: she was about fifteen. She was raped continuously by four or five pirates. The whole ordeal lasted for two hours.

12   The pirates eventually left, but stripped the engine and motor from the boat, and left the refugees stranded in the middle of the ocean. Mrs. L. remembers thinking that "death seemed to approach closer and closer daily," even though the men tried to get the boat moving by using whatever means they could devise. After about seven days and nights adrift at sea, the refugees managed to land on the Malaysian shore where they were finally taken in by the authorities.

13   One of the most notorious incidents that shocked the Vietnamese community in America took place on Kro-Kra Island, located in southern Thailand, where many Vietnamese refugees were captured in 1980. Due to the isolated location of the island, the Vietnamese refugees could not find ways to escape, and almost every female was raped.

14   According to a United Nation High Commissioner of Refugees report, a woman was severely burned when pirates set fire to the hillside where she was hiding in an attempt to force her to come out. Another had stayed for days in a cave, waist-deep in water despite the attack of crabs on her legs.[13] One victim who later settled in America explained, "Thai pirates used steel bars to strike any Vietnamese man who struggled against the attacks on the women."[14]

13. Barry Wain, *The Refused: the Agony of the Indochina Refugees* (New York: Simon and Schuster, 1981), 71.
14. Eve Burton, "Surviving the Flight of Horror: The Story of Refugee Women," *Indochina Issue* (February 1982), I.

Fortunately, some of these women were lucky enough to return to their families. Others were not. And most women were reluctant to press charges against the barbaric pirates in Thailand, because they were afraid that any legal action might delay or jeopardize their departure for resettlement in the new country.

Other problems can plague the women. Some, for instance, suffer from rape-related medical difficulties, such as vaginal disorders, which often interfere with their daily lives. Aside from the physical problems, these women experience long-lasting psychological and emotional problems, including depression and anxiety over unwanted pregnancies and possible reduced chances for a happy marriage.[15]

Most of the Vietnamese women do not want to talk about their experiences with anybody, even their close friends and relatives; they remain silent even after settling in America. Vinh, a rape victim from the Kro-Kra Island incident, says that most people can never understand that what she went through is painful and cannot be described in words.[16] The women are afraid of rejection by their relatives if their experiences became known. But because they are silent about the rapes, no specific report or information is available on the mental health of this group of Vietnamese women. Nevertheless, it is clear to many people that these women do suffer, both physically and mentally, from their trauma. "Perhaps those who suffered silently were more affected by the rape experience than those who spoke more openly," said Eve Burton, a prominent writer on Vietnamese women refugee issues who in recent years sponsored the entry of four Vietnamese rape victims.[17]

Economic Adjustment

Vietnamese women coming to America have experienced fatigue, humiliation, and anger, and continue to face new obstacles here. "Their main problem is feeling helpless and ineffective in coping with reality in this country. They are overwhelmed with the needs of adjustment, especially with their roles in the family," said Dr. Ton That Toai, a psychologist of Prince William County Public School in Virginia, during a personal interview. Thirty percent of his clients are Vietnamese women having psychological problems who have been referred to him by American social workers.

The employment of the Vietnamese wives places these women in a highly stressful situation because the traditional Vietnamese culture is deeply influenced by Confucian doctrine: authority of parent over children, husbands over wives, older children over younger ones. Confucianism also stresses that women have to be submissive: first to their fathers, then later to their husbands.[18] In

15. U.S. Committee for Refugees, *Vietnamese Boat People*, 6.
16. Burton, "Flight of Horror," 2.
17. Ibid., I.
18. Hirayama, "Effects of Employment," 4.

Vietnam, the women are expected to take care of the household, raise the children, and obey their husbands. Although most women in the past were primarily restricted to the home, some had to take outside jobs due to the continuing war in Vietnam. They had to make a living while their husbands were on the battlefields. "Even though my husband was an officer in the navy, his salary was not enough to support the family. Luckily, I was employed before our marriage so I just continued being a nurse," said Mrs. L., one of the more fortunate women who had skills and a good job. Women with a lower level of education had difficulties in becoming self-sufficient or helping out their families. Even though many became shopkeepers, others were trapped in prostitution.

19   When Vietnamese women come to America, more of them drift from their traditional roles in order to help the family financially. This has caused additional cultural stress. The employment of women brings out in the open the conflict between the traditional Vietnamese role of wife and mother, and the role of women in modern American society.[19] Now able to contribute money to the family, the women feel they should have more power in the family than before. Moreover, they want to be treated as equals with their husbands. "The women should have an equal partnership in the marriage. This is America, not Vietnam," said Lan Nguyen during an interview with the author. Lan was a Vietnamese housewife who was able to obtain a technical position in a high-tech company after receiving special training.

20   These drastic changes in the roles of Vietnamese women have disturbed many men. They cannot cope well with the changes in the deeply-rooted Vietnamese customs and traditions; they cannot easily accept their loss of dominance within the family, their declining role as patriarch of the family. "Despite the recent importation of Western-style ways of life and the current feminist movements including the Women's Liberation Movement in the United States, the Vietnamese man in his country is still the boss, [even] if not the big boss anymore," comments Dr. Gia Thuy Vuong, a language and culture specialist.[20] The loss of their home in Vietnam appears to mean also the loss of men's authoritarian role within the family.

21   The husbands have not found it easy to use their working skills in America and consequently have to accept any available job. Approximately 65 percent of the Vietnamese refugees formerly working in white-collar professions have had to enter blue-collar professions in the United States, and then can no longer support their families as they did in Vietnam. Ironically, whereas many men experience downward mobility, many wives experience upward mobility in their work because they are exposed to more occupational opportunities here than in Vietnam. For instance, many electronics companies have been hiring Vietnamese women for electro-mechanical positions. With this type of job, the women

19. Ibid., 13.
20. Gia Thuy Vuong, *Getting to Know the Vietnamese and Their Culture* (New York: Frederick Ungar Publishing Co., 1976), 23.

do not need to speak English well, have a high level of education, or do heavy physical work. Other refugee women enter service jobs, such as beauticians, and some open little shops and restaurants to serve the local Vietnamese community.

Marital Status

The man's loss of status and power, coupled with his downward mobility, has placed severe pressure on the traditional marriage relationship. An increase in spousal abuse, which is accepted to some degree in Vietnam, is a direct result of the stress marriage faces in the transition to a new, modern culture.[21] According to Dr. Ton, violence does exist in the homes of the Vietnamese, but it rarely gets reported. Though women are physically abused by their spouses, they do not want to discuss the experience. Therefore, counselors cannot pursue the matter even though they are aware of it. [22]

In a 1979 survey, marital conflict was found to be one of the top four problems of Vietnamese refugees in America.[22] The divorce rate among Vietnamese couples is increasing markedly. "Women in Vietnam are very dependent," says Thang Cao, a young man who is disturbed by the changes he sees in Vietnamese women.[23] "You can be sure your wife will stay with you forever. Husbands feel safe," he adds. However, in the United States where divorce is more common and acceptable, Vietnamese women are able to end their marriages without suffering as much from gossip or humiliation in the community. [23]

Some divorced husbands have blamed their wives' new roles and new freedom for the break-up of their marriages. During a personal interview, Mr. H., recently divorced after ten years of marriage, gave his reaction to the difficulties associated with the changing roles of women: [24]

> Back in the country, my role was only to bring home money from work, and my wife would take care of the household. Now everything has changed. My wife had to work as hard as I did to support the family. Soon after, she demanded more power at home. In other words, she wanted equal partnership. I am so disappointed! I realized that things are different now, but I could not help feeling the way I do. It is hard to get rid of or change my principles and beliefs which are deeply rooted in me.

Language and Cultural Differences

In addition to problems within the family, Vietnamese women also face adjustment to the outside community. Women may suffer more than men during the resettlement period because most of the responsibility of survival has tradition- [25]

21. Daniel Dinh Phuoc Le, "Vietnamese Refugees' Perceptions and Methods for Coping with Mental Illness" (Ph.D. diss., United States International University, 1979), 41.
22. Davidson, "Women Refugees," 17.
23. John Hubner and Carol Rafferty, "After the Storm," *San Jose Mercury News*, 17 October 1982.

ally fallen on them: they are expected to take care of the children and do all the same household chores they performed in Vietnam. Unfortunately in the new environment and culture, unfamiliar situations prevent women from doing all these tasks as easily as they once did.

26   Most of the older women are not literate because they were never encouraged to go to school in Vietnam. This fact combined with an inability to communicate in English presents a major problem. Because they often do not know how to read the labels on merchandise, every day chores are difficult or even risky when women mistakenly use cleaning fluids in cooking. Their lack of formal education and their limited exposure to Western ways make adjustment in the United States both hard and frustrating. "I can imagine life would be difficult without my husband's help since I cannot speak English well. I feel frustrated when I cannot express myself to Americans. Therefore, at home I always try my best to learn the new language through books or television," said Mrs. L. when she was interviewed for this essay.

27   Inevitably, the women also come face to face with cultural differences. Vietnamese mothers lack familiarity with the new customs and are often misunderstood by the American public. Social workers often conclude inaccurately that these women do not know how to take care of their children properly, because, for example, some women let their children attend school wearing pajamas.[24] The mothers in this case think the attire is quite appropriate, however, because wearing pajamas as street clothes in Vietnam is a common and socially acceptable practice.

28   Confusion about American values and customs contributes to the mental health problems suffered by Vietnamese immigrant women. This confusion can lead to feelings of rejection and then depression. As Mrs. L. said, "I know that there are cultural differences, so I am very careful when I go out. I try to dress properly because I do not want to be looked down upon by the Americans as they occasionally did with the other Vietnamese women down the block." Mental health problems are most frequent among refugees who have limited experience in Western culture and have little formal education or knowledge of English. And it is clear that the majority of Vietnamese immigrant women fall into this category.

Conclusion

29 Past harrowing experiences and present difficulties combine to make resettlement a very strenuous process for Vietnamese women. They face a dichotomy between tradition and modernity. The emotional problems caused by the exodus may not have an immediate effect. After settling in, however, the old problems merge with new ones. "The women have been emotionally distressed constantly

24. Davidson, "Women Refugees," 18.

because their roles change so drastically. In addition, male expectations have not changed. At home, [Vietnamese women] are required to be totally submissive to their husbands, while at work they are respected by co-workers and friends," commented Dr. Ton in our interview. "Many also have problems outside the home in adjusting to the new environment. They are in need of psychological help, but they would not come to see me if they are not constantly pushed by the American social workers," he added. Without help, they usually remain silent and pretend to be fine when they see other Vietnamese.

The Vietnamese culture favors repression of negative or aggressive feelings.[25] Emotional problems are considered a personal matter to be resolved by oneself or within the family. It is very hard to find out exactly how much impact changing roles has on these women's mental health, especially because they are reluctant to reveal their emotional problems. Though the limited studies on Vietnamese women do not emphasize their mental health problems, the phenomenon still remains an issue within the Vietnamese American community, especially among the women.   30

What can be done to help them? The past cannot be undone, but with appropriate and well-conceived programs, the mental health of these women can be improved. They need encouragement to open up and talk about their problems so they can receive help and support in overcoming their difficulties. A small program with specially trained counselors can be a source of relief and information for the women. The program must be promoted so the Vietnamese people can become acquainted with the service. In time a successful program will have the old members coming back to help the new members overcome their hardships. To alleviate the difficulty of adjusting to a new culture and environment, the program could be expanded to teach Vietnamese women about the American way of life and Vietnamese men about the need to be more understanding and compassionate.   31

Vietnamese women hope to be more productive and contribute to their new society, and to enjoy their lives after the long struggle for freedom and happiness. And overall there is a positive outlook for the Vietnamese woman. As Lan Nguyen said, "I would not exchange anything for the life that I have now. A woman now has a chance to lead a happy and meaningful life for herself, instead of devoting it only to her husband and family." ✤   32

RESPONDING

1. In a journal entry, discuss the way you handle stress. Do you feel comfortable talking to others, or do you prefer to keep silent? How does your response to stress compare to the way Luu says Vietnamese women are

25. Hirayama, "Effects of Employment," 144.

expected to respond to stressful situations? How much of your and their behavior is a result of acculturation?

2. Working individually or in a group, discuss the hardships faced by Vietnamese women during their evacuation and resettlement. In your opinion, which problems are the most difficult to cope with: those connected with leaving a familiar culture, those connected with entering an unfamiliar one, other problems? Share your conclusions with the class.

3. According to Luu, one of the major upheavals in Vietnamese family life in the United States has been the changing role of women. Write an essay that explores this change and analyzes the factors in American society that have resulted in changing roles for both men and women.

4. Conduct your own interview of a recent immigrant to the United States, your state, or your city. Write a report for the class investigating the difficulties of moving to a new place and adapting to a new culture.

JOSE ALEJANDRO ROMERO

José Alejandro Romero, a Salvadorean émigré, has witnessed and attempted to protest against the repression and barbarism of El Salvador's right-wing dictatorship. Some of his poetry reflects on the suffering of that country. It is within this context of repression that Romero places the incident at Sumpul, where six hundred men, women, and children were massacred—while a few nursing mothers watched horrified from the shore. As the author explains, "Sumpul is a river dividing El Salvador and Honduras. On May 14, 1980, peasants fleeing to Honduras were pursued by the Salvadoran army for many days. Reaching Sumpul and what they believed would be safety, they faced on the other side the hostile Honduran army. While most of the people were in the middle of the river, which was at that point about 100 meters wide, the two armies opened fire, shooting until everyone in the water was dead. No sign of life remained, only the water mixed with the blood of the dead."

In the poem that follows, the river Sumpul becomes a mirror, for it reflects the pain of those who were helpless witnesses to the massacre, and those whose bodies have found no other grave.

✛

SUMPUL

The afternoon has fallen into black dust,
and from the dust emerges death.
In the red river we swam, desperate to live.
We splashed in its waters and then,
bruised, we were floated by them.
From the river the massacred body arose.
Sumpul drowned in blood,
Sumpul deafened by the shots,
river turned red,
river swollen with anguish,
witnessing river, your hidden heart
containing the anonymous screams of martyrs—
of children, tender shoots,
of mothers, fruiting trees
and old ones ancient oaks.
Facing you is Yankee torture,
murderous sounds and the growl of the dog,
splattering this universe with shrapnel,
splitting open pregnant stars,
slashing the face of the peasant.
Beast, take note:
the worker's face will carry this scar.

River,
We seek your water made holy by force,
and with it anoint our arms,
with reddened eyes.
In a single, slaughtered droplet we watch
the sun, its hopeful yellow;
in its yellow is a future,
a victory, a triumph, a people.
In your winding current
We seek the wide and war-injured reflection of the people
confronting a vast machine;
their last words cursing despotism
their words like weapons, their body a shield,
their ideals, pure light.

I want to respond to the screams of the people,
to fixed eyes shooting off hatred,
to hoist your spirit in the fighting flag of guns.
I salute you with each shot aimed at the enemy
I swear to remember you in our future land,
and in the sky brimming with stars,
and in the first maize field of winter,
and in the waters of every river where I live. ✛

RESPONDING

1. In a journal entry, respond to what the river has witnessed. Were you aware of the historical event presented here? Did prior knowledge or lack of knowledge influence your reaction to the poem? You may want to describe your feelings as you read.

2. Working individually or in a group, describe the speaker in the poem. What is the speaker's situation? Be sure to use specific lines or phrases from the poem to support your interpretation.

3. The author uses poetry to express his feelings about an important event in his country's history. Write a poem about a place or event that is particularly meaningful to you.

BHARATI MUKHERJEE

Born in Calcutta, India, in 1940, Bharati Mukherjee has lived since the 1960s in the United States and Canada. After earning her master's degree from the University of Baroda in 1961 and her doctorate from the University of Iowa in 1969, she has taught English at McGill University in Montreal, Quebec, and Skidmore College in New York; she is currently a professor at the University of California, Berkeley. In addition to contributing stories and essays to journals, Mukherjee has published the novels The Tiger's Daughter *(1972) and* Wife *(1975), as well as the short-story collections* Darkness *(1985) and* The Middleman and Other Stories *(1988). With her husband Clark Blaise, she cowrote* Days and Nights in Calcutta *(1977), a nonfiction work recounting the couple's visit to India in 1973. Her writing has won her awards from many sources, including the Canadian government, the Canadian Arts Council, the Guggenheim Foundation, and the National Endowment for the Arts.*

"Visitors" explores how a person's cultural background helps determine how one behaves and how one can interpret or misinterpret the behavior of others.

✛

VISITORS

1　WHEN VINITA LIVED IN CALCUTTA, she had many admirers. Every morning at ten minutes after nine o'clock when she left home for Loreto College where she majored in French literature, young men with surreptitious hands slipped love notes through the half-open windows of her father's car and were sternly rebuked by the chauffeur. The notes were almost always anonymous; when she read them in class, tucked between the pages of Rimbaud and Baudelaire, the ferocity of passion never failed to thrill and alarm her.

2　For a time after college she worked as a receptionist in the fancy downtown Chowringhee office of a multinational corporation. She had style, she had charm, and everyone genuinely liked her. Especially two junior executives from the fifth floor which was occupied by a company that exported iron manhole covers. If it hadn't been for Vinita's tact, and her ability to make each of the suitors feel that he was the one who made her happier, the two men might have become embittered rivals. She was quietly convivial and on weekdays went, usually in a group of six or eight, for Chinese lunches to the Calcutta Club. Even the club waiters brightened up when they saw Vinita, though she had never actually been heard to say anything more personal to them than, "A lime soda, please, no ice," or "I'll have the Chou En Lai carp."

3　She had known all along that after marriage she would have to leave

Calcutta. Her parents wanted to marry her off to a doctor or engineer of the right caste and class but resident abroad, preferably in America. The groom they finally selected for her was a thirty-five-year-old accountant, Sailen Kumar, a well-mannered and amiable-looking man, a St. Stephen's graduate who had gone on to London University and Harvard and who now worked for a respectable investment house in Manhattan and lived in a two-bedroom condominium with access to gym, pool and sauna across the river. He was successful—and well off, Vinita's parents decided—by anyone's standards. Six days after the wedding, Vinita took an Air India flight to citizenship in the New World.

Marriage suits Vinita. In the months she has been a wife in Guttenberg, New Jersey, she has become even prettier. Her long black hair has a gloss that owes as much to a new sense of well-being as to the new shampoos she tries out and that leave her head smelling of herbs, fruits and flowers. Her surroundings—the sleek Bloomingdale's furniture Sailen had bought just before flying out to find a bride in India, the coordinated linen for bed and bath, and the wide, gleaming appliances in the kitchenette—please her. She finds it hard to believe that she has been gifted the life of grace and ease that she and her Loreto College friends had coveted from reading old copies of *Better Homes and Gardens* in Calcutta. This life of grace and ease has less to do with modern conveniences such as the microwave oven built into a narrow wall which is covered with designer wallpaper, and more to do with moods and traits she recognizes as new in herself. Happiness, expressiveness, bad temper: all these states seem valuable and exciting to her. But she is not sure she deserves this life. She has done nothing exceptional. She has made no brave choices. The decision to start over on a new continent where hard work is more often than not rewarded with comfort has been her parents', not hers. If her father had brought her a proposal and photograph from an upright hydraulics engineer living in a government project site in the wilds of Durgapur or from a rich radiologist with a clinic on a quiet boulevard in South Calcutta, she would have accepted the proposal with the same cheerfulness she has shown Sailen Kumar. She's a little taken aback by the idea of just desserts. Back home good fortune had been exactly that: a matter of luck and fortune, a deity's decision to humor and indulge. She remembered the fables she read as a child in which a silly peasant might find a pitcher of gold *mohurs* on his way to the village tank for his bath. But in America, at least in New Jersey, everyone Vinita meets seems to acknowledge a connection between merit and reward. Everyone looks busy, distraught from overwork. Even the building's doorman; she worries about Castro, the doorman. Such faith in causality can only lead to betrayal.

   Vinita expected married life, especially married life in a new country and with no relatives around, to change her. Overnight she would become mature, complex, fascinating: a wife, instead of a daughter. Thoughts of change did not frighten her. Discreet, dutiful, comfortable with her upper-class status, she had been trained by her mother to stay flexible, to roll with whatever punches the Communist government of Calcutta might deliver. In Vinita's childhood, the city had convulsed through at least two small revolutions. Some nights in Guttenberg, New Jersey, even with her eyes closed, she can see a fresh, male corpse in a monsoon muddy gutter. Her parents still talk of the two boys who had invaded their lawn one heady afternoon of class struggle and pointed pipe-guns at the trembling gardener. Sometimes the designer wallpaper seems to ripple like leaves in a breeze, and she feels herself being watched.

6   But it's not the corpse, not the undernourished child-rebels, who feed her nightmares. It's nothing specific. She considers fear of newness a self-indulgence, quite unworthy of someone who has wanted all along to exchange her native world for an alien one. The slightest possibility of disruption pleases her. But if change has come into her life as Mrs. Sailen Kumar, it has seeped in so gradually that she can't fix it with one admiring stare when she Windexes toothpaste flecks off the bathroom mirror.

7   This afternoon Vinita has three visitors. Two of them are women, Mrs. Leela Mehra and Mrs. Kamila Thapar, wives of civil engineers. They stay just long enough to have spiced tea with onion pakoras and to advise her on which Indian grocers carry the freshest tropical products in the "Little India" block on Lexington. Vinita is convinced the real reason they have come to visit is to check out what changes she, the bride, has made to Sailen's condominium. They have known her husband for almost ten years. Mr. Thapar and Sailen roomed together when both were new to America (she has trouble visualizing the dark-suited, discreetly groomed men as callow foreign students forty pounds lighter with little money and too much ambition). Sailen, while sketching in his bachelor life—all those years when she had not known that the man of her dreams would have only nine fingers—had told her how the Thapars and the Mehras made themselves his substitute family in the new world, how they fed him curries most weekends, made him sleep on their lumpy front room sofas instead of letting him take a late-night bus back to Manhattan, and how the two women hummed bits of old Hindi film songs to tease him into nostalgia. Otherwise, they said, he'd become bad-tempered and self-centered, too American. In Mrs. Mehra's and Mrs. Thapar's presence, Vinita is the intruder.

8   After they leave, Vinita takes out a rubber-banded roll of aerogrammes from a desk built into the wall system. She makes a list of the people she must write today:

1. her parents (a short but vivacious note)
2. her closest Loreto College friend who now works for Air India
3. her married sister in Bombay (it can wait till the weekend)
4. Mother Stella, the Mauritian nun who'd taught her French.

9   Writing letters on the pale blue aerogramme paper makes her feel cheerful and just a little noble. Writing to Mother Stella puts her in a special mood, a world tinged slightly with poetic, even rhapsodic passion. Even lines of Rim-

baud's deemed unsuitable for maidenly Calcutta teenagers were somehow tamed by Mother Stella's exquisite elocution. How preposterous was a passion—*le dos de ces Mains est la place qu'en baisa tout Révolté fier!*—parsed by a half-Indian, French-speaking, Mauritian nun.

She writes her mother, converting each small episode—buying half a dozen cheese Danishes, spraying herself with expensive fragrances from tester atomizers—into grand adventures. When she licks and seals each envelope, she is grateful Sailen agreed to her father's proposal of marriage and that she is now cut off from her moorings. Her letters are intended to please and comfort. She knows that when the postman rings his bicycle bell and keels into the driveway twice a day, the servants, her mother, her sister, her friend and even the nun who has taught her all she knows about literature and good manners run to the front door hoping for a new installment of her idylls in America. But before Vinita can decide what vivacious clichés to end her last letter with, a third visitor arrives at the door and holds out a bright, amateurish poster announcing an Odissi dance recital on the Columbia campus.

"Mrs. Kumar, I thought you would be interested in dance performances," the visitor says. He smiles, but does not step into the tiny hall which is crowded with a pair of Vishnupuri clay horses and a tall, cylindrical Chinese vase that holds umbrellas. "I was afraid that you and Mr. Kumar might not have heard about Rooma Devi coming to Columbia."

"Odissi style?" She knows it is up to her to invite him in or send him away. She has met him, yes, she has talked to him at three, maybe four, cultural evenings organized by one of the Indian Associations in Manhattan. He is a graduate student in history at Columbia.

"Mrs. Kumar, if you don't mind my saying so, the first time I saw you I could tell that you yourself were a dancer. Right?"

She glances at him shyly, and steps back, her slippers grazing the rough clay foot of one of the giant horses. Still she doesn't ask him in. Let him make that decision. In India, she would feel uncomfortable—she knows she would!—if she found herself in an apartment alone with a man not related to her, but the rules are different in Guttenberg. Here one has to size up the situation and make up one's own rules. Or is it, here, that one has to seize the situation?

"You have the grace of a *danseuse*," he says.

Vinita has not heard anyone use the word *danseuse*. She likes the word; it makes her feel elegant and lissom. "I'll have to confess I am. I've danced a bit. But not in years."

She blushes, hoping to pass off for modesty the guilt she feels at having lied. She is not a dancer, not a real dancer. She has studied Rabindra-style dancing for about six years. Her mother, who regarded dancing as necessary a feminine accomplishment as singing and gourmet cooking, had forced the two sisters to take weekly lessons at a fine arts academy in Ballygunge. She looks down at the floor, at his two-tone New Balance running shoes. The shoes deepen her blush. She is in a new country with no rules. No grown man in

India she knows wears gym shoes except for cricket or squash. But there's mud on his New Balances, a half-moon of mud around each toe part. He has taken the bus to Guttenberg, New Jersey, just to make sure that she'll know about the recital. Because he has guessed—he had divined—that she is a *danseuse*.

18   She takes two hesitant steps back, her left hand entwined with the elongated clay neck of the larger horse. Here, as in India, friends stop by without calling, and she is foolish to worry over why the graduate student in his running shoes has come with a poster in the early afternoon. ("All that formality of may-I-come? or hope-we're-not-disturbing-you is for Westerners," the immigrants joke among themselves. She has heard it once already this afternoon from Mrs. Thapar. "We may have minted a bit of money in this country, but that doesn't mean we've let ourselves become Americans. You can see we've remained one hundred percent simple and *deshi* in our customs.") Vinita wants to remain *deshi* too, but being *deshi* and letting in this good-looking young man (a line darts across an imaginary page, enunciated in rotund Mauritian French and Vinita almost giggles: *Le jeune homme dont l'oeil est brillant, la peau brune, Le beau corps de vingt ans qui devrait aller nu . . .* and Vinita blushes again, more deeply), a young man who told her the first time they met, after a movie, that he'd been born in Calcutta but immigrated with his parents when he was just a toddler—letting him in might lead to disproportionate disaster.

19   "It is very kind of you, Mr. Khanna, to bring over Rooma Devi's poster," she says miserably. She has never heard of Rooma Devi. Rooma Devi cannot possibly be a ranking Odissi dancer. Yet Rooma Devi has succeeded in pounding thin whatever tranquility the promise of letter-writing had produced in Vinita.

20   "You remember my name, Mrs. Kumar?" It is not so much a question as an ecstatic exhalation. "But please call me Rajiv. Unless you want to call me Billoo, which was my pet name in India. Just don't call me Bill."

21   She is relieved that Rajiv Khanna is inside the condominium and that the period of indecision is over. He has somehow shut the front door behind him and has suspended his baseball cap on the smaller horse's ear.

22   "Would you like some authentic India-style tea?" she asks. It is the correct thing for an Indian hostess to do, even in New Jersey; to offer the guest something to drink, even if it's just a glass of water. "I am making it exactly like the *chai wallahs.* I am boiling tea leaves in a mixture of milk, water and sugar, and throwing in pinches of cardamom, cloves, cinnamon, etcetera."

23   "I don't want you stuck in the kitchen," he laughs. "I want you to tell me stories about Calcutta. I was only three when Baba took the post-doctoral fellowship at Madison but I still remember what our alley smelled like in July and August." He laughs again, hyper and nervous. "Let's use teabags. You must take advantage of American shortcuts."

24   Rajiv Khanna stalks her into the living room, forcing her to take quicker steps than usual so his New Balances won't catch the thin, stiff leather edges of her Sholapuri slippers. She begins to see Sailen's Bloomingdale decor—the pastel conversation pit made up of modular sofas, the patio-atrium corner

defined by white wicker—the way a hard-up graduate student might, as opulent, tasteful. When Rajiv compliments her artistic touch, she swings back to smile at him, bashful but flattered.

An issue of *Technology Review* on an obviously new coffee table catches his 25 eye, and he lingers in the conversation pit, one knee resting deeply on an ottoman. In that pose, he reminds her of marsh birds she had seen on vacations in rural Bengal. The image automatically makes her pitch her voice low. Her gestures now softly wary, so the bird will not fly off.

She slips off to the kitchenette to make tea. The work counter of butcher's 26 block is a barrier against the unseemly jokes that fate might decide to try out on her. In fact, in the bluish-white fluorescent light that threatens to never burn out, her earlier fears now seem absurd.

"I miss the cultural events of Calcutta," she says chattily. "It's such a lively 27 city. Always some theatrical program, some crafts exhibit, something that touches the heart." From the asylum of the kitchenette, she watches him flip through the pages of Sailen's magazine without actually reading. There's an archness to her posture, she knows. She can feel her body tauten the way it often had in college while Mother Stella sanitized the occasional salacious verse. *On n'est pas sérieux, quand on a dix-sept ans*, Rimbaud said, but now she thinks twenty-five is not a matronly age. Mrs. Mehra and Mrs. Thapar are at least ten years older than her. Sailen had specified to his parents that he wanted a youngish bride, one who could speak fluent English and who could—once he felt he could afford it—bear him two or three children. He has spoken to her of his dream of having a son play in Little League games. Hearing him dream aloud, she assumed that it wasn't so much a son that he wanted as to assimilate, to be a *pukka* American.

Rajiv Khanna ignores her comment. He sits astride the new coffee table 28 (she's distracted with worry that if the glass top breaks, it cannot be replaced; or more accurately, that if the table falls apart she'll have to confess, but confess to what?) and drums his thighs with his fingertips. The fingers are long, the fingers of a poet. No wonder he has not been absorbed by Sailen's *Technology Review*. She waits for him to make small talk, to keep up his part as charming guest.

"I can't believe I went through with it!" It's an outburst, and it confuses 29 her. She busies herself with cups and saucers.

"I can't believe I had the courage!" 30

She steals a look at him, thankful for the cumulous clouds of steam from 31 the boiling water. Courage for what? Instinctively, she smooths down the hair on her crown which she knows from experience turns frizzy in hot, humid weather. Girls should make the best of their looks. She's been taught this by the nuns at school and by her relatives for so long that prettying herself has become a habit, not a vanity. Rajiv approaches her, his gait uneven, nervous; he is a potential invader of her kitchenette-fortress.

"I knew you were special the very first time I saw you. At the India Republic 32

Day celebrations at the Khoranas'. I told myself this is it, this is the goddess of my dreams. I couldn't get you out of my mind."

33   Vinita finishes steeping two Twining teabags in a teapot before responding to the young visitor's outburst. She is not as shocked as she had expected to be. Yes, she has rehearsed moments like this; she has put herself on the television screen, in the roles of afternoon wives taken in passion. Not as shocked as she *should* have been, she worries. A warmth (from Rajiv's compliment? from anxiety? the kettle's steam?) swirls just under her glycerine-and-rose-watered skin. She concentrates on making tea; the brew must be just the right amber color. But tea-making in New Jersey is no challenge. She plucks and dunks each bag repeatedly by its frail string. You give up a little taste, but you grab a little convenience cleaning up. The new world forces you to know what you really want.

34   He barks again. "You haven't discouraged me."

35   She shrinks behind the counter. He shakes an accusatory index finger. She draws the loose end of her sari over her right shoulder so that her arms, her silk-bloused breasts and bare midriff are swathed. But the sari was bought at the Sari Palace on Lexington, and her breasts seem to her to loom and soar, through the Japanese chiffon. The young man has turned her into a siren.

36   "I don't know what you mean." She wants to sound stuffy, but it comes out, she knows, innocent, simpering.

37   "You should have thrown me out minutes ago. You could have refused to let me in. I know you Indian girls. You could have taken the poster and slammed the door in my face. But you didn't!"

38   He is a madman. It's true; he *is* a madman, but she is no siren. She repeats this to herself, a litany against calamity. Because of his windbreaker and his running shoes she has assumed he was just another American, no one to convert her into a crazy emblem. She had assumed that he was the looter of American culture, not hers, and she had envied the looting. Her own transition was slow and wheezing.

39   "You offered to make tea instead." He sounds triumphant.

40   "It was the least I could offer a guest," she retorts. "I haven't lost all my manners because I've moved to a new country. I know some Americans won't even give you a glass of water when you drop in."

41   He is not listening. He blabs, high-pitched angry words undulating from his fleshy lips. Love, it would appear, torments Rajiv. The face, which she had initially considered symmetrical, now devastates her from across the butcher's block counter, the features harsh, moody. His New Balance shoes are anachronistic; he is a lover from the turn-of-the-century novels of Sarat Chandra, the poems of Rimbaud—*Oh! quel Rêve les a saisies . . . un rêve inouï des Asies, Des Khenghavars ou des Sions?*—unmoored by passion. One long-lashed furtive glance from the woman next door, the servant girl, the movie star, and the hero's calamitous fate is sealed. But this is America, she insists. There is no place for

feelings here! We are both a new breed, testing new feelings in new battle-grounds. We must give in to the old world's curb.

"Let's be civilized," she pleads, by which she means, let's be modern and   42
Indian. "Take your cup, and let's sit in the patio. My husband will be here any minute and he'd be so disappointed if you left without seeing him. He thinks you're a brilliant boy." She's pleased at her own diplomacy. She has nipped passion before it can come to full fury, she has flattered his intelligence and she has elevated herself to the role of older sister or youngish aunt.

"Confess!" he demands. "I must mean something special to you. Otherwise   43
you wouldn't have tolerated me this long. You'd have called Mr. Kumar or the police."

"I think you are unwell," she ventures. She hates him for considering her   44
lascivious. She hates herself for not having thought of calling her husband. But what could she have said over the phone to a dark-suited man in an office cubicle concentrating hard on a computer terminal? Please come home and protect me from that Khanna boy who fancies he's in love with me?

He lunges at her. Suddenly the kitchenette counter seems a frail barrier.   45
Tea spurts into a pretty saucer and stains the butcher's block. She has no time to tear off squares of paper towel and wipe up the spill. His right arm snakes toward her, reaches up through the chiffon sari; the snake's jaws, closing on a breast, scratch her hand instead.

"Madman!" she screams. Her side, her breast, her hand, all burn with   46
shame. The snake's jaws have found the breast. She is paralyzed.

"You have no right to play with my feelings, Vinita! Confess at once!"   47

The situation is absolutely preposterous. She has been taught by Mother   48
Stella and by her parents how to deal with revolutions. She can disarm an emaciated Communist pointing a pipe-gun at her pet chihuahua. She can drive her father's new Hindustan Ambassador and she's beginning to drive on week-ends to local shopping malls. But banal calamities, the mad passions of a maladjusted failed American make her shudder.

Rajiv lets go. He picks up his cup and saucer and flounces off to the patio.   49
She watches him curl up on the wicker love seat, his New Balance shoes polluting the new cushions with street germs. He admires Sailen's careful grouping of rare orchids with all the confidence of an invited guest. All but one of the orchids are in their prime this afternoon, and their thick petals glow in the odd New Jersey light. Her breast tingles. It feels warm; it feels recently caressed. She leans her forehead against the fake Ionic column that marks off the alcove for the refrigerator, and wonders if the torment that the madman in her atrium feels is the same torment she too would have suffered if she had the courage to fall in love

At seven-twenty, Sailen comes home. Tonight he has brought Vinod Mehra and   50
Kailash Kapoor with him. They go to the same fitness club after work. Rajiv

Khanna left soon after finishing his cup of tea, so Vinita has had time to bathe at five-thirty as usual (she maintains the Indian habit of bathing twice a day), to put on a purple silk sari she knows looks quite seductive on her, dress her long hair elaborately with silver pins and cook dinner. The dinner includes six courses, not counting the bottled pickles and the store-bought pie for dessert. Cooking a fancy meal has been her self-acknowledged expiation, though in her heart she is sure (why shouldn't she be sure?) that she has committed no transgression. Now seeing the unexpected guests, she is relieved that their visit coincides with the night of her extra effort. What if she had made nothing but *dal*, rice and a vegetable curry? Rumors about Sailen Kumar's bride starving Sailen Kumar would have startled to swirl through highrises in Brooklyn and Rego Park.

51   The men congregate in the atrium. It is quite obviously Sailen's pride and joy; therefore, by extension, it is Vinita's pride and joy, too. She watches him show off his newest acquisitions in plants and flowers. In India, where the gardener and his grandson had taken care of such things, she had thought of blossoms only in terms of interior decoration, how they look against a background of new pink silk drapes, for instance. Now she has to view them differently, as though selecting them at the florist's, nursing them through the winter in overheated rooms and pruning them to look their most gorgeous is self-expression. In fact, she has heard Sailen justify his choice of buying a condominium in New Jersey instead of across the river where the action is by pointing at the atrium. You couldn't afford that in Manhattan, no sir. Unless you were a millionaire. Of course, she knows that Sailen intends to be a millionaire, as do his close friends, especially Vinod Mehra. Everybody in the Indian community knows that Vinod Mehra is likely to reach his goal before he is fifty. He plays the stock market better than most professional brokers. Everybody respects him for being a money wizard.

52   She reminds her husband to fix their guests drinks—"I am knowing so little about shaking cocktails and pouring jiggers, I'm afraid," she apologizes with her infectious laugh—and runs between kitchenette and patio with spiced cashews and deep-fried tidbits like vegetable pakoras. It is obvious that the men find her seductive, charming and inviolable. They alternate between being deferential and being flirtatious. They plague her with questions about local politics in India. They tease her about being a spoiled, rich girl and therefore, a novice cook who makes pakors and samosas. They beg her to sing them a Tagore song (but my harmonium hasn't arrived yet!) because it's already gotten around (from that nice Khanna boy who studies at Columbia, a bright boy, says Sailen) that she must be a talented singer. She is ecstatic; she serves the men and manipulates them with her youth and her beauty and her unmistakable charm. She has no idea that she is on the verge of hysteria. She has no idea.

53   That night in bed, for the first time since she has left Calcutta, she is bothered by insomnia. Within reach, but not touching her, Sailen sleeps on his

stomach. He is breathing through his mouth. She imagines his fleshy lips; they flap like rubber tires. He is a good man, and one day he will be a millionaire. He has never, not once, by gesture or word, made her feel that she is anything but the queen of his heart.

Why then is she moved by an irresistible force to steal out of his bed in the haven of his expensive condominium, and run off into the alien American night where only shame and disaster can await her? 54

RESPONDING

1. Imagine that Vinita had waited to write her letters until after Rajiv Khanna's visit. Consider how her letters might change, and write the letter she might have written to her parents, her closest college friend, her married sister, or Mother Stella. In whom might she confide?

2. Working individually or in a group, list the behavior expected from a traditional Indian woman. How traditional is Vinita? Compare what is required of her by her family and society with what you believe to be required of American women.

3. Continue the story or write an essay that explains how the story might continue. Will Vinita stay with her husband or strike out on her own? Do shame and disaster await her if she leaves her husband? If she remains, how will she feel? Consider what might influence her decision and the gains and losses of either position.

4. Is there a stereotype of a new immigrant? If so, does Vinita fit that stereotype? Explain your answers in an essay that presents the characteristics of the stereotype and compares Vinita with it. If you believe there is no stereotype, compare Vinita with another new immigrant you have read about or know personally.

Naomi Shihab Nye

The poet Naomi Shihab Nye was born in 1952 of an American mother and a Palestinian father in St. Louis, Missouri. She graduated from Trinity University in 1974 and now lives in San Antonio, Texas, where she plays an instrumental role in the state poetry-in-the-schools program. Her works include Different Ways to Pray *(1980),* On the Edge of the Sky *(1981),* Hugging the Jukebox *(1982),* This Same Sky: A Collection of Poems from Around the World *(1993), and* Connected *(1994). Her awards include the Pushcart Prize, the Texas Institute of Letters Poetry Prize, the Charity Fandall Prize for Spoken Poetry from the International Poetry Forum, and the I. B. Lavan Award from the Academy of American Poets.*

The three prose poems that follow reflect on the importance of grandparents, a sense of place, and saved objects in helping the writer fashion an identity.

✚

WHITE COALS

1 SCARCELY ANYTHING BIGGER THAN THE QUESTIONS I didn't ask. What happened to my mouth? I traveled all the way across the ocean with my mouth and couldn't get the questions out. A stiff-haired cat perched on the high stone wall between leafless brambles staring down at me. The cat with his elegant command of two silences. It was *cold.* My grandmother had *bare feet.* She held her feet by a crooked brazier of whitened coals. She turned her hands over and over. In the six years since our last meeting a tiredness had gathered itself, stonelike, in the corners of her eyes. She could say anything she wanted but she didn't want much. Holding her gaze to the floor, she wouldn't look up for pictures. I wanted to describe the silent women on Maunakea Street in Honolulu who sit all day poking needles through the hearts of flowers. The tight purple orchid, its silken lips. I wanted to ask advice: What should we tell our child about his living? But my mouth went heavy, my mouth wouldn't say. It said, Would you like these socks? My grandmother who will never wear a lei, I string you with questions, from a great distance each one flies to your shoulders, pulsing, a bird turned into a flower, folding its wings.

BROKEN CLOCK

1 WHAT DOES TIME LOOK LIKE from your chair? Once you cowered in a ditch as Turkish soldiers on horseback roared past. Your family remembers this when they try to calculate your age. You don't throw anything away. You've saved bits

of a smashed blue plate, a broken clock. Recently my father heard of a blind woman in the next village with a documented age of 106 who had known you all her life. Take me there, he said. He stood in the outer room while the woman's son addressed her loudly. "You remember your friend Khadra Shihab's youngest son Aziz?" The woman shouted back immediately. "You mean that terrible awful boy who broke his mother's heart by going to America? Of course I remember him! How could I forget?"

My father, in the next room, shrinking to the size of a button. Ushered into the woman's presence with a stuck jaw. A peep. "How old is my mother?" She said without hesitating, 104. They always had two years between them. You know if someone else is a little younger than you are, but not much. You know. She remembered, in fact, when Khadra was born, in those other houses, that other world. When they were very young, even then, two years. "And what will you do now?" she asked him. "After so much being away, how does it feel to return? Does anything know you now? Do the trees know you? Does the prayer know you? And where do you go when you leave here? Does this place really let you leave?"

SPEAKING ARABIC

"Why, if I'm part Arab, can't I speak Arabic?" My son, age five, wanting to answer his cousin who calls him to follow her into the kitchen, she shows how she turns the pot of rice and eggplant over onto the silver tray. How the food slips out to stand up like a building. The sizzled pine nuts, poured over the top in a fine fragrant flourish. Then she carries it all on her head into the room where we sit, and we eat with forks from the same giant platter, which I have never gotten used to. The cousins and neighbors file in to say, "Keef ha-lik?"— the door opening into a thousand rooms.

For months in America our son will be placing plates on his head. "This is how Janan would do it."

Why, if we're part anything, does it matter? I had to live in a mostly Mexican-American city to feel what it meant to be part-Arab. It meant Gift. It meant Take the Ribbon and Unwind it Slowly.

Why can't I forget the earnest eyes of the man who said to me in Jordan, "Until you speak Arabic, you will not understand pain"? Ridiculous! I thought. He went on, something to do with the back of the head, an Arab carrying sorrow in the back of the head that only language cracks. A few words couldn't do it. A general passive understanding wasn't enough. At a neighborhood fair in Texas, somewhere between the German Oom-pah Sausage Stand and the Mexican Gorditas booth, I overheard a young man say to his friend, "I wish *I* had a heritage. Sometimes I feel—so lonely for one." And the tall American trees were dangling their thick branches right down over his head.

RESPONDING

1. Write a journal entry about a time you visited family you hadn't seen for a long time or a place where you once lived. How did you feel? Had things changed? Where there adjustments to make?

2. Working individually or in a group, discuss the selections. Are they prose or poetry? Support your opinion with evidence from the readings. Then focus on the individual selections. Fill in the information the reader must supply in order to understand fully each piece. For example, who is speaking? What is taking place? Why did the author expect the reader to fill in many of the narrative details?

3. In "Speaking Arabic," Nye quotes a young American, "'I wish *I* had a heritage. Sometimes I feel—so lonely for one.' And the tall American trees were dangling their thick branches right down over his head" (paragraph 4). In an essay, define and discuss the American heritage. Why do you think the young American feels the way he does?

4. One of the implications of the selection "Speaking Arabic" is that language is an important part of a culture and that until you know the language, you're not really a part of that culture. Do you agree or disagree? Support your argument with evidence from the reading, other sources, and your own observations.

CZESLAW MILOSZ

Czeslaw Milosz, the poet, essayist, and novelist, was born in Lithuania in 1911. He received a law degree from the University of Wilno, Mjuris, in 1934, and in 1961 settled in California to teach Slavic languages at the University of California, Berkeley. He became a naturalized U.S. citizen in 1970. In addition to founding the literary periodical Zegary, *Milosz is a member of the American Association for the Advancement of Slavic Studies as well as the PEN Club in Exile. His critical and historical works published in the United States include* The Captive Mind *(1953),* Native Realm *(1968, tr.)* History of Polish Literature *(1969), and* The Land of Ulro *(1984). Milosz has also published the fictional works* The Usurpers *(1955) and* The Issa Valley *(1955, tr. 1981) and several collections of poetry, among them* Selected Poems *(1973, revised 1981),* Bells in Winter *(1978),* The Witness of Poetry *(1983), and* The Collected Poems 1931–1987 *(1988). He received the Polish PEN Club Award for poetry translation in 1974, a Guggenheim Fellowship in 1976, and the Neustadt International Literary Prize for Literature in 1978. In 1980 Milosz was awarded the Nobel Prize for Literature.*

The essay that follows is Milosz's reflection on what it means to be an émigré, catapulted out of history. The essay also considers how the state of exile or alienation provides a special opportunity for the writer.

ON EXILE

RHYTHM IS AT THE CORE OF HUMAN LIFE. It is, first of all, the rhythm of the organism, ruled by the heartbeat and circulation of blood. As we live in a pulsating, vibrating world, we respond to it and in turn are bound to its rhythm. Without giving much thought to our dependence on the systoles and diastoles of flowing time we move through sunrises and sunsets, through the sequences of four seasons. Repetition enables us to form habits and to accept the world as familiar. Perhaps the need of a routine is deeply rooted in the very structure of our bodies.

In a city or a village which we have known well since our childhood we move in a tamed space, our occupations finding everywhere expected landmarks that favor routine. Transplanted into alien surroundings we are oppressed by the anxiety of indefiniteness, by insecurity. There are too many new shapes and they remain fluid, because the principle of their order through routine cannot be discovered. What I am saying is perhaps just a generalization of my own experience but I hope to be understood as that experience has been shared by many, especially in this century.

3   Among the misfortunes of exile, anxiety of the unfamiliar holds a prominent place. Whoever has found himself as an immigrant in a big foreign city had to cope with a kind of envy at the sight of its inhabitants engaged in purposeful occupations, confidently going to definite, known to them, shops or offices, in a world weaving together a huge fabric of everyday bustle. It is possible that such an observer from the outside would have recourse to special strategies in order to diminish his feeling of alienation. Living in Paris, I was for a long time drawing a line around a few streets in the Latin Quarter, so that I could call a certain area "mine." A restaurant at the corner, a small bookstore, a laundry, a café succeeded each other when I was taking a walk and would give me some assurance through their presence at the points expected in advance.

4   To be lost in a foreign city. Perhaps something more is involved here than a mere inability to find one's way. It once happened to me, also in Paris, a city of my many joyous moments and many misfortunes, when I stepped out of the Métro in a part of the town with which I was acquainted but not too well. I started to walk and suddenly I noticed that there was not even one spot to serve me as a guide mark and I was seized by a sort of fear of height. The houses seemed to turn around and threaten to fall. I lost orientation. And I was quite aware that my indecision of which street to take reflected my loss of orientation in a deeper sense. Exile deprives one of the points of reference that helped us to make projects, choose our goals, to organize our activities. In our native countries we maintained a peculiar relationship with our predecessors, with writers if we were writers, with painters if we were painters, etc., and that was a relationship of both respect and opposition; our driving force was to better them in one or another manner and to add our name to the roster of names remembered by our village, our city, or country. Here, abroad, nothing of that is left, we have been catapulted out of history, which is always the history of a specific area on the map, and we have to cope with, to use an expression of an exile writer, "the unbearable lightness of being."

5   The recovery is slow and never complete. There is a period when we refuse to recognize that our displacement is irrevocable and no political or economic changes in the country of our origin can bring about our return. Then slowly we came to the realization that exile is not just a physical phenomenon of crossing state borders, for it grows on us, transforms us from within, and becomes our fate. The undifferentiated mass of human types, streets, monuments, fashions, trends acquires some distinct features and gradually the strange transforms itself into the familiar. At the same time, however, the memory preserves a topography of our past, and this dual observance keeps us apart from our fellow citizens.

6   "Having left your native land, don't look back, the Erinyes are behind you."

One of the Pythagorean principles, the advice is good but difficult to follow. It is true, the Erinyes are there, behind your back, and their very sight may petrify a mortal. Some say them to be daughters of Earth, others, daughters of Night, in any case they arrive from the depth of the underworld, are winged, and in their hair carry twisting serpents. They are your punishment for your past offenses and you know well that you cannot claim purity whether you are aware of your failings or not. The best protection against the Erinyes would be, indeed, never to look back. And yet it is impossible not to look back, for there, in the land of your ancestors, of your language, of your family, a treasure has been left, more valuable than any riches measured by money, namely, colors, shapes, intonations, details of architecture, everything that shapes one's childhood. By letting your memory speak you wake up the past and by the same token attract the Erinyes; yet man stripped of memory is hardly human or he represents only a very impoverished humanity. Thus a contradiction appears and you have to learn how to live with it.

There is another aspect of exile considered as a specific affliction of the twentieth century. The most famous of the exile writers of the past, Dante, after leaving his native Florence, wandered all his life from one city to another but today those cities can hardly mean "abroad" as they are all situated in Italy. Dante died and was buried in Ravenna which today doesn't seem at all a land distant from his birthplace. Could it happen that with the shrinkage of the planet earth distances but also differences between particular countries grow smaller and smaller? Perhaps it would be possible to visualize a modern pilgrim's wanderings as his going about from one place to another within one country, whether that country is called Europe, a continent, or the world? If this is not so now, there is a certain dynamism inherent in the progress of technology, which pushes in that direction. The twentieth century also brings a quantitative change as befits an era of population explosion. In Dante's time the number of people leaving the towns and villages where they were born was very small. Now hundreds of thousands, even millions, migrate, chased from their homes by war, by harsh economic necessities, or political persecution, and an expatriate, for instance a writer, an artist, an intellectual who left his country for his own, so to say, fastidious reasons, motivated as he was not only by fear of starvation or of the police, cannot isolate his fate from the fate of those masses. Their nomadic existence, the slums they often inhabit, the deserts of dirty streets where their children play are, in a way, his own; he feels solidarity with them and he only wonders whether this is not an image, more and more generalized, of the human condition. For life in exile seems no more limited to a transplantation from one country to another. Industrial centers attract people who leave their peaceful but impoverished rural districts, new towns grow where a few decades ago only cattle were grazing, shacks and barracks of slums surround big capitals. When characterizing the indefiniteness and insecurity inherent in exile one notices that practically everything that is said on the subject applies to the new inhabitants of the urban landscape, even if they have not arrived from foreign lands. Alienation becomes a predicament of too many human beings to be considered an affliction of a special category, and the self-pity of an emigré reflecting on that phenomenon is undermined.

8   Perhaps a loss of harmony with the surrounding space, the inability to feel at home in the world, so oppressing to an expatriate, a refugee, an immigrant, however we call him, paradoxically integrates him in contemporary society and makes him, if he is an artist, understood by all. Even more, to express the existential situation of modern man, one must live in exile of some sort. Are not Samuel Beckett's plays about exile? Time in them is not perceived as a serene repetition favoring a gladly accepted routine; on the contrary, it is empty and destructive, it rushes forward to an illusory goal and closes on itself in a display of futility. Man in those plays cannot enter into a contact with space which is abstract, uniform, deprived of specific objects, in all probability a desert.

9   Writing this I am visited by a tune of an old religious song in Polish which begins: "Exiles of Eve, we beseech Thy help." And indeed an archetypal exclusion from the Garden of Eden repeats itself in our lives, whether Eden be the womb of our mother or the enchanting garden of our early childhood. Centuries of tradition are behind the image of the whole earth as a land of exile, usually presented as a desertic, sterile landscape in which Adam and Eve march, their heads despondently lowered. They were chased from their native realm, their true home where the same rhythm has ruled over their bodies and their surroundings, where no separation and no nostalgia has been known. Looking back, they may see fiery swords guarding the Gates of Paradise. Their nostalgic thinking about a return to the once happy existence is intensified by their awareness of prohibition. And yet they will never completely relinquish the thought of the day when their exile will end. Later, much later on, perhaps that dream will take the shape of a golden city lasting beyond time, of a heavenly Jerusalem.

10   The biblical image favors a cliché according to which exile means looking back towards the country of one's origin. And, indeed, many poems and novels have been written in this century by exiles who describe a region of the world from where they have come as more beautiful than it had been in reality, simply because now it is lost forever. Yet an objection imposes itself here. Displacement creates a distance measured by kilometers or miles, hundreds of thousands of miles. The biblical image is that of a movement in space from the Gates of Eden or, translating this into modern notions, from the borders of a state guarded by armed soldiers. However, distance may be measured not only in miles, but also in months, years, or dozens of years. Assuming this, we may consider the life of every human being as an unrelenting movement from childhood on, through the phases of youth, maturity, and old age. The past of every individual undergoes constant transformations in his or her memory, and

more often than not it acquires the features of an irretrievable land made more and more strange by the flow of time. Thus the difference between a displacement in space and in time is somewhat blurred. We can well imagine an old expatriate who, mediating on the century of his youth, realizes that he is separated from it not only by expanse, but also by the wrinkles on his face and grey hair, marks left by a severe border guard, time. What then is exile if, in this sense, everybody shares that condition?

Nevertheless, the condition of exile in a geographical sense is real enough and 11 those whose fate is to experience it have been using various consolations to make it less depressing. An awareness of its universal character in this century may provide considerable relief and even induce a pride of belonging to an avant garde. In addition, such an awareness draws encouragement from the fact that history knows big countries founded by wanderers, among them, America. An artist and a writer in exile are, however, confronted with the insidious question of his or her creativity or paralysis. An argument has been advanced many times according to which there is a mysterious link between the land of our ancestors, its soil, its light, sounds of its language on the one hand and the creative powers of the individual on the other. It is said that our sources of inspiration risk drying out abroad. And in fact a great number of people who were gifted, brilliant, promising poets, painters, musicians have been leaving their countries only to suffer defeat and to plunge into anonymity that would cover their names forever. There is much truth in the assertion that the native soil possesses a vivifying force, even if we put aside the obvious, namely the mother tongue and its irreplaceable nuances. Fear of sterility is a companion of every expatriate artist and though it visits artists in general, its presence in that particular case is felt more strongly. To calm it, the most useful is to invoke the names of all those who despite the odds have not lost the game. Fundamental works of poetry in some languages, for instance, Polish and Armenian, have been written abroad, owing to the political persecution practiced by foreign occupying powers. Decades spent in Paris far from his native provincial town, Witebsk, didn't discourage Marc Chagall from following his original inspiration and he continued to fly in the sky together with the roofs of huts, with the goats and cows of his childhood and early youth. Isaac Bashevis Singer recreated in America through memory and imagination the life gone forever of the Polish Jews. It is doubtful whether James Joyce's *Ulysses* could have been written in Dublin, it is more probable to assume that his estrangement and his refusal to serve Irish patriotic goals were necessary preconditions for his description of Ireland from afar. And Igor Stravinsky, in spite of malicious rumors, according to which after the "Rites of Spring" his talent, not enlivened by Russia, was on the wane, remained productive and very Russian during his long exile.

In every one of these examples, and they can be multiplied, a pattern is 12 noticeable. A farewell to one's country, to its landscapes, customs and mores throws one into a no man's land comparable perhaps to the desert chosen as a place of contemplation by early Christian hermits. Then the only remedy against the loss of orientation is to create anew one's own North, East, West, and South and posit in that new space a Witebsk or a Dublin elevated to the second power. What has been lost is recuperated on a higher level of vividness and presence.

13   Exile is a test of internal freedom and that freedom is terrifying. Everything depends upon our own resources, of which we are mostly unaware and yet we make decisions assuming our strength will be sufficient. The risk is total, not assuaged by the warmth of a collectivity where the second rate is usually tolerated, regarded as useful and even honored. Now to win or to lose appears in a crude light, for we are alone and loneliness is a permanent affliction of exile. Once Friedrich Nietzsche exalted the freedom of height, of loneliness, of the desert. Freedom of exile is of that lofty sort, though it is imposed by circumstances and, therefore, deprived of bathos. A brief formula may encapsule the outcome of that struggle with our own weakness: exile destroys, but if it fails to destroy you, it makes you stronger.

14   The exodus of people from their countries is a familiar feature in our century and it has been categorized under various names. The Russian Revolution resulted in the appearance of Russian emigrés in the big cities of the West. Soon they were joined by refugees from Hitler's Germany and ex-soldiers from the Spanish Republican army. At the end of World War II a defeated Germany was full of displaced persons called D.P.'s, former slave laborers and survivors of concentration camps, also of Germans expelled from the Eastern provinces. In the subsequent decades a wave of migrations from Central-Eastern Europe has been due to political spasms (the crushed Hungarian uprising, the invasion of Czechoslovakia, the martial law in Poland) or to the economic attractiveness of the capitalist West. Similar names and categories can be found in Africa and Asia, the exodus of the "Boat People" from Vietnam being the most famous case. Though officials, charged with granting or refusing to a newcomer the right to stay, distinguish between ideological and economic motives, reality is more complex than that and a given person has usually been pushed to migrate by a tangle of reasons. One thing is certain: people leave their homelands because life there is difficult to bear.

15   Can we imagine a world in which the phenomenon of exile disappears because it is unnecessary? To envisage such a possibility would mean to disregard the current that seems to carry us in the opposite direction. What is probable is the increase of awareness that whoever looks for happiness in distant lands must be prepared for disillusionment or even for the doubtful reward of one who jumps from the frying pan into the fire. That awareness, of course, would not discourage anybody, for the pain we feel at a given moment is more real than the pain we may endure in the future. This earth with all its charms and beauty is after all the earth of the "exiles of Eve." An old anecdote about

a refugee in a travel agency has not lost its bite: a refugee from war-torn Europe, undecided as to what continent and what state would be far off enough and safe enough, for a while was pensively turning a globe with his finger, then asked, "don't you have something else?" ✥

RESPONDING

1. In a journal entry, write about a time you had to leave a familiar place. The situation may be as dramatic as leaving your homeland or as commonplace as leaving home for kindergarten. How did you feel? Were you apprehensive or excited? What were your expectations? How did reality compare to them?

2. Working individually or in a group, explore the problems a new immigrant would have when coming to the United States. What do you think the most significant problems would be?

3. In an essay, define what Milosz means when he uses the word "exile." Give specific examples from the reading to explain his definition. What connotations does the term have for him? For you?

4. Milosz says, "Exile destroys, but if it fails to destroy you, it makes you stronger" (paragraph 13). Do you agree or disagree? Support your argument with examples from the readings, outside sources, and your own experience.

✥

CONNECTING

Critical Thinking and Writing

1. Most of the readings in this chapter focus on the experiences of immigrants to America. Some of these people left their homelands for better economic opportunities; others were forced to leave because of political conditions. Write an essay classifying the immigrants in this chapter according to their reasons for emigrating.

2. Immigrating to a new country can mean new opportunities or a traumatic change. Using examples from the readings and from your own experience, write

an essay discussing the difficulties of adapting to a new country and a new culture.

3. Cultural expectations can facilitate or inhibit successful adaptation to a new country. Discuss the problems some groups face because of the dramatic differences between their home culture and American culture.

4. Some of the writers in this chapter, for example, Nye and Milosz, explore their personal heritages. In what ways do they use their personal experiences as inspiration for and the content of their professional writing? Are they able to give their personal experiences wider application and appeal?

5. Using examples from the readings in this chapter or from your own readings or a friend's experience, discuss how race, gender, and/or social class help determine the circumstances of a person's life.

6. Working with the class, generate a series of essay questions concerning the issues dealt with in this chapter. Choose one question and answer it in an essay.

7. Compare the reasons that people immigrated to the United States in the 1970s and 1980s with the reasons that immigrants came in the 1870s and 1880s. You might compare a single group, such as the Chinese, or you might compare different groups, such as the Eastern Europeans in the 1800s and recent Latin American immigrants. Consider any changes in conditions that the immigrants encountered after they arrived in the United States.

8. For people such as Rosa in Ozick's story it is impossible to escape the effects of the past. Using examples from the readings, argue whether historical events do or do not shape an individual's or a group's behavior. Focus your discussion by referring to specific historical events such as the Holocaust, the enslavement of African Americans, the internment of Japanese Americans, or the relocation of American Indians.

9. Luu and Mukherjee write about tradition and its influence on individuals. Compare the role of tradition in the lives of the women they present with the women in Ole Edvart Rölvaag, Connie Young Yu, or Piri Thomas.

10. Milosz states that "many poems and novels have been written in this century by exiles who describe a region of the world from where they have come as more beautiful than it had been in reality, simply because now it is lost forever" (paragraph 10). Do you agree or disagree that immigrants often view their homeland unrealistically? Support your argument with examples from the readings and your own knowledge.

11. Many new immigrants see the United States as the Promised Land where they can fulfill the American Dream. What do you think the American Dream means to these people? How does this dream differ from that of the founders of the country? How is it similar?

For Further Research

1. Choose one of the groups represented in this chapter and investigate the history of their immigration and their current situation in the United States. You might consider, for example, the reasons for and difficulties of immigration, economic and social opportunities in the United States, and settlement patterns.

2. Research current United States immigration laws and policies. How does someone immigrate to this country? Who is allowed to enter? What procedures must they follow?

REFERENCES AND ADDITIONAL SOURCES

Anzaldúa, Gloria. *Borderlands: The New Mestiza-La Frontera*. San Francisco: Spinsters/Aunt Lute Book Co., 1987.

Archdeacon, Thomas J. *Becoming American: An Ethnic History*. New York: The Free Press, 1983.

Attwell, David. *J. M. Coetzee: South Africa and the Politics of Writing*. Berkeley: University of California Press, 1993.

Boelhower, William. *Immigrant Autobiography in the United States*. Verona: Essedue Edizioni, 1982.

Brodsky, Joseph. *Less Than One: Selected Essays*. New York: Farrar, Straus & Giroux, 1986.

Bulosan, Carlos. *America Is in the Heart: A Personal History*. Seattle: University of Washington Press, 1943.

Chan, Jeffrey Paul, et al., eds. *The Big Aiiieeeee!: An Anthology of Chinese American and Japanese American Literature*. New York: Meridian, 1991.

Cheung, King-Kok. *Articulate Silences: Hisaye Yamamoto, Maxine Hong Kingston, Joy Kogawa*. Ithaca, N.Y.: Cornell University Press, 1993.

Chin, Frank, et al., eds. *Aiiieeeee: An Anthology of Asian American Writers*. Washington: Howard University Press, 1974.

Colombo, Gary, Robert J. Cullen, and Bonnie Lisle, eds. *Rereading America*. New York: St. Martin's Press, 1989.

Delgado, Asunción Horno. *Breaking Boundaries: Latin Writing and Critical Readings*. Amherst: University of Massachusetts Press, 1989.

De Vos, George, and Lola Romanucci-Ross, eds. *Ethnic Identity: Cultural Continuities and*

Change. Palo Alto, Calif.: Mayfield, 1975; Chicago: University of Chicago Press, 1982, with a new introduction by the authors.

Fanon, Frantz. *The Wretched of the Earth.* New York: Grove Press, 1963.

Fisher, Dexter, ed. *The Third Woman: Minority Women Writers of the United States.* Boston: Houghton Mifflin, 1980.

Gage, Nicholas. *A Place for Us: Eleni's Family in America.* Boston: Houghton Mifflin, 1989.

Gates, Henry Louis, Jr. *Loose Cannons: Notes on the Culture Wars.* New York: Oxford University Press, 1992.

———. *"Race," Writing, and Difference.* Chicago: University of Chicago Press, 1986.

Herrera-Sobek, Maria. *Northward Bound: The Mexican Immigrant Experience in Ballad and Song.* Bloomington, Ind.: Indiana University Press, 1993.

Hwang, David Henry. *Family Devotions. Broken Promises: Four Chinese American Plays.* New York: Avon, 1983.

Iglesias, José. *The Goodbye Land.* New York: Pantheon, 1967.

Kim, Richard E. *Lost Names: Scenes from a Korean Boyhood.* New York: Praeger, 1970.

Kincaid, Jamaica. *A Small Place.* New York: Farrar, Straus & Giroux, 1988.

Marchetti, Gina. *Romance and the "Yellow Peril:" Race, Sex, and Discursive Strategies in Hollywood Fiction.* Berkeley: University of California Press, 1993.

Marshall, Paule. *Brown Girl, Brown Stones.* New York: Random House, 1959.

Mehta, Ved. *Face to Face: An Autobiography.* Boston: Little, Brown, 1957.

Milosz, Czeslaw. *Native Realm: A Search for Self-Definition.* Translated by Catherine S. Leach. Garden City, N.Y.: Doubleday, 1968.

———. *Visions from San Francisco Bay.* Translated by Richard Lourie. New York: Farrar, Straus & Giroux, 1975.

Mirikitani, Janice, ed. *Time to Greez! Incantations from the Third World.* San Francisco: Glide Publications, 1975.

Mukherjee, Bharati. *The Middleman and Other Stories.* New York: Grove Press, 1988.

Orfalea, Gregory, ed. *Wrapping the Grape Leaves: A Sheaf of Contemporary Arab-American Poets.* Washington, D.C.: American-Arab Anti-Discrimination Committee, 1982.

Reed, Ishmael. *Yardbird Lives!* New York: Grove Press, 1978.

Rischin, Moses, ed. *Immigration and the American Tradition.* Indianapolis, Ind.: Bobbs-Merrill, 1976.

Rose, Peter I., Stanley Rochman, and William Julius Wilson, eds. *Through Different Eyes: Black and White Perspectives on American Race Relations.* New York: Oxford University Press, 1973.

Said, Edward, ed. Preface by Edward Said. *Literature and Society*. Baltimore: Johns Hopkins University Press, 1980.

Seller, Maxine. *To Seek America: A History of Ethnic Group Life in the United States*. Englewood Cliffs, N.J.: Ozer, 1977, rev. ed. 1988.

Simonson, Rick, and Scott Walker, eds. *Multicultural Literacy*. Greywolf Annual Five Series. St. Paul: Greywolf, 1988.

Smith, Derek. "A Refugee by Any Other Name: An Examination of the Board of Immigration Appeals' Actions in Asylum Cases." *Virginia Law Review* 75 (1989): 681–721.

Sollors, Werner. *Beyond Ethnicity: Consent and Descent in American Culture*. New York: Oxford University Press, 1986.

Sunoo, Brenda. *Korean American Writing: Selected Material from "Insight," a Korean American Bimonthly*. 1975.

Takaki, Ronald. *A Different Mirror: A History of Multicultural America*. Boston: Little, Brown, 1993.

———, ed. *From Different Shores: Perspectives on Race and Ethnicity in America*. New York: Oxford University Press, 1987.

Tan, Amy. *The Joy Luck Club*. New York: Putnam, 1989.

Todorov, Tzvetan. *The Conquest of America: The Question of the Other*. Translated by Richard Howard. New York: Harper & Row, 1984.

TuSmith, Bonnie. *All My Relatives: Community in Contemporary Ethnic American Literatures*. Ann Arbor, Mich.: The University of Michigan Press, 1993.

INDEX